Deep Learning from first principles – Second Edition

In vectorized Python, R and Octave

This book is dedicated to the memory of my late Mom and Dad who continue to be the force behind all my actions

This book is also dedicated to my wife Shanthi for her support and for giving me the space to work, and finally to my daughter, Shreya, for bringing joy to my life.

Table of Contents

Preface 4
Introduction 6
1. Logistic Regression as a Neural Network 8
2. Implementing a simple Neural Network 23
3. Building a L- Layer Deep Learning Network 48
4. Deep Learning network with the Softmax 85
5. MNIST classification with Softmax 103
6. Initialization, regularization in Deep Learning 121
7. Gradient Descent Optimization techniques 167
8. Gradient Check in Deep Learning 197
1. Appendix A 214
2. Appendix 1 – Logistic Regression as a Neural Network 220
3. Appendix 2 - Implementing a simple Neural Network 227
4. Appendix 3 - Building a L- Layer Deep Learning Network 240
5. Appendix 4 - Deep Learning network with the Softmax 259
6. Appendix 5 - MNIST classification with Softmax 269
7. Appendix 6 - Initialization, regularization in Deep Learning 302
8. Appendix 7 - Gradient Descent Optimization techniques 344
9. Appendix 8 – Gradient Check 405
References 475

Preface

You don't understand anything until you learn it more than one way. **Marvin Minsky**

The last decade and some, has witnessed some remarkable advancements in the area of Deep Learning. This area of AI has proliferated into many branches - Deep Belief Networks, Recurrent Neural Networks, Convolution Neural Networks, Adversorial Networks, Reinforcement Learning, Capsule Networks and the list goes on. These years have also resulted in Deep Learning to move from the research labs and closer to the home, thanks to progress in hardware, strorage and cloud technology.

One common theme when you listen to Deep Learning pundits, is that in order to get a good grasp of the Deep Learning domain, it is essential that you learn to build such a network from scratch. It is towards that end that this book was written.

In this book, I implement Deep Learning Networks from the basics. Each successive chapter builds upon the implementations of the previous chapters so that by chapter 7, I have a full-fledged, generic L-Layer Deep Learning network, with all the bells and whistles. All the necessary derivations required for implementing a multi-layer Deep Learning network is included in the chapters. Detailed derivations for forward propagation and backward propagation cycles with relu, tanh and sigmoid hidden layer units, and sigmoid and softmax output activation units are included. These may serve to jog your memory of all those whose undergrad calculus is a little rusty.

The first chapter derives and implements logisitic regression as a neural network in Python, R and Octave. The second chapter deals with the derivation and implementation of the most primitive neural network, one with just one hidden layer. The third chapter extends on the principles of the 2nd chapter and implements a L-Layer Deep Learning network with the sigmoid activation in vectorized Python, R and Octave. This implementation can include an arbitrary number of hidden units and any number of hidden layers for the sigmoid activation output layer. The fourth chapter introduces the Softmax function required for multi-class classification. The Jacobian of the Softmax and cross-entropy loss is derived and then this implemented to demonstrate multi-class classification of a simple spiral data set. The fifth chapter incorporates the softmax implementation of the fourth chapter into the L-Layer implementation in the 3rd chapter. With this enhancement, the fifth chapter classifies MNIST digits using Softmax output activation unit in a generic L-Layer implementation. The sixth chapter addresses different initialization techniques like He and Xavier. Further, this chapter also discusses and implements L2 regularization and random dropout technique. The seventh chapter looks at gradient descent optimization techniques like learning rate decay, momentum, rmsprop, and adam. The eight chapter discusses a critical technique, that is required to ensure the correctness of the backward propagation implementation. Specifically this chapter discusses and implements 'gradient checking' and also demonstrates how to find bugs in your implementation.

All the chapters include vectorized implementations in Python, R and Octave. The implementations are identical. So, if your are conversant in any one of the languages you can look at the implementations in any other language. It should be a good way to learn the other language.

Note: The functions that are invoked in each of the chapters are included in Appendix 1-Appendix 8.

Feel free to check out the implementations by playing around with the hyper-parameters. A good way to learn is to take the code apart. You could also try to enhance the implementation to include other activation functions like the leaky relu, parametric relu etc. Maybe, you could work on other regularization or gradient descent optimization methods. There may also be opportunities to optimize my code with further vectorization of functions.

This course is largely based on Prof Andrew Ng's Deep Learning Specialization (https://www.coursera.org/specializations/deep-learning).

I would like to thank Prof Andrew Ng and Prof Geoffrey Hinton for making the apparent complexity of the Deep Learning subject into remarkably simple concepts through their courses.

I hope this book sets you off on a exciting and challenging journey into the Deep Learning domain

Tinniam V Ganesh

16 May 2018

Introduction

This is the second edition of my book 'Deep Learning from first principles: Second Edition – In vectorized Python, R and Octave'. Since this book has about 70% code, I wanted to make the code more readable. Hence, in this second edition, I have changed all the code to use the fixed-width font Lucida Console. This makes the code more organized and can be more easily absorbed. I have also included line numbers for all functions and code snippets. Finally, I have corrected some of the typos in the book.

Other books by the author (available on Amazon in paperback and kindle versions)

1. Practical Machine Learning with R and Python: Second Edition – Machine Learning in stereo
2. Beaten by sheer pace: Third Edition – Cricket analytics with yorkr
3. Cricket analytics with cricketr:Third Edition

1. Logistic Regression as a Neural Network

"You don't perceive objects as they are. You perceive them as you are."
"Your interpretation of physical objects has everything to do with the historical trajectory of your brain – and little to do with the objects themselves."
"The brain generates its own reality, even before it receives information coming in from the eyes and the other senses. This is known as the internal model"
David Eagleman - The Brain: The Story of You

This chapter deals with the implementation of Logistic regression as a 2-layer Neural Network i.e. a Neural Network that just has an input layer and an output layer and with no hidden layer. This 2-layer network is implemented in Python, R and Octave languages. I have included Octave, into the mix, as Octave is a close cousin of Matlab. These implementations in Python, R and Octave are equivalent vectorized implementations. Therefore, if you are familiar in any one of the languages, you should be able to look at the corresponding code in the other two. The implementations of the functions invoked in this chapter are in Appendix 1 – Logistic Regression as a Neural Network.

You can also clone/download the vectorized code in Pythin, R and Octave from Github at DeepLearningFromFirstPrinciples '(https://github.com/tvganesh/DeepLearningFromFirstPrinciples/tree/master/Chap1-LogisticRegressionAsNeuralNetwork). To start with, Logistic Regression is performed using sklearn's logistic regression package, for the cancer data set also from sklearn. This is shown below

1. Logistic Regression

```
import numpy as np
import pandas as pd
import os
import matplotlib.pyplot as plt
from sklearn.model_selection import train_test_split
from sklearn.linear_model import LogisticRegression
from sklearn.datasets import make_classification, make_blobs

from sklearn.metrics import confusion_matrix
from matplotlib.colors import ListedColormap
from sklearn.datasets import load_breast_cancer

# Load the cancer data
(X_cancer, y_cancer) = load_breast_cancer(return_X_y = True)
X_train, X_test, y_train, y_test = train_test_split(X_cancer, y_cancer,
                                                    random_state = 0)
```

```python
# Call the Logisitic Regression function
clf = LogisticRegression().fit(X_train, y_train)

#Print accuracy of training and test set
print('Accuracy of Logistic regression classifier on training set: {:.2f}'
      .format(clf.score(X_train, y_train)))
print('Accuracy of Logistic regression classifier on test set: {:.2f}'
      .format(clf.score(X_test, y_test)))
## Accuracy of Logistic regression classifier on training set: 0.96
## Accuracy of Logistic regression classifier on test set: 0.96
```

2. Logistic Regression as a 2-layer Neural Network

In the following section, Logistic Regression is implemented as a 2-layer Neural Network in Python, R and Octave. The same cancer data set from sklearn is used to train and test the Neural Network in Python, R and Octave. This can be represented diagrammatically as below

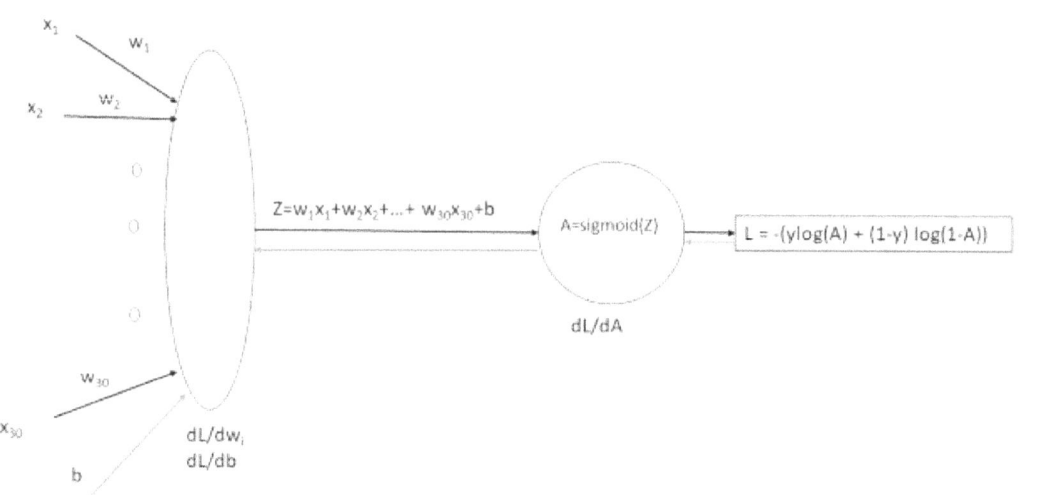

The cancer data set has 30 input features, and the target variable 'output' is either 0 or 1. Hence, the sigmoid activation function will be used in the output layer for classification.

This simple 2-layer Neural Network is shown below.
At the input layer, there are 30 features and the corresponding weights of these inputs which are initialized to small random values.
$$Z = w_1 x_1 + w_2 x_2 + \ldots + w_{30} x_{30} + b$$
where 'b' is the bias term

The Activation function is the sigmoid function which is given by $a = 1/(1 + e^{-z})$
The Loss, when the sigmoid function is used in the output layer, is given by
$$L = -(y \log(a) + (1-y) \log(1-a)) \quad (1)$$

3. Gradient Descent

3.1 Forward propagation

The forward propagation cycle of the Neural Network computes the output Z and the activation the sigmoid activation function. Then using the output 'y' for the given features, the 'Loss' is computed using equation (1) above.

3.2 Backward propagation

The backward propagation cycle determines how the 'Loss' is impacted for small variations from the previous layers up to the input layer. In other words, backward propagation computes the changes in the weights at the input layer, which will minimize the loss at the output layer. Several cycles of gradient descent are performed in the path of steepest descent to find the local minima. In other words, the set of weights and biases, at the input layer, which will result in the lowest loss, is computed by gradient descent. The weights at the input layer are decreased by a parameter known as the 'learning rate'. Too big a 'learning rate' can overshoot the local minima, and too small a 'learning rate' can take a long time to reach the local minima. Gradient Descent iterated through this forward propagation and backward propagation cycle until the loss is minimized. This is done for 'm' training examples.

3.3 Chain rule of differentiation

Let $y = f(u)$
and $u = g(x)$ then by chain rule
$\partial y/\partial x = \partial y/\partial u * \partial u/\partial x$

3.4 Derivative of sigmoid

$\sigma = 1/(1 + e^{-z})$
Let $x = 1 + e^{-z}$ then
$\sigma = 1/x$
$\partial \sigma/\partial x = -1/x^2$ and
$\partial x/\partial z = -e^{-z}$

Using the chain rule of differentiation we get
$\partial \sigma/\partial z = \partial \sigma/\partial x * \partial x/\partial z$
$= -1/(1 + e^{-z})^2 * -e^{-z} = e^{-z}/(1 + e^{-z})^2$
Therefore $\partial \sigma/\partial z = \sigma(1 - \sigma)$ -(2)

The 3 equations for the 2 layer Neural Network representation of Logistic Regression are
$L = -(y * \log(a) + (1 - y) * \log(1 - a))$ -(a)
$a = 1/(1 + e^{-Z})$ -(b)
$Z = w_1 x_1 + w_2 x_2 + \ldots + w_{30} x_{30} + b = Z = \sum_i w_i * x_i + b$ -(c)

Where L is the loss for the sigmoid output activation function

The back-propagation step requires the computation of dL/dw_i and dL/db_i. In the case of regression it would be dE/dw_i and dE/db_i where dE is the Mean Squared Error function.

Computing the derivatives for the Loss function we have
$$dL/da = -(y/a + (1-y)/(1-a)) \quad \text{-(d)}$$
because $d/dx(\log x) = 1/x$
Also from equation (2) we can write
$$da/dZ = a(1-a) \quad \text{-- (e)}$$

By chain rule
$$\partial L/\partial Z = \partial L/\partial a * \partial a/\partial Z$$
therefore substituting the results of (d) & (e) into the equation above we get
$$\partial L/\partial Z = -(y/a + (1-y)/(1-a)) * a(1-a) = a - y \quad \text{(f)}$$

Finally
$$\partial L/\partial w_i = \partial L/\partial a * \partial a/\partial Z * \partial Z/\partial w_i \quad \text{-(g)}$$
$$\partial Z/\partial w_i = x_i \quad \text{-- (h)}$$
and from (f) we have $\partial L/\partial Z = a - y$
Therefore (g) reduces to
$$\partial L/\partial w_i = x_i * (a - y) \quad \text{-(i)}$$

Also
$$\partial L/\partial b = \partial L/\partial a * \partial a/\partial Z * \partial Z/\partial b \quad \text{-(j)}$$
Since
$$\partial Z/\partial b = 1$$
and using (f) in (j) we get
$$\partial L/\partial b = a - y$$

The gradient computes the weights at the input layer and the corresponding bias by using the values of dw_i and db.
$$w_i := w_i - \alpha * dw_i$$
$$b := b - \alpha * db$$

The computation graph representation in the book Deep Learning (http://www.deeplearningbook.org/) : Ian Goodfellow, Yoshua Bengio, Aaron Courville, is very useful to visualize and compute the backward propagation. For the 2-layer Neural Network of Logistic Regression the computation graph is shown below

Computational graph for Neural Network of Logistic Regression

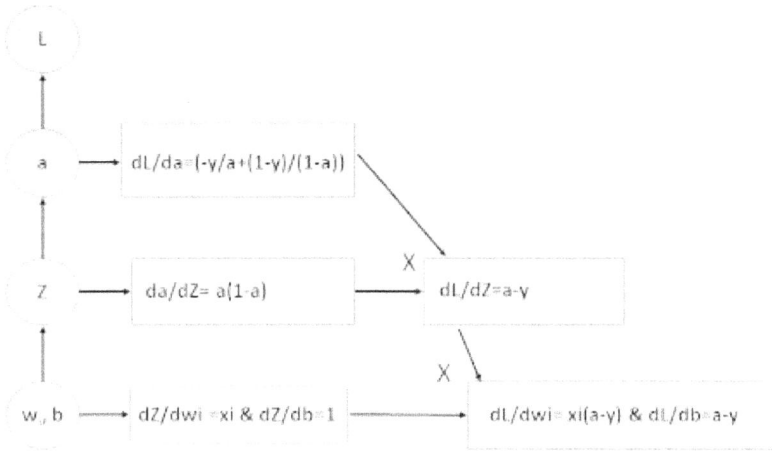

4. Neural Network for Logistic Regression -Python code

```
1  import numpy as np
2  import pandas as pd
3  import os
4  import matplotlib.pyplot as plt
5  from sklearn.model_selection import train_test_split
6
7  # Define the sigmoid function
8  def sigmoid(z):
9      a=1/(1+np.exp(-z))
10     return a
11
12 # Initialize weights and biases
13 def initialize(dim):
14     w = np.zeros(dim).reshape(dim,1)
15     b = 0
16     return w
17
18 # Compute the loss
19 def computeLoss(numTraining,Y,A):
20     loss=-1/numTraining *np.sum(Y*np.log(A) + (1-Y)*(np.log(1-A)))
21     return(loss)
22
23 # Execute the forward propagation
24 def forwardPropagation(w,b,X,Y):
25     # Compute Z
26     Z=np.dot(w.T,X)+b
27     # Determine the number of training samples
28     numTraining=float(len(X))
29     # Compute the output of the sigmoid activation function
30     A=sigmoid(Z)
31     #Compute the loss
32     loss = computeLoss(numTraining,Y,A)
33     # Compute the gradients dZ, dw and db
34     dZ=A-Y
```

```python
        dw=1/numTraining*np.dot(X,dZ.T)
        db=1/numTraining*np.sum(dZ)

        # Return the results as a dictionary
        gradients = {"dw": dw,
                     "db": db}
        loss = np.squeeze(loss)
        return gradients,loss

# Compute Gradient Descent
def gradientDescent(w, b, X, Y, numIerations, learningRate):
        losses=[]
        idx =[]
        # Iterate
        for i in range(numIerations):
            gradients,loss=forwardPropagation(w,b,X,Y)
            #Get the derivates
            dw = gradients["dw"]
            db = gradients["db"]
            w = w-learningRate*dw
            b = b-learningRate*db

            # Store the loss
            if i % 100 == 0:
                idx.append(i)
                losses.append(loss)
        # Set params and grads
        params = {"w": w,
                  "b": b}
        grads = {"dw": dw,
                 "db": db}

        return params, grads, losses,idx

# Predict the output for a training set
def predict(w,b,X):
    size=X.shape[1]
    yPredicted=np.zeros((1,size))
    Z=np.dot(w.T,X)
    # Compute the sigmoid
    A=sigmoid(Z)
    for i in range(A.shape[1]):
        #If the value is > 0.5 then set as 1
        if(A[0][i] > 0.5):
            yPredicted[0][i]=1
        else:
        # Else set as 0
            yPredicted[0][i]=0

    return yPredicted

#Normalize the data
def normalize(x):
    x_norm = None
    x_norm = np.linalg.norm(x,axis=1,keepdims=True)
    x= x/x_norm
    return x


# Run the 2-layer Neural Network on the cancer data set
from sklearn.datasets import load_breast_cancer
# Load the cancer data
(X_cancer, y_cancer) = load_breast_cancer(return_X_y = True)
# Create train and test sets
```

```python
X_train, X_test, y_train, y_test = train_test_split(X_cancer, y_cancer,
                                                    random_state = 0)
# Normalize the data for better performance
X_train1=normalize(X_train)


# Create weight vectors of zeros. The size is the number of features in the
data set=30
w=np.zeros((X_train.shape[1],1))
#w=np.zeros((30,1))
b=0

#Normalize the training data so that gradient descent performs better
X_train1=normalize(X_train)
#Transpose X_train so that we have a matrix as (features, numSamples)
X_train2=X_train1.T

# Reshape to remove the rank 1 array and then transpose
y_train1=y_train.reshape(len(y_train),1)
y_train2=y_train1.T

# Run gradient descent for 4000 times and compute the weights
parameters, grads, costs,idx = gradientDescent(w, b, X_train2, y_train2,
numIerations=4000, learningRate=0.75)
w = parameters["w"]
b = parameters["b"]


# Normalize X_test
X_test1=normalize(X_test)
#Transpose X_train so that we have a matrix as (features, numSamples)
X_test2=X_test1.T

#Reshape y_test
y_test1=y_test.reshape(len(y_test),1)
y_test2=y_test1.T

# Predict the values for
yPredictionTest = predict(w, b, X_test2)
yPredictionTrain = predict(w, b, X_train2)

# Print the accuracy
print("train accuracy: {} %".format(100 - np.mean(np.abs(yPredictionTrain -
y_train2)) * 100))
print("test accuracy: {} %".format(100 - np.mean(np.abs(yPredictionTest -
y_test)) * 100))

# Plot the Costs vs the number of iterations
fig1=plt.plot(idx,costs)
fig1=plt.title("Gradient descent-Cost vs No of iterations")
fig1=plt.xlabel("No of iterations")
fig1=plt.ylabel("Cost")
fig1.figure.savefig("fig1", bbox_inches='tight')
## train accuracy: 90.3755868545 %
## test accuracy: 89.5104895105 %
```
Note: The Accuracy on the training and test set is 90.37% and 89.51%. This is comparatively poorer than the 96%, which the logistic regression of sklearn achieves! But, this is mainly because of the absence of hidden layers which is the real power of neural networks.

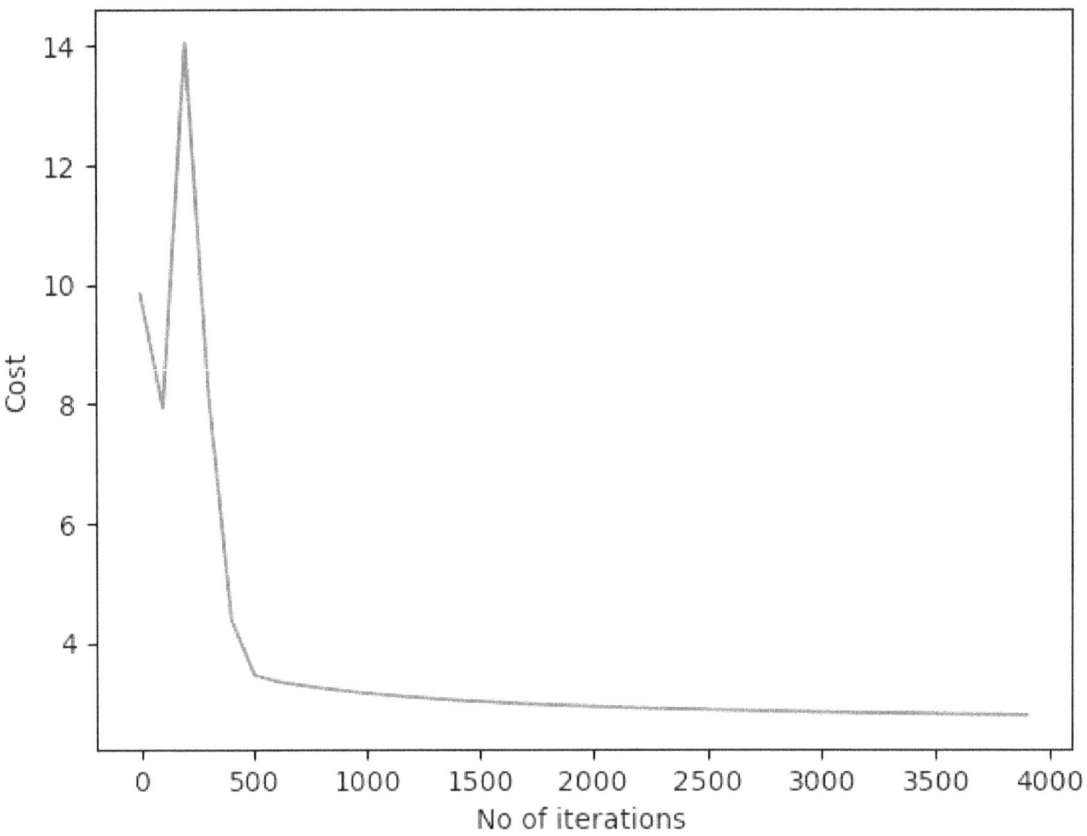

5. Neural Network for Logistic Regression -R code

```
1   source("RFunctions-1.R")
2   # Define the sigmoid function
3   sigmoid <- function(z){
4       a <- 1/(1+ exp(-z))
5       a
6   }
7
8   # Compute the loss
9   computeLoss <- function(numTraining,Y,A){
10      loss <- -1/numTraining* sum(Y*log(A) + (1-Y)*log(1-A))
11      return(loss)
12  }
13
14  # Compute forward propagation
15  forwardPropagation <- function(w,b,X,Y){
16      # Compute Z
17      Z <- t(w) %*% X +b
18      #Set the number of samples
19      numTraining <- ncol(X)
20      # Compute the activation function
21      A=sigmoid(Z)
22
23      #Compute the loss
24      loss <- computeLoss(numTraining,Y,A)
25
```

```r
    # Compute the gradients dZ, dw and db
    dZ<-A-Y
    dw<-1/numTraining * X %*% t(dZ)
    db<-1/numTraining*sum(dZ)

    fwdProp <- list("loss" = loss, "dw" = dw, "db" = db)
    return(fwdProp)
}

# Perform one cycle of Gradient descent
gradientDescent <- function(w, b, X, Y, numIerations, learningRate){
    losses <- NULL
    idx <- NULL
    # Loop through the number of iterations
    for(i in 1:numIerations){
        fwdProp <-forwardPropagation(w,b,X,Y)
        #Get the derivatives
        dw <- fwdProp$dw
        db <- fwdProp$db
        #Perform gradient descent
        w = w-learningRate*dw
        b = b-learningRate*db
        l <- fwdProp$loss
        # Stoe the loss
        if(i %% 100 == 0){
            idx <- c(idx,i)
            losses <- c(losses,l)
        }
    }

    # Return the weights and losses
    gradDescnt <- list("w"=w,"b"=b,"dw"=dw,"db"=db,"losses"=losses,"idx"=idx)
    return(gradDescnt)
}

# Compute the predicted value for input
predict <- function(w,b,X){
    m=dim(X)[2]
    # Create a ector of 0's
    yPredicted=matrix(rep(0,m),nrow=1,ncol=m)
    Z <- t(w) %*% X +b
    # Compute sigmoid
    A=sigmoid(Z)
    for(i in 1:dim(A)[2]){
        # If A > 0.5 set value as 1
        if(A[1,i] > 0.5)
        yPredicted[1,i]=1
      else
        # Else set as 0
        yPredicted[1,i]=0
    }

    return(yPredicted)
}

# Normalize the matrix
normalize <- function(x){
    #Create the norm of the matrix.Perform the Frobenius norm of the matrix
    n<-as.matrix(sqrt(rowSums(x^2)))
    #Sweep by rows by norm. Note '1' in the function which performing on every row
    normalized<-sweep(x, 1, n, FUN="/")
    return(normalized)
}
```

```r
# Run the 2 layer Neural Network on the cancer data set
# Read the data (from sklearn)
cancer <- read.csv("cancer.csv")
# Rename the target variable
names(cancer) <- c(seq(1,30),"output")
# Split as training and test sets
train_idx <- trainTestSplit(cancer,trainPercent=75,seed=5)
train <- cancer[train_idx, ]
test <- cancer[-train_idx, ]

# Set the features
X_train <-train[,1:30]
y_train <- train[,31]
X_test <- test[,1:30]
y_test <- test[,31]
# Create a matrix of 0's with the number of features
w <-matrix(rep(0,dim(X_train)[2]))
b <-0
X_train1 <- normalize(X_train)
X_train2=t(X_train1)

# Reshape  then transpose
y_train1=as.matrix(y_train)
y_train2=t(y_train1)

# Perform gradient descent
gradDescent= gradientDescent(w, b, X_train2, y_train2, numIerations=3000,
learningRate=0.77)
# Normalize X_test
X_test1=normalize(X_test)
#Transpose X_train so that we have a matrix as (features, numSamples)
X_test2=t(X_test1)

#Reshape y_test and take transpose
y_test1=as.matrix(y_test)
y_test2=t(y_test1)

# Use the values of the weights generated from Gradient Descent
yPredictionTest = predict(gradDescent$w, gradDescent$b, X_test2)
yPredictionTrain = predict(gradDescent$w, gradDescent$b, X_train2)

sprintf("Train accuracy: %f",(100 - mean(abs(yPredictionTrain - y_train2)) *
100))
## [1] "Train accuracy: 90.845070"
sprintf("test accuracy: %f",(100 - mean(abs(yPredictionTest - y_test)) *
100))
## [1] "test accuracy: 87.323944"
df <-data.frame(gradDescent$idx, gradDescent$losses)
names(df) <- c("iterations","losses")
ggplot(df,aes(x=iterations,y=losses)) + geom_point() + geom_line(col="blue")
+
    ggtitle("Gradient Descent - Losses vs No of Iterations") +
    xlab("No of iterations") + ylab("Losses")
```

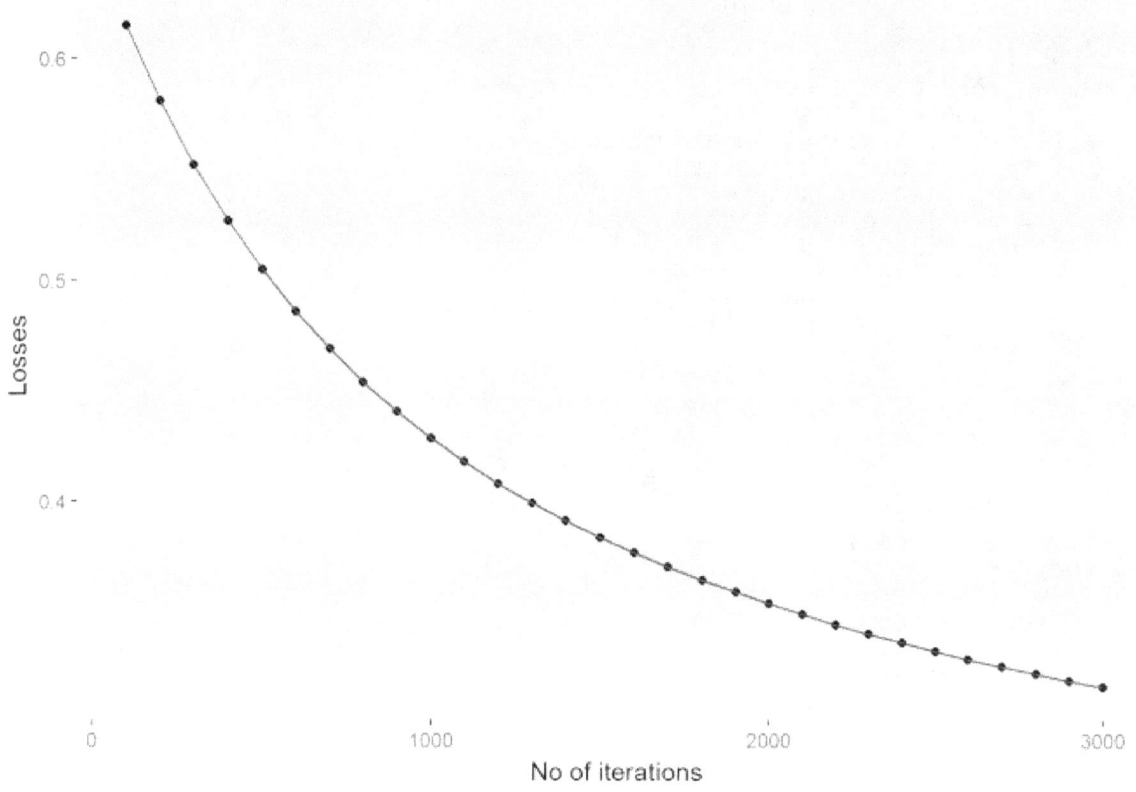

6. Neural Network for Logistic Regression -Octave code

```
1  1;
2  # Define sigmoid function
3  function a = sigmoid(z)
4      a = 1 ./ (1+ exp(-z));
5  end
6
7  # Compute the loss
8  function loss=computeLoss(numtraining,Y,A)
9      loss = -1/numtraining * sum((Y .* log(A)) + (1-Y) .* log(1-A));
10 end
11
12 # Perform forward propagation
13 function [loss,dw,db,dZ] = forwardPropagation(w,b,X,Y)
14     # Compute Z
15     Z = w' * X + b;
16     numtraining = size(X)(1,2);
17     # Compute sigmoid
18     A = sigmoid(Z);
19     #Compute loss. Note this is element wise product
20      loss =computeLoss(numtraining,Y,A);
21     # Compute the gradients dZ, dw and db
22     dZ = A-Y;
23     dw = 1/numtraining* X * dZ';
24    db =1/numtraining*sum(dZ);
25 end
26
27 # Compute Gradient Descent
```

```octave
function [w,b,dw,db,losses,index]=gradientDescent(w, b, X, Y, numIerations, learningRate)
    #Initialize losses and idx
    losses=[];
    index=[];
    # Loop through the number of iterations
    for i=1:numIerations,
        [loss,dw,db,dZ] = forwardPropagation(w,b,X,Y);
        # Perform Gradient descent
        w = w - learningRate*dw;
        b = b - learningRate*db;
        if(mod(i,100) ==0)
            # Append index and loss
            index = [index i];
            losses = [losses loss];
        endif
    end
end

# Determine the predicted value for dataset
function yPredicted = predict(w,b,X)
  m = size(X)(1,2);
  yPredicted=zeros(1,m);
  # Compute Z
  Z = w' * X + b;
  # Compute sigmoid
  A = sigmoid(Z);
  for i=1:size(X)(1,2),
      # Set predicted as 1 if A > 0,5
      if(A(1,i) >= 0.5)
          yPredicted(1,i)=1;
      else
          yPredicted(1,i)=0;
      endif
end
end

# Normalize by dividing each value by the sum of squares
function normalized = normalize(x)
    # Compute Frobenius norm. Square the elements, sum rows and then find square root
    a = sqrt(sum(x .^ 2,2));
     # Perform element wise division
     normalized = x ./ a;
end

# Split into train and test sets
function [X_train,y_train,X_test,y_test] = trainTestSplit(dataset,trainPercent)
    # Create a random index
    ix = randperm(length(dataset));
    # Split into training
    trainSize = floor(trainPercent/100 * length(dataset));
    train=dataset(ix(1:trainSize),:);
    # And test
     test=dataset(ix(trainSize+1:length(dataset)),:);
    X_train = train(:,1:30);
    y_train = train(:,31);
    X_test = test(:,1:30);
   y_test = test(:,31);
end

# Read the data
cancer=csvread("cancer.csv");
```

```
# Split as train and test
[X_train,y_train,X_test,y_test] = trainTestSplit(cancer,75);

#Initialize w and b
w=zeros(size(X_train)(1,2),1);
b=0;

#Normalize training
X_train1=normalize(X_train);
X_train2=X_train1';
y_train1=y_train';

#Perform gradient descent
[w1,b1,dw,db,losses,idx]=gradientDescent(w, b, X_train2, y_train1,
numIerations=3000, learningRate=0.75);

# Normalize X_test
X_test1=normalize(X_test);
#Transpose X_train so that we have a matrix as (features, numSamples)
X_test2=X_test1';
y_test1=y_test';
# Use the values of the weights generated from Gradient Descent
yPredictionTest = predict(w1, b1, X_test2);
yPredictionTrain = predict(w1, b1, X_train2);

#Compute Accouracy
trainAccuracy=100-mean(abs(yPredictionTrain - y_train1))*100
testAccuracy=100- mean(abs(yPredictionTest - y_test1))*100
trainAccuracy = 90.845
testAccuracy = 89.510

graphics_toolkit('gnuplot')
plot(idx,losses);
title ('Gradient descent- Cost vs No of iterations');
xlabel ("No of iterations");
ylabel ("Cost");
```

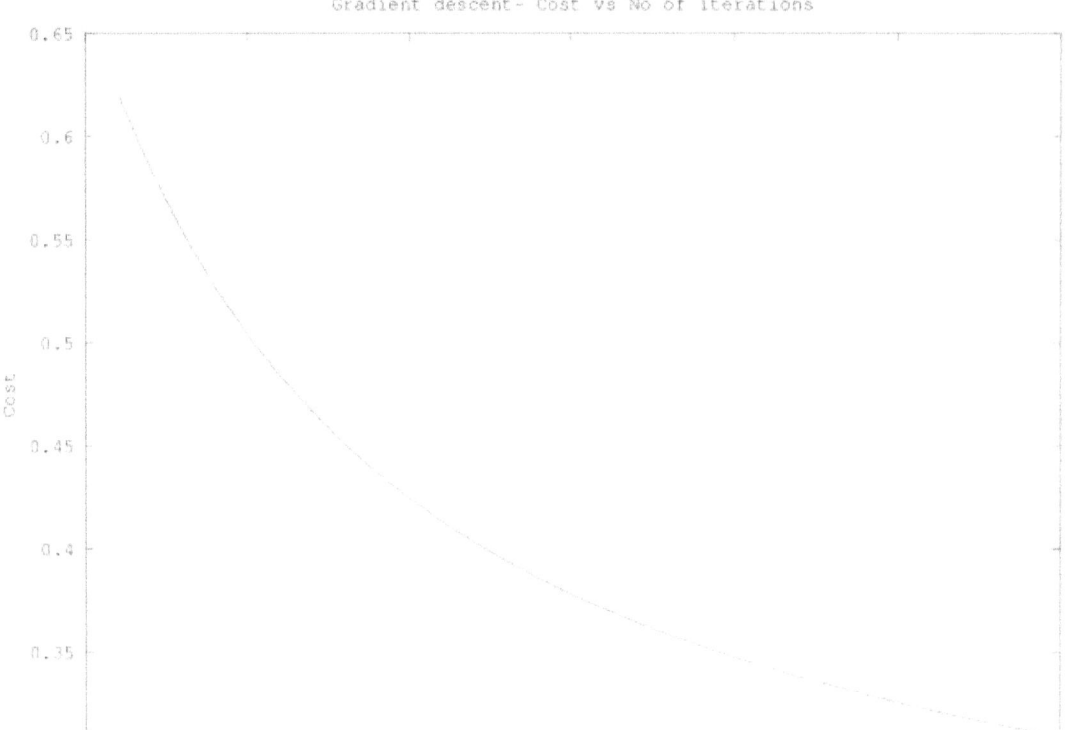

Conclusion
This chapter starts with a simple 2-layer Neural Network implementation of Logistic Regression. Clearly, the performance of this simple Neural Network is comparatively poor to the highly optimized sklearn's Logistic Regression. This is because the above neural network did not have any hidden layers. Deep Learning & Neural Networks achieve extraordinary performance because of the presence of deep hidden layers

2. Implementing a simple Neural Network

"What does the world outside your head really 'look' like? Not only is there no color, there's also no sound: the compression and expansion of air is picked up by the ears and turned into electrical signals. The brain then presents these signals to us as mellifluous tones and swishes and clatters and jangles. Reality is also odorless: there's no such thing as smell outside our brains. Molecules floating through the air bind to receptors in our nose and are interpreted as different smells by our brain. The real world is not full of rich sensory events; instead, our brains light up the world with their own sensuality."
The Brain: The Story of You" by David Eagleman

"The world is Maya, illusory. The ultimate reality, the Brahman, is all-pervading and all-permeating, which is colourless, odourless, tasteless, nameless and formless"
Bhagavad Gita

1. Introduction

In the first chapter, I implemented Logistic Regression, in vectorized Python, R and Octave, with a wannabe Neural Network (a Neural Network with no hidden layers). In this second chapter, I implement a regular, but somewhat primitive Neural Network, (a Neural Network with just 1 hidden layer). This chapter implements classification of manually created datasets, where the different clusters of the 2 classes are not linearly separable.

Neural Network perform well in learning all sorts of non-linear boundaries between classes. Initially logistic regression is used to perform the classification. A simple 3-layer Neural Network is then used on the same data set and the decision boundary plotted. Vanilla logistic regression performs quite poorly. Using SVMs with a radial basis kernel would have performed much better in creating non-linear boundaries. The implementations of the functions invoked in this chapter are in Appendix 2 - Implementing a simple Neural Network

You can clone and fork the vectorized implementations of the 3 layer Neural Network for Python, R and Octave from Github at DeepLearningFromFirstPrinciples (https://github.com/tvganesh/DeepLearningFromFirstPrinciples/tree/master/Chap2-SimpleNeuralNetwork)

2. The 3 layer Neural Network

A simple representation of a 3 layer Neural Network (NN) with 1 hidden layer is shown below.

Neural Network with 1 hidden layer

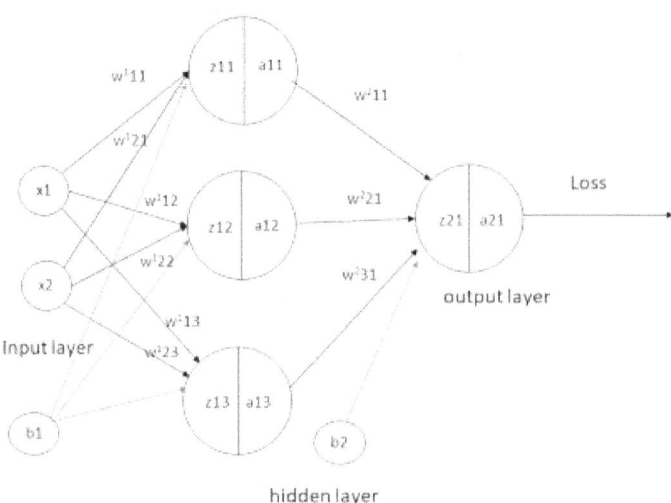

In the above Neural Network, there are two input features at the input layer, three hidden units at the hidden layer and one output layer as it deals with binary classification. The activation unit at the hidden layer can be a tanh, sigmoid, relu etc. At the output layer, the activation is a sigmoid to handle binary classification

Superscript indicates layer '1'

$z_{11} = w^1_{11}x_1 + w^1_{21}x_2 + b_1$
$z_{12} = w^1_{12}x_1 + w^1_{22}x_2 + b_1$
$z_{13} = w^1_{13}x_1 + w^1_{23}x_2 + b_1$

Also $a_{11} = tanh(z_{11})$
$a_{12} = tanh(z_{12})$
$a_{13} = tanh(z_{13})$

Superscript indicates layer '2'

$z_{21} = w^2_{11}a_{11} + w^2_{21}a_{12} + w^2_{31}a_{13} + b_2$
$a_{21} = sigmoid(z_{21})$

Hence

And
$$A1 = \begin{pmatrix} a11 \\ a12 \\ a13 \end{pmatrix} = \begin{pmatrix} tanh(z11) \\ tanh(z12) \\ tanh(z13) \end{pmatrix}$$

Similarly

and $A2 = a_{21} = sigmoid(z_{21})$

These equations can be written as
$Z1 = W1 * X + b1$
$A1 = tanh(Z1)$
$Z2 = W2 * A1 + b2$
$A2 = sigmoid(Z2)$

I) Some important results (a memory refresher!)
$d/dx(e^x) = e^x$ and $d/dx(e^{-x}) = -e^{-x}$ -(a) and
$sinhx = (e^x - e^{-x})/2$ and $coshx = (e^x + e^{-x})/2$

Using (a) we can shown that $d/dx(sinhx) = coshx$ and $d/dx(coshx) = sinhx$ (b)
Now $d/dx(f(x)/g(x)) = (g(x) * d/dx(f(x)) - f(x) * d/dx(g(x)))/g(x)^2$ -(c)
Since $tanhx = z = sinhx/coshx$ and using (c) we get
$tanhx = (coshx * d/dx(sinhx) - sinhx * d/dx(coshx))/cosh^2 x$

Using the values of the derivatives of sinhx and coshx from (b) above we get
$d/dx(tanhx) = (coshx^2 - sinhx2)/coshx2 = 1 - tanhx^2$
Since $tanhx = z$
$d/dx(tanhx) = 1 - tanhx^2 = 1 - z^2$ -(d)

II) Derivatives
The log loss is given below
$L = -(Ylog(A2) + (1 - Y)log(1 - A2))$
$dL/dA2 = -(Y/A2 + (1 - Y)/(1 - A2))$
Since $A2 = sigmoid(Z2)$ therefore $dA2/dZ2 = A2(1 - A2)$ see equation (2) Chapter 1

$Z2 = W2A1 + b2$
Therefore $dZ2/dW2 = A1$ and (e)
$dZ2/db2 = 1$ (f) and
$A1 = tanh(Z1)$ and $dA1/dZ1 = 1 - A1^2$ from (d)
$Z1 = W1X + b1$
$dZ1/dW1 = X$ (g)

$dZ1/db1 = 1$ (h)

III) Back propagation
Using the derivatives from II) we can derive the following results using Chain Rule

$\partial L/\partial Z2 = \partial L/\partial A2 * \partial A2/\partial Z2$
$= -(Y/A2 + (1-Y)/(1-A2)) * A2(1-A2) = A2 - Y$ (i)

$\partial L/\partial W2 = \partial L/\partial A2 * \partial A2/\partial Z2 * \partial Z2/\partial W2$

Using the results of (i) and (e) we get
$= (A2 - Y) * A1$ -(j)

$\partial L/\partial b2 = \partial L/\partial A2 * \partial A2/\partial Z2 * \partial Z2/\partial b2 = (A2 - Y)$ -(k)

And

$\partial L/\partial Z1 = \partial L/\partial A2 * \partial A2/\partial Z2 * \partial Z2/\partial A1 * \partial A1/\partial Z1 = (A2 - Y) * W2 * (1 - A1^2)$

$\partial L/\partial W1 = \partial L/\partial A2 * \partial A2/\partial Z2 * \partial Z2/\partial A1 * \partial A1/\partial Z1 * \partial Z1/\partial W1$

Simplifying we get
$= (A2 - Y) * W2 * (1 - A1^2) * X$ -(l) and

$\partial L/\partial b1 = \partial L/\partial A2 * \partial A2/\partial Z2 * \partial Z2/\partial A1 * dA1/dZ1 * dZ1/db1$
$= (A2 - Y) * W2 * (1 - A1^2)$ -(m)

IV) Gradient Descent
The key computations in the backward cycle are based on the gradient computed above in equations (h), (i),(j) and (k)

$W1 = W1 - learningRate * \partial L/\partial W1$
$b1 = b1 - learningRate * \partial L/\partial b1$
$W2 = W2 - learningRate * \partial L/\partial W2$
$b2 = b2 - learningRate * \partial L/\partial b2$

The weights and biases (W1,b1,W2,b2) are updated for each iteration thus minimizing the loss/cost.

These derivations can be represented pictorially using the computation graph (from the book Deep Learning (http://www.deeplearningbook.org/) by Ian Goodfellow, Joshua Bengio and Aaron

Courville)

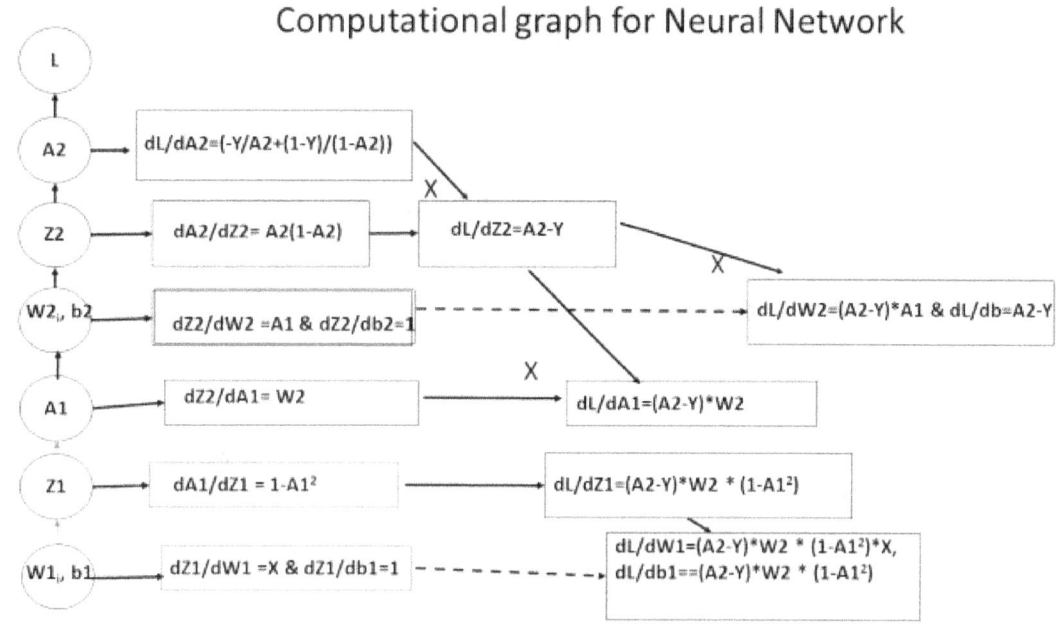

1. Manually create a data set that is not linearly separable

Initially I create a dataset with 2 classes which has around 9 clusters that cannot be separated by linear boundaries. **Note:** *This data set is also saved as data.csv and is used for the R and Octave Neural networks to see how they perform on the same dataset.*

```
1  import numpy as np
2  import matplotlib.pyplot as plt
3  import matplotlib.colors
4  import sklearn.linear_model
5
6  from sklearn.model_selection import train_test_split
7  from sklearn.datasets import make_classification, make_blobs
8  from matplotlib.colors import ListedColormap
9  import sklearn
10 import sklearn.datasets
11
12
13 colors=['black','gold']
14 cmap = matplotlib.colors.ListedColormap(colors)
15 X, y = make_blobs(n_samples = 400, n_features = 2, centers = 7,
16                   cluster_std = 1.3, random_state = 4)
17
18 #Create 2 classes
19 y=y.reshape(400,1)
20 y = y % 2
21
22 #Plot the figure
23 plt.figure()
24 plt.title('Non-linearly separable classes')
```

```
25  plt.scatter(X[:,0], X[:,1], c=y,
26              marker= 'o', s=50,cmap=cmap)
27  plt.savefig('fig1.png', bbox_inches='tight')
```

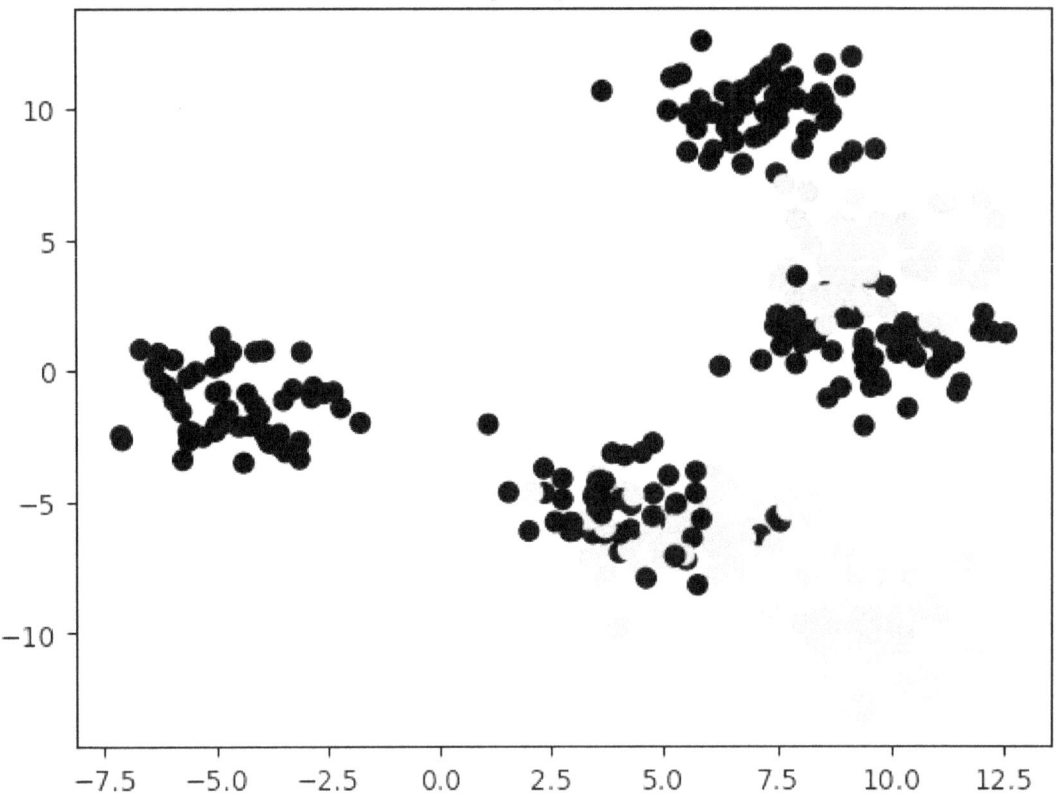

2. Logistic Regression

When classification with logistic regression is performed on the above data set, and the decision boundary is plotted it can be seen that logistic regression performs quite poorly

```
1   import numpy as np
2   import matplotlib.pyplot as plt
3   import matplotlib.colors
4   import sklearn.linear_model
5
6   from sklearn.model_selection import train_test_split
7   from sklearn.datasets import make_classification, make_blobs
8   from matplotlib.colors import ListedColormap
9   import sklearn
10  import sklearn.datasets
11
12  #from DLfunctions import plot_decision_boundary
13  execfile("./DLfunctions.py") # Since import does not work in Rmd!!!
14
15  colors=['black','gold']
16  cmap = matplotlib.colors.ListedColormap(colors)
17  X, y = make_blobs(n_samples = 400, n_features = 2, centers = 7,
18                   cluster_std = 1.3, random_state = 4)
19
```

```
20  #Create 2 classes
21  y=y.reshape(400,1)
22  y = y % 2
23
24  # Train the logistic regression classifier
25  clf = sklearn.linear_model.LogisticRegressionCV();
26  clf.fit(X, y);
27
28  # Plot the decision boundary for logistic regression
29  plot_decision_boundary_n(lambda x: clf.predict(x), X.T, y.T,"fig2.png")
```

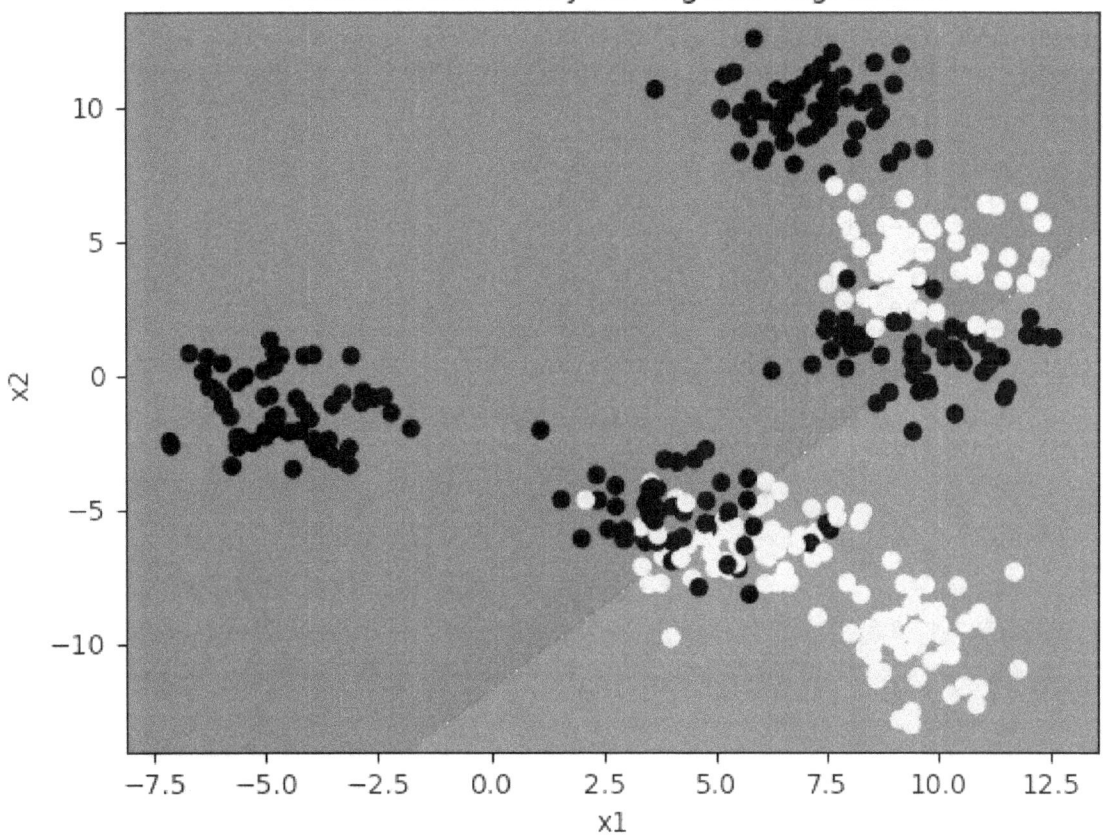

```
30
```

5.1 The 3 layer Neural Network in Python (vectorized)

The vectorized implementation is included below. Note that in the case of Python a learning rate of 0.5 and 3 hidden units performs very well.

```
1  ## Random data set with 9 clusters
2  import numpy as np
3  import matplotlib
4  import matplotlib.pyplot as plt
5  import sklearn.linear_model
6  import pandas as pd
7
8  from sklearn.datasets import make_classification, make_blobs
9  execfile("./DLfunctions.py") # Since import does not work in Rmd!!!
```

```
10
11  X1, Y1 = make_blobs(n_samples = 400, n_features = 2, centers = 9,
12                      cluster_std = 1.3, random_state = 4)
13  #Create 2 classes
14  Y1=Y1.reshape(400,1)
15  Y1 = Y1 % 2
16  X2=X1.T
17  Y2=Y1.T
18
19  # Execute the 3 layer Neural Network
20  parameters,costs = computeNN(X2, Y2, numHidden = 4, learningRate=0.5,
21  numIterations = 10000)
22
23  #Plot the decision boundary
24  plot_decision_boundary(lambda x: predict(parameters, x.T), X2,
25  Y2,str(4),str(0.5),"fig3.png")
26  ## Cost after iteration 0: 0.692669
27  ## Cost after iteration 1000: 0.246650
28  ## Cost after iteration 2000: 0.227801
29  ## Cost after iteration 3000: 0.226809
30  ## Cost after iteration 4000: 0.226518
31  ## Cost after iteration 5000: 0.226331
32  ## Cost after iteration 6000: 0.226194
33  ## Cost after iteration 7000: 0.226085
34  ## Cost after iteration 8000: 0.225994
35  ## Cost after iteration 9000: 0.225915
```

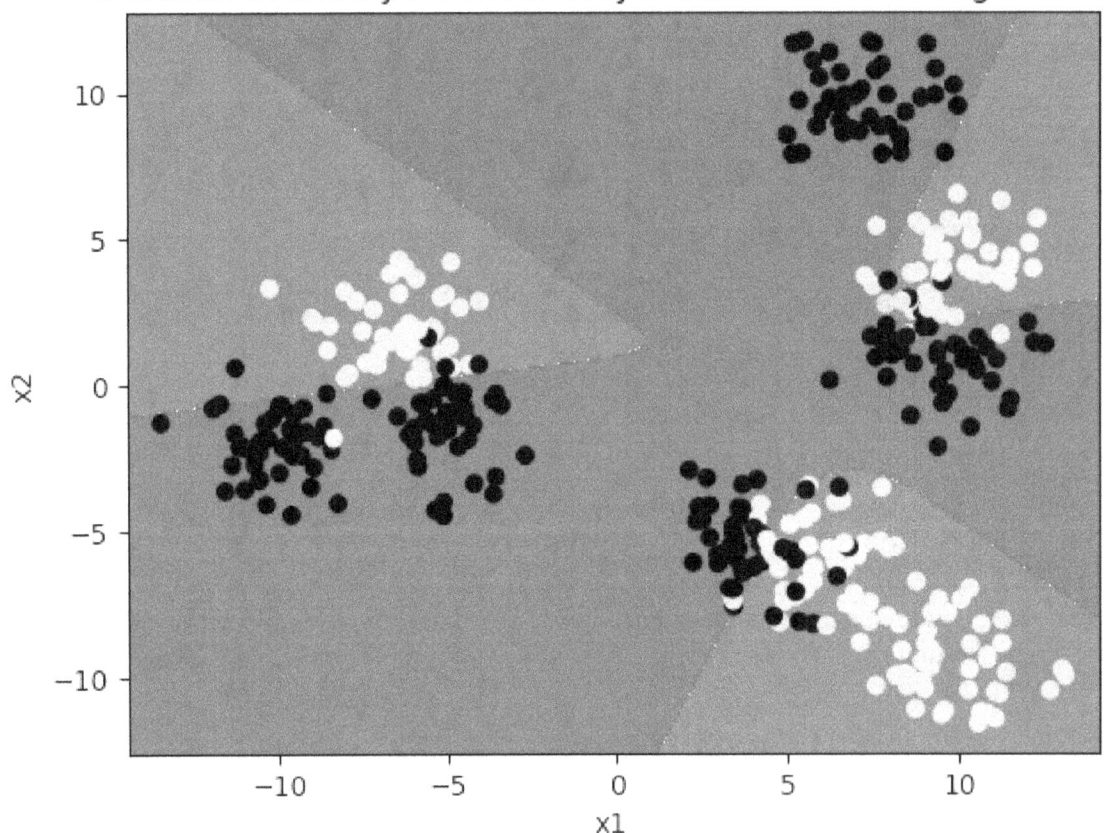

36

It can be seen the the 3 layer Neural Network with a single hidden layer is able to create the non-linear boundary separating the classes

5.2 The 3 layer Neural Network in R (vectorized)

This the dataset created by Python was saved as data.csv. The R code reads this data to see how R performs on the same dataset. The vectorized implementation of a Neural Network in R, was just a little more interesting as R does not have a similar package like 'numpy'. While numpy handles broadcasting implicitly, in R, I had to use the 'sweep' command to broadcast. The implementation is included below. Note that since the initialization with random weights is slightly different, R performs best with a learning rate of 0.1 and with 6 hidden units

```r
source("DLfunctions2_1.R")
z <- as.matrix(read.csv("data.csv",header=FALSE)) #
x <- z[,1:2]
y <- z[,3]
x1 <- t(x)
y1 <- t(y)

# Execute the 3 layer Neural Network
nn <-computeNN(x1, y1, 6, learningRate=0.1,numIterations=10000) # Good
## [1] 0.7075341
## [1] 0.2606695
## [1] 0.2198039
## [1] 0.2091238
## [1] 0.211146
## [1] 0.2108461
## [1] 0.2105351
## [1] 0.210211
## [1] 0.2099104
## [1] 0.2096437
## [1] 0.209409

plotDecisionBoundary(z,nn,6,0.1)
```

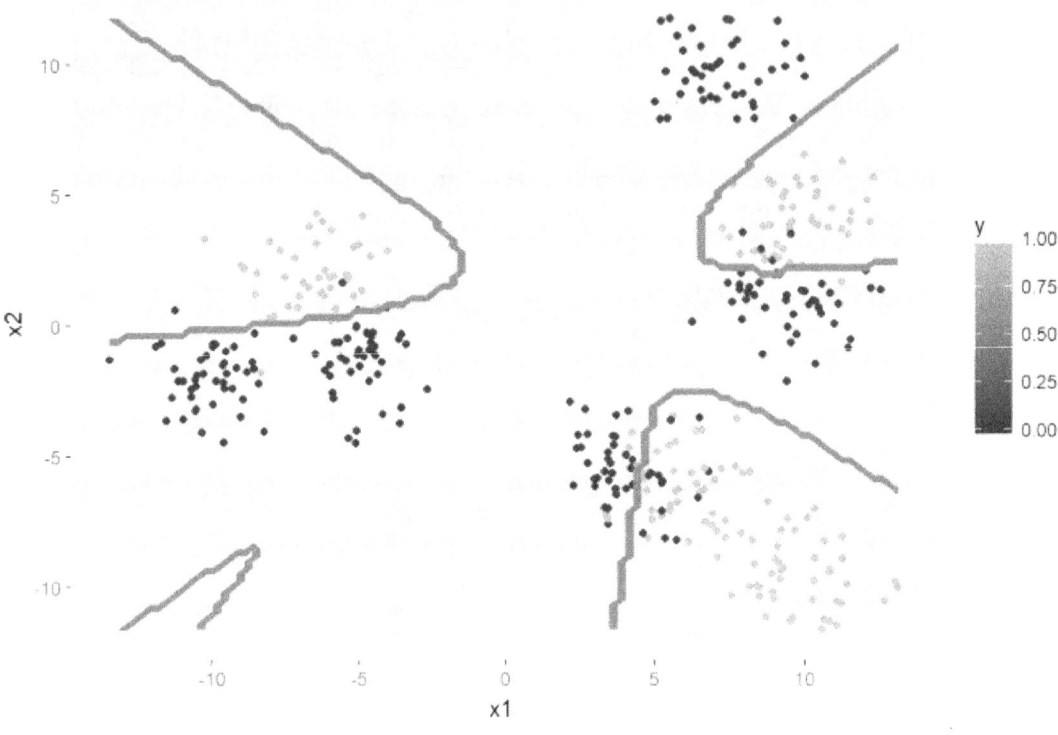

R is also able to create the non-linear boundary.

5.3 The 3 layer Neural Network in Octave (vectorized)

This uses the same dataset (data.csv) that was generated using Python code.

```
1
2  source("DL-function2.m")
3  # Read the data
4  data=csvread("data.csv");
5  X=data(:,1:2);
6  Y=data(:,3);
7
8  # Make sure that the model parameters are correct. Take the transpose of X &
9  Y
10 # Execute the 3 layer Neural Network and plot decision boundary
11 [W1,b1,W2,b2,costs]= computeNN(X', Y',4, learningRate=0.5, numIterations =
12 10000);
```

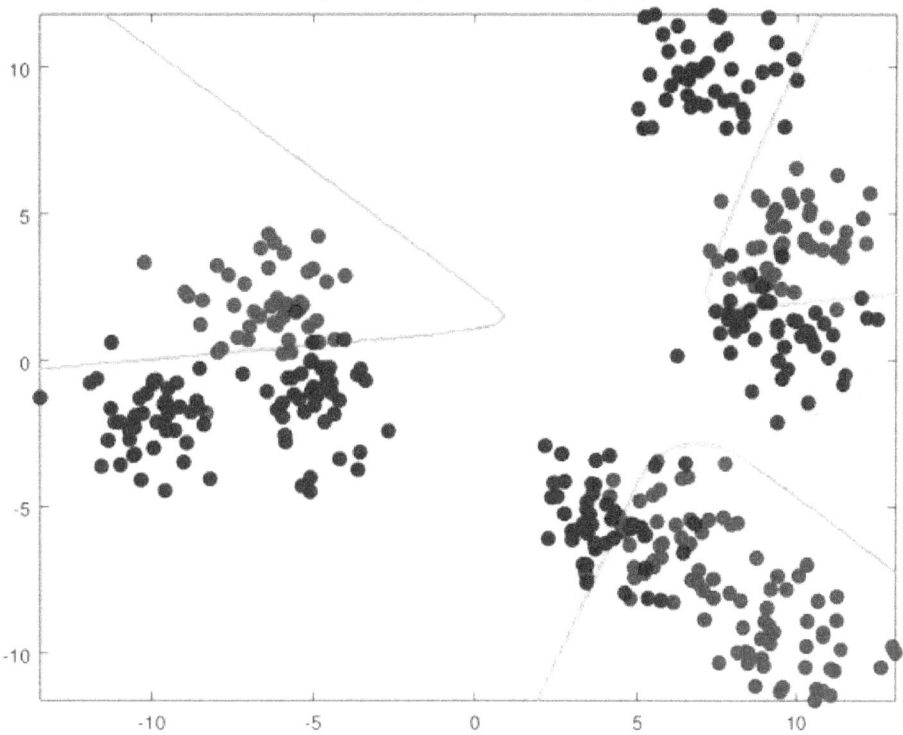

The above plot shows the non-linear boundary created by Octave.

6.1a Performance for different learning rates (Python)

```
1  import numpy as np
2  import matplotlib
3  import matplotlib.pyplot as plt
4  import sklearn.linear_model
5  import pandas as pd
6
7  from sklearn.datasets import make_classification, make_blobs
8  execfile("./DLfunctions.py") # Since import does not work in Rmd!!!
9
10 # Create data
11 X1, Y1 = make_blobs(n_samples = 400, n_features = 2, centers = 9,
12                     cluster_std = 1.3, random_state = 4)
13
14 #Create 2 classes
15 Y1=Y1.reshape(400,1)
16 Y1 = Y1 % 2
17 X2=X1.T
18 Y2=Y1.T
19
20 # Create a list of learning rates
21 learningRate=[0.5,1.2,3.0]
22 df=pd.DataFrame()
23
24 #Compute costs for each learning rate
25 for lr in learningRate:
26     # Execute the 3 layer Neural Network
```

```
27      parameters,costs = computeNN(X2, Y2, numHidden = 4, learningRate=lr,
28 numIterations = 10000)
29      print(costs)
30      df1=pd.DataFrame(costs)
31      df=pd.concat([df,df1],axis=1)
32
33 #Set the iterations
34 iterations=[0,1000,2000,3000,4000,5000,6000,7000,8000,9000]
35
36 #Create data frame
37 #Set index
38 df1=df.set_index([iterations])
39 df1.columns=[0.5,1.2,3.0]
40
41 # Plot cost vs number of iterations for different learning rates
42 fig=df1.plot()
43 fig=plt.title("Cost vs No of Iterations for different learning rates")
44 plt.savefig('fig4.png', bbox_inches='tight')
```

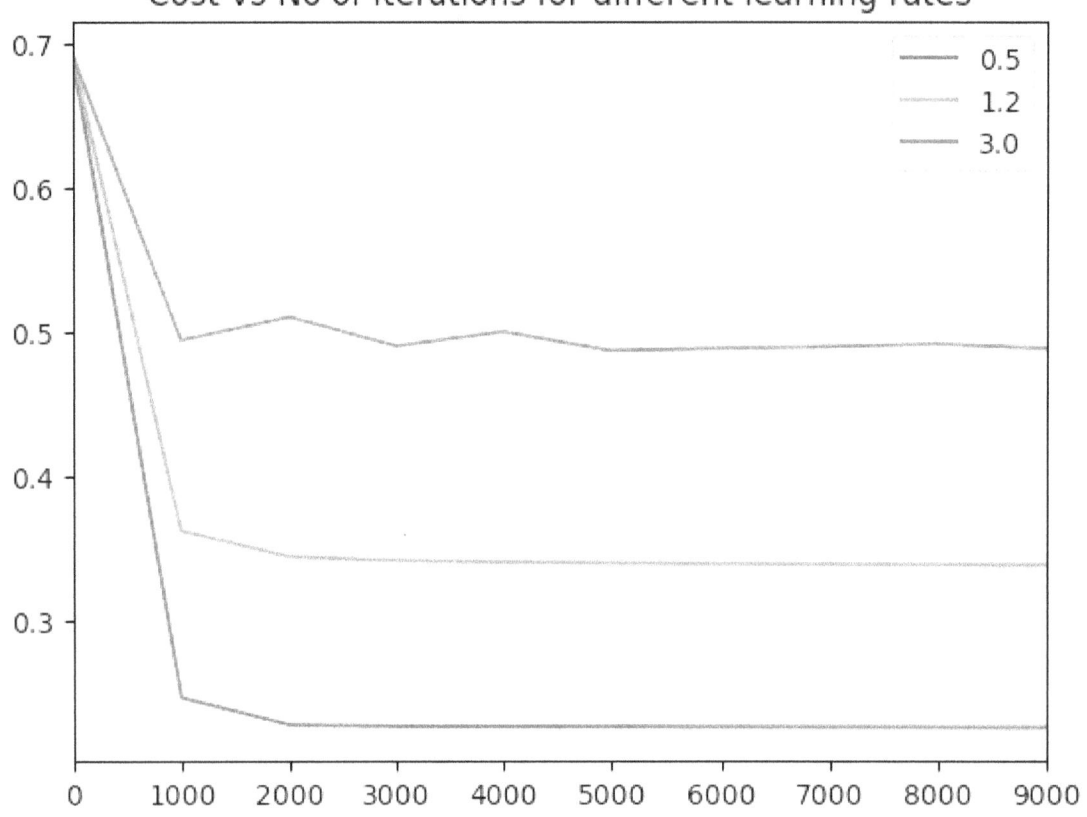

6.1b Performance for different hidden units (Python)

```
1 import numpy as np
2 import matplotlib
3 import matplotlib.pyplot as plt
4 import sklearn.linear_model
5 import pandas as pd
6
7 from sklearn.datasets import make_classification, make_blobs
8 execfile("./DLfunctions.py") # Since import does not work in Rmd!!!
```

```python
#Create data set
X1, Y1 = make_blobs(n_samples = 400, n_features = 2, centers = 9,
                    cluster_std = 1.3, random_state = 4)

#Create 2 classes
Y1=Y1.reshape(400,1)
Y1 = Y1 % 2
X2=X1.T
Y2=Y1.T

# Make a list of hidden unis
numHidden=[3,5,7]
df=pd.DataFrame()
#Compute costs for different hidden units
for numHid in numHidden:
    # Execute the 3 layer Neural Network
    parameters,costs = computeNN(X2, Y2, numHidden = numHid, learningRate=1.2, numIterations = 10000)
    print(costs)
    df1=pd.DataFrame(costs)
    df=pd.concat([df,df1],axis=1)

#Set the iterations
iterations=[0,1000,2000,3000,4000,5000,6000,7000,8000,9000]
#Set index
df1=df.set_index([iterations])

#Plot the cost vs iterations for different number of hidden units
df1.columns=[3,5,7]
#Plot
fig=df1.plot()
fig=plt.title("Cost vs No of Iterations for different no of hidden units")
plt.savefig('fig5.png', bbox_inches='tight')
```

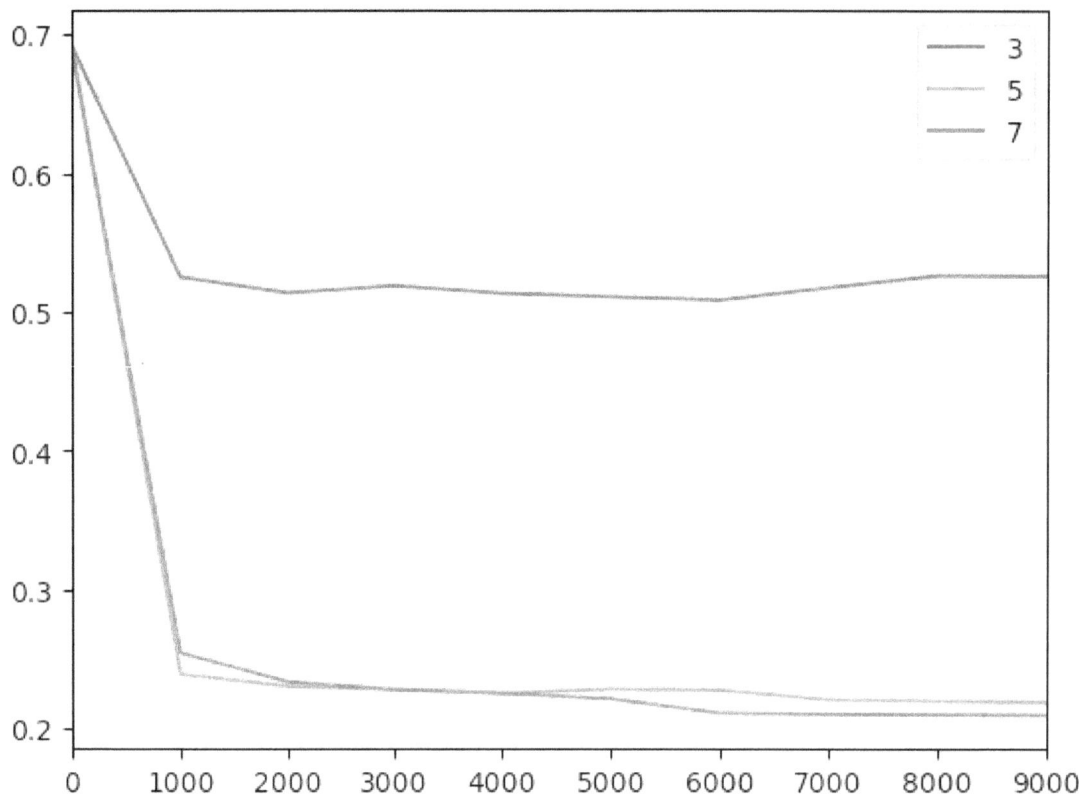

6.2a Performance for different learning rates (R)

```r
source("DLfunctions2_1.R")

# Read data
z <- as.matrix(read.csv("data.csv",header=FALSE)) #
x <- z[,1:2]
y <- z[,3]
x1 <- t(x)
y1 <- t(y)

#Loop through learning rates and compute costs
learningRate <-c(0.1,1.2,3.0)
df <- NULL
for(i in seq_along(learningRate)){
    # Execute the 3 layer Neural Network
    nn <-  computeNN(x1, y1, 6,
learningRate=learningRate[i],numIterations=10000)
    cost <- nn$costs
    df <- cbind(df,cost)

}

#Create dataframe
df <- data.frame(df)
iterations=seq(0,10000,by=1000)
df <- cbind(iterations,df)
names(df) <- c("iterations","0.5","1.2","3.0")

# Reshape the data
```

```r
library(reshape2)
df1 <- melt(df,id="iterations")   # Melt the data

#Plot  the cost vs iterations for different learning rates
ggplot(df1) + geom_line(aes(x=iterations,y=value,colour=variable),size=1)  +
    xlab("Iterations") +
    ylab('Cost') + ggtitle("Cost vs No iterations for  different learning rates")
```

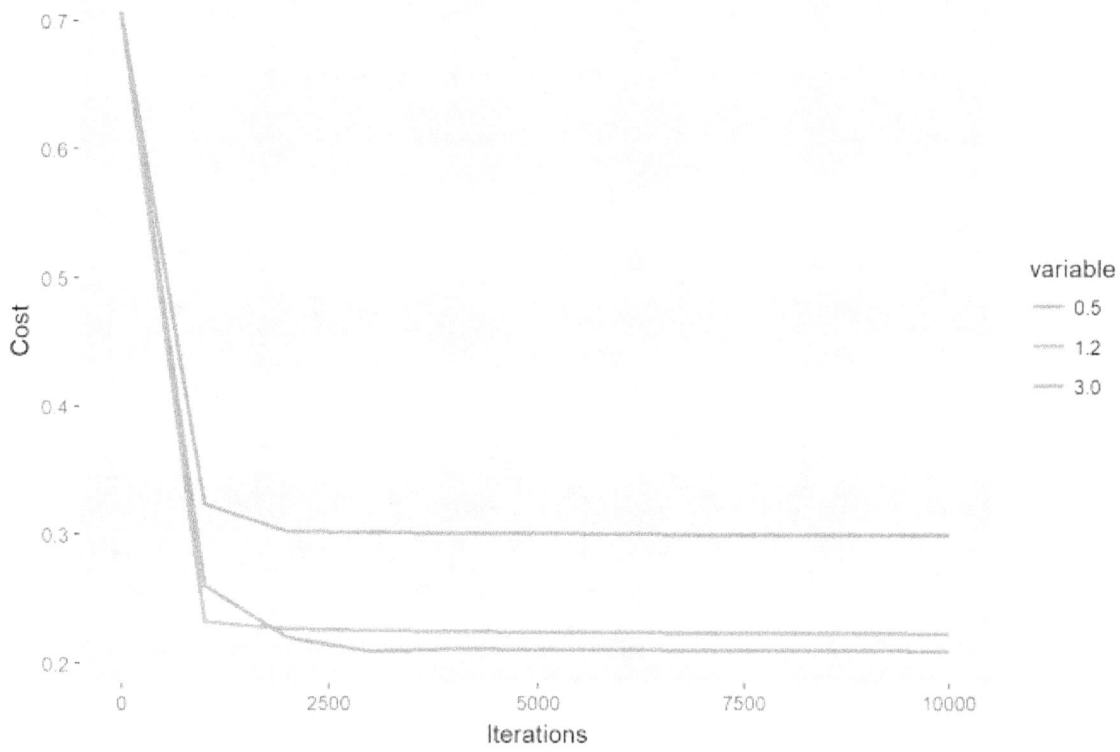

6.2b Performance for different hidden units (R)

```r
source("DLfunctions2_1.R")
# Loop through number of  hidden units
numHidden <-c(4,6,9)
df <- NULL
for(i in seq_along(numHidden)){
    # Execute the 3 layer Neural Network
    nn <-   computeNN(x1, y1, numHidden[i], learningRate=0.1,numIterations=10000)
    cost <- nn$costs
    df <- cbind(df,cost)

}

#Create a dataframe
df <- data.frame(df)
iterations=seq(0,10000,by=1000)
df <- cbind(iterations,df)
names(df) <- c("iterations","4","6","9")
```

```
20  #Reshape the dataframe
21  library(reshape2)
22  # Melt
23  df1 <- melt(df,id="iterations")
24
25  # Plot   cost vs iterations for different number of hidden units
26  ggplot(df1) + geom_line(aes(x=iterations,y=value,colour=variable),size=1)  +
27      xlab("Iterations") +
28      ylab('Cost') + ggtitle("Cost vs No iterations for  different number of
29  hidden units")
```

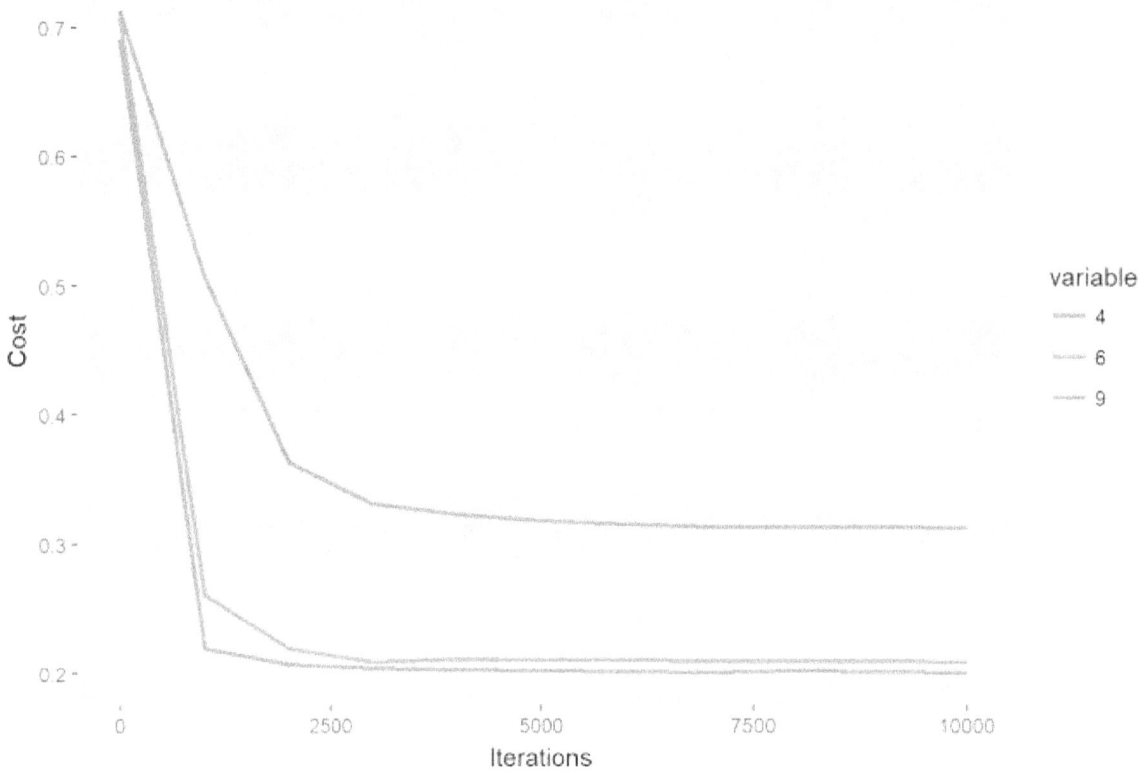

6.3a Performance of the Neural Network for different learning rates (Octave)

```
1  source("DL-function2.m")
2  #Plot cost vs iterations for different learning rates
3  plotLRCostVsIterations()
4  print -djph figa.jpg
```

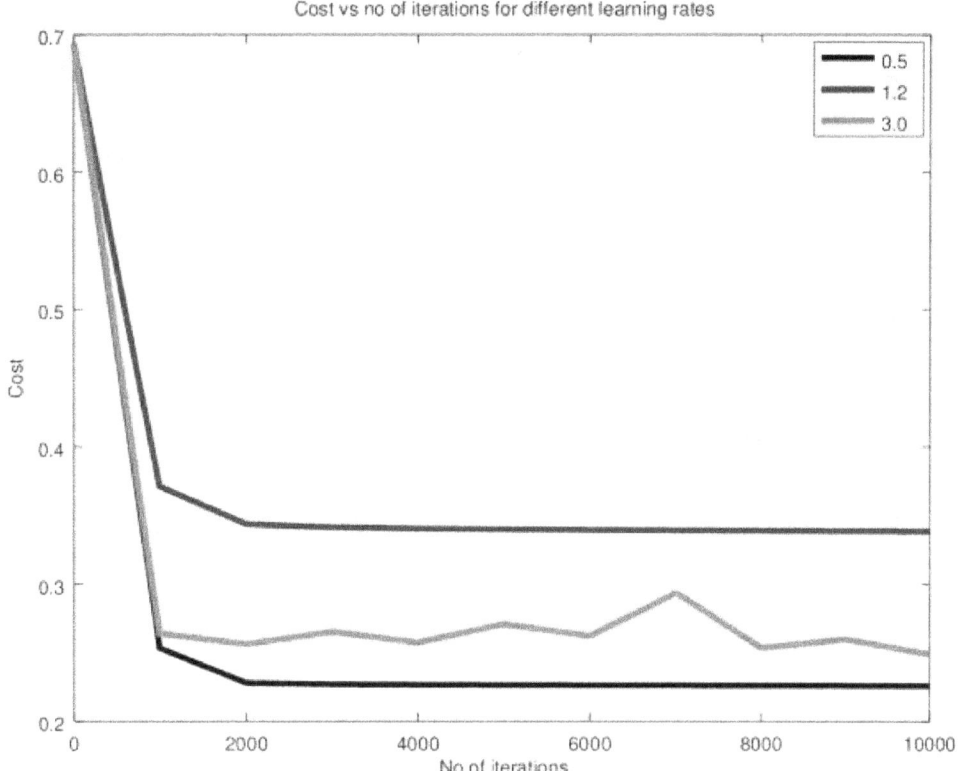

6.3b Performance of the Neural Network for different number of hidden units (Octave)

```
1  source("DL-function2.m")
2  #Plot cost vs Iterations for different number of hidden units
3  plotHiddenCostVsIterations()
4  print -djph figa.jpg
```

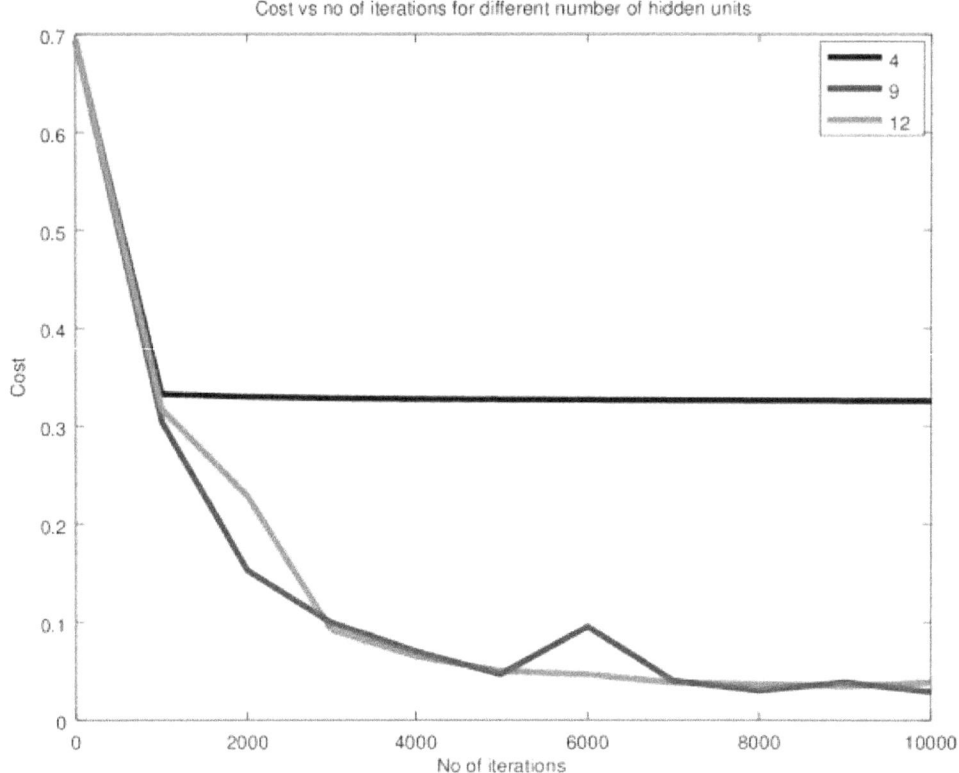

7. Turning the heat on the Neural Network

In this 2nd part, I create a central region of positives and an outside region as negatives. The points are generated using the equation of a circle $(x - a)^2 + (y - b)^2 = R^2$. How does the 3-layer Neural Network perform on this? Here's a look! **Note**: R *and Octave Neural Network constructions also use the same data set.*

8. Manually creating a circular central region

```
import numpy as np
import matplotlib.pyplot as plt
import matplotlib.colors
import sklearn.linear_model

from sklearn.model_selection import train_test_split
from sklearn.datasets import make_classification, make_blobs
from matplotlib.colors import ListedColormap
import sklearn
import sklearn.datasets

colors=['black','gold']
cmap = matplotlib.colors.ListedColormap(colors)
x1=np.random.uniform(0,10,800).reshape(800,1)
x2=np.random.uniform(0,10,800).reshape(800,1)
X=np.append(x1,x2,axis=1)
X.shape

```

```
19  # Create the data set with  (x-a)^2 + (y-b)^2 = R^2
20  # Create a subset of values where squared is <0,4. Perform ravel() to flatten
21  this vector
22  a=(np.power(X[:,0]-5,2) + np.power(X[:,1]-5,2) <= 6).ravel()
23  Y=a.reshape(800,1)
24
25  cmap = matplotlib.colors.ListedColormap(colors)
26
27  #Plot the dataset
28  plt.figure()
29  plt.title('Non-linearly separable classes')
30  plt.scatter(X[:,0], X[:,1], c=Y,
31              marker= 'o', s=15,cmap=cmap)
32  plt.savefig('fig6.png', bbox_inches='tight')
```

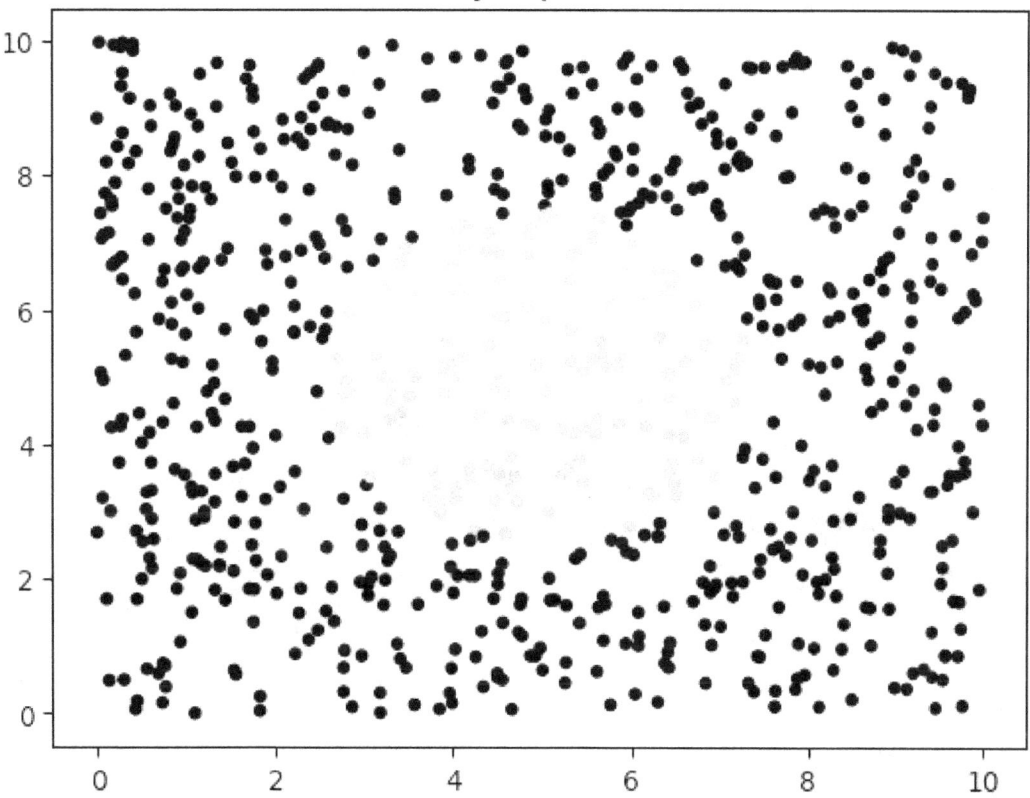

8.1a Decision boundary with hidden units=4 and learning rate = 2.2 (Python)

With the above hyper-parameters, the decision boundary is triangular

```
1  import numpy as np
2  import matplotlib.pyplot as plt
3  import matplotlib.colors
4  import sklearn.linear_model
5
6  execfile("./DLfunctions.py")
7  x1=np.random.uniform(0,10,800).reshape(800,1)
8  x2=np.random.uniform(0,10,800).reshape(800,1)
9  X=np.append(x1,x2,axis=1)
```

```
10  X.shape
11
12  # Create a subset of values where squared is <0,4. Perform ravel() to flatten
13  this vector
14  a=(np.power(X[:,0]-5,2) + np.power(X[:,1]-5,2) <= 6).ravel()
15  Y=a.reshape(800,1)
16
17  X2=X.T
18  Y2=Y.T
19
20  # Execute the 3 layer Neural network
21  parameters,costs = computeNN(X2, Y2, numHidden = 4, learningRate=2.2,
22  numIterations = 10000)
23
24  #Plot the decision boundary
25  plot_decision_boundary(lambda x: predict(parameters, x.T), X2,
26  Y2,str(4),str(2.2),"fig7.png")
27  ## Cost after iteration 0: 0.692836
28  ## Cost after iteration 1000: 0.331052
29  ## Cost after iteration 2000: 0.326428
30  ## Cost after iteration 3000: 0.474887
31  ## Cost after iteration 4000: 0.247989
32  ## Cost after iteration 5000: 0.218009
33  ## Cost after iteration 6000: 0.201034
34  ## Cost after iteration 7000: 0.197030
35  ## Cost after iteration 8000: 0.193507
36  ## Cost after iteration 9000: 0.191949
```

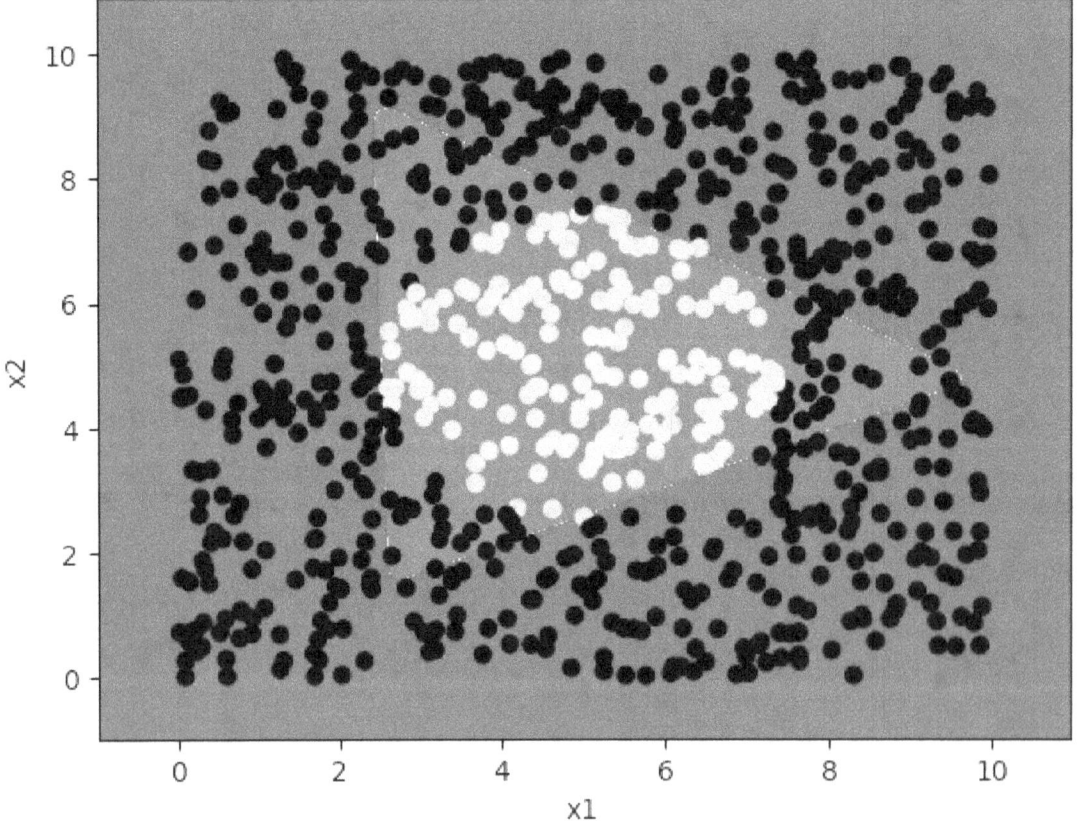

8.1b Decision boundary with hidden units=12 and learning rate = 2.2 (Python)

Increasing the number of hidden units makes the decision boundary much more circular

```
1  import numpy as np
2  import matplotlib.pyplot as plt
3  import matplotlib.colors
4  import sklearn.linear_model
5  execfile("./DLfunctions.py")
6
7  x1=np.random.uniform(0,10,800).reshape(800,1)
8  x2=np.random.uniform(0,10,800).reshape(800,1)
9  X=np.append(x1,x2,axis=1)
10 X.shape
11
12 # Create a subset of values where squared is <0,4. Perform ravel() to flatten
13 this vector
14 a=(np.power(X[:,0]-5,2) + np.power(X[:,1]-5,2) <= 6).ravel()
15 Y=a.reshape(800,1)
16 X2=X.T
17 Y2=Y.T
18
19 # Execute the 3 layer Neural network
20 parameters,costs = computeNN(X2, Y2, numHidden = 12, learningRate=2.2,
21 numIterations = 10000)
22
23 #Plot the decision boundary
24 plot_decision_boundary(lambda x: predict(parameters, x.T), X2,
25 Y2,str(12),str(2.2),"fig8.png")
26 ## Cost after iteration 0: 0.693291
27 ## Cost after iteration 1000: 0.383318
28 ## Cost after iteration 2000: 0.298807
29 ## Cost after iteration 3000: 0.251735
30 ## Cost after iteration 4000: 0.177843
31 ## Cost after iteration 5000: 0.130414
32 ## Cost after iteration 6000: 0.152400
33 ## Cost after iteration 7000: 0.065359
34 ## Cost after iteration 8000: 0.050921
35 ## Cost after iteration 9000: 0.039719
```

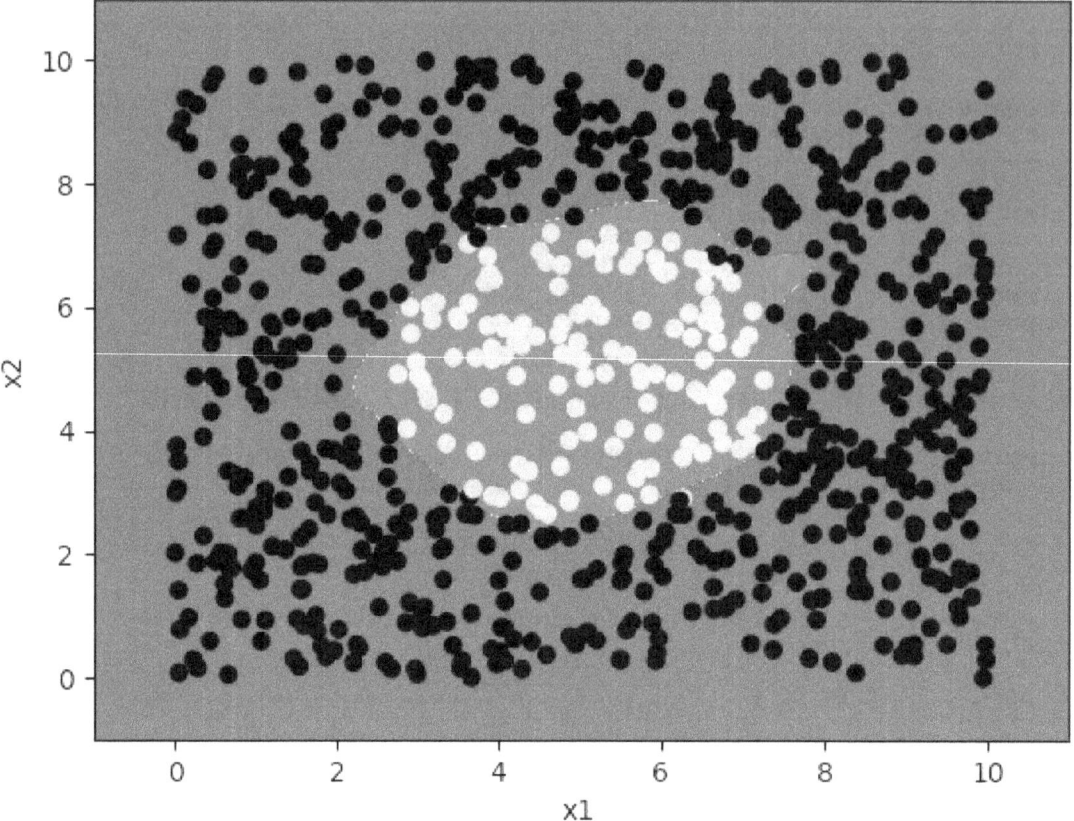

8.2a Decision boundary with hidden units=9 and learning rate = 0.5 (R)

When the number of hidden units is 6 and the learning rate is 0.5, is also a triangular shape in R

```
1  source("DLfunctions2_1.R")
2  z <- as.matrix(read.csv("data1.csv",header=FALSE)) # N
3  x <- z[,1:2]
4  y <- z[,3]
5  x1 <- t(x)
6  y1 <- t(y)
7
8  # Execute the 3 layer Neural network
9  nn <-computeNN(x1, y1, 9, learningRate=0.5,numIterations=10000) # Triangular
10 ## [1] 0.8398838
11 ## [1] 0.3303621
12 ## [1] 0.3127731
13 ## [1] 0.3012791
14 ## [1] 0.3305543
15 ## [1] 0.3303964
16 ## [1] 0.2334615
17 ## [1] 0.1920771
18 ## [1] 0.2341225
19 ## [1] 0.2188118
20 ## [1] 0.2082687
21
22 #Plot the decision boundary
23 plotDecisionBoundary(z,nn,6,0.1)
```

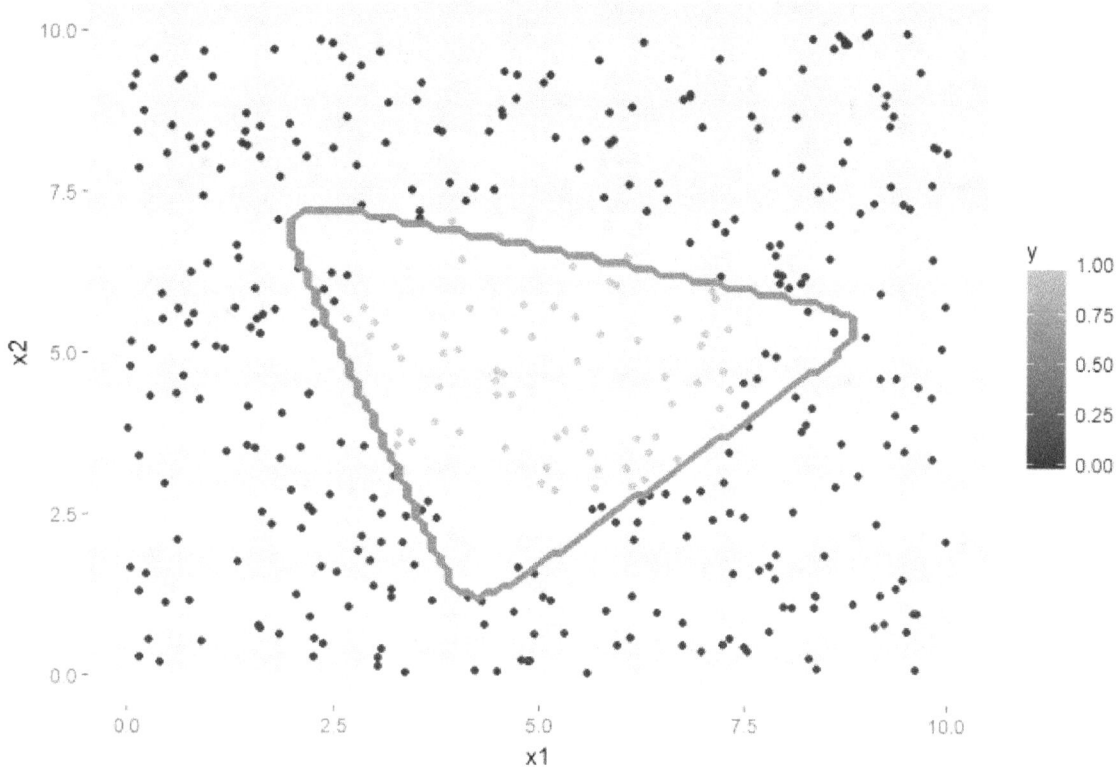

Decision boundary for hidden layer size: 6 learning rate: 0.1

8.2b Decision boundary with hidden units=8 and learning rate = 0.1 (R)

With 8 hidden units the decision boundary is quite circular.

```
source("DLfunctions2_1.R")
z <- as.matrix(read.csv("data1.csv",header=FALSE)) # N
x <- z[,1:2]
y <- z[,3]
x1 <- t(x)
y1 <- t(y)

# Execute the 3 layer Neural network
nn <-computeNN(x1, y1, 8, learningRate=0.1,numIterations=10000) # Hemisphere
## [1] 0.7273279
## [1] 0.3169335
## [1] 0.2378464
## [1] 0.1688635
## [1] 0.1368466
## [1] 0.120664
## [1] 0.111211
## [1] 0.1043362
## [1] 0.09800573
## [1] 0.09126161
## [1] 0.0840379

#Plot the decision boundary
plotDecisionBoundary(z,nn,8,0.1)
```

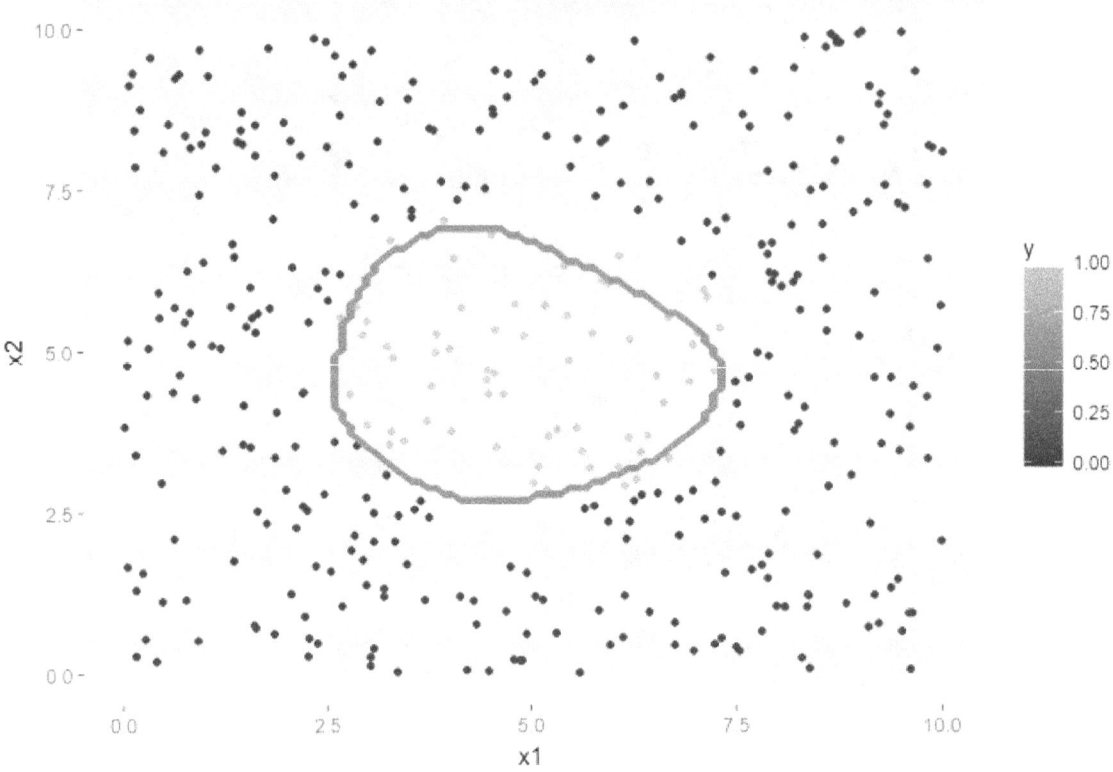

8.3a Decision boundary with hidden units=12 and learning rate = 1.5 (Octave)

```
1  source("DL-function2.m")
2  # Read the data
3  data=csvread("data1.csv");
4  X=data(:,1:2);
5  Y=data(:,3);
6
7  # Make sure that the model parameters are correct. Take the transpose of X &
8  Y
9  # Execute the 3 layer Neural network
10 [W1,b1,W2,b2,costs]= computeNN(X', Y',12, learningRate=1.5, numIterations =
11 10000);
12
13 #Plot the decision boundary
14 plotDecisionBoundary(data, W1,b1,W2,b2)
15 print -djpg fige.jpg
```

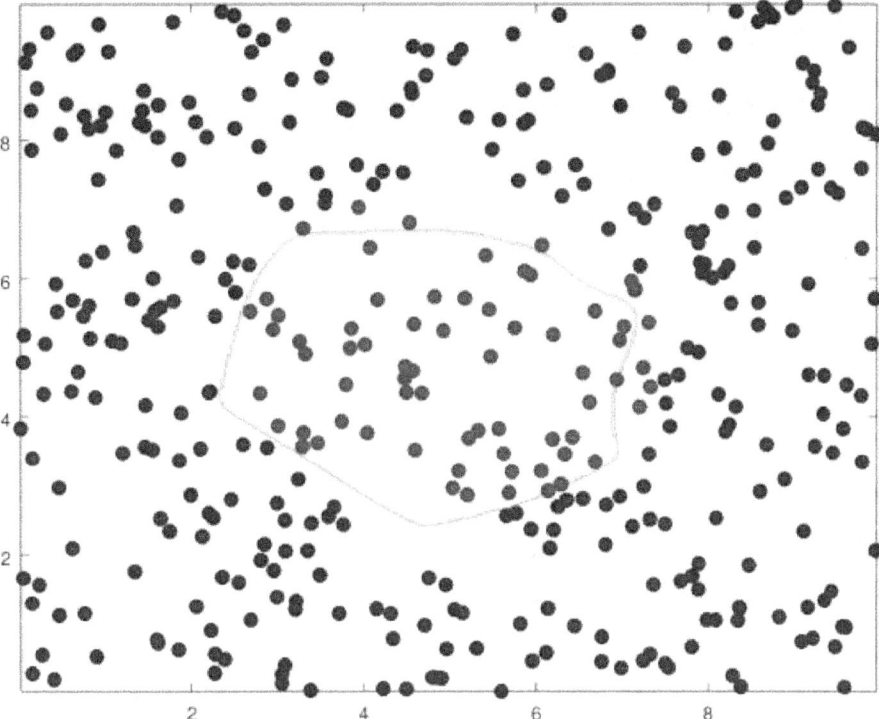

9. Conclusion

This chapter implemented a 3-layer Neural Network to create non-linear boundaries while performing classification. Clearly, the Neural Network performs very well when the number of hidden units and learning rate are varied.

3. Building a L- Layer Deep Learning Network

"Once upon a time, I, Chuang Tzu, dreamt I was a butterfly, fluttering hither and thither, to all intents and purposes a butterfly. I was conscious only of following my fancies as a butterfly, and was unconscious of my individuality as a man. Suddenly, I awoke, and there I lay, myself again. Now I do not know whether I was then a man dreaming I was a butterfly, or whether I am now a butterfly dreaming that I am a man."
from The Brain: The Story of you – David Eagleman

"Thought is a great big vector of neural activity"
Prof Geoffrey Hinton

1. Introduction

This is the third chapter in my series on Deep Learning from first principles in Python, R and Octave. In this third chapter, I implement a multi-layer, Deep Learning (DL) network of arbitrary depth (any number of hidden layers), and arbitrary height (any number of activation units in each hidden layer). The implementation in the 3rd part is for an L-layer Deep Network, but without any regularization, early stopping, momentum or learning rate adaptation techniques. However even this barebones multi-layer DL, is a handful and has enough hyper-parameters to fine-tune and adjust. The implementation of the vectorized L-layer Deep Learning network in Python, R and Octave is quite challenging, as we need to keep track of the indices, layer number and matrix dimensions. Some challenges because of the differences in the languages

1. Python and Octave allow multiple return values to be unpacked in a single statement. With R, unpacking multiple return values from a list, requires the entire to be list returned, and then unpacked separately. I did see that there is a package gsubfn
 https://stackoverflow.com/questions/1826519/how-to-assign-from-a-function-which-returns-more-than-one-value , which does this.
2. Python and R can save and return dissimilar elements from functions using dictionaries or lists respectively. However, there is no real equivalent in Octave. The closest I got to this functionality in Octave, was the 'cell array'. But, the cell array can be accessed only by the index, and not with the key as in a Python dictionary or R list. This makes things just a bit more difficult in Octave.
3. Python and Octave include implicit broadcasting. In R, broadcasting is not implicit, but R has a nifty function, the sweep(), with which we can broadcast either by columns or by rows
4. The closest equivalent of Python's dictionary, or R's list, in Octave is the cell array. However I had to manage separate cell arrays for weights and biases and during gradient descent and separate gradients dW and dB
5. In Python, the rank-1 numpy arrays can be annoying at times. This issue is not present in R and Octave.
The current vectorized implementation supports the relu, sigmoid and tanh activation functions.

While testing with different hyper-parameters namely i) the number of hidden layers, ii) the number of activation units in each layer, iii) the activation function and iv) the number iterations, I found the L-layer Deep Learning Network to be very sensitive to these hyper-parameters. It is not easy to tune the parameters. Adding more hidden layers, or more units per layer, does not help always, and sometimes results in gradient descent getting stuck in some local minima. It does take a fair amount of trial and error and very close observation on how the Deep Learning network performs for logical changes. We then can zero in on the most the optimal solution. A much more detailed approach for tuning hyper-paramaters is discussed in chapter 8. The Python,R and Octave functions used in this chapter are implemented in Appendix 3 - Building a L- Layer Deep Learning Network

Feel free to download/fork my code from Github DeepLearningFromFirstPrinciples (https://github.com/tvganesh/DeepLearningFromFirstPrinciples/tree/master/Chap3-L-LayerDeepLearningNetwork) and play around with the hyper-parameters for your own problems.

2. Derivation of a Multi Layer Deep Learning Network

Let's take a simple 3 layer Neural network with 3 hidden layers and an output layer

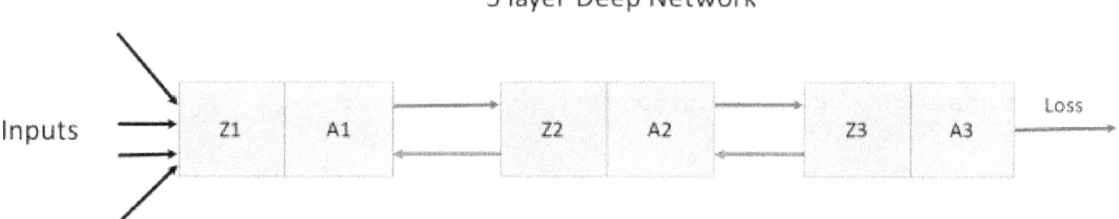

3 layer Deep Network

In the forward propagation cycle the equations are

$Z_1 = W_1 A_0 + b_1$ and $A_1 = g(Z_1)$
$Z_2 = W_2 A_1 + b_2$ and $A_2 = g(Z_2)$
$Z_3 = W_3 A_2 + b_3$ and $A_3 = g(Z_3)$

The loss function is given by
$L = -(y \log A3 + (1-y) \log(1 - A3))$
and $dL/dA3 = -(Y/A_3 + (1-Y)/(1-A_3))$

For a binary classification, the output activation function is the sigmoid function given by $A_3 = 1/(1 + e^{-Z_3})$. Hence
$dA_3/dZ_3 = A_3(1 - A_3)$ see equation (2) in chapter 1
$\partial L/\partial Z_3 = \partial L/\partial A_3 * \partial A_3/\partial Z_3 = A3 - Y$ see equation (f) in chapter 1

and since
$\partial L/\partial A_2 = \partial L/\partial Z_3 * \partial Z_3/\partial A_2 = (A_3 - Y) * W_3$ because $\partial Z_3/\partial A_2 = W_3$ -(1a)

and $\partial L/\partial Z_2 = \partial L/\partial A_2 * \partial A_2/\partial Z_2 = (A_3 - Y) * W_3 * g'(Z_2)$ -(1b)

$\partial L/\partial W_2 = \partial L/\partial Z_2 * A_1$ -(1c)

since $\partial Z_2/\partial W_2 = A_1$

and

$\partial L/\partial b_2 = \partial L/\partial Z_2$ -(1d)

because

$\partial Z_2/\partial b_2 = 1$

Also

$\partial L/\partial A_1 = \partial L/\partial Z_2 * \partial Z_2/\partial A_1 = \partial L/\partial Z_2 * W_2$ – (2a)

$\partial L/\partial Z_1 = \partial L/\partial A_1 * \partial A_1/\partial Z_1 = \partial L/\partial A_1 * W_2 * g'(Z_1)$ – (2b)

$\partial L/\partial W_1 = \partial L/\partial Z_1 * A_0$ – (2c)

$\partial L/\partial b_1 = \partial L/\partial Z_1$ – (2d)

Inspecting the above equations (1a – 1d & 2a-2d), we can discern a pattern in these equations and we can write the equations for any layer 'l' as

$Z_l = W_l A_{l-1} + b_l$ and $A_l = g(Z_l)$

The equations for the backward propagation have the general form

$\partial L/\partial A_l = \partial L/\partial Z_{l+1} * W^{l+1}$

$\partial L/\partial Z_l = \partial L/\partial A_l * g'(Z_l)$

$\partial L/\partial W_l = \partial L/\partial Z_l * A^{l-1}$

$\partial L/\partial b_l = \partial L/\partial Z_l$

Other important results

The derivatives of the activation functions in the implemented Deep Learning network

$g(z) = \text{sigmoid}(z) = 1/(1 + e^{-z}) = a$ $g'(z) = a(1-a)$ – See equation (2) chapter 1

$g(z) = \tanh(z) = a$ $g'(z) = 1 - a^2$ See equation (d) chapter 2

$g(z) = \text{relu}(z) = z$ when $z>0$ and 0 when z 0 and 0 when $z <= 0$

The implementation of the multi-layer vectorized Deep Learning Network for Python, R and Octave is included below. For all these implementations, initially I create the size and configuration of the Deep Learning network with the layer dimensions. So, for example layersDimension Vector 'V' of length L indicating 'L' layers where

V (in Python) = $[c_0, c_1, c_2, \ldots, c_{L-1}]$

V (in R) = $c(c_1, c_2, c_3, \ldots, c_L)$

V (in Octave) = $[c_1 c_2 c_3 \ldots c_L]$

In all of these implementations, the first element is the number of input features to the Deep Learning network and the last element is always a 'sigmoid' activation function since all the problems deal with binary classification.

The number of elements between the first and the last element are the number of hidden layers and the magnitude of each is the number of activation units in each hidden layer, which is specified while actually executing the Deep Learning network using the function L_Layer_DeepModel(), in all the implementations Python, R and Octave

2.1a Classification with Multi-layer Deep Learning Network – Relu activation(Python)

In the code below a 4-layer Neural Network is trained to generate a non-linear boundary between the classes. In the code below the 'Relu' Activation function is used. The number of activation units in each layer is 9. The cost vs iterations is plotted. In addition to the decision boundary. Further, the accuracy, precision, recall and F1 score are also computed

```
1  import os
2  import numpy as np
3  import matplotlib.pyplot as plt
4  import matplotlib.colors
5  import sklearn.linear_model
6
7  from sklearn.model_selection import train_test_split
8  from sklearn.datasets import make_classification, make_blobs
9  from matplotlib.colors import ListedColormap
10 import sklearn
11 import sklearn.datasets
12
13 #from DLfunctions import plot_decision_boundary
14 execfile("./DLfunctions34.py") #
15
16 # Create clusters of 2 classes
17 X1, Y1 = make_blobs(n_samples = 400, n_features = 2, centers = 9,
18                     cluster_std = 1.3, random_state = 4)
19
20 #Create 2 classes
21 Y1=Y1.reshape(400,1)
22 Y1 = Y1 % 2
23 X2=X1.T
24 Y2=Y1.T
25
26 # Set the dimensions of DL Network
27 #   Below we have
28 #   2 - 2 input features
29 #   9,9 - 2 hidden layers with 9 activation units per layer and
30 #   1 - 1 sigmoid activation unit in the output layer as this is a binary
31 classification
32 # The activation in the hidden layer is the 'relu' specified in
33 L_Layer_DeepModel
34
35 layersDimensions = [2, 9, 9,1] #  4-layer model
36
37 # Execute the L-layer Deep Learning network
38 # Hidden layer activation unit - relu
```

```
# Learning rate - 0.3
parameters = L_Layer_DeepModel(X2, Y2,
layersDimensions,hiddenActivationFunc='relu', learning_rate =
0.3,num_iterations = 2500, fig="fig1.png")

#Plot the decision boundary
plot_decision_boundary(lambda x: predict(parameters, x.T),
X2,Y2,str(0.3),"fig2.png")

# Compute the confusion matrix
yhat = predict(parameters,X2)
from sklearn.metrics import confusion_matrix
a=confusion_matrix(Y2.T,yhat.T)

#Print the output
from sklearn.metrics import accuracy_score, precision_score, recall_score,
f1_score
print('Accuracy: {:.2f}'.format(accuracy_score(Y2.T, yhat.T)))
print('Precision: {:.2f}'.format(precision_score(Y2.T, yhat.T)))
print('Recall: {:.2f}'.format(recall_score(Y2.T, yhat.T)))
print('F1: {:.2f}'.format(f1_score(Y2.T, yhat.T)))
## Accuracy: 0.90
## Precision: 0.91
## Recall: 0.87
## F1: 0.89
```

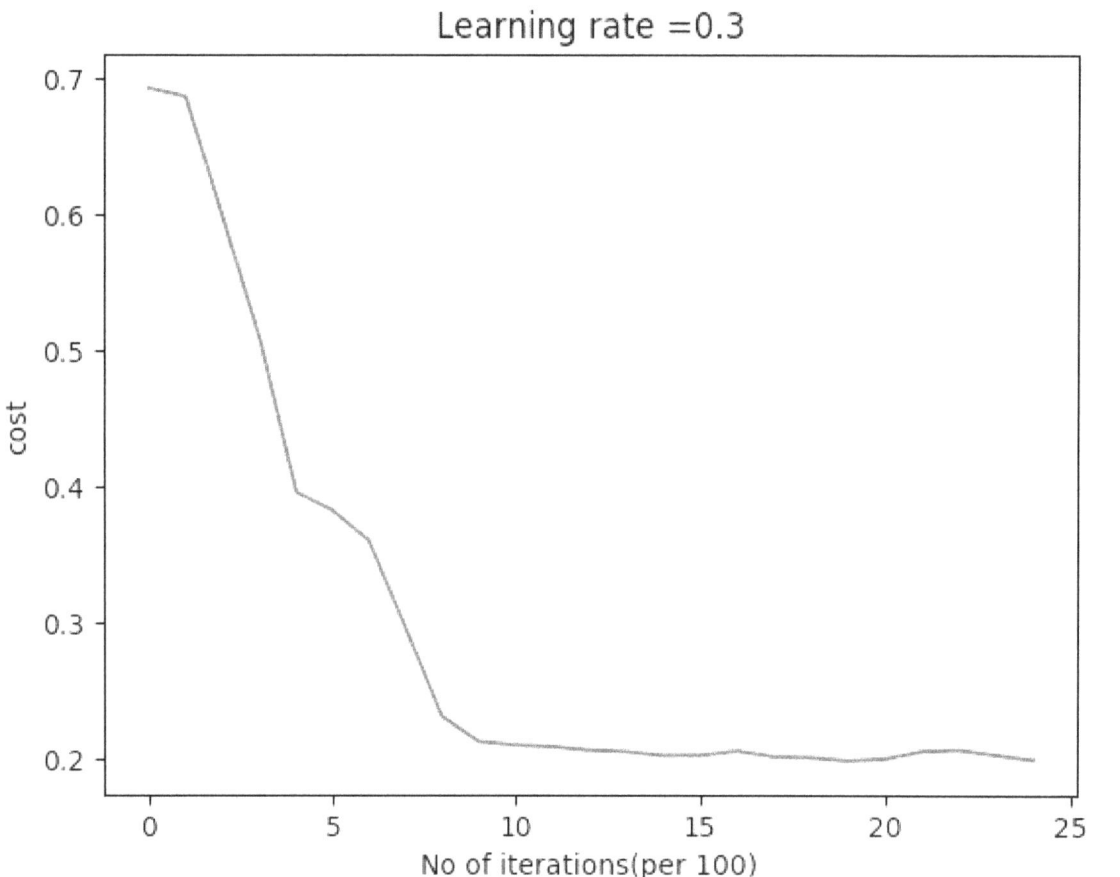

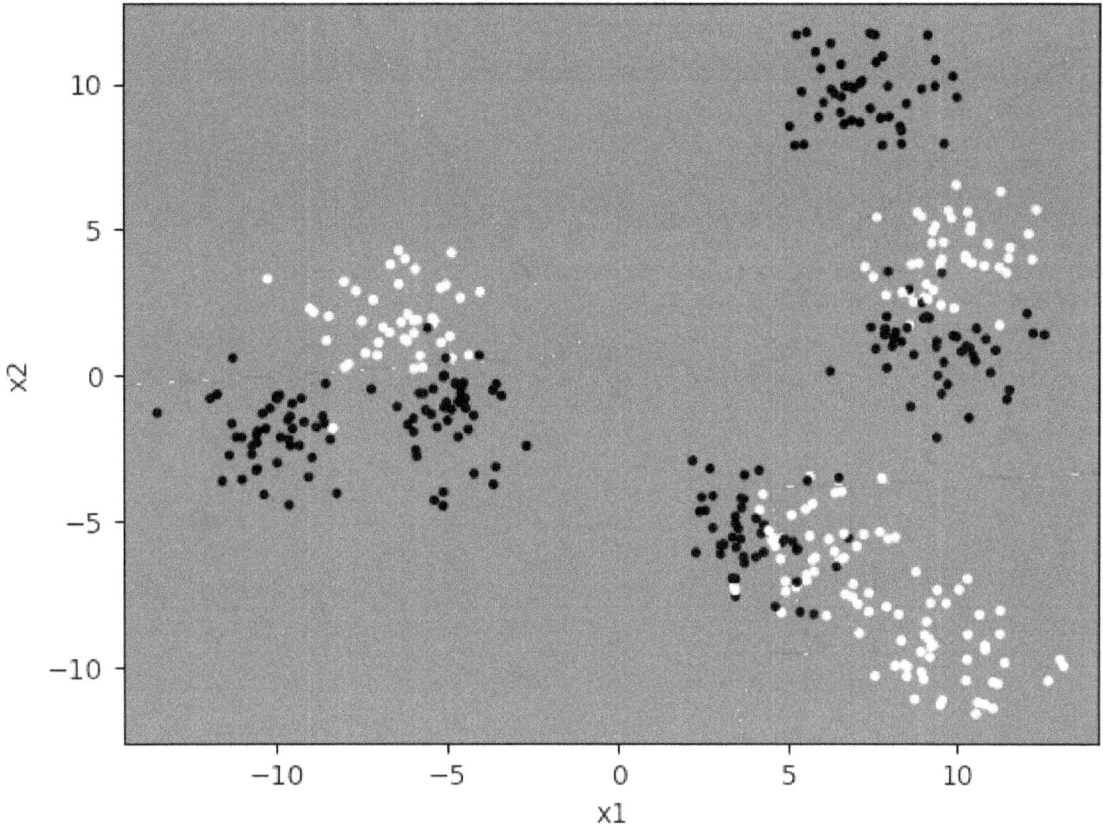

2.1b Classification with Multi-layer Deep Learning Network – Relu activation(R)

In the code below, binary classification is performed on the same dataset (data.csv) as above using the Relu activation function. The DL network is same as above

```
1  library(ggplot2)
2
3  # Read the data
4  z <- as.matrix(read.csv("data.csv",header=FALSE))
5  x <- z[,1:2]
6  y <- z[,3]
7  X1 <- t(x)
8  Y1 <- t(y)
9
10 # Set the dimensions of the Deep Learning network
11 # 2 - No of input features
12 # 9,9 - 2 hidden layers with 9 activation units
13 # 1 - 1 sigmoid activation unit at output layer
14 layersDimensions = c(2, 9, 9,1)
15
16 # Execute the L-layer Deep Learning Neural Network
17 # Hidden layer activation unit - relu
18 # Learning rate - 0.3
19 retvals = L_Layer_DeepModel(X1, Y1, layersDimensions,
20                             hiddenActivationFunc='relu',
```

```
21                            learningRate = 0.3,
22                            numIterations = 5000,
23                            print_cost = True)
24
25
26  library(ggplot2)
27  source("DLfunctions33.R")
28
29  # Get the computed costs
30  costs <- retvals[['costs']]
31  # Create a sequence of iterations
32  numIterations=5000
33  iterations <- seq(0,numIterations,by=1000)
34  df <-data.frame(iterations,costs)
35
36  # Plot the Costs vs number of iterations
37  ggplot(df,aes(x=iterations,y=costs)) + geom_point() +geom_line(color="blue")
38  + xlab('No of iterations') + ylab('Cost') + ggtitle("Cost vs No of
39  iterations")
```

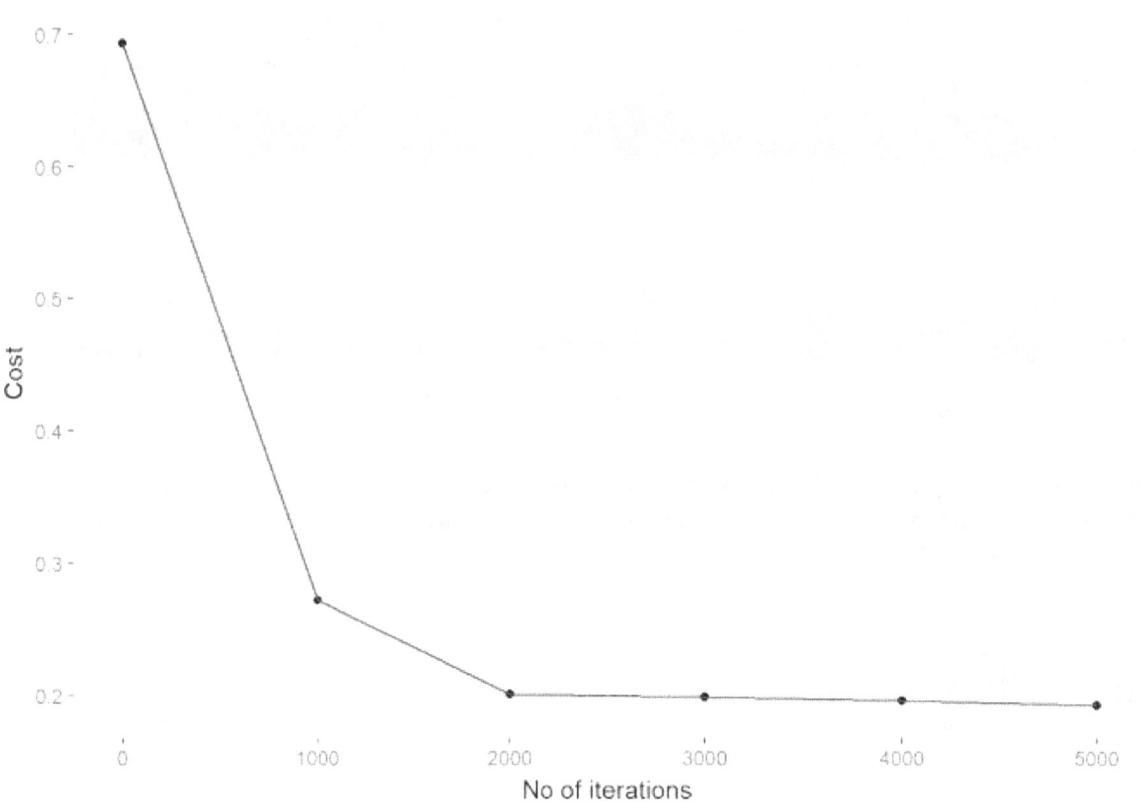

```
1  # Plot the decision boundary
2  plotDecisionBoundary(z,retvals,hiddenActivationFunc="relu",0.3)
```

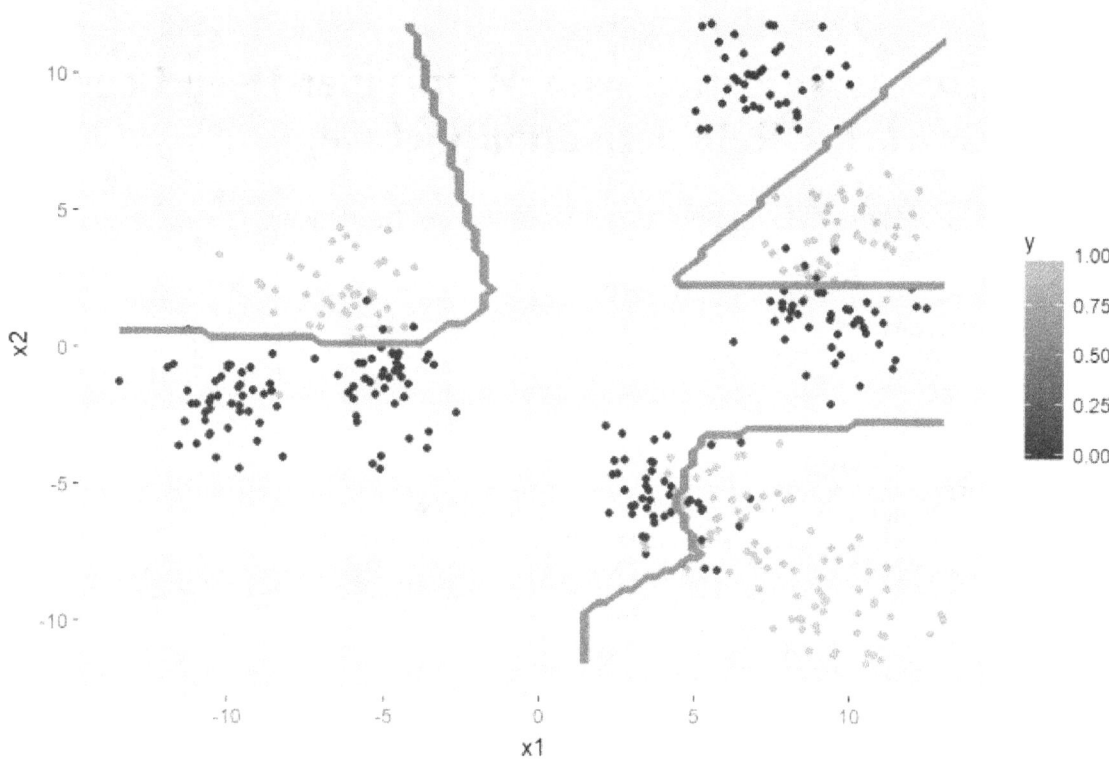

Decision boundary for learning rate: 0.3

```
1  library(caret)
2  # Predict the output for the data values
3  yhat <-predict(retvals$parameters,X1,hiddenActivationFunc="relu")
4  yhat[yhat==FALSE]=0
5  yhat[yhat==TRUE]=1
6  # Compute the confusion matrix
7  confusionMatrix(yhat,Y1)
8  ## Confusion Matrix and Statistics
9  ##
10 ##           Reference
11 ## Prediction   0   1
12 ##          0 201  10
13 ##          1  21 168
14 ##
15 ##                Accuracy : 0.9225
16 ##                  95% CI : (0.8918, 0.9467)
17 ##     No Information Rate : 0.555
18 ##     P-Value [Acc > NIR] : < 2e-16
19 ##
20 ##                   Kappa : 0.8441
21 ##  Mcnemar's Test P-Value : 0.07249
22 ##
23 ##             Sensitivity : 0.9054
24 ##             Specificity : 0.9438
25 ##          Pos Pred Value : 0.9526
26 ##          Neg Pred Value : 0.8889
27 ##              Prevalence : 0.5550
28 ##          Detection Rate : 0.5025
29 ##    Detection Prevalence : 0.5275
30 ##       Balanced Accuracy : 0.9246
31 ##
```

```
32 ##        'Positive' Class : 0
33 ##
```

2.1c Classification with Multi-layer Deep Learning Network – Relu activation(Octave)

Included below is the code for performing classification. Incidentally, Octave does not seem to have implemented the confusion matrix.

```
1  # Read the data
2  data=csvread("data.csv");
3  X=data(:,1:2);
4  Y=data(:,3);
5
6  # Set layer dimensions
7  # 2 - 2 input features
8  # 9 7 - 2 hidden layers with 9 and 7 hidden units
9  # 1 - 1 sigmoid activation unit at output layer
10 layersDimensions = [2 9 7 1]
11
12 # Execute the L-Layer Deep Network
13 # Hidden unit - relu
14 #learning rate - 0.1
15 [weights biases costs]=L_Layer_DeepModel(X', Y', layersDimensions,
16 hiddenActivationFunc='relu',
17 learningRate = 0.1,
18 numIterations = 10000);
19
20 #Plot cost vs iterations
21 plotCostVsIterations(10000,costs);
22
23 #Plot the decision boundary
24 plotDecisionBoundary(data,weights, biases,hiddenActivationFunc="tanh")
```

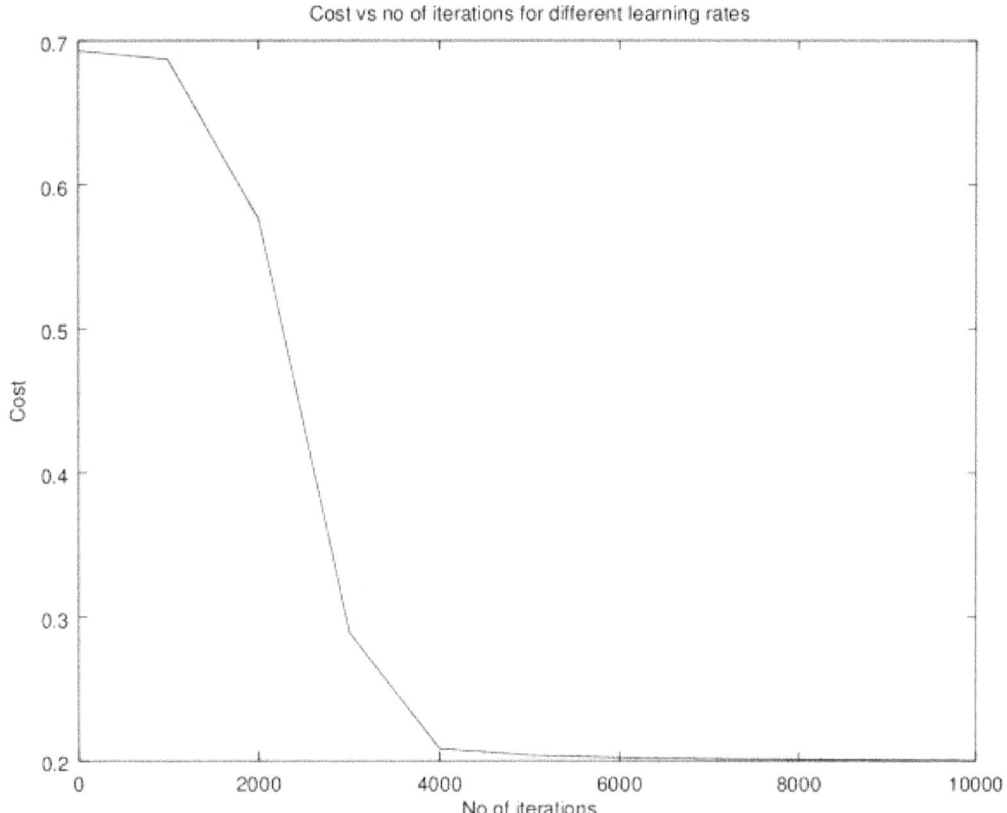

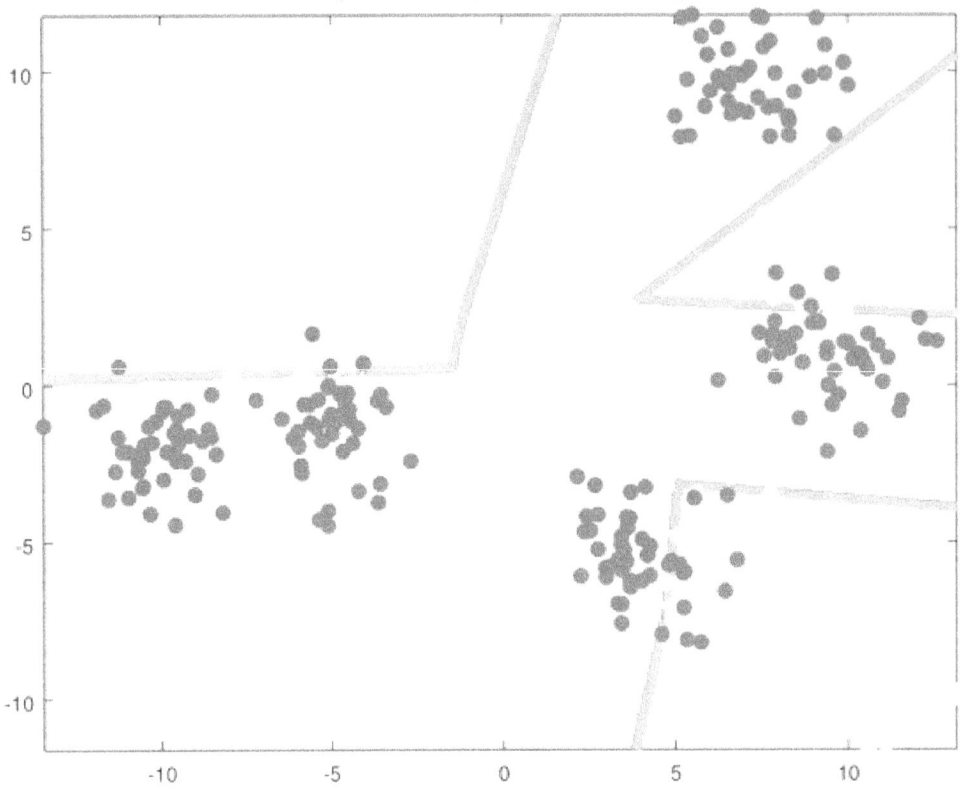

2.2a Classification with Multi-layer Deep Learning Network – Tanh activation(Python)

The code below uses the tanh activation function to perform the same classification. I found the Tanh activation required a simpler Neural Network of 3 layers.

```
1  # Tanh activation
2  import os
3  import numpy as np
4  import matplotlib.pyplot as plt
5  import matplotlib.colors
6  import sklearn.linear_model
7
8  from sklearn.model_selection import train_test_split
9  from sklearn.datasets import make_classification, make_blobs
10 from matplotlib.colors import ListedColormap
11 import sklearn
12 import sklearn.datasets
13 execfile("./DLfunctions34.py")
14
15 # Create the dataset
16 X1, Y1 = make_blobs(n_samples = 400, n_features = 2, centers = 9,
17                    cluster_std = 1.3, random_state = 4)
18
19 #Create 2 classes
```

```
20  Y1=Y1.reshape(400,1)
21  Y1 = Y1 % 2
22  X2=X1.T
23  Y2=Y1.T
24
25  # Set the dimensions of the Neural Network
26  # 2 - input featues
27  # 4 - 1 hidden layer with 4 units
28  # 1 - 1 sigmoid activation unit at output layer
29  layersDimensions = [2, 4, 1] #   3-layer model
30
31  # Execute the L-layer Deep Learning network
32  # hidden layer activation function - tanh
33  # learning rate - 0.5
34  parameters = L_Layer_DeepModel(X2, Y2, layersDimensions,
35  hiddenActivationFunc='tanh', learning_rate = .5,num_iterations =
36  2500,fig="fig3.png")
37
38  #Plot the decision boundary
39  plot_decision_boundary(lambda x: predict(parameters, x.T),
40  X2,Y2,str(0.5),"fig4.png")
```

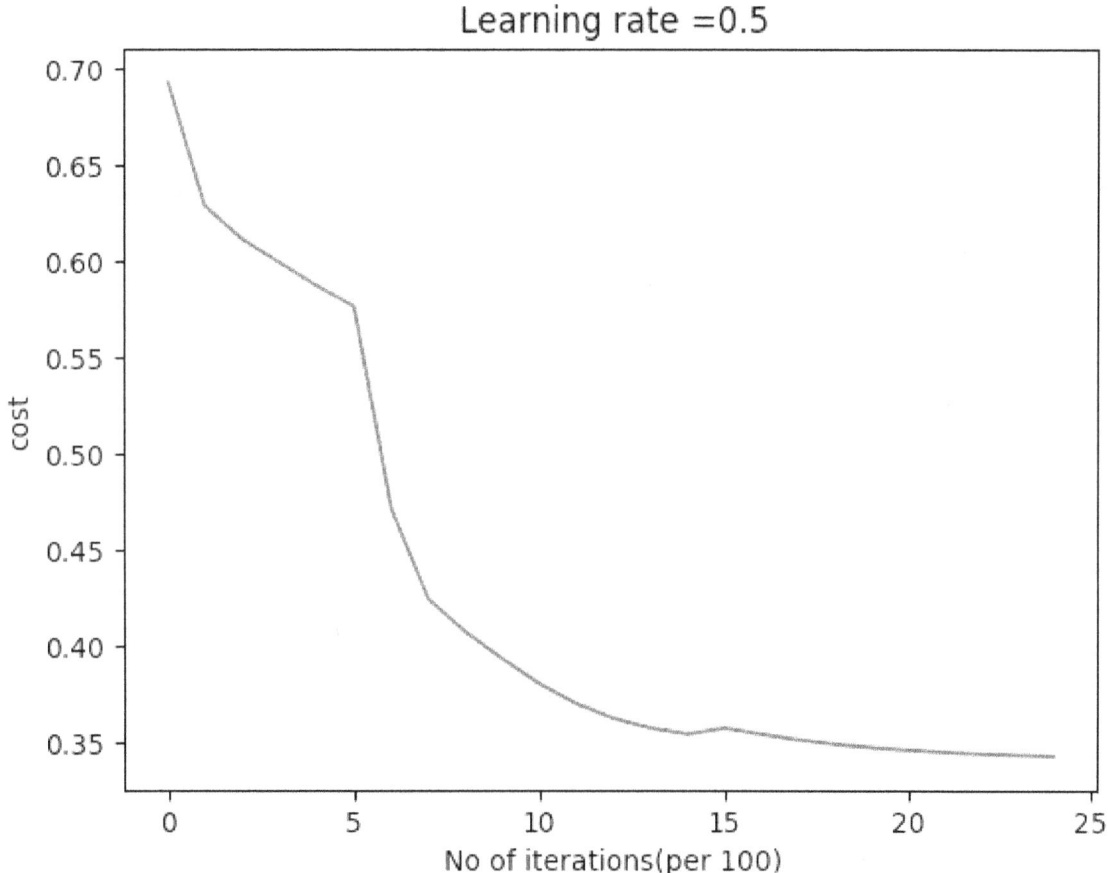

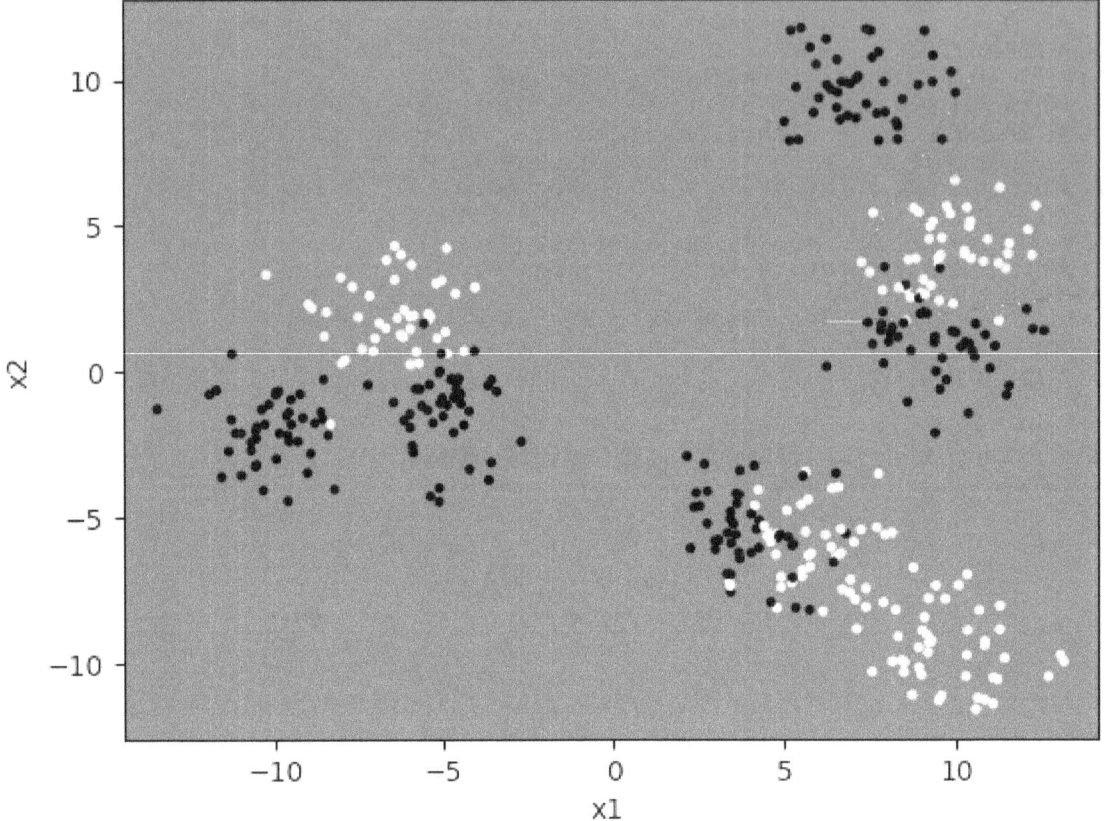

2.2b Classification with Multi-layer Deep Learning Network – Tanh activation(R)

R performs better with a Tanh activation than the Relu as can be seen below

```
1  #Set the dimensions of the Neural Network
2  library(ggplot2)
3
4  # Read the data
5  z <- as.matrix(read.csv("data.csv",header=FALSE))
6  x <- z[,1:2]
7  y <- z[,3]
8  X1 <- t(x)
9  Y1 <- t(y)
10
11 # Set layer dimensions
12 # 2 - 2 inputr features
13 # 9, 9 - 2 hidden layers with 9 activation units
14 # 1 - 1 sigmoid output activation unit
15 layersDimensions = c(2, 9, 9,1)
16
17 # Execute the L-layer  Deep Model
18 # Hidden layer activation function - tanh
19 # learning rate - 0.3
20 retvals = L_Layer_DeepModel(X1, Y1, layersDimensions,
```

```
21                            hiddenActivationFunc='tanh',
22                            learningRate = 0.3,
23                            numIterations = 5000,
24                            print_cost = True)
25
26  # Get the costs
27  costs <- retvals[['costs']]
28  # Set iterations
29  iterations <- seq(0,numIterations,by=1000)
30  df <-data.frame(iterations,costs)
31
32  # Plot Cost vs number of iterations
33  ggplot(df,aes(x=iterations,y=costs)) + geom_point() +geom_line(color="blue")
34  + xlab('No of iterations') + ylab('Cost') + ggtitle("Cost vs No of
35  iterations")
```

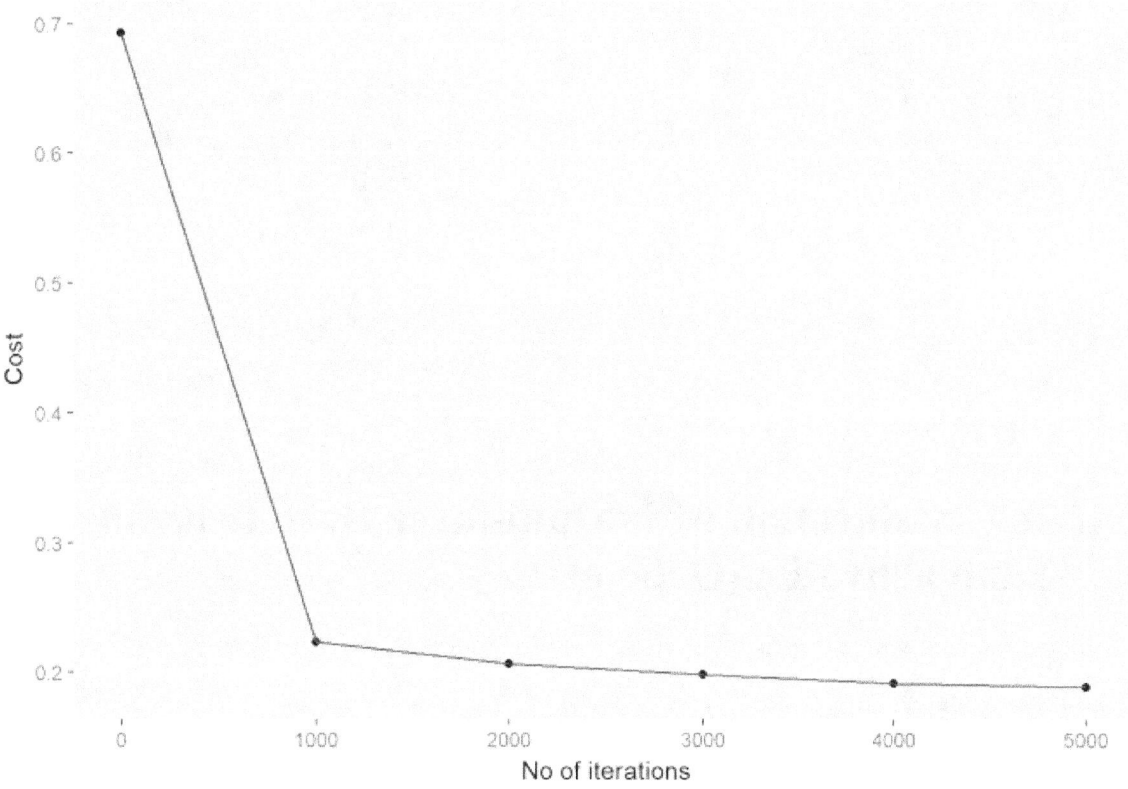

```
1  #Plot the decision boundary
2  plotDecisionBoundary(z,retvals,hiddenActivationFunc="tanh",0.3)
```

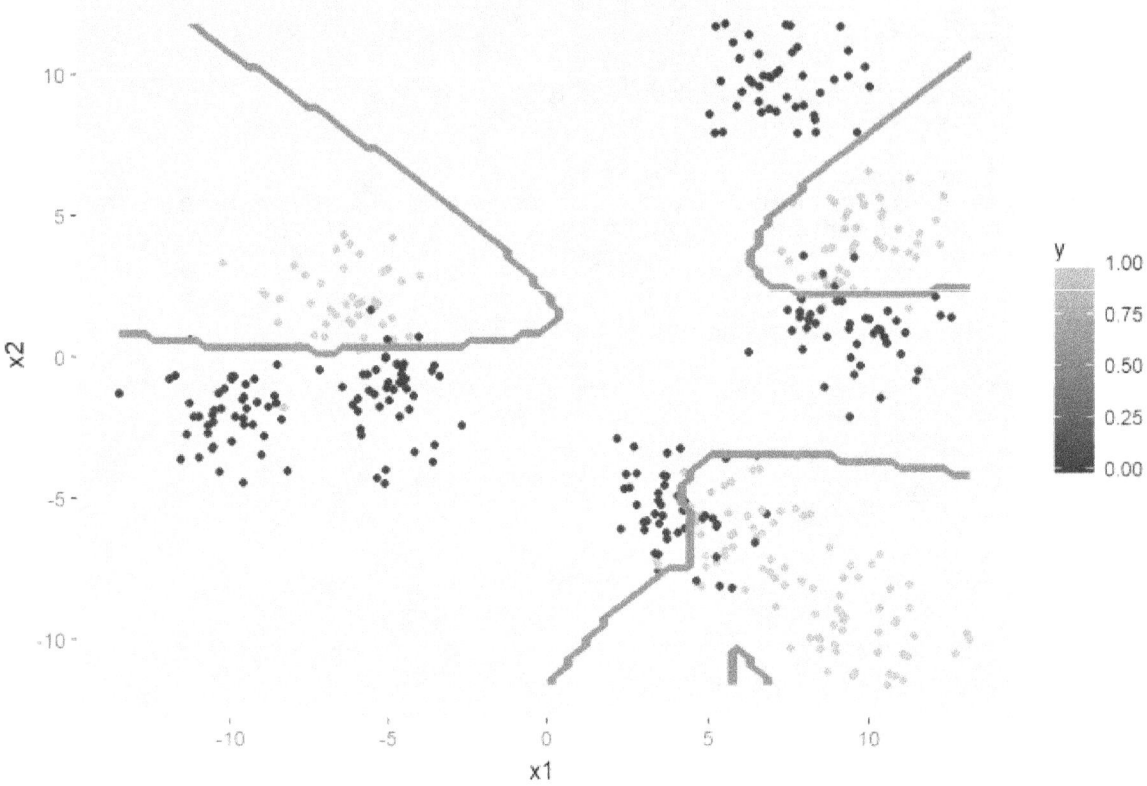

Decision boundary for learning rate: 0.3

2.2c Classification with Multi-layer Deep Learning Network – Tanh activation(Octave)

The code below uses the Tanh activation in the hidden layers for Octave

```
1  # Read the data
2  data=csvread("data.csv");
3  X=data(:,1:2);
4  Y=data(:,3);
5
6  # Set layer dimensions
7  # 2 - input features
8  # 9 7 - 2 hidden layers with 9 and 7 hidden units
9  # 1 - 1 sigmoid unit at output layer
10 layersDimensions = [2 9 7 1] #tanh=-0.5(ok), #relu=0.1 best!
11
12 # Execute the L-Layer Deep Learning Network
13 # hidden layer activation function - tanh
14 # Learning rate - 0.1
15 [weights biases costs]=L_Layer_DeepModel(X', Y', layersDimensions,
16 hiddenActivationFunc='tanh',
17 learningRate = 0.1,
18 numIterations = 10000);
19
20 #Plot cost vs iterations
21 plotCostVsIterations(10000,costs);
```

```
22
23  #Plot the decision boundary
24  plotDecisionBoundary(data,weights, biases,hiddenActivationFunc="tanh")
```

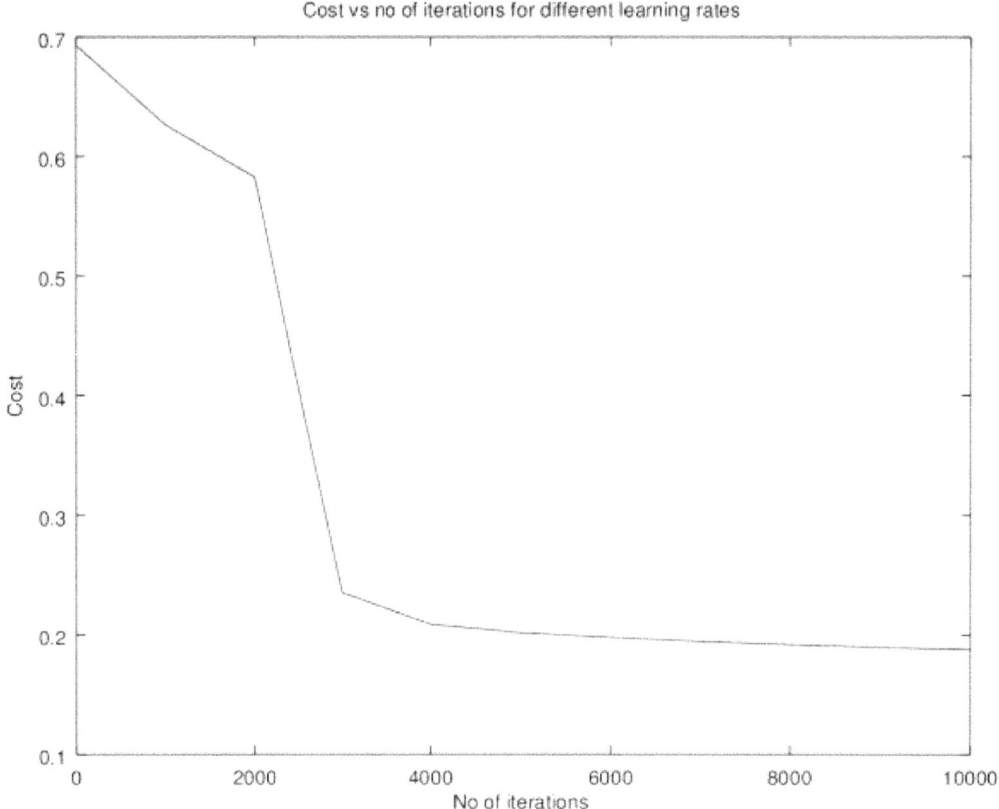

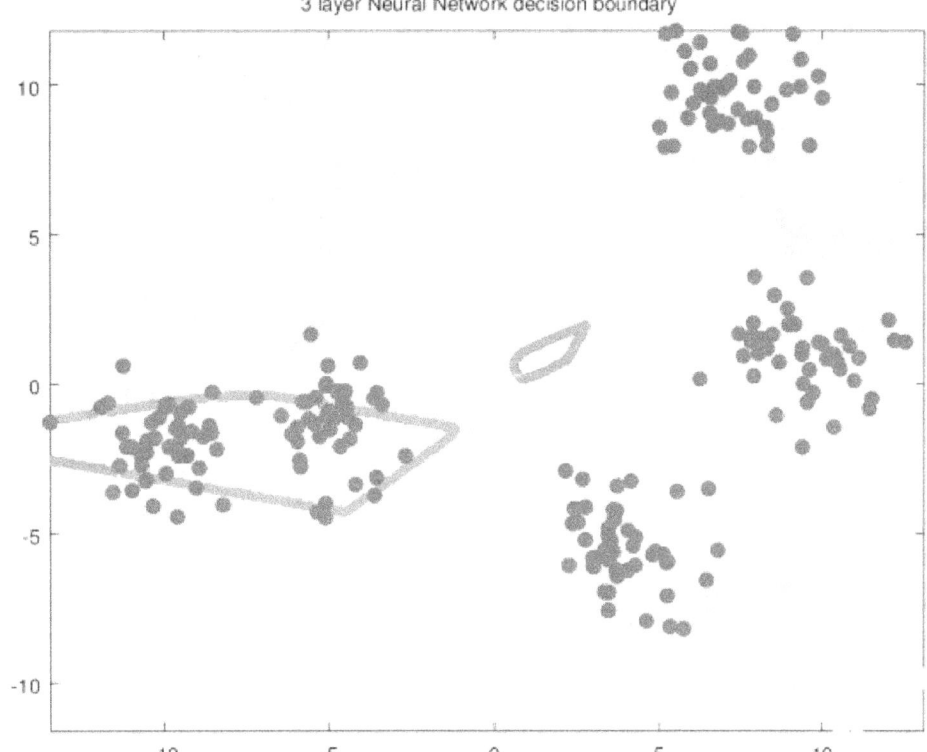

3. Bernoulli's Lemniscate

To make things more interesting, I create a 2D figure of the Bernoulli's lemniscate to perform non-linear classification. The Lemniscate is given by the equation
$(x^2 + y^2)^2 = 2a^2 * (x^2 - y^2)$

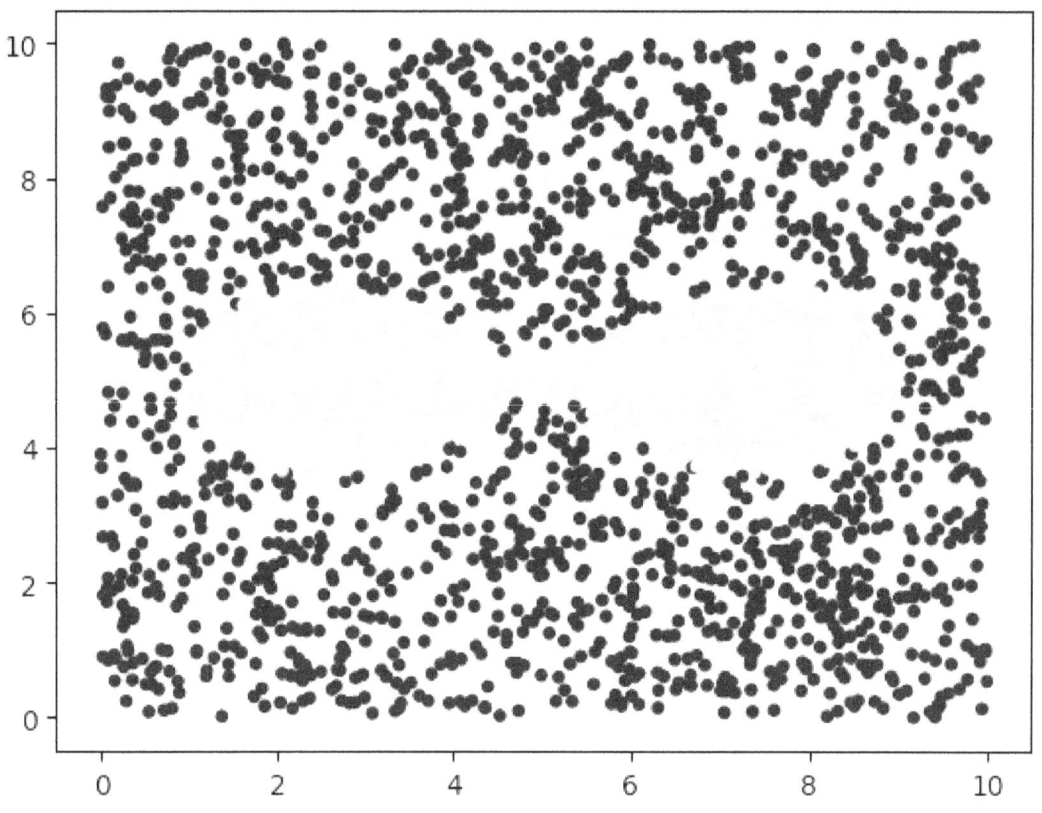

3a. Classifying a lemniscate with Deep Learning Network – Relu activation(Python)

```
1  import os
2  import numpy as np
3  import matplotlib.pyplot as plt
4  os.chdir("C:\\software\\DeepLearning-Posts\\part3")
5  execfile("./DLfunctions33.py")
6
7  # Create data set
8  x1=np.random.uniform(0,10,2000).reshape(2000,1)
9  x2=np.random.uniform(0,10,2000).reshape(2000,1)
10 X=np.append(x1,x2,axis=1)
11 X.shape
12
13 # Create a subset of values where squared is <0.4. Perform ravel() to flatten
14 this vector
15 # Create the equation
16 # (x^{2} + y^{2})^2 - 2a^2*(x^{2}-y^{2}) <= 0
17 a=np.power(np.power(X[:,0]-5,2) + np.power(X[:,1]-5,2),2)
18 b=np.power(X[:,0]-5,2) - np.power(X[:,1]-5,2)
19 c= a - (b*np.power(4,2))  <=0
20 Y=c.reshape(2000,1)
21
22 # Create a scatter plot of the lemniscate
23 plt.scatter(X[:,0], X[:,1], c=Y, marker= 'o', s=15,cmap="viridis")
24 Z=np.append(X,Y,axis=1)
25 plt.savefig("fig50.png",bbox_inches='tight')
26 plt.clf()
```

```python
# Set the data for classification
X2=X.T
Y2=Y.T

# These settings work the best
# Set the Deep Learning layer dimensions for a Relu activation
# 2 - input features
# 7,4 - 2 hidden layers with 7 and 4 hidden units
# 1 - 1 sigmoid activation unit at output layer
layersDimensions = [2,7,4,1]


#Execute the L-layer DL network
# hidden layer activation function - relu
# learning rate - 0.5
parameters = L_Layer_DeepModel(X2, Y2, layersDimensions,
hiddenActivationFunc='relu', learning_rate = 0.5,num_iterations = 10000,
fig="fig5.png")

#Plot the decision boundary
plot_decision_boundary(lambda x: predict(parameters, x.T), X2,
Y2,str(2.2),"fig6.png")

# Compute the Confusion matrix
yhat = predict(parameters,X2)
from sklearn.metrics import confusion_matrix
a=confusion_matrix(Y2.T,yhat.T)

#Print accuracy,precision, recall and F1 score
from sklearn.metrics import accuracy_score, precision_score, recall_score,
f1_score
print('Accuracy: {:.2f}'.format(accuracy_score(Y2.T, yhat.T)))
print('Precision: {:.2f}'.format(precision_score(Y2.T, yhat.T)))
print('Recall: {:.2f}'.format(recall_score(Y2.T, yhat.T)))
print('F1: {:.2f}'.format(f1_score(Y2.T, yhat.T)))
## Accuracy: 0.93
## Precision: 0.77
## Recall: 0.76
## F1: 0.76
```

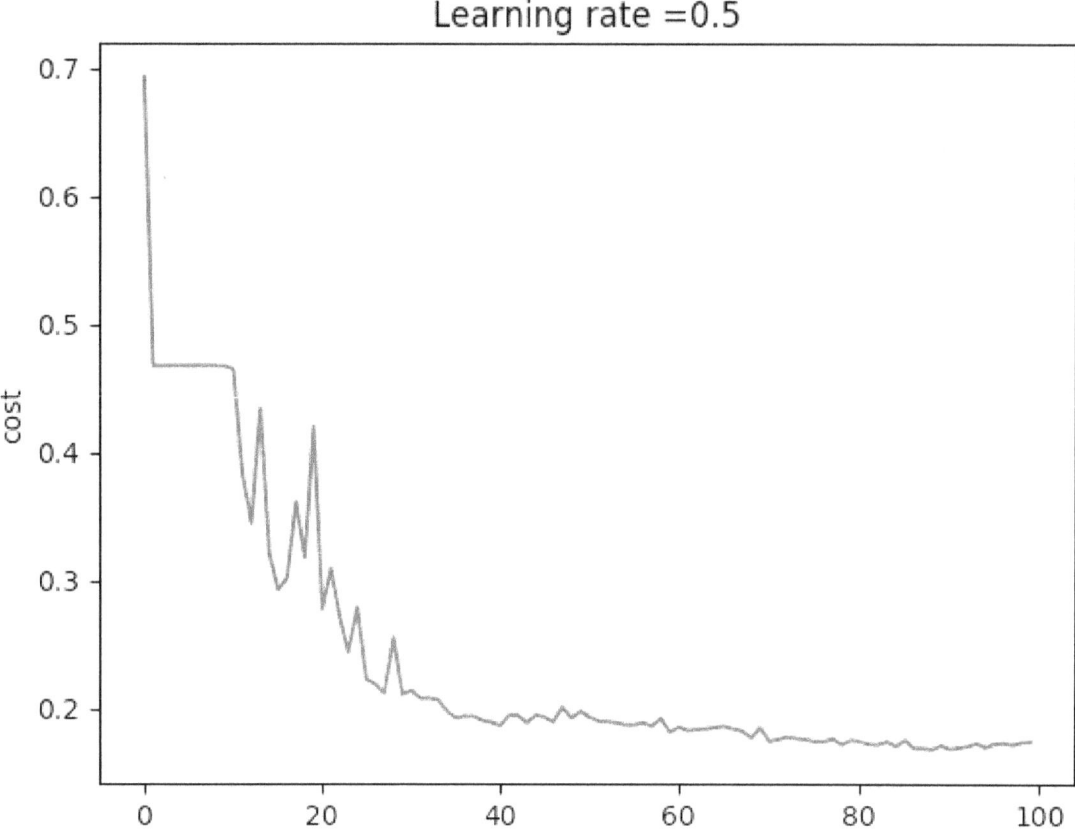

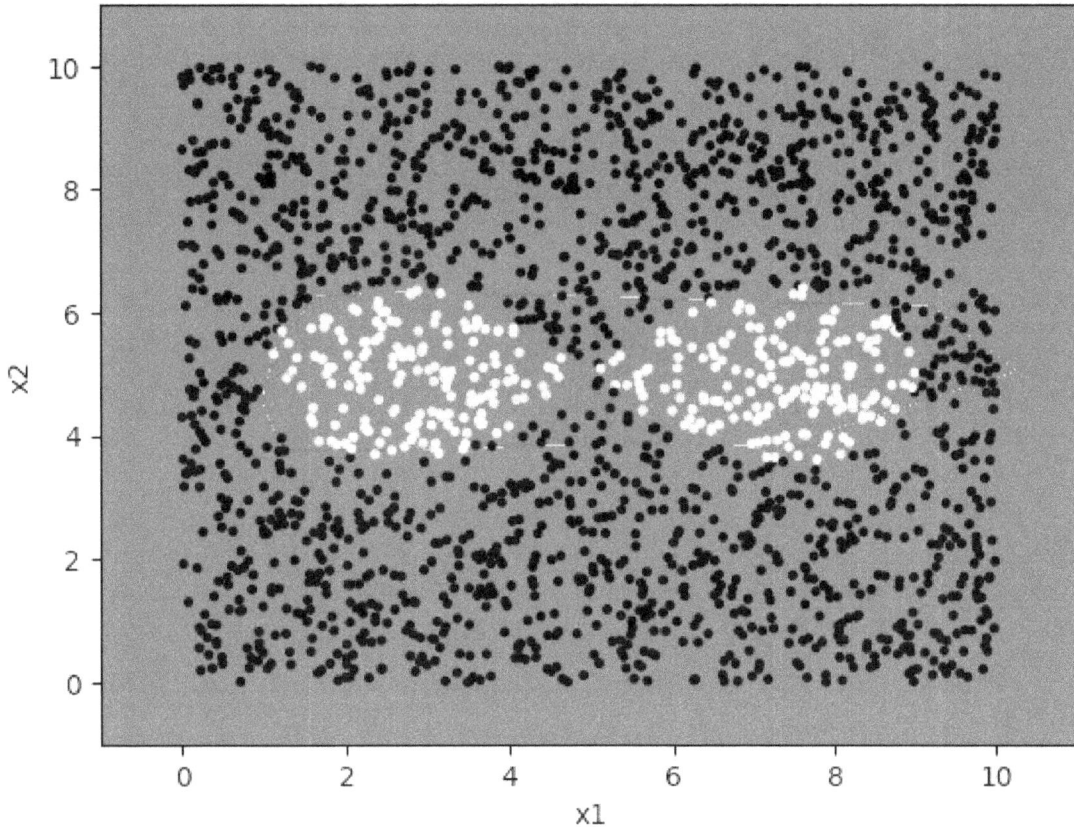

Decision Boundary for learning rate:2.2

We could get better performance by tuning further. Do play around with the code.
Note:: The lemniscate data is saved as a CSV and then read in R and also in Octave.

3b. Classifying a lemniscate with Deep Learning Network – Relu activation(R code)

The R decision boundary for the Bernoulli's lemniscate is shown below

```
1  # Read lemniscate data
2  Z <- as.matrix(read.csv("lemniscate.csv",header=FALSE))
3  Z1=data.frame(Z)
4  
5  # Create a scatter plot of the lemniscate
6  ggplot(Z1,aes(x=V1,y=V2,col=V3)) +geom_point()
7  #Set the data for the DL network
8  X=Z[,1:2]
9  Y=Z[,3]
10 X1=t(X)
11 Y1=t(Y)
12 
13 # Set the layer dimensions for the tanh activation function
14 # 2 - No of input features
15 #5, 4 - 2 hidden layers with 5 and 4 hidden units
```

```r
# 1 - 1 sigmoid output activation function in output layer
layersDimensions = c(2,5,4,1)

# Execute the L layer Deep Learning network
# Activation function in hidden layer - Tanh activation
# learning rate=0.3
retvals = L_Layer_DeepModel(X1, Y1, layersDimensions,
                            hiddenActivationFunc='tanh',
                            learningRate = 0.3,
                            numIterations = 20000, print_cost = True)

# Plot cost vs iteration
costs <- retvals[['costs']]
numIterations = 20000
iterations <- seq(0,numIterations,by=1000)
df <-data.frame(iterations,costs)
ggplot(df,aes(x=iterations,y=costs)) + geom_point() +geom_line(color="blue")
+ xlab('No of iterations') + ylab('Cost') + ggtitle("Cost vs No of
iterations")
```

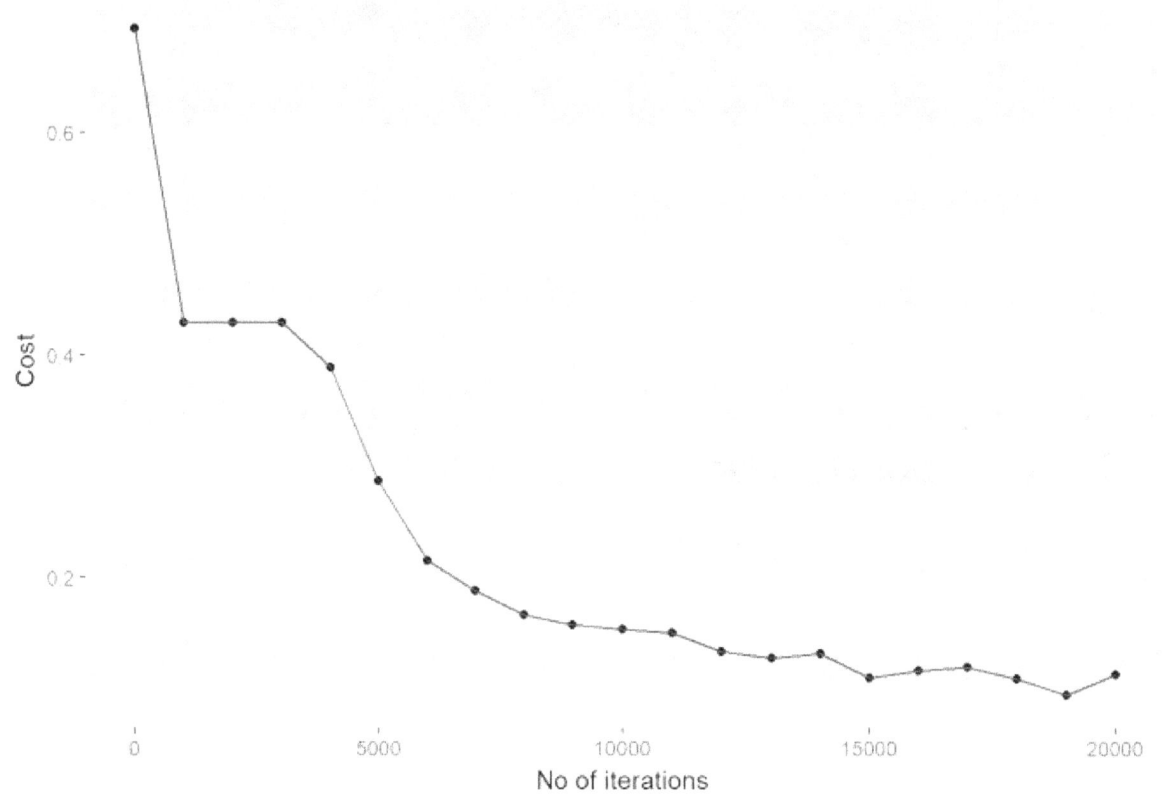

```r
#Plot the decision boundary
plotDecisionBoundary(Z,retvals,hiddenActivationFunc="tanh",0.3)
```

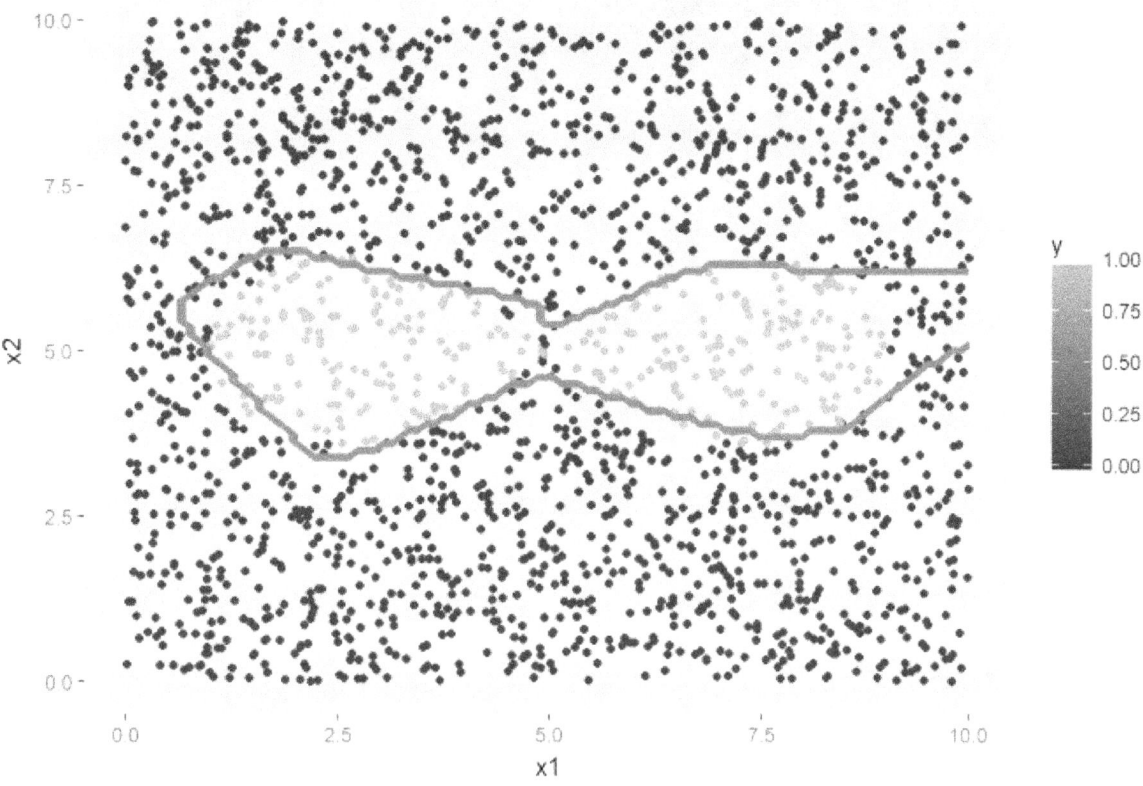

Decision boundary for learning rate: 0.3

3c. Classifying a lemniscate with Deep Learning Network – Relu activation (Octave code)

Octave is used to generate the non-linear lemniscate boundary.

```
# Read the data
data=csvread("lemniscate.csv");
X=data(:,1:2);
Y=data(:,3);

# Set the dimensions of the layers
# 2 - no of input features
# 9 7 - 2 hidden layers with 9 and 7 activation units respectively
# 1 - 1 activation unit in output layer (sigmoid)
layersDimensions = [2 9 7 1]

# Execute the L-layer the DL network
#hidden activation function - relu
# learning rate- 0.20
[weights biases costs]=L_Layer_DeepModel(X', Y', layersDimensions,
hiddenActivationFunc='relu',
learningRate = 0.20,
numIterations = 10000);

#Plot the cost vs iterations
plotCostVsIterations(10000,costs);
```

```
22
23  #Plot the descion boundary
24  plotDecisionBoundary(data,weights, biases,hiddenActivationFunc="relu")
```

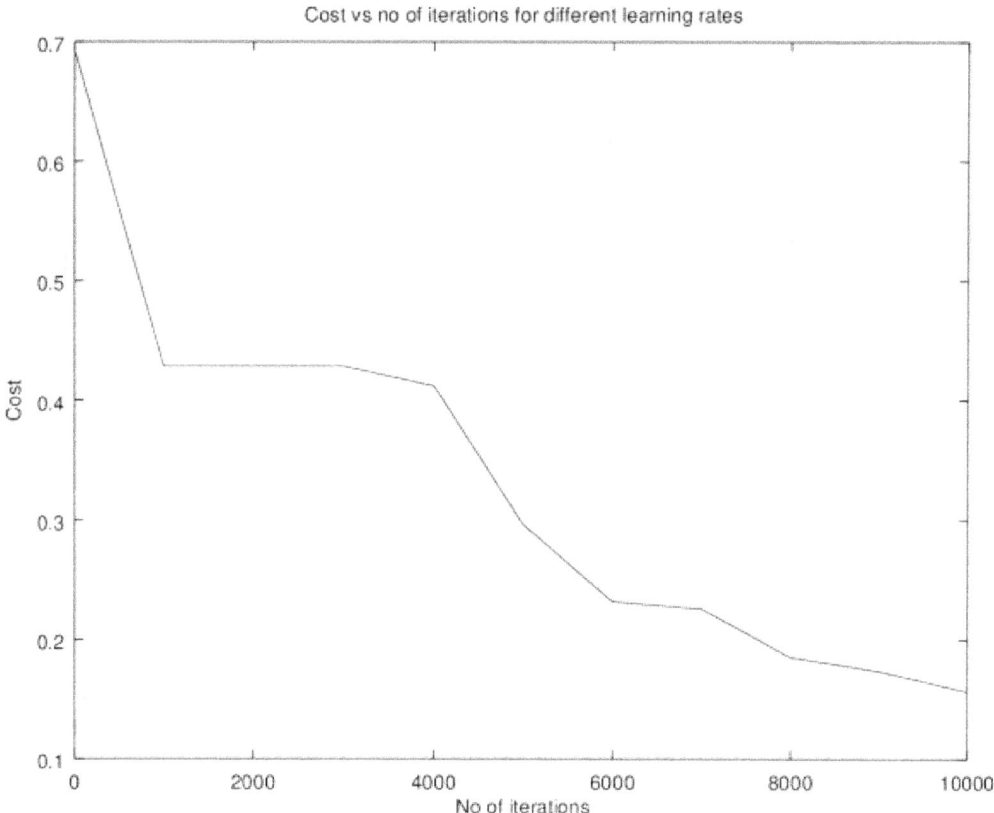

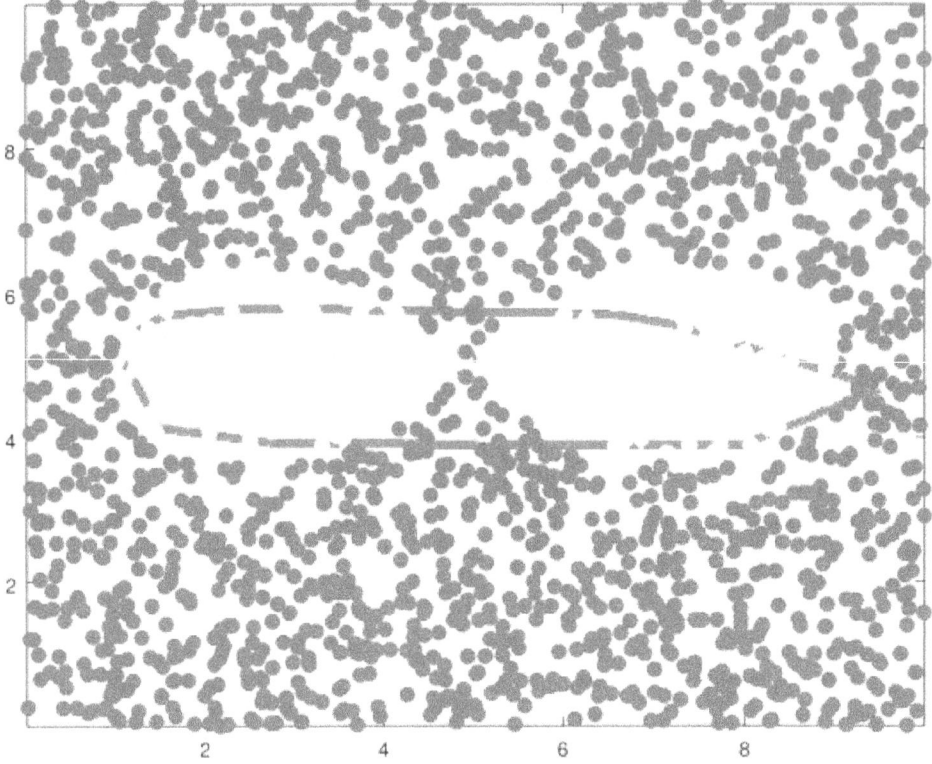

4a. Binary Classification using MNIST – Python code

Finally, I perform a simple classification using the MNIST handwritten digits, which according to Prof Geoffrey Hinton is "the Drosophila of Deep Learning".

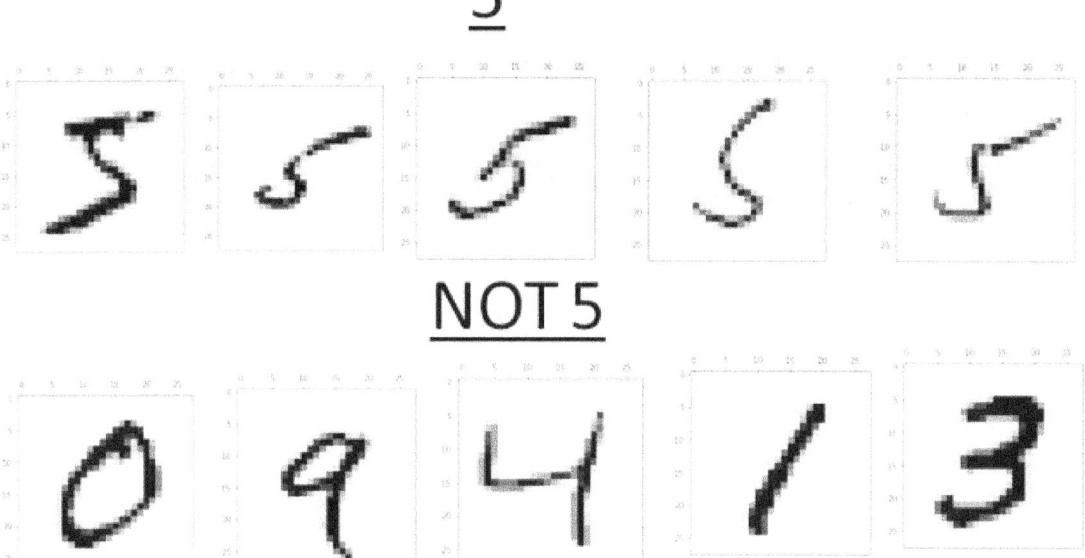

The Python code for reading the MNIST data is taken from Alex Kesling's github link MNIST (https://gist.github.com/akesling/5358964)

In the Python code below, I perform a simple binary classification between the handwritten digit '5' and 'not 5' which is all other digits. I perform the proper classification of all digits using the Softmax classifier in chapter 5.

```
1   import os
2   import numpy as np
3   import matplotlib.pyplot as plt
4   execfile("./DLfunctions34.py")
5
6   #Load MNIST
7   execfile("./load_mnist.py")
8   # Set the training and test data and labels
9   training=list(read(dataset='training',path="./mnist"))
10  test=list(read(dataset='testing',path="./mnist"))
11  lbls=[]
12  pxls=[]
13  print(len(training))
14
15  # Select the first 10000 training data and the labels
16  for i in range(10000):
17          l,p=training[i]
18          lbls.append(l)
19          pxls.append(p)
20  labels= np.array(lbls)
21  pixels=np.array(pxls)
22
23  #  Set y=1  when labels == 5 and 0 otherwise
24  y=(labels==5).reshape(-1,1)
25  X=pixels.reshape(pixels.shape[0],-1)
26
27  # Create the necessary feature and target variable
28  X1=X.T
29  Y1=y.T
30
```

```python
# Create the layer dimensions. The number of features are 28 x 28 = 784 since the 28 x 28
# pixels is flattened to single vector of length 784.
# 784 - No of input features = 28 x28
# 15, 9 - 2 hidden layers with 15 and 9 hidden activation units
# 1 - 1 activation unit in the output layer (sigmoid)
layersDimensions=[784, 15,9,7,1] #

#Execute the L-Layer Deep Learning Network
# hidden activation function - relu
#learning reate - 0.1
parameters = L_Layer_DeepModel(X1, Y1, layersDimensions,
hiddenActivationFunc='relu', learning_rate = 0.1,num_iterations = 1000,
fig="fig7.png")

# Read the Test data and labels
lbls1=[]
pxls1=[]
for i in range(800):
        l,p=test[i]
        lbls1.append(l)
        pxls1.append(p)

testLabels=np.array(lbls1)
testData=np.array(pxls1)

ytest=(testLabels==5).reshape(-1,1)
Xtest=testData.reshape(testData.shape[0],-1)
Xtest1=Xtest.T
Ytest1=ytest.T

# Predict based on test data
yhat = predict(parameters,Xtest1)
from sklearn.metrics import confusion_matrix

#Compute the confusion matrix
a=confusion_matrix(Ytest1.T,yhat.T)

#Print accuracy, precision, recall and F! score
from sklearn.metrics import accuracy_score, precision_score, recall_score, f1_score
print('Accuracy: {:.2f}'.format(accuracy_score(Ytest1.T, yhat.T)))
print('Precision: {:.2f}'.format(precision_score(Ytest1.T, yhat.T)))
print('Recall: {:.2f}'.format(recall_score(Ytest1.T, yhat.T)))
print('F1: {:.2f}'.format(f1_score(Ytest1.T, yhat.T)))

# Plot the Precision-Recall curve
probs=predict_proba(parameters,Xtest1)
from sklearn.metrics import precision_recall_curve

precision, recall, thresholds = precision_recall_curve(Ytest1.T, probs.T)
closest_zero = np.argmin(np.abs(thresholds))
closest_zero_p = precision[closest_zero]
closest_zero_r = recall[closest_zero]

#Plot precision-recall curve
plt.xlim([0.0, 1.01])
plt.ylim([0.0, 1.01])
plt.plot(precision, recall, label='Precision-Recall Curve')
plt.plot(closest_zero_p, closest_zero_r, 'o', markersize = 12, fillstyle = 'none', c='r', mew=3)
plt.xlabel('Precision', fontsize=16)
plt.ylabel('Recall', fontsize=16)
plt.savefig("fig8.png",bbox_inches='tight')
```

```
## Accuracy: 0.99
## Precision: 0.96
## Recall: 0.89
## F1: 0.92
```

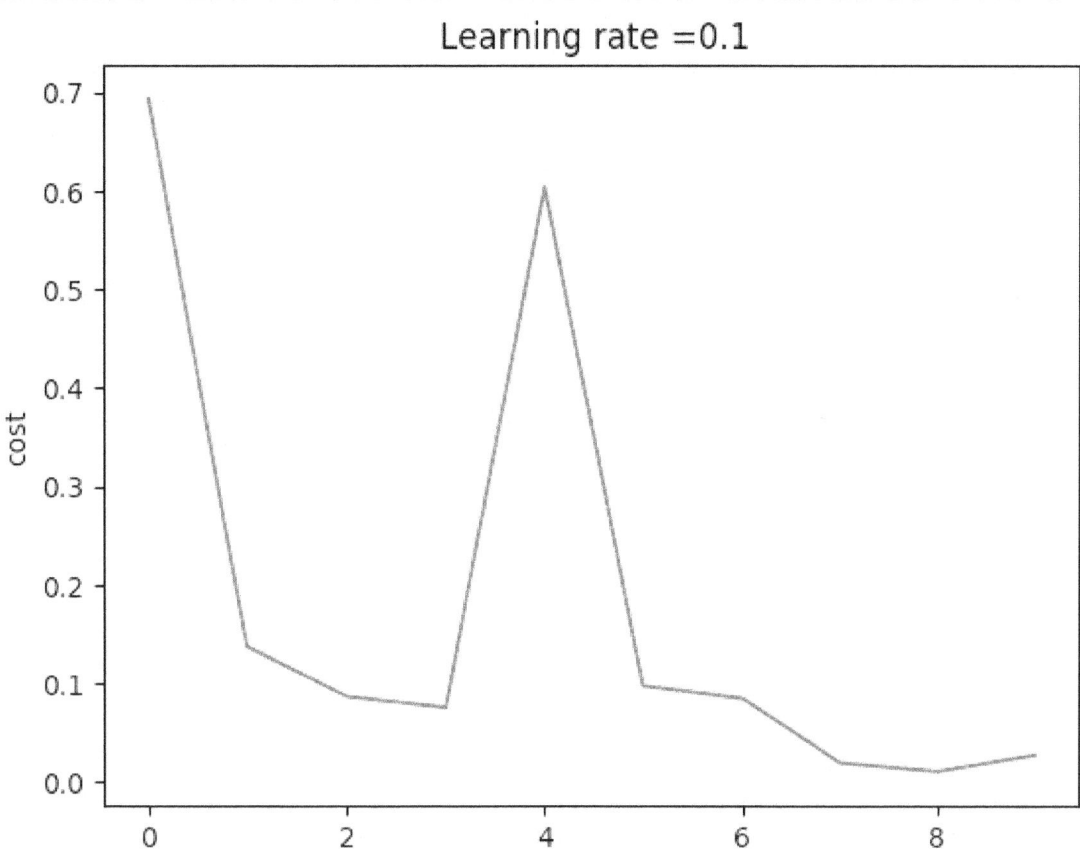

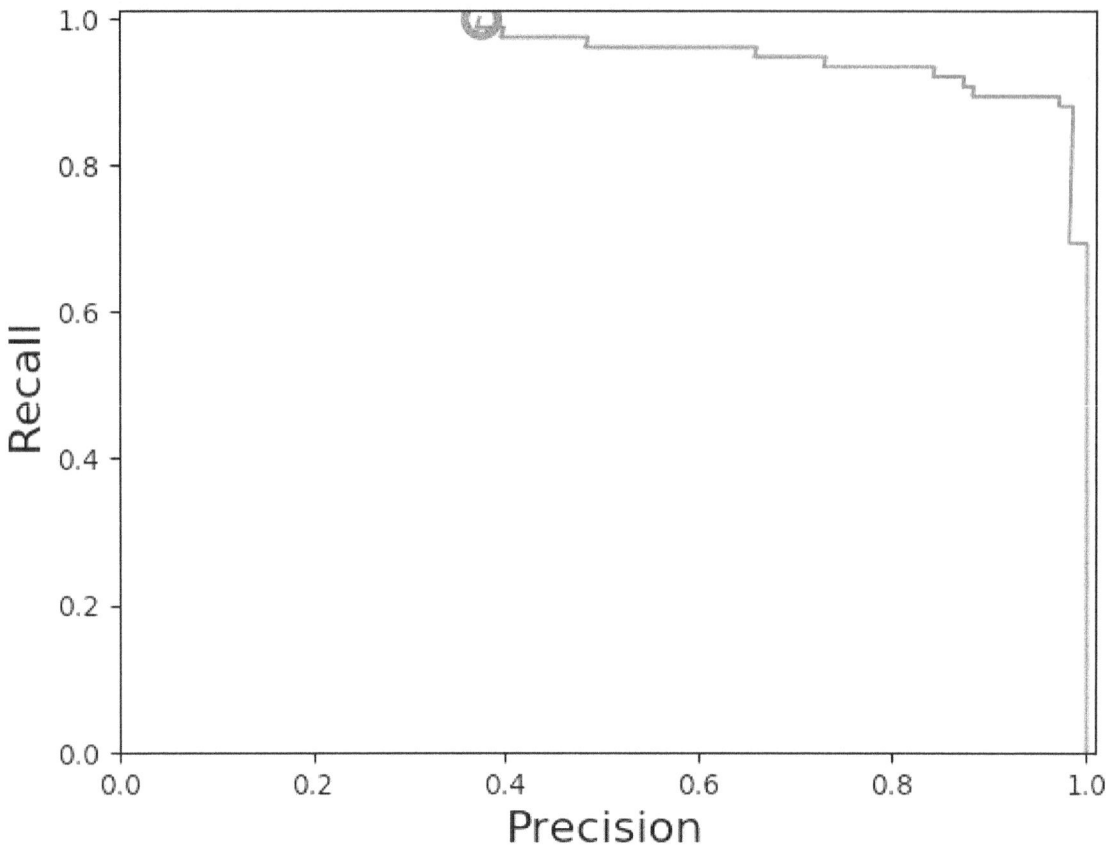

In addition to plotting the Cost vs Iterations, I also plot the Precision-Recall curve to show how the Precision and Recall, which are complementary to each other, vary with respect to the other.

4b. Binary Classification using MNIST – R code

In the R code below the same binary classification of the digit '5' and the 'not 5' is performed. The code to read and display the MNIST data is taken from Brendan O' Connor's github link at MNIST(https://gist.github.com/brendano/39760)

```
1  source("mnist.R")
2  #Load the MNIST data
3  load_mnist()
4  #show_digit(train$x[2,]
5
6  #Set the layer dimensions
7  # 784 - no of input features = 28 x 28
8  # 7, 7, 3 - 3 hidden layers with 7,7,3 activation units
9  # 1 - 1 sigmoid activation unit at output layer
10 layersDimensions=c(784, 7,7,3,1) # Works at 1500
11
12
13 x <- t(train$x)
14 # Choose only 5000 training data
15 x2 <- x[,1:5000]
16
```

```r
17  # Classify the data
18  y <-train$y
19
20  # Set labels for all digits that are 'not 5' to 0
21  y[y!=5] <- 0
22
23  # Set labels of digit 5 as 1
24  y[y==5] <- 1
25
26  # Set the data
27  y1 <- as.matrix(y)
28  y2 <- t(y1)
29
30  # Choose the 1st 5000 data
31  y3 <- y2[,1:5000]
32
33  #Execute the L-Layer Deep Learning Model
34  # hidden activation function - relu
35  # learning rate - 0.3
36  retvals = L_Layer_DeepModel(x2, y3, layersDimensions,
37                              hiddenActivationFunc='tanh',
38                              learningRate = 0.3,
39                              numIterations = 3000, print_cost = True)
40
41  # Setup costs and iterations
42  costs <- retvals[['costs']]
43  numIterations = 3000
44  iterations <- seq(0,numIterations,by=1000)
45  df <-data.frame(iterations,costs)
46
47  # Plot cost vs iterations
48  ggplot(df,aes(x=iterations,y=costs)) + geom_point() +geom_line(color="blue")
49  + xlab('No of iterations') + ylab('Cost') + ggtitle("Cost vs No of
50  iterations")
```

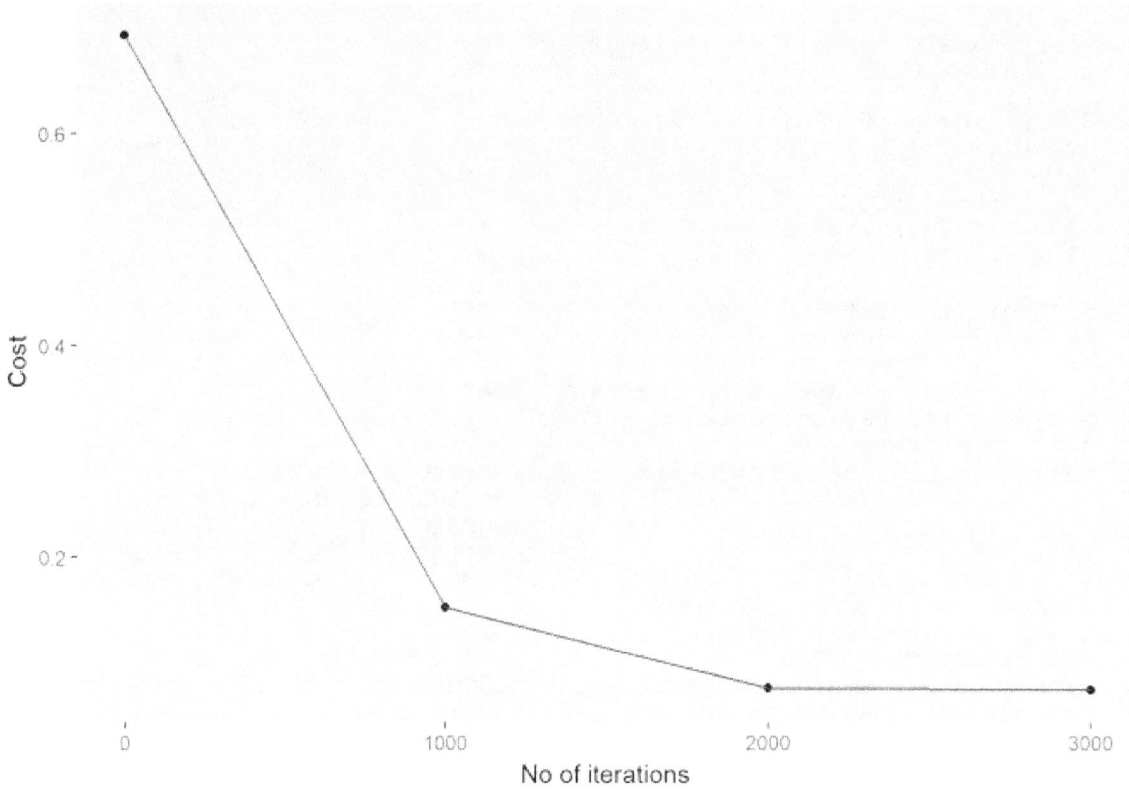

```
1   # Compute probability scores
2   scores <- computeScores(retvals$parameters, x2,hiddenActivationFunc='relu')
3   a=y3==1
4   b=y3==0
5
6   # Compute probabilities of class 0 and class 1
7   class1=scores[a]
8   class0=scores[b]
9
10  # Plot ROC curve
11  pr <-pr.curve(scores.class0=class1,
12          scores.class1=class0,
13         curve=T)
14
15  plot(pr)
```

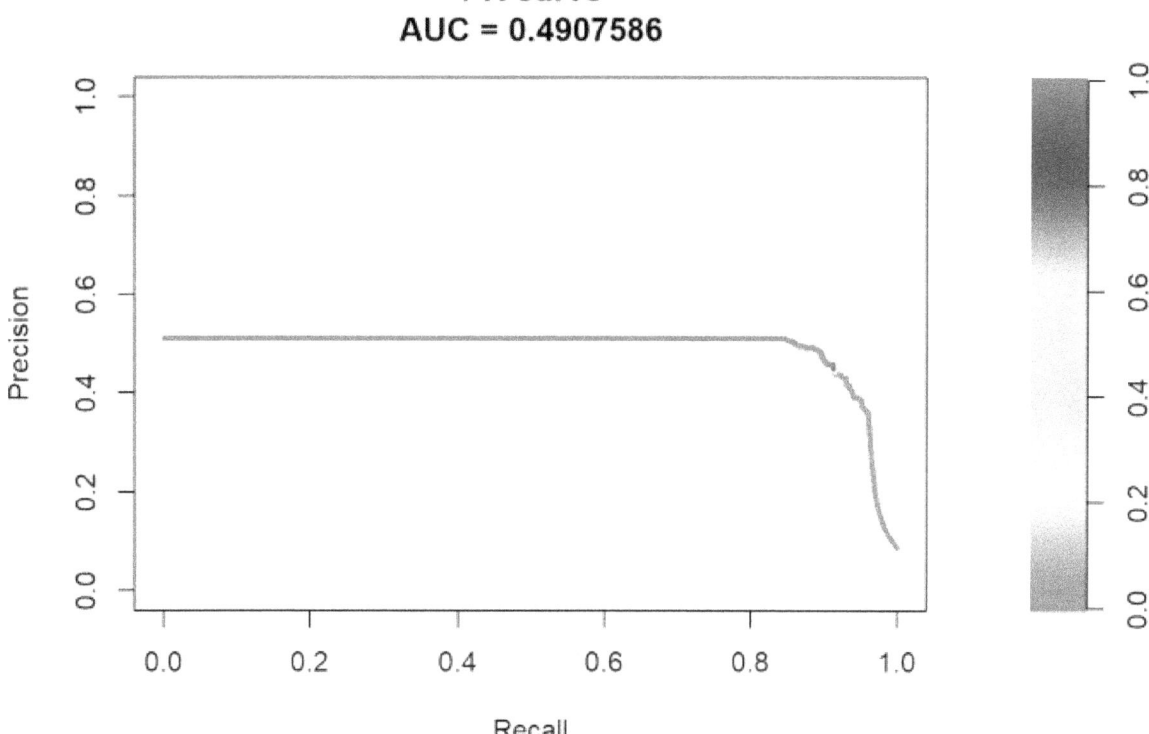

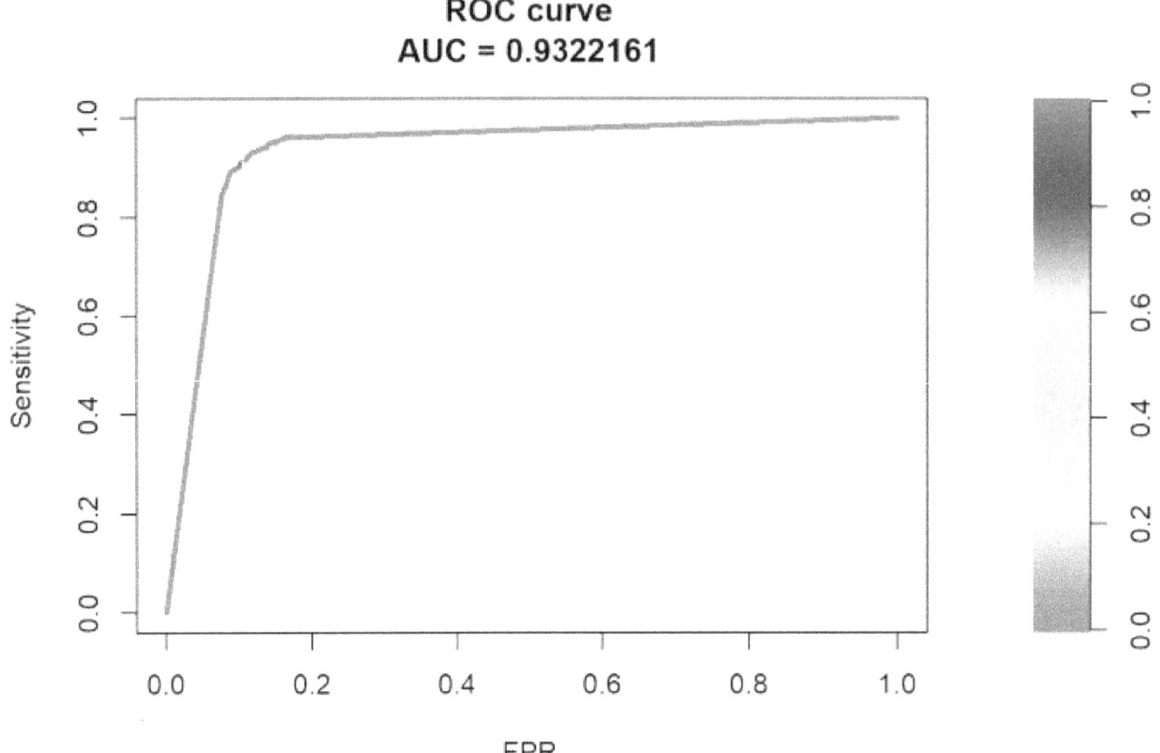

The AUC curve hugs the top left corner and hence the performance of the classifier is quite good.

4c. Binary Classification using MNIST – Octave code

This code to load MNIST data was taken from Daniel E blog (http://daniel-e.github.io/2017-10-20-loading-mnist-handwritten-digits-with-octave-or-matlab/)
Precision recall curves are available in Matlab, but are yet to be implemented in Octave's statistics package.

```
1  # Load the MNIST data
2  load('./mnist/mnist.txt.gz');
3
4  # Classify digits as 5 and not 5
5  # Subset the 'not 5' digits
6  a=(trainY != 5);
7  # Subset '5'
8  b=(trainY == 5);
9  #make a copy of trainY
10 #Set 'not 5' as 0 and '5' as 1
11 y=trainY;
12 y(a)=0;
13 y(b)=1;
14 X=trainX(1:5000,:);
15 Y=y(1:5000);
16
17 # Set the dimensions of layer
18 # 784 - number of input features = 28 x 28
19 # 7, 7, 3 - 3 hidden layers with 7,7, 3 hidden activation units respectively
```

```
20  # 1 - 1 sigmoid activation unit at output layer
21  layersDimensions=[784, 7,7,3,1];
22
23  # Execute the L-Layerthe DL network
24  # hidden activation function - relu
25  #learning rate - 0.1
26  [weights biases costs]=L_Layer_DeepModel(X', Y', layersDimensions,
27  hiddenActivationFunc='relu',
28  learningRate = 0.1,
29  numIterations = 5000);
```

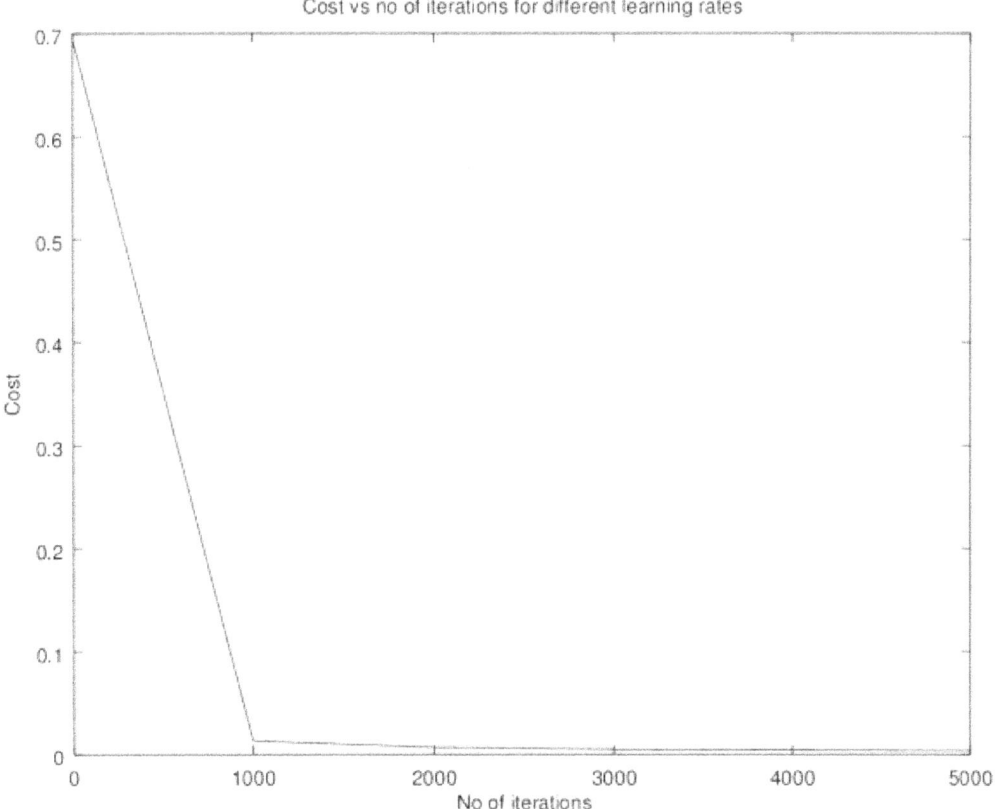

5. Conclusion

It was quite a challenge coding a Deep Learning Network in Python, R and Octave. The Deep Learning network implementation, in this chapter is the 'no-frills' Deep Learning network. It does not include initialization techniques, regularization or gradient optimizations methods. These will be discussed in chapter 6 and chapter 7. This L-layer Deep Learning network will be enhanced in the later chapters. Here are some key learning that I got while playing with different multi-layer networks on different problems

a. Deep Learning Networks come with many levers, the hyper-parameters,
– learning rate
– activation unit
– number of hidden layers
– number of units per hidden layer
– number of iterations while performing gradient descent
b. Deep Networks are very sensitive. A change in any of the hyper-parameter makes it perform very differently
c. Initially I thought adding more hidden layers, or more units per hidden layer will make the DL network better at learning. On the contrary, there is a performance degradation after the optimal DL configuration
d. At a sub-optimal number of hidden layers or number of hidden units, gradient descent seems to get stuck at a local minima
e. There were occasions when the cost came down, only to increase slowly as the number of iterations were increased. Probably early stopping would have helped.
f. I also did come across situations of 'exploding/vanishing gradient'; cost went to Inf/-Inf.

Feel free to fork/clone the code from Github DeepLearningFromFirstPrinciples (https://github.com/tvganesh/DeepLearningFromFirstPrinciples/tree/master/Chap3-L-LayerDeepLearningNetwork) and take the DL network apart and play around with it.

UPGRADE NOW DISMISS MESSAGE

4. Deep Learning network with the Softmax

In this fourth chapter I explore the details of creating a multi-class classifier using the Softmax activation unit in a neural network. This fourth chapter takes a swing at multi-class classification and uses the Softmax as the activation unit in the output layer. Inclusion of the Softmax activation unit in the activation layer requires us to compute the derivative of Softmax, or rather the "Jacobian" of the Softmax function, besides also computing the log loss for this Softmax activation during backward propagation. Since the derivation of the Jacobian of a Softmax and the computation of the Cross Entropy/log loss is very involved, I have implemented a basic neural network with just 1 hidden layer with the Softmax activation at the output layer. I also perform multi-class classification based on the 'spiral' data set from CS231n Convolutional Neural Networks (http://cs231n.github.io/neural-networks-case-study/) Stanford course, to test the performance and correctness of the implementations in Python, R and Octave. The vectorized implementations of the functions in this chapter are at Appendix 4 - Deep Learning network with the Softmax

You can clone download the code for the Python, R and Octave implementations from Github at DeepLearningFromFirstPrinciples (https://github.com/tvganesh/DeepLearningFromFirstPrinciples/tree/master/Chap4-MulticlassDeepLearningNetwork)

The Softmax function takes an N dimensional vector as input and generates a N-dimensional vector as output.
The Softmax function is given by (4a) below
$$S_j = \frac{e^j}{\sum e_k} \quad - (4a)$$
There is a probabilistic interpretation of the Softmax, since the sum of the Softmax values of a set of vectors will always add up to 1, given that each Softmax value is divided by the total of all values.

As mentioned earlier, the Softmax takes a vector input and returns a vector of outputs. For e.g. the Softmax of a vector a= [1, 3, 6], is another vector S= [0.0063, 0.0471, 0.9464]. Notice that vector output is proportional to the input vector. Also, taking the derivative of a vector by another vector, is known as the Jacobian. By the way, The Matrix Calculus You Need For Deep Learning (https://arxiv.org/pdf/1802.01528.pdf) by Terence Parr and Jeremy Howard, is very good paper that distills all the main mathematical concepts for Deep Learning in one place.
Let us take a simple 2 layered neural network with just 2 activation units in the hidden layer is shown below

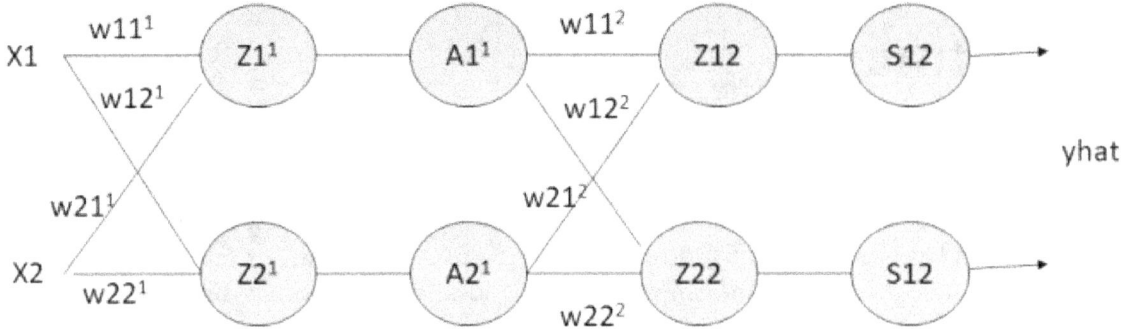

$$Z_1^1 = W_{11}^1 x_1 + W_{21}^1 x_2 + b_1^1$$
$$Z_2^1 = W_{12}^1 x_1 + W_{22}^1 x_2 + b_2^1$$
and
$$A_1^1 = g'(Z_1^1)$$
$$A_2^1 = g'(Z_2^1)$$
where g'() is the activation unit in the hidden layer which can be a relu, sigmoid or a tanh function

Note: The superscript denotes the layer. The equations are applicable for layer 1 of the neural network. For layer 2 with the Softmax activation, the equations are
$$Z_1^2 = W_{11}^2 x_1 + W_{21}^2 x_2 + b_1^2$$
$$Z_2^2 = W_{12}^2 x_1 + W_{22}^2 x_2 + b_2^2$$
and
$$A_1^2 = S(A_1^1)$$
$$A_2^2 = S(A_2^1)$$
where S is the Softmax activation function and using equation (4a) above
$$S = \begin{pmatrix} S(Z_1^2) \\ S(Z_2^2) \end{pmatrix}$$
$$S = \begin{pmatrix} \frac{e^{Z1}}{e^{Z1}+e^{Z2}} \\ \frac{e^{Z2}}{e^{Z1}+e^{Z2}} \end{pmatrix}$$

The Jacobian of the softmax 'S' is given by
$$\begin{pmatrix} \frac{\partial S_1}{\partial Z_1} & \frac{\partial S_1}{\partial Z_2} \\ \frac{\partial S_2}{\partial Z_1} & \frac{\partial S_2}{\partial Z_2} \end{pmatrix} = \begin{pmatrix} \frac{\partial}{\partial Z_1} \frac{e^{Z1}}{e^{Z1}+e^{Z2}} & \frac{\partial}{\partial Z_2} \frac{e^{Z1}}{e^{Z1}+e^{Z2}} \\ \frac{\partial}{\partial Z_1} \frac{e^{Z2}}{e^{Z1}+e^{Z2}} & \frac{\partial}{\partial Z_2} \frac{e^{Z2}}{e^{Z1}+e^{Z2}} \end{pmatrix}$$

Now the 'division-rule' of derivatives is as follows. If u and v are functions of x, then
$$\frac{d}{dx}\frac{u}{v} = \frac{vdu - udv}{v^2}$$
Using this we can compute each element of the above Jacobian matrix It can be seen that when i=j we have
$$\frac{\partial}{\partial Z1} \frac{e^{Z1}}{e^{Z1}+e^{Z2}} = \frac{\sum e^{Z1} - e^{Z1^2}}{\sum^2}$$

and when $i \neq j$
$$\frac{\partial}{\partial Z1} \frac{e^{Z2}}{e^{Z1}+e^{Z2}} = \frac{0-e^{Z1}e^{Z2}}{\Sigma^2}$$

This is of the general form
$$\frac{\partial S_i}{\partial z_i} = S_i(1-S_j) \text{ when i=j}$$
and
$$\frac{\partial S_i}{\partial z_i} = -S_i S_j \text{ when } i \neq j$$

Note: Since the Softmax essentially gives the probability the following notation is also used
$$\frac{\partial p_i}{\partial z_i} = p_i(1-p_j) \text{ when i=j}$$
and
$$\frac{\partial p_i}{\partial z_i} = -p_i p_j \text{ when } i \neq j$$

If you throw the "Kronecker delta" into the equation, then the above equations can be expressed even more concisely as
$$\frac{\partial p_i}{\partial z_i} = p_i(\delta_{ij} - p_j)$$

where $\delta_{ij} = 1$ when i=j and 0 when $i \neq j$

This reduces the Jacobian of the simple 2 output softmax vectors equation (A) as
$$\begin{pmatrix} p_1(1-p_1) & -p_1 p_2 \\ -p_2 p_1 & p_2(1-p_2) \end{pmatrix}$$

The loss of Softmax is given by
$$L = -\sum y_i log(p_i)$$
For the 2 valued Softmax output this is
$$\frac{dL}{dp1} = -\frac{y_1}{p_1}$$
$$\frac{dL}{dp2} = -\frac{y_2}{p_2}$$

Using the chain rule we can write
$$\frac{\partial L}{\partial x_{pq}} = \sum_i \frac{\partial L}{\partial p_i} \frac{\partial p_i}{\partial w_{pq}} \quad (1)$$
In expanded form this is

Also
$$\frac{\partial L}{\partial Z_i} = \sum_i \frac{\partial L}{\partial p} \frac{\partial p}{\partial Z_i}$$
Therefore
$$\frac{\partial L}{\partial z_1} = -\frac{y1}{p1}p1(1-p1) - \frac{y2}{p2} * (-p_2 p_1)$$
Since

$\frac{\partial p_i}{\partial z_i} = p_i(1-p_j)$ when i=j

and

$\frac{\partial p_i}{\partial z_i} = -p_i p_j$ when $i \neq j$

which simplifies to

$\frac{\partial L}{\partial z_1} = -y_1 + y_1 p_1 + y_2 p_1 =$

$p_1 \sum (y_1 + y_2) - y_1$

$\frac{\partial L}{\partial z_1} = p_1 - y_1$

Since

$\sum_i y_i = 1$

Similarly

$\frac{\partial L}{\partial z_2} = -\frac{y_1}{p_1} * (p_1 p_2) - \frac{y_2}{p_2} * p_2(1-p_2)$

$y_1 p_2 + y_2 p_2 - y_2$

$\frac{\partial L}{\partial z_2} = p_2 \sum (y_1 + y_2) - y_2$

$= p_2 - y_2$

In general this is of the form

$\frac{\partial L}{\partial z_i} = p_i - y_i$ - (A)

For e.g. if the probabilities computed were p=[0.1, 0.7, 0.2] then this implies that the class with probability 0.7 is the likely class. This would imply that the 'One hot encoding' for yi would be yi=[0,1,0] therefore the gradient pi-yi = [0.1, -0.3, 0.2]

Note: Further, we could extend this derivation for a Softmax activation output that outputs 3 classes

$$S = \begin{pmatrix} \frac{e^{z_1}}{e^{z_1}+e^{z_2}+e^{z_3}} \\ \frac{e^{z_2}}{e^{z_1}+e^{z_2}+e^{z_3}} \\ \frac{e^{z_3}}{e^{z_1}+e^{z_2}+e^{z_3}} \end{pmatrix}$$

We could derive

$\frac{\partial L}{\partial z_1} = \frac{\partial L}{\partial p_1}\frac{\partial p_1}{\partial z_1} + \frac{\partial L}{\partial p_2}\frac{\partial p_2}{\partial z_1} + \frac{\partial L}{\partial p_3}\frac{\partial p_3}{\partial z_1}$ which similarly reduces to

$\frac{\partial L}{\partial z_1} = -\frac{y_1}{p_1} p_1(1-p_1) - \frac{y_2}{p_2} * (-p_2 p_1) - \frac{y_3}{p_3} * (-p_3 p_1)$

$-y_1 + y_1 p_1 + y_2 p_1 + y_3 p_1 = p_1 \sum (y_1 + y_2 + y_3) - y_1 = p_1 - y_1$

interestingly, despite the lengthy derivations the final result is simple and intuitive!

As seen in in chapter 3, the key equations for forward and backward propagation are

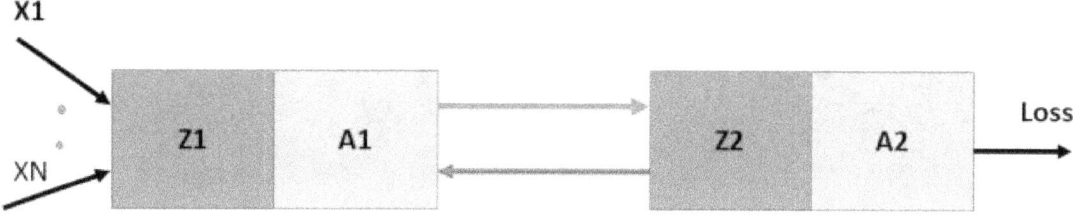

Forward propagation equations layer 1
$Z_1 = W_1 X + b_1$ and $A_1 = g(Z_1)$
Forward propagation equations layer 1
$Z_2 = W_2 A_1 + b_2$ and $A_2 = S(Z_2)$

Using the result (A) in the back propagation equations below we have
Backward propagation equations layer 2
$\partial L/\partial W_2 = \partial L/\partial Z_2 * A_1 = (p_2 - y_2) * A_1$
$\partial L/\partial b_2 = \partial L/\partial Z_2 = p_2 - y_2$
$\partial L/\partial A_1 = \partial L/\partial Z_2 * W_2 = (p_2 - y_2) * W_2$
Backward propagation equations layer 1
$\partial L/\partial W_1 = \partial L/\partial Z_1 * A_0 = (p_1 - y_1) * A_0$
$\partial L/\partial b_1 = \partial L/\partial Z_1 = (p_1 - y_1)$

2. Spiral data set

As I mentioned earlier, I will be using the 'spiral' data from CS231n Convolutional Neural Networks (http://cs231n.github.io/neural-networks-case-study/) to ensure that my vectorized implementations in Python, R and Octave are correct. Here is the 'spiral' data set.

```
1  import numpy as np
2  import matplotlib.pyplot as plt
3  exec(open("././DLfunctions41.py").read())
4
5  # Create an input data set - Taken from CS231n Convolutional Neural networks
6  # http://cs231n.github.io/neural-networks-case-study/
7  N = 100 # number of points per class
8  D = 2 # dimensionality
9  K = 3 # number of classes
10
11 X = np.zeros((N*K,D)) # data matrix (each row = single example)
12 y = np.zeros(N*K, dtype='uint8') # class labels
13 for j in range(K):
14   ix = range(N*j,N*(j+1))
15   r = np.linspace(0.0,1,N) # radius
16   t = np.linspace(j*4,(j+1)*4,N) + np.random.randn(N)*0.2 # theta
17   X[ix] = np.c_[r*np.sin(t), r*np.cos(t)]
18   y[ix] = j
19
20 # Plot the data
21 plt.scatter(X[:, 0], X[:, 1], c=y, s=40, cmap=plt.cm.Spectral)
22 plt.savefig("fig1.png", bbox_inches='tight')
```

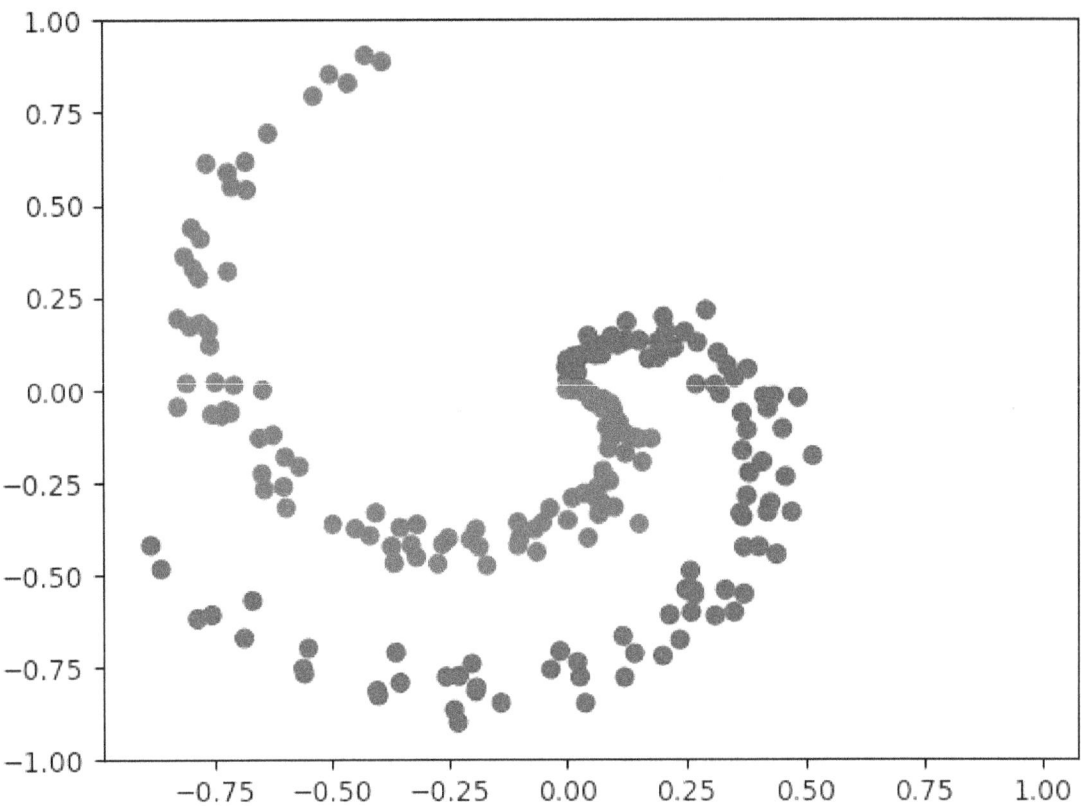

The implementations of the vectorized Python, R and Octave code are shown diagrammatically

below

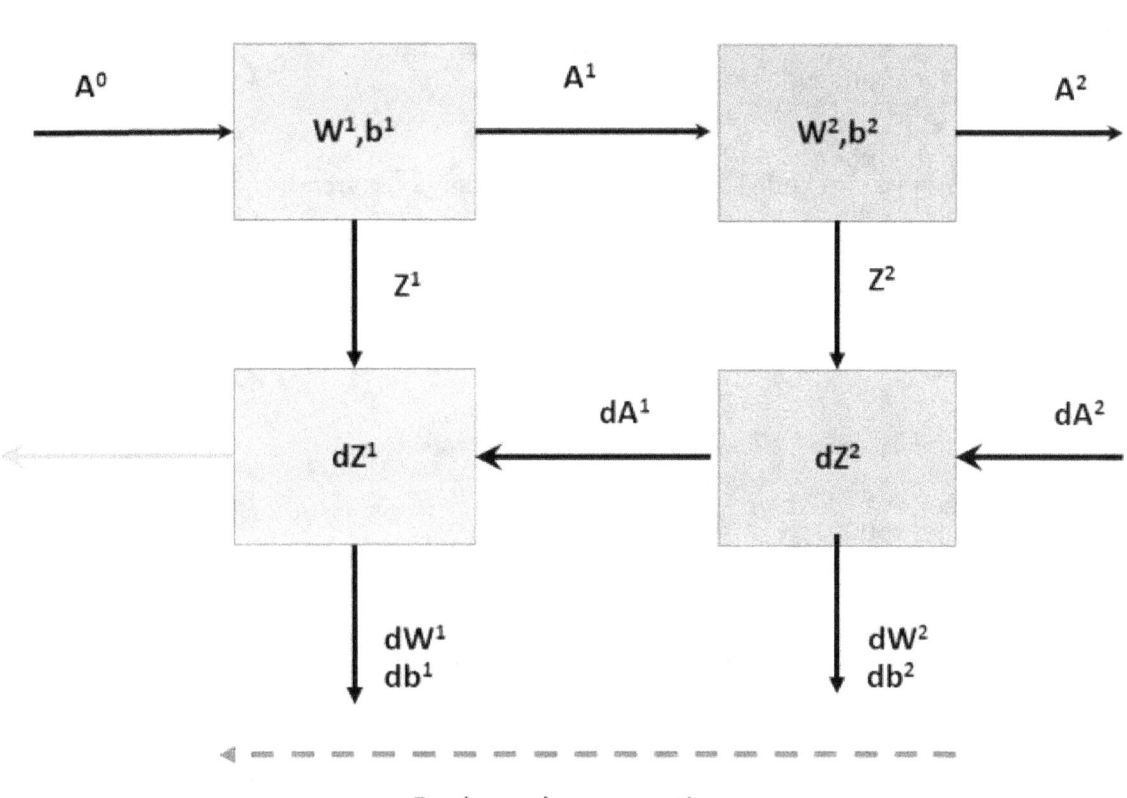

2.1 Multi-class classification with Softmax – Python code

A simple 2-layer Neural network with a single hidden layer, with 100 Relu activation units in the hidden layer and the Softmax activation unit in the output layer is used for multi-class classification. This Deep Learning Network, plots the non-linear boundary of the 3 classes as shown below

```
1  import numpy as np
2  import matplotlib.pyplot as plt
3  import os
4  os.chdir("C:/junk/dl-4/dl-4")
5  exec(open("./../DLfunctions41.py").read())
6
7  # Read the input data
8  N = 100 # number of points per class
9  D = 2 # dimensionality
10 K = 3 # number of classes
11 X = np.zeros((N*K,D)) # data matrix (each row = single example)
12 y = np.zeros(N*K, dtype='uint8') # class labels
13
14 #Loop
15 for j in range(K):
```

```python
16      ix = range(N*j,N*(j+1))
17      r = np.linspace(0.0,1,N) # radius
18      t = np.linspace(j*4,(j+1)*4,N) + np.random.randn(N)*0.2 # theta
19      X[ix] = np.c_[r*np.sin(t), r*np.cos(t)]
20      y[ix] = j
21
22  # Set the number of features, hidden units in hidden layer and number of
23  classess
24  numHidden=100 # No of hidden units in hidden layer
25  numFeats= 2 # dimensionality
26  numOutput = 3 # number of classes
27
28  # Initialize the model
29  parameters=initializeModel(numFeats,numHidden,numOutput)
30  W1= parameters['W1']
31  b1= parameters['b1']
32  W2= parameters['W2']
33  b2= parameters['b2']
34
35  # Set the learning rate
36  learningRate=0.6
37
38  # Initialize losses
39  losses=[]
40
41  # Perform Gradient descent
42  for i in range(10000):
43      # Forward propagation through hidden layer with Relu units
44      A1,cache1= layerActivationForward(X.T,W1,b1,'relu')
45
46      # Forward propagation through output layer with Softmax
47      A2,cache2 = layerActivationForward(A1,W2,b2,'softmax')
48
49      # No of training examples
50      numTraining = X.shape[0]
51      # Compute log probs. Take the log prob of correct class based on output y
52      correct_logprobs = -np.log(A2[range(numTraining),y])
53      # Compute loss
54      loss = np.sum(correct_logprobs)/numTraining
55
56      # Print the loss
57      if i % 1000 == 0:
58          print("iteration %d: loss %f" % (i, loss))
59          losses.append(loss)
60      dA=0
61
62      # Backward  propagation through output layer with Softmax
63      dA1,dW2,db2 = layerActivationBackward(dA, cache2, y,
64  activationFunc='softmax')
65      # Backward  propagation through hidden layer with Relu unit
66      dA0,dW1,db1 = layerActivationBackward(dA1.T, cache1, y,
67  activationFunc='relu')
68
69      #Update paramaters with the learning rate
70      W1 += -learningRate * dW1
71      b1 += -learningRate * db1
72      W2 += -learningRate * dW2.T
73      b2 += -learningRate * db2.T
74
75  #Plot losses vs iterations
76  i=np.arange(0,10000,1000)
77  plt.plot(i,losses)
78
79  plt.xlabel('Iterations')
```

```python
plt.ylabel('Loss')
plt.title('Losses vs Iterations')
plt.savefig("fig2.png", bbox="tight")

#Compute the multi-class Confusion Matrix
from sklearn.metrics import confusion_matrix
from sklearn.metrics import accuracy_score, precision_score, recall_score,
f1_score

# We need to determine the predicted values from the learnt data
# Forward propagation through hidden layer with Relu units
A1,cache1= layerActivationForward(X.T,W1,b1,'relu')

# Forward propagation through output layer with Softmax
A2,cache2 = layerActivationForward(A1,W2,b2,'softmax')
#Compute predicted values from weights and biases
yhat=np.argmax(A2, axis=1)

# Compute the confusion matrix
a=confusion_matrix(y.T,yhat.T)
print("Multi-class Confusion Matrix")
print(a)
## iteration 0: loss 1.098507
## iteration 1000: loss 0.214611
## iteration 2000: loss 0.043622
## iteration 3000: loss 0.032525
## iteration 4000: loss 0.025108
## iteration 5000: loss 0.021365
## iteration 6000: loss 0.019046
## iteration 7000: loss 0.017475
## iteration 8000: loss 0.016359
## iteration 9000: loss 0.015703

## Multi-class Confusion Matrix
## [[ 99   1   0]
##  [  0 100   0]
##  [  0   1  99]]
```

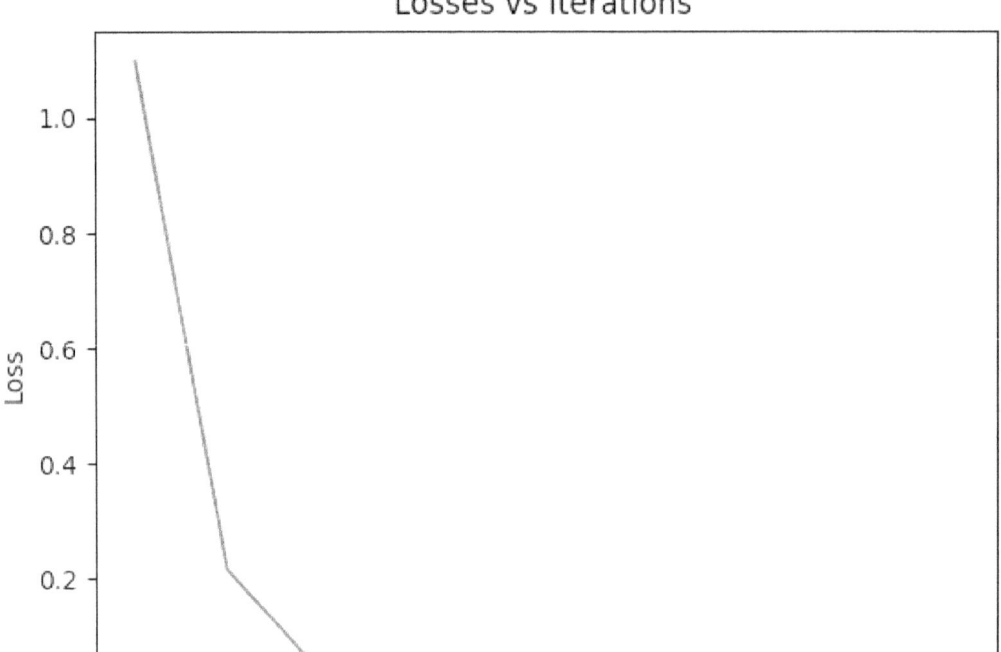

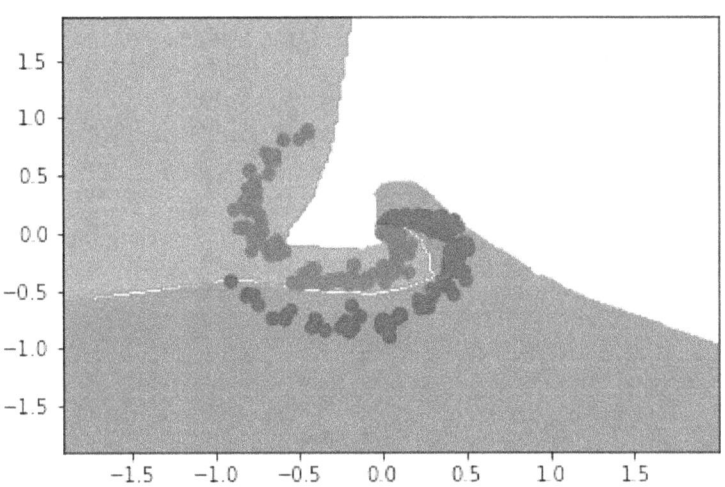

2.2 Multi-class classification with Softmax – R code

The spiral data set created with Python was saved (spiral.csv), and is used as the input with R code. To compute the softmax derivative I create matrices for the One Hot Encoded yi and then stack them before subtracting pi-yi.

```r
library(ggplot2)
library(dplyr)
library(RColorBrewer)
source("DLfunctions41.R")

# Read the spiral dataset
Z <- as.matrix(read.csv("spiral.csv",header=FALSE))
Z1=data.frame(Z)

#Plot the dataset
ggplot(Z1,aes(x=V1,y=V2,col=V3)) +geom_point() +
  scale_colour_gradientn(colours = brewer.pal(10, "Spectral"))
```

```r
# Setup the data
X <- Z[,1:2]
y <- Z[,3]
X1 <- t(X)
Y1 <- t(y)

# Initialize number of features, number of hidden units in hidden layer and
# number of classes
```

```r
numFeats<-2 # No features
numHidden<-100 # No of hidden units
numOutput<-3 # No of classes

# Initialize model
parameters <-initializeModel(numFeats, numHidden,numOutput)

# Get the parameters
w1 <-parameters[['W1']]
b1 <-parameters[['b1']]
w2 <-parameters[['W2']]
b2 <-parameters[['b2']]

# Set the learning rate
learningRate <- 0.5

# Initialize losses
losses <- NULL

# Perform gradient descent
for(i in 0:9000){
        # Forward propagation through hidden layer with Relu units
        retvals <- layerActivationForward(X1,W1,b1,'relu')
        A1 <- retvals[['A']]
        cache1 <- retvals[['cache']]
        forward_cache1 <- cache1[['forward_cache1']]
        activation_cache <- cache1[['activation_cache']]

        # Forward propagation through output layer with Softmax units
        retvals = layerActivationForward(A1,W2,b2,'softmax')
        A2 <- retvals[['A']]
        cache2 <- retvals[['cache']]
        forward_cache2 <- cache2[['forward_cache1']]
        activation_cache2 <- cache2[['activation_cache']]

        # No of training examples
        numTraining <- dim(X)[1]
        dA <-0

        # Select the elements where the y values are 0, 1 or 2 and make a vector
        a=c(A2[y==0,1],A2[y==1,2],A2[y==2,3])

        # Compute probabalities
        correct_probs = -log(a)
        # Compute loss
        loss= sum(correct_probs)/numTraining

        if(i %% 1000 == 0){
                sprintf("iteration %d: loss %f",i, loss)
                print(loss)
        }

        # Backward propagation through output layer with Softmax units
        retvals = layerActivationBackward(dA, cache2, y, activationFunc='softmax')
        dA1 = retvals[['dA_prev']]
        dW2= retvals[['dW']]
        db2= retvals[['db']]

        # Backward propagation through hidden layer with Relu units
        retvals = layerActivationBackward(t(dA1), cache1, y, activationFunc='relu')
        dA0 = retvals[['dA_prev']]
```

```
            dW1= retvals[['dW']]
            db1= retvals[['db']]

            # Update parameters
            W1 <- W1 - learningRate * dW1
            b1 <- b1 - learningRate * db1
            W2 <- W2 - learningRate * t(dW2)
            b2 <- b2 - learningRate * t(db2)
}
## [1] 1.212487
## [1] 0.5740867
## [1] 0.4048824
## [1] 0.3561941
## [1] 0.2509576
## [1] 0.7351063
## [1] 0.2066114
## [1] 0.2065875
## [1] 0.2151943
## [1] 0.1318807


#Create iterations
iterations <- seq(0,10)
df=data.frame(iterations,losses)

# Plot cost vs iterations
ggplot(df,aes(x=iterations,y=losses)) + geom_point() +
geom_line(color="blue") +
    ggtitle("Losses vs iterations") + xlab("Iterations") + ylab("Loss")

#Plot the decision boundary
plotDecisionBoundary(Z,W1,b1,W2,b2)
```

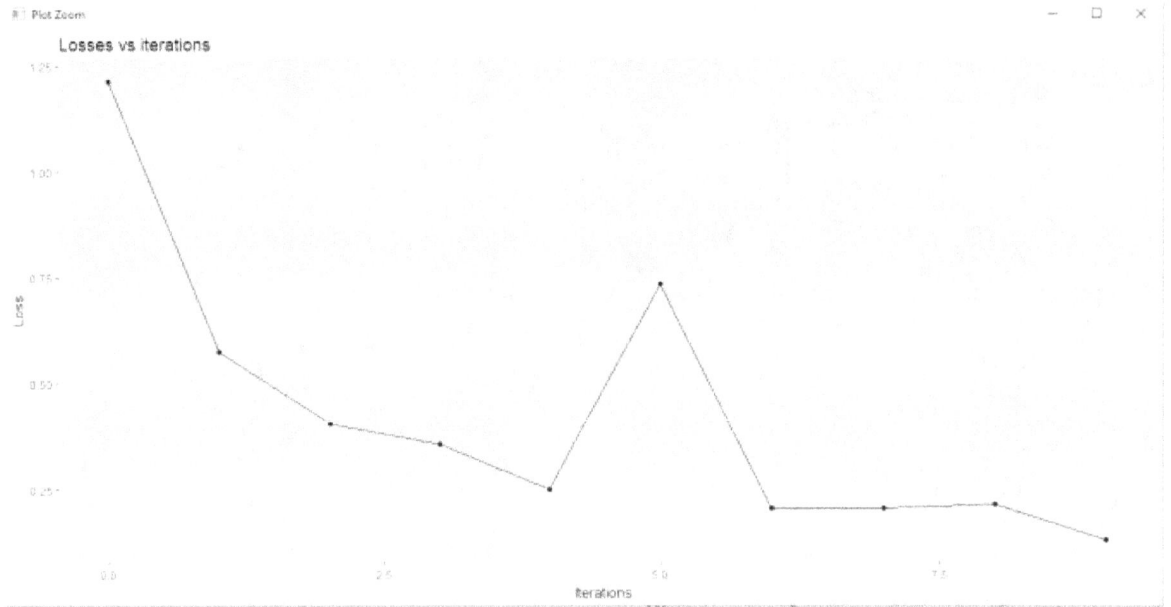

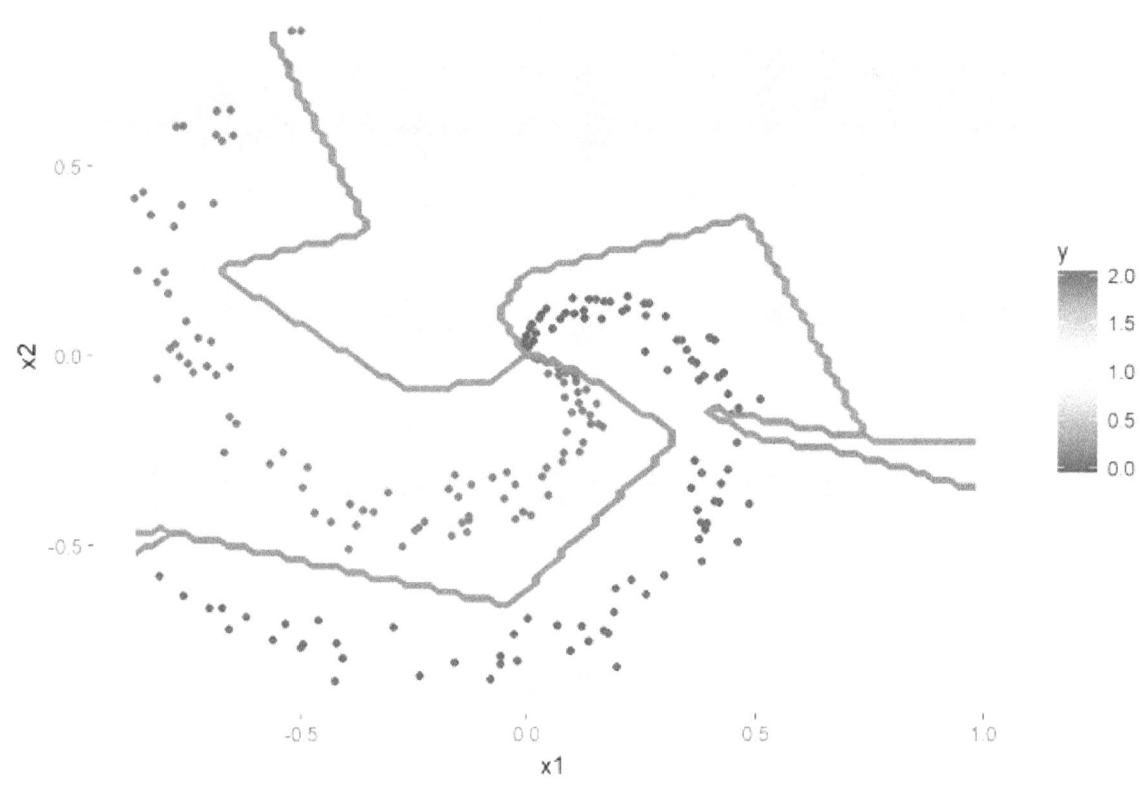

Multi-class Confusion Matrix

```
1  library(caret)
2  library(e1071)
3
4  # Forward propagation through hidden layer with Relu units
5  retvals <- layerActivationForward(X1,W1,b1,'relu')
6  A1 <- retvals[['A']]
7
8  # Forward propagation through output layer with Softmax units
```

```
9  retvals = layerActivationForward(A1,W2,b2,'softmax')
10 A2 <- retvals[['A']]
11 yhat <- apply(A2, 1,which.max) -1
12 Confusion Matrix and Statistics
13           Reference
14 Prediction  0  1  2
15          0 97  0  1
16          1  2 96  4
17          2  1  4 95
18
19 Overall Statistics
20              Accuracy : 0.96
21                95% CI : (0.9312, 0.9792)
22   No Information Rate : 0.3333
23   P-Value [Acc > NIR] : <2e-16
24
25                 Kappa : 0.94
26  Mcnemar's Test P-Value : 0.5724
27 Statistics by Class:
28
29                      Class: 0 Class: 1 Class: 2
30 Sensitivity            0.9700   0.9600   0.9500
31 Specificity            0.9950   0.9700   0.9750
32 Pos Pred Value         0.9898   0.9412   0.9500
33 Neg Pred Value         0.9851   0.9798   0.9750
34 Prevalence             0.3333   0.3333   0.3333
35 Detection Rate         0.3233   0.3200   0.3167
36 Detection Prevalence   0.3267   0.3400   0.3333
37 Balanced Accuracy      0.9825   0.9650   0.9625
```

2.3 Multi-class classification with Softmax – Octave code

A 2-layer neural network with the Softmax activation unit in the output layer is constructed in Octave. The same spiral data (spiral.csv) set is used for Octave also

```
1  source("DL41functions.m")
2  # Read the spiral data
3  data=csvread("spiral.csv");
4  # Setup the data
5  X=data(:,1:2);
6  Y=data(:,3);
7
8  # Set the number of features, number of hidden units in hidden layer and
9  number of classes
10 numFeats=2; #No features
11 numHidden=100; # No of hidden units
12 numOutput=3; # No of classes
13
14 # Initialize model
15 [W1 b1 W2 b2] = initializeModel(numFeats,numHidden,numOutput);
16 # Initialize losses
17 losses=[]
18
19 #Initialize learningRate
20 learningRate=0.5;
21
22 for k =1:10000
23     # Forward propagation through hidden layer with Relu units
24     [A1,cache1 activation_cache1]=
25 layerActivationForward(X',W1,b1,activationFunc ='relu');
```

```octave
    # Forward propagation through output layer with Softmax units
    [A2,cache2 activation_cache2] =
    layerActivationForward(A1,W2,b2,activationFunc='softmax');

    # No of training examples
    numTraining = size(X)(1);
   # Select rows where Y=0,1,and 2 and concatenate to a long vector
   a=[A2(Y==0,1) ;A2(Y==1,2) ;A2(Y==2,3)];

   #Select the correct column for log prob
   correct_probs = -log(a);

   #Compute log loss
    loss= sum(correct_probs)/numTraining;
    if(mod(k,1000) == 0)
       disp(loss);
         losses=[losses loss];
    endif
    dA=0;

    # Backward propagation through output layer with Softmax units
    [dA1 dW2 db2] = layerActivationBackward(dA, cache2,
activation_cache2,Y,activationFunc='softmax');

    # Backward propagation through hidden layer with Relu units
    [dA0,dW1,db1] = layerActivationBackward(dA1', cache1, activation_cache1,
Y,       activationFunc='relu');
    #Update parameters
    W1 += -learningRate * dW1;
    b1 += -learningRate * db1;
    W2 += -learningRate * dW2';
   b2 += -learningRate * db2';
endfor

# Plot Losses vs Iterations
iterations=0:1000:9000
plotCostVsIterations(iterations,losses)

# Plot the decision boundary
plotDecisionBoundary( X,Y,W1,b1,W2,b2)
```

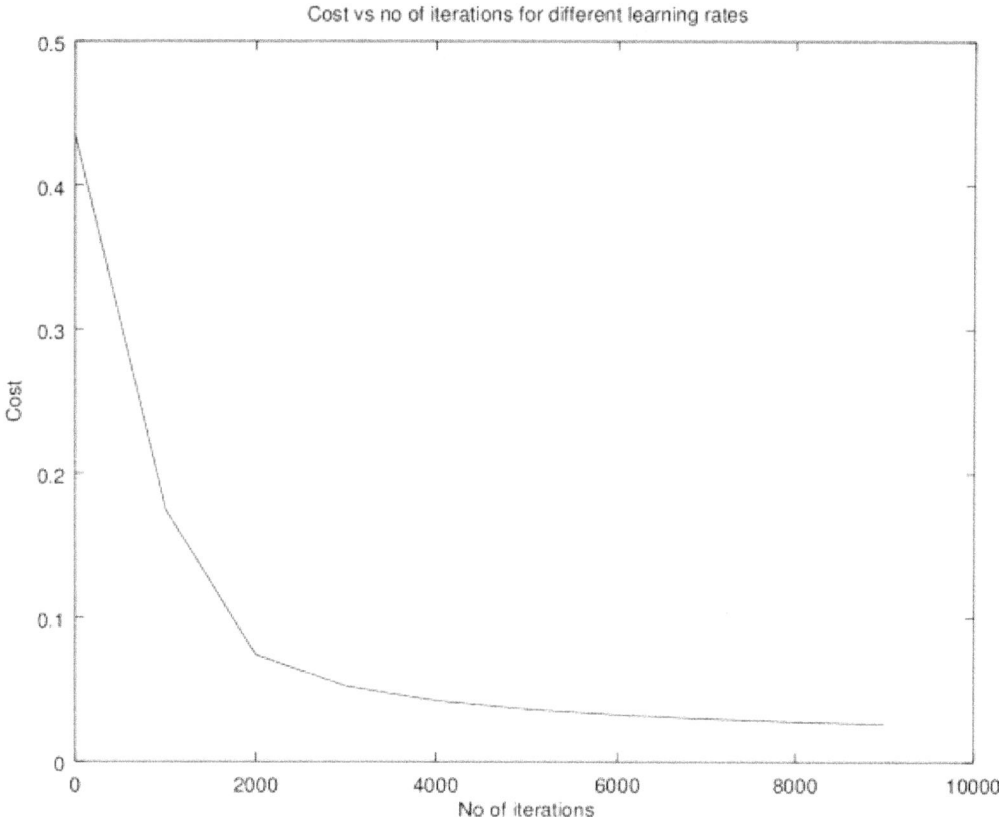

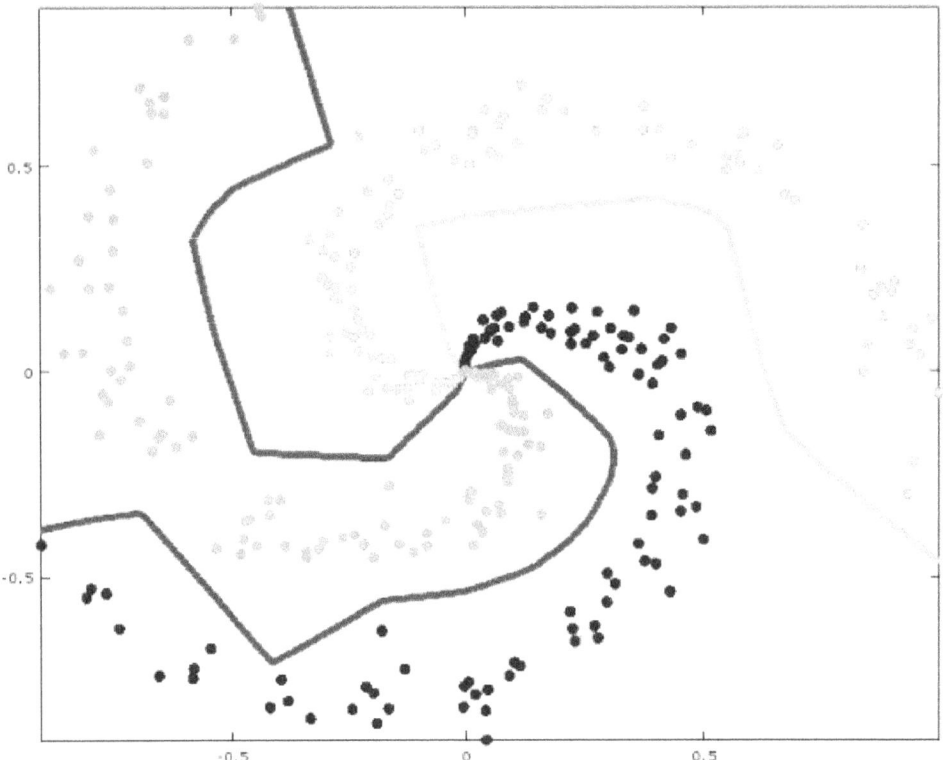

The code for the Python, R and Octave implementations can be downloaded from Github at DeepLearningFromFirstPrinciples (https://github.com/tvganesh/DeepLearningFromFirstPrinciples/tree/master/Chap4-MulticlassDeepLearningNetwork)

Conclusion

In this chapter, I implemented a 2 layer Neural Network with the Softmax classifier. In chapter 3, I implemented a multi-layer Deep Learning Network. The Softmax activation unit is included into into the generalized multi-layer Deep Network along with the other activation units of sigmoid,tanh and relu in chapter 5.

5. MNIST classification with Softmax

a. A robot may not injure a human being or, through inaction, allow a human being to come to harm.
b. A robot must obey orders given it by human beings except where such orders would conflict with the First Law.
c. A robot must protect its own existence as long as such protection does not conflict with the First or Second Law.
   Isaac Asimov's Three Laws of Robotics
Any sufficiently advanced technology is indistinguishable from magic.
   Arthur C Clarke.

1. Introduction

In this 5th chapter on Deep Learning from first Principles in Python, R and Octave, I solve the MNIST data set of handwritten digits (shown below), from the basics. To do this, I construct a L-Layer, vectorized Deep Learning implementation in Python, R and Octave from scratch and classify the MNIST data set. The MNIST training data set contains 60000 handwritten digits from 0-9, and a test set of 10000 digits. MNIST, is a popular dataset for running Deep Learning tests, and has been rightfully termed as the 'drosophila' of Deep Learning, by none other than the venerable Prof Geoffrey Hinton.

This chapter largely builds upon chapter 3, in which I implemented a multi-layer Deep Learning network, with an arbitrary number of hidden layers and activation units per hidden layer and with the sigmoid output layer. To this, I add the derivation of the Jacobian of a Softmax, the Cross entropy loss and the computations of gradient equations for a multi-class Softmax classifier which I had done in chapter 4

By combining the implementations of chapter 3 & 4 I build a generic, L-layer Deep Learning network, with arbitrary number of hidden layers and hidden units, which can do both binary (sigmoid) and multi-class (softmax) classification. The implementations of the functions invoked in this chapter are in Appendix 5 - MNIST classification with Softmax

The generic, vectorized L-Layer Deep Learning Network implementations in Python, R and Octave can be cloned/downloaded from GitHub at DeepLearningFromFirstPrinciples (https://github.com/tvganesh/DeepLearningFromFirstPrinciples/tree/master/Chap5-MNISTMultiClassDLNetwork). This implementation allows for arbitrary number of hidden layers and hidden layer units. The activation function at the hidden layers can be one of sigmoid, relu and tanh. The output activation can do binary classification with the 'sigmoid', function or multi-class classification with 'softmax'. Feel free to download and play around with the code!

Since regular gradient descent on 60,000 training samples on a laptop will result in memory problem on such a large dataset. So, this chapter also implements Stochastic Gradient Descent (SGD) for Python, R and Octave. This chapter also includes the implementation of a numerically stable version of Softmax, to prevent the softmax and its derivative resulting in NaNs.

2. Numerically stable Softmax

The Softmax function $S_j = \frac{e^{Z_j}}{\sum e^{Z_i}}$ can be numerically unstable because of the division of large exponentials. To handle this problem we have to implement stable Softmax function as below

$$S_j = \frac{e^{Z_j}}{\sum e^{Z_i}}$$

Therefore $S_j = \frac{e^{Z_j + D}}{\sum e^{Z_i + D}}$

Here 'D' can be anything. A common choice is
$D = -max(Z_1, Z_2, ..., Z_k)$

Here is the stable Softmax implementation in Python

```python
# A numerically stable Softmax implementation
def stableSoftmax(Z):
    #Compute the softmax of vector x in a numerically stable way.
    shiftZ = Z.T - np.max(Z.T,axis=1).reshape(-1,1)
    exp_scores = np.exp(shiftZ)
    
    # Normalize them for each example
    A = exp_scores / np.sum(exp_scores, axis=1, keepdims=True)
    cache=Z
    return A,cache
```

While trying to create an L-Layer generic Deep Learning network in the 3 languages, I found it useful to ensure that the model executed correctly on smaller datasets. You can run into numerous problems while setting up the matrices, which becomes extremely difficult to debug. So in this post, I run the model on 2 smaller data for sets used in my earlier posts (chapter 3 & chapter 4) , in each of the languages, before running the generic model on MNIST.

Here is a fair warning: - if you think you can dive directly into Deep Learning, with just some basic knowledge of Machine Learning, you are bound to run into serious issues. Moreover, your knowledge will be incomplete. It is essential that you have a good grasp of Machine and Statistical Learning, the different algorithms, the measures and metrics for selecting the models etc. It would help to be conversant with all the ML models, ML concepts, validation techniques, classification measures etc. Check out the internet/books for background.

3.1a Random dataset with sigmoid activation – Python

This random data with 9 clusters, used in chapter 3 was used to test the complete L-layer Deep Learning network with Sigmoid activation.

```
import numpy as np
import matplotlib
import matplotlib.pyplot as plt
import pandas as pd
from sklearn.datasets import make_classification, make_blobs
exec(open("DLfunctions51.py").read()) # Cannot import in Rmd

# Create a random data set with 9 centeres
X1, Y1 = make_blobs(n_samples = 400, n_features = 2, centers = 9,cluster_std
= 1.3, random_state =4)

#Create 2 classes
Y1=Y1.reshape(400,1)
Y1 = Y1 % 2
X2=X1.T
Y2=Y1.T

# Set the dimensions of L -layer DL network
# 2 - number of input features
# 9,9 - 2 hidden layers with 9 activation units
# 1 - 1 activation unit in the output layer
layersDimensions = [2, 9, 9,1] # 4-layer model

# Execute the L-Layer  DL network with hidden activation=relu and sigmoid
output function
parameters = L_Layer_DeepModel(X2, Y2, layersDimensions,
hiddenActivationFunc='relu', outputActivationFunc="sigmoid",learningRate =
0.3,num_iterations = 2500, print_cost = True)
```

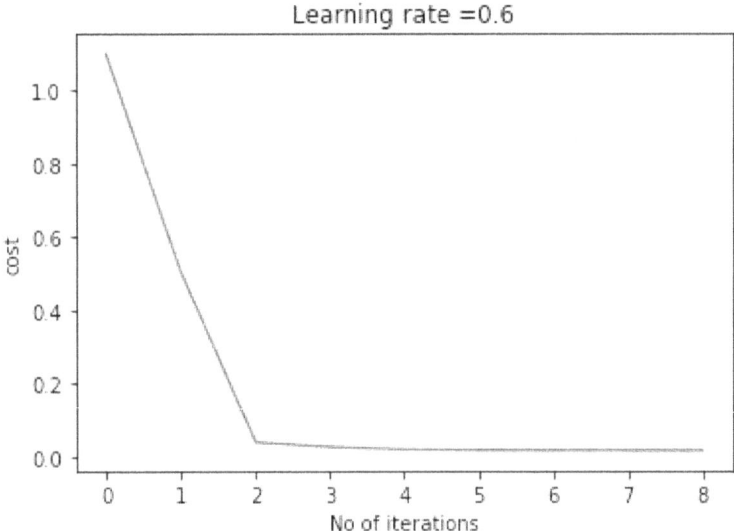

3.1b Spiral dataset with Softmax activation – Python

The Spiral data of chapter 4 was used to test the correct functioning of the complete L-layer Deep Learning network for multi-class classification with Softmax activation.

```
1  import numpy as np
2  import matplotlib
3  import matplotlib.pyplot as plt
4  import pandas as pd
5  from sklearn.datasets import make_classification, make_blobs
6  exec(open("DLfunctions51.py").read())
7
8  # Create an input data set - Taken from CS231n Convolutional Neural networks
9  # http://cs231n.github.io/neural-networks-case-study/
10 N = 100 # number of points per class
11 D = 2 # dimensionality
12 K = 3 # number of classes
13 X = np.zeros((N*K,D)) # data matrix (each row = single example)
14 y = np.zeros(N*K, dtype='uint8') # class labels
15
16 # Loop over K
17 for j in range(K):
18    ix = range(N*j,N*(j+1))
19    r = np.linspace(0.0,1,N) # radius
20    t = np.linspace(j*4,(j+1)*4,N) + np.random.randn(N)*0.2 # theta
21    X[ix] = np.c_[r*np.sin(t), r*np.cos(t)]
22    y[ix] = j
23 X1=X.T
24 Y1=y.reshape(-1,1).T
25
26 Set the parameters of the DL network
27 numHidden=100 # No of hidden units in hidden layer
28 numFeats= 2 # dimensionality
29 numOutput = 3 # number of classes
30 # Set the dimensions of the layers
31 layersDimensions=[numFeats,numHidden,numOutput]
32
33 # Execute the L-layer DL network with hidden activation=relu and softmax
34 output function
```

```
35  parameters = L_Layer_DeepModel(X1, Y1, layersDimensions,
36  hiddenActivationFunc='relu', outputActivationFunc="softmax",learningRate =
37  0.6,num_iterations = 9000, print_cost = True)
38  ## Cost after iteration 0: 1.098759
39  ## Cost after iteration 1000: 0.112666
40  ## Cost after iteration 2000: 0.044351
41  ## Cost after iteration 3000: 0.027491
42  ## Cost after iteration 4000: 0.021898
43  ## Cost after iteration 5000: 0.019181
44  ## Cost after iteration 6000: 0.017832
45  ## Cost after iteration 7000: 0.017452
46  ## Cost after iteration 8000: 0.017161
```

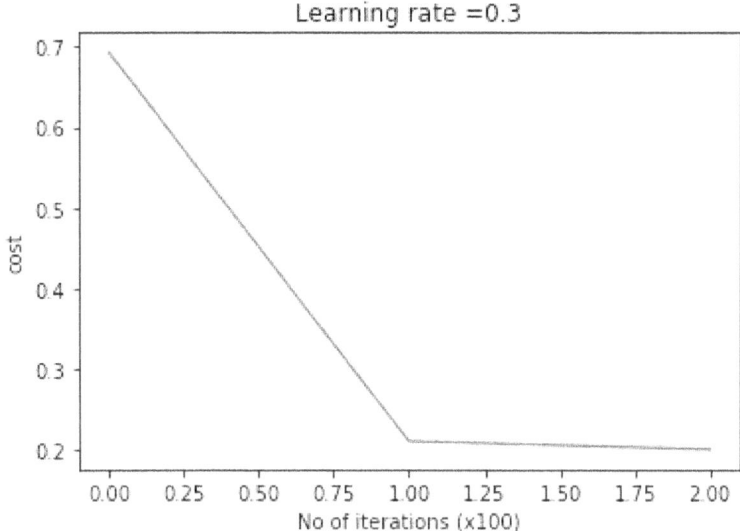

3.1c MNIST dataset with Softmax activation – Python

In the code below, I execute Stochastic Gradient Descent on the MNIST training data of 60000. I used a mini-batch size of 1000. Python takes about 40 minutes to crunch the data. In addition, I also compute the Confusion Matrix and other metrics like Accuracy, Precision and Recall for the MNIST data set. I get an accuracy of 0.93 on the MNIST test set. This accuracy can be improved by choosing more hidden layers or more hidden units and possibly tweaking the learning rate and the number of epochs.

```
1   import numpy as np
2   import matplotlib
3   import matplotlib.pyplot as plt
4   import pandas as pd
5   import math
6   from sklearn.datasets import make_classification, make_blobs
7   from sklearn.metrics import confusion_matrix
8   from sklearn.metrics import accuracy_score, precision_score, recall_score,
9   f1_score
10  exec(open("DLfunctions51.py").read())
11  exec(open("load_mnist.py").read())
12
13  # Read the MNIST training and test sets
14  training=list(read(dataset='training',path=".\\mnist"))
15  test=list(read(dataset='testing',path=".\\mnist"))
```

```python
# Create labels and pixel arrays
lbls=[]
pxls=[]
print(len(training))
#for i in range(len(training)):
for i in range(60000):
        l,p=training[i]
        lbls.append(l)
        pxls.append(p)
labels= np.array(lbls)
pixels=np.array(pxls)
y=labels.reshape(-1,1)
X=pixels.reshape(pixels.shape[0],-1)
X1=X.T
Y1=y.T

# Set the dimensions of the layers. The MNIST data is 28x28 pixels= 784
# Hence input layer is 784. For the 10 digits the Softmax classifier
# has to handle 10 outputs
# 784 - No of input features- 28 x27
# 15,9 - 2 hidden layers with 15 & 9 hidden units
#10 - 10 outputs at the output layer for 10 digits
layersDimensions=[784, 15,9,10] # Works very well,lr=0.01,mini_batch =1000,
total=20000
np.random.seed(1)
costs = []

# Execute the L-Layer Deep Learning network with Stochastic Gradient Descent
# with Learning Rate=0.01, mini batch size=1000
# number of epochs=3000
# hidden units= relu
# output activation unit =softmax
parameters = L_Layer_DeepModel_SGD(X1, Y1, layersDimensions,
hiddenActivationFunc='relu', outputActivationFunc="softmax",learningRate =
0.01 ,mini_batch_size =1000, num_epochs = 3000, print_cost = True)

# Compute the Confusion Matrix on Training set
# Compute the training accuracy, precision and recall
proba=predict_proba(parameters, X1,outputActivationFunc="softmax")
#A2, cache = forwardPropagationDeep(X1, parameters)
#proba=np.argmax(A2, axis=0).reshape(-1,1)
a=confusion_matrix(Y1.T,proba)
print(a)
from sklearn.metrics import accuracy_score, precision_score, recall_score,
f1_score
print('Accuracy: {:.2f}'.format(accuracy_score(Y1.T, proba)))
print('Precision: {:.2f}'.format(precision_score(Y1.T,
proba,average="micro")))
print('Recall: {:.2f}'.format(recall_score(Y1.T, proba,average="micro")))

# Read the test data
lbls=[]
pxls=[]
print(len(test))

# Loop
for i in range(10000):
        l,p=test[i]
        lbls.append(l)
        pxls.append(p)
testLabels= np.array(lbls)
testPixels=np.array(pxls)
ytest=testLabels.reshape(-1,1)
Xtest=testPixels.reshape(testPixels.shape[0],-1)
```

```
X1test=Xtest.T
Y1test=ytest.T

# Compute the Confusion Matrix on Test set
# Compute the test accuracy, precision and recall
probaTest=predict_proba(parameters, X1test,outputActivationFunc="softmax")
#A2, cache = forwardPropagationDeep(X1, parameters)
#proba=np.argmax(A2, axis=0).reshape(-1,1)
a=confusion_matrix(Y1test.T,probaTest)

# Print accuracy, recall, precison and the 10-digit confusion matrix
from sklearn.metrics import accuracy_score, precision_score, recall_score, f1_score
print('Accuracy: {:.2f}'.format(accuracy_score(Y1test.T, probaTest)))
print('Precision: {:.2f}'.format(precision_score(Y1test.T, probaTest,average="micro")))
print('Recall: {:.2f}'.format(recall_score(Y1test.T, probaTest,average="micro")))

##1.  Confusion Matrix of Training set
##        0     1     2     3     4     5     6     7     8     9
## [[5854    0   19    2   10    7    0    1   24    6]
##  [   1 6659   30   10    5    3    0   14   20    0]
##  [  20   24 5805   18    6   11    2   32   37    3]
##  [   5    4  175 5783    1   27    1   58   60   17]
##  [   1   21    9    0 5780    0    5    2   12   12]
##  [  29    9   21  224    6 4824   18   17  245   28]
##  [   5    4   22    1   32   12 5799    0   43    0]
##  [   3   13  148  154   18    3    0 5883    4   39]
##  [  11   34   30   21   13   16    4    7 5703   12]
##  [  10    4    1   32  135   14    1   92  134 5526]]

##2. Accuracy, Precision, Recall of  Training set
## Accuracy: 0.96
## Precision: 0.96
## Recall: 0.96

##3. Confusion Matrix of Test set
##        0     1     2     3     4     5     6     7     8     9
## [[ 954    1    8    0    3    3    2    4    4    1]
##  [   0 1107    6    5    0    0    1    2   14    0]
##  [  11    7  957   10    5    0    5   20   16    1]
##  [   2    3   37  925    3   13    0    8   18    1]
##  [   2    6    1    1  944    0    7    3    4   14]
##  [  12    5    4   45    2  740   24    8   42   10]
##  [   8    4    4    2   16    9  903    0   12    0]
##  [   4   10   27   18    5    1    0  940    1   22]
##  [  11   13    6   13    9   10    7    2  900    3]
##  [   8    5    1    7   50    7    0   20   29  882]]
##4. Accuracy, Precision, Recall of  Training set
## Accuracy: 0.93
## Precision: 0.93
## Recall: 0.93
```

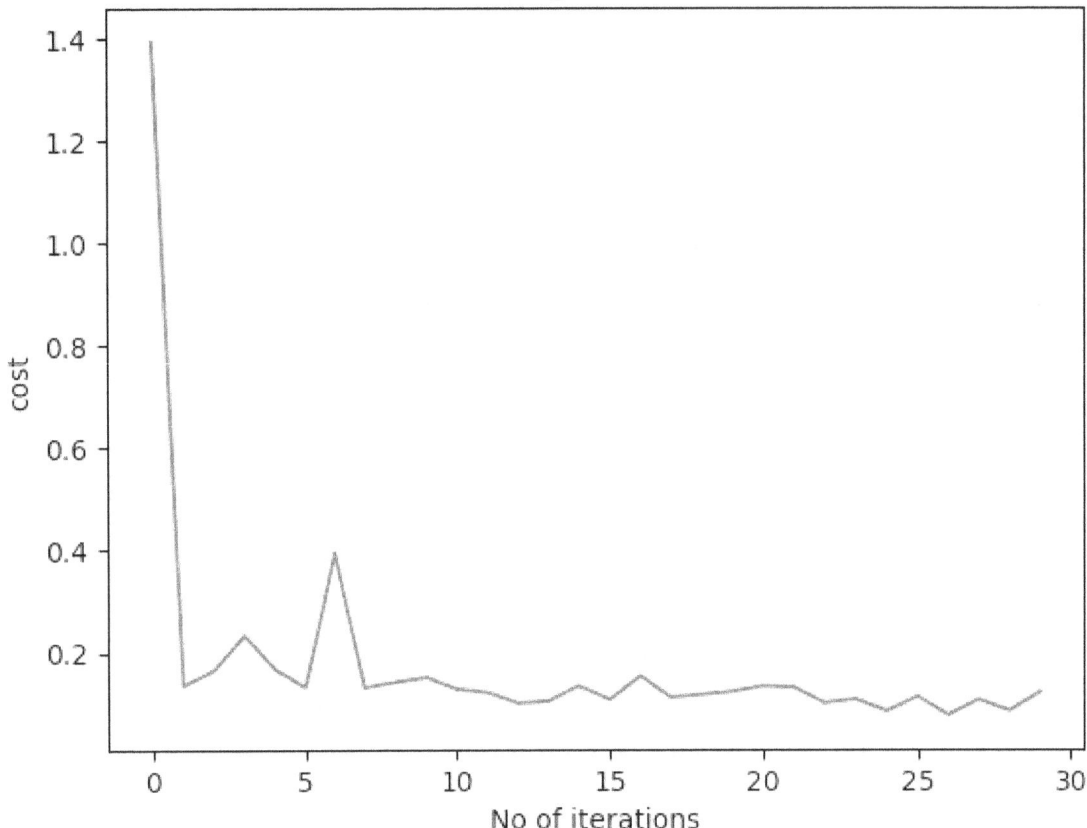

3.2a Random dataset with sigmoid activation – R code

The random data set used in the Python code above which was saved as a csv(data.csv). The code is used to test the L -Layer DL network with sigmoid Activation in R.

```
1  source("DLfunctions5.R")
2
3  # Read the random data set
4  z <- as.matrix(read.csv("data.csv",header=FALSE))
5  x <- z[,1:2]
6  y <- z[,3]
7  X <- t(x)
8  Y <- t(y)
9
10 # Set the dimensions of the layers
11 # 2 - number of input features]
12 #9, 9 - 2 hidden layers with 9 hidden units each
13 # 1 - 1 activation unit in the output layer
14 layersDimensions = c(2, 9, 9,1)
15
16 # Execute a L-Layer DL network on the data set with relu hidden unit
17 activation
18 # sigmoid activation unit in the output layer
19 retvals = L_Layer_DeepModel(X, Y, layersDimensions,
20                             hiddenActivationFunc='relu',
```

```
21                         outputActivationFunc="sigmoid",
22                         learningRate = 0.3,
23                         numIterations = 5000,
24                         print_cost = True)
25
26 #Plot the cost vs iterations
27 iterations <- seq(0,5000,1000)
28 costs=retvals$costs
29 df=data.frame(iterations,costs)
30 ggplot(df,aes(x=iterations,y=costs)) + geom_point() + geom_line(color="blue")
31  + ggtitle("Costs vs iterations") + xlab("Iterations") + ylab("Loss")
```

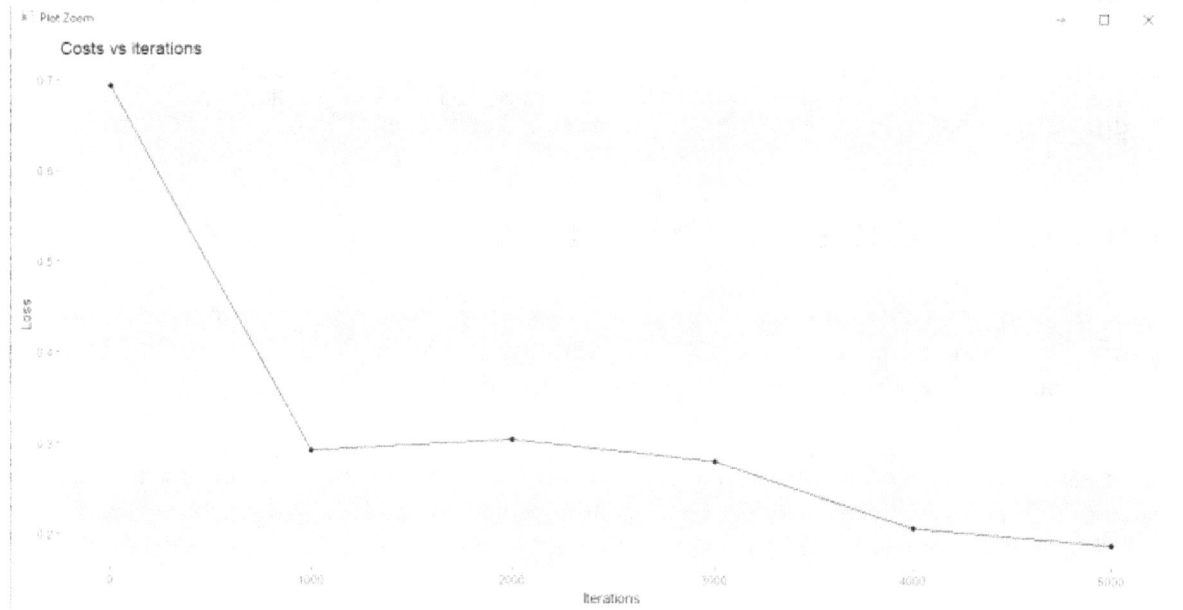

3.2b Spiral dataset with Softmax activation – R

The spiral data set used in the Python code above(spiral.csv) , is reused to test multi-class classification with Softmax.

```
1  source("DLfunctions5.R")
2  Z <- as.matrix(read.csv("spiral.csv",header=FALSE))
3
4  # Setup the data
5  X <- Z[,1:2]
6  y <- Z[,3]
7  X <- t(X)
8  Y <- t(y)
9
10 # Initialize number of features, number of hidden units in hidden layer and
11 # number of classes
12 numFeats<-2 # No features
13 numHidden<-100 # No of hidden units
14 numOutput<-3 # No of classes
15
16 # Set the layer dimensions
17 layersDimensions = c(numFeats,numHidden,numOutput)
18
```

```
19  # Execute the L-Layer Deep Learning network with relu activation unit for
20  hidden layer
21  # and softmax activation in the output
22  retvals = L_Layer_DeepModel(X, Y, layersDimensions,
23                              hiddenActivationFunc='relu',
24                              outputActivationFunc="softmax",
25                              learningRate = 0.5,
26                              numIterations = 9000,
27                              print_cost = True)
28
29
30  #Plot cost vs iterations
31  iterations <- seq(0,9000,1000)
32  costs=retvals$costs
33  df=data.frame(iterations,costs)
34  ggplot(df,aes(x=iterations,y=costs)) + geom_point() + geom_line(color="blue")
35  +  ggtitle("Costs vs iterations") + xlab("Iterations") + ylab("Costs")
```

3.2c MNIST dataset with Softmax activation – R

The code below executes a L –Layer Deep Learning network with Softmax output activation, to classify the 10 handwritten digits from MNIST with Stochastic Gradient Descent. The 32768 random samples from the data set was used to train the data.

Having said that, the Confusion Matrix in R dumps a lot of interesting statistics! There is a bunch of statistical measures for each class. For e.g. the Balanced Accuracy for the digits '6' and '9' is around 50%. Looks like, the classifier is confused by the fact that 6 is inverted 9 and vice-versa. The accuracy on the Test data set is just around 75%. I could have played around with the number of layers, number of hidden units, learning rates, epochs etc to get a much higher accuracy. But since each test took about 8+ hours, I may work on this, some other day!

```
1   source("DLfunctions5.R")
2   source("mnist.R")
3
4   #Load the mnist data
5   load_mnist()
6   show_digit(train$x[2,])
7   #Set the layer dimensions
8   layersDimensions=c(784, 15,9, 10) # Works at 1500
9   x <- t(train$x)
10  X <- x[,1:60000]
11  y <-train$y
12  y1 <- y[1:60000]
13  y2 <- as.matrix(y1)
14  Y=t(y2)
15
16  # Subset 32768 random samples from MNIST
17  permutation = c(sample(2^15))
18  # Randomly shuffle the training data
19  X1 = X[, permutation]
20  y1 = Y[1, permutation]
21  y2 <- as.matrix(y1)
22  Y1=t(y2)
23
24  # Execute Stochastic Gradient Descent on the entire training set
25  # with 'relu' activiation in the hidden layer 'softmax' activation and
```

```
# learning rate =0.05
retvalsSGD= L_Layer_DeepModel_SGD(X1, Y1, layersDimensions,
                        hiddenActivationFunc='relu',
                        outputActivationFunc="softmax",
                        learningRate = 0.05,
                        mini_batch_size = 512,
                        num_epochs = 1,
                        print_cost = True)
```

```
# Compute the Confusion Matrix
library(caret)
library(e1071)
predictions=predictProba(retvalsSGD[['parameters']],
X,hiddenActivationFunc='relu',
                outputActivationFunc="softmax")
confusionMatrix(predictions,Y)

# Confusion Matrix on the Training set
> confusionMatrix(predictions,Y)
Confusion Matrix and Statistics

          Reference
Prediction    0    1    2    3    4    5    6    7    8    9
         0 5738    1   21    5   16   17    7   15    9   43
         1    5 6632   21   24   25    3    2   33   13  392
         2   12   32 5747  106   25   28    3   27   44 4779
         3    0   27   12 5715    1   21    1   20    1   13
         4   10    5   21   18 5677    9   17   30   15  166
         5  142   21   96  136   93 5306 5884   43   60  413
         6    0    0    0    0    0    0    0    0    0    0
         7    6    9   13   13    3    4    0 6085    0   55
         8    8   12    7   43    1   32    2    7 5703   69
         9    2    3   20   71    1    1    2    5    6   19

Overall Statistics
                  Accuracy : 0.777
                    95% CI : (0.7737, 0.7804)
       No Information Rate : 0.1124
       P-Value [Acc > NIR] : < 2.2e-16

                     Kappa : 0.7524
```

Mcnemar's Test P-Value : NA

Statistics by Class:

	Class: 0	Class: 1	Class: 2	Class: 3	Class: 4	Class: 5	Class: 6
Sensitivity	0.96877	0.9837	0.96459	0.93215	0.97176	0.97879	0.00000
Specificity	0.99752	0.9903	0.90644	0.99822	0.99463	0.87380	1.00000
Pos Pred Value	0.97718	0.9276	0.53198	0.98348	0.95124	0.43513	NaN
Neg Pred Value	0.99658	0.9979	0.99571	0.99232	0.99695	0.99759	0.90137
Prevalence	0.09872	0.1124	0.09930	0.10218	0.09737	0.09035	0.09863
Detection Rate	0.09563	0.1105	0.09578	0.09525	0.09462	0.08843	0.00000
Detection Prevalence	0.09787	0.1192	0.18005	0.09685	0.09947	0.20323	0.00000
Balanced Accuracy	0.98314	0.9870	0.93551	0.96518	0.98319	0.92629	0.50000

	Class: 7	Class: 8	Class: 9
Sensitivity	0.9713	0.97471	0.0031938
Specificity	0.9981	0.99666	0.9979464
Pos Pred Value	0.9834	0.96924	0.1461538
Neg Pred Value	0.9967	0.99727	0.9009521
Prevalence	0.1044	0.09752	0.0991500
Detection Rate	0.1014	0.09505	0.0003167
Detection Prevalence	0.1031	0.09807	0.0021667
Balanced Accuracy	0.9847	0.98568	0.5005701

Confusion Matrix on the Training set xtest <- t(test$x) Xtest <- xtest[,1:10000] ytest <-test$y ytest1 <- ytest[1:10000] ytest2 <- as.matrix(ytest1) Ytest=t(ytest2)

Confusion Matrix and Statistics

```
          Reference
Prediction    0    1    2    3    4    5    6    7    8    9
         0  950    2    2    3    0    6    9    4    7    6
         1    3 1110    4    2    9    0    3   12    5   74
         2    2    6  965   21    9   14    5   16   12  789
         3    1    2    9  908    2   16    0   21    2    6
         4    0    1    9    5  938    1    8    6    8   39
         5   19    5   25   35   20  835  929    8   54   67
         6    0    0    0    0    0    0    0    0    0    0
         7    4    4    7   10    2    4    0  952    5    6
         8    1    5    8   14    2   16    2    3  876   21
         9    0    0    3   12    0    0    2    6    5    1
```

Overall Statistics

```
               Accuracy : 0.7535
                 95% CI : (0.7449, 0.7619)
    No Information Rate : 0.1135
    P-Value [Acc > NIR] : < 2.2e-16

                  Kappa : 0.7262
 Mcnemar's Test P-Value : NA
```

Statistics by Class:

	Class: 0	Class: 1	Class: 2	Class: 3	Class: 4	Class: 5	Class: 6

97	Sensitivity	0.9694	0.9780	0.9351	0.8990	0.9552	0.9361
98	0.0000						
99	Specificity	0.9957	0.9874	0.9025	0.9934	0.9915	0.8724
100	1.0000						
101	Pos Pred Value	0.9606	0.9083	0.5247	0.9390	0.9241	0.4181
102	NaN						
103	Neg Pred Value	0.9967	0.9972	0.9918	0.9887	0.9951	0.9929
104	0.9042						
105	Prevalence	0.0980	0.1135	0.1032	0.1010	0.0982	0.0892
106	0.0958						
107	Detection Rate	0.0950	0.1110	0.0965	0.0908	0.0938	0.0835
108	0.0000						
109	Detection Prevalence	0.0989	0.1222	0.1839	0.0967	0.1015	0.1997
110	0.0000						
111	Balanced Accuracy	0.9825	0.9827	0.9188	0.9462	0.9733	0.9043
112	0.5000						

		Class: 7	Class: 8	Class: 9
114	Sensitivity	0.9261	0.8994	0.0009911
115	Specificity	0.9953	0.9920	0.9968858
116	Pos Pred Value	0.9577	0.9241	0.0344828
117	Neg Pred Value	0.9916	0.9892	0.8989068
118	Prevalence	0.1028	0.0974	0.1009000
119	Detection Rate	0.0952	0.0876	0.0001000
120	Detection Prevalence	0.0994	0.0948	0.0029000
121	Balanced Accuracy	0.9607	0.9457	0.4989384

3.3a Random dataset with sigmoid activation – Octave

The Octave code below uses the random data set used by Python(data.csv). The code below implements a L-Layer Deep Learning with Sigmoid Activation.

```
source("DL5functions.m")

# Read the data
data=csvread("data.csv");

#Set up the data
X=data(:,1:2);
Y=data(:,3);

#Set the layer dimensions
# 2 - 2 input features
# 9 7 - 2 hidden layers with 9 and 7 activation units
# 1 - 1 sigmoid activation at output layer
layersDimensions = [2 9 7  1]; #tanh=-0.5(ok),

# Execute L-layer Deep Learning Network
# with relu as hidden unit and sigmoid as output activation and
# learning rate 0.1
[weights biases costs]=L_Layer_DeepModel(X', Y', layersDimensions,
                      hiddenActivationFunc='relu',
                      outputActivationFunc="sigmoid",
                      learningRate = 0.1,
                      numIterations = 10000);

# Plot cost vs iterations
plotCostVsIterations(10000,costs);
```

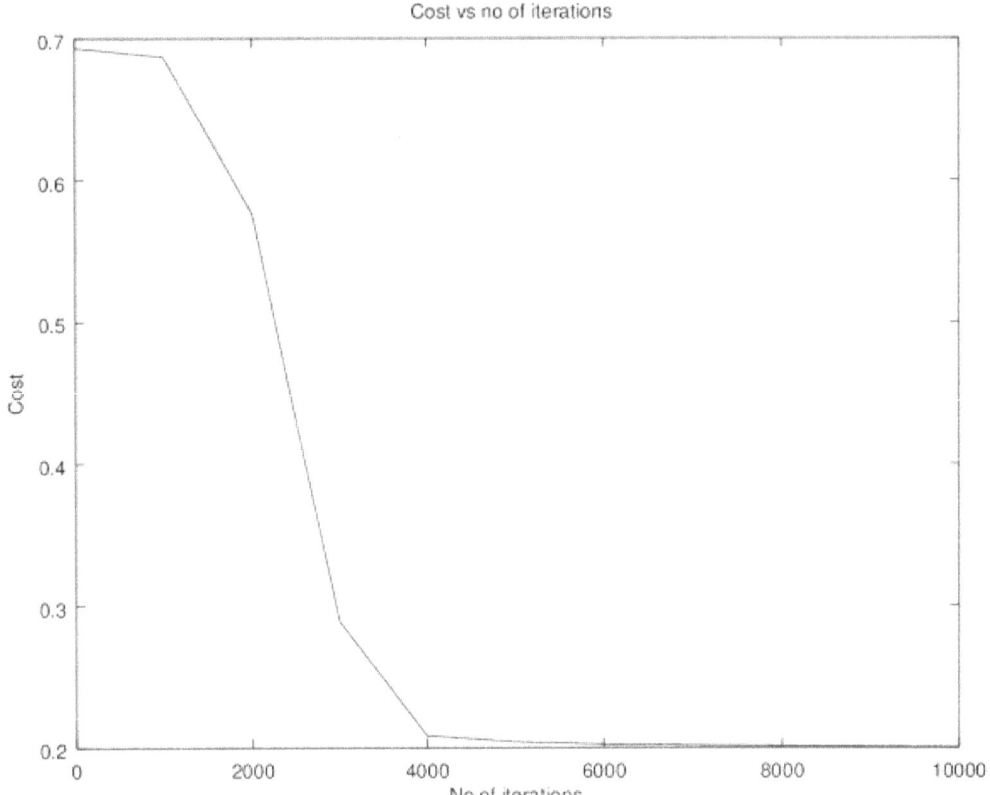

3.3b Spiral dataset with Softmax activation – Octave

The code below uses the spiral data set used by Python above(spiral.csv). The code below implements a L-Layer Deep Learning with Softmax Activation.

```
1  # Read the data
2  data=csvread("spiral.csv");
3
4  # Setup the data
5  X=data(:,1:2);
6  Y=data(:,3);
7
8  # Set the number of features, number of hidden units in hidden layer and
9  number of classess
10 numFeats=2; #No features
11 numHidden=100; # No of hidden units
12 numOutput=3; # No of  classes
13 # Set the layer dimensions
14 layersDimensions = [numFeats numHidden  numOutput];
15
16 #Execute the L-Layer Deep Learning network with 'relu' activation
17 # in the hidden layer and softmax activation unit at the output layer
18 # with learning rate=0.1
19 [weights biases costs]=L_Layer_DeepModel(X', Y', layersDimensions,
20                        hiddenActivationFunc='relu',
21                        outputActivationFunc="softmax",
```

```
22                          learningRate = 0.1,
23                          numIterations = 10000);
```

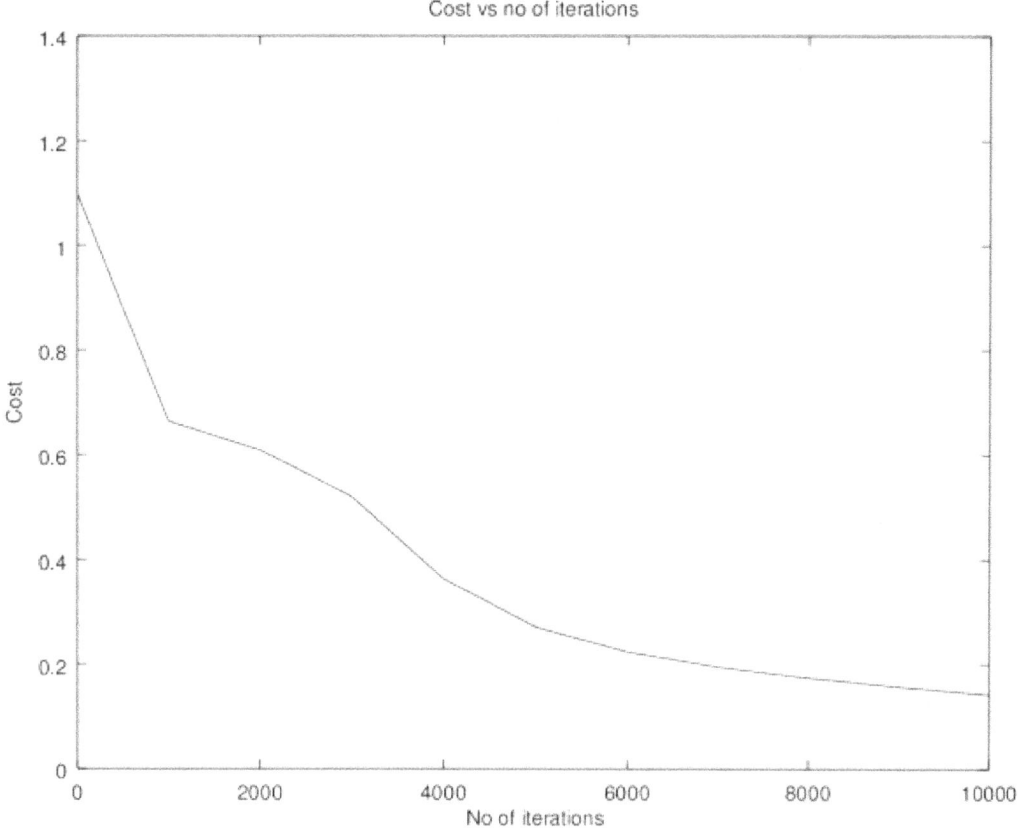

3.3c MNIST dataset with Softmax activation – Octave

The code below implements a L-Layer Deep Learning Network in Octave with Softmax output activation unit, for classifying the 10 handwritten digits in the MNIST dataset. Unfortunately, Octave can only index to around 10000 training at a time, and I was getting an error '*error: out of memory or dimension too large for Octave's index type error: called from...*', when I tried to create a batch size of 20000. So, I had to come with a work around to create a batch size of 10000 (randomly) and then use a mini-batch of 1000 samples and execute Stochastic Gradient Descent. The performance was good. Octave takes about 15 minutes, on a batch size of 10000 and a mini batch of 1000.

```
1   # Pseudo code that could be used since Octave only allows 10K batches
2   # at a time
3   # Randomly create weights
4   [weights biases] = initialize_weights()
5   for i=1:k
6       # Create a random permutation and create a random batch
7       permutation = randperm(10000);
8       X=trainX(permutation,:);
9       Y=trainY(permutation,:);
10
11      # Compute weights from SGD and update weights in the next batch update
```

```
12          [weights biases
13  costs]=L_Layer_DeepModel_SGD(X,Y,mini_bactch=1000,weights, biases,...);
14       ...
15  Endfor
16
17  # Load the MNIST data
18  load('./mnist/mnist.txt.gz');
19
20  #Create a random permutatation from 60K
21  permutation = randperm(10000);
22  disp(length(permutation));
23
24  # Use this 10K as the batch
25  X=trainX(permutation,:);
26  Y=trainY(permutation,:);
27
28  # Set layer dimensions
29  # 784 - Number of input features - 28 x28
30  # 15 9 - 2 hidden layers with 15 and 9 activation units
31  # 10 - 10 activation units at the output layer
32  layersDimensions=[784, 15, 9, 10];
33
34  # Run Stochastic Gradient descent with batch size=10K and
35  mini_batch_size=1000
36  # with 'relu' activation in hidden layer and 'softmax' activation at the
37  output layer
38  [weights biases costs]=L_Layer_DeepModel_SGD(X', Y', layersDimensions,
39                          hiddenActivationFunc='relu',
40                          outputActivationFunc="softmax",
41                          learningRate = 0.01,
42                          mini_batch_size = 2000, num_epochs = 5000);
```

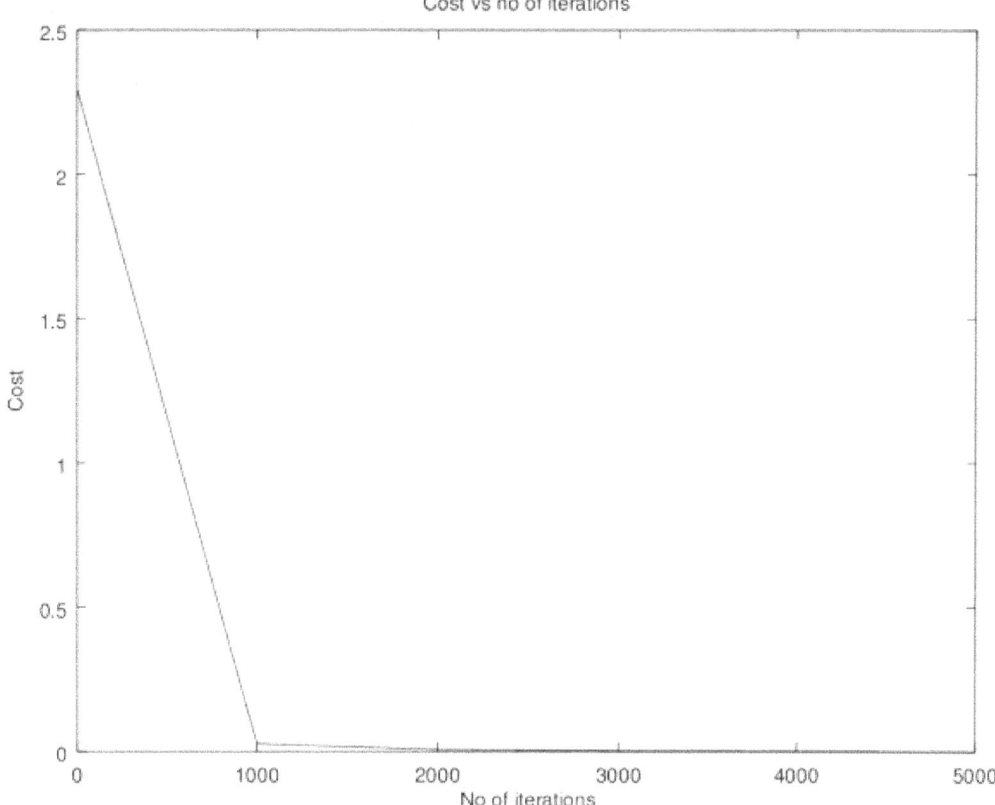

4. Final thoughts

Here are some of my final thoughts after working on Python, R and Octave in this series and in other projects

1. Python, with its highly optimized numpy library, is ideally suited for creating Deep Learning Models, which have a lot of matrix manipulations. Python is a real workhorse when it comes to Deep Learning computations.
2. R is somewhat clunky in comparison to its cousin Python in handling matrices or in returning multiple values. But R's statistical libraries, dplyr, and ggplot are really superior to the Python peers. Also, I find R handles dataframes, much better than Python.
3. Octave is a no-nonsense, minimalist language which is very efficient in handling matrices. It is ideally suited for implementing Machine Learning and Deep Learning from scratch. But, Octave has its problems and cannot handle large matrix sizes, and also lacks the statistical libaries of R and Python. They possibly exist in its sibling, Matlab

5. Conclusion

Building a Deep Learning Network from scratch is quite challenging, time-consuming but nevertheless an exciting task. While the statements in the different languages for manipulating matrices, summing up columns, finding columns which have ones don't take more than a single statement, extreme care has to be taken to ensure that the statements work well for any dimension. The lessons learnt from creating L-Layer Deep Learning network are many and well worth it. Give it a try!

6. Initialization, regularization in Deep Learning

"Today you are You, that is truer than true. There is no one alive who is Youer than You."
Dr. Seuss

"Explanations exist; they have existed for all time; there is always a well-known solution to every human problem — neat, plausible, and wrong."
H L Mencken

1. Introduction

In this 6th chapter of 'Deep Learning from first principles', I look at a couple of different initialization techniques used in Deep Learning, L2 regularization and the 'dropout' method. Specifically, I implement "He" initialization" & "Xavier" Initialization.

In addition I also implement L2 regularization and finally dropout. Hence, my generic L-Layer Deep Learning network includes these additional enhancements for enabling/disabling initialization methods, regularization or dropout in the algorithm. It already included sigmoid & softmax output activation for binary and multi-class classification, besides allowing relu, tanh and sigmoid activation for hidden units. The Python,R and Octave functions used in this chapter are implemented in Appendix 6 - Initialization, regularization in Deep Learning

This code for Python, R and Octave can be cloned/downloaded from Github at DeepLearningFromFirstPrinciples (https://github.com/tvganesh/DeepLearningFromFirstPrinciples/tree/master/Chap6-DLInitializationRegularization)

2. Initialization techniques

The usual initialization technique is to generate Gaussian or uniform random numbers and multiply it by a small value like 0.01. Two techniques which are used to speed up convergence is the 'He' (https://www.cv-foundation.org/openaccess/content_iccv_2015/papers/He_Delving_Deep_into_ICCV_2015_paper.pdf) initialization or Xavier (https://www.cv-foundation.org/openaccess/content_iccv_2015/papers/He_Delving_Deep_into_ICCV_2015_paper.pdf) . These initialization techniques enable gradient descent to converge faster.

1.1a Default initialization – Python

This technique just initializes the weights to small random values based on Gaussian or uniform distribution

```
1   import numpy as np
2   import matplotlib
3   import matplotlib.pyplot as plt
4   import sklearn.linear_model
5   import pandas as pd
6   import sklearn
7   import sklearn.datasets
8   exec(open("DLfunctions61.py").read())
9
10  #Load the data
11  train_X, train_Y, test_X, test_Y = load_dataset()
12
13  # Set the layers dimensions
14  # 2 - number of input features
15  # 7 - 1 hidden layer 7 hidden units
16  # 1 - 1 sigmoid activation unit at the output layer
17  layersDimensions = [2,7,1]
18
19  # Train a L-layer deep learning network with random initialization
20  # hidden Activation function - relu
21  # output activation function - sigmoid
22  # learning rate - 0.6
23  parameters = L_Layer_DeepModel(train_X, train_Y, layersDimensions,
24  hiddenActivationFunc='relu', outputActivationFunc="sigmoid",learningRate =
25  0.6, num_iterations = 9000, initType="default", print_cost =
26  True,figure="fig1.png")
27
28  # Clear the plot
29  plt.clf()
30  plt.close()
31
32  # Plot the decision boundary
33  plot_decision_boundary(lambda x: predict(parameters, x.T), train_X,
34  train_Y,str(0.6),figure1="fig2.png")
```

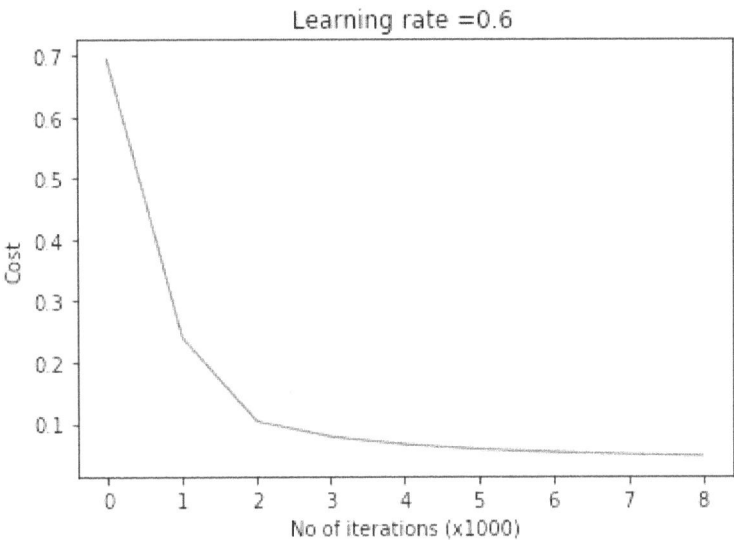

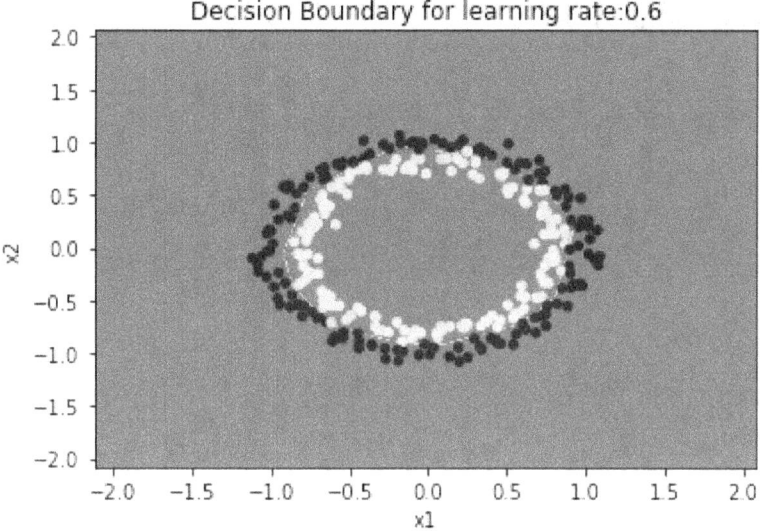

1.1b He initialization – Python

'He' initialization attributed to 'He et al' https://www.cv-foundation.org/openaccess/content_iccv_2015/papers/He_Delving_Deep_into_ICCV_2015_paper.pdf , multiplies the random weights by

$$\sqrt{\frac{2}{dimension\ of\ previous\ layer}}$$

```python
import numpy as np
import matplotlib
import matplotlib.pyplot as plt
import sklearn.linear_model
import pandas as pd
import sklearn
import sklearn.datasets
exec(open("DLfunctions61.py").read())

#Load the data
train_X, train_Y, test_X, test_Y = load_dataset()
# Set the layers dimensions
# 2 - number of input features
# 7 - 1 hidden layer 7 hidden units
# 1 - 1 sigmoid activation unit at the output layer
layersDimensions = [2,7,1]

# Train a L-layer deep learning network with He initialization
# hidden Activation function - relu
# output activation function - sigmoid
# learning rate - 0.6
parameters = L_Layer_DeepModel(train_X, train_Y, layersDimensions,
hiddenActivationFunc='relu', outputActivationFunc="sigmoid", learningRate
=0.6,    num_iterations = 10000,initType="He",print_cost = True,
figure="fig3.png")

# Clear plot
plt.clf()
plt.close()

# Plot the decision boundary
```

```
32  plot_decision_boundary(lambda x: predict(parameters, x.T), train_X,
33  train_Y,str(0.6),figure1="fig4.png")
```

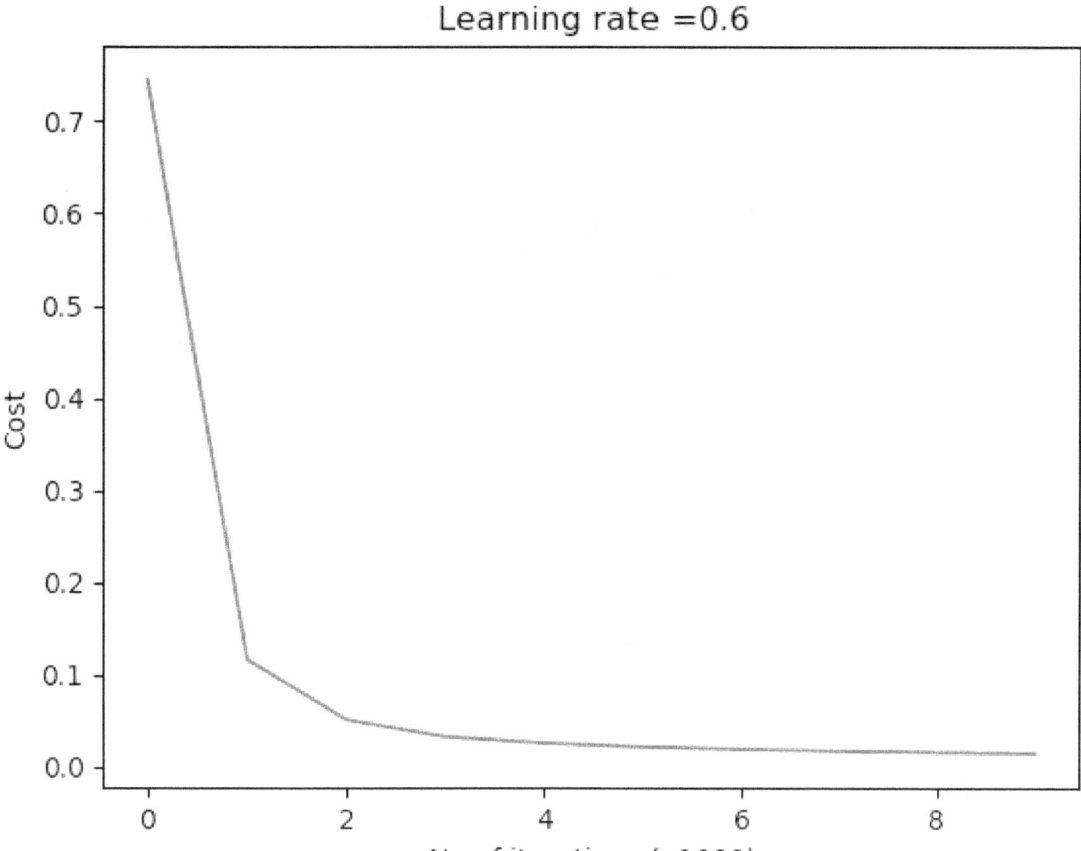

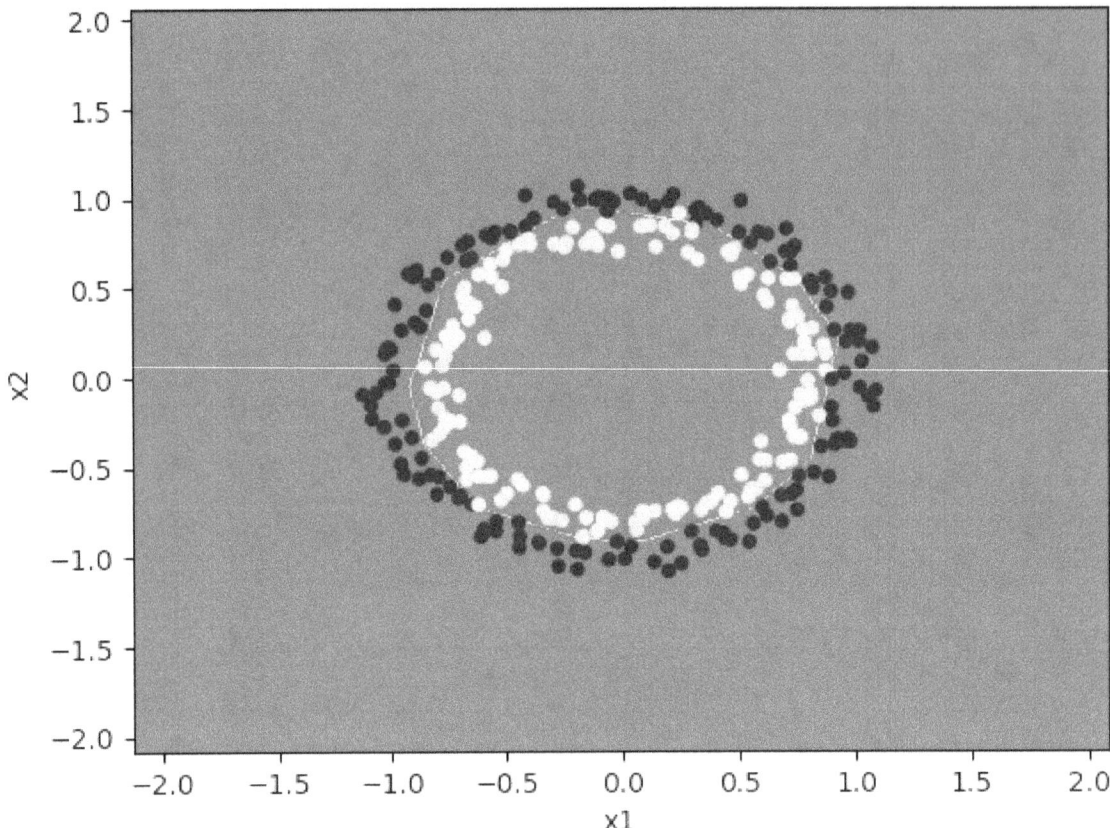

1.1c Xavier initialization – Python

'Xavier' (http://proceedings.mlr.press/v9/glorot10a/glorot10a.pdf) initialization multiply the random weights by

$$\sqrt{\frac{1}{dimension\ of\ previous\ layer}}$$

```
1  import numpy as np
2  import matplotlib
3  import matplotlib.pyplot as plt
4  import sklearn.linear_model
5  import pandas as pd
6  import sklearn
7  import sklearn.datasets
8  exec(open("DLfunctions61.py").read())
9
10 #Load the data
11 train_X, train_Y, test_X, test_Y = load_dataset()
12
13 # Set the layers dimensions
14 # 2 - number of input features
15 # 7 - 1 hidden layer 7 hidden units
16 # 1 - 1 sigmoid activation unit at the output layer
17 layersDimensions = [2,7,1]
18
19 # Train a L-layer Deep Learning network with Xavier initialization
20 # hidden Activation function - relu
```

```
# output activation function - sigmoid
# learning rate - 0.6
parameters = L_Layer_DeepModel(train_X, train_Y, layersDimensions,
hiddenActivationFunc='relu', outputActivationFunc="sigmoid",
                               learningRate = 0.6,num_iterations = 10000,
initType="Xavier",print_cost = True,
                               figure="fig5.png")

# Plot the decision boundary
plot_decision_boundary(lambda x: predict(parameters, x.T), train_X,
train_Y,str(0.6),figure1="fig6.png")
```

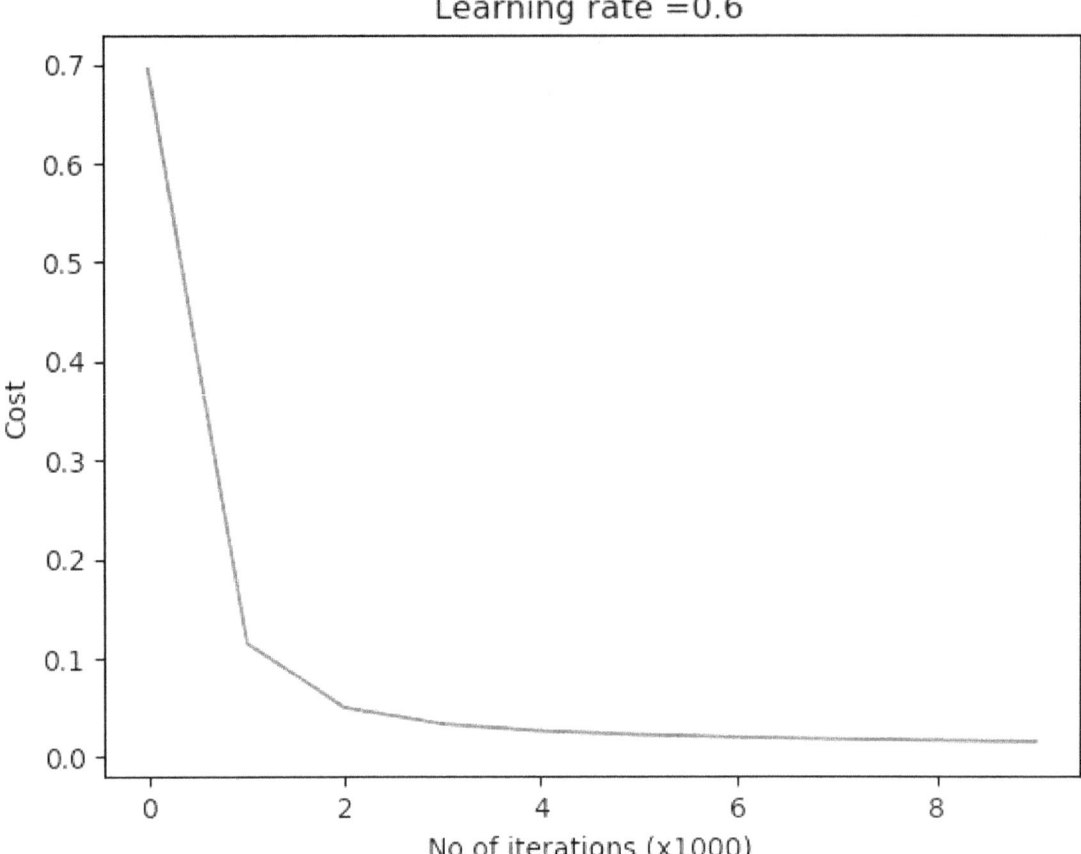

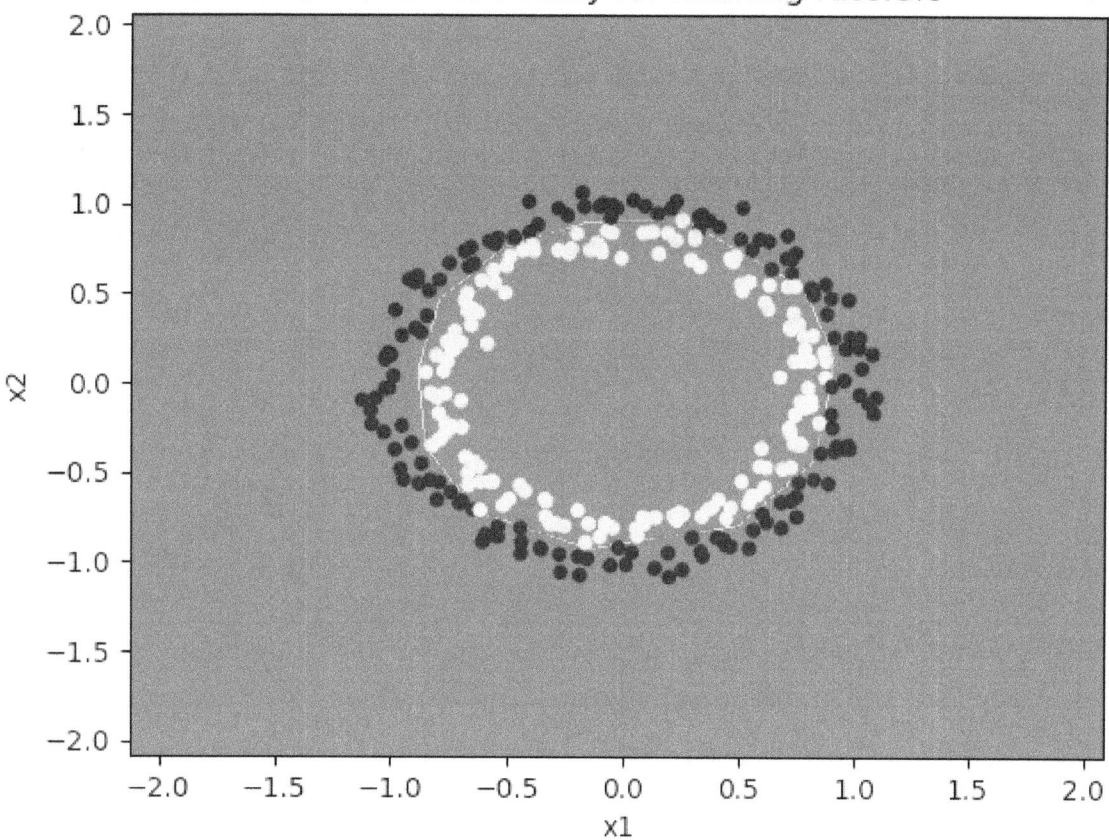

1.2a Default initialization – R

```
1  source("DLfunctions61.R")
2  #Load the data
3  z <- as.matrix(read.csv("circles.csv",header=FALSE))
4  x <- z[,1:2]
5  y <- z[,3]
6  X <- t(x)
7  Y <- t(y)
8
9  #Set the layer dimensions
10 # 2 - number of input features
11 # 11 - 1 hidden layer 11 hidden units
12 # 1 - 1 sigmoid activation unit at the output layer
13 layersDimensions = c(2,11,1)
14
15 # Train a L-layer deep learning network
16 # hidden Activation function - relu
17 # output activation function - sigmoid
18 # learning rate - 0.5
19 retvals = L_Layer_DeepModel(X, Y, layersDimensions,
20                             hiddenActivationFunc='relu',
21                             outputActivationFunc="sigmoid",
22                             learningRate = 0.5,
23                             numIterations = 8000,
24                             initType="default",
25                             print_cost = True)
```

```
#Plot the cost vs iterations
iterations <- seq(0,8000,1000)

# Plot cost vs iterations
costs=retvals$costs
df=data.frame(iterations,costs)
ggplot(df,aes(x=iterations,y=costs)) + geom_point() + geom_line(color="blue")
+  ggtitle("Costs vs iterations") + xlab("No of iterations") + ylab("Cost")
```

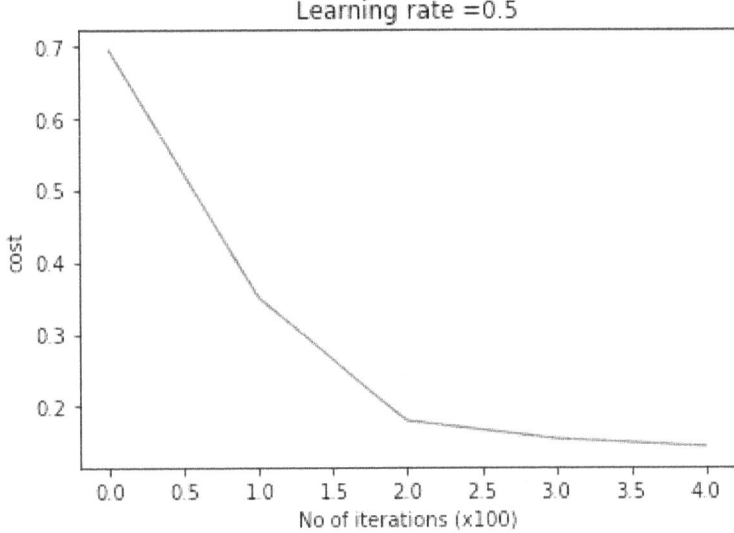

```
# Plot the decision boundary
plotDecisionBoundary(z,retvals,hiddenActivationFunc="relu",lr=0.5)
```

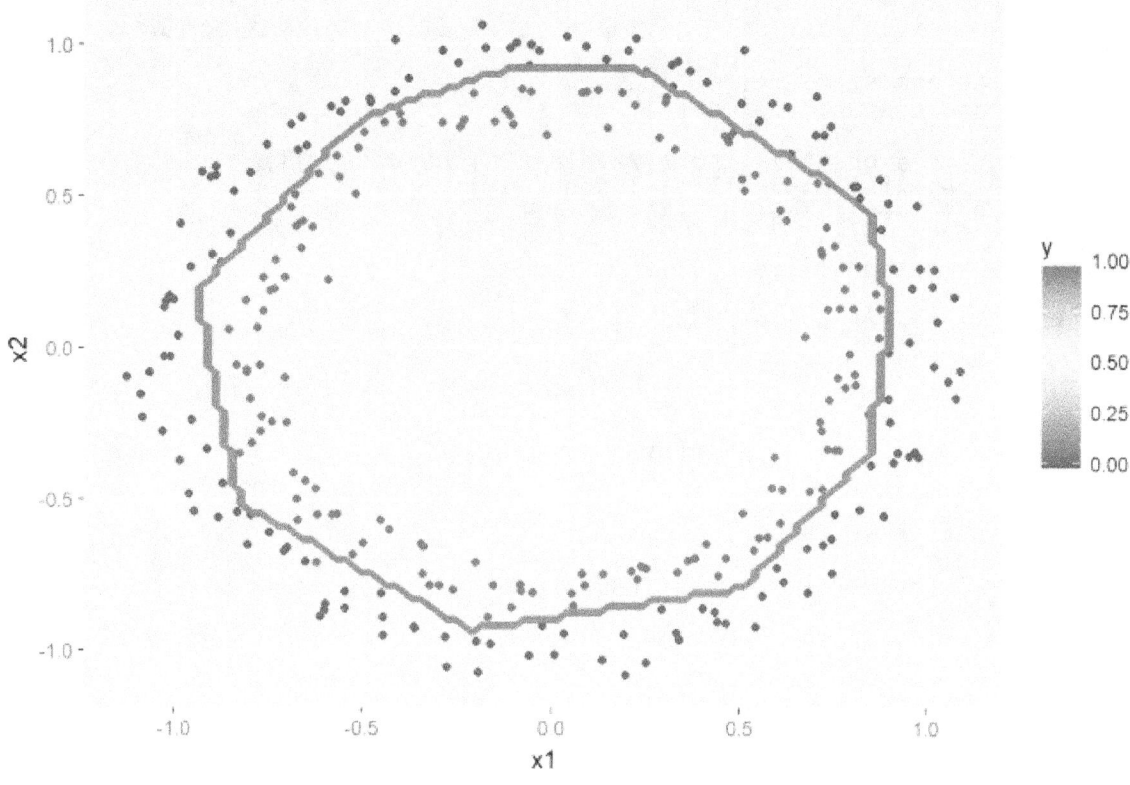

Decision boundary for learning rate: 0.5

1.2b He initialization – R

The code for 'He' initialization in R is included below

```
1  # He Initialization model for L layers
2  # Input: List of units in each layer
3  # Returns: Initial weights and biases matrices for all layers
4  # He initialization multiplies the random numbers with
5  sqrt(2/layerDimensions[previouslayer])
6
7  HeInitializeDeepModel <- function(layerDimensions){
8      set.seed(2)
9
10     # Initialize empty list
11     layerParams <- list()
12
13     # Note the Weight matrix at layer 'l' is a matrix of size (l,l-1)
14     # The Bias is a vectors of size (l,1)
15
16     # Loop through the layer dimension from 1.. L
17     # Indices in R start from 1
18     for(l in 2:length(layersDimensions)){
19
20         # Initialize a matrix of small random numbers of size l x l-1
21         # Create random numbers of size  l x l-1
22         w=rnorm(layersDimensions[l]*layersDimensions[l-1])
23
```

```
24          # Create a weight matrix of size l x l-1 with this initial weights
25 and
26          # Add to list W1,W2... WL
27          # He initialization - Divide by sqrt(2/layerDimensions[previous
28 layer])
29          layerParams[[paste('W',l-1,sep="")]] =
30 matrix(w,nrow=layersDimensions[l],
31
32 ncol=layersDimensions[l-1])*sqrt(2/layersDimensions[l-1])
33          layerParams[[paste('b',l-1,sep="")]] =
34 matrix(rep(0,layersDimensions[l]),
35
36 nrow=layersDimensions[l],ncol=1)
37      }
38      return(layerParams)
39 }
```

The code in R below uses He initialization to learn the data

```
1  source("DLfunctions61.R")
2  # Load the data
3  z <- as.matrix(read.csv("circles.csv",header=FALSE))
4  x <- z[,1:2]
5  y <- z[,3]
6  X <- t(x)
7  Y <- t(y)
8
9  # Set the layer dimensions
10 # 2 - number of input features
11 # 11 - 1 hidden layer 11 hidden units
12 # 1 - 1 sigmoid activation unit at the output layer
13 layersDimensions = c(2,11,1)
14
15 # Train a L-layer Deep learning network with He initialization
16 # hidden Activation function - relu
17 # output activation function - sigmoid
18 # learning rate - 0.5
19 retvals = L_Layer_DeepModel(X, Y, layersDimensions,
20                             hiddenActivationFunc='relu',
21                             outputActivationFunc="sigmoid",
22                             learningRate = 0.5,
23                             numIterations = 9000,
24                             initType="He",
25                             print_cost = True)
26
27 #Plot the cost vs iterations
28 iterations <- seq(0,9000,1000)
29 costs=retvals$costs
30 df=data.frame(iterations,costs)
31 ggplot(df,aes(x=iterations,y=costs)) + geom_point() + geom_line(color="blue")
32 + ggtitle("Costs vs iterations") + xlab("No of iterations") + ylab("Cost")
```

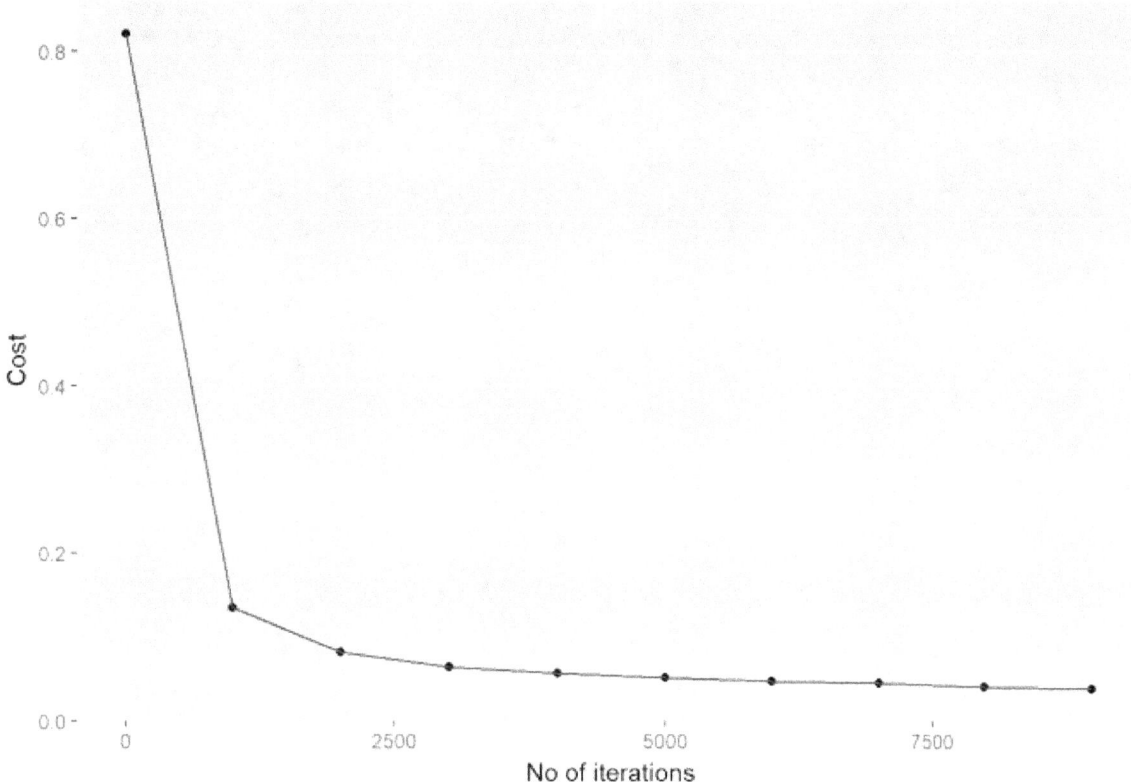

```
1  # Plot the decision boundary
2  plotDecisionBoundary(z,retvals,hiddenActivationFunc="relu",0.5,lr=0.5)
```

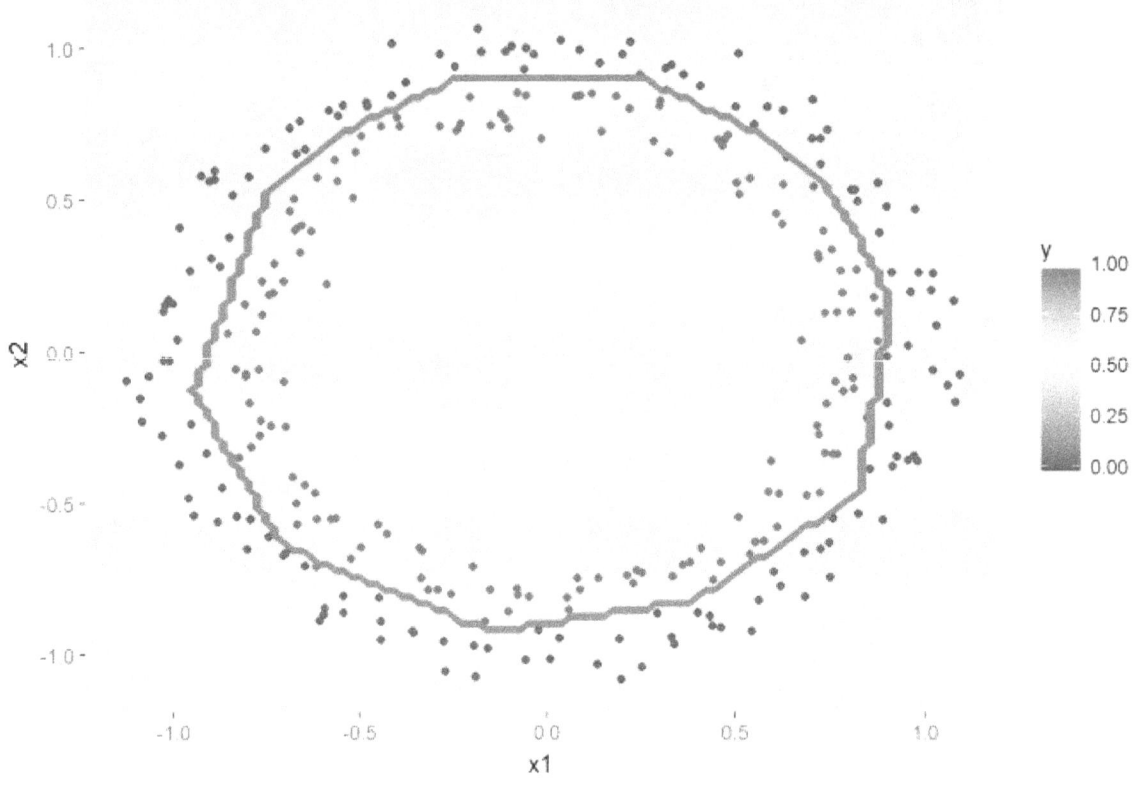

1.2c Xavier initialization – R

```
1  ## Xav initialization
2  # Set the layer dimensions
3  # 2 - number of input features
4  # 11 - 1 hidden layer 11 hidden units
5  # 1 - 1 sigmoid activation unit at the output layer
6  layersDimensions = c(2,11,1)
7
8  # Train a deep learning network with Xavier initialization
9  # hidden Activation function - relu
10 # output activation function - sigmoid
11 # learning rate - 0.5
12 retvals = L_Layer_DeepModel(X, Y, layersDimensions,
13                      hiddenActivationFunc='relu',
14                      outputActivationFunc="sigmoid",
15                      learningRate = 0.5,
16                      numIterations = 9000,
17                      initType="Xav",
18                      print_cost = True)
19
20 #Plot the cost vs iterations
21 iterations <- seq(0,9000,1000)
22 costs=retvals$costs
23 df=data.frame(iterations,costs)
24 ggplot(df,aes(x=iterations,y=costs)) + geom_point() + geom_line(color="blue")
25 + ggtitle("Costs vs iterations") + xlab("No of iterations") + ylab("Cost")
```

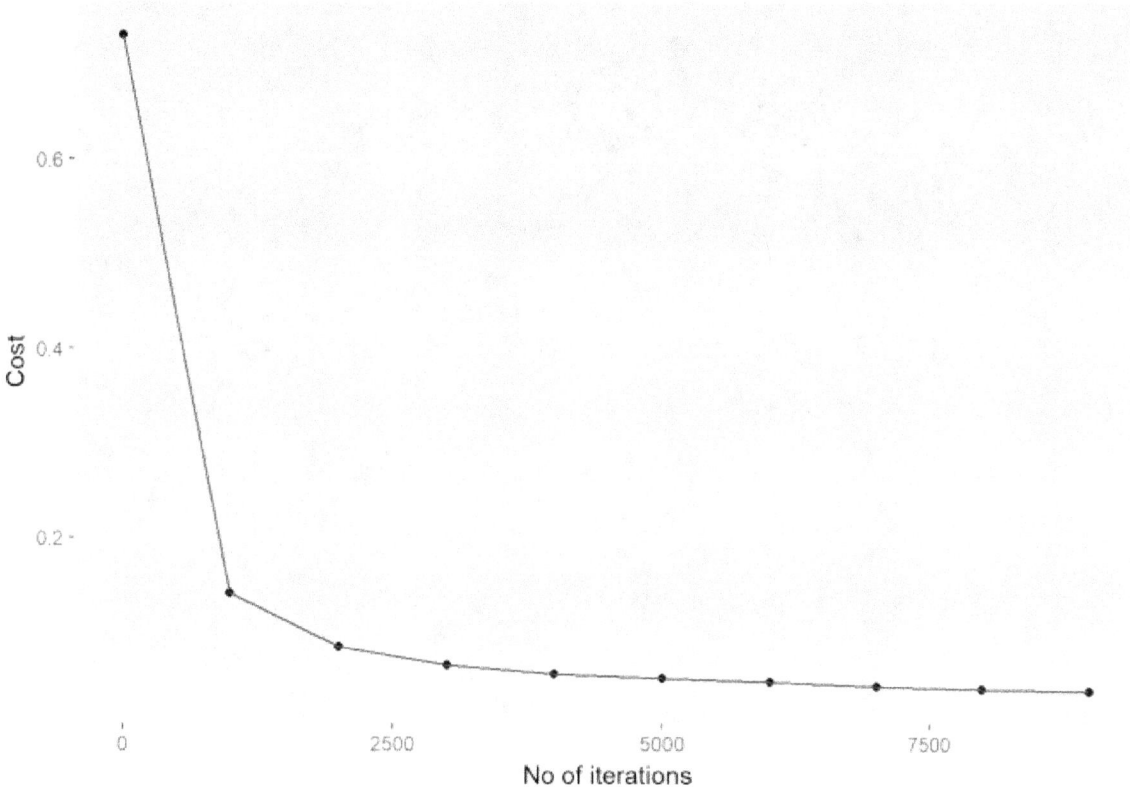

```
1  # Plot the decision boundary
2  plotDecisionBoundary(z,retvals,hiddenActivationFunc="relu",0.5)
```

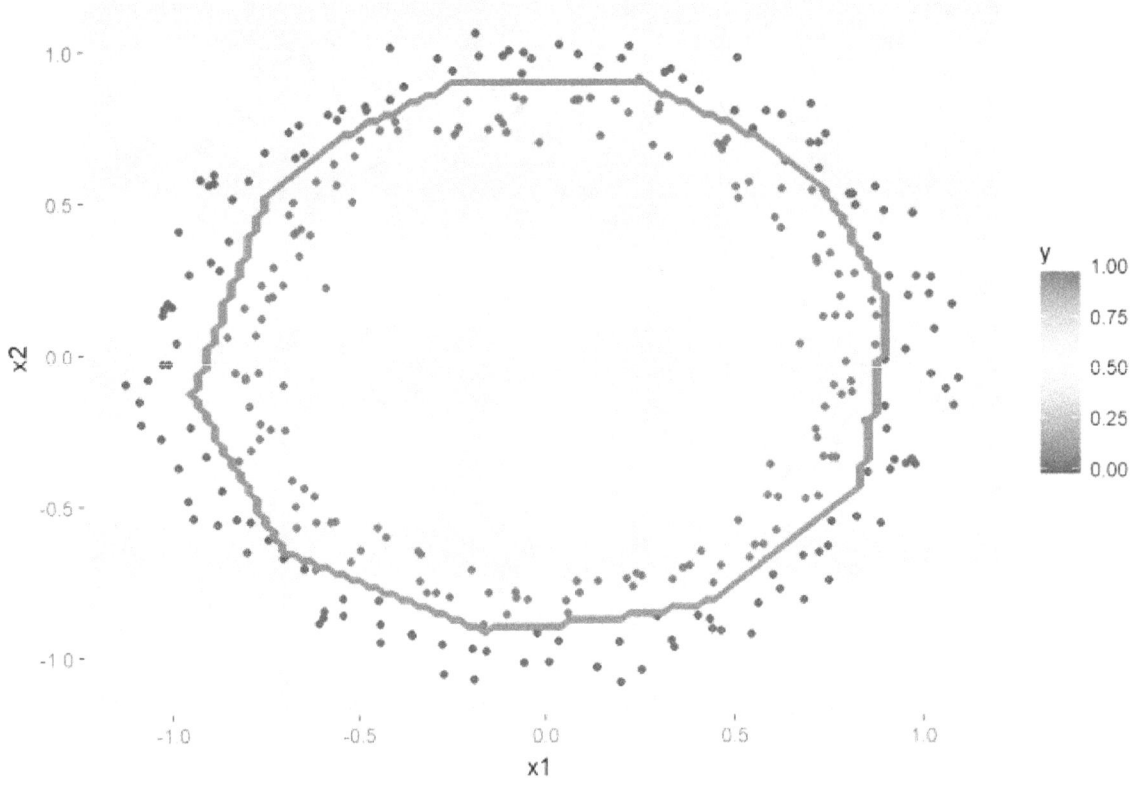
Decision boundary for learning rate: 0.5

1.3a Default initialization – Octave

```
1  source("DL61functions.m")
2  # Read the data
3  data=csvread("circles.csv");
4
5  X=data(:,1:2);
6  Y=data(:,3);
7  # Set the layer dimensions
8  # 2 - number of input features
9  # 11 - 1 hidden layer 11 hidden units
10 # 1 - 1 sigmoid activation unit at the output layer
11 layersDimensions = [2 11  1];
12
13 # Train a L-layer deep learning network with deafault initialization
14 # hidden Activation function - relu
15 # output activation function - sigmoid
16 # learning rate - 0.5
17 [weights biases costs]=L_Layer_DeepModel(X', Y', layersDimensions,
18                         hiddenActivationFunc='relu',
19                         outputActivationFunc="sigmoid",
20                         learningRate = 0.5,
21                         lambd=0,
22                         keep_prob=1,
23                         numIterations = 10000,
24                         initType="default");
25
26 # Plot cost vs iterations
27 plotCostVsIterations(10000,costs)
28
```

```
29  #Plot decision boundary
30  plotDecisionBoundary(data,weights, biases,keep_prob=1,
31  hiddenActivationFunc="relu")
```

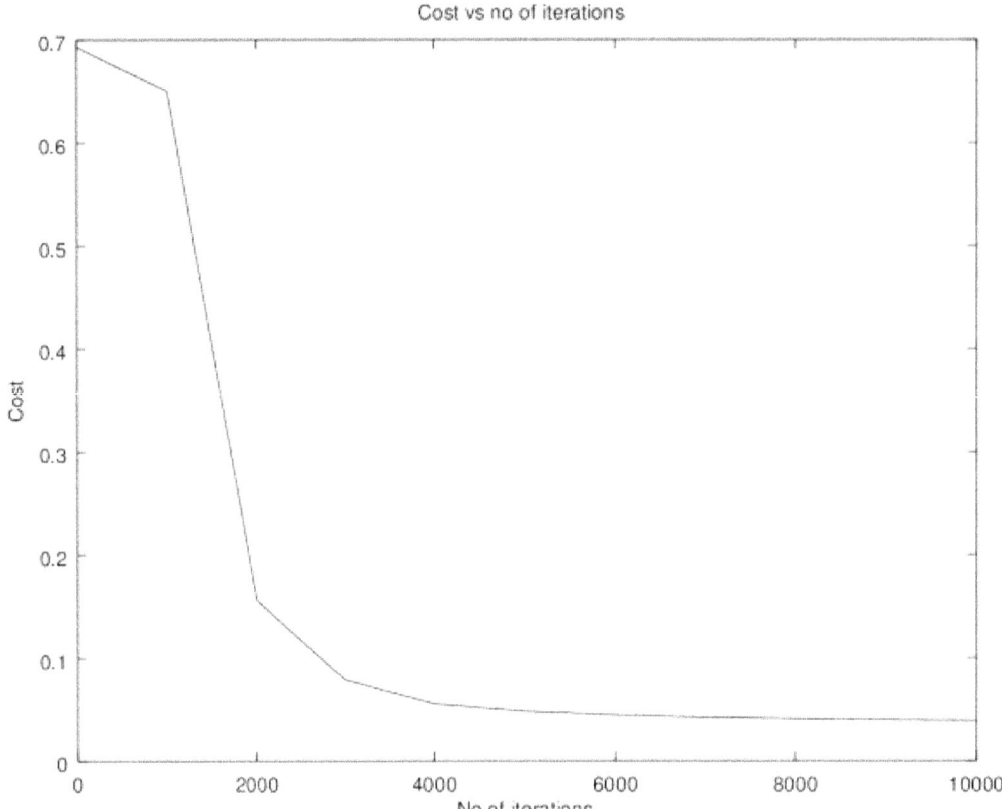

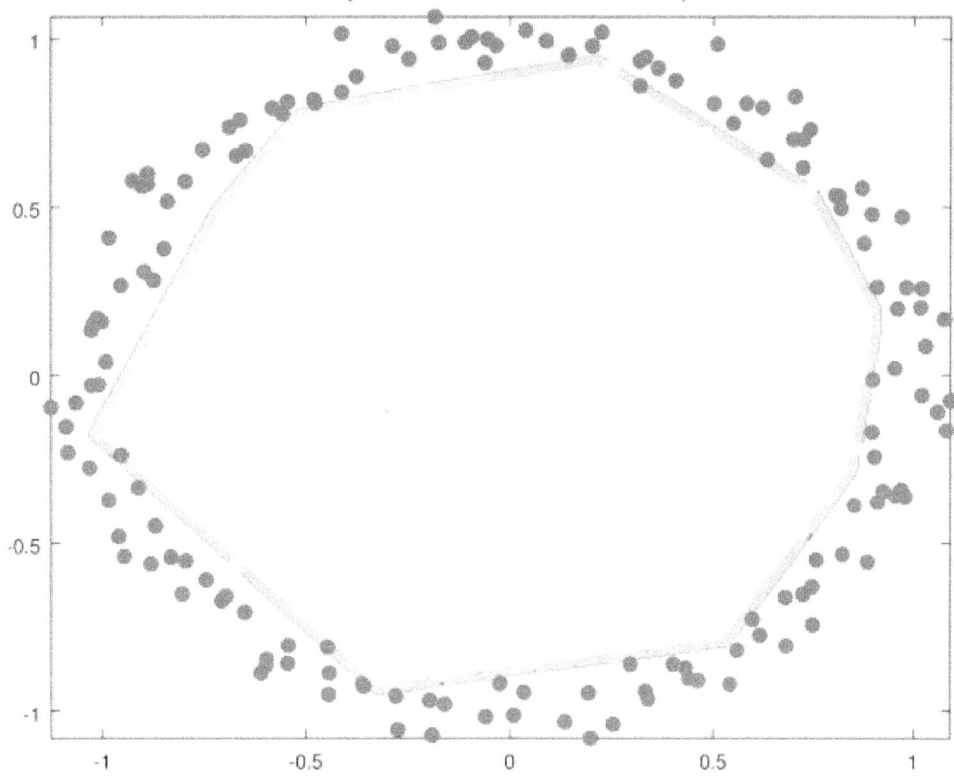

1.3b He initialization – Octave

```
1   source("DL61functions.m")
2   #Load data
3   data=csvread("circles.csv");
4   X=data(:,1:2);
5   Y=data(:,3);
6
7   # Set the layer dimensions
8   # 2 - number of input features
9   # 11 - 1 hidden layer 11 hidden units
10  # 1 - 1 sigmoid activation unit at the output layer
11  layersDimensions = [2 11  1];
12
13  # Train a L-layer deep learning network with He initialization
14  # hidden Activation function - relu
15  # output activation function - sigmoid
16  # learning rate - 0.5
17  [weights biases costs]=L_Layer_DeepModel(X', Y', layersDimensions,
18                           hiddenActivationFunc='relu',
19                           outputActivationFunc="sigmoid",
20                           learningRate = 0.5,
21                           lambd=0,
22                           keep_prob=1,
23                           numIterations = 8000,
24                           initType="He");
25
26  # Plot cost vs iterations
27  plotCostVsIterations(8000,costs)
```

```
28
29  #Plot decision boundary
30  plotDecisionBoundary(data,weights,
31  biases,keep_prob=1,hiddenActivationFunc="relu")
```

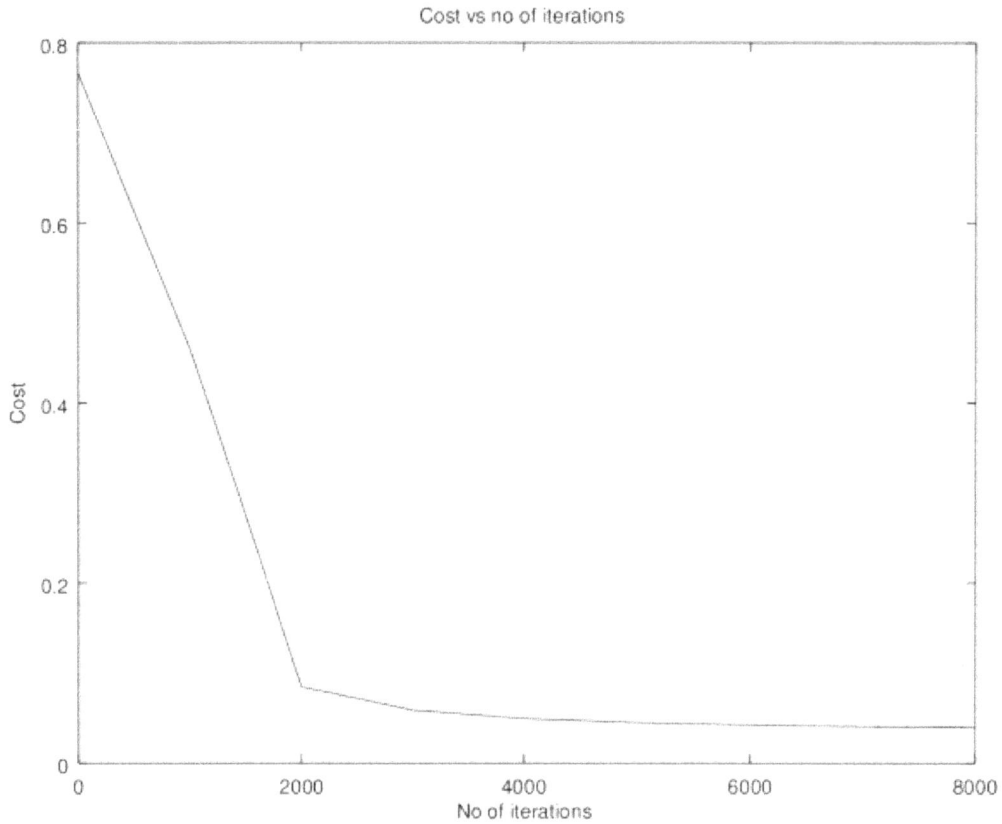

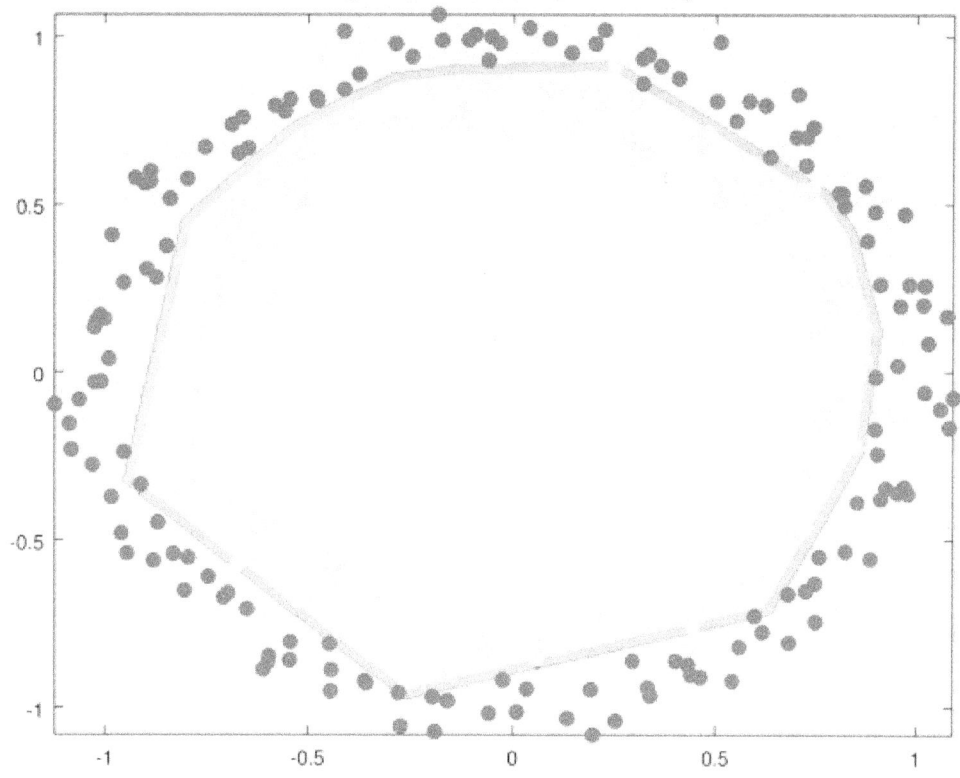

1.3c Xavier initialization – Octave

The code snippet for Xavier initialization in Octave is shown below

```octave
1  source("DL61functions.m")
2  # Xavier Initialization for L layers
3  # Input: List of units in each layer
4  # Returns: Initial weights and biases matrices for all layers
5  function [W b] = XavInitializeDeepModel(layerDimensions)
6      rand ("seed", 3);
7      # note the Weight matrix at layer 'l' is a matrix of size (l,l-1)
8      # The Bias is a vectors of size (l,1)
9
10     # Loop through the layer dimension from 1.. L
11     # Create cell arrays for Weights and biases
12
13     for l =2:size(layerDimensions)(2)
14         W{l-1} = rand(layerDimensions(l),layerDimensions(l-1))*
15 sqrt(1/layerDimensions(l-1)); #  Multiply by .01
16         b{l-1} = zeros(layerDimensions(l),1);
17
18     endfor
19 end
```

The Octave code below uses Xavier initialization

```
source("DL61functions.m")
#Load data
data=csvread("circles.csv");
X=data(:,1:2);
Y=data(:,3);

#Set layer dimensions
# 2 - number of input features
# 11 - 1 hidden layer 11 hidden units
# 1 - 1 sigmoid activation unit at the output layer
layersDimensions = [2 11 1]

# Train a L-layer deep learning network with Xavier initialization
# hidden Activation function - relu
# output activation function - sigmoid
# learning rate - 0.5
[weights biases costs]=L_Layer_DeepModel(X', Y', layersDimensions,
hiddenActivationFunc='relu',
outputActivationFunc="sigmoid",
learningRate = 0.5,
lambd=0,
keep_prob=1,
numIterations = 8000,
initType="Xav");

#Plot cost vs iterations
plotCostVsIterations(8000,costs)

# Plot decision boundary
plotDecisionBoundary(data,weights,
biases,keep_prob=1,hiddenActivationFunc="relu")
```

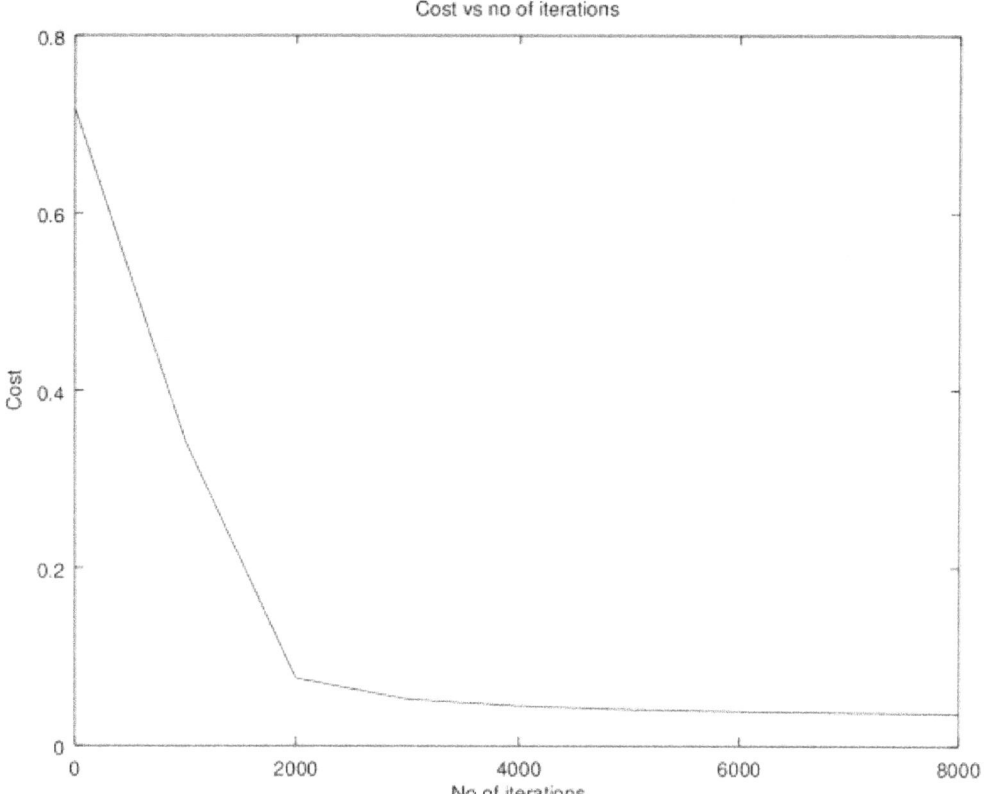

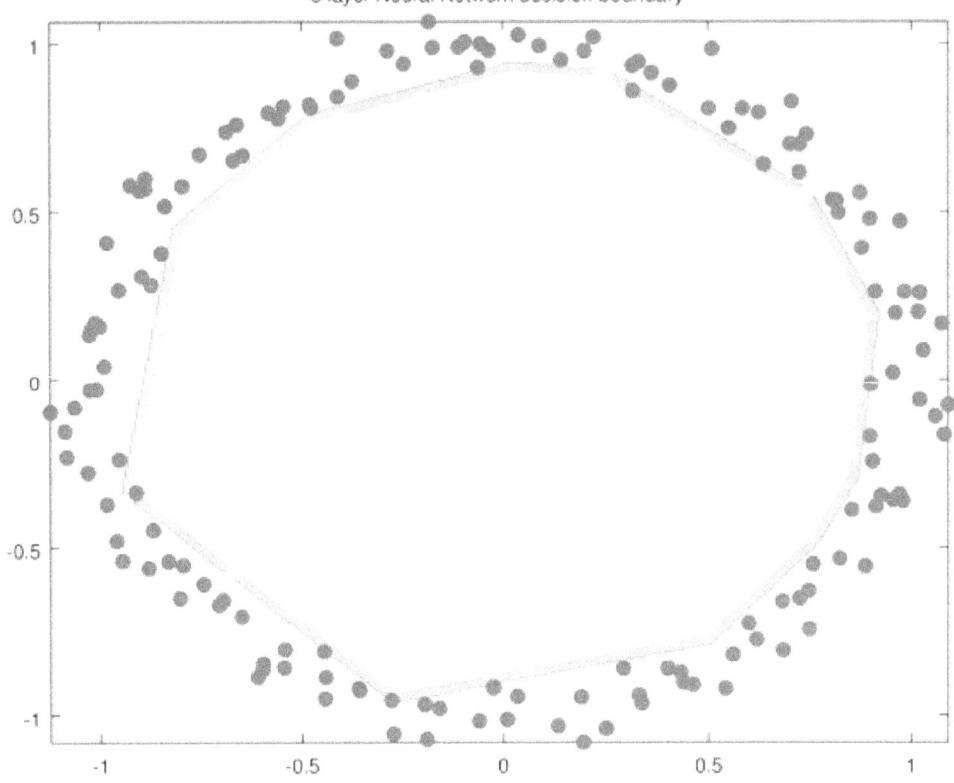

2.1a Regularization : Circles data – Python

The cross-entropy cost for Logistic classification is given as
$$J = \frac{1}{m}\sum_{i=1}^{m} y^i log((a^L)^{(i)}) - (1-y^i)log((a^L)^{(i)})$$

```
1  import numpy as np
2  import matplotlib
3  import matplotlib.pyplot as plt
4  import sklearn.linear_model
5  import pandas as pd
6  import sklearn
7  import sklearn.datasets
8  exec(open("DLfunctions61.py").read())
9
10 #Load the data
11 train_X, train_Y, test_X, test_Y = load_dataset()
12
13 # Set the layers dimensions
14 # 2 - number of input features
15 # 7 - 1 hidden layer 7 hidden units
16 # 1 - 1 sigmoid activation unit at the output layer
17 layersDimensions = [2,7,1]
```

```
# Train a L-layer deep learning network with default initialization
# hidden Activation function - relu
# output activation function - sigmoid
# learning rate - 0.6
# lambd=0.1
parameters = L_Layer_DeepModel(train_X, train_Y, layersDimensions,
hiddenActivationFunc='relu',  outputActivationFunc="sigmoid",learningRate =
0.6, lambd=0.1, num_iterations = 9000,    initType="default", print_cost =
True,figure="fig7.png")

# Clear the plot
plt.clf()
plt.close()

# Plot the decision boundary
plot_decision_boundary(lambda x: predict(parameters, x.T), train_X,
train_Y,str(0.6),figure1="fig8.png")

plt.clf()
plt.close()
```

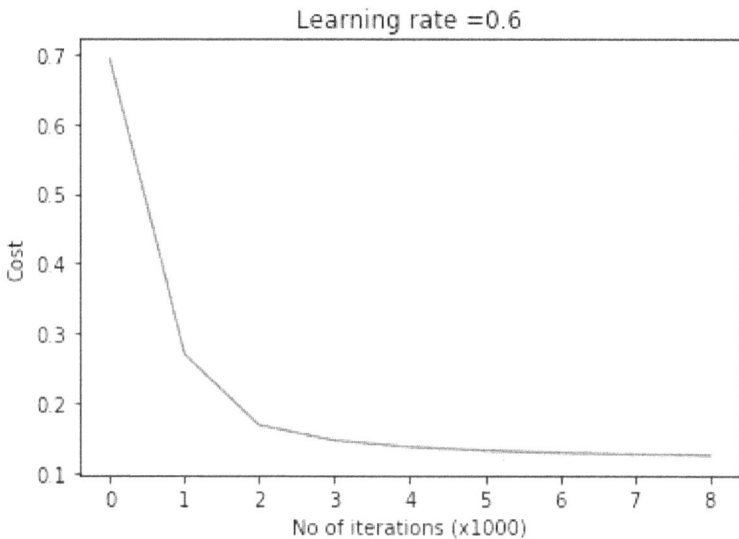

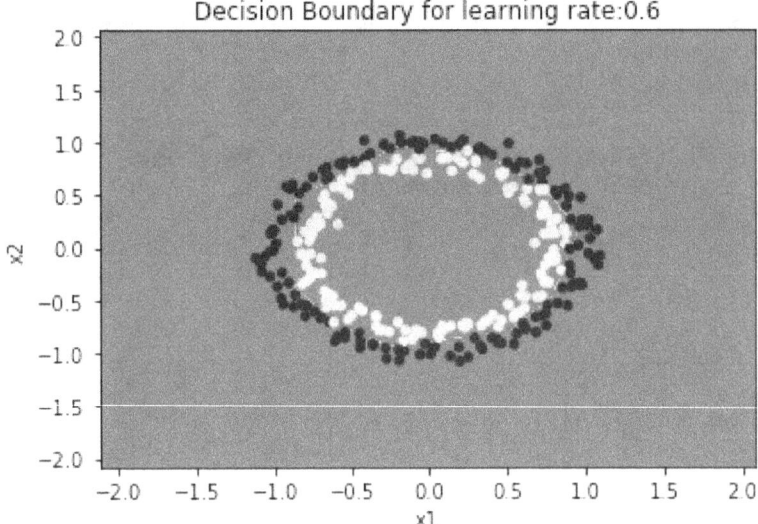

2.1b Regularization: Spiral data – Python

```
1  import numpy as np
2  import matplotlib
3  import matplotlib.pyplot as plt
4  import sklearn.linear_model
5  import pandas as pd
6  import sklearn
7  import sklearn.datasets
8  exec(open("DLfunctions61.py").read())
9
10 N = 100 # number of points per class
11 D = 2 # dimensionality
12 K = 3 # number of classes
13 X = np.zeros((N*K,D)) # data matrix (each row = single example)
14 y = np.zeros(N*K, dtype='uint8') # class labels
15 for j in range(K):
16   ix = range(N*j,N*(j+1))
17   r = np.linspace(0.0,1,N) # radius
18   t = np.linspace(j*4,(j+1)*4,N) + np.random.randn(N)*0.2 # theta
19   X[ix] = np.c_[r*np.sin(t), r*np.cos(t)]
20   y[ix] = j
21
22
23 # Plot the data
24 plt.scatter(X[:, 0], X[:, 1], c=y, s=40, cmap=plt.cm.Spectral)
25 plt.clf()
26 plt.close()
27
28 #Set layer dimensions
29 # 2 - number of input features
30 # 100 - 1 hidden layer 100 hidden units
31 # 3 -3 classes with softmax unit at the output layer
32 layersDimensions = [2,100,3]
33 y1=y.reshape(-1,1).T
34
35 # Train a L-layer deep learning network
36 # hidden Activation function - relu
37 # output activation function - softmax
38 # learning rate - 1
```

```
39  # lambd=1e-3
40  parameters = L_Layer_DeepModel(X.T, y1, layersDimensions,
41  hiddenActivationFunc='relu', outputActivationFunc="softmax",   learningRate =
42  1,lambd=1e-3, num_iterations = 5000, print_cost = True,figure="fig9.png")
43
44  plt.clf()
45  plt.close()
46
47  # Plot decision boundary
48  W1=parameters['W1']
49  b1=parameters['b1']
50  W2=parameters['W2']
51  b2=parameters['b2']
52  plot_decision_boundary1(X, y1,W1,b1,W2,b2,figure2="fig10.png")
```

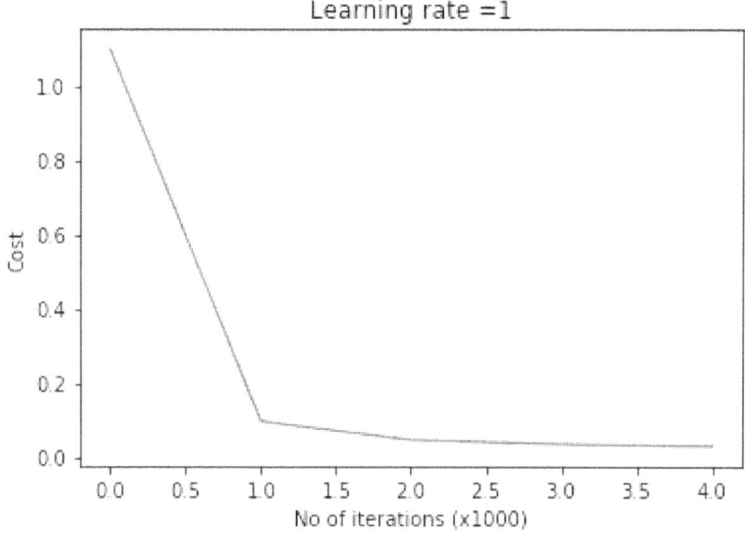

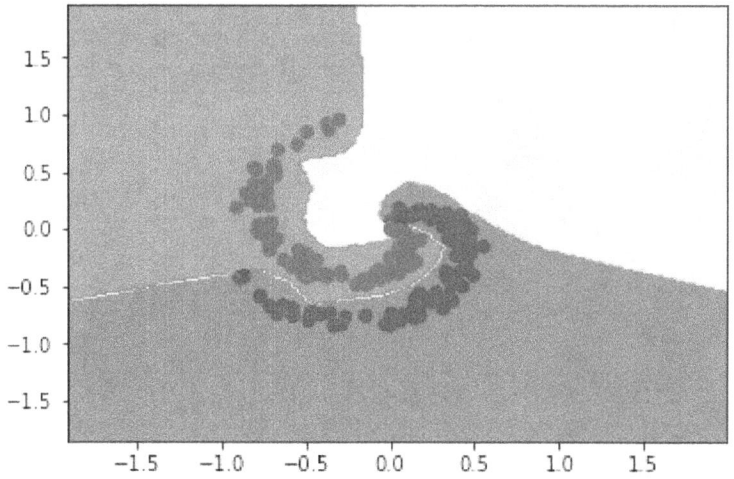

2.2a Regularization: Circles data – R

```r
source("DLfunctions61.R")
#Load data
df=read.csv("circles.csv",header=FALSE)
z <- as.matrix(read.csv("circles.csv",header=FALSE))
x <- z[,1:2]
y <- z[,3]
X <- t(x)
Y <- t(y)

#Set layer dimensions
# 2 - number of input features
# 11 - 1 hidden layer 11 hidden units
# 1 - 1 sigmoid activation unit at the output layer
layersDimensions = c(2,11,1)

# Train a L-layer deep learning network
# hidden Activation function - relu
# output activation function - sigmoid
# learning rate - 0.6
# lambd=0.1
retvals = L_Layer_DeepModel(X, Y, layersDimensions,
                            hiddenActivationFunc='relu',
                            outputActivationFunc="sigmoid",
                            learningRate = 0.5,
                            lambd=0.1,
                            numIterations = 9000,
                            initType="default",
                            print_cost = True)

#Plot the cost vs iterations
iterations <- seq(0,9000,1000)
costs=retvals$costs
df=data.frame(iterations,costs)
ggplot(df,aes(x=iterations,y=costs)) + geom_point() + geom_line(color="blue")
+ ggtitle("Costs vs iterations") + xlab("No of iterations") + ylab("Cost")
```

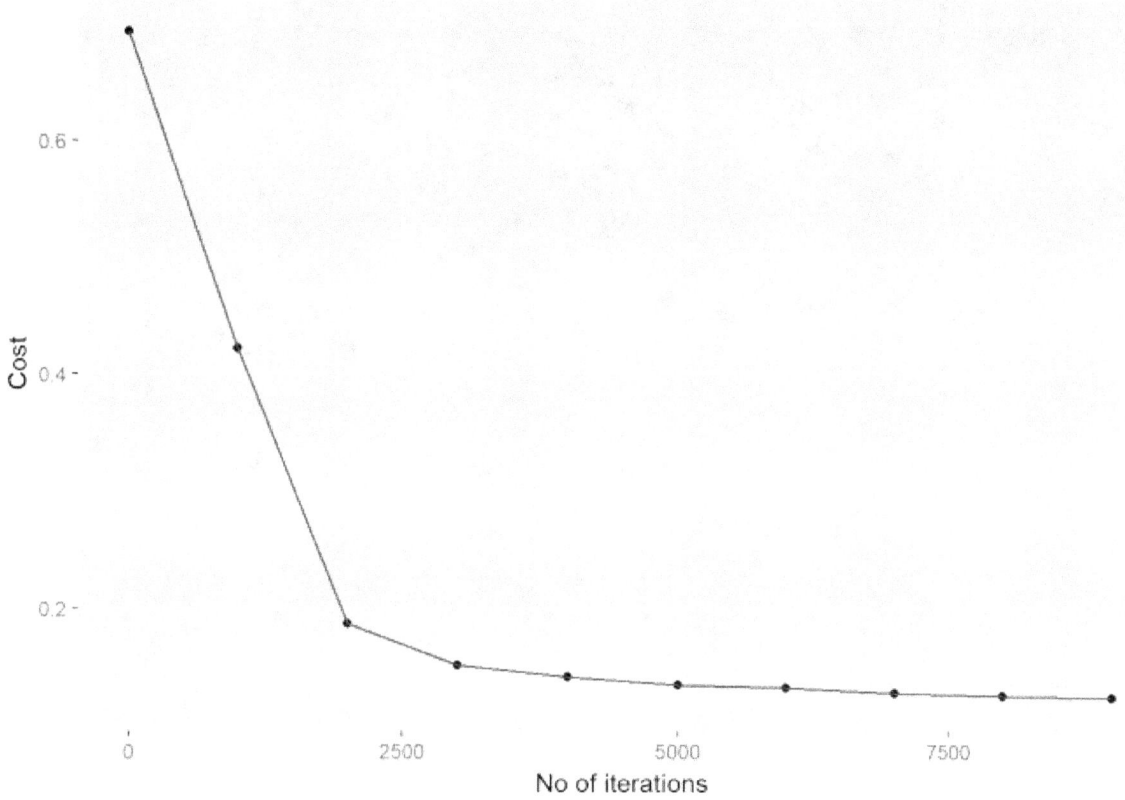

```
1  # Plot the decision boundary
2  plotDecisionBoundary(z,retvals,hiddenActivationFunc="relu",0.5)
```

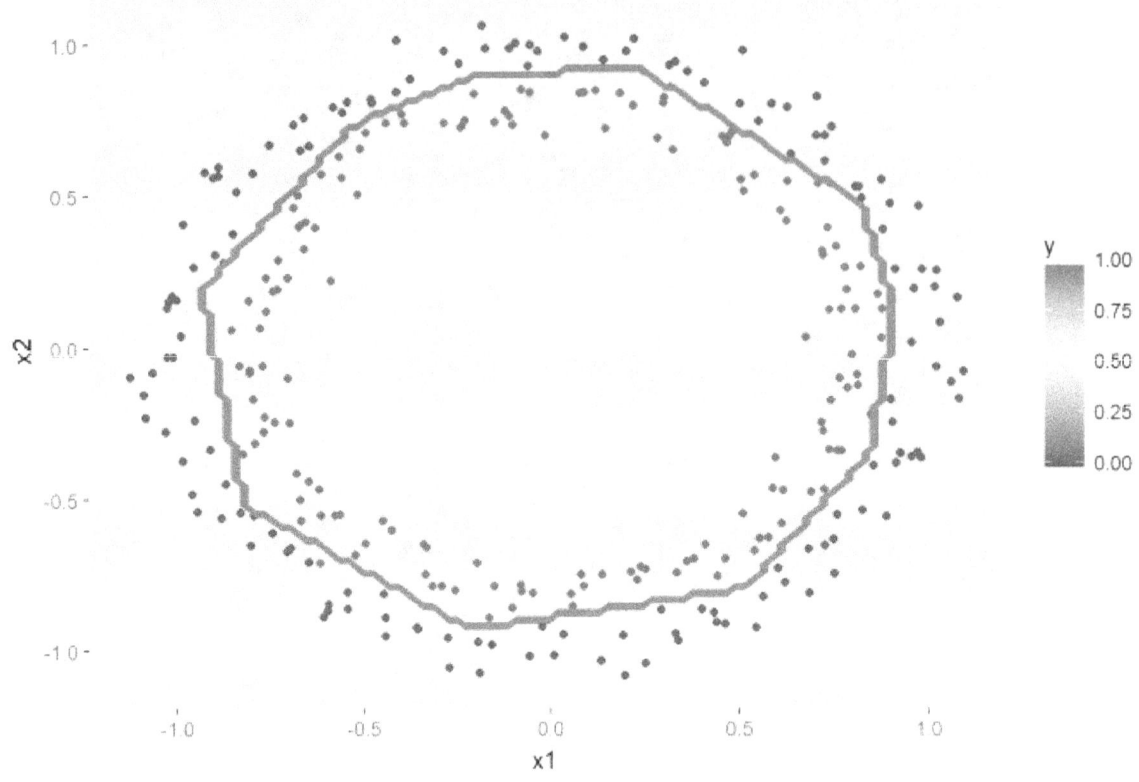

Decision boundary for learning rate: 0.5

2.2b Regularization:Spiral data – R

```
1  # Read the spiral dataset
2  #Load the data
3  source("DLfunctions61.R")
4  Z <- as.matrix(read.csv("spiral.csv",header=FALSE))
5
6  # Setup the data
7  X <- Z[,1:2]
8  y <- Z[,3]
9  X <- t(X)
10 Y <- t(y)
11
12 # Set layer dimensions
13 layersDimensions = c(2, 100, 3)
14 # 2 - number of input features
15 # 100 - 1 hidden layer 100 hidden units
16 # 3 - 3 softmax classes at the output layer
17
18 # Train a L-layer deep learning network
19 # hidden Activation function - relu
20 # output activation function - sigmoid
21 # learning rate - 0.5
22 # lambd=0.01
23 retvals = L_Layer_DeepModel(X, Y, layersDimensions,
24         hiddenActivationFunc='relu',
25         outputActivationFunc="softmax",
26         learningRate = 0.5,
27         lambd=0.01,
28         numIterations = 9000,
```

```
29            print_cost = True)
30 parameters<-retvals$parameters
31
32 #Plot decision boundary
33 plotDecisionBoundary1(Z,parameters)
```

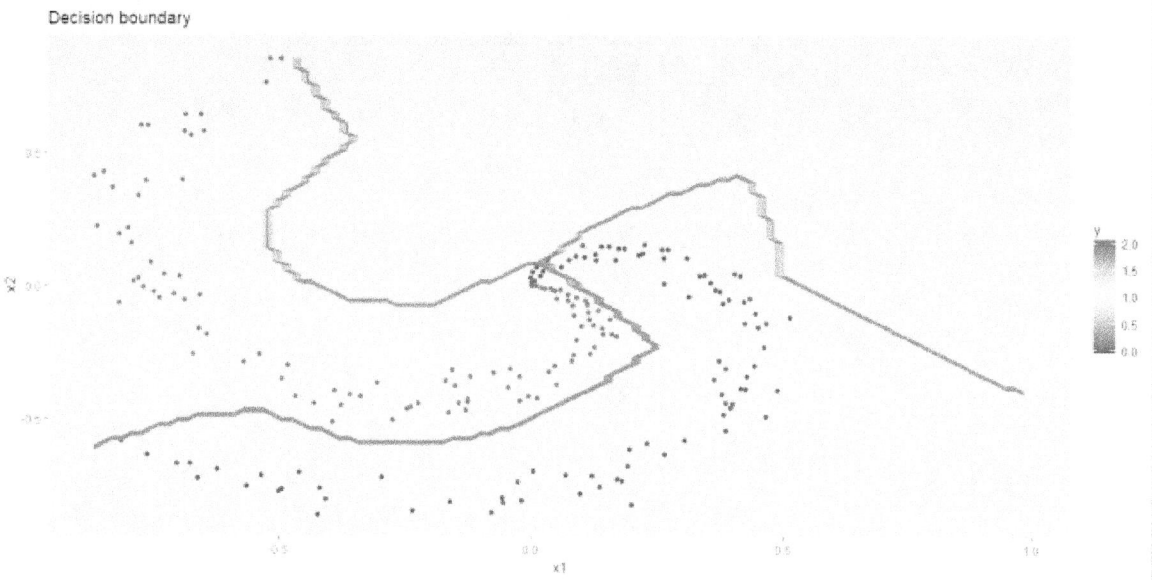

2.3a Regularization: Circles data – Octave

```
1  #
2  source("DL61functions.m")
3  #Load data
4  data=csvread("circles.csv");
5  X=data(:,1:2);
6  Y=data(:,3);
7
8  # Set layer dimensions
9  # 2 - number of input features
10 # 11 - 1 hidden layer 11 hidden units
11 # 1 - 1 sigmoid activation unit at the output layer
12 layersDimensions = [2 11  1]; #tanh=-0.5(ok), #relu=0.1 best!
13
14 # Train a L-layer deep learning network
15 # hidden Activation function - relu
16 # output activation function - sigmoid
17 # learning rate - 0.5
18 # lambd=0.2
19 [weights biases costs]=L_Layer_DeepModel(X', Y', layersDimensions,
20                           hiddenActivationFunc='relu',
21                           outputActivationFunc="sigmoid",
22                           learningRate = 0.5,
23                           lambd=0.2,
24                           keep_prob=1,
25                           numIterations = 8000,
26                           initType="default");
27
28 #Plot cost vs iterations
29 plotCostVsIterations(8000,costs)
30
31 #Plot decision boundary
32 plotDecisionBoundary(data,weights,
33 biases,keep_prob=1,hiddenActivationFunc="relu")
```

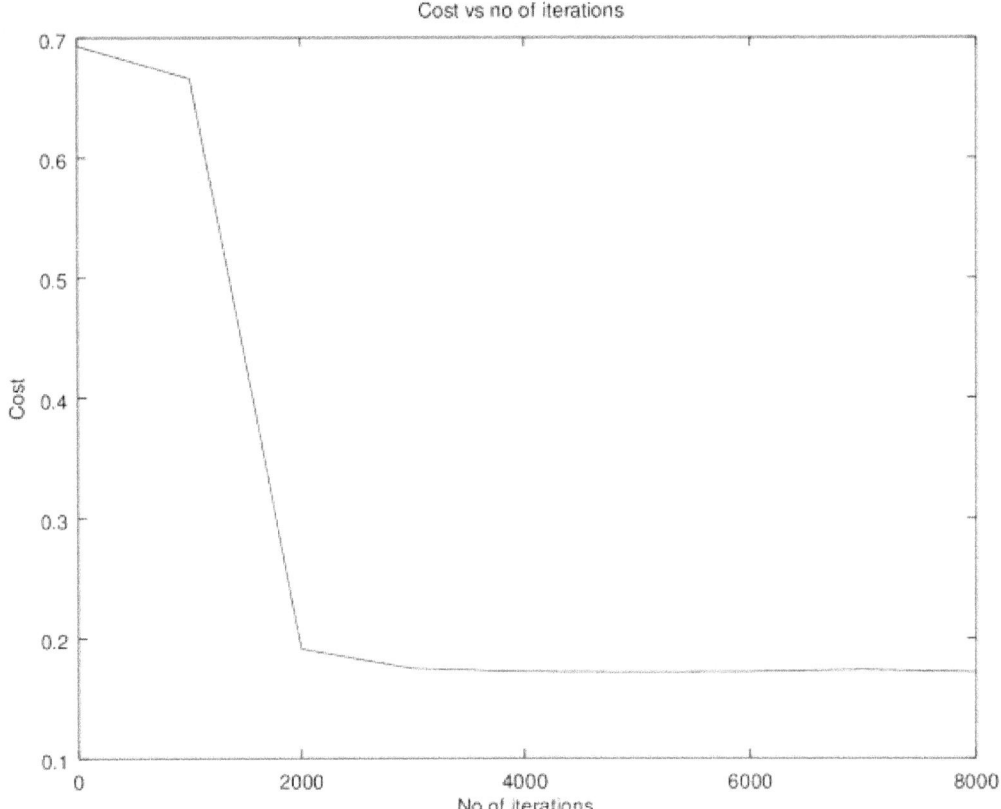

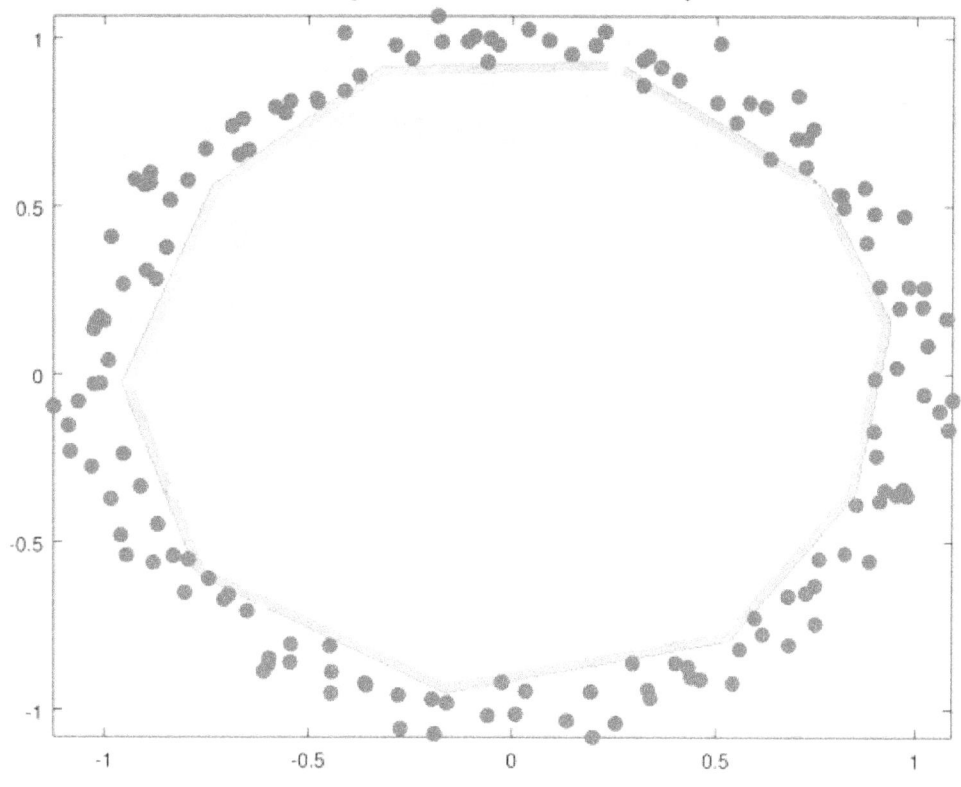

2.3b Regularization:Spiral data 2 – Octave

```
#
source("DL61functions.m")
data=csvread("spiral.csv");

# Setup the data
X=data(:,1:2);
Y=data(:,3);

# Set layer dimensions
# 2 - number of input features
# 100 - 1 hidden layer 100 hidden units
# 3 -3 classes with softmax activation unit at the output layer
layersDimensions = [2 100 3]

# Train a L-layer deep learning network
# hidden Activation function - relu
# output activation function - sigmoid
# learning rate - 0.6
# lambd=0.2
[weights biases costs]=L_Layer_DeepModel(X', Y', layersDimensions,
                               hiddenActivationFunc='relu',
                               outputActivationFunc="softmax",
                               learningRate = 0.6,
                               lambd=0.2,
                               keep_prob=1,
                               numIterations = 10000);
```

```
27
28  #Plot cost vs iterations
29  plotCostVsIterations(10000,costs)
30
31  #Plot decision boundary
32  plotDecisionBoundary1(data,weights,
33  biases,keep_prob=1,hiddenActivationFunc="relu")
```

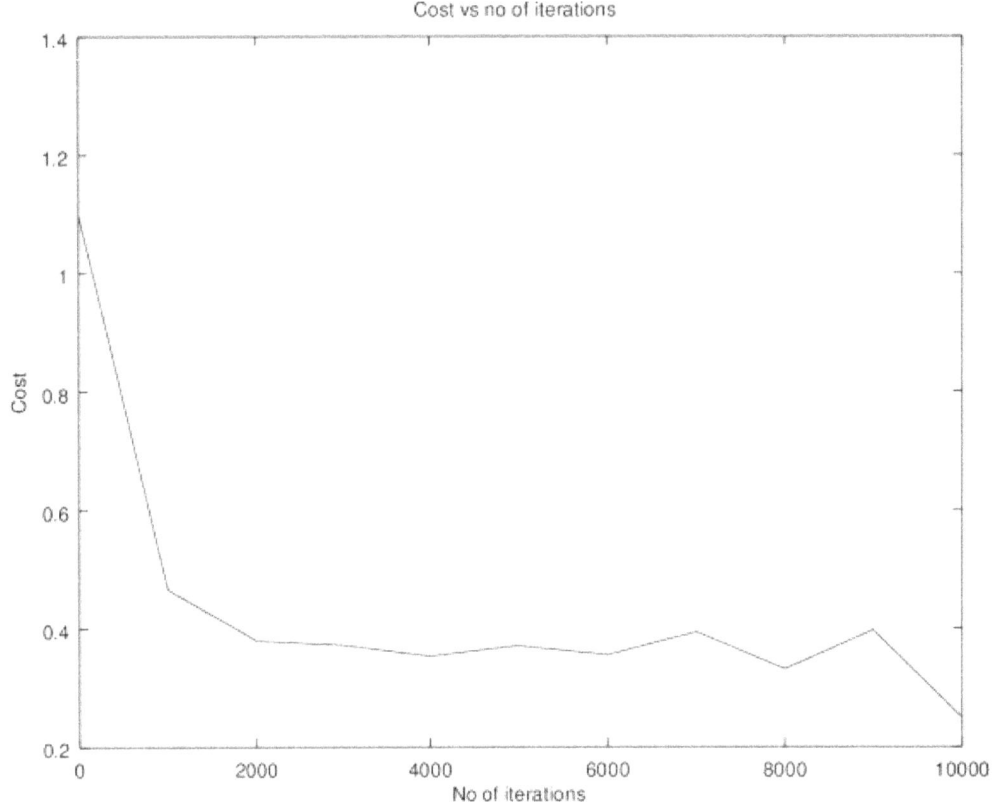

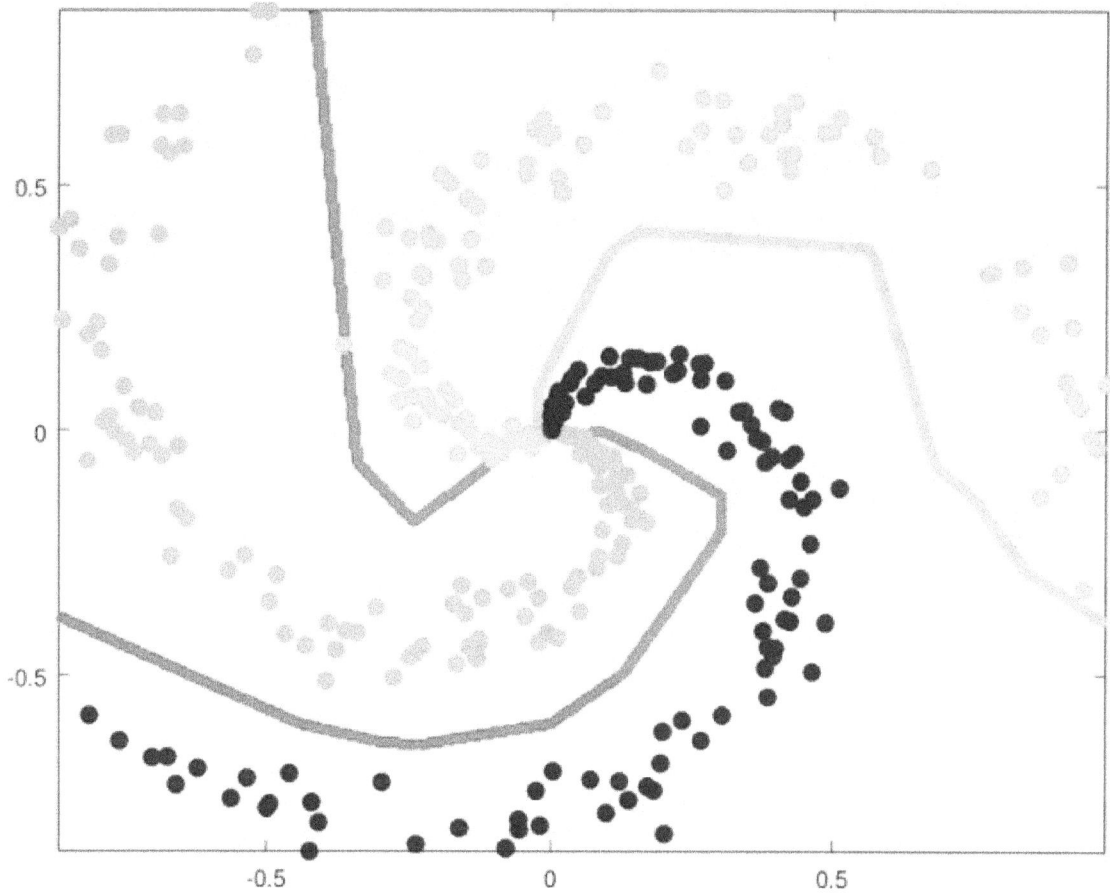

3.1a Dropout: Circles data – Python

The 'dropout' regularization technique was used with great effectiveness, to prevent overfitting by Alex Krizhevsky, Ilya Sutskever and Prof Geoffrey E. Hinton in the 'Imagenet classification with Deep Convolutional Neural Networks' (https://www.nvidia.cn/content/tesla/pdf/machine-learning/imagenet-classification-with-deep-convolutional-nn.pdf)

The technique of dropout works by dropping a random set of activation units in each hidden layer, based on a 'keep_prob' criteria in the forward propagation cycle. Here is the code for Octave. A 'dropoutMat' is created for each layer which specifies which units to drop **Note**: The same 'dropoutMat has to be used which computing the gradients in the backward propagation cycle. Hence the dropout matrices are stored in a cell array.

```
1  for l =1:L-1
2     ...
3     D=rand(size(A)(1),size(A)(2));
4     D = (D < keep_prob) ;
5     # Zero out some hidden units
6     A= A .* D;
7     # Divide by keep_prob to keep the expected value of A the same
8     A = A ./ keep_prob;
9     # Store D in a dropoutMat cell array
10    dropoutMat{l}=D;
11    ...
12 endfor
```

In the backward propagation cycle we have
```
for l =(L-1):-1:1
         ...
         D = dropoutMat{l};
         # Zero out the dAl based on same dropout matrix
         dAl= dAl .* D;
         # Divide by keep_prob to maintain the expected value
         dAl = dAl ./ keep_prob;
         ...
    endfor
```

```python
#
import numpy as np
import matplotlib
import matplotlib.pyplot as plt
import sklearn.linear_model
import pandas as pd
import sklearn
import sklearn.datasets
exec(open("DLfunctions61.py").read())

#Load the data
train_X, train_Y, test_X, test_Y = load_dataset()

# Set the layers dimensions
# 2 - number of input features
# 7 - 1 hidden layer 7 hidden units
# 1 - 1 sigmoid activation unit at the output layer
layersDimensions = [2,7,1]

# Train a L-layer deep learning network
# hidden Activation function - relu
# output activation function - sigmoid
# learning rate - 0.6
#keep_prob=0.7
parameters = L_Layer_DeepModel(train_X, train_Y, layersDimensions,
hiddenActivationFunc='relu',    outputActivationFunc="sigmoid",learningRate =
0.6, keep_prob=0.7, num_iterations = 9000,    initType="default", print_cost
= True,figure="fig11.png")

# Clear the plot
plt.clf()
plt.close()

# Plot the decision boundary
plot_decision_boundary(lambda x: predict(parameters, x.T,keep_prob=0.7),
train_X, train_Y,str(0.6),figure1="fig12.png")
```

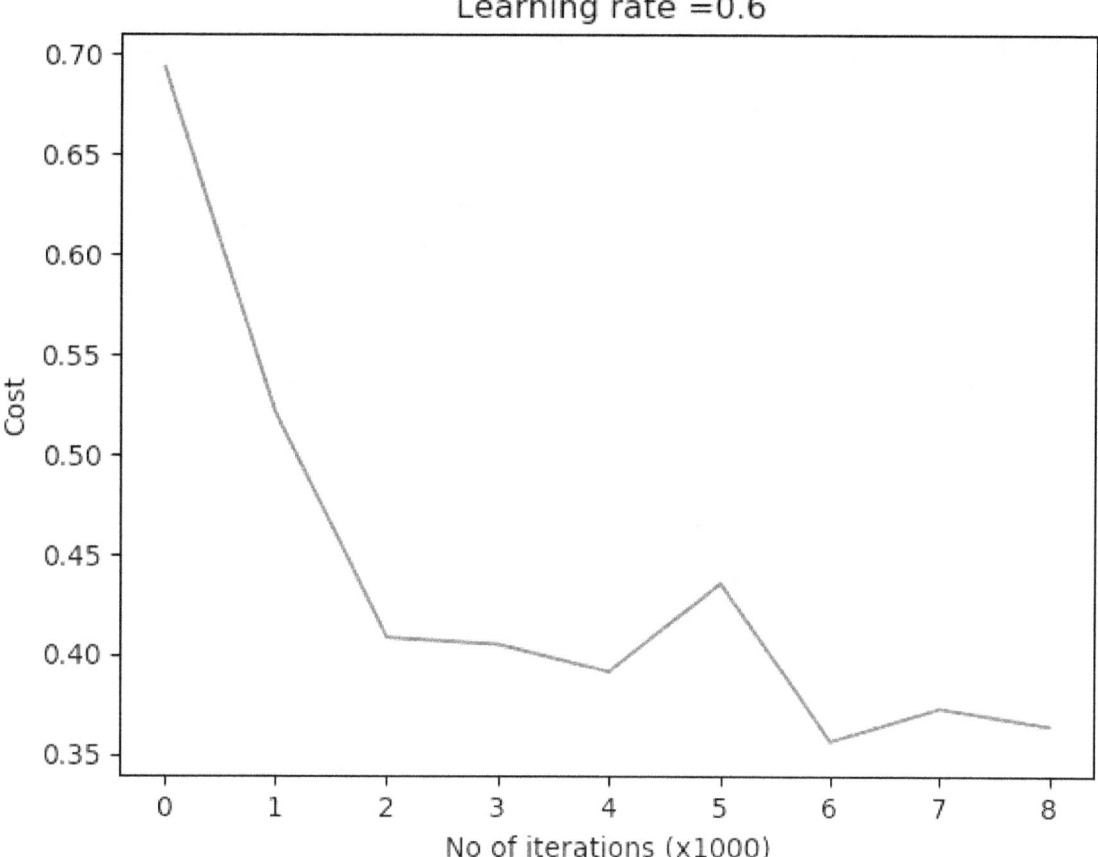

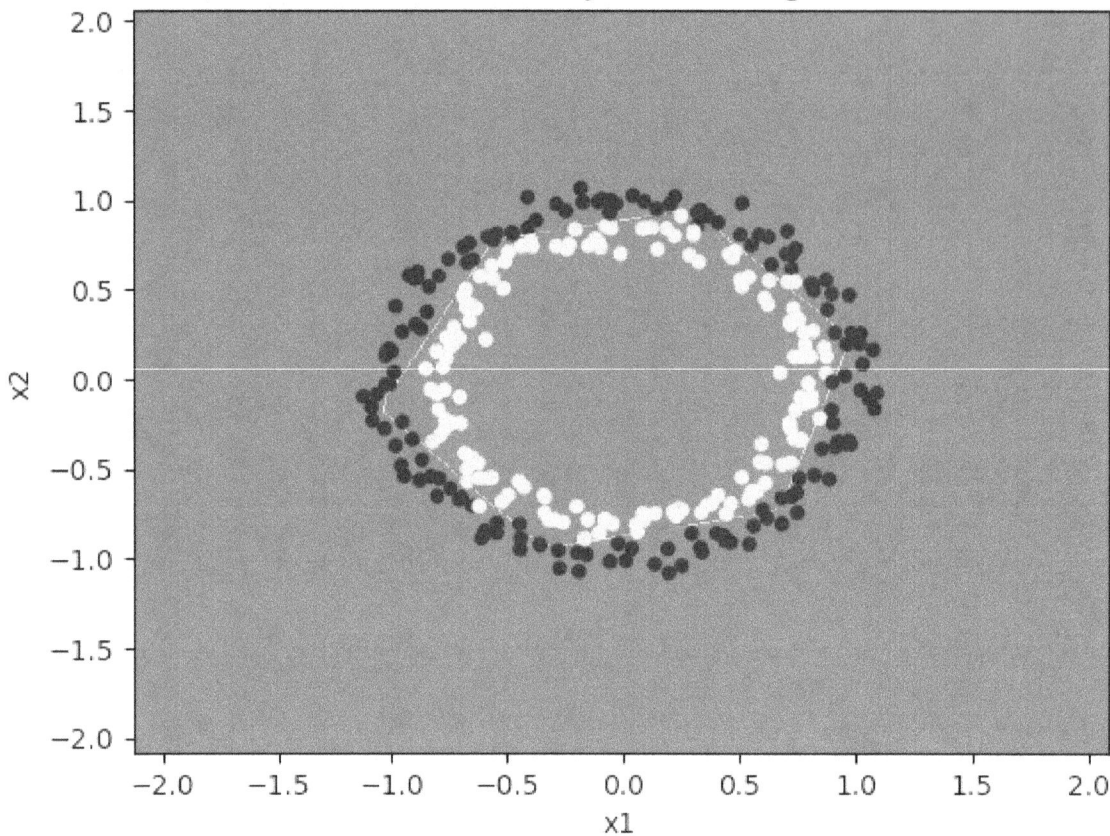

3.1b Dropout: Spiral data – Python

```
1  import numpy as np
2  import matplotlib
3  import matplotlib.pyplot as plt
4  import sklearn.linear_model
5  import pandas as pd
6  import sklearn
7  import sklearn.datasets
8  exec(open("DLfunctions61.py").read())
9  # Create an input data set - Taken from CS231n Convolutional Neural networks,
10 # http://cs231n.github.io/neural-networks-case-study/
11
12
13 N = 100 # number of points per class
14 D = 2 # dimensionality
15 K = 3 # number of classes
16 X = np.zeros((N*K,D)) # data matrix (each row = single example)
17 y = np.zeros(N*K, dtype='uint8') # class labels
18 for j in range(K):
19    ix = range(N*j,N*(j+1))
20    r = np.linspace(0.0,1,N) # radius
21    t = np.linspace(j*4,(j+1)*4,N) + np.random.randn(N)*0.2 # theta
22    X[ix] = np.c_[r*np.sin(t), r*np.cos(t)]
23    y[ix] = j
24
25
```

```python
26  # Plot the data
27  plt.scatter(X[:, 0], X[:, 1], c=y, s=40, cmap=plt.cm.Spectral)
28  plt.clf()
29  plt.close()
30
31  #Set layer dimensions
32  # 2 - number of input features
33  # 100 - 1 hidden layer 100 hidden units
34  # 3 -3 classes with softmax activation unit at the output layer
35  layersDimensions = [2,100,3]
36  y1=y.reshape(-1,1).T
37
38  # Train a L-layer deep learning network
39  # hidden Activation function - relu
40  # output activation function - softmax
41  # learning rate - 1
42  #keep_prob=0.9
43  parameters = L_Layer_DeepModel(X.T, y1, layersDimensions,
44  hiddenActivationFunc='relu', outputActivationFunc="softmax",   learningRate =
45  1,keep_prob=0.9, num_iterations = 5000, print_cost = True,figure="fig13.png")
46
47  plt.clf()
48  plt.close()
49  W1=parameters['W1']
50  b1=parameters['b1']
51  W2=parameters['W2']
52  b2=parameters['b2']
53
54  #Plot decision boundary
55  plot_decision_boundary1(X, y1,W1,b1,W2,b2,figure2="fig14.png")
```

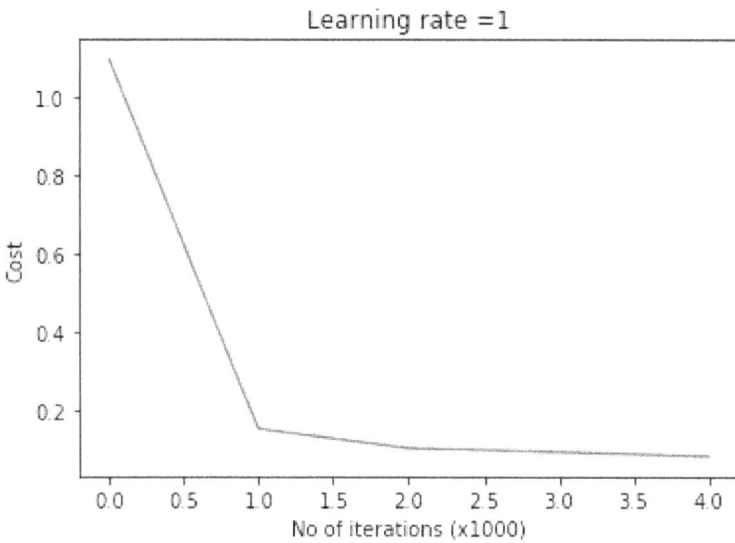

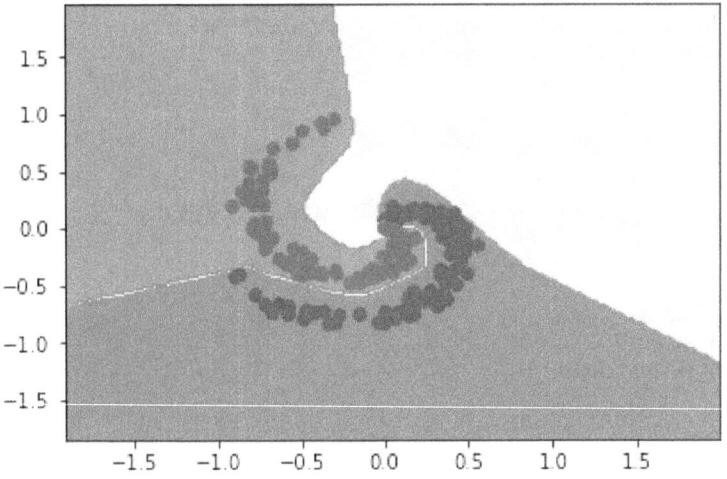

3.2a Dropout: Circles data – R

```
1  source("DLfunctions61.R")
2  #Load data
3  df=read.csv("circles.csv",header=FALSE)
4  z <- as.matrix(read.csv("circles.csv",header=FALSE))
5
6  x <- z[,1:2]
7  y <- z[,3]
8  X <- t(x)
9  Y <- t(y)
10
11 # Set layer dimensions
12 # 2 - number of input features
13 # 11 - 1 hidden layer 11 hidden units
14 # 1 - 1 sigmoid activation unit at the output layer
15 layersDimensions = c(2,11,1)
16
17 # Train a L-layer deep learning network
18 # hidden Activation function - relu
19 # output activation function - sigmoid
20 # learning rate - 0.5
21 # keep_prob=0.8
22 retvals = L_Layer_DeepModel(X, Y, layersDimensions,
23                             hiddenActivationFunc='relu',
24                             outputActivationFunc="sigmoid",
25                             learningRate = 0.5,
26                             keep_prob=0.8,
27                             numIterations = 9000,
28                             initType="default",
29                             print_cost = True)
30
31 # Plot the decision boundary
32 plotDecisionBoundary(z,retvals,keep_prob=0.6,
33 hiddenActivationFunc="relu",0.5)
```

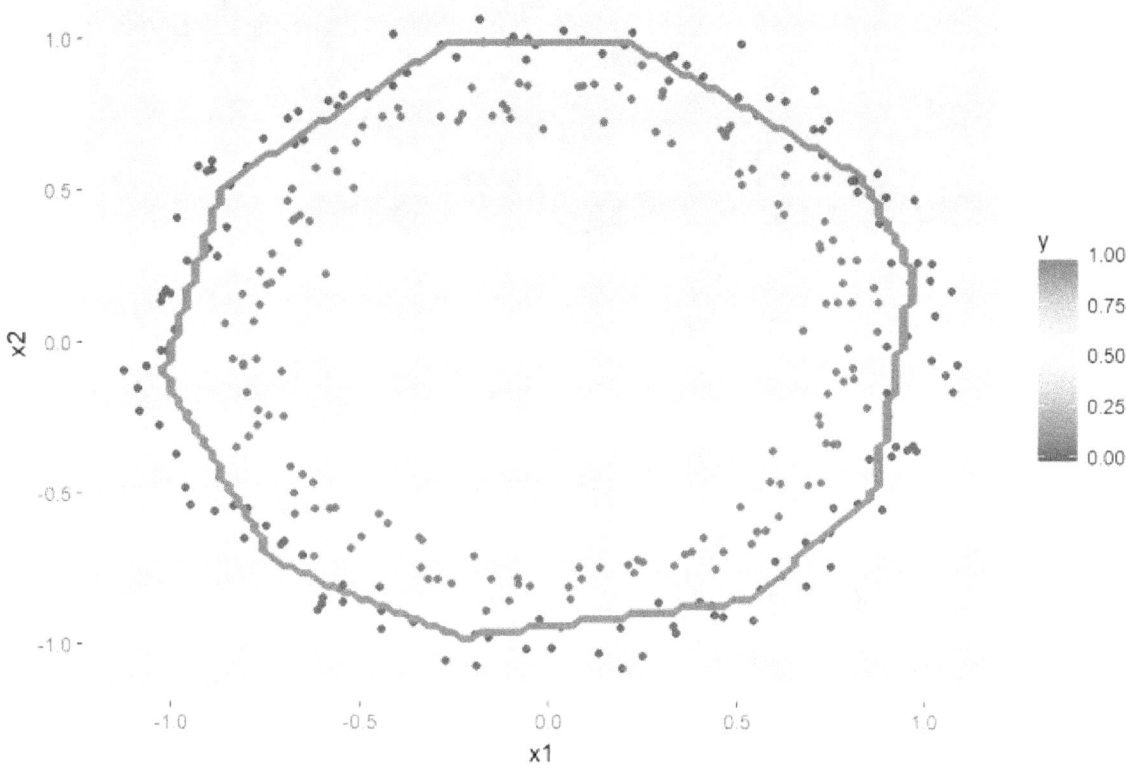

Decision boundary for learning rate: 0.5

3.2b Dropout: Spiral data – R

```r
# Read the spiral dataset
source("DLfunctions61.R")
# Load data
Z <- as.matrix(read.csv("spiral.csv",header=FALSE))

# Setup the data
X <- Z[,1:2]
y <- Z[,3]
X <- t(X)
Y <- t(y)

# Train a L-layer deep learning network
# hidden Activation function - relu
# output activation function - softmax
# learning rate - 0.1
#keep_prob=0.9
retvals = L_Layer_DeepModel(X, Y, layersDimensions,
                            hiddenActivationFunc='relu',
                            outputActivationFunc="softmax",
                            learningRate = 0.1,
                            keep_prob=0.90,
                            numIterations = 9000,
                            print_cost = True)

parameters<-retvals$parameters
#Plot decision boundary
plotDecisionBoundary1(Z,parameters)
```

3.3a Dropout: Circles data – Octave

```
1   data=csvread("circles.csv");
2
3   X=data(:,1:2);
4   Y=data(:,3);
5
6   # Set layer dimensions
7   # 2 - number of input features
8   # 11 - 1 hidden layer 11 hidden units
9   # 1 - 1 sigmoid activation unit at the output layer
10  layersDimensions = [2 11  1];
11
12  # Train a L-layer deep learning network
13  # hidden Activation function - relu
14  # output activation function - sigmoid
15  # learning rate - 0.5
16  # keep_prob=0.8
17  [weights biases costs]=L_Layer_DeepModel(X', Y', layersDimensions,
18                          hiddenActivationFunc='relu',
19                          outputActivationFunc="sigmoid",
20                          learningRate = 0.5,
21                          lambd=0,
22                          keep_prob=0.8,
23                          numIterations = 10000,
24                          initType="default");
25
26  #Plot cost vs iterations
27  plotCostVsIterations(10000,costs)
28
29  #Plot decision boundary
30  plotDecisionBoundary1(data,weights, biases,keep_prob=1,
31  hiddenActivationFunc="relu")
32
```

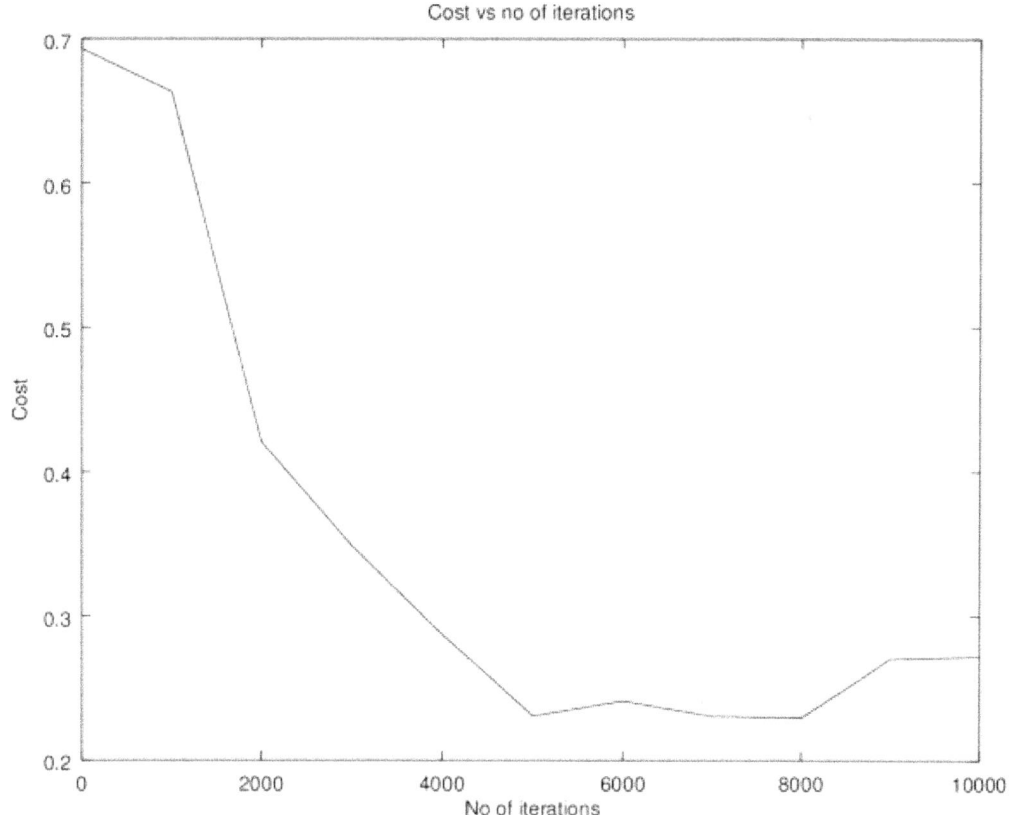

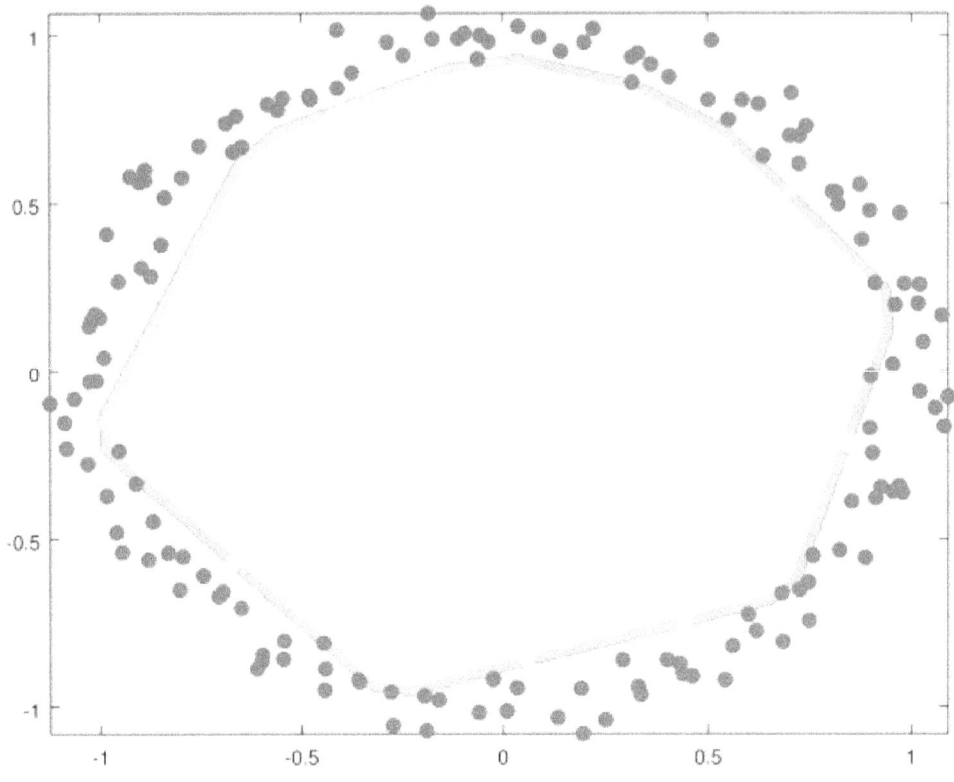

3 layer Neural Network decision boundary

3.3b Dropout Spiral data – Octave

```
1  source("DL61functions.m")
2  data=csvread("spiral.csv");
3
4  # Setup the data
5  X=data(:,1:2);
6  Y=data(:,3);
7
8  # Set layer dimensions
9  layersDimensions = [numFeats numHidden  numOutput];
10
11 # Train a L-layer deep learning network
12 # hidden Activation function - relu
13 # output activation function - softmax
14 # learning rate - 0.1
15 #keep_prob=0.8
16 [weights biases costs]=L_Layer_DeepModel(X', Y', layersDimensions,
17                          hiddenActivationFunc='relu',
18                          outputActivationFunc="softmax",
19                          learningRate = 0.1,
20                          lambd=0,
21                          keep_prob=0.8,
22                          numIterations = 10000);
23
24 #Plot cost vs iterations
25 plotCostVsIterations(10000,costs)
26
```

```
27  #Plot decision boundary
28  plotDecisionBoundary1(data,weights, biases,keep_prob=1,
29  hiddenActivationFunc="relu")
```

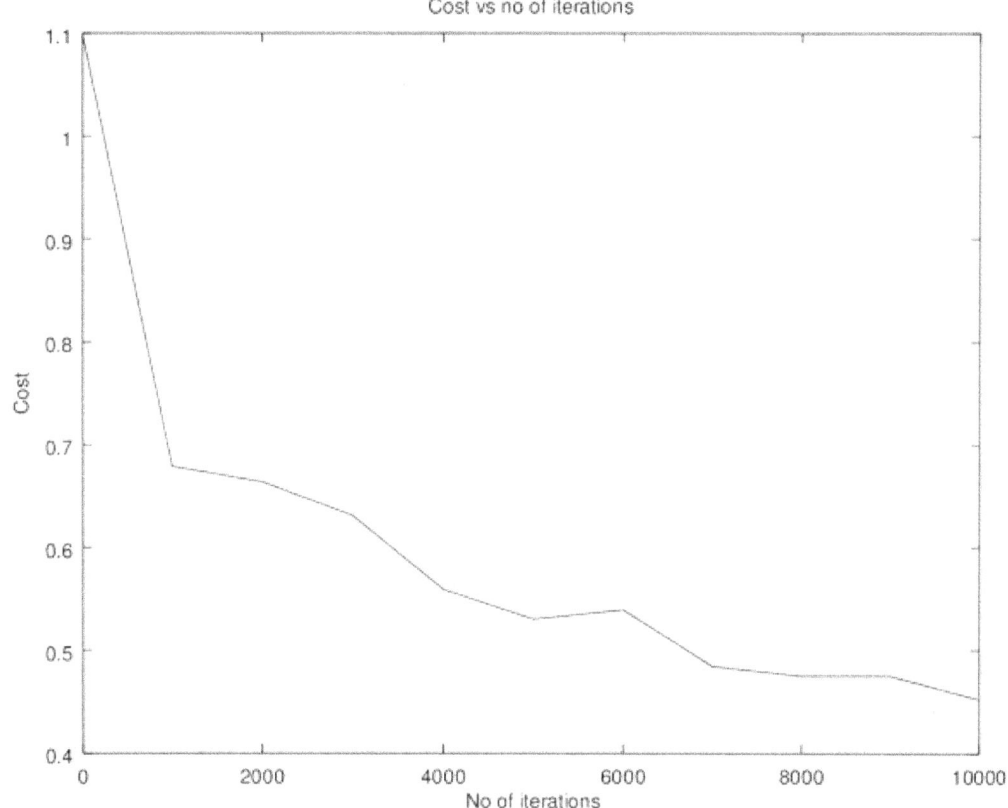

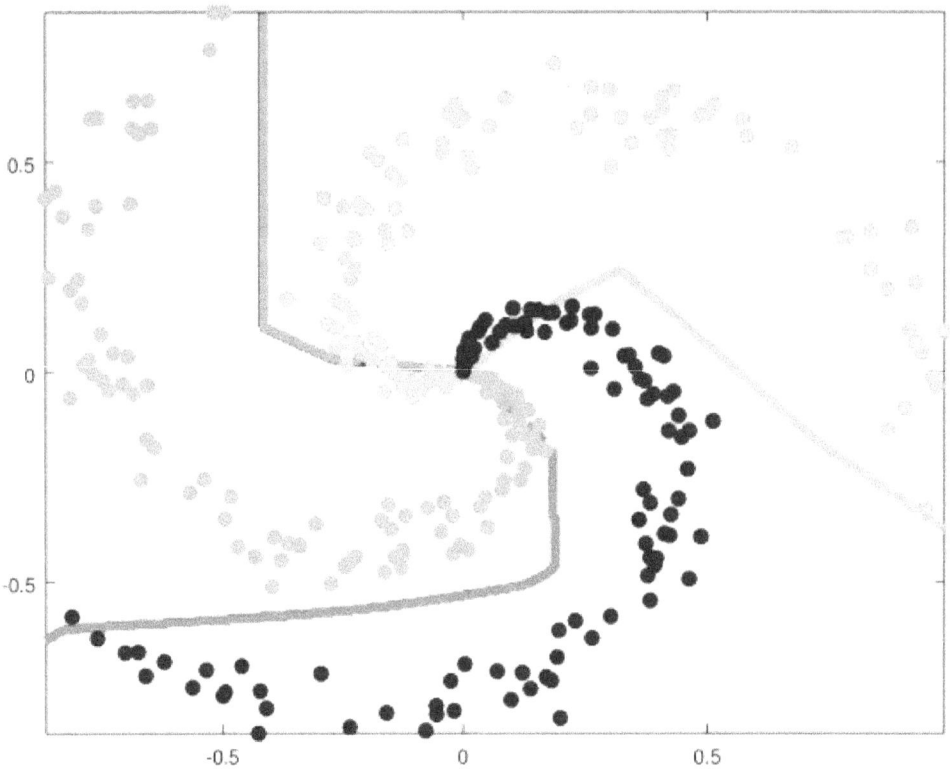

4. Conclusion
This post further enhances my earlier L-Layer generic implementation of a Deep Learning network to include options for initialization techniques, L2 regularization or dropout regularization

7. Gradient Descent Optimization techniques

Artificial Intelligence is the new electricity. – Prof Andrew Ng
Most of human and animal learning is unsupervised learning. If intelligence was a cake, unsupervised learning would be the cake, supervised learning would be the icing on the cake, and reinforcement learning would be the cherry on the cake. We know how to make the icing and the cherry, but we don't know how to make the cake. We need to solve the unsupervised learning problem before we can even think of getting to true AI. – Yann LeCun, March 14, 2016 (Facebook)

1. Introduction

In this chapter 7 of 'Deep Learning from first principles, I implement optimization methods used in Stochastic Gradient Descent (SGD) to speed up the convergence. Specifically, I discuss and implement the following gradient descent optimization techniques

a. Vanilla Stochastic Gradient Descent
b. Learning rate decay
c. Momentum method
d. RMSProp
e. Adaptive Moment Estimation (Adam)

This chapter, further enhances my generic L-Layer Deep Learning Network implementations in vectorized Python, R and Octave to also include the Stochastic Gradient Descent optimization techniques. These vectorized implementation are in Appendix 7 - Gradient Descent Optimization techniques

You can clone/download the code from Github at DeepLearningFromFirstPrinciples (https://github.com/tvganesh/DeepLearningFromFirstPrinciples/tree/master/Chap7-DLGradientDescentOptimization) Incidentally, a good discussion of the various optimizations methods used in Stochastic Gradient Optimization techniques can be seen at Sebastian Ruder's blog (http://ruder.io/optimizing-gradient-descent/)

Note: The vectorized Python, R and Octave implementations in this chapter, only a 1024 random training samples were used. This was to reduce the computation time. You are free to use the entire data set (60000 training data) for the computation.

This chapter is largely based of on Prof Andrew Ng's Deep Learning Specialization (https://www.coursera.org/specializations/deep-learning). All the optimization techniques discussed here use Stochastic Gradient Descent and are based on the technique of exponentially weighted average method. So, for example if we had some time series data $\theta_1, \theta_2, \theta_3 \ldots \theta_t$ then we can represent the exponentially average value at time 't' as a sequence of the previous value c_{t-1} and θ_t as shown below

$$c_t = \beta c_{t-1} + (1-\beta)\theta_t$$

Here c_t represent the average of the data set over $\frac{1}{1-\beta}$ By choosing different values of β, we can average over a larger or smaller number of the data points.

We can write the equations as follows
$$c_t = \beta c_{t-1} + (1-\beta)\theta_t$$
$$c_{t-1} = \beta c_{t-2} + (1-\beta)\theta_{t-1}$$
$$c_{t-2} = \beta c_{t-3} + (1-\beta)\theta_{t-2}$$
and
$$c_{t-k} = \beta c_{t-(k+1)} + (1-\beta)\theta_{t-k}$$

By substitution we have
$$c_t = (1-\beta)\theta_t + \beta c_{t-1}$$
$$c_t = (1-\beta)\theta_t + \beta((1-\beta)\theta_{t-1}) + \beta c_{t-2}$$
$$c_t = (1-\beta)\theta_t + \beta((1-\beta)\theta_{t-1}) + \beta((1-\beta)\theta_{t-2} + \beta c_{t-3})$$

Hence it can be seen that the c_t is the weighted sum over the previous values θ_k, which is an exponentially decaying function.

1.1a. Stochastic Gradient Descent (Vanilla) – Python

```
1  import numpy as np
2  import matplotlib
3  import matplotlib.pyplot as plt
4  import sklearn.linear_model
5  import pandas as pd
6  import sklearn
7  import sklearn.datasets
8  exec(open("DLfunctions7.py").read())
9  exec(open("load_mnist.py").read())
10
11 # Read the MNIST training data and labels
12 training=list(read(dataset='training',path=".\\mnist"))
13 test=list(read(dataset='testing',path=".\\mnist"))
14 lbls=[]
15 pxls=[]
16
17 #Loop
18 for i in range(60000):
19         l,p=training[i]
20         lbls.append(l)
21         pxls.append(p)
22 labels= np.array(lbls)
23 pixels=np.array(pxls)
24 y=labels.reshape(-1,1)
25 X=pixels.reshape(pixels.shape[0],-1)
```

```
26  X1=X.T
27  Y1=y.T
28
29  # Create a list of 1024 random numbers.
30  permutation = list(np.random.permutation(2**10))
31
32  # Subset 1024 training samples from the data
33  X2 = X1[:, permutation]
34  Y2 = Y1[:, permutation].reshape((1,2**10))
35
36  # Set the layer dimensions
37  # 784 - number of input features (28 x28)
38  # 15, 9 - 2 hidden layers with 15, 9 hidden units respectively
39  # 10 - 10 output classes with softmax activation unit at the output layer
40  layersDimensions=[784, 15,9,10]
41
42  # Execute the L-Layer Deep Network to perform SGD with regular gradient
43  descent
44  # hidden Activation function - relu
45  # output activation function - softmax
46  # learning rate - 0.01
47  # optimizer="gd"  # gradient descent
48  # mini_batch_size = 512
49  parameters = L_Layer_DeepModel_SGD(X2, Y2, layersDimensions,
50  hiddenActivationFunc='relu',
51
52  outputActivationFunc="softmax",learningRate = 0.01 ,
53                                    optimizer="gd",  mini_batch_size =512,
54  num_epochs = 1000, print_cost = True,figure="fig1.png")
```

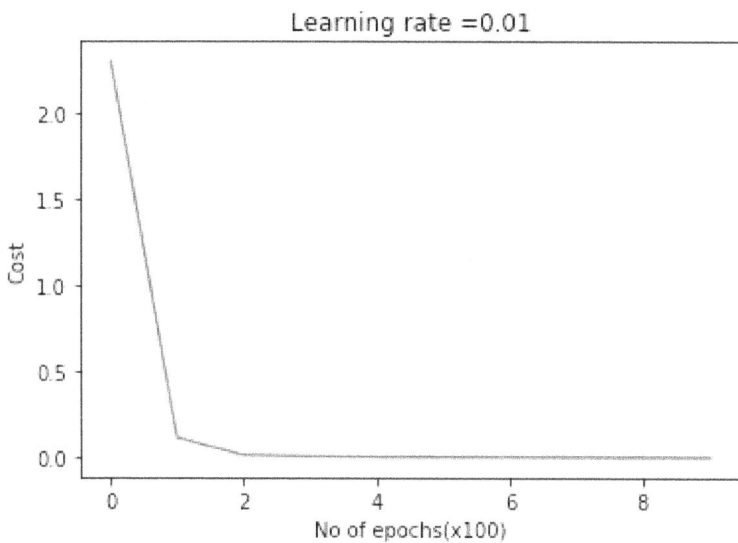

1.1b. Stochastic Gradient Descent (Vanilla) – R

```
1  source("mnist.R")
2  source("DLfunctions7.R")
3
4  #Load and read MNIST data
5  load_mnist()
6  x <- t(train$x)
7  X <- x[,1:60000]
8  y <-train$y
```

```r
y1 <- y[1:60000]
y2 <- as.matrix(y1)
Y=t(y2)

# Subset 1024 random samples from MNIST
permutation = c(sample(2^10))

# Randomly shuffle the training data
X1 = X[, permutation]
y1 = Y[1, permutation]
y2 <- as.matrix(y1)
Y1=t(y2)

# Set layer dimensions
# 784 - number of input features (28 x28)
# 15, 9 - 2 hidden layers with 15, 9 hidden units respectively
# 10 - 10 output classes with softmax activation unit at the output layer
layersDimensions=c(784, 15,9, 10)

# Execute the L-Layer Deep Network to perform SGD with regular gradient
descent
# hidden Activation function - tanh
# output activation function - softmax
# learning rate - 0.05
# optimizer="gd"  # gradient descent
# mini_batch_size = 512
retvalsSGD= L_Layer_DeepModel_SGD(X1, Y1, layersDimensions,
                            hiddenActivationFunc='tanh',
                            outputActivationFunc="softmax",
                            learningRate = 0.05,
                            optimizer="gd",
                            mini_batch_size = 512,
                            num_epochs = 5000,
                            print_cost = True)

#Plot the cost vs number of epochs
iterations <- seq(0,5000,1000)
costs=retvalsSGD$costs
df=data.frame(iterations,costs)
ggplot(df,aes(x=iterations,y=costs)) + geom_point() + geom_line(color="blue")
+ ggtitle("Costs vs no of epochs") + xlab("No of epochss") + ylab("Cost")
```

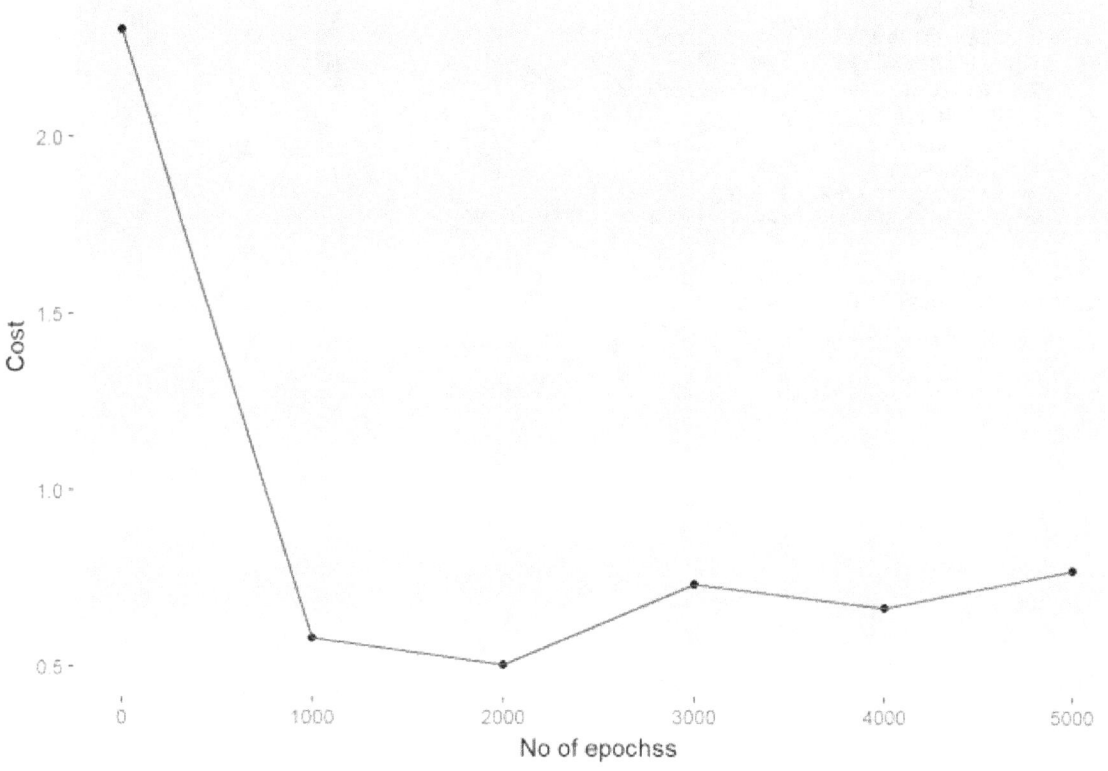

1.1c. Stochastic Gradient Descent (Vanilla) – Octave

```
1  source("DL7functions.m")
2  #Load and read MNIST
3  load('./mnist/mnist.txt.gz');
4  #Create a random permutatation from 1024
5  permutation = randperm(1024);
6  disp(length(permutation));
7
8  # Use this 1024 as the mini-batch
9  X=trainX(permutation,:);
10 Y=trainY(permutation,:);
11
12 # Set layer dimensions
13 # 784 - number of input features (28 x28)
14 # 15, 9 - 2 hidden layers with 15, 9 hidden units respectively
15 # 10 - 10 output classes with softmax activation unit at the output layer
16 layersDimensions=[784, 15, 9, 10];
17
18 # Execute the L-Layer Deep Network to perform SGD with regular gradient
19 descent
20 # hidden Activation function - relu
21 # output activation function - softmax
22 # learning rate - 0.005
23 # optimizer="gd"   # gradient descent
24 # mini_batch_size = 512
25 [weights biases costs]=L_Layer_DeepModel_SGD(X', Y', layersDimensions,
26         hiddenActivationFunc='relu',
27         outputActivationFunc="softmax",
28         learningRate = 0.005,
```

```
29          lrDecay=true,
30          decayRate=1,
31           lambd=0,
32          keep_prob=1,
33          optimizer="gd",
34          beta=0.9,
35          beta1=0.9,
36          beta2=0.999,
37          epsilon=10^-8,
38          mini_batch_size = 512,
39          num_epochs = 5000);
40
41  #Plot cost vs number epochs
42  plotCostVsEpochs(5000,costs);
```

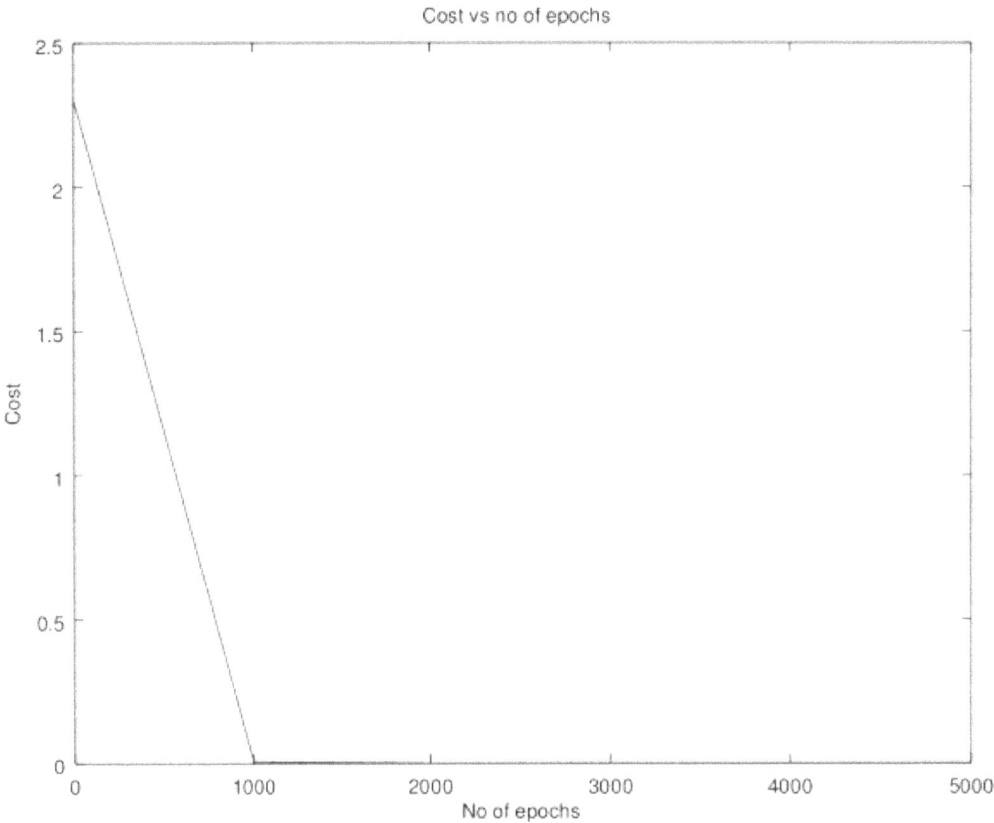

2.1. Stochastic Gradient Descent with Learning rate decay

Since in Stochastic Gradient Descent, with each epoch, we use slight different samples, the gradient descent algorithm, oscillates across the ravines and wanders around the minima, when a fixed learning rate is used. In this technique of 'learning rate decay' the learning rate is slowly decreased with the number of epochs and becomes smaller and smaller, so that gradient descent can take smaller steps towards the minima.

There are several techniques employed in learning rate decay

a) Exponential decay: $\alpha = decayRate^{epochNum} * \alpha_0$

b) 1/t decay: $\alpha = \frac{\alpha_0}{1+decayRate*epochNum}$

c) $\alpha = \frac{decayRate}{\sqrt{(epochNum)}} * \alpha_0$

In my implementation I have used the 'exponential decay'. The code snippet for Python is shown below

```
1  if lrDecay == True:
2      #decay the learning rate exponentially
3      learningRate = np.power(decayRate,(num_epochs/1000)) * learningRate
```

2.1a. Stochastic Gradient Descent with Learning rate decay – Python

```
1   import numpy as np
2   import matplotlib
3   import matplotlib.pyplot as plt
4   import sklearn.linear_model
5   import pandas as pd
6   import sklearn
7   import sklearn.datasets
8   exec(open("DLfunctions7.py").read())
9   exec(open("load_mnist.py").read())
10
11  # Read the MNIST data
12  training=list(read(dataset='training',path=".\\mnist"))
13  test=list(read(dataset='testing',path=".\\mnist"))
14  lbls=[]
15  pxls=[]
16  for i in range(60000):
17          l,p=training[i]
18          lbls.append(l)
19          pxls.append(p)
20  labels= np.array(lbls)
21  pixels=np.array(pxls)
22  y=labels.reshape(-1,1)
23  X=pixels.reshape(pixels.shape[0],-1)
24  X1=X.T
25  Y1=y.T
26
27  # Create a list of random numbers of 1024
28  permutation = list(np.random.permutation(2**10))
29
```

```
30  # Subset 1024 from the data
31  X2 = X1[:, permutation]
32  Y2 = Y1[:, permutation].reshape((1,2**10))
33
34  # Set layer dimensions
35  # 784 - number of input features (28 x28)
36  # 15, 9 - 2 hidden layers with 15, 9 hidden units respectively
37  # 10 - 10 output classes with softmax activation unit at the output layer
38  layersDimensions=[784, 15,9,10]
39
40  # Execute the L-layer Deep Learning network using SGD with learning rate
41  decay
42  # hidden Activation function - relu
43  # output activation function - softmax
44  # learning rate - 0.01
45  # lrDecay=True
46  # decayRate=0.9999
47  # optimizer="gd"   # gradient descent
48  # mini_batch_size = 512
49  parameters = L_Layer_DeepModel_SGD(X2, Y2, layersDimensions,
50  hiddenActivationFunc='relu',
51  outputActivationFunc="softmax",
52  learningRate = 0.01 , lrDecay=True, decayRate=0.9999,
53  optimizer="gd", mini_batch_size =512, num_epochs = 1000, print_cost =
54  True,figure="fig2.png")
```

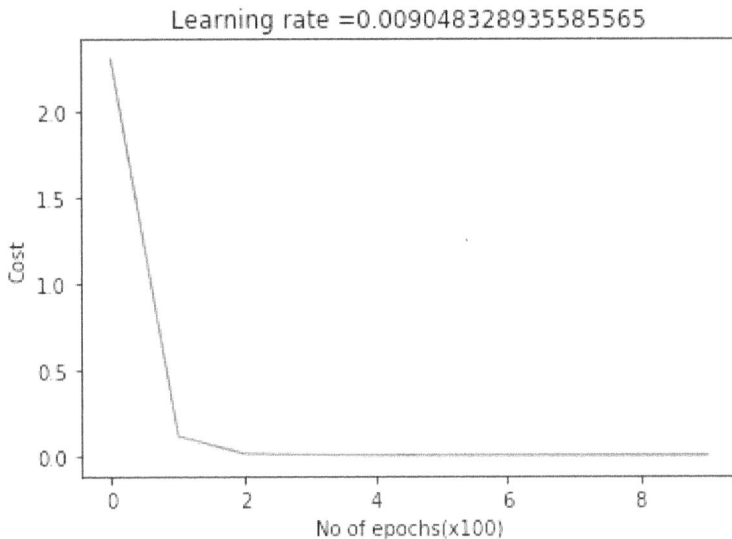

2.1b. Stochastic Gradient Descent with Learning rate decay – R

```
1   source("mnist.R")
2   source("DLfunctions7.R")
3
4   # Read and load MNIST
5   load_mnist()
6   x <- t(train$x)
7   X <- x[,1:60000]
8   y <-train$y
9   y1 <- y[1:60000]
10  y2 <- as.matrix(y1)
```

```r
Y=t(y2)

# Subset 1024 random samples from MNIST
permutation = c(sample(2^10))

# Randomly shuffle the training data
X1 = X[, permutation]
y1 = Y[1, permutation]
y2 <- as.matrix(y1)
Y1=t(y2)

# Set layer dimensions
# 784 - number of input features (28 x28)
# 15, 9 - 2 hidden layers with 15, 9 hidden units respectively
# 10 - 10 output classes with softmax activation unit at the output layer
layersDimensions=c(784, 15,9, 10)

# Execute the L-layer Deep Learning network using SGD with learning rate decay
# hidden Activation function - tanh
# output activation function - softmax
# learning rate - 0.05
# lrDecay=TRUE
# decayRate=0.9999
# optimizer="gd"  # gradient descent
# mini_batch_size = 512
retvalsSGD= L_Layer_DeepModel_SGD(X1, Y1, layersDimensions,
                                  hiddenActivationFunc='tanh',
                                  outputActivationFunc="softmax",
                                  learningRate = 0.05,
                                  lrDecay=TRUE,
                                  decayRate=0.9999,
                                  optimizer="gd",
                                  mini_batch_size = 512,
                                  num_epochs = 5000,
                                  print_cost = True)

#Plot the cost vs number of  epochs
iterations <- seq(0,5000,1000)
costs=retvalsSGD$costs
df=data.frame(iterations,costs)
ggplot(df,aes(x=iterations,y=costs)) + geom_point() + geom_line(color="blue")
+  ggtitle("Costs vs number of epochs") + xlab("No of epochs") + ylab("Cost")
```

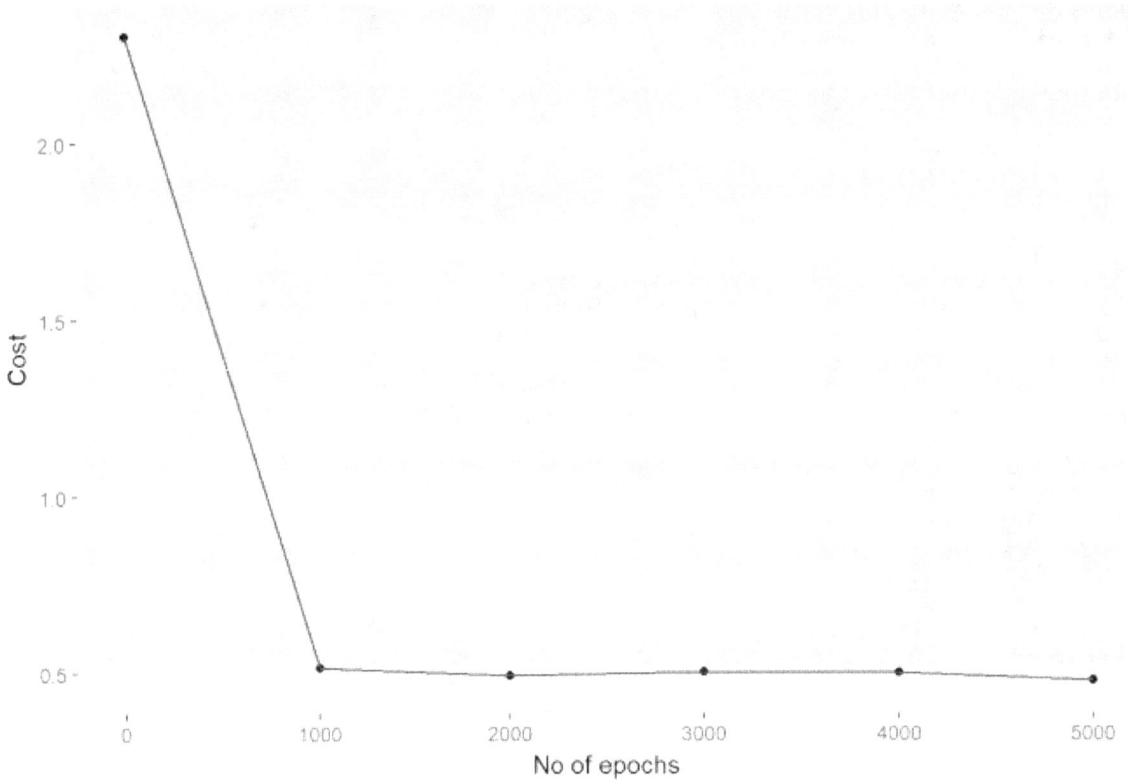

2.1c. Stochastic Gradient Descent with Learning rate decay – Octave

```
1  source("DL7functions.m")
2  #Load and read MNIST
3  load('./mnist/mnist.txt.gz');
4
5  #Create a random permutatation from 1024
6  permutation = randperm(1024);
7  disp(length(permutation));
8
9  # Use this 1024 as the batch
10 X=trainX(permutation,:);
11 Y=trainY(permutation,:);
12
13 # Set layer dimensions
14 # 784 - number of input features (28 x28)
15 # 15, 9 - 2 hidden layers with 15, 9 hidden units respectively
16 # 10 - 10 output classes with softmax activation unit at the output layer
17 layersDimensions=[784, 15, 9, 10];
18
19 # Execute the L-layer Deep Learning network using SGD with learning rate
20 decay
21 # hidden Activation function - relu
22 # output activation function - softmax
23 # learning rate - 0.01
24 # lrDecay=true
25 # decayRate=0.999
```

```
26  # optimizer="gd"   # gradient descent
27  # mini_batch_size = 512
28    [weights biases costs]=L_Layer_DeepModel_SGD(X', Y', layersDimensions,
29          hiddenActivationFunc='relu',
30          outputActivationFunc="softmax",
31          learningRate = 0.01,
32          lrDecay=true,
33          decayRate=0.999,
34          lambd=0,
35          keep_prob=1,
36          optimizer="gd",
37          beta=0.9,
38          beta1=0.9,
39          beta2=0.999,
40          epsilon=10^-8,
41          mini_batch_size = 512,
42          num_epochs = 5000);
43
44  # Plot cost vs number of epochs
45  plotCostVsEpochs(5000,costs)
```

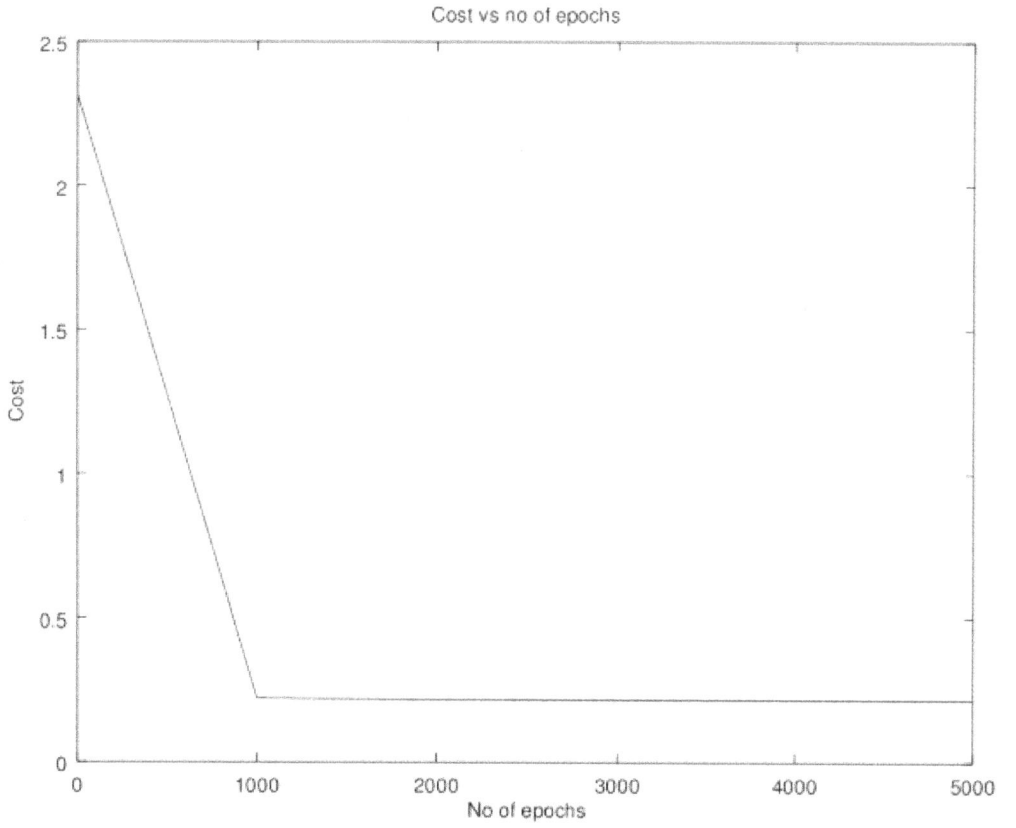

3.1. Stochastic Gradient Descent with Momentum

Stochastic Gradient Descent with Momentum uses the exponentially weighted average method discussed above and hence moves faster into the ravine than across it. The equations are

$$v_{dW}^l = \beta v_{dW}^l + (1-\beta)dW^l$$
$$v_{db}^l = \beta v_{db}^l + (1-\beta)db^l$$
$$W^l = W^l - \alpha v_{dW}^l$$
$$b^l = b^l - \alpha v_{db}^l$$ where

v_{dW} and v_{db} are the momentum terms which are exponentially weighted with the corresponding gradients 'dW' and 'db' at the corresponding layer 'l' The code snippet for Stochastic Gradient Descent with momentum in R is shown below

```r
# Perform Gradient Descent with momentum
# Input : Weights and biases
#        : beta
#        : gradients
#        : learning rate
#        : outputActivationFunc - Activation function at hidden layer
sigmoid/softmax
#output : Updated weights after 1 iteration
gradientDescentWithMomentum  <- function(parameters, gradients,v, beta,
learningRate,outputActivationFunc="sigmoid"){

    L = length(parameters)/2 # number of layers in the neural network
    # Update rule for each parameter. Use a for loop.
    for(l in 1:(L-1)){

        # Compute velocities
        # v['dWk'] = beta *v['dWk'] + (1-beta)*dwk
        v[[paste("dW",l, sep="")]] = beta*v[[paste("dW",l, sep="")]] +
            (1-beta) * gradients[[paste('dW',l,sep="")]]
        v[[paste("db",l, sep="")]] = beta*v[[paste("db",l, sep="")]] +
            (1-beta) * gradients[[paste('db',l,sep="")]]
        #Update parameters with velocities
        parameters[[paste("W",l,sep="")]] = parameters[[paste("W",l,sep="")]] -
            learningRate* v[[paste("dW",l, sep="")]]
        parameters[[paste("b",l,sep="")]] = parameters[[paste("b",l,sep="")]] -
            learningRate* v[[paste("db",l, sep="")]]
    }

    # Compute for the Lth layer if output activation is sigmoid
    if(outputActivationFunc=="sigmoid"){
        v[[paste("dW",L, sep="")]] = beta*v[[paste("dW",L, sep="")]] +
            (1-beta) * gradients[[paste('dW',L,sep="")]]
        v[[paste("db",L, sep="")]] = beta*v[[paste("db",L, sep="")]] +
            (1-beta) * gradients[[paste('db',L,sep="")]]

        parameters[[paste("W",L,sep="")]] = parameters[[paste("W",L,sep="")]] -
            learningRate* v[[paste("dW",l, sep="")]]
        parameters[[paste("b",L,sep="")]] = parameters[[paste("b",L,sep="")]] -
            learningRate* v[[paste("db",l, sep="")]]

    }else if (outputActivationFunc=="softmax"){ #If output activation is Softmax
        v[[paste("dW",L, sep="")]] = beta*v[[paste("dW",L, sep="")]] +
            (1-beta) * t(gradients[[paste('dW',L,sep="")]])
        v[[paste("db",L, sep="")]] = beta*v[[paste("db",L, sep="")]] +
```

```
50                (1-beta) * t(gradients[[paste('db',L,sep="")]])
51            parameters[[paste("W",L,sep="")]] = parameters[[paste("W",L,sep="")]]
52 -
53                learningRate* t(gradients[[paste("dW",L,sep="")]])
54            parameters[[paste("b",L,sep="")]] = parameters[[paste("b",L,sep="")]]
55 -
56                learningRate* t(gradients[[paste("db",L,sep="")]])
57     }
58     return(parameters)
59 }
60
```

3.1a. Stochastic Gradient Descent with Momentum- Python

```
1  import numpy as np
2  import matplotlib
3  import matplotlib.pyplot as plt
4  import sklearn.linear_model
5  import pandas as pd
6  import sklearn
7  import sklearn.datasets
8
9  # Read and load data and labels
10 exec(open("DLfunctions7.py").read())
11 exec(open("load_mnist.py").read())
12 training=list(read(dataset='training',path=".\\mnist"))
13 test=list(read(dataset='testing',path=".\\mnist"))
14 lbls=[]
15 pxls=[]
16 for i in range(60000):
17         l,p=training[i]
18         lbls.append(l)
19         pxls.append(p)
20 labels= np.array(lbls)
21 pixels=np.array(pxls)
22 y=labels.reshape(-1,1)
23 X=pixels.reshape(pixels.shape[0],-1)
24 X1=X.T
25 Y1=y.T
26
27 # Create a list of random numbers of 1024
28 permutation = list(np.random.permutation(2**10))
29 # Subset 1024 random samples from the data
30 X2 = X1[:, permutation]
31 Y2 = Y1[:, permutation].reshape((1,2**10))
32
33 # Set layer dimensions
34 # 784 - number of input features (28 x28)
35 # 15, 9 - 2 hidden layers with 15, 9 hidden units respectively
36 # 10 - 10 output classes with softmax activation unit at the output layer
37 layersDimensions=[784, 15,9,10]
38
39 # Execute the L-Layer Deep Learning network using SGD with momentum
40 # hidden Activation function - relu
41 # output activation function - softmax
42 # learning rate - 0.01
43 # optimizer="momentum"
44 # beta =0.9
```

```
45  # mini_batch_size = 512
46  parameters = L_Layer_DeepModel_SGD(X2, Y2, layersDimensions,
47  hiddenActivationFunc='relu',
48  outputActivationFunc="softmax",learningRate = 0.01 ,
49  optimizer="momentum", beta=0.9,
50  mini_batch_size =512, num_epochs = 1000, print_cost = True,figure="fig3.png")
```

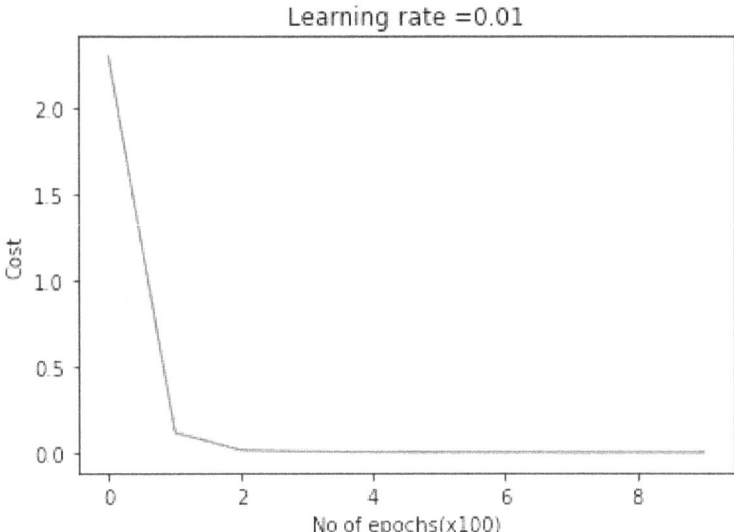

3.1b. Stochastic Gradient Descent with Momentum- R

```
1   source("mnist.R")
2   source("DLfunctions7.R")
3   load_mnist()
4   x <- t(train$x)
5   X <- x[,1:60000]
6   y <-train$y
7   y1 <- y[1:60000]
8   y2 <- as.matrix(y1)
9   Y=t(y2)
10
11  # Subset 1024 random samples from MNIST
12  permutation = c(sample(2^10))
13
14  # Randomly shuffle the training data
15  X1 = X[, permutation]
16  y1 = Y[1, permutation]
17  y2 <- as.matrix(y1)
18  Y1=t(y2)
19
20  # Set layer dimensions
21  # 784 - number of input features (28 x28)
22  # 15, 9 - 2 hidden layers with 15, 9 hidden units respectively
23  # 10 - 10 output classes with softmax activation unit at the output layer
24  layersDimensions=c(784, 15,9, 10)
25
26  # Execute the L-Layer Deep Learning network using SGD with momentum
27  # hidden Activation function - tanh
28  # output activation function - softmax
29  # learning rate - 0.05
30  # optimizer="momentum"
31  # beta =0.9
```

```
32  # mini_batch_size = 512
33  retvalsSGD= L_Layer_DeepModel_SGD(X1, Y1, layersDimensions,
34                                    hiddenActivationFunc='tanh',
35                                    outputActivationFunc="softmax",
36                                    learningRate = 0.05,
37                                    optimizer="momentum",
38                                    beta=0.9,
39                                    mini_batch_size = 512,
40                                    num_epochs = 5000,
41                                    print_cost = True)
42
43  #Plot the cost vs number of epochs
44  iterations <- seq(0,5000,1000)
45  costs=retvalsSGD$costs
46  df=data.frame(iterations,costs)
47  ggplot(df,aes(x=iterations,y=costs)) + geom_point() + geom_line(color="blue")
48  +  ggtitle("Costs vs number of epochs") + xlab("No of epochs") + ylab("Cost")
```

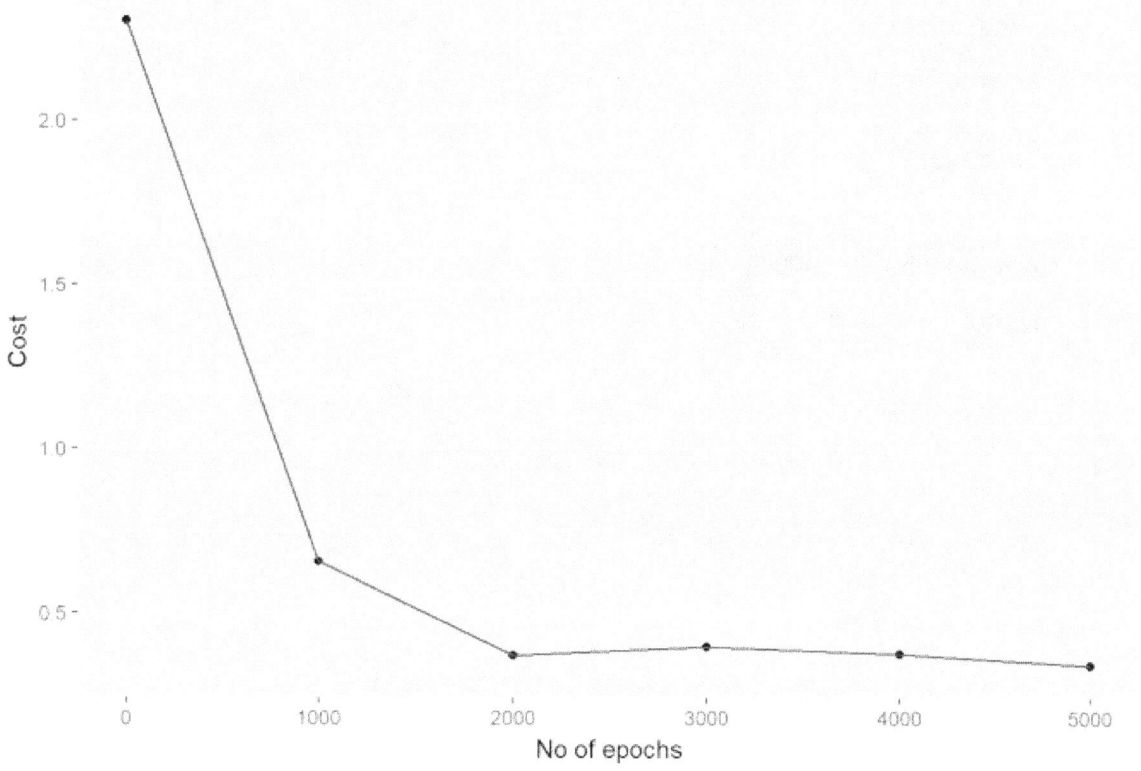

3.1c. Stochastic Gradient Descent with Momentum- Octave

```
1   source("DL7functions.m")
2
3   #Load and read MNIST
4   load('./mnist/mnist.txt.gz');
5
6   #Create a random permutatation from 60K
7   permutation = randperm(1024);
8   disp(length(permutation));
9
10  # Use this 1024 as the batch
```

```
11  X=trainX(permutation,:);
12  Y=trainY(permutation,:);
13
14  # Set layer dimensions
15  # 784 - number of input features (28 x28)
16  # 15, 9 - 2 hidden layers with 15, 9 hidden units respectively
17  # 10 - 10 output classes with softmax activation unit at the output layer
18  layersDimensions=[784, 15, 9, 10];
19
20  # Execute the L-Layer Deep Learning network using SGD with momentum
21  # hidden Activation function - relu
22  # output activation function - softmax
23  # learning rate - 0.01
24  # optimizer="momentum"
25  # beta =0.9
26  # mini_batch_size = 512
27    [weights biases costs]=L_Layer_DeepModel_SGD(X', Y', layersDimensions,
28            hiddenActivationFunc='relu',
29            outputActivationFunc="softmax",
30            learningRate = 0.01,
31            lrDecay=false,
32            decayRate=1,
33            lambd=0,
34            keep_prob=1,
35            optimizer="momentum",
36            beta=0.9,
37            beta1=0.9,
38            beta2=0.999,
39            epsilon=10^-8,
40            mini_batch_size = 512,
41            num_epochs = 5000);
42
43  #Plot the cost vs number of epochs
44  plotCostVsEpochs(5000,costs)
```

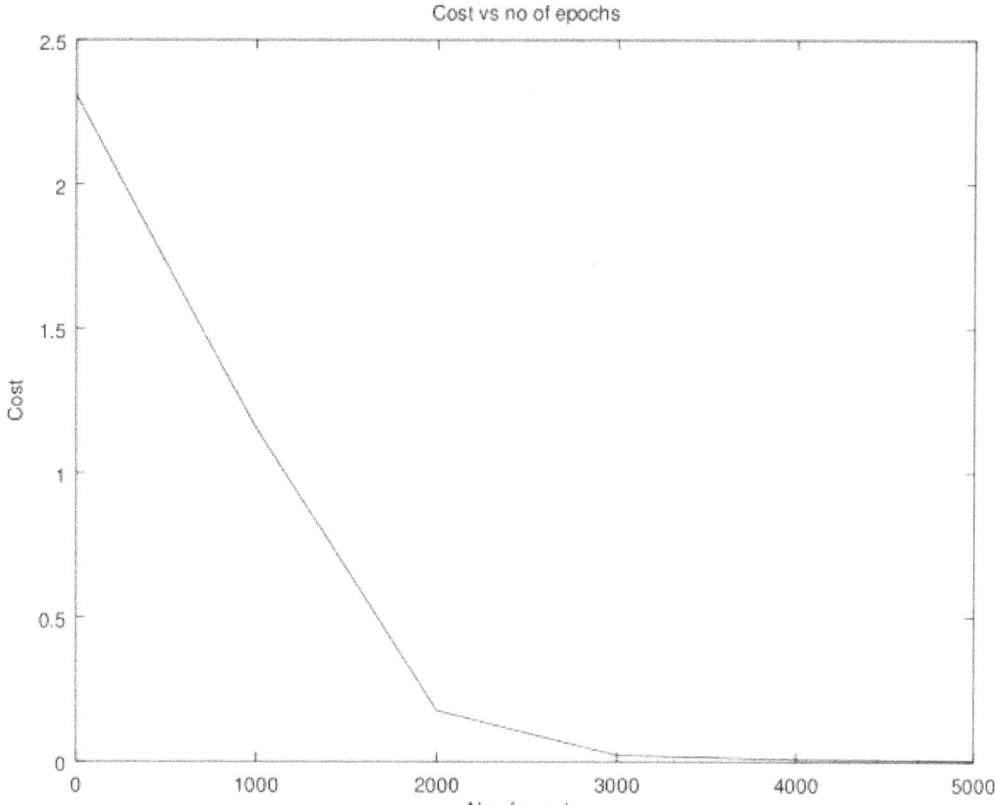

4.1. Stochastic Gradient Descent with RMSProp

Stochastic Gradient Descent with RMSProp tries to move faster towards the minima while dampening the oscillations across the ravine.
The equations are

$$s^l_{dW} = \beta_1 s^l_{dW} + (1 - \beta_1)(dW^l)^2$$
$$s^l_{db} = \beta_1 s^l_{db} + (1 - \beta_1)(db^l)^2$$
$$W^l = W^l - \frac{\alpha s^l_{dW}}{\sqrt{(s^l_{dW} + \epsilon)}}$$
$$b^l = b^l - \frac{\alpha s^l_{db}}{\sqrt{(s^l_{db} + \epsilon)}}$$

where s_{dW} and s_{db} are the RMSProp terms which are exponentially weighted with the corresponding gradients 'dW' and 'db' at the corresponding layer 'l'

The code snippet in Octave is shown below

```
1  # Update parameters with RMSProp
2  # Input : parameters
3  #       : gradients
4  #       : s
```

```octave
5  #           : beta
6  #           : learningRate
7  #output : Updated parameters RMSProp
8
9  function [weights biases] = gradientDescentWithRMSProp(weights,
10 biases,gradsDW,gradsDB, sdW, sdB, beta1, epsilon,
11 learningRate,outputActivationFunc="sigmoid")
12     L = size(weights)(2); # number of layers in the neural network
13
14     # Update rule for each parameter.
15     for l=1:(L-1)
16         sdW{l} =  beta1*sdW{l} + (1 -beta1) * gradsDW{l} .* gradsDW{l};
17         sdB{l} =  beta1*sdB{l} + (1 -beta1) * gradsDB{l} .* gradsDB{l};
18         weights{l} = weights{l} - learningRate* gradsDW{l} ./ sqrt(sdW{l} +
19 epsilon);
20         biases{l} = biases{l} -  learningRate* gradsDB{l} ./ sqrt(sdB{l} +
21 epsilon);
22     endfor
23
24     #Update for Lth layer is output is sigmoid
25     if (strcmp(outputActivationFunc,"sigmoid"))
26         sdW{L} =  beta1*sdW{L} + (1 -beta1) * gradsDW{L} .* gradsDW{L};
27         sdB{L} =  beta1*sdB{L} + (1 -beta1) * gradsDB{L} .* gradsDB{L};
28         weights{L} = weights{L} -learningRate* gradsDW{L} ./ sqrt(sdW{L}
29 +epsilon);
30         biases{L} = biases{L} -learningRate* gradsDB{L} ./ sqrt(sdB{L} +
31 epsilon);
32     elseif (strcmp(outputActivationFunc,"softmax")) #Update for Lth layer is
33 output is softmax
34         sdW{L} =  beta1*sdW{L} + (1 -beta1) * gradsDW{L}' .* gradsDW{L}';
35         sdB{L} =  beta1*sdB{L} + (1 -beta1) * gradsDB{L}' .* gradsDB{L}';
36         weights{L} = weights{L} -learningRate* gradsDW{L}' ./ sqrt(sdW{L}
37 +epsilon);
38         biases{L} = biases{L} -learningRate* gradsDB{L}' ./ sqrt(sdB{L} +
39 epsilon);
40     endif
41 end
```

4.1a. Stochastic Gradient Descent with RMSProp – Python

```python
1  import numpy as np
2  import matplotlib
3  import matplotlib.pyplot as plt
4  import sklearn.linear_model
5  import pandas as pd
6  import sklearn
7  import sklearn.datasets
8  exec(open("DLfunctions7.py").read())
9  exec(open("load_mnist.py").read())
10
11 # Read and load MNIST
12 training=list(read(dataset='training',path=".\\mnist"))
13 test=list(read(dataset='testing',path=".\\mnist"))
14 lbls=[]
15 pxls=[]
16 for i in range(60000):
17     l,p=training[i]
18     lbls.append(l)
```

```
19          pxls.append(p)
20   labels= np.array(lbls)
21   pixels=np.array(pxls)
22   y=labels.reshape(-1,1)
23   X=pixels.reshape(pixels.shape[0],-1)
24   X1=X.T
25   Y1=y.T
26
27   print("X1=",X1.shape)
28   print("y1=",Y1.shape)
29
30   # Create a list of random numbers of 1024
31   permutation = list(np.random.permutation(2**10))
32   # Subset 1024 from the data
33   X2 = X1[:, permutation]
34   Y2 = Y1[:, permutation].reshape((1,2**10))
35
36   # Set layer dimensions
37   # 784 - number of input features (28 x28)
38   # 15, 9 - 2 hidden layers with 15, 9 hidden units respectively
39   # 10 - 10 output classes with softmax activation unit at the output layer
40   layersDimensions=[784, 15,9,10]
41
42   # Execute the L-layer Deep learning network using SGD with RMSProp
43   # hidden Activation function - relu
44   # output activation function - softmax
45   # learning rate - 0.01
46   # optimizer="rmsprop"
47   # beta1 =0.7
48   # epsilon=1e-8
49   # mini_batch_size = 512
50   parameters = L_Layer_DeepModel_SGD(X2, Y2, layersDimensions,
51   hiddenActivationFunc='relu',
52   outputActivationFunc="softmax",learningRate = 0.01 ,
53   optimizer="rmsprop", beta1=0.7, epsilon=1e-8,
54   mini_batch_size =512, num_epochs = 1000, print_cost = True,figure="fig4.png")
```

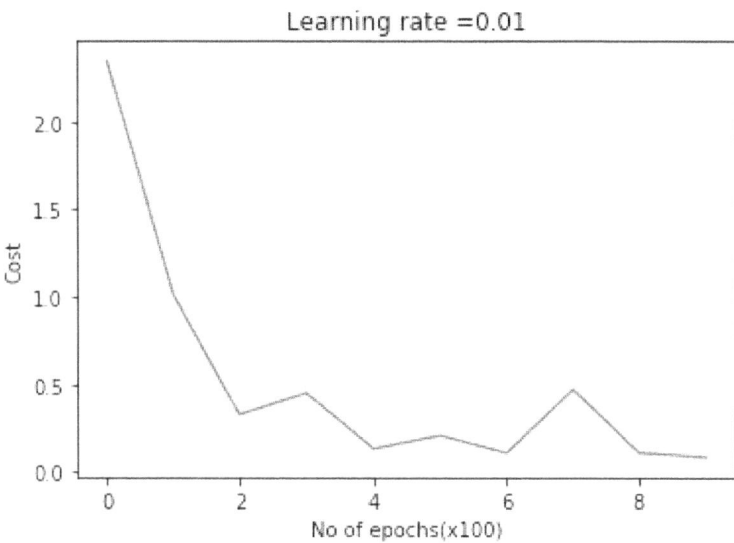

4.1b. Stochastic Gradient Descent with RMSProp – R

```
1   source("mnist.R")
```

```r
source("DLfunctions7.R")
load_mnist()
x <- t(train$x)
X <- x[,1:60000]
y <-train$y
y1 <- y[1:60000]
y2 <- as.matrix(y1)
Y=t(y2)

# Subset 1024 random samples from MNIST
permutation = c(sample(2^10))

# Randomly shuffle the training data
X1 = X[, permutation]
y1 = Y[1, permutation]
y2 <- as.matrix(y1)
Y1=t(y2)

# Set layer dimensions
# 784 - number of input features (28 x28)
# 15, 9 - 2 hidden layers with 15, 9 hidden units respectively
# 10 - 10 output classes with softmax activation unit at the output layer
layersDimensions=c(784, 15,9, 10)

# Execute the L-layer Deep learning network using SGD with RMSProp
# hidden Activation function - tanh
# output activation function - softmax
# learning rate - 0.001
# optimizer="rmsprop"
# beta1 =0.9
# epsilon=1e-8
# mini_batch_size = 512
retvalsSGD= L_Layer_DeepModel_SGD(X1, Y1, layersDimensions,
                                    hiddenActivationFunc='tanh',
                                    outputActivationFunc="softmax",
                                    learningRate = 0.001,
                                    optimizer="rmsprop",
                                    beta1=0.9,
                                    epsilon=10^-8,
                                    mini_batch_size = 512,
                                    num_epochs = 5000 ,
                                    print_cost = True)

#Plot the cost vs number of epochs
iterations <- seq(0,5000,1000)
costs=retvalsSGD$costs
df=data.frame(iterations,costs)
ggplot(df,aes(x=iterations,y=costs)) + geom_point() + geom_line(color="blue")
+  ggtitle("Costs vs number of epochs") + xlab("No of epochs") + ylab("Cost")
```

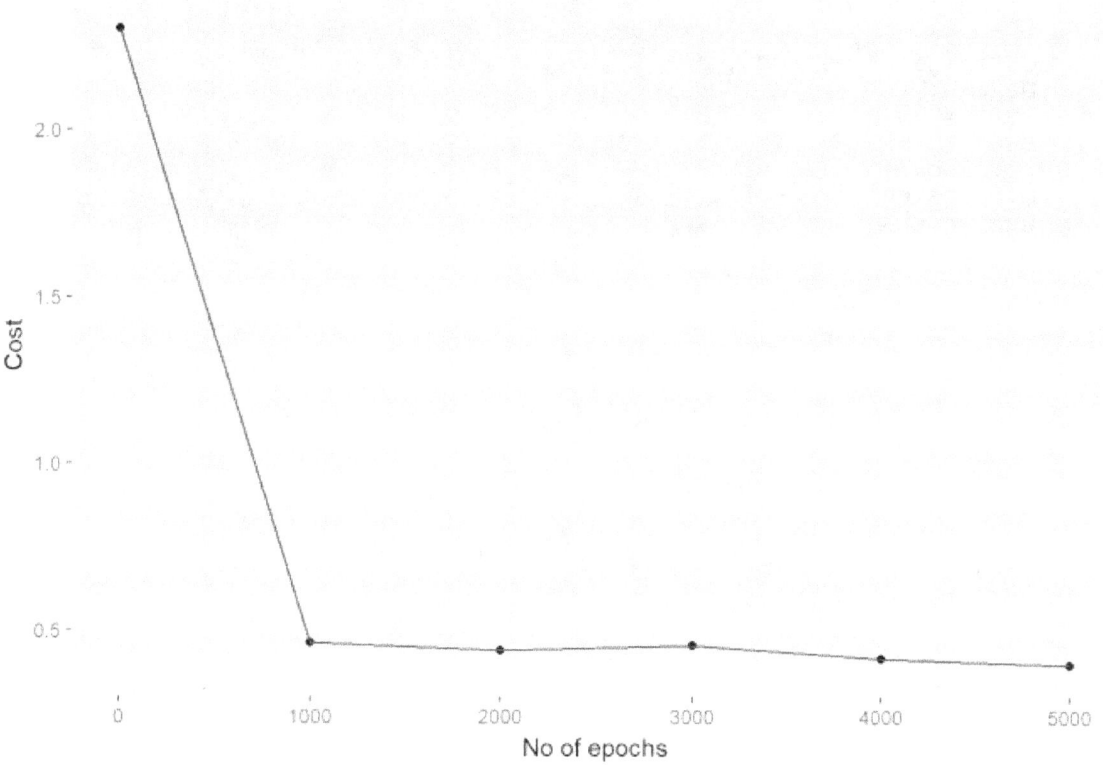

4.1c. Stochastic Gradient Descent with RMSProp – Octave

```
1   source("DL7functions.m")
2   load('./mnist/mnist.txt.gz');
3   #Create a random permutatation from 1024
4   permutation = randperm(1024);
5
6   # Use this 1024 as the batch
7   X=trainX(permutation,:);
8   Y=trainY(permutation,:);
9
10  # Set layer dimensions
11  # Set layer dimensions
12  # 784 - number of input features (28 x28)
13  # 15, 9 - 2 hidden layers with 15, 9 hidden units respectively
14  # 10 - 10 output classes with softmax activation unit at the output layer
15  layersDimensions=[784, 15, 9, 10];
16
17  # Execute the L-layer Deep learning network using SGD with RMSProp
18  # hidden Activation function - relu
19  # output activation function - softmax
20  # learning rate - 0.005
21  # optimizer="rmsprop"
22  # beta1 =0.9
23  # epsilon=1
24  # mini_batch_size = 512
25    [weights biases costs]=L_Layer_DeepModel_SGD(X', Y', layersDimensions,
26          hiddenActivationFunc='relu',
27          outputActivationFunc="softmax",
28          learningRate = 0.005,
```

```
29          lrDecay=false,
30          decayRate=1,
31          lambd=0,
32          keep_prob=1,
33          optimizer="rmsprop",
34          beta=0.9,
35          beta1=0.9,
36          beta2=0.999,
37          epsilon=1,
38          mini_batch_size = 512,
39          num_epochs = 5000);
40
41 #Plot cost vs number of epochs
42 plotCostVsEpochs(5000,costs)
```

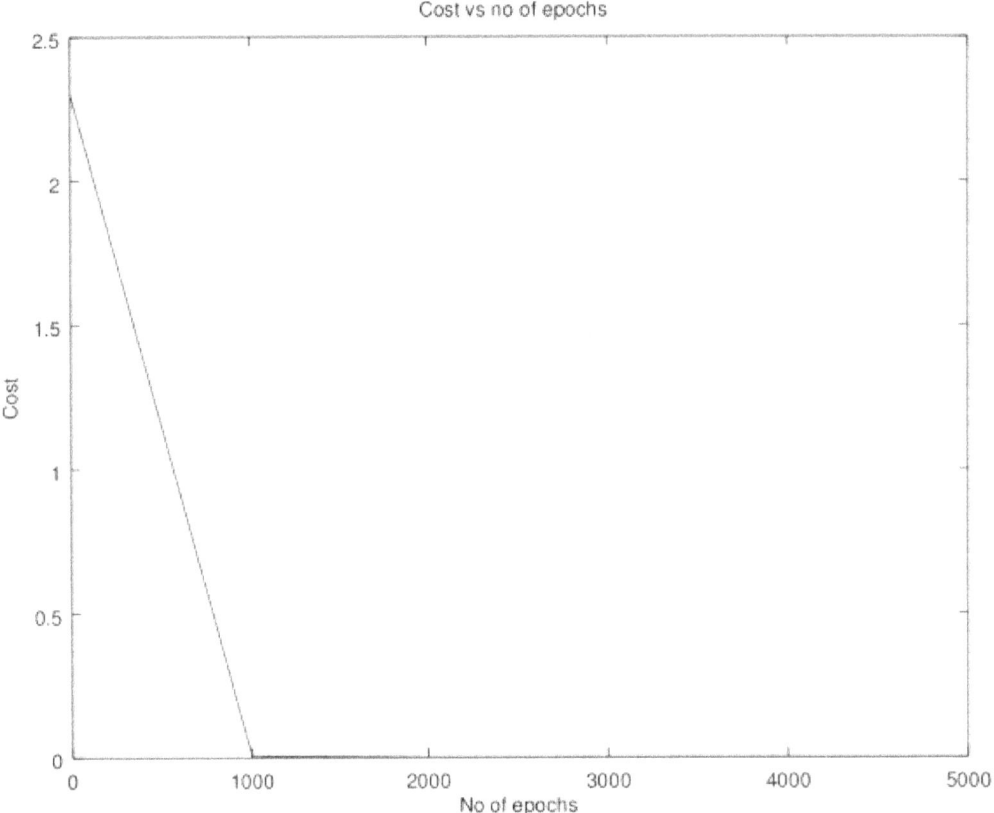

5.1. Stochastic Gradient Descent with Adam

Adaptive Moment Estimate is a combination of the momentum (1st moment) and RMSProp (2nd moment). The equations for Adam are below

The moving average for the 1st moment
$$v^l_{dW} = \beta_1 v^l_{dW} + (1-\beta_1)dW^l$$
$$v^l_{db} = \beta_1 v^l_{db} + (1-\beta_1)db^l$$

The bias corrections for the 1st moment
$$vCorrected^l_{dW} = \frac{v^l_{dW}}{1-\beta_1^t}$$
$$vCorrected^l_{db} = \frac{v^l_{db}}{1-\beta_1^t}$$

Similarly, the moving average for the 2nd moment- RMSProp
$$s^l_{dW} = \beta_2 s^l_{dW} + (1-\beta_2)(dW^l)^2$$
$$s^l_{db} = \beta_2 s^l_{db} + (1-\beta_2)(db^l)^2$$

The bias corrections for the 2nd moment
$$sCorrected^l_{dW} = \frac{s^l_{dW}}{1-\beta_2^t}$$
$$sCorrected^l_{db} = \frac{s^l_{db}}{1-\beta_2^t}$$

The Adam Gradient Descent is given by
$$W^l = W^l - \frac{\alpha\, vCorrected^l_{dW}}{\sqrt{(s^l_{dW}+\epsilon)}}$$
$$b^l = b^l - \frac{\alpha\, vCorrected^l_{db}}{\sqrt{(s^l_{db}+\epsilon)}}$$

The code snippet of Adam in R is included be

```
# Perform Gradient Descent with Adam
# Input : weights and biases
#                : beta1
#                : epsilon
#                : gradients
#                : learning rate
#                : outputActivationFunc - Activation function at hidden layer
sigmoid/softmax
#output : Updated weights after 1 iteration
gradientDescentwithAdam   <- function(parameters, gradients,v, s, t,
                          beta1=0.9, beta2=0.999, epsilon=10^-8,
learningRate=0.1,outputActivationFunc="sigmoid"){

    L = length(parameters)/2 # number of layers in the neural network
    v_corrected <- list()
    s_corrected <- list()
    # Update rule for each parameter.
    for(l in 1:(L-1)){
        # v['dWk'] = beta *v['dWk'] + (1-beta)*dWk
        v[[paste("dw",l, sep="")]] = beta1*v[[paste("dw",l, sep="")]] +
            (1-beta1) * gradients[[paste('dw',l,sep="")]]
        v[[paste("db",l, sep="")]] = beta1*v[[paste("db",l, sep="")]] +
            (1-beta1) * gradients[[paste('db',l,sep="")]]

        # Compute bias-corrected first moment estimate.
        v_corrected[[paste("dw",l, sep="")]] = v[[paste("dw",l, sep="")]]/(1-beta1^t)
        v_corrected[[paste("db",l, sep="")]] = v[[paste("db",l, sep="")]]/(1-beta1^t)
```

```
        # Element wise multiply of gradients
        s[[paste("dw",l, sep="")]] = beta2*s[[paste("dw",l, sep="")]] +
            (1-beta2) * gradients[[paste('dw',l,sep="")]] *
gradients[[paste('dw',l,sep="")]]
        s[[paste("db",l, sep="")]] = beta2*s[[paste("db",l, sep="")]] +
            (1-beta2) * gradients[[paste('db',l,sep="")]] *
gradients[[paste('db',l,sep="")]]

        # Compute bias-corrected second moment estimate.
        s_corrected[[paste("dw",l, sep="")]] = s[[paste("dw",l, sep="")]]/(1-
beta2^t)
        s_corrected[[paste("db",l, sep="")]] = s[[paste("db",l, sep="")]]/(1-
beta2^t)

        # Update parameters.
        d1=sqrt(s_corrected[[paste("dw",l, sep="")]]+epsilon)
        d2=sqrt(s_corrected[[paste("db",l, sep="")]]+epsilon)

        parameters[[paste("W",l,sep="")]] = parameters[[paste("W",l,sep="")]]
-
            learningRate * v_corrected[[paste("dw",l, sep="")]]/d1
        parameters[[paste("b",l,sep="")]] = parameters[[paste("b",l,sep="")]]
-
            learningRate*v_corrected[[paste("db",l, sep="")]]/d2
    }
    # Compute for the Lth layer for sigmoid activation
    if(outputActivationFunc=="sigmoid"){
        v[[paste("dw",L, sep="")]] = beta1*v[[paste("dw",L, sep="")]] +
            (1-beta1) * gradients[[paste('dw',L,sep="")]]
        v[[paste("db",L, sep="")]] = beta1*v[[paste("db",L, sep="")]] +
            (1-beta1) * gradients[[paste('db',L,sep="")]]

        # Compute bias-corrected first moment estimate.
        v_corrected[[paste("dw",L, sep="")]] = v[[paste("dw",L, sep="")]]/(1-
beta1^t)
        v_corrected[[paste("db",L, sep="")]] = v[[paste("db",L, sep="")]]/(1-
beta1^t)

        # Element wise multiply of gradients
        s[[paste("dw",L, sep="")]] = beta2*s[[paste("dw",L, sep="")]] +
            (1-beta2) * gradients[[paste('dw',L,sep="")]] *
gradients[[paste('dw',L,sep="")]]
        s[[paste("db",L, sep="")]] = beta2*s[[paste("db",L, sep="")]] +
            (1-beta2) * gradients[[paste('db',L,sep="")]] *
gradients[[paste('db',L,sep="")]]

        # Compute bias-corrected second moment estimate.
        s_corrected[[paste("dw",L, sep="")]] = s[[paste("dw",L, sep="")]]/(1-
beta2^t)
        s_corrected[[paste("db",L, sep="")]] = s[[paste("db",L, sep="")]]/(1-
beta2^t)

        # Update parameters.
        d1=sqrt(s_corrected[[paste("dw",L, sep="")]]+epsilon)
        d2=sqrt(s_corrected[[paste("db",L, sep="")]]+epsilon)

        parameters[[paste("W",L,sep="")]] = parameters[[paste("W",L,sep="")]]
-
            learningRate * v_corrected[[paste("dw",L, sep="")]]/d1
        parameters[[paste("b",L,sep="")]] = parameters[[paste("b",L,sep="")]]
-
            learningRate*v_corrected[[paste("db",L, sep="")]]/d2
```

```
94        }else if (outputActivationFunc=="softmax"){ #Compute for the Lth layer
95  for softmax activation
96          v[[paste("dW",L, sep="")]] = beta1*v[[paste("dW",L, sep="")]] +
97              (1-beta1) * t(gradients[[paste('dW',L,sep="")]])
98          v[[paste("db", L,  sep="")]] = beta1*v[[paste("db",L, sep="")]] +
99              (1-beta1) * t(gradients[[paste('db',L,sep="")]])
100
101         # Compute bias-corrected first moment estimate.
102         v_corrected[[paste("dW",L, sep="")]] = v[[paste("dW",L, sep="")]]/(1-
103 beta1^t)
104         v_corrected[[paste("db",L, sep="")]] = v[[paste("db",L, sep="")]]/(1-
105 beta1^t)
106
107         # Element wise multiply of gradients
108         s[[paste("dW",L,  sep="")]] = beta2*s[[paste("dW",L, sep="")]] +
109             (1-beta2) * t(gradients[[paste('dW',L,sep="")]]) *
110 t(gradients[[paste('dW',L,sep="")]])
111         s[[paste("db",L,  sep="")]] = beta2*s[[paste("db",L, sep="")]] +
112             (1-beta2) * t(gradients[[paste('db',L,sep="")]]) *
113 t(gradients[[paste('db',L,sep="")]])
114
115         # Compute bias-corrected second moment estimate.
116         s_corrected[[paste("dW",L, sep="")]] = s[[paste("dW",L, sep="")]]/(1-
117 beta2^t)
118         s_corrected[[paste("db",L, sep="")]] = s[[paste("db",L, sep="")]]/(1-
119 beta2^t)
120
121         # Update parameters.
122         d1=sqrt(s_corrected[[paste("dW",L, sep="")]]+epsilon)
123         d2=sqrt(s_corrected[[paste("db",L, sep="")]]+epsilon)
124
125         parameters[[paste("W",L,sep="")]] = parameters[[paste("W",L,sep="")]]
126 -
127             learningRate * v_corrected[[paste("dW",L, sep="")]]/d1
128         parameters[[paste("b",L,sep="")]] = parameters[[paste("b",L,sep="")]]
129 -
130             learningRate*v_corrected[[paste("db",L, sep="")]]/d2
131     }
132     return(parameters)
133 }
```

5.1a. Stochastic Gradient Descent with Adam – Python

```
1  import numpy as np
2  import matplotlib
3  import matplotlib.pyplot as plt
4  import sklearn.linear_model
5  import pandas as pd
6  import sklearn
7  import sklearn.datasets
8
9  exec(open("DLfunctions7.py").read())
10
11 #Load MNIST
12 exec(open("load_mnist.py").read())
13 training=list(read(dataset='training',path=".\\mnist"))
14 test=list(read(dataset='testing',path=".\\mnist"))
15 lbls=[]
16 pxls=[]
```

```
17  print(len(training))
18  #for i in range(len(training)):
19  for i in range(60000):
20          l,p=training[i]
21          lbls.append(l)
22          pxls.append(p)
23  labels= np.array(lbls)
24  pixels=np.array(pxls)
25  y=labels.reshape(-1,1)
26  X=pixels.reshape(pixels.shape[0],-1)
27  X1=X.T
28  Y1=y.T
29
30
31  # Create a list of random numbers of 1024
32  permutation = list(np.random.permutation(2**10))
33  # Subset 1024 from the data
34  X2 = X1[:, permutation]
35  Y2 = Y1[:, permutation].reshape((1,2**10))
36
37  # Set layer dimensions
38  # 784 - number of input features (28 x28)
39  # 15, 9 - 2 hidden layers with 15, 9 hidden units respectively
40  # 10 - 10 output classes with softmax activation unit at the output layer
41  layersDimensions=[784, 15,9,10]
42
43  #Execute a L-layer Deep Learning network using SGD with Adam optimization
44  # hidden Activation function - relu
45  # output activation function - softmax
46  # learning rate - 0.01
47  # optimizer="adam"
48  # beta1 =0.9
49  # beta2=0.9
50  # epsilon=1e-8
51  # mini_batch_size = 512
52  parameters = L_Layer_DeepModel_SGD(X2, Y2, layersDimensions,
53  hiddenActivationFunc='relu',
54  outputActivationFunc="softmax",learningRate = 0.01 ,
55  optimizer="adam", beta1=0.9, beta2=0.9, epsilon = 1e-8,
56  mini_batch_size =512, num_epochs = 1000, print_cost = True,
57  figure="fig5.png")
```

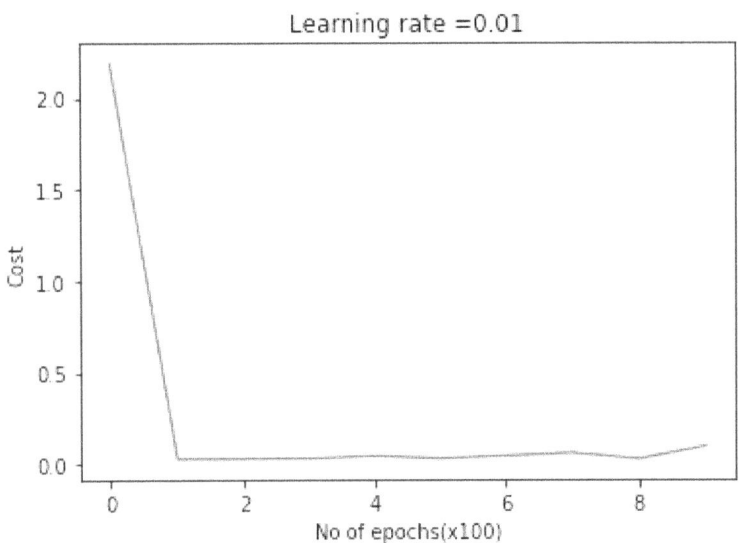

5.1b. Stochastic Gradient Descent with Adam – R

```r
source("mnist.R")
source("DLfunctions7.R")
load_mnist()
x <- t(train$x)
X <- x[,1:60000]
y <-train$y
y1 <- y[1:60000]
y2 <- as.matrix(y1)
Y=t(y2)

# Subset 1024 random samples from MNIST
permutation = c(sample(2^10))
# Randomly shuffle the training data
X1 = X[, permutation]
y1 = Y[1, permutation]
y2 <- as.matrix(y1)
Y1=t(y2)

# Set layer dimensions
# 784 - number of input features (28 x28)
# 15, 9 - 2 hidden layers with 15,9 hidden units respectively
# 10 - 10 output classes with softmax activation unit at the output layer
layersDimensions=c(784, 15,9, 10)

#Execute a L-layer Deep Learning network using SGD with Adam optimization
# hidden Activation function - tanh
# output activation function - softmax
# learning rate - 0.005
# optimizer="adam"
# beta1 =0.7
# beta2=0.9
# epsilon=1e-8
# mini_batch_size = 512
retvalsSGD= L_Layer_DeepModel_SGD(X1, Y1, layersDimensions,
                                  hiddenActivationFunc='tanh',
                                  outputActivationFunc="softmax",
                                  learningRate = 0.005,
                                  optimizer="adam",
                                  beta1=0.7,
                                  beta2=0.9,
                                  epsilon=10^-8,
                                  mini_batch_size = 512,
                                  num_epochs = 5000 ,
                                  print_cost = True)

#Plot the cost vs number of epochs
iterations <- seq(0,5000,1000)
costs=retvalsSGD$costs
df=data.frame(iterations,costs)
ggplot(df,aes(x=iterations,y=costs)) + geom_point() + geom_line(color="blue")
+   ggtitle("Costs vs number of epochs") + xlab("No of epochs") + ylab("Cost")
```

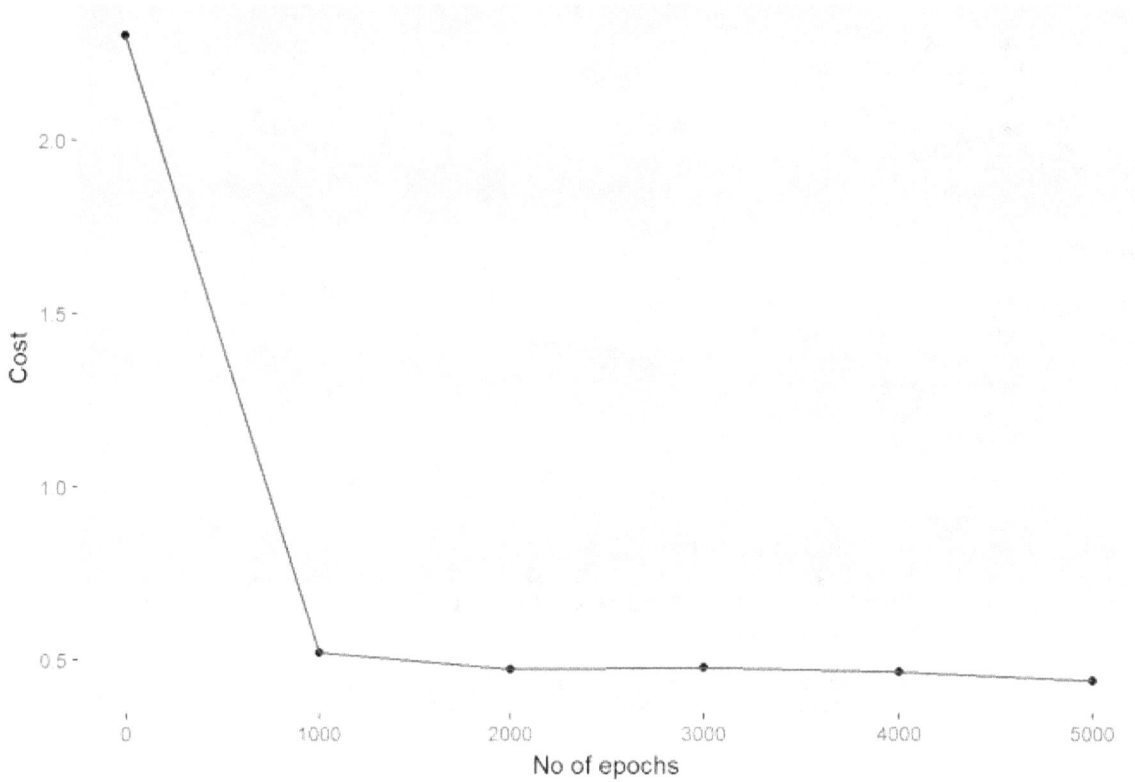

5.1c. Stochastic Gradient Descent with Adam – Octave

```
1   source("DL7functions.m")
2   load('./mnist/mnist.txt.gz');
3   #Create a random permutatation from 1024
4   permutation = randperm(1024);
5   disp(length(permutation));
6
7   # Use this 1024 as the batch
8   X=trainX(permutation,:);
9   Y=trainY(permutation,:);
10  # Set layer dimensions
11  # 784 - number of input features (28 x28)
12  # 15, 9 - 2 hidden layers with 15,9 hidden units respectively
13  # 10 - 10 output classes with softmax activation unit at the output layer
14  layersDimensions=[784, 15, 9, 10];
15
16  # Note the high value for epsilon.
17  #Otherwise GD with Adam does not seem to converge
18  #Execute a L-layer Deep Learning network using SGD with Adam optimization
19  # hidden Activation function - relu
20  # output activation function - softmax
21  # learning rate - 0.01
22  # optimizer="adam"
23  # beta1 =0.9
24  # beta2=0.9
25  # epsilon=100
26  # mini_batch_size = 512
27    [weights biases costs]=L_Layer_DeepModel_SGD(X', Y', layersDimensions,
28                          hiddenActivationFunc='relu',
```

```
29                         outputActivationFunc="softmax",
30                         learningRate = 0.1,
31                         lrDecay=false,
32                         decayRate=1,
33                         lambd=0,
34                         keep_prob=1,
35                         optimizer="adam",
36                         beta=0.9,
37                         beta1=0.9,
38                         beta2=0.9,
39                         epsilon=100,
40                         mini_batch_size = 512,
41                         num_epochs = 5000);
42
43 #Plot cost vs number of epochs
44 plotCostVsEpochs(5000,costs)
```

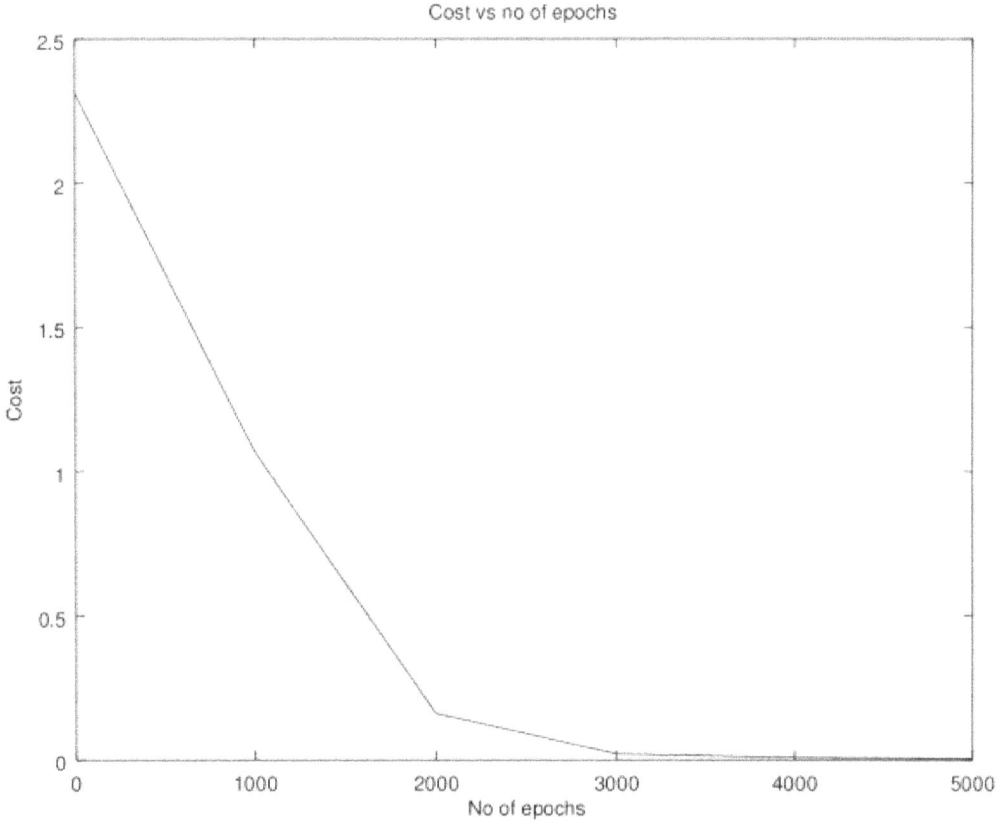

6.Conclusion

In this chapter I discuss and implement several Stochastic Gradient Descent optimization methods. The implementation of these methods enhance my already existing generic L-Layer Deep Learning Network implementation in vectorized Python, R and Octave.

8. Gradient Check in Deep Learning

You don't understand anything until you learn it more than one way. Marvin Minsky
No computer has ever been designed that is ever aware of what it's doing; but most of the time, we aren't either. Marvin Minsky
A wealth of information creates a poverty of attention. Herbert Simon

In this final chapter, I discuss and implement a key functionality needed while building Deep Learning networks viz. 'Gradient Checking'. Gradient Checking is an important method to check the correctness of your implementation, specifically the forward propagation and the backward propagation cycles of an implementation. In addition, I also discuss some tips for tuning hyper-parameters of a Deep Learning network based on my experience.

This chapter implements a critical function for ensuring the correctness of a L-Layer Deep Learning network implementation using Gradient Checking
Gradient Checking is based on the following approach. One iteration of Gradient Descent computes and updates the parameters θ by doing
$$\theta := \theta - \frac{d}{d\theta} J(\theta)$$.

To minimize the cost we will need to minimize $J(\theta)$

Let $g(\theta)$ be a function that computes the derivative $\frac{d}{d\theta} J(\theta)$. Gradient Checking allows us to numerically evaluate the implementation of the function $g(\theta)$ and verify its correctness.
We know the derivative of a function is given by
$$\frac{d}{d\theta} J(\theta) = lim-> 0 \frac{J(\theta+\epsilon) - J(\theta-\epsilon)}{2*\epsilon}$$

Note: The above derivative is based on the 2-sided derivative. The 1-sided derivative is given by
$$\frac{d}{d\theta} J(\theta) = lim-> 0 \frac{J(\theta+\epsilon) - J(\theta)}{\epsilon}$$
Gradient Checking is based on the 2-sided derivative because the error is of the order $O(\epsilon^2)$ as opposed $O(\epsilon)$ for the 1-sided derivative.

Hence Gradient Check uses the 2-sided derivative as follows.
$$g(\theta) = lim-> 0 \frac{J(\theta+\epsilon) - J(\theta-\epsilon)}{2*\epsilon}$$

In Gradient Check the following is done
A) Run one normal cycle of your implementation by doing the following
a) Compute the output activation by running 1 cycle of forward propagation
b) Compute the cost using the output activation
c) Compute the gradients using backpropagation (grad)

B) Perform gradient check steps as below
a) Set θ. Flatten all 'weights' and 'bias' matrices and vectors to a column vector.
b) Initialize $\theta+$ by nudging θ up by adding ϵ ($\theta + \epsilon$)
c) Perform forward propagation with $\theta+$
d) Compute cost with $\theta+$ i.e. $J(\theta+)$

e) Initialize $\theta-$ by nudging θ down by subtracting ϵ $(\theta - \epsilon)$
f) Perform forward propagation with $\theta-$
g) Compute cost with $\theta-$ i.e. $J(\theta-)$
h) Compute $\frac{d}{d\theta}J(\theta)$ or 'gradapprox' as $\frac{J(\theta+)-J(\theta-)}{2\epsilon}$ using the 2 sided derivative.
i) Compute L2norm or the Euclidean distance between 'grad' and 'gradapprox'.

If the difference is of the order of 10^{-5} or 10^{-7} the implementation is correct. In the Deep Learning Specialization (https://www.coursera.org/specializations/deep-learning) Prof Andrew Ng mentions that if the difference is of the order of 10^{-7} then the implementation is correct. A difference of 10^{-5} is also ok. Anything more than that is a cause of worry and you should look at your code more closely. To see more details click Gradient checking and advanced optimization (http://ufldl.stanford.edu/wiki/index.php/Gradient_checking_and_advanced_optimization) The implementations of the functions invoked in this chapter are in Appendix 8 – Gradient Check

You can clone/download the code from Github at DeepLearningFromFirstPrinciples (https://github.com/tvganesh/DeepLearningFromFirstPrinciples/tree/master/Chap8-DLGradientCheck)

After spending a better part of 3 days, I now realize how critical Gradient Check is for ensuring the correctness of your implementation. Initially I was getting very high difference and did not know how to understand the results or debug my implementation. After many hours of staring at the results, I was able to finally arrive at a way, to localize issues in the implementation. In fact, I did catch a small bug in my Python code, which did not exist in the R and Octave implementations. I will demonstrate this below

1.1a Gradient Check – Sigmoid Activation – Python

```
1  import numpy as np
2  import matplotlib
3
4  exec(open("DLfunctions8.py").read())
5  exec(open("testcases.py").read())
6
7  #Load the circles data set
8  train_X, train_Y, test_X, test_Y = load_dataset()
9
10 #Set layer dimensions
11 # 2 - number of input features
12 # 4 -  1 hidden layer with 4 activation units
13 # 1 - 1 sigmoid activation unit at the output layer
14 layersDimensions = [2,4,1]
15
16 # Initialize parameters
17 parameters = initializeDeepModel(layersDimensions)
18
19 #Perform forward propagation
20 AL, caches, dropoutMat = forwardPropagationDeep(train_X, parameters,
21 keep_prob=1, hiddenActivationFunc="relu",outputActivationFunc="sigmoid")
22
23 #Compute cost
24 cost = computeCost(AL, train_Y, outputActivationFunc="sigmoid")
25 print("cost=",cost)
```

```python
#Perform backprop and get gradients
gradients = backwardPropagationDeep(AL, train_Y, caches, dropoutMat, lambd=0,
keep_prob=1,
hiddenActivationFunc="relu",outputActivationFunc="sigmoid")

# Set values
epsilon = 1e-7
outputActivationFunc="sigmoid"

# Set-up variables
# Flatten parameters to a vector
parameters_values, _ = dictionary_to_vector(parameters)

#Flatten gradients to a vector
grad = gradients_to_vector(parameters,gradients)
num_parameters = parameters_values.shape[0]

#Initialize J_plus, J_minus and gradapprox
J_plus = np.zeros((num_parameters, 1))
J_minus = np.zeros((num_parameters, 1))
gradapprox = np.zeros((num_parameters, 1))

# Compute gradapprox using 2-sided derivative
for i in range(num_parameters):

    # Compute J_plus[i].
    thetaplus = np.copy(parameters_values)
    thetaplus[i][0] = thetaplus[i][0] + epsilon
    AL, caches, dropoutMat = forwardPropagationDeep(train_X,
vector_to_dictionary(parameters,thetaplus), keep_prob=1,
hiddenActivationFunc="relu",outputActivationFunc=outputActivationFunc)
    J_plus[i] = computeCost(AL, train_Y,
outputActivationFunc=outputActivationFunc)


    # Compute J_minus[i].
    thetaminus = np.copy(parameters_values)
    thetaminus[i][0] = thetaminus[i][0] - epsilon
    AL, caches, dropoutMat  = forwardPropagationDeep(train_X,
vector_to_dictionary(parameters,thetaminus), keep_prob=1,
hiddenActivationFunc="relu",outputActivationFunc=outputActivationFunc)
    J_minus[i] = computeCost(AL, train_Y,
outputActivationFunc=outputActivationFunc)

    # Compute gradapprox[i]
    gradapprox[i] = (J_plus[i] - J_minus[i])/(2*epsilon)

# Compare gradapprox to  gradients from backprop by computing euclidean
difference.
numerator = np.linalg.norm(grad-gradapprox)
denominator = np.linalg.norm(grad) +  np.linalg.norm(gradapprox)
difference = numerator/denominator

#Check the difference
if difference > 1e-5:
    print ("\033[93m" + "There is a mistake in the backward propagation!
difference = " + str(difference) + "\033[0m")
else:
    print ("\033[92m" + "Your backward propagation works perfectly fine!
difference = " + str(difference) + "\033[0m")
print(difference)
print("\n")
```

```python
# The technique below can be used to identify
# which of the parameters are in error

# Covert grad to dictionary
m=vector_to_dictionary2(parameters,grad)
print("Gradients from backprop")
print(m)
print("\n")

# Convert gradapprox to dictionary
n=vector_to_dictionary2(parameters,gradapprox)
print("Gradapprox from gradient check")
print(n)
## (300, 2)
## (300,)
## cost= 0.6931455556341791
## [Your backward propagation works perfectly fine! difference = 1.1604150683743381e-06[0m
## 1.1604150683743381e-06
##
##
## Gradients from backprop
## {'dw1': array([[-6.19439955e-06, -2.06438046e-06],
##         [-1.50165447e-05,  7.50401672e-05],
##         [ 1.33435433e-04,  1.74112143e-04],
##         [-3.40909024e-05, -1.38363681e-04]]), 'db1': array([[ 7.31333221e-07],
##         [ 7.98425950e-06],
##         [ 8.15002817e-08],
##         [-5.69821155e-08]]), 'dw2': array([[2.73416304e-04, 2.96061451e-04, 7.51837363e-05, 1.01257729e-04]]), 'db2': array([[-7.22232235e-06]])}
##
##
## Gradapprox from gradient check
## {'dw1': array([[-6.19448937e-06, -2.06501483e-06],
##         [-1.50168766e-05,  7.50399742e-05],
##         [ 1.33435485e-04,  1.74112391e-04],
##         [-3.40910633e-05, -1.38363765e-04]]), 'db1': array([[ 7.31081862e-07],
##         [ 7.98472399e-06],
##         [ 8.16013923e-08],
##         [-5.71764858e-08]]), 'dw2': array([[2.73416290e-04, 2.96061509e-04, 7.51831930e-05, 1.01257891e-04]]), 'db2': array([[-7.22255589e-06]])}
```

1.1b Gradient Check – Softmax Activation – Python (Error!!)

In the code below I show, how I managed to spot a bug in your implementation

```python
import numpy as np
exec(open("DLfunctions8.py").read())

# Create spiral dataset
N = 100 # number of points per class
D = 2 # dimensionality
K = 3 # number of classes
X = np.zeros((N*K,D)) # data matrix (each row = single example)
y = np.zeros(N*K, dtype='uint8') # class labels
for j in range(K):
    ix = range(N*j,N*(j+1))
```

```
    r = np.linspace(0.0,1,N) # radius
    t = np.linspace(j*4,(j+1)*4,N) + np.random.randn(N)*0.2 # theta
    X[ix] = np.c_[r*np.sin(t), r*np.cos(t)]
    y[ix] = j


# Plot the data
#plt.scatter(X[:, 0], X[:, 1], c=y, s=40, cmap=plt.cm.Spectral)

# Set layer dimensions
# 2 - number of input features
# 3 -  1 hidden layer with 3 activation units
# 3 - 3 classes with softmax  activation unit at the output layer
layersDimensions = [2,3,3]

# Set params
y1=y.reshape(-1,1).T
train_X=X.T
train_Y=y1

# Initialize the model
parameters = initializeDeepModel(layersDimensions)

#Compute forward prop
AL, caches, dropoutMat = forwardPropagationDeep(train_X, parameters,
keep_prob=1,

hiddenActivationFunc="relu",outputActivationFunc="softmax")

#Compute cost
cost = computeCost(AL, train_Y, outputActivationFunc="softmax")
print("cost=",cost)

#Compute gradients from backprop
gradients = backwardPropagationDeep(AL, train_Y, caches, dropoutMat, lambd=0,
keep_prob=1,

hiddenActivationFunc="relu",outputActivationFunc="softmax")

# Note the transpose of the gradients for Softmax has to be taken
L= len(parameters)//2
print(L)
gradients['dW'+str(L)]=gradients['dW'+str(L)].T
gradients['db'+str(L)]=gradients['db'+str(L)].T

# Perform gradient check
gradient_check_n(parameters, gradients, train_X, train_Y, epsilon = 1e-
7,outputActivationFunc="softmax")

cost= 1.0986187818144022
There is a mistake in the backward propagation! difference =
0.7100295155692544
0.7100295155692544


Gradients from backprop
{'dW1': array([[ 0.00050125,  0.00045194],
       [ 0.00096392,  0.00039641],
       [-0.00014276, -0.00045639]]), 'db1': array([[ 0.00070082],
       [-0.00224399],
       [ 0.00052305]]), 'dW2': array([[-8.40953794e-05, -9.52657769e-04, -
1.10269379e-04],
       [-7.45469382e-04,  9.49795606e-04,  2.29045434e-04],
       [ 8.29564761e-04,  2.86216305e-06, -1.18776055e-04]]),
```

```
76        'db2': array([[-0.00253808],
77           [-0.00505508],
78           [ 0.00759315]])}
79
80
81   Gradapprox from gradient check
82   {'dW1': array([[ 0.00050125,  0.00045194],
83          [ 0.00096392,  0.00039641],
84          [-0.00014276, -0.00045639]]), 'db1': array([[ 0.00070082],
85          [-0.00224399],
86          [ 0.00052305]]), 'dW2': array([[-8.40960634e-05, -9.52657953e-04, -
87   1.10268461e-04],
88          [-7.45469242e-04,  9.49796908e-04,  2.29045671e-04],
89          [ 8.29565305e-04,  2.86104473e-06, -1.18776100e-04]]),
90       'db2': array([[-8.46211989e-06],
91          [-1.68487446e-05],
92          [ 2.53108645e-05]])}
```

Gradient Check gives a high value of the difference of 0.7100295. Inspecting the Gradients and Gradapprox we can see there is a very big discrepancy in db2. After I went over my code I discovered that my computation in the function layerActivationBackward for Softmax was

```
1   # Erroneous code
2       if activationFunc == 'softmax':
3           dW = 1/numtraining * np.dot(A_prev,dZ)
4           db = np.sum(dZ, axis=0, keepdims=True)
5           dA_prev = np.dot(dZ,W)
6
7   instead of
8
9       # Fixed code
10      if activationFunc == 'softmax':
11          dW = 1/numtraining * np.dot(A_prev,dZ)
12          db = 1/numtraining *  np.sum(dZ, axis=0, keepdims=True)
13          dA_prev = np.dot(dZ,W)
```

After fixing this error when I ran the Gradient Check as shown below

1.1c Gradient Check – Softmax Activation – Python (Corrected!!)

```
1   import numpy as np
2   exec(open("DLfunctions8.py").read())
3
4   # Create Spiral dataset
5   N = 100 # number of points per class
6   D = 2 # dimensionality
7   K = 3 # number of classes
8   X = np.zeros((N*K,D)) # data matrix (each row = single example)
9   y = np.zeros(N*K, dtype='uint8') # class labels
10  for j in range(K):
11    ix = range(N*j,N*(j+1))
12    r = np.linspace(0.0,1,N) # radius
13    t = np.linspace(j*4,(j+1)*4,N) + np.random.randn(N)*0.2 # theta
14    X[ix] = np.c_[r*np.sin(t), r*np.cos(t)]
15    y[ix] = j
```

```python
# Plot the data
#plt.scatter(X[:, 0], X[:, 1], c=y, s=40, cmap=plt.cm.Spectral)
# Set layer dimensions
# 2 - number of input features
# 3 -  1 hidden layer with 3 activation units
# 3 - 3 classes with softmax  activation unit at the output layer
layersDimensions = [2,3,3]
y1=y.reshape(-1,1).T
train_X=X.T
train_Y=y1

# Initialize model
parameters = initializeDeepModel(layersDimensions)

#Perform forward prop
AL, caches, dropoutMat = forwardPropagationDeep(train_X, parameters,
keep_prob=1,

hiddenActivationFunc="relu",outputActivationFunc="softmax")

#Compute cost
cost = computeCost(AL, train_Y, outputActivationFunc="softmax")
print("cost=",cost)

#Compute gradients from backprop
gradients = backwardPropagationDeep(AL, train_Y, caches, dropoutMat, lambd=0,
keep_prob=1,

hiddenActivationFunc="relu",outputActivationFunc="softmax")

# Note the transpose of the gradients for Softmax has to be taken
L= len(parameters)//2
print(L)
gradients['dW'+str(L)]=gradients['dW'+str(L)].T
gradients['db'+str(L)]=gradients['db'+str(L)].T

#Perform gradient check
gradient_check_n(parameters, gradients, train_X, train_Y, epsilon = 1e-
7,outputActivationFunc="softmax")
## cost= 1.0986193170234435
## 2
## [92mYour backward propagation works perfectly fine! difference =
5.268804859613151e-07[0m
## 5.268804859613151e-07
##
##
## Gradients from backprop
## {'dW1': array([[ 0.00053206,  0.00038987],
##        [ 0.00093941,  0.00038077],
##        [-0.00012177, -0.0004692 ]]), 'db1': array([[ 0.00072662],
##        [-0.00210198],
##        [ 0.00046741]]), 'dW2': array([[-7.83441270e-05, -9.70179498e-04, -
1.08715815e-04],
##        [-7.70175008e-04,  9.54478237e-04,  2.27690198e-04],
##        [ 8.48519135e-04,  1.57012608e-05, -1.18974383e-04]]), 'db2':
array([[-8.52190476e-06],
##        [-1.69954294e-05],
##        [ 2.55173342e-05]])}
##
##
## Gradapprox from gradient check
## {'dW1': array([[ 0.00053206,  0.00038987],
```

```
80 ##            [ 0.00093941,  0.00038077],
81 ##            [-0.00012177, -0.0004692 ]]), 'db1': array([[ 0.00072662],
82 ##            [-0.00210198],
83 ##            [ 0.00046741]]), 'dW2': array([[-7.83439980e-05, -9.70180603e-04, -
84 1.08716369e-04],
85 ##            [-7.70173925e-04,  9.54478718e-04,  2.27690089e-04],
86 ##            [ 8.48520143e-04,  1.57018842e-05, -1.18973720e-04]]), 'db2':
87 array([[-8.52096171e-06],
88 ##            [-1.69964043e-05],
89 ##            [ 2.55162558e-05]])}
```

1.2a Gradient Check – Sigmoid Activation – R

```r
source("DLfunctions8.R")
z <- as.matrix(read.csv("circles.csv",header=FALSE))

x <- z[,1:2]
y <- z[,3]
X <- t(x)
Y <- t(y)

#Set layer dimensions
layersDimensions = c(2,5,1)

#Initialize model
parameters = initializeDeepModel(layersDimensions)

#Perform forward prop
retvals = forwardPropagationDeep(X, parameters,keep_prob=1,
hiddenActivationFunc="relu",
                            outputActivationFunc="sigmoid")
AL <- retvals[['AL']]
caches <- retvals[['caches']]
dropoutMat <- retvals[['dropoutMat']]

#Compute cost
cost <- computeCost(AL, Y,outputActivationFunc="sigmoid",
                numClasses=layersDimensions[length(layersDimensions)])
print(cost)
## [1] 0.6931447

# Perform backward propagation and get gradients
gradients = backwardPropagationDeep(AL, Y, caches, dropoutMat, lambd=0,
keep_prob=1, hiddenActivationFunc="relu",

outputActivationFunc="sigmoid",numClasses=layersDimensions[length(layersDimen
sions)])

# Set values
epsilon = 1e-07
outputActivationFunc="sigmoid"

#Convert parameter list to vector
parameters_values = list_to_vector(parameters)

#Convert gradient list to vector
grad = gradients_to_vector(parameters,gradients)
num_parameters = dim(parameters_values)[1]

#Initialize J_plus, J_minus and gradapprox
J_plus = matrix(rep(0,num_parameters),
                nrow=num_parameters,ncol=1)
```

```r
J_minus = matrix(rep(0,num_parameters),
                 nrow=num_parameters,ncol=1)
gradapprox = matrix(rep(0,num_parameters),
                    nrow=num_parameters,ncol=1)

# Compute J_plus, J_minus and
for(i in 1:num_parameters){

    # Compute J_plus[i].
    thetaplus = parameters_values
    thetaplus[i][1] = thetaplus[i][1] + epsilon
    retvals = forwardPropagationDeep(X, vector_to_list(parameters,thetaplus),
keep_prob=1,
hiddenActivationFunc="relu",outputActivationFunc=outputActivationFunc)

    AL <- retvals[['AL']]
    J_plus[i] = computeCost(AL, Y, outputActivationFunc=outputActivationFunc)


    # Compute J_minus[i].
     thetaminus = parameters_values
     thetaminus[i][1] = thetaminus[i][1] - epsilon
     retvals  = forwardPropagationDeep(X,
vector_to_list(parameters,thetaminus), keep_prob=1,
hiddenActivationFunc="relu",outputActivationFunc=outputActivationFunc)
    AL <- retvals[['AL']]
    J_minus[i] = computeCost(AL, Y,
outputActivationFunc=outputActivationFunc)

    # Compute gradapprox[i]
    gradapprox[i] = (J_plus[i] - J_minus[i])/(2*epsilon)
}
# Compare gradapprox to backprop gradients by computing Euclidean difference.
#Compute L2Norm
numerator = L2NormVec(grad-gradapprox)
denominator = L2NormVec(grad) +  L2NormVec(gradapprox)
difference =  numerator/denominator

# Output difference
if(difference > 1e-5){
    cat("There is a mistake, the difference is too high",difference)
} else{
    cat("The implementations works perfectly", difference)
}
## The implementations works perfectly 1.279911e-06

#  Technique to check gradients
print("Gradients from backprop")
## [1] "Gradients from backprop"
vector_to_list2(parameters,grad)
## $dW1
##                [,1]          [,2]
## [1,] -7.641588e-05 -3.427989e-07
## [2,] -9.049683e-06  6.906304e-05
## [3,]  3.401039e-06 -1.503914e-04
## [4,]  1.535226e-04 -1.686402e-04
## [5,] -6.029292e-05 -2.715648e-04
##
## $db1
##                [,1]
## [1,]  6.930318e-06
## [2,] -3.283117e-05
## [3,]  1.310647e-05
## [4,] -3.454308e-05
```

```
## [5,] -2.331729e-08
##
## $dw2
##                 [,1]         [,2]         [,3]         [,4]         [,5]
## [1,] 0.0001612356 0.0001113475 0.0002435824 0.000362149 2.874116e-05
##
## $db2
##              [,1]
## [1,] -1.16364e-05
print("Grad approx from gradient check")
## [1] "Grad approx from gradient check"
vector_to_list2(parameters,gradapprox)
## $dW1
##                [,1]          [,2]
## [1,] -7.641554e-05 -3.430589e-07
## [2,] -9.049428e-06  6.906253e-05
## [3,]  3.401168e-06 -1.503919e-04
## [4,]  1.535228e-04 -1.686401e-04
## [5,] -6.029288e-05 -2.715650e-04
##
## $db1
##                [,1]
## [1,]  6.930012e-06
## [2,] -3.283096e-05
## [3,]  1.310618e-05
## [4,] -3.454237e-05
## [5,] -2.275957e-08
##
## $dW2
##                 [,1]         [,2]         [,3]         [,4]         [,5]
## [1,] 0.0001612355 0.0001113476 0.0002435829 0.0003621486 2.87409e-05
##
## $db2
##              [,1]
## [1,] -1.16368e-05
```

1.2b Gradient Check – Softmax Activation – R

```
source("DLfunctions8.R")
Z <- as.matrix(read.csv("spiral.csv",header=FALSE))

# Setup the data
X <- Z[,1:2]
y <- Z[,3]
X <- t(X)
Y <- t(y)

# Set layer dimensions
# 2 - number of input features
# 3 -  1 hidden layer with 3 activation units
# 3 - 3 classes with softmax  activation unit at the output layer
layersDimensions = c(2, 3, 3)

#Initialize model
parameters = initializeDeepModel(layersDimensions)

#Perform forward propagation
retvals = forwardPropagationDeep(X, parameters,keep_prob=1,
hiddenActivationFunc="relu",
                                  outputActivationFunc="softmax")
AL <- retvals[['AL']]
```

```r
caches <- retvals[['caches']]
dropoutMat <- retvals[['dropoutMat']]

#Compute cost
cost <- computeCost(AL, Y,outputActivationFunc="softmax",
                    numClasses=layersDimensions[length(layersDimensions)])
print(cost)
## [1] 1.098618

# Perform Backward propagation.
gradients = backwardPropagationDeep(AL, Y, caches, dropoutMat, lambd=0,
keep_prob=1, hiddenActivationFunc="relu",
outputActivationFunc="softmax",numClasses=layersDimensions[length(layersDimensions)])

# Need to take transpose of the last layer for Softmax
L=length(parameters)/2
gradients[[paste('dW',L,sep="")]]=t(gradients[[paste('dW',L,sep="")]])
gradients[[paste('db',L,sep="")]]=t(gradients[[paste('db',L,sep="")]])

#Perform gradient check
gradient_check_n(parameters, gradients, X, Y,
                 epsilon = 1e-7,outputActivationFunc="softmax")
## The implementations works perfectly 3.903011e-07[1] "Gradients from
backprop"
## $dW1
##                [,1]            [,2]
## [1,] 0.0007962367 -0.0001907606
## [2,] 0.0004444254  0.0010354412
## [3,] 0.0003078611  0.0007591255
##
## $db1
##                [,1]
## [1,] -0.0017305136
## [2,]  0.0005393734
## [3,]  0.0012484550
##
## $dW2
##                [,1]            [,2]            [,3]
## [1,] -3.515627e-04  7.487283e-04 -3.971656e-04
## [2,] -6.381521e-05 -1.257328e-06  6.507254e-05
## [3,] -1.719479e-04 -4.857264e-04  6.576743e-04
##
## $db2
##                [,1]
## [1,] -5.536383e-06
## [2,] -1.824656e-05
## [3,]  2.378295e-05
##
## [1] "Grad approx from gradient check"
## $dW1
##                [,1]            [,2]
## [1,] 0.0007962364 -0.0001907607
## [2,] 0.0004444256  0.0010354406
## [3,] 0.0003078615  0.0007591250
##
## $db1
##                [,1]
## [1,] -0.0017305135
## [2,]  0.0005393741
## [3,]  0.0012484547
##
## $dW2
##                [,1]            [,2]            [,3]
```

```
## [1,]  -3.515632e-04  7.487277e-04 -3.971656e-04
## [2,]  -6.381451e-05 -1.257883e-06  6.507239e-05
## [3,]  -1.719469e-04 -4.857270e-04  6.576739e-04
##
## $db2
##                  [,1]
## [1,] -5.536682e-06
## [2,] -1.824652e-05
## [3,]  2.378209e-05
```

1.3a Gradient Check – Sigmoid Activation – Octave

```
source("DL8functions.m")

# Read circles data
data=csvread("circles.csv");
X=data(:,1:2);
Y=data(:,3);

#Set layer dimensions
# 2 - number of input features
# 5 -  1 hidden layer with 5 activation units
# 1 - 1 sigmoid activation unit at the output layer
layersDimensions = [2 5  1];

#Initialize model
[weights biases] = initializeDeepModel(layersDimensions);

#Perform forward prop
[AL forward_caches activation_caches droputMat] = forwardPropagationDeep(X',
weights, biases,keep_prob=1,
                  hiddenActivationFunc="relu",
outputActivationFunc="sigmoid");

#Compute cost
cost = computeCost(AL,
Y',outputActivationFunc=outputActivationFunc,numClasses=layersDimensions(size
(layersDimensions)(2)));
disp(cost);

#Compute gradients from cost
[gradsDA gradsDW gradsDB] = backwardPropagationDeep(AL, Y',
activation_caches,forward_caches, droputMat, lambd=0, keep_prob=1,
                                hiddenActivationFunc="relu",
outputActivationFunc="sigmoid",

numClasses=layersDimensions(size(layersDimensions)(2)));

#Set values
epsilon = 1e-07;
outputActivationFunc="sigmoid";

# Convert paramters cell array to vector
parameters_values = cellArray_to_vector(weights, biases);

#Convert gradient cell array to vector
grad = gradients_to_vector(gradsDW,gradsDB);
num_parameters = size(parameters_values)(1);

#Initialize J_plus, J_minus and gradapprox
J_plus = zeros(num_parameters, 1);
J_minus = zeros(num_parameters, 1);
```

```octave
gradapprox = zeros(num_parameters, 1);

# Compute gradapprox
for i = 1:num_parameters

    # Compute J_plus[i].
    thetaplus = parameters_values;
    thetaplus(i,1) = thetaplus(i,1) + epsilon;
    [weights1 biases1] =vector_to_cellArray(weights, biases,thetaplus);
    [AL forward_caches activation_caches droputMat] =
forwardPropagationDeep(X', weights1, biases1, keep_prob=1,
hiddenActivationFunc="relu",outputActivationFunc=outputActivationFunc);
    J_plus(i) = computeCost(AL, Y',
outputActivationFunc=outputActivationFunc);

    # Compute J_minus[i].
    thetaminus = parameters_values;
    thetaminus(i,1) = thetaminus(i,1) - epsilon ;
    [weights1 biases1] = vector_to_cellArray(weights, biases,thetaminus);
    [AL forward_caches activation_caches droputMat]   =
forwardPropagationDeep(X',weights1, biases1, keep_prob=1,

hiddenActivationFunc="relu",outputActivationFunc=outputActivationFunc);
    J_minus(i) = computeCost(AL, Y',
outputActivationFunc=outputActivationFunc);

    # Compute gradapprox[i]
    gradapprox(i) = (J_plus(i) - J_minus(i))/(2*epsilon);

endfor

#Compute L2Norm or the Euclidean distance between gradients and gradapprox
numerator = L2NormVec(grad-gradapprox);
denominator = L2NormVec(grad) +  L2NormVec(gradapprox);
difference =  numerator/denominator;
disp(difference);

#Check difference
if difference > 1e-04
   printf("There is a mistake in the implementation ");
   disp(difference);
else
   printf("The implementation works perfectly");
       disp(difference);
endif

# Technique to compare the weights and biases and localize issue
# Convert grad to cell Array
[weights1 biases1] = vector_to_cellArray(weights, biases,grad);
printf("Gradients from back propagation");
disp(weights1);
disp(biases1);

# Convert gradapprox to cell array
[weights2 biases2] = vector_to_cellArray(weights, biases,gradapprox);
printf("Gradients from gradient check");

# Display
disp(weights2);
disp(biases2);

0.69315
1.4893e-005
The implementation works perfectly 1.4893e-005
```

```
Gradients from back propagation
{
[1,1] =
5.0349e-005  2.1323e-005
8.8632e-007  1.8231e-006
9.3784e-005  1.0057e-004
1.0875e-004 -1.9529e-007
5.4502e-005  3.2721e-005
[1,2] =
1.0567e-005  6.0615e-005  4.6004e-005  1.3977e-004  1.0405e-004
}
{
[1,1] =
-1.8716e-005
1.1309e-009
4.7686e-005
1.2051e-005
-1.4612e-005
[1,2] = 9.5808e-006
}
Gradients from gradient check
{
[1,1] =
5.0348e-005  2.1320e-005
8.8485e-007  1.8219e-006
9.3784e-005  1.0057e-004
1.0875e-004 -1.9762e-007
5.4502e-005  3.2723e-005
[1,2] =
[1,2] =
1.0565e-005  6.0614e-005  4.6007e-005  1.3977e-004  1.0405e-004
}
{
[1,1] =
-1.8713e-005
1.1102e-009
4.7687e-005
1.2048e-005
-1.4609e-005
[1,2] = 9.5790e-006
}
```

1.3b Gradient Check – Softmax Activation – Octave

```
source("DL8functions.m")
data=csvread("spiral.csv");

# Setup the data
X=data(:,1:2);
Y=data(:,3);

# Set the layer dimensions
# 2 - number of input features
# 3 -  1 hidden layer with 3 activation units
# 3 - 3 classes with softmax  activation unit at the output
layerlayersDimensions = [2 3  3];
```

```octave
[weights biases] = initializeDeepModel(layersDimensions);

# Run forward prop
[AL forward_caches activation_caches droputMat] = forwardPropagationDeep(X',
weights, biases,keep_prob=1,
                 hiddenActivationFunc="relu",
outputActivationFunc="softmax");

# Compute cost
cost = computeCost(AL,
Y',outputActivationFunc=outputActivationFunc,numClasses=layersDimensions(size
(layersDimensions)(2)));
disp(cost);

# Perform backward prop
[gradsDA gradsDW gradsDB] = backwardPropagationDeep(AL, Y',
activation_caches,forward_caches, droputMat, lambd=0, keep_prob=1,
                            hiddenActivationFunc="relu",
outputActivationFunc="softmax",

numClasses=layersDimensions(size(layersDimensions)(2)));

#Take transpose of last layer for Softmax
L=size(weights)(2);
gradsDW{L}= gradsDW{L}';
gradsDB{L}= gradsDB{L}';

#Perform gradient check
difference= gradient_check_n(weights, biases, gradsDW,gradsDB, X, Y, epsilon
= 1e-7,

outputActivationFunc="softmax",numClasses=layersDimensions(size(layersDimensi
ons)(2)));
1.0986
The implementation works perfectly!   2.0021e-005
Gradients from back propagation
{
  [1,1] =
    -7.1590e-005   4.1375e-005
    -1.9494e-004  -5.2014e-005
    -1.4554e-004   5.1699e-005
  [1,2] =
     3.3129e-004   1.9806e-004  -1.5662e-005
    -4.9692e-004  -3.7756e-004  -8.2318e-005
     1.6562e-004   1.7950e-004   9.7980e-005
}
{
  [1,1] =
    -3.0856e-005
    -3.3321e-004
    -3.8197e-004
  [1,2] =
     1.2046e-006
     2.9259e-007
    -1.4972e-006
}
Gradients from gradient check
{
  [1,1] =
    -7.1586e-005   4.1377e-005
    -1.9494e-004  -5.2013e-005
    -1.4554e-004   5.1695e-005
     3.3129e-004   1.9806e-004  -1.5664e-005
    -4.9692e-004  -3.7756e-004  -8.2316e-005
```

```
77          1.6562e-004   1.7950e-004   9.7979e-005
78  }
79  {
80    [1,1] =
81       -3.0852e-005
82       -3.3321e-004
83       -3.8197e-004
84    [1,2] =
85       1.1902e-006
86       2.8200e-007
87       -1.4644e-006
88  }
89
```

2. Tip for tuning hyperparameters

Deep Learning Networks come with a large number of hyper parameters which require tuning. The hyper parameters are

1. α -learning rate
2. Number of layers
3. Number of hidden units
4. Number of iterations
5. Momentum – β – 0.9
6. RMSProp – β_1 – 0.9
7. Adam – β_1, β_2 and ϵ
8. learning rate decay
9. mini batch size
10. Initialization method – He, Xavier
11. Regularization

– Among the above the most critical learning rate α. Rather than just trying out random values, it may help to try out values on a logarithmic scale. So, we could try out values -0.01,0.1,1.0,10 etc. If we find that the cost is between 0.01 and 0.1 we could use the bisection technique so we can try 0.05. If we need to be bigger than 0.01 and 0.05 we could try 0.03 and then keep halving the distance etc.
– The performance of Momentum and RMSProp are very good and work well with values 0.9. Even with this, it is better to try out values of 1-β in the logarithmic range. So, 1-β could 0.001,0.01,0.1 and hence β would be 0.999,0.99 or 0.9
– Increasing the number of hidden units or number of hidden layers needs to be done gradually. I have noticed that increasing number of hidden layers heavily does not improve performance and sometimes degrades it.
– Sometimes, I tend to increase the number of iterations if I think I see a steady decrease in the cost for a certain learning rate
– It may also help to add learning rate decay if you see there is an oscillation while it decreases.
– Xavier and He initializations also help in a fast convergence and are worth trying out.

3. Final thoughts

As I come to a close in this Deep Learning Series from first principles in Python, R and Octave, I must admit that I learnt a lot in the process.

* Building a L-layer, vectorized Deep Learning Network in Python, R and Octave was extremely challenging but very rewarding
* One benefit of building vectorized versions in Python, R and Octave was that I was looking at each function that I was implementing thrice, and hence I was able to fix any bugs in any of the languages
* In addition since I built the generic L-Layer DL network with all the bells and whistles, layer by layer I further had an opportunity to look at all the functions in each successive post.
* Each language has its advantages and disadvantages. From the performance perspective I think Python is the best, followed by Octave and then R
* Interesting, I noticed that even if small bugs creep into your implementation, the DL network does learn and does generate a valid set of weights and biases, however this may not be an optimum solution. In one case of an inadvertent bug, I was not updating the weights in the final layer of the DL network. Yet, using all the other layers, the DL network was able to come with a reasonable solution (maybe like random dropout, remaining units can still learn the data!)
* Having said that, the Gradient Check method discussed and implemented in this post can be very useful in ironing out bugs.

4. Conclusion

These months when I was writing the chapters and the also churning up the code in Python, R and Octave were very hectic. There have been times when I found that implementations of some function to be extremely demanding and I almost felt like giving up. There have been other times when I had to spend quite some time on an intractable DL network which would not respond to changes in hyper-parameters. All in all, it was a great learning experience.

Hope you enjoyed this detailed derivations and the implementation!!!

1. Appendix A

Neural NetworksThe mechanics of backpropagation

The initial work in the 'Backpropagation Algorithm' started in the 1980's and led to an explosion of interest in Neural Networks and the application of backpropagation

The 'Backpropagation' algorithm computes the minimum of an error function with respect to the weights in the Neural Network. It uses the method of gradient descent. The combination of weights in a multi-layered neural network, which minimizes the error/cost function, is considered a solution of the learning problem.

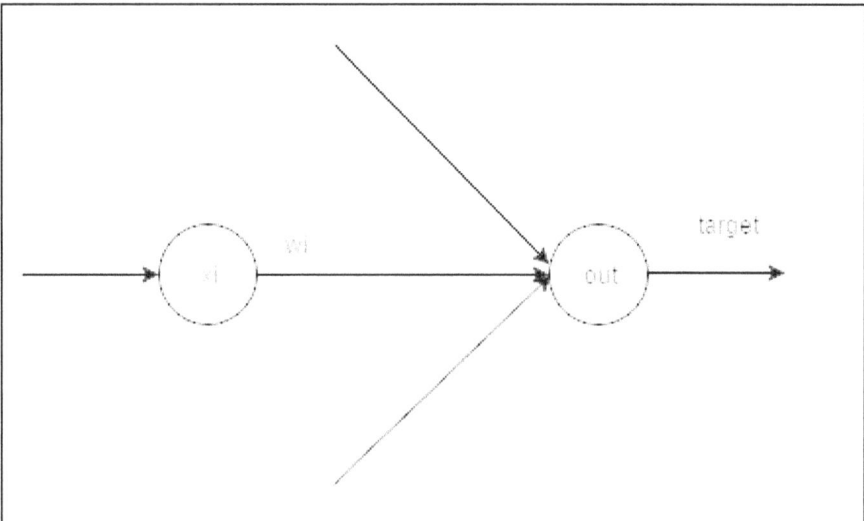

In the Neural Network above
$out_{o1} = \sum_i w_i * x_i$
$E = 1/2(target - out)^2$
$\partial E/\partial out = 1/2 * 2 * (target - out) * -1 = -(target - out)$
$\partial E/\partial w_i = \partial E/\partial y * \partial y/\partial w_i$
$\partial E/\partial w_i = -(target - out) * x_i$

Perceptrons and single layered neural networks can only classify, if the sample space is linearly separable. For non-linear decision boundaries, a multi layered neural network with backpropagation is required to generate more complex boundaries.The backpropagation algorithm, computes the minimum of the error function in weight space using the method of gradient descent. This computation of the gradient requires the activation function to be both differentiable and continuous. Hence, the sigmoid or logistic function is typically chosen as the activation function at every layer.
This post looks at a 3 layer neural network with 1 input, 1 hidden and 1 output. To a large extent this post is based on Matt Mazur's detailed "A step by step backpropagation example" (https://www.coursera.org/learn/neural-networks/home), and Prof Hinton's "Neural Networks for

Machine Learning"(https://www.coursera.org/learn/neural-networks/home/welcome) at Coursera and a few other sources.

While Matt Mazur's post uses example values, I generate the formulas for the gradient derivatives for each weight in the hidden and input layers. I intend to implement a vector version of backpropagation in Octave, R and Python. Therefore, this post is a prequel to that.

The 3-layer neural network is as below

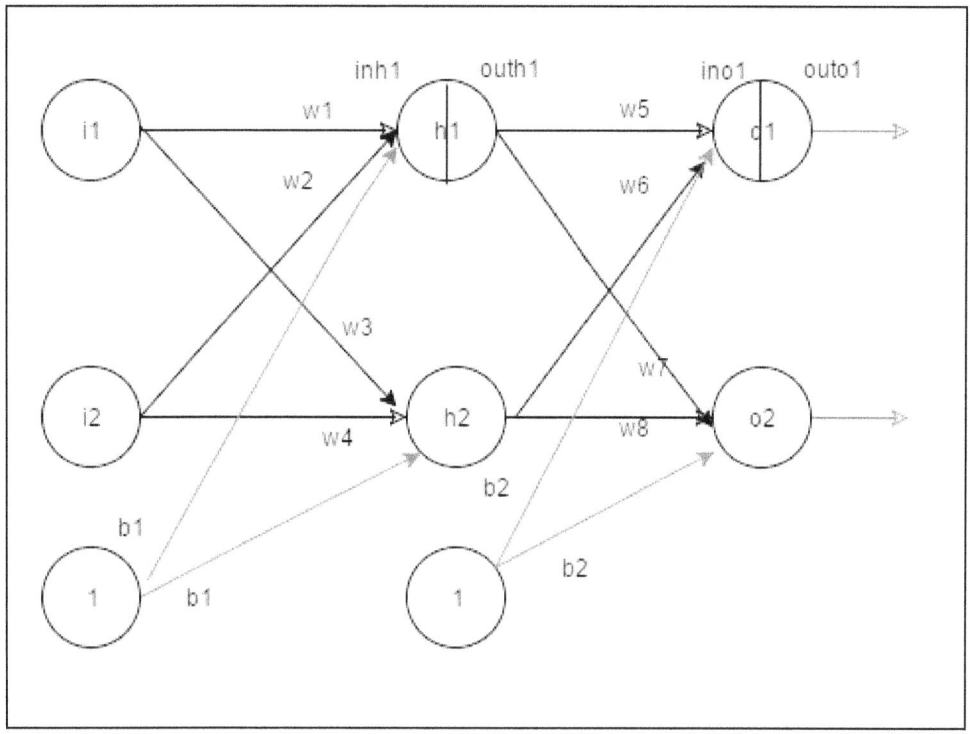

Some basic derivations which are used in backpropagation

Chain rule of differentiation
Let y=f(u)
and u=g(x) then
$\partial y/\partial x = \partial y/\partial u * \partial u/\partial x$

An important result
$y = 1/(1 + e^{-z})$
Let $x = 1 + e^{-z}$ then
$y = 1/x$
$\partial y/\partial x = -1/x^2$
$\partial x/\partial z = -e^{-z}$
Using the chain rule of differentiation we get
$\partial y/\partial z = \partial y/\partial x * \partial x/\partial z$

$$= -1/(1+e^{-z})^2 * -e^{-z} = e^{-z}/(1+e^{-z})^2$$
Therefore $\partial y/\partial z = y(1-y)$ -(A)

1) Feed forward network
The net output at the 1st hidden layer
$in_{h1} = w_1 i_1 + w_2 i_2 + b_1$
$in_{h2} = w_3 i_1 + w_4 i_2 + b_1$

The sigmoid/logistic function function is used to generate the activation outputs for each hidden layer. The sigmoid is chosen because it is continuous and has a continuous derivative

$out_{h1} = 1/1 + e^{-in_{h1}}$
$out_{h2} = 1/1 + e^{-in_{h2}}$

The net output at the output layer
$in_{o1} = w_5 out_{h1} + w_6 out_{h2} + b_2$
$in_{o2} = w_7 out_{h1} + w_8 out_{h2} + b_2$

Total error
$E_{total} = 1/2 \sum (target - output)^2$
$E_{total} = E_{o1} + E_{o2}$
$E_{total} = 1/2(target_{o1} - out_{o1})^2 + 1/2(target_{o2} - out_{o2})^2$

2) The backwards pass
In the backward pass we need to compute how the squared error changes with changing weight. i.e we compute $\partial E_{total}/\partial w_i$ for each weight w_i. This is shown below
A squared error is assumed

Error gradient with w_5

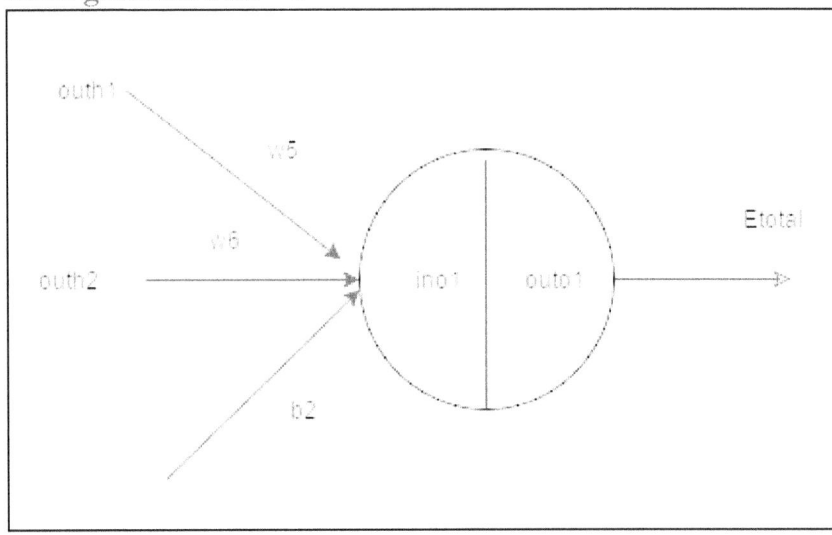

$\partial E_{total}/\partial w_5 = \partial E_{total}/\partial out_{o1} * \partial out_{o1}/\partial in_{o1} * \partial in_{o1}/\partial w_5$ -(B)

Since
$$E_{total} = 1/2 \sum (target - output)^2$$
$$E_{total} = 1/2(target_{o1} - out_{o1})^2 + 1/2(target_{o2} - out_{o2})^2$$
$$\partial E_{total}/\partial out_{o1} = \partial E_{o1}/\partial out_{o1} + \partial E_{o2}/\partial out_{o1}$$
$$\partial E_{total}/\partial out_{o1} = \partial/\partial_{out_{o1}}[1/2(target_{01} - out_{01})^2 - 1/2(target_{02} - out_{02})^2]$$
$$\partial E_{total}/\partial out_{o1} = 2 * 1/2 * (target_{01} - out_{01}) * -1 + 0$$

Now considering the 2nd term in (B)
$$\partial out_{o1}/\partial in_{o1} = \partial/\partial in_{o1}[1/(1 + e^{-in_{o1}})]$$

Using result (A)
$$\partial out_{o1}/\partial in_{o1} = \partial/\partial in_{o1}[1/(1 + e^{-in_{o1}})] = out_{o1}(1 - out_{o1})$$

The 3rd term in (B)
$$\partial in_{o1}/\partial w_5 = \partial/\partial w_5[w_5 * out_{h1} + w_6 * out_{h2}] = out_{h1}$$
$$\partial E_{total}/\partial w_5 = -(target_{o1} - out_{o1}) * out_{o1} * (1 - out_{o1}) * out_{h1}$$

Having computed $\partial E_{total}/\partial w_5$, we now perform gradient descent, by computing a new weight, assuming a learning rate α
$$w_5^+ = w_5 - \alpha * \partial E_{total}/\partial w_5$$

If we do this for $\partial E_{total}/\partial w_6$ we would get
$$\partial E_{total}/\partial w_6 = -(target_{o2} - out_{o2}) * out_{o2} * (1 - out_{o2}) * out_{h2}$$

3) Hidden layer

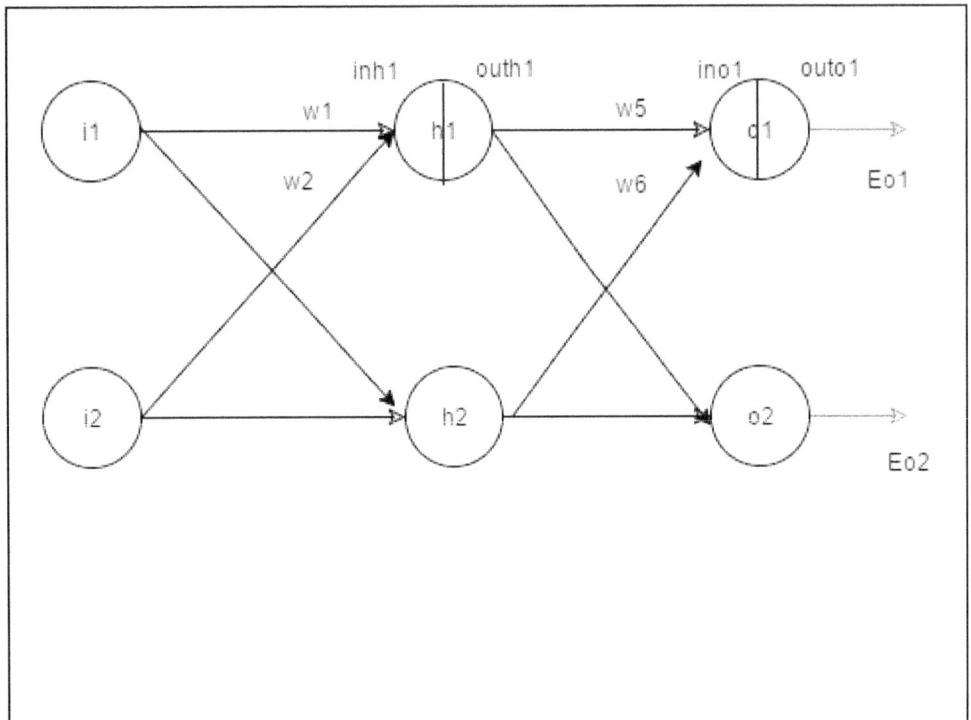

Text

We now compute how the total error changes for a change in weight w_1
$$\partial E_{total}/\partial w_1 = \partial E_{total}/\partial out_{h1} * \partial out_{h1}/\partial in_{h1} * \partial in_{h1}/\partial w_1 \text{ (C)}$$

Using
$E_{total} = E_{o1} + E_{o2}$ we get
$$\partial E_{total}/\partial w_1 = (\partial E_{o1}/\partial out_{h1} + \partial E_{o2}/\partial out_{h1}) * \partial out_{h1}/\partial in_{h1} * \partial in_{h1}/\partial w_1$$
$$\partial E_{total}/\partial w_1 = (\partial E_{o1}/\partial out_{h1} + \partial E_{o2}/\partial out_{h1}) * out_{h1} * (1 - out_{h1}) * i_1 \partial w_1 \text{ (D)}$$

Considering the 1st term in (C)
$$\partial E_{total}/\partial out_{h1} = \partial E_{o1}/\partial out_{h1} + \partial E_{o2}/\partial out_{h1}$$

Now
$$\partial E_{o1}/\partial out_{h1} = \partial E_{o1}/\partial out_{o1} * \partial out_{o1}/\partial in_{o1} * \partial in_{o1}/\partial out_{h1} \text{ (E)}$$
$$\partial E_{o2}/\partial out_{h1} = \partial E_{o2}/\partial out_{o2} * \partial out_{o2}/\partial in_{o2} * \partial in_{o2}/\partial out_{h1} \text{ (F)}$$

which gives the following

$$\partial E_{o1}/\partial out_{o1} * \partial out_{o1}/\partial in_{o1} * \partial in_{o1}/\partial out_{h1} = -(target_{o1} - out_{o1}) * out_{o1}(1 - out_{o1}) * w_5$$

$$\partial E_{o2}/\partial out_{o2} * \partial out_{o2}/\partial in_{o2} * \partial in_{o2}/\partial out_{h1} = -(target_{o2} - out_{o2}) * out_{o2}(1 - out_{o2}) * w_6$$

Combining (D), (E) & (F) we get

$$\partial E_{total}/\partial w_1 = -[(target_{o1} - out_{o1}) * out_{o1}(1 - out_{o1}) * w_5 + (target_{o2} - out_{o2}) * out_{o2}(1 - out_{o2}) * w_6] * out_{h1} * (1 - out_{h1}) * i_1$$

This can be represented as

$$\partial E_{total}/\partial w_1 = -\sum_i [(target_{oi} - out_{oi}) * out_{oi}(1 - out_{oi}) * w_j] * out_{h1} * (1 - out_{h1}) * i_1$$

With this derivative a new value of w_1 is computed
$$w_1^+ = w_1 - \alpha * \partial E_{total}/\partial w_1$$

Hence there are 2 important results
At the output layer we have
a) $\partial E_{total}/\partial w_j = -(target_{oi} - out_{oi}) * out_{oi} * (1 - out_{oi}) * out_{hi}$
At each hidden layer we compute
b) $\partial E_{total}/\partial w_k = -\sum_i [(target_{oi} - out_{oi}) * out_{oi}(1 - out_{oi}) * w_j] * out_{hk} * (1 - out_{hk}) * i_k$

Backpropagation was very successful in the early years, but the algorithm does have its problems for e.g the issue of the 'vanishing' and 'exploding' gradient. Yet it is a key development in Neural Networks, and the issues with the backprop gradients have been addressed through techniques such as the momentum method and adaptive learning rate etc.

In this post. I derive the weights at the output layer and the hidden layer. As I already mentioned above, I intend to implement a vector version of the backpropagation algorithm in Octave, R and Python in the days to come.

2. Appendix 1 – Logistic Regression as a Neural Network

1.1 Python functions

```
#######################################################################
###################
#
# Created by: Tinniam V Ganesh
# Date : 4 Jan 2018
# File: DLfunctions1.py
#
#######################################################################
###################

import numpy as np
import pandas as pd
import os
import matplotlib.pyplot as plt
from sklearn.model_selection import train_test_split

# Define the sigmoid function
def sigmoid(z):
    a=1/(1+np.exp(-z))
    return a

# Initialize weights and biases
def initialize(dim):
    w = np.zeros(dim).reshape(dim,1)
    b = 0
    return w

# Compute the loss
# Inputs: numTraining
#       : Y
#       : A
# Ouputs : loss
def computeLoss(numTraining,Y,A):
    loss=-1/numTraining *np.sum(Y*np.log(A) + (1-Y)*(np.log(1-A)))
    return(loss)

# Execute the forward propagation
# Inputs: w
#       : b
#       : X
#       : Y
# Ouputs : gradients, loss (dict)
def forwardPropagation(w,b,X,Y):
    # Compute Z
    Z=np.dot(w.T,X)+b
    # Determine the number of training samples
    numTraining=float(len(X))
    # Compute the output of the sigmoid activation function
    A=sigmoid(Z)
    #Compute the loss
    loss = computeLoss(numTraining,Y,A)
    # Compute the gradients dZ, dw and db
    dZ=A-Y
    dw=1/numTraining*np.dot(X,dZ.T)
```

```python
            db=1/numTraining*np.sum(dZ)

        # Return the results as a dictionary
        gradients = {"dw": dw,
                     "db": db}
        loss = np.squeeze(loss)
        return gradients,loss

# Compute Gradient Descent
# Inputs: w
#       : b
#       : X
#       : Y
#       : numIerations
#       : learningRate
# Ouputs : params, grads, losses,idx
def gradientDescent(w, b, X, Y, numIerations, learningRate):
    losses=[]
    idx =[]
    # Iterate
    for i in range(numIerations):
        gradients,loss=forwardPropagation(w,b,X,Y)
        #Get the derivates
        dw = gradients["dw"]
        db = gradients["db"]
        w = w-learningRate*dw
        b = b-learningRate*db

        # Store the loss
        if i % 100 == 0:
            idx.append(i)
            losses.append(loss)
        # Set params and grads
        params = {"w": w,
                  "b": b}
        grads = {"dw": dw,
                 "db": db}

    return params, grads, losses,idx

# Predict the output for a training set
# Inputs: w
#       : b
#       : X
# Ouputs : yPredicted
def predict(w,b,X):
    size=X.shape[1]
    yPredicted=np.zeros((1,size))
    Z=np.dot(w.T,X)
    # Compute the sigmoid
    A=sigmoid(Z)
    for i in range(A.shape[1]):
        #If the value is > 0.5 then set as 1
        if(A[0][i] > 0.5):
            yPredicted[0][i]=1
        else:
        # Else set as 0
            yPredicted[0][i]=0

    return yPredicted

#Normalize the data
# Predict the output for a training set
# Inputs: x
```

```
# Ouputs : x (normalized)
def normalize(x):
    x_norm = None
    x_norm = np.linalg.norm(x,axis=1,keepdims=True)
    x= x/x_norm
    return x
```

1.2 R

```
################################################################################
########
#
# Created by: Tinniam V Ganesh
# Date : 4 Jan 2018
# File: DLfunctions1.py
#
################################################################################
########
source("RFunctions-1.R")

# Define the sigmoid function
sigmoid <- function(z){
    a <- 1/(1+ exp(-z))
    a
}


# Compute the loss
# Inputs: numTraining
#       : Y
#       : A
# Ouputs : loss
computeLoss <- function(numTraining,Y,A){
    loss <- -1/numTraining* sum(Y*log(A) + (1-Y)*log(1-A))
    return(loss)
}

# Compute forward propagation
# Inputs: w
#       : b
#       : X
#       : Y
# Ouputs : fwdProp (list)
forwardPropagation <- function(w,b,X,Y){
    # Compute Z
    Z <- t(w) %*% X +b
    #Set the number of samples
    numTraining <- ncol(X)
    # Compute the activation function
    A=sigmoid(Z)

    #Compute the loss
    loss <- computeLoss(numTraining,Y,A)

    # Compute the gradients dZ, dw and db
    dZ<-A-Y
    dw<-1/numTraining * X %*% t(dZ)
    db<-1/numTraining*sum(dZ)

```

```r
        fwdProp <- list("loss" = loss, "dw" = dw, "db" = db)
        return(fwdProp)
}

# Perform one cycle of Gradient descent
# Compute Gradient Descent
# Inputs: w
#       : b
#       : X
#       : Y
#       : numIerations
#       : learningRate
# Ouputs : gradDescnt (list)
gradientDescent <- function(w, b, X, Y, numIerations, learningRate){
    losses <- NULL
    idx <- NULL
    # Loop through the number of iterations
    for(i in 1:numIerations){
        fwdProp <-forwardPropagation(w,b,X,Y)
        #Get the derivatives
        dw <- fwdProp$dw
        db <- fwdProp$db
        #Perform gradient descent
        w = w-learningRate*dw
        b = b-learningRate*db
        l <- fwdProp$loss
        # Stoe the loss
        if(i %% 100 == 0){
            idx <- c(idx,i)
            losses <- c(losses,l)
        }
    }

    # Return the weights and losses
    gradDescnt <-
list("w"=w,"b"=b,"dw"=dw,"db"=db,"losses"=losses,"idx"=idx)
    return(gradDescnt)
}

# Compute the predicted value for input
# Predict the output for a training set
# Inputs: w
#       : b
#       : X
# Ouputs : yPredicted
predict <- function(w,b,X){
    m=dim(X)[2]
    # Create a ector of 0's
    yPredicted=matrix(rep(0,m),nrow=1,ncol=m)
    Z <- t(w) %*% X +b
    # Compute sigmoid
    A=sigmoid(Z)
    for(i in 1:dim(A)[2]){
        # If A > 0.5 set value as 1
        if(A[1,i] > 0.5)
            yPredicted[1,i]=1
        else
            # Else set as 0
            yPredicted[1,i]=0
    }

    return(yPredicted)
}
```

```r
# Normalize the matrix
# Predict the output for a training set
# Inputs: x
# Ouputs : normalized
normalize <- function(x){
    #Create the norm of the matrix.Perform the Frobenius norm of the matrix
    n<-as.matrix(sqrt(rowSums(x^2)))
    #Sweep by rows by norm. Note '1' in the function which performing on every row
    normalized<-sweep(x, 1, n, FUN="/")
    return(normalized)
```

1.3 Octave

```octave
###########################################################################
####################
#
# Created by: Tinniam V Ganesh
# Date : 4 Jan 2018
# File: DLfunctions.m
#
###########################################################################
####################
1;
# Define sigmoid function
function a = sigmoid(z)
  a = 1 ./ (1+ exp(-z));
end

# Compute the loss
# Inputs: numTraining
#       : Y
#       : A
# Ouputs : loss
function loss=computeLoss(numtraining,Y,A)
   loss = -1/numtraining * sum((Y .* log(A)) + (1-Y) .* log(1-A));
end

# Perform forward propagation
# Inputs: w
#       : b
#       : X
#       : Y
# Ouputs : loss,dw,db,dZ
function [loss,dw,db,dZ] = forwardPropagation(w,b,X,Y)
  % Compute Z
  Z = w' * X + b;
  numtraining = size(X)(1,2);
  # Compute sigmoid
  A = sigmoid(Z);

  #Compute loss. Note this is element wise product
  loss =computeLoss(numtraining,Y,A);
  # Compute the gradients dZ, dw and db
   dZ = A-Y;
   dw = 1/numtraining* X * dZ';
   db =1/numtraining*sum(dZ);

end
```

```octave
# Compute Gradient Descent
# Inputs: w
#       : b
#       : X
#       : Y
#       : numIerations
#       : learningRate
# Ouputs : w,b,dw,db,losses,index
function [w,b,dw,db,losses,index]=gradientDescent(w, b, X, Y,
numIerations, learningRate)
  #Initialize losses and idx
  losses=[];
  index=[];
  # Loop through the number of iterations
  for i=1:numIerations,
     [loss,dw,db,dZ] = forwardPropagation(w,b,X,Y);
     # Perform Gradient descent
     w = w - learningRate*dw;
     b = b - learningRate*db;
     if(mod(i,100) ==0)
        # Append index and loss
        index = [index i];
        losses = [losses loss];
     endif

  end
end

# Determine the predicted value for dataset
# Inputs: w
#       : b
#       : X
# Ouputs : yPredicted
function yPredicted = predict(w,b,X)
   m = size(X)(1,2);
   yPredicted=zeros(1,m);
   # Compute Z
   Z = w' * X + b;
   # Compute sigmoid
   A = sigmoid(Z);
   for i=1:size(X)(1,2),
      # Set predicted as 1 if A > 0,5
      if(A(1,i) >= 0.5)
         yPredicted(1,i)=1;
       else
         yPredicted(1,i)=0;
       endif
    end
end

# Normalize by dividing each value by the sum of squares
# Predict the output for a training set
# Inputs: x
# Ouputs : normalized
function normalized = normalize(x)
    # Compute Frobenius norm. Square the elements, sum rows and then find
square root
    a = sqrt(sum(x .^ 2,2));
    # Perform element wise division
    normalized = x ./ a;
end

# Split into train and test sets
```

```octave
# Predict the output for a training set
# Inputs: dataset
#        :trainPercent
# Ouputs : X_train,y_train,X_test,y_test
function [X_train,y_train,X_test,y_test] =
trainTestSplit(dataset,trainPercent)
    # Create a random index
    ix = randperm(length(dataset));
    # Split into training
    trainSize = floor(trainPercent/100 * length(dataset));
    train=dataset(ix(1:trainSize),:);
    # And test
    test=dataset(ix(trainSize+1:length(dataset)),:);
    X_train = train(:,1:30);
    y_train = train(:,31);
    X_test = test(:,1:30);
    y_test = test(:,31);
end
```

3. Appendix 2 - Implementing a simple Neural Network

2.1 Python

```
1  ########################################################################
2  ################
3  #
4  # Created by: Tinniam V Ganesh
5  # Date : 11 Jan 2018
6  # File: DLfunctions.py
7  #
8  ########################################################################
9  ################
10 import numpy as np
11 import matplotlib
12 import matplotlib.pyplot as plt
13
14 # Conmpute the sigmoid of a vector
15 # Inputs: z
16 # Ouputs : a
17 def sigmoid(z):
18     a=1/(1+np.exp(-z))
19     return a
20
21 # Compute the model shape given the dataset
22 # Input : X
23 #         Y
24 # Returns: modelParams
25 def getModelShape(X,Y):
26     numTraining= X.shape[1] # No of training examples
27     numFeats=X.shape[0]     # No of input features
28     numHidden=4             # No of units in hidden layer
29     numOutput=Y.shape[0]    # No of output units
30     # Create a dcitionary of values
31
32 modelParams={"numTraining":numTraining,"numFeats":numFeats,"numHidden":numHid
33 den,"numOutput":numOutput}
34     return(modelParams)
35
36
37 # Initialize the model
38 # Input : number of features
39 #         number of hidden units
40 #         number of units in output
41 # Returns: Weight and bias matrices and vectors
42 def initializeModel(numFeats,numHidden,numOutput):
43     np.random.seed(2)
44     W1=np.random.randn(numHidden,numFeats)*0.01 #  Multiply by .01
45     b1=np.zeros((numHidden,1))
46     W2=np.random.randn(numOutput,numHidden)*0.01
47     b2=np.zeros((numOutput,1))
48
49     # Create a dictionary of the neural network parameters
50     nnParameters={'W1':W1,'b1':b1,'W2':W2,'b2':b2}
51     return(nnParameters)
52
53 # Compute the forward propoagation through the neural network
54 # Input : X
```

```python
 55  #               nnParameters
 56  # Returns : The Activation of 2nd layer
 57  #            : Output and activation of layer 1 & 2
 58  def forwardPropagation(X,nnParameters):
 59      # Get the parameters
 60      W1=nnParameters["W1"]
 61      b1=nnParameters["b1"]
 62      W2=nnParameters["W2"]
 63      b2=nnParameters["b2"]
 64
 65      # Compute Z1 of the input layer
 66      Z1=np.dot(W1,X)+b1
 67      # Compute the output A1 with the tanh activation function. The tanh
 68  activation function
 69      # performs better than the sigmoid function
 70      A1=np.tanh(Z1)
 71
 72      # Compute Z2 of the 2nd  layer
 73      Z2=np.dot(W2,A1)+b2
 74      # Compute the output A1 with the tanh activation function. The tanh
 75  activation function
 76      # performs better than the sigmoid function
 77      A2=sigmoid(Z2)
 78      cache={'Z1':Z1,'A1':A1,'Z2':Z2,'A2':A2}
 79      return A2,cache
 80
 81  # Compute the cost
 82  # Input : A2
 83  #         :Y
 84  # Output: cost
 85  def computeCost(A2,Y):
 86      m= float(Y.shape[1])
 87      # Element wise multiply for logprobs
 88      cost=-1/m *np.sum(Y*np.log(A2) + (1-Y)*(np.log(1-A2)))
 89      cost = np.squeeze(cost)
 90      return cost
 91
 92  # Compute the backpropoagation for 1 cycle
 93  # Input : Neural Network parameters - weights and biases
 94  #         # Z and Activations of 2 layers
 95  #         # Input features
 96  #         # Output values Y
 97  # Returns: Gradients
 98  def backPropagation(nnParameters, cache, X, Y):
 99      numtraining=float(X.shape[1])
100      # Get parameters
101      W1=nnParameters["W1"]
102      W2=nnParameters["W2"]
103
104      #Get the NN cache
105      A1=cache["A1"]
106      A2=cache["A2"]
107
108      # Compute gradients
109      dZ2 = A2 - Y
110      dW2 = 1/numtraining *np.dot(dZ2,A1.T)
111      db2 = 1/numtraining *np.sum(dZ2,axis=1,keepdims=True)
112      dZ1 = np.multiply(np.dot(W2.T,dZ2), (1 - np.power(A1, 2)))
113      dW1 = 1/numtraining* np.dot(dZ1,X.T)
114      db1 = 1/numtraining *np.sum(dZ1,axis=1,keepdims=True)
115
116      # Create a dictionary
117      gradients = {"dW1": dW1,
118                   "db1": db1,
```

```python
                          "dW2": dW2,
                          "db2": db2}
    return gradients

# Perform Gradient Descent
# Input : Weights and biases
#         : gradients
#         : learning rate
#output : Updated weights after 1 iteration
def gradientDescent(nnParameters, gradients, learningRate):
    W1 = nnParameters['W1']
    b1 = nnParameters['b1']
    W2 = nnParameters['W2']
    b2 = nnParameters['b2']
    dW1 = gradients["dW1"]
    db1 = gradients["db1"]
    dW2 = gradients["dW2"]
    db2 = gradients["db2"]
    W1 = W1-learningRate*dW1
    b1 = b1-learningRate*db1
    W2 = W2-learningRate*dW2
    b2 = b2-learningRate*db2
    # Update the Neural Network parametrs
    updatedNNParameters = {"W1": W1,
                  "b1": b1,
                  "W2": W2,
                  "b2": b2}

    return updatedNNParameters

# Compute the Neural Network  by minimizing the cost
# Input : Input data X,
#         Output Y
#         No of hidden units in hidden layer
#         No of iterations
# Returns  Updated weight and bias vectors of the neural network
def computeNN(X, Y, numHidden, learningRate, numIterations = 10000):
    np.random.seed(3)
    modelParams = getModelShape(X, Y)
    numFeats=modelParams['numFeats']
    numOutput=modelParams['numOutput']

    costs=[]

    nnParameters = initializeModel(numFeats,numHidden,numOutput)
    W1 = nnParameters['W1']
    b1 = nnParameters['b1']
    W2 = nnParameters['W2']
    b2 = nnParameters['b2']
    # Perform gradient descent
    for i in range(0, numIterations):
        # Evaluate forward prop to compute activation at output layer
        A2, cache =  forwardPropagation(X, nnParameters)
        # Compute cost from Activation at output and Y
        cost = computeCost(A2, Y)
        # Perform backprop to compute gradients
        gradients = backPropagation(nnParameters, cache, X, Y)
        # Use gradients to update the weights for each iteration.
        nnParameters = gradientDescent(nnParameters, gradients,learningRate)
        # Print the cost every 1000 iterations
        if i % 1000 == 0:
            costs.append(cost)
            print ("Cost after iteration %i: %f" %(i, cost))
    return nnParameters,costs
```

```python
# Compute the predicted value for a given input
# Input : Neural Network parameters
#       : Input data
def predict(nnParameters, X):
    A2, cache = forwardPropagation(X, nnParameters)
    predictions = (A2>0.5)
    return predictions

# Plot a decision boundary
# Input : Input Model,
#         X
#         Y
#         Fig to be saved as
# Returns Null
def plot_decision_boundary_n(model, X, y,fig):
    # Set min and max values and give it some padding
    x_min, x_max = X[0, :].min() - 1, X[0, :].max() + 1
    y_min, y_max = X[1, :].min() - 1, X[1, :].max() + 1
    colors=['black','gold']
    cmap = matplotlib.colors.ListedColormap(colors)
    h = 0.01
    # Generate a grid of points with distance h between them
    xx, yy = np.meshgrid(np.arange(x_min, x_max, h), np.arange(y_min, y_max, h))
    # Predict the function value for the whole grid
    Z = model(np.c_[xx.ravel(), yy.ravel()])
    Z = Z.reshape(xx.shape)
    # Plot the contour and training examples
    plt.contourf(xx, yy, Z, cmap=plt.cm.Spectral)
    plt.ylabel('x2')
    plt.xlabel('x1')
    plt.scatter(X[0, :], X[1, :], c=y, cmap=cmap)
    plt.title("Decision Boundary for logistic regression")
    plt.savefig(fig, bbox_inches='tight')

# Plot a decision boundary
# Input : Input Model,
#         X
#         Y
#         sz - Num of hiden units
#         lr - Learning rate
#         Fig to be saved as
# Returns Null
def plot_decision_boundary(model, X, y,sz,lr,fig):
    # Set min and max values and give it some padding
    x_min, x_max = X[0, :].min() - 1, X[0, :].max() + 1
    y_min, y_max = X[1, :].min() - 1, X[1, :].max() + 1
    colors=['black','gold']
    cmap = matplotlib.colors.ListedColormap(colors)
    h = 0.01
    # Generate a grid of points with distance h between them
    xx, yy = np.meshgrid(np.arange(x_min, x_max, h), np.arange(y_min, y_max, h))
    # Predict the function value for the whole grid
    Z = model(np.c_[xx.ravel(), yy.ravel()])
    Z = Z.reshape(xx.shape)
    # Plot the contour and training examples
    plt.contourf(xx, yy, Z, cmap=plt.cm.Spectral)
    plt.ylabel('x2')
    plt.xlabel('x1')
    plt.scatter(X[0, :], X[1, :], c=y, cmap=cmap)
    plt.title("Decision Boundary for hidden layer size:" + sz +" and learning rate:"+lr)
```

```
           plt.savefig(fig, bbox_inches='tight')
```

2.2 R

```r
################################################################################
################
#
# Created by: Tinniam V Ganesh
# Date : 11 Jan 2018
# File: DLfunctions2_1.R
#
################################################################################
################
library(ggplot2)

# Sigmoid function
sigmoid <- function(z){
    a <- 1/(1+ exp(-z))
    a
}

# Compute the model shape given the dataset
# Input : X - features
#         Y - output
#
# Returns: no of training samples, no features, no hidden, no output
getModelShape <- function(X,Y){
    numTraining <- dim(X)[2] # No of training examples
    numFeats <- dim(X)[1]    # No of input features
    numHidden<-4             # No of units in hidden layer
    # If Y is a row vector set numOutput as 1
    if(is.null(dim(Y)))
        numOutput <-1        # No of output units
    else
        numOutput <- dim(Y)[1]
    # Create a list of values
    modelParams <-
list("numTraining"=numTraining,"numFeats"=numFeats,"numHidden"=numHidden,
                    "numOutput"=numOutput)
    return(modelParams)
}


# Initialize the model
# Input : number of features
#         number of hidden units
#         number of units in output
# Returns: Weight and bias matrices and vectors
initializeModel <- function(numFeats,numHidden,numOutput){
    set.seed(2)
    w= rnorm(numHidden*numFeats)*0.01
    W1<-matrix(w,nrow=numHidden,ncol=numFeats) # Multiply by .01
    b1<-matrix(rep(0,numHidden),nrow=numHidden,ncol=1)
    w= rnorm(numOutput*numHidden)
    W2<-matrix(w,nrow=numOutput,ncol=numHidden)
    b2<- matrix(rep(0,numOutput),nrow=numOutput,ncol=1)

    # Create a list of the neural network parameters
    nnParameters<- list('W1'=W1,'b1'=b1,'W2'=W2,'b2'=b2)
```

```r
    return(nnParameters)
}


#Compute the forward propagation through the neural network
# Input : Features
#           Weight and bias matrices and vectors
# Returns : The Activation of 2nd layer
#            : Output and activation of layer 1 & 2

forwardPropagation <- function(X,nnParameters){
    # Get the parameters
    W1<-nnParameters$W1
    b1<-nnParameters$b1
    W2<-nnParameters$W2
    b2<-nnParameters$b2

    z <- W1 %*% X

    # Broadcast the bias vector for each row. Use 'sweep' The value '1' for MARGIN
    # indicates sweep each row by this value( add a column vector to each row).
    # If we want to sweep by column use '2'for MARGIN. Here a row vector is added to
    # column (braodcasting!)

    Z1 <-sweep(z,1,b1,'+')
    # Compute the output A1 with the tanh activation function. The tanh activation function
    # performs better than the sigmoid function

    A1<-tanh(Z1)

    # Compute Z2 of the 2nd  layer
    z <- W2 %*% A1
    # Broadcast the bias vector for each row. Use 'sweep'
    Z2 <- sweep(z,1,b2,'+')
    # Compute the output A1 with the tanh activation function. The tanh activation function
    # performs better than the sigmoid function
    A2<-sigmoid(Z2)
    cache <- list('Z1'=Z1,'A1'=A1,'Z2'=Z2,'A2'=A2)
    return(list('A2'=A2, 'cache'=cache))
}

# Compute the cost
# Input : Activation of 2nd layer
#            : Output from data
# Output: cost
computeCost <- function(A2,Y){
    m= length(Y)
    cost=-1/m*sum(Y*log(A2) + (1-Y)*log(1-A2))
    #cost=-1/m*sum(a+b)
    return(cost)
}


# Compute the backpropoagation for 1 cycle
# Input : Neural Network parameters - weights and biases
#           # Z and Activations of 2 layers
#           # Input features
#           # Output values Y
# Returns: Gradients
```

```r
backPropagation <- function(nnParameters, cache, X, Y){
    numtraining<- dim(X)[2]
    # Get parameters
    W1<-nnParameters$W1
    W2<-nnParameters$W2

    #Get the NN cache
    A1<-cache$A1
    A2<-cache$A2


    dZ2 <- A2 - Y
    dW2 <-   1/numtraining * dZ2 %*% t(A1)
    db2 <- 1/numtraining * rowSums(dZ2)
    dZ1 <-   t(W2) %*% dZ2 * (1 - A1^2)
    dW1 = 1/numtraining*  dZ1 %*% t(X)
    db1 = 1/numtraining * rowSums(dZ1)

    gradients <- list("dW1"= dW1, "db1"= db1, "dW2"= dW2, "db2"= db2)
    return(gradients)
}



# Gradient descent
# Perform Gradient Descent
# Input : Weights and biases
#        : gradients
#        : learning rate
#output : Updated weights after 1 iteration
gradientDescent <- function(nnParameters, gradients, learningRate){
    W1 <- nnParameters$W1
    b1 <- nnParameters$b1
    W2 <- nnParameters$W2
    b2 <- nnParameters$b2
    dW1<-gradients$dW1
    db1 <- gradients$db1
    dW2 <- gradients$dW2
    db2 <-gradients$db2
    W1 <- W1-learningRate*dW1
    b1 <- b1-learningRate*db1
    W2 <- W2-learningRate*dW2
    b2 <- b2-learningRate*db2
    updatedNNParameters <- list("W1"= W1, "b1"= b1, "W2"= W2, "b2"= b2)
    return(updatedNNParameters)
}

# Compute the Neural Network  by minimizing the cost
# Input : Input data X,
#         Output Y
#         No of hidden units in hidden layer
#         No of iterations
# Returns  Updated weight and bias vectors of the neural network
computeNN <- function(X, Y, numHidden, learningRate, numIterations = 10000){

    modelParams <- getModelShape(X, Y)
    numFeats<-modelParams$numFeats
    numOutput<-modelParams$numOutput
    costs=NULL
    nnParameters <- initializeModel(numFeats,numHidden,numOutput)
    W1 <- nnParameters$W1
    b1<-nnParameters$b1
    W2<-nnParameters$W2
    b2<-nnParameters$b2
```

```r
        # Perform gradient descent
        for(i in 0: numIterations){

            # Evaluate forward prop to compute activation at output layer
            #print("Here")
            fwdProp =  forwardPropagation(X, nnParameters)
            # Compute cost from Activation at output and Y
            cost = computeCost(fwdProp$A2, Y)
            # Perform backprop to compute gradients
            gradients = backPropagation(nnParameters, fwdProp$cache, X, Y)
            # Use gradients to update the weights for each iteration.
            nnParameters = gradientDescent(nnParameters, gradients,learningRate)
            # Print the cost every 1000 iterations
            if(i%%1000 == 0){
                costs=c(costs,cost)
                print(cost)
            }
        }

    nnVals <- list("nnParameter"=nnParameters,"costs"=costs)
    return(nnVals)
}
# Predict the output
predict <- function(parameters, X){

    fwdProp <- forwardPropagation(X, parameters)
    predictions <- fwdProp$A2>0.5

    return (predictions)
}

# Plot a decision boundary
# This function uses the contour method
drawBoundary <- function(z,nn){
    # Find the minimum and maximum of the 2 fatures
    xmin<-min(z[,1])
    xmax<-max(z[,1])
    ymin<-min(z[,2])
    ymax<-max(z[,2])

    a=seq(xmin,xmax,length=100)
    b=seq(ymin,ymax,length=100)
    grid <- expand.grid(x=a, y=b)
    grid1 <-t(grid)
    q <-predict(nn$nnParameter,grid1)
    # Works
    contour(a, b, z=matrix(q, nrow=100), levels=0.5,
            col="black", drawlabels=FALSE, lwd=2,xlim=range(2,10))
    points(z[,1],z[,2],col=ifelse(z[,3]==1, "coral",
"cornflowerblue"),pch=18)
}

# Plot a decision boundary
# This function uses ggplot2
plotDecisionBoundary <- function(z,nn,sz,lr){
    xmin<-min(z[,1])
    xmax<-max(z[,1])
    ymin<-min(z[,2])
    ymax<-max(z[,2])


    a=seq(xmin,xmax,length=100)
    b=seq(ymin,ymax,length=100)
    grid <- expand.grid(x=a, y=b)
```

```r
        colnames(grid) <- c('x1', 'x2')
        grid1 <-t(grid)
        q <-predict(nn$nnParameter,grid1)
        q1 <- t(data.frame(q))
        q2 <- as.numeric(q1)
        grid2 <- cbind(grid,q2)
        colnames(grid2) <- c('x1', 'x2','q2')

        z1 <- data.frame(z)
        names(z1) <- c("x1","x2","y")
        atitle=paste("Decision boundary for hidden layer size:",sz,"learning rate:",lr)
        ggplot(z1) +
            geom_point(data = z1, aes(x = x1, y = x2, color = y)) +
            stat_contour(data = grid2, aes(x = x1, y = x2, z = q2,color=q2), alpha = 0.9)+
            ggtitle(atitle)
}

# Plot a decision boundary
# This function uses ggplot2 and stat_contour
plotBoundary <- function(z,nn){
    xmin<-min(z[,1])
    xmax<-max(z[,1])
    ymin<-min(z[,2])
    ymax<-max(z[,2])


    a=seq(xmin,xmax,length=100)
    b=seq(ymin,ymax,length=100)
    grid <- expand.grid(x=a, y=b)
    colnames(grid) <- c('x1', 'x2')
    grid1 <-t(grid)
    q <-predict(nn$nnParameter,grid1)
    q1 <- t(data.frame(q))
    q2 <- as.numeric(q1)
    grid2 <- cbind(grid,q2)
    colnames(grid2) <- c('x1', 'x2','q2')

    z1 <- data.frame(z)
    names(z1) <- c("x1","x2","y")
    data.plot <- ggplot() +
        geom_point(data = z1, aes(x = x1, y = x2, color = y)) +
        coord_fixed() +

        xlab('x1') +
        ylab('x2')
    print(data.plot)

    data.plot + stat_contour(data = grid2, aes(x = x1, y = x2, z = q2), alpha = 0.9)
}
```

2.3 Octave

```
################################################################################
################
```

```octave
#
# Created by: Tinniam V Ganesh
# Date : 11 Jan 2018
# File: DLfunctions2.m
#
###########################################################################
################
1;
# Define sigmoid function
function a = sigmoid(z)
  a = 1 ./ (1+ exp(-z));
end

# Compute the loss
# Inputs: numTraining
#       : Y
#       : A
# Ouputs : loss
function loss=computeLoss(numtraining,Y,A)
   loss = -1/numtraining * sum((Y .* log(A)) + (1-Y) .* log(1-A));
end

# Compute the model shape given the dataset
# Inputs: X
#       : Y
# Ouputs : n_x,m,n_h,n_y
function [n_x,m,n_h,n_y] = getModelShape(X,Y)
    m= size(X)(2);
    n_x=size(X)(1);
    n_h=4;
    n_y=size(Y)(1);
end

# Initialize model
# Inputs: n_x
#       : n_h
#       : n_y
# Ouputs : W1,b1,W2,b2
function [W1,b1,W2,b2] = modelInit(n_x,n_h,n_y)
    rand ("seed", 2);
    W1=rand(n_h,n_x)*0.01; # Set the initial values to a small number
    b1=zeros(n_h,1);
    W2=rand(n_y,n_h)*0.01;
    b2=zeros(n_y,1);

end

# Compute the forward propoagation through the neural network
# Input : Features
#         Weight and bias matrices and vectors
# Returns : The Activation of 2nd layer
#         : Output and activation of layer 1 & 2
function [Z1,A1,Z2,A2]= forwardPropagation(X,W1,b1,W2,b2)
    # Get the parameters

    # Determine the number of training samples
    m=size(X)(2);
    # Compute Z1 of the input layer
    # Octave also handles broadcasting like Python!!
    Z1=W1 * X +b1;
    # Compute the output A1 with the tanh activation function. The tanh activation function
    # performs better than the sigmoid function
    A1=tanh(Z1);
```

```octave
    # Compute Z2 of the input layer
    Z2=W2 * A1+b2;
    # Compute the output A1 with the tanh activation function. The tanh
activation function
    # performs better than the sigmoid function
    A2=sigmoid(Z2);

end

# Compute the cost
# Input : Activation of 2nd layer
#        : Output from data
# Output: cost
function [cost] = computeCost(A,Y)
    numTraining= size(Y)(2);
    # Element wise multiply for logprobs
    cost = -1/numTraining * sum((Y .* log(A)) + (1-Y) .* log(1-A));
end


# Compute the backpropoagation for 1 cycle
# Input : Neural Network parameters - weights and biases
#         # Z and Activations of 2 layers
#         # Input features
#         # Output values Y
# Returns: Gradients
function [dW1,db1,dW2,db2]= backPropagation(W1,W2,A1,A2, X, Y)
    numTraining=size(X)(2);

    dZ2 = A2 - Y;
    dW2 = 1/numTraining * dZ2 * A1';
    db2 = 1/numTraining * sum(dZ2);

    dZ1 =  W2' * dZ2 .* (1 - power(A1, 2));
    dW1 = 1/numTraining *   dZ1 * X';
    # Note the '2' in the next statement indicates that a row sum has to done
, 2nd dimension
    db1 = 1/numTraining * sum(dZ1,2);

end

# Perform Gradient Descent
# Input : Weights and biases
#        : gradients
#        : learning rate
#output : Updated weights after 1 iteration
function [W1,b1,W2,b2]= gradientDescent(W1,b1,W2,b2, dW1,db1,dW2,db2,
learningRate)
    W1 = W1-learningRate*dW1;
    b1 = b1-learningRate*db1;
    W2 = W2-learningRate*dW2;
    b2 = b2-learningRate*db2;
end


# Compute the Neural Network  by minimizing the cost
# Input : Input data X,
#         Output Y
#         No of hidden units in hidden layer
#         No of iterations
# Returns   Updated weight and bias vectors of the neural network
function [W1,b1,W2,b2,costs]= computeNN(X, Y,numHidden, learningRate,
numIterations = 10000)
```

```octave
    [numFeats,numTraining,n_h,numOutput] = getModelShape(X, Y);

    costs=[];

    [W1,b1,W2,b2] = modelInit(numFeats,numHidden,numOutput) ;
    #W1 =[-0.00416758, -0.00056267; -0.02136196,  0.01640271; -0.01793436, -0.00841747;   0.00502881 -0.01245288];
    #W2=[-0.01057952, -0.00909008,  0.00551454,  0.02292208];
    #b1=[0;0;0;0];
    #b2=[0];
    # Perform gradient descent
    for i =0:numIterations
        # Evaluate forward prop to compute activation at output layer
        [Z1,A1,Z2,A2] =  forwardPropagation(X, W1,b1,W2,b2);
        # Compute cost from Activation at output and Y
        cost = computeCost(A2, Y);
        # Perform backprop to compute gradients
        [dW1,db1,dW2,db2] = backPropagation(W1,W2,A1,A2, X, Y);
        # Use gradients to update the weights for each iteration.

        [W1,b1,W2,b2] = gradientDescent(W1,b1,W2,b2, dW1,db1,dW2,db2,learningRate);
        # Print the cost every 1000 iterations
        if ( mod(i,1000) == 0)
            costs =[costs cost];
            #disp ("Cost after iteration"), disp(i),disp(cost);
        endif
    endfor
end

# Compute the predicted value for a given input
# Input : Neural Network parameters
#       : Input data
# Output : predictions
function [predictions]= predict(W1,b1,W2,b2, X)
    [Z1,A1,Z2,A2] = forwardPropagation(X, W1,b1,W2,b2);
    predictions = (A2>0.5);
end

# Plot the decision boundary
function plotDecisionBoundary(data,W1,b1,W2,b2)
    %Plot a non-linear decision boundary learned by the SVM
    colormap ("default");

    % Make classification predictions over a grid of values
    x1plot = linspace(min(data(:,1)), max(data(:,1)), 400)';
    x2plot = linspace(min(data(:,2)), max(data(:,2)), 400)';
    [X1, X2] = meshgrid(x1plot, x2plot);
    vals = zeros(size(X1));
    # Plot the prediction for the grid
    for i = 1:size(X1, 2)
       gridPoints = [X1(:, i), X2(:, i)];
       vals(:, i)=predict(W1,b1,W2,b2,gridPoints');
    endfor

    scatter(data(:,1),data(:,2),8,c=data(:,3),"filled");
    % Plot the boundary
    hold on
    #contour(X1, X2, vals, [0 0], 'LineWidth', 2);
    contour(X1, X2, vals);
    title ({"3 layer Neural Network decision boundary"});
    hold off;
```

```octave
195  end
196
197  # Plot the cost vs iterations
198  function plotLRCostVsIterations()
199      data=csvread("data.csv");
200
201      X=data(:,1:2);
202      Y=data(:,3);
203      lr=[0.5,1.2,3]
204      col='kbm'
205      for i=1:3
206          [W1,b1,W2,b2,costs]= computeNN(X', Y',4, learningRate=lr(i),
207  numIterations = 10000);
208          iterations = 1000*[0:10];
209          hold on;
210          plot(iterations,costs,color=col(i),"linewidth", 3);
211          hold off;
212          title ("Cost vs no of iterations for different learning rates");
213          xlabel("No of iterations")
214          ylabel("Cost")
215          legend('0.5','1.2','3.0')
216      endfor
217  end
218
219  # Plot the cost vs number of hidden units
220  function plotHiddenCostVsIterations()
221      data=csvread("data1.csv");
222
223      X=data(:,1:2);
224      Y=data(:,3);
225      hidden=[4,9,12]
226      col='kbm'
227      for i=1:3
228          [W1,b1,W2,b2,costs]= computeNN(X', Y',hidden(i), learningRate=1.5,
229  numIterations = 10000);
230          iterations = 1000*[0:10];
231          hold on;
232          plot(iterations,costs,color=col(i),"linewidth", 3);
233          hold off;
234          title ("Cost vs no of iterations for different number of hidden
235  units");
236          xlabel("No of iterations")
237          ylabel("Cost")
238          legend('4','9','12')
239      endfor
240  end
```

4. Appendix 3 - Building a L- Layer Deep Learning Network

3.1 Python

```python
# -*- coding: utf-8 -*-
"""
###########################################################################
################################
#
# File: DLfunctions34.py
# Developer: Tinniam V Ganesh
# Date : 30 Jan 2018
#
###########################################################################
############################
@author: Ganesh
"""

import numpy as np
import matplotlib.pyplot as plt
import matplotlib
import matplotlib.pyplot as plt
from matplotlib import cm


# Conmpute the sigmoid of a vector. Also return Z
def sigmoid(Z):
    A=1/(1+np.exp(-Z))
    cache=Z
    return A,cache

# Conmpute the Relu of a vector
def relu(Z):
    A = np.maximum(0,Z)
    cache=Z
    return A,cache

# Conmpute the tanh of a vector
def tanh(Z):
    A = np.tanh(Z)
    cache=Z
    return A,cache

# Compute the detivative of Relu
# g'(z) = 1 if z >0 and 0 otherwise
def reluDerivative(dA, cache):
```

```python
44      Z = cache
45      dZ = np.array(dA, copy=True) # just converting dz to a correct object.
46      # When z <= 0, you should set dz to 0 as well.
47      dZ[Z <= 0] = 0
48      return dZ
49
50  # Compute the derivative of sigmoid
51  # Derivative g'(z) = a* (1-a)
52  def sigmoidDerivative(dA, cache):
53      Z = cache
54      s = 1/(1+np.exp(-Z))
55      dZ = dA * s * (1-s)
56      return dZ
57
58  # Compute the derivative of tanh
59  # Derivative g'(z) = 1- a^2
60  def tanhDerivative(dA, cache):
61      Z = cache
62      a = np.tanh(Z)
63      dZ = dA * (1 - np.power(a, 2))
64      return dZ
65
66
67  # Initialize the model
68  # Input : number of features
69  #         number of hidden units
70  #         number of units in output
71  # Returns: Weight and bias matrices and vectors
72  def initializeModel(numFeats,numHidden,numOutput):
73      np.random.seed(1)
74      W1=np.random.randn(numHidden,numFeats)*0.01 #  Multiply by .01
75      b1=np.zeros((numHidden,1))
76      W2=np.random.randn(numOutput,numHidden)*0.01
77      b2=np.zeros((numOutput,1))
78
79      # Create a dictionary of the neural network parameters
80      nnParameters={'W1':W1,'b1':b1,'W2':W2,'b2':b2}
81      return(nnParameters)
82
83
84  # Initialize model for L layers
85  # Input : List of units in each layer
86  # Returns: Initial weights and biases matrices for all layers
87  def initializeDeepModel(layerDimensions):
88      np.random.seed(3)
89      # note the Weight matrix at layer 'l' is a matrix of size (l,l-1)
90      # The Bias is a vectors of size (l,1)
91
92      # Loop through the layer dimension from 1.. L. Initialize an empty
93  dictionary
94      layerParams = {}
95      for l in range(1,len(layerDimensions)):
96          # Append to dictionary
97          layerParams['W' + str(l)] =
98  np.random.randn(layerDimensions[l],layerDimensions[l-1])*0.01 #  Multiply by
99  .01
100         layerParams['b' + str(l)] = np.zeros((layerDimensions[l],1))
101
102     return(layerParams)
103
104
105 # Compute the activation at a layer 'l' for forward prop in a Deep Network
106 # Input : A_prec - Activation of previous layer
107 #         W,b - Weight and bias matrices and vectors
```

```python
#            activationFunc - Activation function - sigmoid, tanh, relu etc
# Returns : The Activation of this layer
#       :
# Z = W * X + b
# A = sigmoid(Z), A= Relu(Z), A= tanh(Z)
def layerActivationForward(A_prev, W, b, activationFunc):

    # Compute Z
    Z = np.dot(W,A_prev) + b
    forward_cache = (A_prev, W, b)
    # Compute the activation for sigmoid
    if activationFunc == "sigmoid":
        A, activation_cache = sigmoid(Z)
    # Compute the activation for Relu
    elif activationFunc == "relu":
        A, activation_cache = relu(Z)
    # Compute the activation for tanh
    elif activationFunc == 'tanh':
        A, activation_cache = tanh(Z)
    # Cache the forward-cache and activation_cache
    cache = (forward_cache, activation_cache)
    return A, cache



# Compute the forward propagation for layers 1..L
# Input : X - Input Features
#         paramaters: Weights and biases
#         hiddenActivationFunc - Activation function at hidden layers
Relu/tanh
# Returns : AL
#           caches
# The forward propagtion uses the Relu/tanh activation from layer 1..L-1 and
sigmoid actiovation at layer L
def forwardPropagationDeep(X, parameters,hiddenActivationFunc='relu'):
    caches = []
    # Set A to X (A0)
    A = X
    L = int(len(parameters)/2) # number of layers in the neural network
    # Loop through from layer 1 to upto layer L
    for l in range(1, L):
        A_prev = A
        A, cache = layerActivationForward(A_prev, parameters['W'+str(l)],
parameters['b'+str(l)], activationFunc = hiddenActivationFunc)
        caches.append(cache)

    # Since this is binary classification use the sigmoid activation function
in
    # last layer
    AL, cache = layerActivationForward(A, parameters['W'+str(L)],
parameters['b'+str(L)], activationFunc = "sigmoid")
    caches.append(cache)

    return AL, caches


# Compute the cost
# Input : Activation of last layer
#       : Output from data
# Output: cost
def computeCost(AL,Y):
    m= float(Y.shape[1])
    # Element wise multiply for logprobs
    cost=-1/m *np.sum(Y*np.log(AL) + (1-Y)*(np.log(1-AL)))
```

```python
        cost = np.squeeze(cost)
        return cost

# Compute the backpropoagation for tnrough 1 layer
# Input : Neural Network parameters - dA
#         # cache - forward_cache & activation_cache
#         # Input features
#         # Output values Y
# Returns: Gradients
# dL/dWi= dL/dZi*A1-1
# dl/dbl = dL/dZl
# dL/dZ_prev=dL/dZl*W
def layerActivationBackward(dA, cache, activationFunc):
    forward_cache, activation_cache = cache

    # Compute derivative based on activation function
    if activationFunc == "relu":
        dZ = reluDerivative(dA, activation_cache)
    elif activationFunc == "sigmoid":
        dZ = sigmoidDerivative(dA, activation_cache)
    elif activationFunc == "tanh":
        dZ = tanhDerivative(dA, activation_cache)

    # Compute gradients
    A_prev, W, b = forward_cache
    numtraining = float(A_prev.shape[1])
    dW = 1/numtraining *(np.dot(dZ,A_prev.T))
    db = 1/numtraining * np.sum(dZ, axis=1, keepdims=True)
    dA_prev = np.dot(W.T,dZ)
    return dA_prev, dW, db

# Compute the backpropoagation for 1 cycle, through all layers
# Input : AL: Output of L layer Network - weights
#         # Y  Real output
#         # caches -- list of caches containing:
#         every cache of layerActivationForward() with "relu"/"tanh"
#         #(it's caches[l], for l in range(L-1) i.e l = 0...L-2)
#         #the cache of layerActivationForward() with "sigmoid" (it's caches[L-1])
#         hiddenActivationFunc - Activation function at hidden layers
#
#    Returns:
#     gradients -- A dictionary with the gradients
#                  gradients["dA" + str(l)] = ...
#                  gradients["dW" + str(l)] = ...

def backwardPropagationDeep(AL, Y, caches,hiddenActivationFunc='relu'):
    #initialize the gradients
    gradients = {}

    # Set the number of layers
    L = len(caches)
    m = float(AL.shape[1])
    Y = Y.reshape(AL.shape) # after this line, Y is the same shape as AL

    # Initializing the backpropagation
    # dl/dAL= -(y/a + (1-y)/(1-a)) - At the output layer
    dAL = - (np.divide(Y, AL) - np.divide(1 - Y, 1 - AL))

    # Since this is a binary classification the activation at output is sigmoid
    # Get the gradients at the last layer
    current_cache = caches[L-1]
```

```python
        gradients["dA" + str(L)], gradients["dW" + str(L)], gradients["db" + str(L)] = layerActivationBackward(dAL, current_cache, activationFunc = "sigmoid")

    # Traverse in the reverse direction
    for l in reversed(range(L-1)):
        # Compute the gradients for L-1 to 1 for Relu/tanh
        current_cache = caches[l]
        dA_prev_temp, dW_temp, db_temp = layerActivationBackward(gradients['dA'+str(l+2)], current_cache, activationFunc = hiddenActivationFunc)
        gradients["dA" + str(l + 1)] = dA_prev_temp
        gradients["dW" + str(l + 1)] = dW_temp
        gradients["db" + str(l + 1)] = db_temp


    return gradients

# Perform Gradient Descent
# Input : Weights and biases
#        : gradients
#        : learning rate
#output : Updated weights after 1 iteration
def gradientDescent(parameters, gradients, learningRate):

    L = len(parameters) / 2

    # Update rule for each parameter.
    for l in range(L):
        parameters["W" + str(l+1)] = parameters['W'+str(l+1)] -learningRate*gradients['dW' + str(l+1)]
        parameters["b" + str(l+1)] = parameters['b'+str(l+1)] -learningRate*gradients['db' + str(l+1)]

    return parameters


#  Execute a L layer Deep learning model
# Input : X - Input features
#        : Y output
#        : layersDimensions - Dimension of layers
#        : hiddenActivationFunc - Activation function at hidden layer relu /tanh
#        : learning rate
#        : num of iterations
#output : Updated weights  and biases

def L_Layer_DeepModel(X, Y, layersDimensions, hiddenActivationFunc='relu', learning_rate = .3, num_iterations = 10000, fig="figx.png"):#lr was 0.009

    np.random.seed(1)
    costs = []

    #Initialize paramaters
    parameters = initializeDeepModel(layersDimensions)

    #  Perform gradient descent
    for i in range(0, num_iterations):
        # Perform one cycle of forward propagation
        AL, caches = forwardPropagationDeep(X, parameters,hiddenActivationFunc)

        # Compute cost.
        cost = computeCost(AL, Y)
```

```
            # Compute gradients through 1 cycle of backprop
            gradients = backwardPropagationDeep(AL, Y, caches,hiddenActivationFunc)

            # Update parameters.
            parameters = gradientDescent(parameters, gradients, learning_rate)

            # Store the costs
            if i % 100 == 0:
                print ("Cost after iteration %i: %f" %(i, cost))
            if i % 100 == 0:
                costs.append(cost)

    # plot the cost
    fig1=plt.plot(np.squeeze(costs))
    fig1=plt.ylabel('cost')
    fig1=plt.xlabel('No of iterations(per 100)')
    fig1=plt.title("Learning rate =" + str(learning_rate))
    #plt.show()
    fig1.figure.savefig(fig,bbox_inches='tight')
    plt.clf()

    return parameters


# Plot a decision boundary
# Input : Input Model,
#         X
#         Y
#         sz - Num of hiden units
#         lr - Learning rate
#         Fig to be saved as
# Returns Null
def plot_decision_boundary(model, X, y,lr,fig):
    # Set min and max values and give it some padding
    x_min, x_max = X[0, :].min() - 1, X[0, :].max() + 1
    y_min, y_max = X[1, :].min() - 1, X[1, :].max() + 1
    colors=['black','yellow']
    cmap = matplotlib.colors.ListedColormap(colors)
    h = 0.01
    # Generate a grid of points with distance h between them
    xx, yy = np.meshgrid(np.arange(x_min, x_max, h), np.arange(y_min, y_max, h))
    # Predict the function value for the whole grid
    Z = model(np.c_[xx.ravel(), yy.ravel()])
    Z = Z.reshape(xx.shape)
    # Plot the contour and training examples
    fig2=plt.contourf(xx, yy, Z, cmap="coolwarm")
    fig2=plt.ylabel('x2')
    fig2=plt.xlabel('x1')
    fig2=plt.scatter(X[0, :], X[1, :], c=y, s=7,cmap=cmap)
    fig2=plt.title("Decision Boundary for learning rate:"+lr)
    fig2.figure.savefig(fig, bbox_inches='tight')
    plt.clf()

# Predict the output for given input
# Input : parameters
#       : X
# Output: predictions
def predict(parameters, X):
    A2, cache = forwardPropagationDeep(X, parameters)
    predictions = (A2>0.5)
    return predictions
```

```python
# Predict the probability scores for given data
# Input : parameters
#       : X
# Output: probability of output
def predict_proba(parameters, X):
    A2, cache = forwardPropagationDeep(X, parameters)
    proba=A2
    return proba


# Plot a decision boundary
# Input : Input Model,
#         X
#         Y
#         sz - Num of hiden units
#         lr - Learning rate
#         Fig to be saved as
# Returns Null
def plot_decision_surface(model, X, y,sz,lr,fig):
    # Set min and max values and give it some padding
    x_min, x_max = X[0, :].min() - 1, X[0, :].max() + 1
    y_min, y_max = X[1, :].min() - 1, X[1, :].max() + 1
    z_min, z_max = X[2, :].min() - 1, X[2, :].max() + 1
    colors=['black','gold']
    cmap = matplotlib.colors.ListedColormap(colors)
    h = 3
    # Generate a grid of points with distance h between them
    xx, yy, zz = np.meshgrid(np.arange(x_min, x_max, h), np.arange(y_min, y_max, h), np.arange(z_min, z_max, h))
    # Predict the function value for the whole grid
    a=np.c_[xx.ravel(), yy.ravel(), zz.ravel()]

    Z = predict(parameters,a.T)
    Z = Z.reshape(xx.shape)
    # Plot the contour and training examples
    #plt.contourf(xx, yy, Z, cmap=plt.cm.Spectral)
    ax = plt.axes(projection='3d')
    ax.contour3D(xx, yy, Z, 50, cmap='binary')
    #plt.ylabel('x2')
    #plt.xlabel('x1')
    plt.scatter(X[0, :], X[1, :], c=y, cmap=cmap)
    plt.title("Decision Boundary for hidden layer size:" + sz +" and learning rate:"+lr)
    plt.show()

def plotSurface(X,parameters):

    #xx, yy, zz = np.meshgrid(np.arange(10), np.arange(10), np.arange(10))
    x_min, x_max = X[0, :].min() - 1, X[0, :].max() + 1
    y_min, y_max = X[1, :].min() - 1, X[1, :].max() + 1
    z_min, z_max = X[2, :].min() - 1, X[2, :].max() + 1
    colors=['red']
    cmap = matplotlib.colors.ListedColormap(colors)
    h = 1
    xx, yy, zz = np.meshgrid(np.arange(x_min, x_max, h), np.arange(y_min, y_max, h),
                                  np.arange(z_min, z_max, h))
    # For the meh grid values predict a model
    a=np.c_[xx.ravel(), yy.ravel(), zz.ravel()]
    Z = predict(parameters,a.T)
    r=Z.T
    r1=r.reshape(xx.shape)
    # Find teh values for which the repdiction is 1
```

```
427         xx1=xx[r1]
428         yy1=yy[r1]
429         zz1=zz[r1]
430         # Plot these values
431         ax = plt.axes(projection='3d')
432         #ax.plot_trisurf(xx1, yy1, zz1, cmap='bone', edgecolor='none');
433         ax.scatter3D(xx1, yy1,zz1, c=zz1,s=10,cmap=cmap)
434         #ax.plot_surface(xx1, yy1, zz1, 'gray')
```

3.2 R

```
1  ###########################################################################
2  ###############################
3  #
4  # File    : DLfunctions33.R
5  # Author  : Tinniam V Ganesh
6  # Date    : 30 Jan 2018
7  #
8  ###########################################################################
9  ############################
10 library(ggplot2)
11 library(PRROC)
12 library(dplyr)
13
14 # Compute the sigmoid of a vector
15 sigmoid <- function(Z){
16     A <- 1/(1+ exp(-Z))
17     cache<-Z
18     retvals <- list("A"=A,"Z"=Z)
19     return(retvals)
20
21 }
22
23 # Compute the Relu of a vector
24 relu   <-function(Z){
25     A <- apply(Z, 1:2, function(x) max(0,x))
26     cache<-Z
27     retvals <- list("A"=A,"Z"=Z)
28     return(retvals)
29 }
30
31 # Compute the tanh activation of a vector
32 tanhActivation <- function(Z){
33     A <- tanh(Z)
34     cache<-Z
35     retvals <- list("A"=A,"Z"=Z)
36     return(retvals)
37 }
38
39 # Compute the detivative of Relu
40 # g'(z) = 1 if z >0 and 0 otherwise
41 reluDerivative   <-function(dA, cache){
42     Z <- cache
43     dZ <- dA
44     # Create a logical matrix of values > 0
45     a <- Z > 0
46     # When z <= 0, you should set dz to 0 as well. Perform an element wise
47 multiple
48     dZ <- dZ * a
49     return(dZ)
50 }
```

```r
# Compute the derivative of sigmoid
# Derivative g'(z) = a* (1-a)
sigmoidDerivative   <- function(dA, cache){
    Z <- cache
    s <- 1/(1+exp(-Z))
    dZ <- dA * s * (1-s)
    return(dZ)
}

# Compute the derivative of tanh
# Derivative g'(z) = 1- a^2
tanhDerivative   <- function(dA, cache){
    Z = cache
    a = tanh(Z)
    dZ = dA * (1 - a^2)
    return(dZ)
}

# Initialize model for L layers
# Input : List of units in each layer
# Returns: Initial weights and biases matrices for all layers
initializeDeepModel <- function(layerDimensions){
    set.seed(2)

    # Initialize empty list
    layerParams <- list()

    # Note the Weight matrix at layer 'l' is a matrix of size (l,l-1)
    # The Bias is a vectors of size (l,1)

    # Loop through the layer dimension from 1.. L
    # Indices in R start from 1
    for(l in 2:length(layersDimensions)){
        # Initialize a matrix of small random numbers of size l x l-1
        # Create random numbers of size   l x l-1
        w=rnorm(layersDimensions[l]*layersDimensions[l-1])*0.01

        # Create a weight matrix of size l x l-1 with this initial weights and
        # Add to list W1,W2... WL
        layerParams[[paste('W',l-1,sep="")]] = matrix(w,nrow=layersDimensions[l],
ncol=layersDimensions[l-1])
        layerParams[[paste('b',l-1,sep="")]] = matrix(rep(0,layersDimensions[l]),
nrow=layersDimensions[l],ncol=1)
    }
    return(layerParams)
}


# Compute the activation at a layer 'l' for forward prop in a Deep Network
# Input : A_prec - Activation of previous layer
#         W,b - Weight and bias matrices and vectors
#         activationFunc - Activation function - sigmoid, tanh, relu etc
# Returns(list) : The Activation of this layer
#             :
# Z = W * X + b
# A = sigmoid(Z), A= Relu(Z), A= tanh(Z)
layerActivationForward <- function(A_prev, W, b, activationFunc){
```

```r
115        # Compute Z
116        z = W %*% A_prev
117        # Broadcast the bias 'b' by column
118        Z <-sweep(z,1,b,'+')
119
120        forward_cache <- list("A_prev"=A_prev, "W"=W, "b"=b)
121        # Compute the activation for sigmoid
122        if(activationFunc == "sigmoid"){
123            vals = sigmoid(Z)
124        } else if (activationFunc == "relu"){ # Compute the activation for relu
125            vals = relu(Z)
126        } else if(activationFunc == 'tanh'){ # Compute the activation for tanh
127            vals = tanhActivation(Z)
128        }
129        # Create a list of forward and activation cache
130        cache <- list("forward_cache"=forward_cache,
131 "activation_cache"=vals[['Z']])
132        retvals <- list("A"=vals[['A']],"cache"=cache)
133        return(retvals)
134 }
135
136 # Compute the forward propagation for layers 1..L
137 # Input : X - Input Features
138 #         paramaters: Weights and biases
139 # Returns (list) : AL
140 #         caches
141 # The forward prooagtion uses the Relu/tanh activation from layer 1..L-1 and
142 sigmoid actiovation at layer L
143 forwardPropagationDeep <- function(X,
144 parameters,hiddenActivationFunc='relu'){
145     caches <- list()
146     # Set A to X (A0)
147     A <- X
148     L <- length(parameters)/2 # number of layers in the neural network
149     # Loop through from layer 1 to upto layer L
150     for(l in 1:(L-1)){
151         A_prev <- A
152         # Zi = Wi x Ai-1 + bi   and Ai = g(Zi)
153         # Set W and b for layer 'l'
154         # Loop throug from w1,W2... WL-1
155         W <- parameters[[paste("W",l,sep="")]]
156         b <- parameters[[paste("b",l,sep="")]]
157
158         # Compute the forward propagation through layer 'l' using the
159 activation function
160         actForward <- layerActivationForward(A_prev,
161                                              W,
162                                              b,
163                                              activationFunc =
164 hiddenActivationFunc)
165         A <- actForward[['A']]
166         # Append the cache A_prev,W,b, Z
167         caches[[l]] <-actForward
168     }
169
170     # Since this is binary classification use the sigmoid activation function
171 in
172     # last layer
173     # Set the weights and biases for the last layer
174     W <- parameters[[paste("W",L,sep="")]]
175     b <- parameters[[paste("b",L,sep="")]]
176     # Compute the sigmoid activation
177     actForward = layerActivationForward(A, W, b, activationFunc = "sigmoid")
178     AL <- actForward[['A']]
```

```r
        # Append the output of this forward propagation through the last layer
        caches[[L]] <- actForward
        # Create a list of the final output and the caches
        fwdPropDeep <- list("AL"=AL,"caches"=caches)
        return(fwdPropDeep)

}


# Compute the cost
# Input : Activation of last layer
#         : Output from data
# Output: cost
computeCost <- function(AL,Y){
        # Element wise multiply for logprobs
        m= length(Y)
        cost=-1/m*sum(Y*log(AL) + (1-Y)*log(1-AL))
        #cost=-1/m*sum(a+b)
        return(cost)
}


# Compute the backpropagation through a layer
# Input : Neural Network parameters - dA
#             # cache - forward_cache & activation_cache
#             # Input features
#             # Output values Y
# Returns: Gradients as list
# dL/dWi= dL/dZi*Al-1
# dl/dbl = dL/dZl
# dL/dZ_prev=dL/dZl*W
layerActivationBackward  <- function(dA, cache, activationFunc){
        # Get A_prev,W,b
        forward_cache <-cache[['forward_cache']]
        # Get Z
        activation_cache <- cache[['activation_cache']]
        if(activationFunc == "relu"){
            dZ <- reluDerivative(dA, activation_cache)
        } else if(activationFunc == "sigmoid"){
            dZ <- sigmoidDerivative(dA, activation_cache)
        } else if(activationFunc == "tanh"){
            dZ <- tanhDerivative(dA, activation_cache)
        }
        A_prev <- forward_cache[['A_prev']]
        W <- forward_cache[['W']]
        b <- forward_cache[['b']]
        numtraining = dim(A_prev)[2]
        dW = 1/numtraining * dZ %*% t(A_prev)
        db = 1/numtraining * rowSums(dZ)
        dA_prev = t(W) %*% dZ
        retvals <- list("dA_Prev"=dA_prev,"dW"=dW,"db"=db)
        return(retvals)
}

# Compute the backpropagation for 1 cycle through all layers
# Input : AL: Output of L layer Network - weights
#            # Y  Real output
#            # caches -- list of caches containing:
#            every cache of layerActivationForward() with "relu"/"tanh"
#            #(it's caches[l], for l in range(L-1) i.e l = 0...L-2)
#            #the cache of layerActivationForward() with "sigmoid" (it's caches[L-1])
#            hiddenActivationFunc - Activation function at hidden layers
#
```

```r
#     Returns:
#        gradients -- A list with the gradients
#                     gradients["dA" + str(l)] = ...
#
backwardPropagationDeep <- function(AL, Y,
caches,hiddenActivationFunc='relu'){
    #initialize the gradients
    gradients = list()
    # Set the number of layers
    L = length(caches)
    numTraining = dim(AL)[2]

    # Initializing the backpropagation
    # dl/dAL= -(y/a) - ((1-y)/(1-a)) - At the output layer
    dAL = -( (Y/AL) -(1 - Y)/(1 - AL))

    # Since this is a binary classification the activation at output is
sigmoid
    # Get the gradients at the last layer
    # Inputs: "AL, Y, caches".
    # Outputs: "gradients["dAL"], gradients["dWL"], gradients["dbL"]
    # Start with Layer L
    # Get the current cache
    current_cache = caches[[L]]$cache
    #gradients["dA" + str(L)], gradients["dW" + str(L)], gradients["db" +
str(L)] = layerActivationBackward(dAL, current_cache, activationFunc =
"sigmoid")
    retvals <-  layerActivationBackward(dAL, current_cache, activationFunc =
"sigmoid")
    # Create gradients as lists
    gradients[[paste("dA",L,sep="")]] <- retvals[['dA_Prev']]
    gradients[[paste("dW",L,sep="")]] <- retvals[['dW']]
    gradients[[paste("db",L,sep="")]] <- retvals[['db']]


    # Traverse in the reverse direction
    for(l in (L-1):1){
        # Compute the gradients for L-1 to 1 for Relu/tanh
        # Inputs: "gradients["dA" + str(l + 2)], caches".
        # Outputs: "gradients["dA" + str(l + 1)] , gradients["dW" + str(l +
1)] , gradients["db" + str(l + 1)]
        current_cache = caches[[l]]$cache
        retvals =
layerActivationBackward(gradients[[paste('dA',l+1,sep="")]],
                                        current_cache,
                                        activationFunc =
hiddenActivationFunc)

        gradients[[paste("dA",l,sep="")]] <-retvals[['dA_Prev']]
        gradients[[paste("dW",l,sep="")]] <- retvals[['dW']]
        gradients[[paste("db",l,sep="")]] <- retvals[['db']]
    }

    return(gradients)
}


# Perform Gradient Descent
# Input : Weights and biases
#       : gradients
#       : learning rate
#output : Updated weights after 1 iteration as a list
gradientDescent  <- function(parameters, gradients, learningRate){

```

```r
        L = length(parameters)/2 # number of layers in the neural network

        # Update rule for each parameter. Use a for loop.
        for(l in 1:L){
            parameters[[paste("W",l,sep="")]] = parameters[[paste("W",l,sep="")]]  -
                learningRate* gradients[[paste("dW",l,sep="")]]
            parameters[[paste("b",l,sep="")]] = parameters[[paste("b",l,sep="")]]  -
                learningRate* gradients[[paste("db",l,sep="")]]
        }
        return(parameters)
}


# Execute a L layer Deep learning model
# Input : X - Input features
#       : Y output
#       : layersDimensions - Dimension of layers
#       : hiddenActivationFunc - Activation function at hidden layer relu /tanh
#       : learning rate
#       : num of iterations
#output : Updated weights and biases
L_Layer_DeepModel <- function(X, Y, layersDimensions,
                              hiddenActivationFunc='relu',
                              learningRate = .3,
                              numIterations = 10000, print_cost=False){
    #Initialize costs vector as NULL
    costs <- NULL

    # Parameters initialization.
    parameters = initializeDeepModel(layersDimensions)

    # Loop (gradient descent)
    for( i in 0:numIterations){
        # Forward propagation: [LINEAR -> RELU]*(L-1) -> LINEAR -> SIGMOID.
        retvals = forwardPropagationDeep(X, parameters,hiddenActivationFunc)
        AL <- retvals[['AL']]
        caches <- retvals[['caches']]

        # Compute cost.
        cost <- computeCost(AL, Y)

        # Backward propagation.
        gradients = backwardPropagationDeep(AL, Y, caches,hiddenActivationFunc)

        # Update parameters.
        parameters = gradientDescent(parameters, gradients, learningRate)


        if(i%%1000 == 0){
            costs=c(costs,cost)
            print(cost)
        }
    }

    retvals <- list("parameters"=parameters,"costs"=costs)

    return(retvals)
}

# Predict the output for given input
```

```r
# Input : parameters
#       : X
# Output: predictions
predict <- function(parameters, X,hiddenActivationFunc='relu'){
    
    fwdProp <- forwardPropagationDeep(X, parameters,hiddenActivationFunc)
    predictions <- fwdProp$AL>0.5
    
    return (predictions)
}

# Plot a decision boundary
# This function uses ggplot2
plotDecisionBoundary <- function(z,retvals,hiddenActivationFunc,lr){
    # Find the minimum and maximum for the data
    xmin<-min(z[,1])
    xmax<-max(z[,1])
    ymin<-min(z[,2])
    ymax<-max(z[,2])
    
    # Create a grid of values
    a=seq(xmin,xmax,length=100)
    b=seq(ymin,ymax,length=100)
    grid <- expand.grid(x=a, y=b)
    colnames(grid) <- c('x1', 'x2')
    grid1 <-t(grid)
    # Predict the output for this grid
    q <-predict(retvals$parameters,grid1,hiddenActivationFunc)
    q1 <- t(data.frame(q))
    q2 <- as.numeric(q1)
    grid2 <- cbind(grid,q2)
    colnames(grid2) <- c('x1', 'x2','q2')
    
    z1 <- data.frame(z)
    names(z1) <- c("x1","x2","y")
    atitle=paste("Decision boundary for learning rate:",lr)
    # Plot the contour of the boundary
    ggplot(z1) +
        geom_point(data = z1, aes(x = x1, y = x2, color = y)) +
        stat_contour(data = grid2, aes(x = x1, y = x2, z = q2,color=q2),
alpha = 0.9)+
        ggtitle(atitle)
}

# Predict the probability  scores for given data set
# Input : parameters
#       : X
# Output: probability of output
computeScores <- function(parameters, X,hiddenActivationFunc='relu'){
    
    fwdProp <- forwardPropagationDeep(X, parameters,hiddenActivationFunc)
    scores <- fwdProp$AL
    
    return (scores)
}
```

3.3 Octave

```octave
################################################################################
###############################
#
# File: DLfunctions3.m
# Developer: Tinniam V Ganesh
# Date : 30 Jan 2018
#
################################################################################
#############################
1;
# Define sigmoid function
function [A,cache] = sigmoid(Z)
   A = 1 ./ (1+ exp(-Z));
   cache=Z;
end

# Define Relu function
function [A,cache] = relu(Z)
   A = max(0,Z);
   cache=Z;
end

# Define Relu function
function [A,cache] = tanhAct(Z)
   A = tanh(Z);
   cache=Z;
end

# Define Relu Derivative
function [dZ] = reluDerivative(dA,cache)
   Z = cache;
   dZ = dA;
   # Get elements that are greater than 0
   a = (Z > 0);
   # Select only those elements where Z > 0
   dZ = dZ .* a;
end

# Define Sigmoid Derivative
function [dZ] = sigmoidDerivative(dA,cache)
   Z = cache;
   s = 1 ./ (1+ exp(-Z));
   dZ = dA .* s .* (1-s);
end

# Define Tanh Derivative
function [dZ] = tanhDerivative(dA,cache)
   Z = cache;
   a = tanh(Z);
   dZ = dA .* (1 - a .^ 2);
end

# Initialize the model
# Input : number of features
#         number of hidden units
#         number of units in output
# Returns: Weight and bias matrices and vectors


# Initialize model for L layers
# Input : Vector of units in each layer
# Returns: Initial weights and biases matrices for all layers as a cell array
function [W b] = initializeDeepModel(layerDimensions)
     rand ("seed", 3);
```

```octave
        # note the Weight matrix at layer 'l' is a matrix of size (l,l-1)
        # The Bias is a vectors of size (l,1)

        # Loop through the layer dimension from 1.. L
        # Create cell arrays for Weights and biases

        for l =2:size(layerDimensions)(2)
             W{l-1} = rand(layerDimensions(l),layerDimensions(l-1))*0.01; # Multiply by .01
             b{l-1} = zeros(layerDimensions(l),1);

        endfor
end

# Compute the activation at a layer 'l' for forward prop in a Deep Network
# Input : A_prec - Activation of previous layer
#         W,b - Weight and bias matrices and vectors
#         activationFunc - Activation function - sigmoid, tanh, relu etc
# Returns : A, forward_cache, activation_cache
#         :
# Z = W * X + b
# A = sigmoid(Z), A= Relu(Z), A= tanh(Z)
function [A forward_cache activation_cache] = layerActivationForward(A_prev, W, b, activationFunc)

    # Compute Z
    Z = W * A_prev +b;
    # Create a cell array
    forward_cache = {A_prev  W  b};
    # Compute the activation for sigmoid
    if (strcmp(activationFunc,"sigmoid"))
        [A activation_cache] = sigmoid(Z);
    elseif (strcmp(activationFunc, "relu"))    # Compute the activation for Relu
        [A activation_cache] = relu(Z);
    elseif(strcmp(activationFunc,'tanh'))       # Compute the activation for tanh
        [A activation_cache] = tanhAct(Z);
    endif

end

# Compute the forward propagation for layers 1..L
# Input : X - Input Features
#         paramaters: Weights and biases
#         hiddenActivationFunc - Activation function at hidden layers Relu/tanh
# Returns : AL, forward_caches, activation_caches as a cell array
# The forward propoagtion uses the Relu/tanh activation from layer 1..L-1 and sigmoid actiovation at layer L
function [AL forward_caches activation_caches] = forwardPropagationDeep(X, weights,biases, hiddenActivationFunc='relu')
    # Create an empty cell array
    forward_caches = {};
    activation_caches = {};
    # Set A to X (A0)
    A = X;
    L = length(weights); # number of layers in the neural network
    # Loop through from layer 1 to upto layer L
    for l =1:L-1
        A_prev = A;
        # Zi = Wi x Ai-1 + bi   and Ai = g(Zi)
        W = weights{l};
        b = biases{l};
```

```octave
            [A forward_cache activation_cache] = layerActivationForward(A_prev,
W,b, activationFunc=hiddenActivationFunc);
            forward_caches{l}=forward_cache;
            activation_caches{l} = activation_cache;
        endfor
        # Since this is binary classification use the sigmoid activation function in
        # last layer
        W = weights{L};
        b = biases{L};
        [AL, forward_cache activation_cache] = layerActivationForward(A, W,b,
activationFunc = "sigmoid");
        forward_caches{L}=forward_cache;
        activation_caches{L} = activation_cache;

end

# Compute the cost
# Input : Activation of last layer
#        : Output from data
# Output: cost
function [cost]= computeCost(AL,Y)
    numTraining= size(Y)(2);
    # Element wise multiply for logprobs
    cost = -1/numTraining * sum((Y .* log(AL)) + (1-Y) .* log(1-AL));
end

# Compute the layerActivationBackward
# Input : Neural Network parameters - dA
#         # cache - forward_cache & activation_cache
# Returns: dA_prev, dW, db
# dL/dWi= dL/dZi*Al-1
# dl/dbl = dL/dZl
# dL/dZ_prev=dL/dZl*W
function [dA_prev dW db] =  layerActivationBackward(dA, forward_cache,
activation_cache, activationFunc)

    if (strcmp(activationFunc,"relu"))
        dZ = reluDerivative(dA, activation_cache);
    elseif (strcmp(activationFunc,"sigmoid"))
        dZ = sigmoidDerivative(dA, activation_cache);
    elseif(strcmp(activationFunc, "tanh"))
        dZ = tanhDerivative(dA, activation_cache);
    endif
    A_prev = forward_cache{1};
    W =forward_cache{2};
    b = forward_cache{3};
    numTraining = size(A_prev)(2);
    dW = 1/numTraining * dZ * A_prev';
    db = 1/numTraining * sum(dZ,2);
    dA_prev = W'*dZ;

end


# Compute the backpropoagation for 1 cycle
# Input : AL: Output of L layer Network - weights
#         # Y  Real output
#         # activation_caches
#         # forward_caches
#         every cache of layerActivationForward() with "relu"/"tanh"
#         #(it's caches[l], for l in range(L-1) i.e l = 0...L-2)
#         #the cache of layerActivationForward() with "sigmoid" (it's caches[L-1])
```

```octave
#             hiddenActivationFunc - Activation function at hidden layers
#
#    Returns (cell array): gradsDA,gradsDW, gradsDB
function [gradsDA gradsDW gradsDB]= backwardPropagationDeep(AL, Y,
activation_caches,forward_caches,hiddenActivationFunc='relu')


    # Set the number of layers
    L = length(activation_caches);
    m = size(AL)(2);

    # Initializing the backpropagation
    # dl/dAL= -(y/a + (1-y)/(1-a)) - At the output layer
    dAL = -((Y ./ AL) - (1 - Y) ./ ( 1 - AL));

    # Since this is a binary classification the activation at output is
sigmoid
    # Get the gradients at the last layer
    # Inputs: "AL, Y, caches".
    # Outputs: "gradients["dAL"], gradients["dWL"], gradients["dbL"]
    activation_cache = activation_caches{L};
    forward_cache = forward_caches(L);
    # Note the cell array includes an array of forward caches. To get to this
we need to include the index {1}
    [dA dW db] = layerActivationBackward(dAL, forward_cache{1},
activation_cache, activationFunc = "sigmoid");
    gradsDA{L}= dA;
    gradsDW{L}= dW;
    gradsDB{L}= db;

    # Traverse in the reverse direction
    for l =(L-1):-1:1
        # Compute the gradients for L-1 to 1 for Relu/tanh
        # Inputs: "gradients["dA" + str(l + 2)], caches".
        # Outputs: "gradients["dA" + str(l + 1)] , gradients["dW" + str(l +
1)] , gradients["db" + str(l + 1)]
        activation_cache = activation_caches{l};
        forward_cache = forward_caches(l);

        #dA_prev_temp, dW_temp, db_temp =
layerActivationBackward(gradients['dA'+str(l+1)], current_cache,
activationFunc = "relu")
        # dAl the dervative of the activation of the lth layer,is the first
element
        dAl= gradsDA{l+1};
        [dA_prev_temp, dW_temp, db_temp] = layerActivationBackward(dAl,
forward_cache{1}, activation_cache,  activationFunc = hiddenActivationFunc);
        gradsDA{l}= dA_prev_temp;
        gradsDW{l}= dW_temp;
        gradsDB{l}= db_temp;
    endfor

end


# Perform Gradient Descent
# Input : Weights and biases
#       : gradients
#       : learning rate
#output : Updated weights and biases after 1 iteration
function [weights biases] = gradientDescent(weights, biases,gradsW,gradsB,
learningRate)

    L = size(weights)(2); # number of layers in the neural network
```

```octave
        # Update rule for each parameter.
    for l=1:L
        weights{l} = weights{l} -learningRate* gradsW{l};
        biases{l} = biases{l} -learningRate* gradsB{l};
    endfor
end


#   Execute a L layer Deep learning model
# Input : X - Input features
#         : Y output
#         : layersDimensions - Dimension of layers
#         : hiddenActivationFunc - Activation function at hidden layer relu /tanh
#         : learning rate
#         : num of iterations
#output : Updated weights and biases
function [weights biases costs] = L_Layer_DeepModel(X, Y, layersDimensions, hiddenActivationFunc='relu', learning_rate = .3, num_iterations = 10000)#lr was 0.009

    rand ("seed", 1);
    costs = [] ;

    # Parameters initialization.
    [weights biases] = initializeDeepModel(layersDimensions);

    # Loop (gradient descent)
    for i = 0:num_iterations
        # Forward propagation: [LINEAR -> RELU]*(L-1) -> LINEAR -> SIGMOID.
        [AL forward_caches activation_caches] = forwardPropagationDeep(X, weights, biases,hiddenActivationFunc);

        # Compute cost.
        cost = computeCost(AL, Y);

        # Backward propagation.
        [gradsDA gradsDW gradsDB] = backwardPropagationDeep(AL, Y, activation_caches,forward_caches,hiddenActivationFunc);

        # Update parameters.
        [weights biases] = gradientDescent(weights,biases, gradsDW,gradsDB,learning_rate);


          # Print the cost every 1000 iterations
        if ( mod(i,1000) == 0)
           costs =[costs cost];
           #disp ("Cost after iteration"), disp(i),disp(cost);
           printf("Cost after iteration i=%i cost=%d\n",i,cost);
        endif
     endfor

end

 #Plot cost vs iterations
 function plotCostVsIterations(maxIterations,costs)
     iterations=[0:1000:maxIterations];
     plot(iterations,costs);
     title ("Cost vs no of iterations for different learning rates");
     xlabel("No of iterations");
     ylabel("Cost");
end;
```

```octave
# Compute the predicted value for a given input
# Input : Neural Network parameters
#       : Input data
function [predictions]= predict(weights, biases,
X,hiddenActivationFunc="relu")
    [AL forward_caches activation_caches] = forwardPropagationDeep(X,
weights, biases,hiddenActivationFunc);
    predictions = (AL>0.5);
end

# Plot the decision boundary
function plotDecisionBoundary(data,weights,
biases,hiddenActivationFunc="relu")
    %Plot a non-linear decision boundary learned by the SVM
    colormap ("summer");

    % Make classification predictions over a grid of values
    x1plot = linspace(min(data(:,1)), max(data(:,1)), 400)';
    x2plot = linspace(min(data(:,2)), max(data(:,2)), 400)';
    [X1, X2] = meshgrid(x1plot, x2plot);
    vals = zeros(size(X1));
    # Plot the prediction for the grid
    for i = 1:size(X1, 2)
        gridPoints = [X1(:, i), X2(:, i)];
        vals(:, i)=predict(weights,
biases,gridPoints',hiddenActivationFunc=hiddenActivationFunc);
    endfor

    scatter(data(:,1),data(:,2),8,c=data(:,3),"filled");
    % Plot the boundary
    hold on
    #contour(X1, X2, vals, [0 0], 'LineWidth', 2);
    contour(X1, X2, vals,"linewidth",4);
    title ({"3 layer Neural Network decision boundary"});
    hold off;

end

# Compute scores
function [AL]= scores(weights, biases, X,hiddenActivationFunc="relu")
    [AL forward_caches activation_caches] = forwardPropagationDeep(X,
weights, biases,hiddenActivationFunc);
end
```

5. Appendix 4 - Deep Learning network with the Softmax

4.1 Python

```python
# -*- coding: utf-8 -*-
```

```python
"""
################################################################################
###############################
#
# File: DLfunctions41.py
# Developer: Tinniam V Ganesh
# Date : 26 Feb 2018
#
################################################################################
###############################
@author: Ganesh
"""

import numpy as np
import matplotlib.pyplot as plt
import matplotlib
import matplotlib.pyplot as plt
from matplotlib import cm

# Conmpute the Relu of a vector
def relu(Z):
    A = np.maximum(0,Z)
    cache=Z
    return A,cache

# Conmpute the softmax of a vector
def softmax(Z):
    # get unnormalized probabilities
    exp_scores = np.exp(Z.T)
    # normalize them for each example
    A = exp_scores / np.sum(exp_scores, axis=1, keepdims=True)
    cache=Z
    return A,cache

# Compute the derivative of Relu
def reluDerivative(dA, cache):
    Z = cache
    dZ = np.array(dA, copy=True) # just converting dz to a correct object.
    # When z <= 0, you should set dz to 0 as well.
    dZ[Z <= 0] = 0
    return dZ


# Compute the derivative of softmax
def softmaxDerivative(dA,  cache,y,numTraining):
      # Note : dA not used. dL/dZ = dL/dA * dA/dZ = pi-yi
      Z = cache
      # Compute softmax
      exp_scores = np.exp(Z.T)
      # normalize them for each example
      probs = exp_scores / np.sum(exp_scores, axis=1, keepdims=True)

      # compute the gradient on scores
      dZ = probs
      # dZ = pi- yi
      dZ[range(int(numTraining)),y] -= 1
      return(dZ)


# Initialize the model
# Input : number of features
#         number of hidden units
#         number of units in output
# Returns: Weight and bias matrices and vectors
```

```python
def initializeModel(numFeats,numHidden,numOutput):
    np.random.seed(1)
    W1=np.random.randn(numHidden,numFeats)*0.01 #   Multiply by .01
    b1=np.zeros((numHidden,1))
    W2=np.random.randn(numOutput,numHidden)*0.01
    b2=np.zeros((numOutput,1))

    # Create a dictionary of the neural network parameters
    nnParameters={'W1':W1,'b1':b1,'W2':W2,'b2':b2}
    return(nnParameters)



# Compute the activation at a layer 'l' for forward prop in a Deep Network
# Input : A_prec - Activation of previous layer
#         W,b - Weight and bias matrices and vectors
#         activationFunc - Activation function - sigmoid, tanh, relu etc
# Returns : A, cache
#         :
# Z = W * X + b
# A = sigmoid(Z), A= Relu(Z), A= tanh(Z)
def layerActivationForward(A_prev, W, b, activationFunc):

    # Compute Z
    Z = np.dot(W,A_prev) + b
    forward_cache = (A_prev, W, b)
    # Compute the activation for sigmoid
    if activationFunc == "sigmoid":
        A, activation_cache = sigmoid(Z)
    # Compute the activation for Relu
    elif activationFunc == "relu":
        A, activation_cache = relu(Z)
    # Compute the activation for tanh
    elif activationFunc == 'tanh':
        A, activation_cache = tanh(Z)
    # Compute the activation for softmax
    elif activationFunc == 'softmax':
        A, activation_cache = softmax(Z)
    cache = (forward_cache, activation_cache)
    return A, cache

# Compute the backpropoagation for 1 cycle
# Input : Neural Network parameters - dA
#         # cache - forward_cache & activation_cache
#         # y
#         # activationFunc
# Returns: dA_prev, dW, db
# dL/dWi= dL/dZi*Al-1
# dl/dbl = dL/dZl
# dL/dZ_prev=dL/dZl*W
def layerActivationBackward(dA, cache, y, activationFunc):
    forward_cache, activation_cache = cache
    A_prev, W, b = forward_cache
    numtraining = float(A_prev.shape[1])
    if activationFunc == "relu":
        dZ = reluDerivative(dA, activation_cache)
    elif activationFunc == "sigmoid":
        dZ = sigmoidDerivative(dA, activation_cache)
    elif activationFunc == "tanh":
        dZ = tanhDerivative(dA, activation_cache)
    elif activationFunc == "softmax":
        dZ = softmaxDerivative(dA, activation_cache,y,numtraining)

    if activationFunc == 'softmax':
```

```
                dW = 1/numtraining * np.dot(A_prev,dZ)
                db = np.sum(dZ, axis=0, keepdims=True)
                dA_prev = np.dot(dZ,W)
        else:
            #print(numtraining)
            dW = 1/numtraining *(np.dot(dZ,A_prev.T))
            #print("dW=",dW)
            db = 1/numtraining * np.sum(dZ, axis=1, keepdims=True)
            #print("db=",db)
            dA_prev = np.dot(W.T,dZ)
    return dA_prev, dW, db


# Plot a decision boundary
# Input : Input Model,
#         X
#         Y
#         w1
#         b1
#         w2
#         fig
# Returns Null
def plot_decision_boundary(X, y,W1,b1,W2,b2,fig1):
    #plot_decision_boundary(lambda x: predict(parameters, x.T),
x1,y1.T,str(0.3),"fig2.png")
    h = 0.02
    x_min, x_max = X[:, 0].min() - 1, X[:, 0].max() + 1
    y_min, y_max = X[:, 1].min() - 1, X[:, 1].max() + 1
    xx, yy = np.meshgrid(np.arange(x_min, x_max, h),
                         np.arange(y_min, y_max, h))
    Z = np.dot(np.maximum(0, np.dot(np.c_[xx.ravel(), yy.ravel()], W1.T) +
b1.T), W2.T) + b2.T
    Z = np.argmax(Z, axis=1)
    Z = Z.reshape(xx.shape)

    fig = plt.figure()
    plt.contourf(xx, yy, Z, cmap=plt.cm.Spectral, alpha=0.8)
    plt.scatter(X[:, 0], X[:, 1], c=y, s=40, cmap=plt.cm.Spectral)
    plt.xlim(xx.min(), xx.max())
    plt.ylim(yy.min(), yy.max())
```

4.2 R

```
###########################################################################
###############################
#
# File: DLfunctions41.R
# Developer: Tinniam V Ganesh
# Date : 26 Feb 2018
#
###########################################################################
###############################

# Compute the Relu of a vector
relu    <-function(Z){
    A <- apply(Z, 1:2, function(x) max(0,x))
    cache<-Z
```

```r
15      retvals <- list("A"=A,"Z"=Z)
16      return(retvals)
17 }
18
19 # Compute the softmax of a vector
20 softmax    <- function(Z){
21      # get unnormalized probabilities
22      exp_scores = exp(t(Z))
23      # normalize them for each example
24      A = exp_scores / rowSums(exp_scores)
25      retvals <- list("A"=A,"Z"=Z)
26      return(retvals)
27 }
28
29 # Compute the detivative of Relu
30 reluDerivative    <-function(dA, cache){
31      Z <- cache
32      dZ <- dA
33      # Create a logical matrix of values > 0
34      a <- Z > 0
35      # When z <= 0, you should set dz to 0 as well. Perform an element wise
36 multiple
37      dZ <- dZ * a
38      return(dZ)
39 }
40
41 # Compute the detivative of softmax
42 softmaxDerivative    <- function(dA, cache ,y,numTraining){
43      # Note : dA not used. dL/dZ = dL/dA * dA/dZ = pi-yi
44      Z <- cache
45      # Compute softmax
46      exp_scores = exp(t(Z))
47      # normalize them for each example
48      probs = exp_scores / rowSums(exp_scores)
49      # Get the number of 0, 1 and 2 classes and store in a,b,c
50      a=sum(y==0)
51      b=sum(y==1)
52      c=sum(y==2)
53      # Create a yi matrix based on yi for each class
54      m= matrix(rep(c(1,0,0),a),nrow=a,ncol=3,byrow=T)
55      n= matrix(rep(c(0,1,0),b),nrow=b,ncol=3,byrow=T)
56      o= matrix(rep(c(0,0,1),c),nrow=c,ncol=3,byrow=T)
57      # Stack them vertically
58      yi=rbind(m,n,o)
59
60      dZ = probs-yi
61      return(dZ)
62 }
63
64 # Initialize the model
65 # Input : number of features
66 #         number of hidden units
67 #         number of units in output
68 # Returns: list of Weight and bias matrices and vectors
69 initializeModel <- function(numFeats,numHidden,numOutput){
70      set.seed(2)
71      a<-rnorm(numHidden*numFeats)*0.01 #  Multiply by .01
72      W1 <- matrix(a,nrow=numHidden,ncol=numFeats)
73      a<-rnorm(numHidden*1)
74      b1 <- matrix(a,nrow=numHidden,ncol=1)
75      a<-rnorm(numOutput*numHidden)*0.01
76      W2 <- matrix(a,nrow=numOutput,ncol=numHidden)
77      a<-rnorm(numOutput*1)
78      b2 <- matrix(a,nrow=numOutput,ncol=1)
```

```r
        parameters <- list("W1"=W1,"b1"=b1,"W2"=W2,"b2"=b2)
        return(parameters)

}
# Compute the activation at a layer 'l' for forward prop in a Deep Network
# Input : A_prev - Activation of previous layer
#         W,b - Weight and bias matrices and vectors
#         activationFunc - Activation function - sigmoid, tanh, relu etc
# Returns : A list of  forward_cache, activation_cache, cache
# Z = W * X + b
# A = sigmoid(Z), A= Relu(Z), A= tanh(Z)
layerActivationForward <- function(A_prev, W, b, activationFunc){

    # Compute Z
    z = W %*% A_prev
    Z <-sweep(z,1,b,'+')

    forward_cache <- list("A_prev"=A_prev, "W"=W, "b"=b)
    # Compute the activation for sigmoid
    if(activationFunc == "sigmoid"){
        vals = sigmoid(Z)
    } else if (activationFunc == "relu"){ # Compute the activation for relu
        vals = relu(Z)
    } else if(activationFunc == 'tanh'){ # Compute the activation for tanh
        vals = tanhActivation(Z)
    } else if(activationFunc == 'softmax'){
        vals = softmax(Z)
    }

    cache <- list("forward_cache"=forward_cache,
"activation_cache"=vals[['Z']])
    retvals <- list("A"=vals[['A']],"cache"=cache)
    return(retvals)
}



# Compute the backpropagation for 1 cycle
# Input : Neural Network parameters - dA
#         # cache - forward_cache & activation_cache
#         # y
#         # activationFunc
# Returns: Gradients - a list of dA_prev, dW, db
# dL/dWi= dL/dZi*Al-1
# dl/dbl = dL/dZl
# dL/dZ_prev=dL/dZl*W
layerActivationBackward  <- function(dA, cache, y, activationFunc){
    # Get A_prev,w,b
    forward_cache <-cache[['forward_cache']]
    activation_cache <- cache[['activation_cache']]
    A_prev <- forward_cache[['A_prev']]
    numtraining = dim(A_prev)[2]
    # Get Z

    if(activationFunc == "relu"){
        dZ <- reluDerivative(dA, activation_cache)
    } else if(activationFunc == "sigmoid"){
        dZ <- sigmoidDerivative(dA, activation_cache)
    } else if(activationFunc == "tanh"){
        dZ <- tanhDerivative(dA, activation_cache)
    } else if(activationFunc == "softmax"){
        dZ <- softmaxDerivative(dA,  activation_cache,y,numtraining)
    }
```

```r
        # Check if softmax
        if (activationFunc == 'softmax'){
            W <- forward_cache[['W']]
            b <- forward_cache[['b']]
            dW = 1/numtraining * A_prev%*%dZ
            db = 1/numtraining* matrix(colSums(dZ),nrow=1,ncol=3)
            dA_prev = dZ %*%W
        } else {
            W <- forward_cache[['W']]
            b <- forward_cache[['b']]
            numtraining = dim(A_prev)[2]
            dW = 1/numtraining * dZ %*% t(A_prev)
            db = 1/numtraining * rowSums(dZ)
            dA_prev = t(W) %*% dZ
        }
        retvals <- list("dA_prev"=dA_prev,"dW"=dW,"db"=db)
        return(retvals)
}



# Plot a decision boundary for Softmax output activation
# This function uses ggplot2
plotDecisionBoundary <- function(Z,w1,b1,w2,b2){
    xmin<-min(Z[,1])
    xmax<-max(Z[,1])
    ymin<-min(Z[,2])
    ymax<-max(Z[,2])

    # Create a grid of points
    a=seq(xmin,xmax,length=100)
    b=seq(ymin,ymax,length=100)
    grid <- expand.grid(x=a, y=b)
    colnames(grid) <- c('x1', 'x2')
    grid1 <-t(grid)


    # Predict the output based on the grid of points
    retvals <- layerActivationForward(grid1,w1,b1,'relu')
    A1 <- retvals[['A']]
    cache1 <- retvals[['cache']]
    forward_cache1 <- cache1[['forward_cache1']]
    activation_cache <- cache1[['activation_cache']]

    retvals = layerActivationForward(A1,w2,b2,'softmax')
    A2 <- retvals[['A']]
    cache2 <- retvals[['cache']]
    forward_cache2 <- cache2[['forward_cache1']]
    activation_cache2 <- cache2[['activation_cache']]

    # From the  softmax probabilities pick the one with the highest probability
    q= apply(A2,1,which.max)

    q1 <- t(data.frame(q))
    q2 <- as.numeric(q1)
    grid2 <- cbind(grid,q2)
    colnames(grid2) <- c('x1', 'x2','q2')

    z1 <- data.frame(Z)
    names(z1) <- c("x1","x2","y")
    atitle=paste("Decision boundary")
    ggplot(z1) +
```

```r
            geom_point(data = z1, aes(x = x1, y = x2, color = y)) +
            stat_contour(data = grid2, aes(x = x1, y = x2, z = q2,color=q2), alpha = 0.9)+
            ggtitle(atitle) + scale_colour_gradientn(colours = brewer.pal(10, "Spectral"))
}

# Predict the output
computeScores <- function(parameters, X,hiddenActivationFunc='relu'){
    
    fwdProp <- forwardPropagationDeep(X, parameters,hiddenActivationFunc)
    scores <- fwdProp$AL
    
    return (scores)
}
```

4.3 Octave

```octave
###############################################################################
##############################
#
# File: DLfunctions41.m
# Developer: Tinniam V Ganesh
# Date : 26 Feb 2018
#
###############################################################################
##############################
1;

# Define Relu function
function [A,cache] = relu(Z)
  A = max(0,Z);
  cache=Z;
end


# Define Softmax function
function [A,cache] = softmax(Z)
    # get unnormalized probabilities
    exp_scores = exp(Z');
    # normalize them for each example
    A = exp_scores ./ sum(exp_scores,2);
    cache=Z;
end

# Define Relu Derivative
function [dZ] = reluDerivative(dA,cache)
  Z = cache;
  dZ = dA;
  # Get elements that are greater than 0
  a = (Z > 0);
  # Select only those elements where Z > 0
  dZ = dZ .* a;
end


# Define Softmax Derivative
function [dZ] = softmaxDerivative(dA,cache,Y)
```

```octave
    Z = cache;
    # get unnormalized probabilities
    exp_scores = exp(Z');
    # normalize them for each example
    probs = exp_scores ./ sum(exp_scores,2);

    # dZ = pi- yi
    a=sum(Y==0);
    b=sum(Y==1);
    c=sum(Y==2);
    m= repmat([1 0 0],a,1);
    n= repmat([0 1 0],b,1);
    o= repmat([0 0 1],c,1);
    yi=[m;n;o];
    dZ=probs-yi;

end

# Initialize the model
# Input : number of features
#         number of hidden units
#         number of units in output
# Returns: Weight and bias matrices and vectors
function [W1 b1 W2 b2] = initializeModel(numFeats,numHidden,numOutput)
    rand ("seed", 3);
    W1=rand(numHidden,numFeats)*0.01; #  Multiply by .01
    b1=zeros(numHidden,1);
    W2=rand(numOutput,numHidden)*0.01;
    b2=zeros(numOutput,1);
 end



# Compute the activation at a layer 'l' for forward prop in a Deep Network
# Input : A_prev - Activation of previous layer
#         W,b - Weight and bias matrices and vectors
#         activationFunc - Activation function - sigmoid, tanh, relu etc
# Returns : A, forward_cache, activation_cache
# Z = W * X + b
# A = sigmoid(Z), A= Relu(Z), A= tanh(Z)
function [A forward_cache activation_cache] = layerActivationForward(A_prev,
W, b, activationFunc)

    # Compute Z
    Z = W * A_prev +b;
    # Create a cell array
    forward_cache = {A_prev  W  b};
    # Compute the activation for sigmoid
    if (strcmp(activationFunc,"sigmoid"))
        [A activation_cache] = sigmoid(Z);
    elseif (strcmp(activationFunc, "relu"))   # Compute the activation for Relu
        [A activation_cache] = relu(Z);
    elseif(strcmp(activationFunc,'tanh'))      # Compute the activation for tanh
        [A activation_cache] = tanhAct(Z);
     elseif(strcmp(activationFunc,'softmax'))       # Compute the activation for softmax
        [A activation_cache] = softmax(Z);

    endif

end
```

```octave
# Compute the backpropoagation for 1 cycle
# Input : Neural Network parameters - dA
#          # cache - forward_cache & activation_cache
#          # Input features
#          # Output values Y
# Returns: dA_prev, dW, db
# dL/dWi= dL/dZi*Al-1
# dl/dbl = dL/dZl
# dL/dZ_prev=dL/dZl*W
function [dA_prev dW db] =  layerActivationBackward(dA, forward_cache,
activation_cache, Y, activationFunc)

    if (strcmp(activationFunc,"relu"))
        dZ = reluDerivative(dA, activation_cache);
    elseif (strcmp(activationFunc,"sigmoid"))
        dZ = sigmoidDerivative(dA, activation_cache);
    elseif(strcmp(activationFunc, "tanh"))
        dZ = tanhDerivative(dA, activation_cache);
    elseif(strcmp(activationFunc, "softmax"))
        dZ = softmaxDerivative(dA, activation_cache,Y);
    endif
    A_prev = forward_cache{1};
    numTraining = size(A_prev)(2);

    # If activation is softmax
    if(strcmp(activationFunc, "softmax"))
      W =forward_cache{2};
      b = forward_cache{3};
      dW = 1/numTraining * A_prev * dZ;
      db = 1/numTraining * sum(dZ,1);
      dA_prev = dZ*W;
    else
      W =forward_cache{2};
      b = forward_cache{3};
      dW = 1/numTraining * dZ * A_prev';
      db = 1/numTraining * sum(dZ,2);
      dA_prev = W'*dZ;
    endif
end

 # Plot cost vs iterations
 function plotCostVsIterations(iterations,costs)

    plot(iterations,costs);
    title ("Cost vs no of iterations for different learning rates");
    xlabel("No of iterations");
    ylabel("Cost");
    print -dpng "figo2.png"
end;

# Plot softmax decision boundary
function plotDecisionBoundary( X,Y,W1,b1,W2,b2)
    % Make classification predictions over a grid of values
    x1plot = linspace(min(X(:,1)), max(X(:,1)), 400)';
    x2plot = linspace(min(X(:,2)), max(X(:,2)), 400)';
    [X1, X2] = meshgrid(x1plot, x2plot);
    vals = zeros(size(X1));

    for i = 1:size(X1, 2)
            gridPoints = [X1(:, i), X2(:, i)];
            [A1,cache1 activation_cache1]=
layerActivationForward(gridPoints',W1,b1,activationFunc ='relu');
```

```
170            [A2,cache2 activation_cache2] =
171 layerActivationForward(A1,w2,b2,activationFunc='softmax');
172            [l m] = max(A2, [ ], 2);
173            vals(:, i)= m;
174     endfor
175
176     scatter(X(:,1),X(:,2),8,c=Y,"filled");
177     % Plot the boundary
178     hold on
179     contour(X1, X2, vals,"linewidth",4);
180     print -dpng "fig-o1.png"
181 end
```

6. Appendix 5 - MNIST classification with Softmax

5.1 Python

```python
# -*- coding: utf-8 -*-
"""
###########################################################################
###############################
#
# File: DLfunctions41.py
# Developer: Tinniam V Ganesh
# Date : 23 Mar 2018
#
###########################################################################
###############################
@author: Ganesh
"""

import numpy as np
import matplotlib.pyplot as plt
import matplotlib
import matplotlib.pyplot as plt
from matplotlib import cm
import math

# Conmpute the sigmoid of a vector
def sigmoid(Z):
    A=1/(1+np.exp(-Z))
    cache=Z
    return A,cache

# Conmpute the Relu of a vector
def relu(Z):
    A = np.maximum(0,Z)
    cache=Z
    return A,cache

# Conmpute the tanh of a vector
def tanh(Z):
    A = np.tanh(Z)
    cache=Z
    return A,cache

# Conmpute the softmax of a vector
def softmax(Z):
    # get unnormalized probabilities
    exp_scores = np.exp(Z.T)
    # normalize them for each example
    A = exp_scores / np.sum(exp_scores, axis=1, keepdims=True)
    cache=Z
    return A,cache

# Conmpute the Stable Softmax of a vector
def stableSoftmax(Z):
    #Compute the softmax of vector x in a numerically stable way.
    shiftZ = Z.T - np.max(Z.T,axis=1).reshape(-1,1)
    exp_scores = np.exp(shiftZ)

    # normalize them for each example
    A = exp_scores / np.sum(exp_scores, axis=1, keepdims=True)
    cache=Z
    return A,cache

# Compute the derivative of Relu
def reluDerivative(dA, cache):

    Z = cache
    dZ = np.array(dA, copy=True) # just converting dz to a correct object.
```

```python
        # When z <= 0, you should set dz to 0 as well.
        dZ[Z <= 0] = 0
        return dZ

# Compute the derivative of Sigmoid
def sigmoidDerivative(dA, cache):
    Z = cache
    s = 1/(1+np.exp(-Z))
    dZ = dA * s * (1-s)
    return dZ

# Compute the derivative of tanh
def tanhDerivative(dA, cache):
    Z = cache
    a = np.tanh(Z)
    dZ = dA * (1 - np.power(a, 2))
    return dZ

# Compute the derivative of Softmax
def softmaxDerivative(dA, cache,y,numTraining):
        # Note : dA not used. dL/dZ = dL/dA * dA/dZ = pi-yi
        Z = cache
        # Compute softmax
        exp_scores = np.exp(Z.T)
        # normalize them for each example
        probs = exp_scores / np.sum(exp_scores, axis=1, keepdims=True)

        # compute the gradient on scores
        dZ = probs

        # dZ = pi- yi
        dZ[range(int(numTraining)),y[:,0]] -= 1
        return(dZ)

# Compute the derivative of Stable Softmax
def stableSoftmaxDerivative(dA, cache,y,numTraining):
        # Note : dA not used. dL/dZ = dL/dA * dA/dZ = pi-yi
        Z = cache
        # Compute stable softmax
        shiftZ = Z.T - np.max(Z.T,axis=1).reshape(-1,1)
        exp_scores = np.exp(shiftZ)
        # normalize them for each example
        probs = exp_scores / np.sum(exp_scores, axis=1, keepdims=True)
        #print(probs)
        # compute the gradient on scores
        dZ = probs

        # dZ = pi- yi
        dZ[range(int(numTraining)),y[:,0]] -= 1
        return(dZ)


# Initialize the model
# Input : number of features
#         number of hidden units
#         number of units in output
# Returns: nnParameters dict
def initializeModel(numFeats,numHidden,numOutput):
    np.random.seed(1)
    W1=np.random.randn(numHidden,numFeats)*0.01 #  Multiply by .01
    b1=np.zeros((numHidden,1))
    W2=np.random.randn(numOutput,numHidden)*0.01
    b2=np.zeros((numOutput,1))

```

```python
        # Create a dictionary of the neural network parameters
        nnParameters={'W1':W1,'b1':b1,'W2':W2,'b2':b2}
        return(nnParameters)


# Initialize model for L layers
# Input : List of units in each layer
# Returns: Z, cache
def initializeDeepModel(layerDimensions):
    np.random.seed(3)
    # note the Weight matrix at layer 'l' is a matrix of size (l,l-1)
    # The Bias is a vectors of size (l,1)

    # Loop through the layer dimension from 1.. L
    layerParams = {}
    for l in range(1,len(layerDimensions)):
        layerParams['W' + str(l)] = np.random.randn(layerDimensions[l],layerDimensions[l-1])*0.01 #  Multiply by .01
        layerParams['b' + str(l)] = np.zeros((layerDimensions[l],1))

    return(layerParams)
return Z, cache

# Compute the activation at a layer 'l' for forward prop in a Deep Network
# Input : A_prev - Activation of previous layer
#         W,b - Weight and bias matrices and vectors
#         activationFunc - Activation function - sigmoid, tanh, relu etc
# Returns : A, cache
#         :
# Z = W * X + b
# A = sigmoid(Z), A= Relu(Z), A= tanh(Z)
def layerActivationForward(A_prev, W, b, activationFunc):

    # Compute Z
    Z = np.dot(W,A_prev) + b
    forward_cache = (A_prev, W, b)
    # Compute the activation for sigmoid
    if activationFunc == "sigmoid":
        A, activation_cache = sigmoid(Z)
    # Compute the activation for Relu
    elif activationFunc == "relu":
        A, activation_cache = relu(Z)
    # Compute the activation for tanh
    elif activationFunc == 'tanh':
        A, activation_cache = tanh(Z)
    elif activationFunc == 'softmax':
        A, activation_cache = stableSoftmax(Z)

    cache = (forward_cache, activation_cache)
    return A, cache

# Compute the forward propagation for layers 1..L
# Input : X - Input Features
#         paramaters: Weights and biases
#         hiddenActivationFunc - Activation function at hidden layers Relu/tanh
#         outputActivationFunc - Activation function at output - sigmoid/softmax
# Returns : AL
#           caches
# The forward propoagtion uses the Relu/tanh activation from layer 1..L-1 and sigmoid actiovation at layer L
```

```python
def forwardPropagationDeep(X,
parameters,hiddenActivationFunc='relu',outputActivationFunc='sigmoid'):
    caches = []
    # Set A to X (A0)
    A = X
    L = int(len(parameters)/2) # number of layers in the neural network
    # Loop through from layer 1 to upto layer L
    for l in range(1, L):
        A_prev = A
        # Zi = Wi x Ai-1 + bi   and Ai = g(Zi)
        #A, cache = layerActivationForward(A_prev, parameters['W'+str(l)],
parameters['b'+str(l)], activationFunc = "relu")
        A, cache = layerActivationForward(A_prev, parameters['W'+str(l)],
parameters['b'+str(l)], activationFunc = hiddenActivationFunc)
        caches.append(cache)
        #print("l=",l)
        #print(A)

    # Since this is binary classification use the sigmoid activation function in
    # last layer
    AL, cache = layerActivationForward(A, parameters['W'+str(L)],
parameters['b'+str(L)], activationFunc = outputActivationFunc)
    caches.append(cache)

    return AL, caches


# Compute the cost
# Input : AL-Activation of last layer
#       : Y
#       :outputActivationFunc - Activation function at output -
sigmoid/softmax
# Output: cost
def computeCost(AL,Y,outputActivationFunc="sigmoid"):

    if outputActivationFunc=="sigmoid":
        m= float(Y.shape[1])
        # Element wise multiply for logprobs
        cost=-1/m *np.sum(Y*np.log(AL) + (1-Y)*(np.log(1-AL)))
        cost = np.squeeze(cost)
    elif outputActivationFunc=="softmax":
        # Note:Take transpose of Y for softmax
        Y=Y.T
        m= float(len(Y))
        # Compute log probs. Take the log prob of correct class based on
output y
        correct_logprobs = -np.log(AL[range(int(m)),Y.T])
        # Conpute loss
        cost = np.sum(correct_logprobs)/m
    return cost

# Compute the backpropoagation for 1 cycle
# Input : Neural Network parameters - dA
#         # cache - forward_cache & activation_cache
#         # Y
#         # activationFunc # relu, tanh, sigmoid,softmax
# Returns: dA_prev, dW, db
# dL/dWi= dL/dZi*Ai-1
# dl/dbl = dL/dZl
# dL/dZ_prev=dL/dZl*W
def layerActivationBackward(dA, cache, Y, activationFunc):
    forward_cache, activation_cache = cache
    A_prev, W, b = forward_cache
```

```python
        numtraining = float(A_prev.shape[1])
        #print("n=",numtraining)
        #print("no=",numtraining)
        if activationFunc == "relu":
            dZ = reluDerivative(dA, activation_cache)
        elif activationFunc == "sigmoid":
            dZ = sigmoidDerivative(dA, activation_cache)
        elif activationFunc == "tanh":
            dZ = tanhDerivative(dA, activation_cache)
        elif activationFunc == "softmax":
            dZ = stableSoftmaxDerivative(dA, activation_cache,Y,numtraining)

        if activationFunc == 'softmax':
            dW = 1/numtraining * np.dot(A_prev,dZ)
            db = 1/numtraining * np.sum(dZ, axis=0, keepdims=True)
            dA_prev = np.dot(dZ,W)
        else:
            #print(numtraining)
            dW = 1/numtraining *(np.dot(dZ,A_prev.T))
            #print("dW=",dW)
            db = 1/numtraining * np.sum(dZ, axis=1, keepdims=True)
            #print("db=",db)
            dA_prev = np.dot(W.T,dZ)


    return dA_prev, dW, db

# Compute the backpropoagation for 1 cycle
# Input : AL: Output of L layer Network - weights
#         # Y  Real output
#         # caches -- list of caches containing:
#         every cache of layerActivationForward() with "relu"/"tanh"
#         #(it's caches[l], for l in range(L-1) i.e l = 0...L-2)
#         #the cache of layerActivationForward() with "sigmoid" (it's caches[L-1])
#         hiddenActivationFunc - Activation function at hidden layers - relu/sigmoid/tanh
#         outputActivationFunc - Activation function at output - sigmoid/softmax
#
#    Returns:
#      gradients -- A dictionary with the gradients
#                   gradients["dA" + str(l)] = ...
#                   gradients["dW" + str(l)] = ...
#                   gradients["db" + str(l)]
def backwardPropagationDeep(AL, Y, caches,hiddenActivationFunc='relu',outputActivationFunc="sigmoid"):
    #initialize the gradients
    gradients = {}
    # Set the number of layers
    L = len(caches)
    m = float(AL.shape[1])

    if outputActivationFunc == "sigmoid":
        Y = Y.reshape(AL.shape) # after this line, Y is the same shape as AL
        # Initializing the backpropagation
        # dl/dAL= -(y/a + (1-y)/(1-a)) - At the output layer
        dAL = - (np.divide(Y, AL) - np.divide(1 - Y, 1 - AL))
    else:
        dAL =0
        Y=Y.T


    # Since this is a binary classification the activation at output is sigmoid
```

```python
        # Get the gradients at the last layer
        # Inputs: "AL, Y, caches".
        # Outputs: "gradients["dAL"], gradients["dWL"], gradients["dbL"]
        current_cache = caches[L-1]
        gradients["dA" + str(L)], gradients["dW" + str(L)], gradients["db" + str(L)] = layerActivationBackward(dAL, current_cache, Y, activationFunc = outputActivationFunc)

        # Note dA for softmax is the transpose
        if outputActivationFunc == "softmax":
            gradients["dA" + str(L)] = gradients["dA" + str(L)].T
        # Traverse in the reverse direction
        for l in reversed(range(L-1)):
            # Compute the gradients for L-1 to 1 for Relu/tanh
            # Inputs: "gradients["dA" + str(l + 2)], caches".
            # Outputs: "gradients["dA" + str(l + 1)] , gradients["dW" + str(l + 1)] , gradients["db" + str(l + 1)]
            current_cache = caches[l]

            #dA_prev_temp, dW_temp, db_temp = layerActivationBackward(gradients['dA'+str(l+2)], current_cache, activationFunc = "relu")
            dA_prev_temp, dW_temp, db_temp = layerActivationBackward(gradients['dA'+str(l+2)], current_cache, Y, activationFunc = hiddenActivationFunc)
            gradients["dA" + str(l + 1)] = dA_prev_temp
            gradients["dW" + str(l + 1)] = dW_temp
            gradients["db" + str(l + 1)] = db_temp


    return gradients

# Perform Gradient Descent
# Input : Weights and biases
#       : gradients
#       : learning rate
#       : outputActivationFunc - Activation function at output - sigmoid/softmax
#return : parameters
def gradientDescent(parameters, gradients, learningRate,outputActivationFunc="sigmoid"):

    L = int(len(parameters) / 2)
    # Update rule for each parameter.
    for l in range(L-1):
        parameters["W" + str(l+1)] = parameters['W'+str(l+1)] -learningRate* gradients['dW' + str(l+1)]
        parameters["b" + str(l+1)] = parameters['b'+str(l+1)] -learningRate* gradients['db' + str(l+1)]

    if outputActivationFunc=="sigmoid":
        parameters["W" + str(L)] = parameters['W'+str(L)] -learningRate* gradients['dW' + str(L)]
        parameters["b" + str(L)] = parameters['b'+str(L)] -learningRate* gradients['db' + str(L)]
    elif outputActivationFunc=="softmax":
        parameters["W" + str(L)] = parameters['W'+str(L)] -learningRate* gradients['dW' + str(L)].T
        parameters["b" + str(L)] = parameters['b'+str(L)] -learningRate* gradients['db' + str(L)].T


    return parameters
```

```python
#   Execute a L layer Deep learning model
# Input : X1 - Input features
#         : Y1 output
#         : layersDimensions - Dimension of layers
#         : hiddenActivationFunc - Activation function at hidden layer relu /tanh/sigmoid
#         : outputActivationFunc - sigmoid/softmax
#         : learning rate
#         : num of iteration
# output : parameters

def L_Layer_DeepModel(X1, Y1, layersDimensions, hiddenActivationFunc='relu',
outputActivationFunc="sigmoid", learningRate = .3, num_iterations = 10000,
print_cost=False):#lr was 0.009

    np.random.seed(1)
    costs = []

    # Parameters initialization.
    parameters = initializeDeepModel(layersDimensions)

    # Loop (gradient descent)
    for i in range(0, num_iterations):
        # Forward propagation: [LINEAR -> RELU]*(L-1) -> LINEAR -> SIGMOID.
        #AL, caches = forwardPropagationDeep(X, parameters,hiddenActivationFunc)

        # Compute cost.
        #cost = computeCost(AL, Y)

        # Backward propagation.
        #gradients = backwardPropagationDeep(AL, Y, caches,hiddenActivationFunc)

        ## Update parameters.
        #parameters = gradientDescent(parameters, gradients, learning_rate)

        AL, caches = forwardPropagationDeep(X1,
parameters,hiddenActivationFunc="relu",outputActivationFunc=outputActivationFunc)

        # Compute cost
        cost = computeCost(AL, Y1,outputActivationFunc=outputActivationFunc)
        #print("Y1=",Y1.shape)
        # Backward propagation.
        gradients = backwardPropagationDeep(AL, Y1,
caches,hiddenActivationFunc="relu",outputActivationFunc=outputActivationFunc)

        # Update parameters.
        parameters = gradientDescent(parameters, gradients,
learningRate=learningRate,outputActivationFunc=outputActivationFunc)


        # Print the cost every 100 training example
        if print_cost and i % 1000 == 0:
            print ("Cost after iteration %i: %f" %(i, cost))
        if print_cost and i % 1000 == 0:
            costs.append(cost)

    # plot the cost
    plt.plot(np.squeeze(costs))
    plt.ylabel('cost')
    plt.xlabel('No of iterations (x100)')
```

```python
            plt.title("Learning rate =" + str(learningRate))
        #plt.show()
        plt.savefig("fig1",bbox_inches='tight')

    return parameters

#  Execute a L layer Deep learning model Stoachastic Gradient Descent
# Input : X1 - Input features
#         : Y1- output
#         : layersDimensions - Dimension of layers
#         : hiddenActivationFunc - Activation function at hidden layer relu
/tanh/sigmoid
#         : outputActivationFunc - Activation function at output -
sigmoid/softmax
#         : learning rate
#         : mini_batch_size
#         : num_epochs
#output : parameters
def L_Layer_DeepModel_SGD(X1, Y1, layersDimensions,
hiddenActivationFunc='relu', outputActivationFunc="sigmoid",learningRate =
.3, mini_batch_size = 64, num_epochs = 2500, print_cost=False):#lr was 0.009

    np.random.seed(1)
    costs = []

    # Parameters initialization.
    parameters = initializeDeepModel(layersDimensions)
    seed=10
   # Loop for number of epochs
    for i in range(num_epochs):
         # Define the random minibatches. We increment the seed to reshuffle
differently the dataset after each epoch
        seed = seed + 1
        minibatches = random_mini_batches(X1, Y1, mini_batch_size, seed)

        batch=0
        # Loop through each mini batch
        for minibatch in minibatches:
            #print("batch=",batch)
            batch=batch+1
            # Select a minibatch
            (minibatch_X, minibatch_Y) = minibatch

            # Perfrom forward propagation
            AL, caches = forwardPropagationDeep(minibatch_X,
parameters,hiddenActivationFunc="relu",outputActivationFunc=outputActivationF
unc)

            # Compute cost
            cost = computeCost(AL,
minibatch_Y,outputActivationFunc=outputActivationFunc)
            #print("minibatch_Y=",minibatch_Y.shape)
            # Backward propagation.
            gradients = backwardPropagationDeep(AL, minibatch_Y,
caches,hiddenActivationFunc="relu",outputActivationFunc=outputActivationFunc)

            # Update parameters.
            parameters = gradientDescent(parameters, gradients,
learningRate=learningRate,outputActivationFunc=outputActivationFunc)

        # Print the cost every 1000 epoch
        if print_cost and i % 100 == 0:
            print ("Cost after epoch %i: %f" %(i, cost))
        if print_cost and i % 100 == 0:
```

```python
            costs.append(cost)

        # plot the cost
    plt.plot(np.squeeze(costs))
    plt.ylabel('cost')
    plt.xlabel('No of iterations')
    plt.title("Learning rate =" + str(learningRate))
        #plt.show()
    plt.savefig("fig1",bbox_inches='tight')

    return parameters


# Create random mini batches
# Input : X - Input features
#       : Y- output
#       : miniBatchSizes
#       : seed
#output : mini_batches
def random_mini_batches(X, Y, miniBatchSize = 64, seed = 0):

    np.random.seed(seed)
    # Get number of training samples
    m = X.shape[1]
    # Initialize mini batches
    mini_batches = []

    # Create  a list of random numbers < m
    permutation = list(np.random.permutation(m))
    # Randomly shuffle the training data
    shuffled_X = X[:, permutation]
    shuffled_Y = Y[:, permutation].reshape((1,m))

    # Compute number of mini batches
    numCompleteMinibatches = math.floor(m/miniBatchSize)

   # For the number of mini batches
    for k in range(0, numCompleteMinibatches):

        # Set the start and end of each mini batch
        mini_batch_X = shuffled_X[:, k*miniBatchSize : (k+1) * miniBatchSize]
        mini_batch_Y = shuffled_Y[:, k*miniBatchSize : (k+1) * miniBatchSize]

        mini_batch = (mini_batch_X, mini_batch_Y)
        mini_batches.append(mini_batch)


    #if m % miniBatchSize != 0:. The batch does not evenly divide by the mini batch
    if m % miniBatchSize != 0:
        l=math.floor(m/miniBatchSize)*miniBatchSize
        # Set the start and end of last mini batch
        m=l+m % miniBatchSize
        mini_batch_X = shuffled_X[:,l:m]
        mini_batch_Y = shuffled_Y[:,l:m]

        mini_batch = (mini_batch_X, mini_batch_Y)
        mini_batches.append(mini_batch)

    return mini_batches

# Plot a decision boundary
# Input : Input Model,
#          X
```

```python
#              Y
#              lr - Learning rate
#              Fig to be saved as
# Returns Null
def plot_decision_boundary(model, X, y,lr,fig):
    # Set min and max values and give it some padding
    x_min, x_max = X[0, :].min() - 1, X[0, :].max() + 1
    y_min, y_max = X[1, :].min() - 1, X[1, :].max() + 1
    colors=['black','yellow']
    cmap = matplotlib.colors.ListedColormap(colors)
    h = 0.01
    # Generate a grid of points with distance h between them
    xx, yy = np.meshgrid(np.arange(x_min, x_max, h), np.arange(y_min, y_max, h))
    # Predict the function value for the whole grid
    Z = model(np.c_[xx.ravel(), yy.ravel()])
    Z = Z.reshape(xx.shape)
    # Plot the contour and training examples
    plt.contourf(xx, yy, Z, cmap="coolwarm")
    plt.ylabel('x2')
    plt.xlabel('x1')
    plt.scatter(X[0, :], X[1, :], c=y, s=7,cmap=cmap)
    plt.title("Decision Boundary for learning rate:"+lr)
    #plt.show()
    plt.savefig(fig, bbox_inches='tight')

def predict(parameters, X):
    A2, cache = forwardPropagationDeep(X, parameters)
    predictions = (A2>0.5)
    return predictions

def predict_proba(parameters, X,outputActivationFunc="sigmoid"):
    A2, cache = forwardPropagationDeep(X, parameters)
    if outputActivationFunc=="sigmoid":
        proba=A2
    elif outputActivationFunc=="softmax":
        proba=np.argmax(A2, axis=0).reshape(-1,1)
        print("A2=",A2.shape)
    return proba


# Plot a decision boundary
# Input : Input Model,
#          X
#          Y
#          sz - Num of hiden units
#          lr - Learning rate
#          Fig to be saved as
# Returns Null
def plot_decision_surface(model, X, y,sz,lr,fig):
    # Set min and max values and give it some padding
    x_min, x_max = X[0, :].min() - 1, X[0, :].max() + 1
    y_min, y_max = X[1, :].min() - 1, X[1, :].max() + 1
    z_min, z_max = X[2, :].min() - 1, X[2, :].max() + 1
    colors=['black','gold']
    cmap = matplotlib.colors.ListedColormap(colors)
    h = 3
    # Generate a grid of points with distance h between them
    xx, yy, zz = np.meshgrid(np.arange(x_min, x_max, h), np.arange(y_min, y_max, h), np.arange(z_min, z_max, h))
    # Predict the function value for the whole grid
    a=np.c_[xx.ravel(), yy.ravel(), zz.ravel()]

    Z = predict(parameters,a.T)
```

```
640        Z = Z.reshape(xx.shape)
641        # Plot the contour and training examples
642        #plt.contourf(xx, yy, Z, cmap=plt.cm.Spectral)
643        fig = plt.figure()
644        ax = plt.axes(projection='3d')
645        ax.contour3D(xx, yy, Z, 50, cmap='binary')
646        #plt.ylabel('x2')
647        #plt.xlabel('x1')
648        plt.scatter(X[0, :], X[1, :], c=y, cmap=cmap)
649        plt.title("Decision Boundary for hidden layer size:" + sz +" and learning
650 rate:"+lr)
651        plt.show()
652
653 def plotSurface(X,parameters):
654
655        #xx, yy, zz = np.meshgrid(np.arange(10), np.arange(10), np.arange(10))
656        x_min, x_max = X[0, :].min() - 1, X[0, :].max() + 1
657        y_min, y_max = X[1, :].min() - 1, X[1, :].max() + 1
658        z_min, z_max = X[2, :].min() - 1, X[2, :].max() + 1
659        colors=['red']
660        cmap = matplotlib.colors.ListedColormap(colors)
661        h = 1
662        xx, yy, zz = np.meshgrid(np.arange(x_min, x_max, h), np.arange(y_min,
663 y_max, h),
664                                 np.arange(z_min, z_max, h))
665        # For the meh grid values predict a model
666        a=np.c_[xx.ravel(), yy.ravel(), zz.ravel()]
667        Z = predict(parameters,a.T)
668        r=Z.T
669        r1=r.reshape(xx.shape)
670        # Find teh values for which the repdiction is 1
671        xx1=xx[r1]
672        yy1=yy[r1]
673        zz1=zz[r1]
674        # Plot these values
675        ax = plt.axes(projection='3d')
676        #ax.plot_trisurf(xx1, yy1, zz1, cmap='bone', edgecolor='none');
677        ax.scatter3D(xx1, yy1,zz1, c=zz1,s=10,cmap=cmap)
678        #ax.plot_surface(xx1, yy1, zz1, 'gray')
```

5.2 R

```
 1 ##############################################################################
 2 ###############################
 3 #
 4 # File    : DLfunctions5.R
 5 # Author  : Tinniam V Ganesh
 6 # Date    : 22 Mar 2018
 7 #
 8 ##############################################################################
 9 ############################
10 library(ggplot2)
11 library(PRROC)
12 library(dplyr)
13
14 # Compute the sigmoid of a vector
15 sigmoid <- function(Z){
```

```r
16      A <- 1/(1+ exp(-Z))
17      cache<-Z
18      retvals <- list("A"=A,"Z"=Z)
19      return(retvals)
20
21  }
22
23  # Compute the Relu(old) of a vector (performance hog!)
24  reluOld     <-function(Z){
25      A <- apply(Z, 1:2, function(x) max(0,x))
26      cache<-Z
27      retvals <- list("A"=A,"Z"=Z)
28      return(retvals)
29  }
30
31  # Compute the Relu (current) of a vector (much better performance!)
32  relu    <-function(Z){
33          # Perform relu. Set values less that equal to 0 as 0
34      Z[Z<0]=0
35      A=Z
36      cache<-Z
37      retvals <- list("A"=A,"Z"=Z)
38      return(retvals)
39  }
40
41  # Compute the tanh activation of a vector
42  tanhActivation <- function(Z){
43      A <- tanh(Z)
44      cache<-Z
45      retvals <- list("A"=A,"Z"=Z)
46      return(retvals)
47  }
48
49  # Conmpute the softmax of a vector
50  softmax    <- function(Z){
51      # get unnormalized probabilities
52      exp_scores = exp(t(Z))
53      # normalize them for each example
54      A = exp_scores / rowSums(exp_scores)
55      retvals <- list("A"=A,"Z"=Z)
56      return(retvals)
57  }
58
59  # Compute the detivative of Relu
60  # g'(z) = 1 if z >0 and 0 otherwise
61  reluDerivative    <-function(dA, cache){
62      Z <- cache
63      dZ <- dA
64      # Create a logical matrix of values > 0
65      a <- Z > 0
66      # When z <= 0, you should set dz to 0 as well. Perform an element wise
67  multiple
68      dZ <- dZ * a
69      return(dZ)
70  }
71
72  # Compute the derivative of sigmoid
73  # Derivative g'(z) = a* (1-a)
74  sigmoidDerivative    <- function(dA, cache){
75      Z <- cache
76      s <- 1/(1+exp(-Z))
77      dZ <- dA * s * (1-s)
78      return(dZ)
79  }
```

```r
# Compute the derivative of tanh
# Derivative g'(z) = 1- a^2
tanhDerivative   <- function(dA, cache){
  Z = cache
  a = tanh(Z)
  dZ = dA * (1 - a^2)
  return(dZ)
}

# This function is used in computing the softmax derivative
# Populate a matrix of 1s in rows where Y==1
# This may need to be extended for K classes. Currently
# supports K=3 & K=10
popMatrix <- function(Y,numClasses){
    a=rep(0,times=length(Y))
    Y1=matrix(a,nrow=length(Y),ncol=numClasses)
    #Set the rows and columns as 1's where Y is the class value
    if(numClasses==3){
        Y1[Y==0,1]=1
        Y1[Y==1,2]=1
        Y1[Y==2,3]=1
    } else if (numClasses==10){
        Y1[Y==0,1]=1
        Y1[Y==1,2]=1
        Y1[Y==2,3]=1
        Y1[Y==3,4]=1
        Y1[Y==4,5]=1
        Y1[Y==5,6]=1
        Y1[Y==6,7]=1
        Y1[Y==7,8]=1
        Y1[Y==8,9]=1
        Y1[Y==9,0]=1
    }
    return(Y1)
}

# Compute the softmax derivative
softmaxDerivative   <- function(dA, cache ,y,numTraining,numClasses){
  # Note : dA not used. dL/dZ = dL/dA * dA/dZ = pi-yi
  Z <- cache
  # Compute softmax
  exp_scores = exp(t(Z))
  # normalize them for each example
  probs = exp_scores / rowSums(exp_scores)
  # Create a matrix of zeros
  Y1=popMatrix(y,numClasses)
  dZ = probs-Y1
  return(dZ)
}


# Initialize model for L layers
# Input : Vector of units in each layer
# Returns: Initial weights and biases matrices for all layers
initializeDeepModel <- function(layerDimensions){
  set.seed(2)

  # Initialize empty list
  layerParams <- list()

  # Note the Weight matrix at layer 'l' is a matrix of size (l,l-1)
  # The Bias is a vectors of size (l,1)
```

```r
144      # Loop through the layer dimension from 1.. L
145      # Indices in R start from 1
146      for(l in 2:length(layersDimensions)){
147        # Initialize a matrix of small random numbers of size l x l-1
148        # Create random numbers of size   l x l-1
149        w=rnorm(layersDimensions[l]*layersDimensions[l-1])*0.01
150
151        # Create a weight matrix of size l x l-1 with this initial weights and
152        # Add to list W1,W2... WL
153        layerParams[[paste('W',l-1,sep="")]] = matrix(w,nrow=layersDimensions[l],
154                                                 ncol=layersDimensions[l-1])
155        layerParams[[paste('b',l-1,sep="")]] = matrix(rep(0,layersDimensions[l]),
156
157 nrow=layersDimensions[l],ncol=1)
158      }
159    return(layerParams)
160 }
161
162
163 # Compute the activation at a layer 'l' for forward prop in a Deep Network
164 # Input : A_prev - Activation of previous layer
165 #         W,b - Weight and bias matrices and vectors
166 #         activationFunc - Activation function - sigmoid, tanh, relu etc
167 # Returns : forward_cache, activation_cache, cache
168 #          :
169 # Z = W * X + b
170 # A = sigmoid(Z), A= Relu(Z), A= tanh(Z)
171 layerActivationForward <- function(A_prev, W, b, activationFunc){
172
173    # Compute Z
174    z = W %*% A_prev
175    # Broadcast the bias 'b' by column
176    Z <-sweep(z,1,b,'+')
177
178    forward_cache <- list("A_prev"=A_prev, "W"=W, "b"=b)
179    # Compute the activation for sigmoid
180    if(activationFunc == "sigmoid"){
181      vals = sigmoid(Z)
182    } else if (activationFunc == "relu"){ # Compute the activation for relu
183      vals = relu(Z)
184    } else if(activationFunc == 'tanh'){ # Compute the activation for tanh
185      vals = tanhActivation(Z)
186    } else if(activationFunc == 'softmax'){
187      vals = softmax(Z)
188    }
189    # Create a list of forward and activation cache
190    cache <- list("forward_cache"=forward_cache,
191 "activation_cache"=vals[['Z']])
192    retvals <- list("A"=vals[['A']],"cache"=cache)
193    return(retvals)
194 }
195
196 # Compute the forward propagation for layers 1..L
197 # Input : X - Input Features
198 #         parameters: Weights and biases
199 #         hiddenActivationFunc - relu/sigmoid/tanh
200 #         outputActivationFunc - Activation function at hidden layer
201 sigmoid/softmax
202 # Returns : AL
203 #           caches
204 # The forward propagtion uses the Relu/tanh activation from layer 1..L-1 and
205 sigmoid actiovation at layer L
206 forwardPropagationDeep <- function(X, parameters,hiddenActivationFunc='relu',
207                                     outputActivationFunc='sigmoid'){
```

```r
    caches <- list()
    # Set A to X (A0)
    A <- X
    L <- length(parameters)/2 # number of layers in the neural network
    # Loop through from layer 1 to upto layer L
    for(l in 1:(L-1)){
       A_prev <- A
       # Zi = Wi x Ai-1 + bi   and Ai = g(Zi)
       # Set W and b for layer 'l'
       # Loop throug from W1,W2... WL-1
       W <- parameters[[paste("W",l,sep="")]]
       b <- parameters[[paste("b",l,sep="")]]
       # Compute the forward propagation through layer 'l' using the activation
function
       actForward <- layerActivationForward(A_prev,
                                            W,
                                            b,
                                            activationFunc =
hiddenActivationFunc)
       A <- actForward[['A']]
       # Append the cache A_prev,W,b, Z
       caches[[l]] <-actForward
    }

    # Since this is binary classification use the sigmoid activation function
in
    # last layer
    # Set the weights and biases for the last layer
    W <- parameters[[paste("W",L,sep="")]]
    b <- parameters[[paste("b",L,sep="")]]
    # Compute the sigmoid activation
    actForward = layerActivationForward(A, W, b, activationFunc =
outputActivationFunc)
    AL <- actForward[['A']]
    # Append the output of this forward propagation through the last layer
    caches[[L]] <- actForward
    # Create a list of the final output and the caches
    fwdPropDeep <- list("AL"=AL,"caches"=caches)
    return(fwdPropDeep)


}

# Function pickColumns(). This function is in computeCost()
# Pick columns
# Input : AL
#         : Y
#         : numClasses
# Output: a
pickColumns <- function(AL,Y,numClasses){
     if(numClasses==3){
         # Select the elements where the y values are 0, 1 or 2 and make a
vector
         a=c(AL[Y==0,1],AL[Y==1,2],AL[Y==2,3])
     }
     else if (numClasses==10){
         # Select the elements where the y values are 0,1,2..,9
         a=c(AL[Y==0,1],AL[Y==1,2],AL[Y==2,3],AL[Y==3,4],AL[Y==4,5],
             AL[Y==5,6],AL[Y==6,7],AL[Y==7,8],AL[Y==8,9],AL[Y==9,10])
     }
     return(a)
}


# Compute the cost
```

```r
# Input : AL
#       : Y
#       : outputActivationFunc - Activation function at hidden layer
sigmoid/softmax
#       : numClasses
# Output: cost
computeCost <- function(AL,Y,outputActivationFunc="sigmoid",numClasses=3){
  if(outputActivationFunc=="sigmoid"){
    m= length(Y)
    cost=-1/m*sum(Y*log(AL) + (1-Y)*log(1-AL))
  }else if (outputActivationFunc=="softmax"){
    # Pick columns
    m= length(Y)
    a =pickColumns(AL,Y,numClasses)
    # Take log
    correct_probs = -log(a)
    # Compute loss
    cost= sum(correct_probs)/m
  }
  #cost=-1/m*sum(a+b)
  return(cost)
}


# Compute the backpropagation through a layer
# Input : Neural Network parameters - dA
#         # cache - forward_cache & activation_cache
#         # Output values Y
#         # activationFunc
#         # numClasses
# Returns: Gradients - dA_prev, dW,db
# dL/dWi= dL/dZi*Al-1
# dl/dbl = dL/dZl
# dL/dZ_prev=dL/dZl*W

layerActivationBackward  <- function(dA, cache, Y,
activationFunc,numClasses){
  # Get A_prev,W,b
  forward_cache <-cache[['forward_cache']]
  activation_cache <- cache[['activation_cache']]
  A_prev <- forward_cache[['A_prev']]
  numtraining = dim(A_prev)[2]
  # Get Z
  activation_cache <- cache[['activation_cache']]
  if(activationFunc == "relu"){
    dZ <- reluDerivative(dA, activation_cache)
  } else if(activationFunc == "sigmoid"){
    dZ <- sigmoidDerivative(dA, activation_cache)
  } else if(activationFunc == "tanh"){
    dZ <- tanhDerivative(dA, activation_cache)
  } else if(activationFunc == "softmax"){
    dZ <- softmaxDerivative(dA,  activation_cache,Y,numtraining,numClasses)
  }
  # Check if softmax
  if (activationFunc == 'softmax'){
    W <- forward_cache[['W']]
    b <- forward_cache[['b']]
    dW = 1/numtraining * A_prev%*%dZ
    db = 1/numtraining* matrix(colSums(dZ),nrow=1,ncol=numClasses)
    dA_prev = dZ %*%W
  } else {
    W <- forward_cache[['W']]
    b <- forward_cache[['b']]
    numtraining = dim(A_prev)[2]
```

```r
        dW = 1/numtraining * dZ %*% t(A_prev)
        db = 1/numtraining * rowSums(dZ)
        dA_prev = t(W) %*% dZ
    }
    retvals <- list("dA_prev"=dA_prev,"dW"=dW,"db"=db)
    return(retvals)
}

# Compute the backpropagation for 1 cycle through all layers
# Input  : AL: Output of L layer Network - weights
#        # Y  Real output
#        # caches -- list of caches containing:
#          every cache of layerActivationForward() with "relu"/"tanh"
#          #(it's caches[l], for l in range(L-1) i.e l = 0...L-2)
#          #the cache of layerActivationForward() with "sigmoid" (it's caches[L-1])
#          hiddenActivationFunc - Activation function at hidden layers - relu/tanh/sigmoid
#          outputActivationFunc - Activation function at hidden layer sigmoid/softmax
#          numClasses
#   Returns:
#     gradients -- listwith the gradients
#                  gradients["dA" + str(l)]
#                  gradients["dW" + str(l)]
#                  gradients["db" + str(l)]
backwardPropagationDeep <- function(AL, Y, caches,hiddenActivationFunc='relu',
                                    outputActivationFunc="sigmoid",numClasses){
    #initialize the gradients
    gradients = list()
    # Set the number of layers
    L = length(caches)
    numTraining = dim(AL)[2]
    
    if(outputActivationFunc == "sigmoid")
       # Initializing the backpropagation
       # dl/dAL= -(y/a) - ((1-y)/(1-a)) - At the output layer
       dAL = -( (Y/AL) -(1 - Y)/(1 - AL))
    else if(outputActivationFunc == "softmax"){
       dAL=0
       Y=t(Y)
    }
    
    # Get the gradients at the last layer
    # Inputs: "AL, Y, caches".
    # Outputs: "gradients["dAL"], gradients["dWL"], gradients["dbL"]
    # Start with Layer L
    # Get the current cache
    current_cache = caches[[L]]$cache
    #gradients["dA" + str(L)], gradients["dW" + str(L)], gradients["db" + str(L)] = layerActivationBackward(dAL, current_cache, activationFunc = "sigmoid")
    retvals <-   layerActivationBackward(dAL, current_cache, Y, activationFunc = outputActivationFunc,numClasses)
    # Create gradients as lists
    #Note: Take the transpose of dA
    if(outputActivationFunc =="sigmoid")
        gradients[[paste("dA",L,sep="")]] <- retvals[['dA_prev']]
    else if(outputActivationFunc =="softmax")
       gradients[[paste("dA",L,sep="")]] <- t(retvals[['dA_prev']])
    gradients[[paste("dW",L,sep="")]] <- retvals[['dW']]
    gradients[[paste("db",L,sep="")]] <- retvals[['db']]
```

```r
    # Traverse in the reverse direction
    for(l in (L-1):1){
        # Compute the gradients for L-1 to 1 for Relu/tanh
        # Inputs: "gradients["dA" + str(l + 2)], caches".
        # Outputs: "gradients["dA" + str(l + 1)] , gradients["dW" + str(l + 1)] ,
gradients["db" + str(l + 1)]
        current_cache = caches[[l]]$cache

        retvals = layerActivationBackward(gradients[[paste('dA',l+1,sep="")]],
                                        current_cache,
                                        activationFunc = hiddenActivationFunc)

        gradients[[paste("dA",l,sep="")]] <-retvals[['dA_prev']]
        gradients[[paste("dW",l,sep="")]] <- retvals[['dW']]
        gradients[[paste("db",l,sep="")]] <- retvals[['db']]
    }

    return(gradients)
}


# Perform Gradient Descent
# Input : weights and biases
#       : gradients
#       : learning rate
#       : outputActivationFunc - Activation function at hidden layer
sigmoid/softmax
# output : parameters
gradientDescent  <- function(parameters, gradients,
learningRate,outputActivationFunc="sigmoid"){

    L = length(parameters)/2 # number of layers in the neural network

    # Update rule for each parameter. Use a for loop.
    for(l in 1:(L-1)){
        parameters[[paste("W",l,sep="")]] = parameters[[paste("W",l,sep="")]] -
            learningRate* gradients[[paste("dW",l,sep="")]]
        parameters[[paste("b",l,sep="")]] = parameters[[paste("b",l,sep="")]] -
            learningRate* gradients[[paste("db",l,sep="")]]
    }
    if(outputActivationFunc=="sigmoid"){
        parameters[[paste("W",L,sep="")]] = parameters[[paste("W",L,sep="")]] -
            learningRate* gradients[[paste("dW",L,sep="")]]
        parameters[[paste("b",L,sep="")]] = parameters[[paste("b",L,sep="")]] -
            learningRate* gradients[[paste("db",L,sep="")]]

    }else if (outputActivationFunc=="softmax"){
        parameters[[paste("W",L,sep="")]] = parameters[[paste("W",L,sep="")]] -
            learningRate* gradients[[paste("dW",L,sep="")]]
        parameters[[paste("b",L,sep="")]] = parameters[[paste("b",L,sep="")]] -
            learningRate* gradients[[paste("db",L,sep="")]]
    }
    return(parameters)
}


# Execute a L layer Deep learning model
# Input : X - Input features
#       : Y output
#       : layersDimensions - Dimension of layers
#       : hiddenActivationFunc - Activation function at hidden layer relu
/tanh/sigmoid
#       : outputActivationFunc - Activation function at hidden layer
sigmoid/softmax
```

```
#              : learning rate
#              : num of iterations
#output : Updated weights after each   iteration

L_Layer_DeepModel <- function(X, Y, layersDimensions,
                              hiddenActivationFunc='relu',
                              outputActivationFunc= 'sigmoid',
                              learningRate = 0.5,
                              numIterations = 10000,
                              print_cost=False){
  #Initialize costs vector as NULL
  costs <- NULL

  # Parameters initialization.
  parameters = initializeDeepModel(layersDimensions)


  # Loop (gradient descent)
  for( i in 0:numIterations){
     # Forward propagation: [LINEAR -> RELU]*(L-1) -> LINEAR -> SIGMOID/SOFTMAX.
     retvals = forwardPropagationDeep(X, parameters,hiddenActivationFunc,

outputActivationFunc=outputActivationFunc)
     AL <- retvals[['AL']]
     caches <- retvals[['caches']]

     # Compute cost.
     cost <- computeCost(AL,
Y,outputActivationFunc=outputActivationFunc,numClasses=layersDimensions[3])

     # Backward propagation.
     gradients = backwardPropagationDeep(AL, Y, caches,hiddenActivationFunc,

outputActivationFunc=outputActivationFunc,numClasses=layersDimensions[3])

     # Update parameters.
     parameters = gradientDescent(parameters, gradients, learningRate,
                                  outputActivationFunc=outputActivationFunc)


     if(i%%1000 == 0){
       costs=c(costs,cost)
       print(cost)
     }
  }

  retvals <- list("parameters"=parameters,"costs"=costs)

  return(retvals)
}

# Execute a L layer Deep learning model with Stochastic Gradient descent
# Input : X - Input features
#         : Y output
#         : layersDimensions - Dimension of layers
#         : hiddenActivationFunc - Activation function at hidden layer relu /tanh/sigmoid
#         : outputActivationFunc - Activation function at hidden layer sigmoid/softmax
#         : learning rate
#         : mini_batch_size
#         : num of epochs
#output : Updated weights after each   iteration
```

```r
L_Layer_DeepModel_SGD <- function(X, Y, layersDimensions,
                                  hiddenActivationFunc='relu',
                                  outputActivationFunc= 'sigmoid',
                                  learningRate = .3,
                                  mini_batch_size = 64,
                                  num_epochs = 2500,
                                  print_cost=False){

    set.seed(1)
    #Initialize costs vector as NULL
    costs <- NULL

    # Parameters initialization.
    parameters = initializeDeepModel(layersDimensions)
    seed=10

    # Loop for number of epochs
    for( i in 0:num_epochs){
        seed=seed+1
        minibatches = random_mini_batches(X, Y, mini_batch_size, seed)

        for(batch in 1:length(minibatches)){

            mini_batch_X=minibatches[[batch]][['mini_batch_X']]
            mini_batch_Y=minibatches[[batch]][['mini_batch_Y']]
            # Forward propagation:
            retvals = forwardPropagationDeep(mini_batch_X,
parameters,hiddenActivationFunc,

outputActivationFunc=outputActivationFunc)
            AL <- retvals[['AL']]
            caches <- retvals[['caches']]

            # Compute cost.
            cost <- computeCost(AL,
mini_batch_Y,outputActivationFunc=outputActivationFunc,numClasses=layersDimen
sions[length(layersDimensions)])

            # Backward propagation.
            gradients = backwardPropagationDeep(AL, mini_batch_Y,
caches,hiddenActivationFunc,

outputActivationFunc=outputActivationFunc,numClasses=layersDimensions[length(
layersDimensions)])

            # Update parameters.
            parameters = gradientDescent(parameters, gradients, learningRate,

outputActivationFunc=outputActivationFunc)
        }

        if(i%%100 == 0){
            costs=c(costs,cost)
            print(cost)
        }
    }

    retvals <- list("parameters"=parameters,"costs"=costs)

    return(retvals)
}

# Predict the output for given input
# Input : parameters
```

```r
#          : X
#          : hiddenActivationFunc
# Output: predictions
predict <- function(parameters, X,hiddenActivationFunc='relu'){
    
    fwdProp <- forwardPropagationDeep(X, parameters,hiddenActivationFunc)
    predictions <- fwdProp$AL>0.5
    
    return (predictions)
}

# Predict the output
predictProba <- function(parameters, X,hiddenActivationFunc,
                        outputActivationFunc){
    retvals = forwardPropagationDeep(X, parameters,hiddenActivationFunc,
                                    outputActivationFunc="softmax")
    if(outputActivationFunc =="sigmoid")
        predictions <- retvals$AL>0.5
    else if (outputActivationFunc =="softmax")
        predictions <- apply(retvals$AL, 1,which.max) -1
    
    return (predictions)
}

# Plot a decision boundary
# This function uses ggplot2
plotDecisionBoundary <- function(z,retvals,hiddenActivationFunc,lr){
  # Find the minimum and maximum for the data
  xmin<-min(z[,1])
  xmax<-max(z[,1])
  ymin<-min(z[,2])
  ymax<-max(z[,2])
  
  # Create a grid of values
  a=seq(xmin,xmax,length=100)
  b=seq(ymin,ymax,length=100)
  grid <- expand.grid(x=a, y=b)
  colnames(grid) <- c('x1', 'x2')
  grid1 <-t(grid)
  # Predict the output for this grid
  q <-predict(retvals$parameters,grid1,hiddenActivationFunc)
  q1 <- t(data.frame(q))
  q2 <- as.numeric(q1)
  grid2 <- cbind(grid,q2)
  colnames(grid2) <- c('x1', 'x2','q2')
  
  z1 <- data.frame(z)
  names(z1) <- c("x1","x2","y")
  atitle=paste("Decision boundary for learning rate:",lr)
  # Plot the contour of the boundary
  ggplot(z1) +
     geom_point(data = z1, aes(x = x1, y = x2, color = y)) +
     stat_contour(data = grid2, aes(x = x1, y = x2, z = q2,color=q2), alpha = 0.9)+
     ggtitle(atitle)
}

# Predict the probability  scores for given data set
# Input : parameters
#          : X
# Output: probability of output
computeScores <- function(parameters, X,hiddenActivationFunc='relu'){
    
    fwdProp <- forwardPropagationDeep(X, parameters,hiddenActivationFunc)
```

```r
      scores <- fwdProp$AL

    return (scores)
}

# Create random mini batches
# Input : X - Input features
#         : Y- output
#         : miniBatchSize
#         : seed
#output : mini_batches
random_mini_batches <- function(X, Y, miniBatchSize = 64, seed = 0){


    set.seed(seed)
    # Get number of training samples
    m = dim(X)[2]
    # Initialize mini batches
    mini_batches = list()

    # Create  a list of random numbers < m
    permutation = c(sample(m))
    # Randomly shuffle the training data
    shuffled_X = X[, permutation]
    shuffled_Y = Y[1, permutation]

    # Compute number of mini batches
    numCompleteMinibatches = floor(m/miniBatchSize)
    batch=0
    for(k in 0:(numCompleteMinibatches-1)){
        batch=batch+1
        # Set the lower and upper bound of the mini batches
        lower=(k*miniBatchSize)+1
        upper=((k+1) * miniBatchSize)
        mini_batch_X = shuffled_X[, lower:upper]
        mini_batch_Y = shuffled_Y[lower:upper]
        # Add it to the list of mini batches
        mini_batch =
list("mini_batch_X"=mini_batch_X,"mini_batch_Y"=mini_batch_Y)
        mini_batches[[batch]] =mini_batch

    }

    # If the batch size does not divide evenly with mini batc size
    if(m %% miniBatchSize != 0){
        p=floor(m/miniBatchSize)*miniBatchSize
        # Set the start and end of last batch
        q=p+m %% miniBatchSize
        mini_batch_X = shuffled_X[,(p+1):q]
        mini_batch_Y = shuffled_Y[(p+1):q]
    }
    # Return the list of mini batches
    mini_batch =
list("mini_batch_X"=mini_batch_X,"mini_batch_Y"=mini_batch_Y)
    mini_batches[[batch]]=mini_batch

    return(mini_batches)
}
```

5.3 Octave

```octave
##############################################################################
###############################
#
# File: DLfunctions5.m
# Developer: Tinniam V Ganesh
# Date : 23 Mar 2018
#
##############################################################################
###############################
1;
# Define sigmoid function
function [A,cache] = sigmoid(Z)
  A = 1 ./ (1+ exp(-Z));
  cache=Z;
end

# Define Relu function
function [A,cache] = relu(Z)
  A = max(0,Z);
  cache=Z;
end

# Define Relu function
function [A,cache] = tanhAct(Z)
  A = tanh(Z);
  cache=Z;
end

# Define Softmax function
function [A,cache] = softmax(Z)
    # get unnormalized probabilities
    exp_scores = exp(Z');
    # normalize them for each example
    A = exp_scores ./ sum(exp_scores,2);
    cache=Z;
end

# Define Stable Softmax function
function [A,cache] = stableSoftmax(Z)
    # Normalize by max value in each row
    shiftZ = Z' - max(Z',[],2);
    exp_scores = exp(shiftZ);
    # normalize them for each example
    A = exp_scores ./ sum(exp_scores,2);
    #disp("sm")
    #disp(A);
    cache=Z;
end

# Define Relu Derivative
function [dZ] = reluDerivative(dA,cache)
  Z = cache;
  dZ = dA;
  # Get elements that are greater than 0
  a = (Z > 0);
  # Select only those elements where Z > 0
  dZ = dZ .* a;
end

# Define Sigmoid Derivative
function [dZ] = sigmoidDerivative(dA,cache)
  Z = cache;
  s = 1 ./ (1+ exp(-Z));
  dZ = dA .* s .* (1-s);
```

```octave
65  end
66
67  # Define Tanh Derivative
68  function [dZ] = tanhDerivative(dA,cache)
69      Z = cache;
70      a = tanh(Z);
71      dZ = dA .* (1 - a .^ 2);
72  end
73
74  # Populate a matrix with 1s in rows where Y=1
75  # This function may need to be modified if K is not 3, 10
76  # This function is used in computing the softmax derivative
77  function [Y1] = popMatrix(Y,numClasses)
78      Y1=zeros(length(Y),numClasses);
79      if(numClasses==3) # For 3 output classes
80          Y1(Y==0,1)=1;
81          Y1(Y==1,2)=1;
82          Y1(Y==2,3)=1;
83      elseif(numClasses==10) # For 10 output classes
84          Y1(Y==0,1)=1;
85          Y1(Y==1,2)=1;
86          Y1(Y==2,3)=1;
87          Y1(Y==3,4)=1;
88          Y1(Y==4,5)=1;
89          Y1(Y==5,6)=1;
90          Y1(Y==6,7)=1;
91          Y1(Y==7,8)=1;
92          Y1(Y==8,9)=1;
93          Y1(Y==9,10)=1;
94
95      endif
96  end
97
98  # Define Softmax Derivative
99  function [dZ] = softmaxDerivative(dA,cache,Y, numClasses)
100     Z = cache;
101     # get unnormalized probabilities
102     shiftZ = Z' - max(Z',[],2);
103     exp_scores = exp(shiftZ);
104
105     # normalize them for each example
106     probs = exp_scores ./ sum(exp_scores,2);
107     # dZ = pi- yi
108     yi=popMatrix(Y,numClasses);
109     dZ=probs-yi;
110
111 end
112
113 # Define Stable Softmax Derivative
114 function [dZ] = stableSoftmaxDerivative(dA,cache,Y, numClasses)
115     Z = cache;
116     # get unnormalized probabilities
117     exp_scores = exp(Z');
118     # normalize them for each example
119     probs = exp_scores ./ sum(exp_scores,2);
120     # dZ = pi- yi
121     yi=popMatrix(Y,numClasses);
122     dZ=probs-yi;
123
124 end
125
126 # Initialize model for L layers
127 # Input : List of units in each layer
128 # Returns: Initial weights and biases matrices for all layers
```

```octave
function [W b] = initializeDeepModel(layerDimensions)
    rand ("seed", 3);
    # note the Weight matrix at layer 'l' is a matrix of size (l,l-1)
    # The Bias is a vectors of size (l,1)

    # Loop through the layer dimension from 1.. L
    # Create cell arrays for Weights and biases

    for l =2:size(layerDimensions)(2)
        W{l-1} = rand(layerDimensions(l),layerDimensions(l-1))*0.01; # Multiply by .01
        b{l-1} = zeros(layerDimensions(l),1);

    endfor
end

# Compute the activation at a layer 'l' for forward prop in a Deep Network
# Input : A_prev - Activation of previous layer
#         W,b - Weight and bias matrices and vectors
#         activationFunc - Activation function - sigmoid, tanh, relu etc
# Returns : A, forward_cache, activation_cache
#         :
# Z = W * X + b
# A = sigmoid(Z), A= Relu(Z), A= tanh(Z)
function [A forward_cache activation_cache] = layerActivationForward(A_prev, W, b, activationFunc)

    # Compute Z
    Z = W * A_prev +b;
    # Create a cell array
    forward_cache = {A_prev  W  b};
    # Compute the activation for sigmoid
    if (strcmp(activationFunc,"sigmoid"))
        [A activation_cache] = sigmoid(Z);
    elseif (strcmp(activationFunc, "relu"))   # Compute the activation for Relu
        [A activation_cache] = relu(Z);
    elseif(strcmp(activationFunc,'tanh'))     # Compute the activation for tanh
        [A activation_cache] = tanhAct(Z);
    elseif(strcmp(activationFunc,'softmax'))    # Compute the activation for tanh
        #[A activation_cache] = softmax(Z);
        [A activation_cache] = stableSoftmax(Z);
    endif

end

# Compute the forward propagation for layers 1..L
# Input : X - Input Features
#         paramaters: Weights and biases
#         hiddenActivationFunc - Activation function at hidden layers Relu/tanh
#         outputActivationFunc- sigmoid/softmax
# Returns : AL, forward_caches, activation_caches
# The forward propoagtion uses the Relu/tanh activation from layer 1..L-1 and sigmoid actiovation at layer L
function [AL forward_caches activation_caches] = forwardPropagationDeep(X, weights,biases,
                                                    hiddenActivationFunc='relu', outputActivationFunc='sigmoid')
    # Create an empty cell array
    forward_caches = {};
    activation_caches = {};
```

```octave
        # Set A to X (A0)
        A = X;
        L = length(weights); # number of layers in the neural network
        # Loop through from layer 1 to upto layer L
        for l =1:L-1
            A_prev = A;
            # Zi = Wi x Ai-1 + bi   and Ai = g(Zi)
            W = weights{l};
            b = biases{l};
            [A forward_cache activation_cache] = layerActivationForward(A_prev, W,b, activationFunc=hiddenActivationFunc);
            forward_caches{l}=forward_cache;
            activation_caches{l} = activation_cache;
        endfor
        # Since this is binary classification use the sigmoid activation function in
        # last layer
        W = weights{L};
        b = biases{L};
        [AL, forward_cache activation_cache] = layerActivationForward(A, W,b, activationFunc = outputActivationFunc);
        forward_caches{L}=forward_cache;
        activation_caches{L} = activation_cache;

end

# Pick columns where Y==1
# This function is used in computeCost
function [a] = pickColumns(AL,Y,numClasses)
    if(numClasses==3)
        a=[AL(Y==0,1) ;AL(Y==1,2) ;AL(Y==2,3)];
    elseif (numClasses==10)
        a=[AL(Y==0,1) ;AL(Y==1,2) ;AL(Y==2,3);AL(Y==3,4);AL(Y==4,5);
           AL(Y==5,6); AL(Y==6,7);AL(Y==7,8);AL(Y==8,9);AL(Y==9,10)];
    endif
end


# Compute the cost
# Input : AL
#       : Y
#       : outputActivationFunc- sigmoid/softmax
#       : numClasses
# Output: cost
function [cost]= computeCost(AL, Y, outputActivationFunc="sigmoid",numClasses)
    if(strcmp(outputActivationFunc,"sigmoid"))
        numTraining= size(Y)(2);
        # Element wise multiply for logprobs
        cost = -1/numTraining * sum((Y .* log(AL)) + (1-Y) .* log(1-AL));
    elseif(strcmp(outputActivationFunc,'softmax'))
        numTraining = size(Y)(2);
        Y=Y';
        # Select rows where Y=0,1,and 2 and concatenate to a long vector
        #a=[AL(Y==0,1) ;AL(Y==1,2) ;AL(Y==2,3)];
        a =pickColumns(AL,Y,numClasses);

        #Select the correct column for log prob
         correct_probs = -log(a);
         #Compute log loss
         cost= sum(correct_probs)/numTraining;
     endif
end
```

```octave
# Compute the backpropoagation for 1 cycle
# Input : Neural Network parameters - dA
#          # cache - forward_cache & activation_cache
#          # Input features
#          # Output values Y
#          # activationFunc- sigmoid/softmax/tanh
#          # numClasses
# Returns: Gradients
# dL/dWi= dL/dZi*Al-1
# dl/dbl = dL/dzl
# dL/dZ_prev=dL/dZl*w
function [dA_prev dW db] = layerActivationBackward(dA, forward_cache, activation_cache, Y, activationFunc,numClasses)

    A_prev = forward_cache{1};
    W =forward_cache{2};
    b = forward_cache{3};
    numTraining = size(A_prev)(2);
    if (strcmp(activationFunc,"relu"))
        dZ = reluDerivative(dA, activation_cache);
    elseif (strcmp(activationFunc,"sigmoid"))
        dZ = sigmoidDerivative(dA, activation_cache);
    elseif(strcmp(activationFunc, "tanh"))
        dZ = tanhDerivative(dA, activation_cache);
    elseif(strcmp(activationFunc, "softmax"))
        #dZ = softmaxDerivative(dA, activation_cache,Y,numClasses);
        dZ = stableSoftmaxDerivative(dA, activation_cache,Y,numClasses);
    endif

    # Check if softmax
    if (strcmp(activationFunc,"softmax"))
      W =forward_cache{2};
      b = forward_cache{3};
      dW = 1/numTraining * A_prev * dZ;
      db = 1/numTraining * sum(dZ,1);
      dA_prev = dZ*W;
    else
      W =forward_cache{2};
      b = forward_cache{3};
      dW = 1/numTraining * dZ * A_prev';
      db = 1/numTraining * sum(dZ,2);
      dA_prev = W'*dZ;
    endif

end


# Compute the backpropoagation for 1 cycle
# Input : AL: Output of L layer Network - weights
#         # Y  Real output
#         # caches -- list of caches containing:
#         every cache of layerActivationForward() with "relu"/"tanh"
#         #(it's caches[l], for l in range(L-1) i.e l = 0...L-2)
#         #the cache of layerActivationForward() with "sigmoid" (it's caches[L-1])
#         # hiddenActivationFunc - Activation function at hidden layers
#         # outputActivationFunc- sigmoid/softmax
#         # numClasses
#
#    Returns:
#     gradients -- A dictionary with the gradients
#                  gradients["dA" + str(l)] = ...
#                  gradients["dW" + str(l)] = ...
#                  gradients["db" + str(l)] = ...
```

```octave
function [gradsDA gradsDW gradsDB]= backwardPropagationDeep(AL, Y, 
activation_caches,forward_caches,

hiddenActivationFunc='relu',outputActivationFunc="sigmoid",numClasses)


    # Set the number of layers
    L = length(activation_caches);
    m = size(AL)(2);

    if (strcmp(outputActivationFunc,"sigmoid"))
       # Initializing the backpropagation
       # dl/dAL= -(y/a + (1-y)/(1-a)) - At the output layer
       dAL = -((Y ./ AL) - (1 - Y) ./ ( 1 - AL));
    elseif (strcmp(outputActivationFunc,"softmax"))
       dAL=0;
       Y=Y';
    endif


    # Since this is a binary classification the activation at output is
sigmoid
    # Get the gradients at the last layer
    # Inputs: "AL, Y, caches".
    # Outputs: "gradients["dAL"], gradients["dWL"], gradients["dbL"]
    activation_cache = activation_caches{L};
    forward_cache = forward_caches(L);
    # Note the cell array includes an array of forward caches. To get to this
we need to include the index {1}
    [dA dW db] = layerActivationBackward(dAL, forward_cache{1}, 
activation_cache, Y, activationFunc = outputActivationFunc,numClasses);
    if (strcmp(outputActivationFunc,"sigmoid"))
         gradsDA{L}= dA;
    elseif (strcmp(outputActivationFunc,"softmax"))
         gradsDA{L}= dA';#Note the transpose
    endif
    gradsDW{L}= dW;
    gradsDB{L}= db;

    # Traverse in the reverse direction
    for l =(L-1):-1:1
        # Compute the gradients for L-1 to 1 for Relu/tanh
        # Inputs: "gradients["dA" + str(l + 2)], caches".
        # Outputs: "gradients["dA" + str(l + 1)] , gradients["dW" + str(l +
1)] , gradients["db" + str(l + 1)]
        activation_cache = activation_caches{l};
        forward_cache = forward_caches(l);

        #dA_prev_temp, dW_temp, db_temp = 
layerActivationBackward(gradients['dA'+str(l+1)], current_cache,
activationFunc = "relu")
        # dAl the dervative of the activation of the lth layer,is the first
element
        dAl= gradsDA{l+1};
        [dA_prev_temp, dW_temp, db_temp] = layerActivationBackward(dAl,
forward_cache{1}, activation_cache, Y, activationFunc = 
hiddenActivationFunc,numClasses);
        gradsDA{l}= dA_prev_temp;
        gradsDW{l}= dW_temp;
        gradsDB{l}= db_temp;

    endfor
```

```octave
end


# Perform Gradient Descent
# Input : Weights and biases
#        : gradients
#        : learning rate
#        : outputActivationFunc
#output : weights, biases
function [weights biases] = gradientDescent(weights, biases,gradsW,gradsB,
learningRate,outputActivationFunc="sigmoid")

    L = size(weights)(2); # number of layers in the neural network

    # Update rule for each parameter.
    for l=1:(L-1)
        weights{l} = weights{l} -learningRate* gradsW{l};
        biases{l} = biases{l} -learningRate* gradsB{l};
    endfor


    if (strcmp(outputActivationFunc,"sigmoid"))
        weights{L} = weights{L} -learningRate* gradsW{L};
        biases{L} = biases{L} -learningRate* gradsB{L};
     elseif (strcmp(outputActivationFunc,"softmax"))
        weights{L} = weights{L} -learningRate* gradsW{L}';
        biases{L} = biases{L} -learningRate* gradsB{L}';
     endif


end


# Execute a L layer Deep learning model
# Input : X - Input features
#        : Y output
#        : layersDimensions - Dimension of layers
#        : hiddenActivationFunc - Activation function at hidden layer relu
/tanh
#        : outputActivationFunc - Activation function at hidden layer
sigmoid/softmax
#        : learning rate
#        : num of iterations
#output : Updated weights and biases after each  iteration
function [weights biases costs] = L_Layer_DeepModel(X, Y, layersDimensions,
hiddenActivationFunc='relu',  outputActivationFunc="sigmoid",learning_rate =
.3, num_iterations = 10000)#lr was 0.009

    rand ("seed", 1);
    costs = [] ;

    # Parameters initialization.
    [weights biases] = initializeDeepModel(layersDimensions);

    # Loop (gradient descent)
    for i = 0:num_iterations
        # Forward propagation: [LINEAR -> RELU]*(L-1) -> LINEAR -> SIGMOID.
        [AL forward_caches activation_caches] = forwardPropagationDeep(X,
weights, biases,hiddenActivationFunc,
outputActivationFunc=outputActivationFunc);

        # Compute cost.
```

```octave
            cost = computeCost(AL,
Y,outputActivationFunc=outputActivationFunc,numClasses=layersDimensions(size(
layersDimensions)(2)));

            # Backward propagation.
            [gradsDA gradsDW gradsDB] = backwardPropagationDeep(AL, Y,
activation_caches,forward_caches,hiddenActivationFunc,
outputActivationFunc=outputActivationFunc,

numClasses=layersDimensions(size(layersDimensions)(2)));
            # Update parameters.
            [weights biases] = gradientDescent(weights,biases,
gradsDW,gradsDB,learning_rate,outputActivationFunc=outputActivationFunc);


            # Print the cost every 1000 iterations
           if ( mod(i,1000) == 0)
              costs =[costs cost];
              #disp ("Cost after iteration"), disp(i),disp(cost);
              printf("Cost after iteration i=%i cost=%d\n",i,cost);
           endif
       endfor

end

# Execute a L layer Deep learning model with Stochastic Gradient descent
# Input : X - Input features
#        : Y output
#        : layersDimensions - Dimension of layers
#        : hiddenActivationFunc - Activation function at hidden layer relu
/tanh
#        : outputActivationFunc - Activation function at hidden layer
sigmoid/softmax
#        : learning rate
#        : mini_batch_size
#        : num of epochs
#output : Updated weights and biases after each  iteration
function [weights biases costs] = L_Layer_DeepModel_SGD(X, Y,
layersDimensions, hiddenActivationFunc='relu',
outputActivationFunc="sigmoid",learning_rate = .3,
                      mini_batch_size = 64, num_epochs = 2500)#lr was 0.009

    rand ("seed", 1);
    costs = [] ;

    # Parameters initialization.
    [weights biases] = initializeDeepModel(layersDimensions);
    seed=10;
    # Loop (gradient descent)
    for i = 0:num_epochs
        seed = seed + 1;
        [mini_batches_X  mini_batches_Y] = random_mini_batches(X, Y,
mini_batch_size, seed);

        minibatches=length(mini_batches_X);
        for batch=1:minibatches
            X=mini_batches_X{batch};
            Y=mini_batches_Y{batch};
            # Forward propagation: [LINEAR -> RELU]*(L-1) -> LINEAR ->
SIGMOID/SOFTMAX.
            [AL forward_caches activation_caches] =
forwardPropagationDeep(X, weights, biases,hiddenActivationFunc,
outputActivationFunc=outputActivationFunc);
            #disp(batch);
```

```octave
                        #disp(size(X));
                        #disp(size(Y));

                        # Compute cost.
                        cost = computeCost(AL,
Y,outputActivationFunc=outputActivationFunc,numClasses=layersDimensions(size(
layersDimensions)(2)));

                        #disp(cost);
                        # Backward propagation.
                        [gradsDA gradsDW gradsDB] = backwardPropagationDeep(AL, Y,
activation_caches,forward_caches,hiddenActivationFunc,
outputActivationFunc=outputActivationFunc,

numClasses=layersDimensions(size(layersDimensions)(2)));
                        # Update parameters.
                        [weights biases] = gradientDescent(weights,biases,
gradsDW,gradsDB,learning_rate,outputActivationFunc=outputActivationFunc);

               endfor
               # Print the cost every 1000 iterations
               if ( mod(i,1000) == 0)
                   costs =[costs cost];
                   #disp ("Cost after iteration"), disp(i),disp(cost);
                   printf("Cost after iteration i=%i cost=%d\n",i,cost);
               endif
          endfor

end

  # Plot cost vs iterations
  function plotCostVsIterations(maxIterations,costs)
       iterations=[0:1000:maxIterations];
       plot(iterations,costs);
       title ("Cost vs no of iterations ");
       xlabel("No of iterations");
       ylabel("Cost");
       print -dpng figure23.jpg
end;

# Compute the predicted value for a given input
# Input : Neural Network parameters
#       : Input data
function [predictions]= predict(weights, biases,
X,hiddenActivationFunc="relu")
     [AL forward_caches activation_caches] = forwardPropagationDeep(X,
weights, biases,hiddenActivationFunc);
     predictions = (AL>0.5);
end

# Plot the decision boundary
function plotDecisionBoundary(data,weights,
biases,hiddenActivationFunc="relu")
     %Plot a non-linear decision boundary learned by the SVM
     colormap ("summer");

     % Make classification predictions over a grid of values
     x1plot = linspace(min(data(:,1)), max(data(:,1)), 400)';
     x2plot = linspace(min(data(:,2)), max(data(:,2)), 400)';
     [X1, X2] = meshgrid(x1plot, x2plot);
     vals = zeros(size(X1));
     # Plot the prediction for the grid
     for i = 1:size(X1, 2)
        gridPoints = [X1(:, i), X2(:, i)];
```

```octave
        vals(:, i)=predict(weights, biases,gridPoints',hiddenActivationFunc=hiddenActivationFunc);
    endfor

    scatter(data(:,1),data(:,2),8,c=data(:,3),"filled");
    % Plot the boundary
    hold on
    #contour(X1, X2, vals, [0 0], 'LineWidth', 2);
    contour(X1, X2, vals,"linewidth",4);
    title ({"3 layer Neural Network decision boundary"});
    hold off;
    print -dpng figure32.jpg

end

# Compute scores
function [AL]= scores(weights, biases, X,hiddenActivationFunc="relu")
    [AL forward_caches activation_caches] = forwardPropagationDeep(X, weights, biases,hiddenActivationFunc);
end

# Create Random mini batches. Return cell arrays with the mini batches
# Input : X, Y
#         : Size of minibatch
#         : seed
#Output : mini batches X & Y
function [mini_batches_X  mini_batches_Y]= random_mini_batches(X, Y, miniBatchSize = 64, seed = 0)

    rand ("seed", seed);
    # Get number of training samples
    m = size(X)(2);


    # Create  a list of random numbers < m
    permutation = randperm(m);
    # Randomly shuffle the training data
    shuffled_X = X(:, permutation);
    shuffled_Y = Y(:, permutation);

    # Compute number of mini batches
    numCompleteMinibatches = floor(m/miniBatchSize);
    batch=0;
    for k = 0:(numCompleteMinibatches-1)
        #Set the start and end of each mini batch
        batch=batch+1;
        lower=(k*miniBatchSize)+1;
        upper=(k+1) * miniBatchSize;
        mini_batch_X = shuffled_X(:, lower:upper);
        mini_batch_Y = shuffled_Y(:, lower:upper);

        # Create cell arrays
        mini_batches_X{batch} = mini_batch_X;
        mini_batches_Y{batch} = mini_batch_Y;
    endfor

    # If the batc size does not cleanly divide with number of mini batches
    if mod(m ,miniBatchSize) != 0
        # Set the start and end of the last mini batch
        l=floor(m/miniBatchSize)*miniBatchSize;
        m=l+ mod(m,miniBatchSize);
        mini_batch_X = shuffled_X(:,(l+1):m);
        mini_batch_Y = shuffled_Y(:,(l+1):m);
```

```
639            batch=batch+1;
640            mini_batches_X{batch} = mini_batch_X;
641            mini_batches_Y{batch} = mini_batch_Y;
642        endif
643 end
```

7. Appendix 6 - Initialization, regularization in Deep Learning

6.1 Python

```
1   # -*- coding: utf-8 -*-
2   ##########################################################################
3   ###############################
4   #
5   # File: DLfunctions61.py
6   # Developer: Tinniam V Ganesh
7   # Date : 16 Apr 2018
8   #
9   ##########################################################################
10  ###########################
11  import numpy as np
12  import matplotlib.pyplot as plt
13  import matplotlib
14  import matplotlib.pyplot as plt
15  from matplotlib import cm
16  import math
17  import sklearn
18  import sklearn.datasets
19
20  # Conmpute the sigmoid of a vector
21  def sigmoid(Z):
22      A=1/(1+np.exp(-Z))
23      cache=Z
24      return A,cache
25
26  # Conmpute the Relu of a vector
27  def relu(Z):
28      A = np.maximum(0,Z)
29      cache=Z
30      return A,cache
31
32  # Conmpute the tanh of a vector
33  def tanh(Z):
34      A = np.tanh(Z)
35      cache=Z
36      return A,cache
37
38  # Conmpute the softmax of a vector
39  def softmax(Z):
40      # get unnormalized probabilities
41      exp_scores = np.exp(Z.T)
42      # normalize them for each example
43      A = exp_scores / np.sum(exp_scores, axis=1, keepdims=True)
44      cache=Z
45      return A,cache
46
47  # Conmpute the Stable Softmax of a vector
```

```python
48  def stableSoftmax(z):
49      #Compute the softmax of vector x in a numerically stable way.
50      shiftZ = Z.T - np.max(Z.T,axis=1).reshape(-1,1)
51      exp_scores = np.exp(shiftZ)
52
53      # normalize them for each example
54      A = exp_scores / np.sum(exp_scores, axis=1, keepdims=True)
55      cache=Z
56      return A,cache
57
58  # Compute the detivative of Relu
59  def reluDerivative(dA, cache):
60
61      Z = cache
62      dZ = np.array(dA, copy=True) # just converting dz to a correct object.
63      # When z <= 0, you should set dz to 0 as well.
64      dZ[Z <= 0] = 0
65      return dZ
66
67  # Compute the derivative of sigmoid
68  def sigmoidDerivative(dA, cache):
69      Z = cache
70      s = 1/(1+np.exp(-Z))
71      dZ = dA * s * (1-s)
72      return dZ
73
74  # Compute the derivative of tanh
75  def tanhDerivative(dA, cache):
76      Z = cache
77      a = np.tanh(Z)
78      dZ = dA * (1 - np.power(a, 2))
79      return dZ
80
81  # Compute the derivative of softmax
82  def softmaxDerivative(dA, cache,y,numTraining):
83      # Note : dA not used. dL/dZ = dL/dA * dA/dZ = pi-yi
84      Z = cache
85      # Compute softmax
86      exp_scores = np.exp(Z.T)
87      # normalize them for each example
88      probs = exp_scores / np.sum(exp_scores, axis=1, keepdims=True)
89
90      # compute the gradient on scores
91      dZ = probs
92
93      # dZ = pi- yi
94      dZ[range(int(numTraining)),y[:,0]] -= 1
95      return(dZ)
96
97  # Compute the derivative of Stable Softmax
98  def stableSoftmaxDerivative(dA, cache,y,numTraining):
99      # Note : dA not used. dL/dZ = dL/dA * dA/dZ = pi-yi
100     Z = cache
101     # Compute stable softmax
102     shiftZ = Z.T - np.max(Z.T,axis=1).reshape(-1,1)
103     exp_scores = np.exp(shiftZ)
104     # normalize them for each example
105     probs = exp_scores / np.sum(exp_scores, axis=1, keepdims=True)
106     #print(probs)
107     # compute the gradient on scores
108     dZ = probs
109
110     # dZ = pi- yi
111     dZ[range(int(numTraining)),y[:,0]] -= 1
```

```python
            return(dZ)


# Initialize the model
# Input : number of features
#         number of hidden units
#         number of units in output
# Returns: Weight and bias matrices and vectors
def initializeModel(numFeats,numHidden,numOutput):
    np.random.seed(1)
    w1=np.random.randn(numHidden,numFeats)*0.01 #  Multiply by .01
    b1=np.zeros((numHidden,1))
    w2=np.random.randn(numOutput,numHidden)*0.01
    b2=np.zeros((numOutput,1))

    # Create a dictionary of the neural network parameters
    nnParameters={'W1':w1,'b1':b1,'W2':w2,'b2':b2}
    return(nnParameters)


# Initialize model for L layers
# Input : List of units in each layer
# Returns: Initial weights and biases matrices for all layers
def initializeDeepModel(layerDimensions):
    np.random.seed(3)
    # note the Weight matrix at layer 'l' is a matrix of size (l,l-1)
    # The Bias is a vectors of size (l,1)

    # Loop through the layer dimension from 1.. L
    layerParams = {}
    for l in range(1,len(layerDimensions)):
        layerParams['W' + str(l)] =
np.random.randn(layerDimensions[l],layerDimensions[l-1])*0.01 #  Multiply by
.01
        layerParams['b' + str(l)] = np.zeros((layerDimensions[l],1))

    return(layerParams)
    return Z, cache

# He Initialization model for L layers
# Input : List of units in each layer
# Returns: Initial weights and biases matrices for all layers
# He initilization multiplies the random numbers with
sqrt(2/layerDimensions[l-1])
def HeInitializeDeepModel(layerDimensions):
    np.random.seed(3)
    # note the Weight matrix at layer 'l' is a matrix of size (l,l-1)
    # The Bias is a vectors of size (l,1)

    # Loop through the layer dimension from 1.. L
    layerParams = {}
    for l in range(1,len(layerDimensions)):
        layerParams['W' + str(l)] = np.random.randn(layerDimensions[l],
                    layerDimensions[l-1])*np.sqrt(2/layerDimensions[l-1])
        layerParams['b' + str(l)] = np.zeros((layerDimensions[l],1))

    return(layerParams)
    return Z, cache

# Xavier Initialization model for L layers
# Input : List of units in each layer
# Returns: Initial weights and biases matrices for all layers
# Xavier initilization multiplies the random numbers with
sqrt(1/layerDimensions[l-1])
```

```python
def XavInitializeDeepModel(layerDimensions):
    np.random.seed(3)
    # note the Weight matrix at layer 'l' is a matrix of size (l,l-1)
    # The Bias is a vectors of size (l,1)

    # Loop through the layer dimension from 1.. L
    layerParams = {}
    for l in range(1,len(layerDimensions)):
        layerParams['W' + str(l)] = np.random.randn(layerDimensions[l],
                    layerDimensions[l-1])*np.sqrt(1/layerDimensions[l-1])
        layerParams['b' + str(l)] = np.zeros((layerDimensions[l],1))

    return(layerParams)
    return Z, cache

# Compute the activation at a layer 'l' for forward prop in a Deep Network
# Input : A_prev - Activation of previous layer
#         W,b - Weight and bias matrices and vectors
#         keep_prob
#         activationFunc - Activation function - sigmoid, tanh, relu etc
# Returns : The Activation of this layer
#         :
# Z = W * X + b
# A = sigmoid(Z), A= Relu(Z), A= tanh(Z)
def layerActivationForward(A_prev, W, b, keep_prob=1, activationFunc="relu"):

    # Compute Z
    Z = np.dot(W,A_prev) + b
    forward_cache = (A_prev, W, b)
    # Compute the activation for sigmoid
    if activationFunc == "sigmoid":
        A, activation_cache = sigmoid(Z)
    # Compute the activation for Relu
    elif activationFunc == "relu":
        A, activation_cache = relu(Z)
    # Compute the activation for tanh
    elif activationFunc == 'tanh':
        A, activation_cache = tanh(Z)
    elif activationFunc == 'softmax':
        A, activation_cache = stableSoftmax(Z)

    cache = (forward_cache, activation_cache)
    return A, cache

# Compute the forward propagation for layers 1..L
# Input : X - Input Features
#         parameters: Weights and biases
#         keep_prob
#         hiddenActivationFunc - Activation function at hidden layers
Relu/tanh
#         outputActivationFunc - Activation function at output -
sigmoid/softmax
# Returns : AL
#           caches
#           dropoutMat
# The forward propoagtion uses the Relu/tanh activation from layer 1..L-1 and
sigmoid actiovation at layer L
def forwardPropagationDeep(X, parameters,keep_prob=1,
hiddenActivationFunc='relu',outputActivationFunc='sigmoid'):
    caches = []
    #initialize the dropout matrix
    dropoutMat = {}
    # Set A to X (A0)
    A = X
```

```python
        L = int(len(parameters)/2)  # number of layers in the neural network
        # Loop through from layer 1 to upto layer L
        for l in range(1, L):
            A_prev = A
            # Zi = Wi x Ai-1 + bi   and Ai = g(Zi)
            A, cache = layerActivationForward(A_prev, parameters['W'+str(l)],
parameters['b'+str(l)], keep_prob, activationFunc = hiddenActivationFunc)

            # Randomly drop some activation units
            # Create a matrix as the same shape as A
            D = np.random.rand(A.shape[0],A.shape[1])
            D = (D < keep_prob)
            # We need to use the same 'dropout' matrix in backward propagation
            # Save the dropout matrix for use in backprop
            dropoutMat["D" + str(l)] =D
            A= np.multiply(A,D)
            A = np.divide(A,keep_prob)

            caches.append(cache)


    # Since this is binary classification use the sigmoid activation function in
    # last layer
    AL, cache = layerActivationForward(A, parameters['W'+str(L)],
parameters['b'+str(L)], activationFunc = outputActivationFunc)
    caches.append(cache)

    return AL, caches, dropoutMat


# Compute the cost
# Input : parameters
#       : AL
#       : Y
#       :outputActivationFunc - Activation function at output - sigmoid/softmax/tanh
# Output: cost
def computeCost(parameters,AL,Y,outputActivationFunc="sigmoid"):
    if outputActivationFunc=="sigmoid":
        m= float(Y.shape[1])
        # Element wise multiply for logprobs
        cost=-1/m *np.sum(Y*np.log(AL) + (1-Y)*(np.log(1-AL)))
        cost = np.squeeze(cost)
    elif outputActivationFunc=="softmax":
        # Take transpose of Y for softmax
        Y=Y.T
        m= float(len(Y))
        # Compute log probs. Take the log prob of correct class based on output y
        correct_logprobs = -np.log(AL[range(int(m)),Y.T])
        # Conpute loss
        cost = np.sum(correct_logprobs)/m
    return cost


# Compute the cost with regularization
# Input : parameters
#       : AL
#       : Y
#       : lambd
#       :outputActivationFunc - Activation function at output - sigmoid/softmax/tanh
# Output: cost
```

```python
def computeCostWithReg(parameters,AL,Y,lambd,
outputActivationFunc="sigmoid"):
    if outputActivationFunc=="sigmoid":
        m= float(Y.shape[1])
        # Element wise multiply for logprobs
        cost=-1/m *np.sum(Y*np.log(AL) + (1-Y)*(np.log(1-AL)))
        cost = np.squeeze(cost)

        # Regularization cost
        L= int(len(parameters)/2)
        L2RegularizationCost=0
        for l in range(L):
            L2RegularizationCost+=np.sum(np.square(parameters['W'+str(l+1)]))

        L2RegularizationCost = (lambd/(2*m))*L2RegularizationCost
        cost = cost +  L2RegularizationCost

    elif outputActivationFunc=="softmax":
        # Take transpose of Y for softmax
        Y=Y.T
        m= float(len(Y))
        # Compute log probs. Take the log prob of correct class based on output y
        correct_logprobs = -np.log(AL[range(int(m)),Y.T])
        # Conpute loss
        cost = np.sum(correct_logprobs)/m

                # Regularization cost
        L= int(len(parameters)/2)
        L2RegularizationCost=0
        for l in range(L):
            L2RegularizationCost+=np.sum(np.square(parameters['W'+str(l+1)]))

        L2RegularizationCost = (lambd/(2*m))*L2RegularizationCost
        cost = cost +  L2RegularizationCost

    return cost

# Compute the backpropoagation for 1 cycle with dropout included
# Input : Neural Network parameters - dA
#         # cache - forward_cache & activation_cache
#         # Input features
#         # keep_prob
#         # Output values Y
# Returns: Gradients
# dL/dWi= dL/dZi*Al-1
# dl/dbl = dL/dZl
# dL/dZ_prev=dL/dZl*W
def layerActivationBackward(dA, cache, Y, keep_prob=1,
activationFunc="relu"):
    forward_cache, activation_cache = cache
    A_prev, W, b = forward_cache
    numtraining = float(A_prev.shape[1])
    #print("n=",numtraining)
    #print("no=",numtraining)
    if activationFunc == "relu":
        dZ = reluDerivative(dA, activation_cache)
    elif activationFunc == "sigmoid":
        dZ = sigmoidDerivative(dA, activation_cache)
    elif activationFunc == "tanh":
        dZ = tanhDerivative(dA, activation_cache)
    elif activationFunc == "softmax":
        dZ = stableSoftmaxDerivative(dA, activation_cache,Y,numtraining)
```

```python
        if activationFunc == 'softmax':
            dW = 1/numtraining * np.dot(A_prev,dZ)
            db = 1/numtraining * np.sum(dZ, axis=0, keepdims=True)
            dA_prev = np.dot(dZ,W)
        else:
            #print(numtraining)
            dW = 1/numtraining *(np.dot(dZ,A_prev.T))
            #print("dW=",dW)
            db = 1/numtraining * np.sum(dZ, axis=1, keepdims=True)
            #print("db=",db)
            dA_prev = np.dot(W.T,dZ)

    return dA_prev, dW, db


# Compute the backpropoagation with regularization for 1 cycle
# Input : dA-Neural Network parameters
#         # cache - forward_cache & activation_cache
#         # Output values Y
#         # lambd
#         # activationFunc
# Returns dA_prev, dW, db
# Returns: Gradients
# dL/dWi= dL/dZi*Al-1
# dl/dbl = dL/dZl
# dL/dZ_prev=dL/dZl*W
def layerActivationBackwardWithReg(dA, cache, Y, lambd, activationFunc):
    forward_cache, activation_cache = cache
    A_prev, W, b = forward_cache
    numtraining = float(A_prev.shape[1])
    #print("n=",numtraining)
    #print("no=",numtraining)
    if activationFunc == "relu":
        dZ = reluDerivative(dA, activation_cache)
    elif activationFunc == "sigmoid":
        dZ = sigmoidDerivative(dA, activation_cache)
    elif activationFunc == "tanh":
        dZ = tanhDerivative(dA, activation_cache)
    elif activationFunc == "softmax":
        dZ = stableSoftmaxDerivative(dA, activation_cache,Y,numtraining)

    if activationFunc == 'softmax':
        # Add the regularization factor
        dW = 1/numtraining * np.dot(A_prev,dZ) +  (lambd/numtraining) * W.T
        db = 1/numtraining * np.sum(dZ, axis=0, keepdims=True)
        dA_prev = np.dot(dZ,W)
    else:
        # Add the regularization factor
        dW = 1/numtraining *(np.dot(dZ,A_prev.T)) + (lambd/numtraining) * W
        #print("dW=",dW)
        db = 1/numtraining * np.sum(dZ, axis=1, keepdims=True)
        #print("db=",db)
        dA_prev = np.dot(W.T,dZ)
    return dA_prev, dW, db

# Compute the backpropoagation for 1 cycle
# Input : AL: Output of L layer Network - weights
#         # Y  Real output
#         # caches -- list of caches containing:
#         # dropoutMat
#         # lambd
#         # keep_prob
#         every cache of layerActivationForward() with "relu"/"tanh"
#         #(it's caches[l], for l in range(L-1) i.e l = 0...L-2)
```

```
#           #the cache of layerActivationForward() with "sigmoid" (it's caches[L-
1])
#         # hiddenActivationFunc - Activation function at hidden layers -
relu/sigmoid/tanh
#           #outputActivationFunc - Activation function at output -
sigmoid/softmax
#
#    Returns:
#      gradients -- A dictionary with the gradients
#                   gradients["dA" + str(l)] = ...
#                   gradients["dW" + str(l)] = ...

def backwardPropagationDeep(AL, Y, caches, dropoutMat, lambd=0, keep_prob=1,
hiddenActivationFunc='relu',outputActivationFunc="sigmoid"):
    #initialize the gradients
    gradients = {}
    # Set the number of layers
    L = len(caches)
    m = float(AL.shape[1])

    if outputActivationFunc == "sigmoid":
        Y = Y.reshape(AL.shape) # after this line, Y is the same shape as AL
        # Initializing the backpropagation
        # dl/dAL= -(y/a + (1-y)/(1-a)) - At the output layer
        dAL = - (np.divide(Y, AL) - np.divide(1 - Y, 1 - AL))
    else:
        dAL =0
        Y=Y.T

    # Since this is a binary classification the activation at output is
sigmoid
    # Get the gradients at the last layer
    # Inputs: "AL, Y, caches".
    # Outputs: "gradients["dAL"], gradients["dWL"], gradients["dbL"]
    current_cache = caches[L-1]
    if lambd==0:
        gradients["dA" + str(L)], gradients["dW" + str(L)], gradients["db" +
str(L)] = layerActivationBackward(dAL, current_cache,
                                                Y, activationFunc =
outputActivationFunc)
    else: #Regularization
        gradients["dA" + str(L)], gradients["dW" + str(L)], gradients["db" +
str(L)] = layerActivationBackwardWithReg(dAL, current_cache,
                                                Y, lambd, activationFunc =
outputActivationFunc)

    # Note dA for softmax is the transpose
    if outputActivationFunc == "softmax":
        gradients["dA" + str(L)] = gradients["dA" + str(L)].T
    # Traverse in the reverse direction
    for l in reversed(range(L-1)):
        # Compute the gradients for L-1 to 1 for Relu/tanh
        # Inputs: "gradients["dA" + str(l + 2)], caches".
        # Outputs: "gradients["dA" + str(l + 1)] , gradients["dW" + str(l +
1)] , gradients["db" + str(l + 1)]
        current_cache = caches[l]

        #dA_prev_temp, dW_temp, db_temp =
layerActivationBackward(gradients['dA'+str(l+2)], current_cache,
activationFunc = "relu")
        if lambd==0:

            # In the reverse direction use the dame dropout matrix
            # Random dropout
```

```python
                    # Multiply dA'l' with the dropoutMat and divide to keep the
expected value same
                    D = dropoutMat["D" + str(l+1)]
                    # Drop some dAl's
                    gradients['dA'+str(l+2)]= np.multiply(gradients['dA'+str(l+2)],D)
                    # Divide by keep_prob to keep expected value same
                    gradients['dA'+str(l+2)] = np.divide(gradients['dA'+str(l+2)],keep_prob)

                    dA_prev_temp, dW_temp, db_temp = layerActivationBackward(gradients['dA'+str(l+2)], current_cache, Y, keep_prob=1, activationFunc = hiddenActivationFunc)

            else:
                    dA_prev_temp, dW_temp, db_temp = layerActivationBackwardWithReg(gradients['dA'+str(l+2)], current_cache, Y, lambd, activationFunc = hiddenActivationFunc)

            gradients["dA" + str(l + 1)] = dA_prev_temp
            gradients["dW" + str(l + 1)] = dW_temp
            gradients["db" + str(l + 1)] = db_temp


    return gradients

# Perform Gradient Descent
# Input : Weights and biases
#         : gradients
#         : learning rate
#         : outputActivationFunc - Activation function at output - sigmoid/softmax
#output : Updated weights after 1 iteration
def gradientDescent(parameters, gradients, learningRate,outputActivationFunc="sigmoid"):

    L = int(len(parameters) / 2)
    # Update rule for each parameter.
    for l in range(L-1):
        parameters["W" + str(l+1)] = parameters['W'+str(l+1)] -learningRate* gradients['dW' + str(l+1)]
        parameters["b" + str(l+1)] = parameters['b'+str(l+1)] -learningRate* gradients['db' + str(l+1)]

    if outputActivationFunc=="sigmoid":
        parameters["W" + str(L)] = parameters['W'+str(L)] -learningRate* gradients['dW' + str(L)]
        parameters["b" + str(L)] = parameters['b'+str(L)] -learningRate* gradients['db' + str(L)]
    elif outputActivationFunc=="softmax":
        parameters["W" + str(L)] = parameters['W'+str(L)] -learningRate* gradients['dW' + str(L)].T
        parameters["b" + str(L)] = parameters['b'+str(L)] -learningRate* gradients['db' + str(L)].T
    return parameters




#  Execute a L layer Deep learning model
# Input : X - Input features
#         : Y output
#         : layersDimensions - Dimension of layers
```

```python
#          : hiddenActivationFunc - Activation function at hidden layer relu
/tanh/sigmoid
#          : outputActivationFunc - Activation function at output layer
sigmoid/softmax
#          : learning rate
#          : lambd
#          : keep_prob
#          : num of iteration
#          : initType
#output : parameters
def L_Layer_DeepModel(X1, Y1, layersDimensions, hiddenActivationFunc='relu',
outputActivationFunc="sigmoid",
                      learningRate = .3,   lambd=0, keep_prob=1,
num_iterations = 10000,initType="default",
print_cost=False,figure="figa.png"):

    np.random.seed(1)
    costs = []

    # Parameters initialization.
    if initType == "He":
       parameters = HeInitializeDeepModel(layersDimensions)
    elif initType == "Xavier" :
       parameters = XavInitializeDeepModel(layersDimensions)
    else: #Default
       parameters = initializeDeepModel(layersDimensions)
    # Loop (gradient descent)
    for i in range(0, num_iterations):

        AL, caches, dropoutMat = forwardPropagationDeep(X1, parameters,
keep_prob,
hiddenActivationFunc="relu",outputActivationFunc=outputActivationFunc)

        # Regularization parameter is 0
        if lambd==0:
            # Compute cost
            cost = computeCost(parameters,AL, Y1,
outputActivationFunc=outputActivationFunc)
        # Include L2 regularization
        else:
           # Compute cost
            cost = computeCostWithReg(parameters,AL, Y1, lambd,
outputActivationFunc=outputActivationFunc)

        # Backward propagation.
        gradients = backwardPropagationDeep(AL, Y1, caches, dropoutMat,
lambd, keep_prob,
hiddenActivationFunc="relu",outputActivationFunc=outputActivationFunc)

        # Update parameters.
        parameters = gradientDescent(parameters, gradients,
learningRate=learningRate,outputActivationFunc=outputActivationFunc)


        # Print the cost every 100 training example
        if print_cost and i % 1000 == 0:
            print ("Cost after iteration %i: %f" %(i, cost))
        if print_cost and i % 1000 == 0:
            costs.append(cost)

    # plot the cost
    plt.plot(np.squeeze(costs))
    plt.ylabel('Cost')
    plt.xlabel('No of iterations (x1000)')
```

```python
            plt.title("Learning rate =" + str(learningRate))
            plt.savefig(figure,bbox_inches='tight')
            #plt.show()
            plt.clf()
            plt.close()



    return parameters

#  Execute a L layer Deep learning model Stoachastic Gradient Descent
# Input : X1 - Input features
#        : Y1- output
#        : layersDimensions - Dimension of layers
#        : hiddenActivationFunc - Activation function at hidden layer relu
/tanh/sigmoid
#        : outputActivationFunc - Activation function at output -
sigmoid/softmax
#        : learning rate
#        : mini_batch_size
#        : num_epochs
#output : parameters

def L_Layer_DeepModel_SGD(X1, Y1, layersDimensions,
hiddenActivationFunc='relu', outputActivationFunc="sigmoid",learningRate =
.3, mini_batch_size = 64, num_epochs = 2500, print_cost=False):#lr was 0.009

    np.random.seed(1)
    costs = []

    # Parameters initialization.
    parameters = initializeDeepModel(layersDimensions)
    seed=10
    # Loop for number of epochs
    for i in range(num_epochs):
        # Define the random minibatches. We increment the seed to reshuffle
differently the dataset after each epoch
        seed = seed + 1
        minibatches = random_mini_batches(X1, Y1, mini_batch_size, seed)

        batch=0
        # Loop through each mini batch
        for minibatch in minibatches:
            #print("batch=",batch)
            batch=batch+1
            # Select a minibatch
            (minibatch_X, minibatch_Y) = minibatch

            # Perfrom forward propagation
            AL, caches = forwardPropagationDeep(minibatch_X,
parameters,hiddenActivationFunc="relu",outputActivationFunc=outputActivationF
unc)

            # Compute cost
            cost = computeCost(AL,
minibatch_Y,outputActivationFunc=outputActivationFunc)
            #print("minibatch_Y=",minibatch_Y.shape)
            # Backward propagation.
            gradients = backwardPropagationDeep(AL, minibatch_Y,
caches,hiddenActivationFunc="relu",outputActivationFunc=outputActivationFunc)

            # Update parameters.
            parameters = gradientDescent(parameters, gradients,
learningRate=learningRate,outputActivationFunc=outputActivationFunc)
```

```python
            # Print the cost every 1000 epoch
            if print_cost and i % 100 == 0:
                print ("Cost after epoch %i: %f" %(i, cost))
            if print_cost and i % 100 == 0:
                costs.append(cost)

    # plot the cost
    plt.plot(np.squeeze(costs))
    plt.ylabel('cost')
    plt.xlabel('No of iterations')
    plt.title("Learning rate =" + str(learningRate))
    #plt.show()
    plt.savefig("fig1",bbox_inches='tight')
    plt.close()
    return parameters


# Create random mini batches
# Input : X - Input features
#         : Y- output
#         : miniBatchSizes
#         : seed
#output : mini_batches
def random_mini_batches(X, Y, miniBatchSize = 64, seed = 0):

    np.random.seed(seed)
    # Get number of training samples
    m = X.shape[1]
    # Initialize mini batches
    mini_batches = []

    # Create  a list of random numbers < m
    permutation = list(np.random.permutation(m))
    # Randomly shuffle the training data
    shuffled_X = X[:, permutation]
    shuffled_Y = Y[:, permutation].reshape((1,m))

    # Compute number of mini batches
    numCompleteMinibatches = math.floor(m/miniBatchSize)

    # For the number of mini batches
    for k in range(0, numCompleteMinibatches):

        # Set the start and end of each mini batch
        mini_batch_X = shuffled_X[:, k*miniBatchSize : (k+1) * miniBatchSize]
        mini_batch_Y = shuffled_Y[:, k*miniBatchSize : (k+1) * miniBatchSize]

        mini_batch = (mini_batch_X, mini_batch_Y)
        mini_batches.append(mini_batch)


    #if m % miniBatchSize != 0:. The batch does not evenly divide by the mini batch
    if m % miniBatchSize != 0:
        l=math.floor(m/miniBatchSize)*miniBatchSize
        # Set the start and end of last mini batch
        m=l+m % miniBatchSize
        mini_batch_X = shuffled_X[:,l:m]
        mini_batch_Y = shuffled_Y[:,l:m]

        mini_batch = (mini_batch_X, mini_batch_Y)
        mini_batches.append(mini_batch)

```

```python
        return mini_batches

# Plot a decision boundary
# Input : Input Model,
#           X
#           Y
#           sz - Num of hiden units
#           lr - Learning rate
#           Fig to be saved as
# Returns Null
def plot_decision_boundary(model, X, y,lr,figure1="figb.png"):
    print("plot")
    # Set min and max values and give it some padding
    x_min, x_max = X[0, :].min() - 1, X[0, :].max() + 1
    y_min, y_max = X[1, :].min() - 1, X[1, :].max() + 1
    colors=['black','gold']
    cmap = matplotlib.colors.ListedColormap(colors)
    h = 0.01
    # Generate a grid of points with distance h between them
    xx, yy = np.meshgrid(np.arange(x_min, x_max, h), np.arange(y_min, y_max, h))
    # Predict the function value for the whole grid
    Z = model(np.c_[xx.ravel(), yy.ravel()])
    Z = Z.reshape(xx.shape)
    # Plot the contour and training examples
    plt.contourf(xx, yy, Z, cmap="coolwarm")
    plt.ylabel('x2')
    plt.xlabel('x1')
    x=X.T
    y=y.T.reshape(300,)
    plt.scatter(x[:, 0], x[:, 1], c=y, s=20);
    print(X.shape)
    plt.title("Decision Boundary for learning rate:"+lr)
    plt.savefig(figure1, bbox_inches='tight')
    #plt.show()


def predict(parameters, X,keep_prob=1,hiddenActivationFunc="relu",outputActivationFunc="sigmoid"):
    A2, cache,dropoutMat = forwardPropagationDeep(X, parameters, keep_prob=1, hiddenActivationFunc="relu",outputActivationFunc=outputActivationFunc)
    predictions = (A2>0.5)
    return predictions

def predict_proba(parameters, X,outputActivationFunc="sigmoid"):
    A2, cache = forwardPropagationDeep(X, parameters)
    if outputActivationFunc=="sigmoid":
       proba=A2
    elif outputActivationFunc=="softmax":
       proba=np.argmax(A2, axis=0).reshape(-1,1)
       print("A2=",A2.shape)
    return proba

# Plot a decision boundary
# Input : Input Model,
#           X
#           Y
#           sz - Num of hiden units
#           lr - Learning rate
#           Fig to be saved as
# Returns Null
def plot_decision_boundary1(X, y,W1,b1,W2,b2,figure2="figc.png"):
    #plot_decision_boundary(lambda x: predict(parameters, x.T), x1,y1.T,str(0.3),"fig2.png")
```

```
        h = 0.02
        x_min, x_max = X[:, 0].min() - 1, X[:, 0].max() + 1
        y_min, y_max = X[:, 1].min() - 1, X[:, 1].max() + 1
        xx, yy = np.meshgrid(np.arange(x_min, x_max, h),
                             np.arange(y_min, y_max, h))
        Z = np.dot(np.maximum(0, np.dot(np.c_[xx.ravel(), yy.ravel()], W1.T) +
b1.T), W2.T) + b2.T
        Z = np.argmax(Z, axis=1)
        Z = Z.reshape(xx.shape)

        fig = plt.figure()
        plt.contourf(xx, yy, Z, cmap=plt.cm.Spectral, alpha=0.8)
        print(X.shape)
        y1=y.reshape(300,)
        plt.scatter(X[:, 0], X[:, 1], c=y1, s=40, cmap=plt.cm.Spectral)
        plt.xlim(xx.min(), xx.max())
        plt.ylim(yy.min(), yy.max())
        plt.savefig(figure2, bbox_inches='tight')

# Load the circles data set
def load_dataset():
    np.random.seed(1)
    train_X, train_Y = sklearn.datasets.make_circles(n_samples=300,
noise=.05)
    np.random.seed(2)
    test_X, test_Y = sklearn.datasets.make_circles(n_samples=100, noise=.05)
    # Visualize the data
    print(train_X.shape)
    print(train_Y.shape)
    print("load")
    #plt.scatter(train_X[:, 0], train_X[:, 1], c=train_Y, s=40,
cmap=plt.cm.Spectral);
    train_X = train_X.T
    train_Y = train_Y.reshape((1, train_Y.shape[0]))
    test_X = test_X.T
    test_Y = test_Y.reshape((1, test_Y.shape[0]))
    return train_X, train_Y, test_X, test_Y
```

6.2 R

```
#################################################################
################################
#
# File    : DLfunctions6.R
# Author  : Tinniam V Ganesh
# Date    : 16 Apr 2018
#
#################################################################
############################
library(ggplot2)
library(PRROC)
library(dplyr)

# Compute the sigmoid of a vector
sigmoid <- function(Z){
  A <- 1/(1+ exp(-Z))
  cache<-Z
  retvals <- list("A"=A,"Z"=Z)
```

```r
19      return(retvals)
20
21  }
22
23  # Compute the Relu(old) of a vector (performance hog!)
24  reluOld    <-function(Z){
25      A <- apply(Z, 1:2, function(x) max(0,x))
26      cache<-Z
27      retvals <- list("A"=A,"Z"=Z)
28      return(retvals)
29  }
30
31  # Compute the Relu of a vector (performs better!)
32  relu    <-function(Z){
33         # Perform relu. Set values less that equal to 0 as 0
34         Z[Z<0]=0
35         A=Z
36         cache<-Z
37         retvals <- list("A"=A,"Z"=Z)
38         return(retvals)
39  }
40
41  # Compute the tanh activation of a vector
42  tanhActivation <- function(Z){
43      A <- tanh(Z)
44      cache<-Z
45      retvals <- list("A"=A,"Z"=Z)
46      return(retvals)
47  }
48
49  # Conmpute the softmax of a vector
50  softmax     <- function(Z){
51      # get unnormalized probabilities
52      exp_scores = exp(t(Z))
53      # normalize them for each example
54      A = exp_scores / rowSums(exp_scores)
55      retvals <- list("A"=A,"Z"=Z)
56      return(retvals)
57  }
58
59  # Compute the detivative of Relu
60  # g'(z) = 1 if z >0 and 0 otherwise
61  reluDerivative      <-function(dA, cache){
62      Z <- cache
63      dZ <- dA
64      # Create a logical matrix of values > 0
65      a <- Z > 0
66      # When z <= 0, you should set dz to 0 as well. Perform an element wise
67  multiple
68      dZ <- dZ * a
69      return(dZ)
70  }
71
72  # Compute the derivative of sigmoid
73  # Derivative g'(z) = a* (1-a)
74  sigmoidDerivative     <- function(dA, cache){
75      Z <- cache
76      s <- 1/(1+exp(-z))
77      dZ <- dA * s * (1-s)
78      return(dZ)
79  }
80
81  # Compute the derivative of tanh
82  # Derivative g'(z) = 1- a^2
```

```r
tanhDerivative   <- function(dA, cache){
  Z = cache
  a = tanh(Z)
  dZ = dA * (1 - a^2)
  return(dZ)
}

# This function is used in computing the softmax derivative
# Populate a matrix of 1s in rows where Y==1
# This may need to be extended for K classes. Currently
# supports K=3 & K=10
popMatrix <- function(Y,numClasses){
     a=rep(0,times=length(Y))
     Y1=matrix(a,nrow=length(Y),ncol=numClasses)
     #Set the rows and columns as 1's where Y is the class value
     if(numClasses==3){
         Y1[Y==0,1]=1
         Y1[Y==1,2]=1
         Y1[Y==2,3]=1
     } else if (numClasses==10){
         Y1[Y==0,1]=1
         Y1[Y==1,2]=1
         Y1[Y==2,3]=1
         Y1[Y==3,4]=1
         Y1[Y==4,5]=1
         Y1[Y==5,6]=1
         Y1[Y==6,7]=1
         Y1[Y==7,8]=1
         Y1[Y==8,9]=1
         Y1[Y==9,0]=1
     }
     return(Y1)
}

# Compute the softmax derivative
softmaxDerivative    <- function(dA, cache ,y,numTraining,numClasses){
  # Note : dA not used. dL/dZ = dL/dA * dA/dZ = pi-yi
  Z <- cache
  # Compute softmax
  exp_scores = exp(t(Z))
  # normalize them for each example
  probs = exp_scores / rowSums(exp_scores)
  # Create a matrix of zeros
  Y1=popMatrix(y,numClasses)
  #a=rep(0,times=length(Y))
  #Y1=matrix(a,nrow=length(Y),ncol=numClasses)
  #Set the rows and columns as 1's where Y is the class value
  dZ = probs-Y1
  return(dZ)
}

# Initialize model for L layers
# Input : List of units in each layer
# Returns: Initial weights and biases matrices for all layers
initializeDeepModel <- function(layerDimensions){
  set.seed(2)

  # Initialize empty list
  layerParams <- list()

  # Note the Weight matrix at layer 'l' is a matrix of size (l,l-1)
  # The Bias is a vectors of size (l,1)

  # Loop through the layer dimension from 1.. L
```

```r
    # Indices in R start from 1
    for(l in 2:length(layersDimensions)){
      # Initialize a matrix of small random numbers of size l x l-1
      # Create random numbers of size  l x l-1
      w=rnorm(layersDimensions[l]*layersDimensions[l-1])*0.01
      # Create a weight matrix of size l x l-1 with this initial weights and
      # Add to list W1,W2... WL
      layerParams[[paste('W',l-1,sep="")]] = matrix(w,nrow=layersDimensions[l],
                                        ncol=layersDimensions[l-1])
      layerParams[[paste('b',l-1,sep="")]] = matrix(rep(0,layersDimensions[l]),

nrow=layersDimensions[l],ncol=1)
    }
    return(layerParams)
}

# He Initialization model for L layers
# Input : Vector of units in each layer
# Returns: Initial weights and biases matrices for all layers
# He initilization multiplies the random numbers with
sqrt(2/layerDimensions[previouslayer])
HeInitializeDeepModel <- function(layerDimensions){
    set.seed(2)

    # Initialize empty list
    layerParams <- list()

    # Note the Weight matrix at layer 'l' is a matrix of size (l,l-1)
    # The Bias is a vectors of size (l,1)

    # Loop through the layer dimension from 1.. L
    # Indices in R start from 1
    for(l in 2:length(layersDimensions)){
        # Initialize a matrix of small random numbers of size l x l-1
        # Create random numbers of size  l x l-1
        w=rnorm(layersDimensions[l]*layersDimensions[l-1])

        # Create a weight matrix of size l x l-1 with this initial weights and
        # Add to list W1,W2... WL
        # He initialization - Divide by sqrt(2/layerDimensions[previous layer])
        layerParams[[paste('W',l-1,sep="")]] = matrix(w,nrow=layersDimensions[l],

ncol=layersDimensions[l-1])*sqrt(2/layersDimensions[l-1])
        layerParams[[paste('b',l-1,sep="")]] = matrix(rep(0,layersDimensions[l]),

nrow=layersDimensions[l],ncol=1)
    }
    return(layerParams)
}

# XavInitializeDeepModel Initialization model for L layers
# Input : Vrctor of units in each layer
# Returns: Initial weights and biases matrices for all layers
# He initilization multiplies the random numbers with
sqrt(1/layerDimensions[previouslayer])
XavInitializeDeepModel <- function(layerDimensions){
    set.seed(2)

    # Initialize empty list
    layerParams <- list()
```

```r
        # Note the Weight matrix at layer 'l' is a matrix of size (l,l-1)
        # The Bias is a vectors of size (l,1)

        # Loop through the layer dimension from 1.. L
        # Indices in R start from 1
        for(l in 2:length(layersDimensions)){
            # Initialize a matrix of small random numbers of size l x l-1
            # Create random numbers of size  l x l-1
            w=rnorm(layersDimensions[l]*layersDimensions[l-1])

            # Create a weight matrix of size l x l-1 with this initial weights and
            # Add to list W1,W2... WL
            # He initialization - Divide by sqrt(2/layerDimensions[previous layer])
            layerParams[[paste('W',l-1,sep="")]] = matrix(w,nrow=layersDimensions[l],
ncol=layersDimensions[l-1])*sqrt(1/layersDimensions[l-1])
            layerParams[[paste('b',l-1,sep="")]] = matrix(rep(0,layersDimensions[l]),
nrow=layersDimensions[l],ncol=1)
        }
    return(layerParams)
}


# Compute the activation at a layer 'l' for forward prop in a Deep Network
# Input : A_prev - Activation of previous layer
#         W,b - Weight and bias matrices and vectors
#         activationFunc - Activation function - sigmoid, tanh, relu etc
# Returns : The Activation of this layer
#         :
# Z = W * X + b
# A = sigmoid(Z), A= Relu(Z), A= tanh(Z)
layerActivationForward <- function(A_prev, W, b, activationFunc){

  # Compute Z
  z = W %*% A_prev
  # Broadcast the bias 'b' by column
  Z <-sweep(z,1,b,'+')

  forward_cache <- list("A_prev"=A_prev, "W"=W, "b"=b)
  # Compute the activation for sigmoid
  if(activationFunc == "sigmoid"){
    vals = sigmoid(Z)
  } else if (activationFunc == "relu"){ # Compute the activation for relu
    vals = relu(Z)
  } else if(activationFunc == 'tanh'){ # Compute the activation for tanh
    vals = tanhActivation(Z)
  } else if(activationFunc == 'softmax'){
    vals = softmax(Z)
  }
  # Create a list of forward and activation cache
  cache <- list("forward_cache"=forward_cache, "activation_cache"=vals[['Z']])
  retvals <- list("A"=vals[['A']],"cache"=cache)
  return(retvals)
}


# Compute the forward propagation for layers 1..L
```

```r
# Input : X - Input Features
#         parameters: Weights and biases
#         keep_prob
#         hiddenActivationFunc - relu/sigmoid/tanh
#         outputActivationFunc - Activation function at hidden layer
sigmoid/softmax
# Returns : AL
#           caches
#           dropoutMat
# The forward propoagtion uses the Relu/tanh activation from layer 1..L-1 and
sigmoid actiovation at layer L
forwardPropagationDeep <- function(X, parameters,keep_prob=1,
hiddenActivationFunc='relu',
                                                  outputActivationFunc='sigmoid'){
  caches <- list()
  dropoutMat <- list()
  # Set A to X (A0)
  A <- X
  L <- length(parameters)/2 # number of layers in the neural network
  # Loop through from layer 1 to upto layer L
  for(l in 1:(L-1)){
    A_prev <- A
    # Zi = Wi x Ai-1 + bi   and Ai = g(Zi)
    # Set W and b for layer 'l'
    # Loop throug from W1,W2... WL-1
    W <- parameters[[paste("W",l,sep="")]]
    b <- parameters[[paste("b",l,sep="")]]
    # Compute the forward propagation through layer 'l' using the activation
function
    actForward <- layerActivationForward(A_prev,
                                          W,
                                          b,
                                          activationFunc =
hiddenActivationFunc)
    A <- actForward[['A']]
    # Append the cache A_prev,W,b, Z
    caches[[l]] <-actForward

    # Randomly drop some activation units
    # Create a matrix as the same shape as A
    set.seed(1)
    i=dim(A)[1]
    j=dim(A)[2]
    a<-rnorm(i*j)
    # Normalize a between 0 and 1
    a = (a - min(a))/(max(a) - min(a))
    # Create a matrix of D
    D <- matrix(a,nrow=i, ncol=j)
    # Find D which is less than equal to keep_prob
    D <- D < keep_prob
    # Remove some A's
    A <- A * D
    # Divide by keep_prob to keep expected value same
    A <- A/keep_prob
    dropoutMat[[paste("D",l,sep="")]] <- D
  }

  # Since this is binary classification use the sigmoid activation function in
  # last layer
  # Set the weights and biases for the last layer
  W <- parameters[[paste("W",L,sep="")]]
  b <- parameters[[paste("b",L,sep="")]]
  # Compute the sigmoid activation
```

```
339     actForward = layerActivationForward(A, W, b, activationFunc =
340 outputActivationFunc)
341     AL <- actForward[['A']]
342     # Append the output of this forward propagation through the last layer
343     caches[[L]] <- actForward
344     # Create a list of the final output and the caches
345     fwdPropDeep <- list("AL"=AL,"caches"=caches,"dropoutMat"=dropoutMat)
346     return(fwdPropDeep)
347
348 }
349
350 # Function pickColumns(). This function is in computeCost()
351 # Pick columns
352 # Input : AL
353 #         : Y
354 #         : numClasses
355 # Output: a
356 pickColumns <- function(AL,Y,numClasses){
357     if(numClasses==3){
358         a=c(AL[Y==0,1],AL[Y==1,2],AL[Y==2,3])
359     }
360     else if (numClasses==10){
361         a=c(AL[Y==0,1],AL[Y==1,2],AL[Y==2,3],AL[Y==3,4],AL[Y==4,5],
362             AL[Y==5,6],AL[Y==6,7],AL[Y==7,8],AL[Y==8,9],AL[Y==9,10])
363     }
364     return(a)
365 }
366
367
368 # Compute the cost
369 # Input : AL-Activation of last layer
370 #         : Y-Output from data
371 #         : outputActivationFunc - Activation function at hidden layer
372 sigmoid/softmax
373 #         : numClasses
374 # Output: cost
375 computeCost <- function(AL,Y,outputActivationFunc="sigmoid",numClasses=3){
376     if(outputActivationFunc=="sigmoid"){
377         m= length(Y)
378         cost=-1/m*sum(Y*log(AL) + (1-Y)*log(1-AL))
379
380
381     }else if (outputActivationFunc=="softmax"){
382         # Select the elements where the y values are 0, 1 or 2 and make a vector
383         # Pick columns
384         #a=c(AL[Y==0,1],AL[Y==1,2],AL[Y==2,3])
385         m= length(Y)
386         a =pickColumns(AL,Y,numClasses)
387         #a = c(A2[y=k,k+1])
388         # Take log
389         correct_probs = -log(a)
390         # Compute loss
391         cost= sum(correct_probs)/m
392     }
393     #cost=-1/m*sum(a+b)
394     return(cost)
395 }
396
397
398 # Compute the cost with Regularization
399 # Input : parameters
400 #         : AL-Activation of last layer
401 #         : Y-Output from data
402 #         : lambd
```

```r
#          : outputActivationFunc - Activation function at hidden layer
sigmoid/softmax
#          : numClasses
# Output: cost
computeCostWithReg <- function(parameters, AL,Y,lambd,
outputActivationFunc="sigmoid",numClasses=3){

            if(outputActivationFunc=="sigmoid"){
            m= length(Y)
            cost=-1/m*sum(Y*log(AL) + (1-Y)*log(1-AL))

            # Regularization cost
            L <- length(parameters)/2
            L2RegularizationCost=0
            for(l in 1:L){
                L2RegularizationCost = L2RegularizationCost +
                            sum(parameters[[paste("W",l,sep="")]]^2)
            }
            L2RegularizationCost = (lambd/(2*m))*L2RegularizationCost
            cost = cost +  L2RegularizationCost

        }else if (outputActivationFunc=="softmax"){
            # Select the elements where the y values are 0, 1 or 2 and make a vector
            # Pick columns
            #a=c(AL[Y==0,1],AL[Y==1,2],AL[Y==2,3])
            m= length(Y)
            a =pickColumns(AL,Y,numClasses)
            #a = c(A2[y=k,k+1])
            # Take log
            correct_probs = -log(a)
            # Compute loss
            cost= sum(correct_probs)/m

            # Regularization cost
            L <- length(parameters)/2
            L2RegularizationCost=0
            # Add L2 norm
            for(l in 1:L){
                L2RegularizationCost = L2RegularizationCost +
                    sum(parameters[[paste("W",l,sep="")]]^2)
            }
            L2RegularizationCost = (lambd/(2*m))*L2RegularizationCost
            cost = cost +  L2RegularizationCost
        }
     return(cost)
}

# Compute the backpropagation through a layer
# Input : Neural Network parameters - dA
#         # cache - forward_cache & activation_cache
#         # Output values Y
#         # activationFunc
#         # numClasses
# Returns: Gradients
# dL/dWi= dL/dZi*Al-1
# dl/dbl = dL/dZl
# dL/dZ_prev=dL/dZl*W

layerActivationBackward  <- function(dA, cache, Y,
activationFunc,numClasses){
   # Get A_prev,W,b
   forward_cache <-cache[['forward_cache']]
   activation_cache <- cache[['activation_cache']]
```

```r
    A_prev <- forward_cache[['A_prev']]
    numtraining = dim(A_prev)[2]
    # Get Z
    activation_cache <- cache[['activation_cache']]
    if(activationFunc == "relu"){
      dZ <- reluDerivative(dA, activation_cache)
    } else if(activationFunc == "sigmoid"){
      dZ <- sigmoidDerivative(dA, activation_cache)
    } else if(activationFunc == "tanh"){
      dZ <- tanhDerivative(dA, activation_cache)
    } else if(activationFunc == "softmax"){
      dZ <- softmaxDerivative(dA, activation_cache,Y,numtraining,numClasses)
    }

    if (activationFunc == 'softmax'){
      W <- forward_cache[['W']]
      b <- forward_cache[['b']]
      dW = 1/numtraining * A_prev%*%dZ
      db = 1/numtraining* matrix(colSums(dZ),nrow=1,ncol=numClasses)
      dA_prev = dZ %*%W
    } else {
      W <- forward_cache[['W']]
      b <- forward_cache[['b']]
      numtraining = dim(A_prev)[2]

      dW = 1/numtraining * dZ %*% t(A_prev)
      db = 1/numtraining * rowSums(dZ)
      dA_prev = t(W) %*% dZ
    }
    retvals <- list("dA_prev"=dA_prev,"dW"=dW,"db"=db)
    return(retvals)
}

# Compute the backpropagation through a layer with Regularization
# Input : dA-Neural Network parameters
#         # cache - forward_cache & activation_cache
#         # Output values Y
#         # lambd
#         # activationFunc
#         # numClasses
# Returns: Gradients
# dL/dWi= dL/dZi*Al-1
# dl/dbl = dL/dZl
# dL/dZ_prev=dL/dZl*W
layerActivationBackwardwithReg  <- function(dA, cache, Y, lambd,
activationFunc,numClasses){
    # Get A_prev,W,b
    forward_cache <-cache[['forward_cache']]
    activation_cache <- cache[['activation_cache']]
    A_prev <- forward_cache[['A_prev']]
    numtraining = dim(A_prev)[2]
    # Get Z
    activation_cache <- cache[['activation_cache']]
    if(activationFunc == "relu"){
        dZ <- reluDerivative(dA, activation_cache)
    } else if(activationFunc == "sigmoid"){
        dZ <- sigmoidDerivative(dA, activation_cache)
    } else if(activationFunc == "tanh"){
        dZ <- tanhDerivative(dA, activation_cache)
    } else if(activationFunc == "softmax"){
        dZ <- softmaxDerivative(dA,
activation_cache,Y,numtraining,numClasses)
    }

```

```r
    if (activationFunc == 'softmax'){
        W <- forward_cache[['W']]
        b <- forward_cache[['b']]
        # Add the regularization factor
        dW = 1/numtraining * A_prev%*%dZ  + (lambd/numtraining) * t(W)
        db = 1/numtraining* matrix(colSums(dZ),nrow=1,ncol=numClasses)
        dA_prev = dZ %*%W
    } else {
        W <- forward_cache[['W']]
        b <- forward_cache[['b']]
        numtraining = dim(A_prev)[2]
        # Add the regularization factor
        dW = 1/numtraining * dZ %*% t(A_prev) + (lambd/numtraining) * W
        db = 1/numtraining * rowSums(dZ)
        dA_prev = t(W) %*% dZ
    }
    retvals <- list("dA_prev"=dA_prev,"dW"=dW,"db"=db)
    return(retvals)
}

# Compute the backpropagation for 1 cycle through all layers
# Input : AL: Output of L layer Network - weights
#         Y  Real output
#         caches -- list of caches containing:
#         every cache of layerActivationForward() with "relu"/"tanh"
#         #(it's caches[l], for l in range(L-1) i.e l = 0...L-2)
#         #the cache of layerActivationForward() with "sigmoid" (it's caches[L-1])
#         dropoutMat
#         lambd
#         keep_prob
#         hiddenActivationFunc - Activation function at hidden layers - relu/tanh/sigmoid
#         outputActivationFunc - Activation function at hidden layer sigmoid/softmax
#         numClasses
#   Returns:
#     gradients -- A dictionary with the gradients
#                   gradients["dA" + str(l)]
#                   gradients["dW" + str(l)]
#                   gradients["db" + str(l)]
backwardPropagationDeep <- function(AL, Y, caches,dropoutMat, lambd=0,
keep_prob=0,  hiddenActivationFunc='relu',
                                    outputActivationFunc="sigmoid",numClasses){
    #initialize the gradients
    gradients = list()
    # Set the number of layers
    L = length(caches)
    numTraining = dim(AL)[2]

    if(outputActivationFunc == "sigmoid")
        # Initializing the backpropagation
        # dl/dAL= -(y/a) - ((1-y)/(1-a)) - At the output layer
        dAL = -( (Y/AL) -(1 - Y)/(1 - AL))
    else if(outputActivationFunc == "softmax"){
      dAL=0
      Y=t(Y)
    }

    # Get the gradients at the last layer
    # Inputs: "AL, Y, caches".
    # Outputs: "gradients["dAL"], gradients["dWL"], gradients["dbL"]
    # Start with Layer L
    # Get the current cache
```

```
595    current_cache = caches[[L]]$cache
596    if (lambd==0){
597       retvals <-  layerActivationBackward(dAL, current_cache, Y,
598                                          activationFunc =
599 outputActivationFunc,numClasses)
600    } else {
601        retvals = layerActivationBackwardWithReg(dAL, current_cache, Y, lambd,
602                                          activationFunc =
603 outputActivationFunc,numClasses)
604    }
605
606
607
608    #Note: Take the transpose of dA
609    if(outputActivationFunc =="sigmoid")
610        gradients[[paste("dA",L,sep="")]] <- retvals[['dA_prev']]
611    else if(outputActivationFunc =="softmax")
612      gradients[[paste("dA",L,sep="")]] <- t(retvals[['dA_prev']])
613      gradients[[paste("dW",L,sep="")]] <- retvals[['dW']]
614     gradients[[paste("db",L,sep="")]] <- retvals[['db']]
615
616    # Traverse in the reverse direction
617    for(l in (L-1):1){
618      # Compute the gradients for L-1 to 1 for Relu/tanh
619      # Inputs: "gradients["dA" + str(l + 2)], caches".
620      # Outputs: "gradients["dA" + str(l + 1)] , gradients["dW" + str(l + 1)] ,
621 gradients["db" + str(l + 1)]
622      current_cache = caches[[l]]$cache
623      if (lambd==0){
624         # Get the dropout matrix
625         D <-dropoutMat[[paste("D",l,sep="")]]
626         # Multiply gradient with dropout matrix
627         gradients[[paste('dA',l+1,sep="")]] =
628 gradients[[paste('dA',l+1,sep="")]] *D
629         # Divide by keep_prob to keep expected value same
630         gradients[[paste('dA',l+1,sep="")]] =
631 gradients[[paste('dA',l+1,sep="")]]/keep_prob
632         retvals =
633 layerActivationBackward(gradients[[paste('dA',l+1,sep="")]],
634                                          current_cache, Y,
635                                          activationFunc = hiddenActivationFunc)
636      } else {
637         retvals =
638 layerActivationBackwardWithReg(gradients[[paste('dA',l+1,sep="")]],
639                                          current_cache, Y, lambd,
640                                          activationFunc =
641 hiddenActivationFunc)
642      }
643
644      gradients[[paste("dA",l,sep="")]] <-retvals[['dA_prev']]
645      gradients[[paste("dW",l,sep="")]] <- retvals[['dW']]
646      gradients[[paste("db",l,sep="")]] <- retvals[['db']]
647    }
648
649
650
651    return(gradients)
652 }
653
654
655 # Perform Gradient Descent
656 # Input : Weights and biases
657 #       : gradients
658 #       : learning rate
```

```r
#         : outputActivationFunc - Activation function at hidden layer sigmoid/softmax
#output : Updated weights after 1 iteration
gradientDescent   <- function(parameters, gradients,
learningRate,outputActivationFunc="sigmoid"){

  L = length(parameters)/2 # number of layers in the neural network

  # Update rule for each parameter. Use a for loop.
  for(l in 1:(L-1)){
    parameters[[paste("W",l,sep="")]] = parameters[[paste("W",l,sep="")]] -
      learningRate* gradients[[paste("dW",l,sep="")]]
    parameters[[paste("b",l,sep="")]] = parameters[[paste("b",l,sep="")]] -
      learningRate* gradients[[paste("db",l,sep="")]]
  }
  if(outputActivationFunc=="sigmoid"){
    parameters[[paste("W",L,sep="")]] = parameters[[paste("W",L,sep="")]] -
      learningRate* gradients[[paste("dW",L,sep="")]]
    parameters[[paste("b",L,sep="")]] = parameters[[paste("b",L,sep="")]] -
      learningRate* gradients[[paste("db",L,sep="")]]

  }else if (outputActivationFunc=="softmax"){
    parameters[[paste("W",L,sep="")]] = parameters[[paste("W",L,sep="")]] -
      learningRate* t(gradients[[paste("dW",L,sep="")]])
    parameters[[paste("b",L,sep="")]] = parameters[[paste("b",L,sep="")]] -
      learningRate* t(gradients[[paste("db",L,sep="")]])
  }
  return(parameters)
}


# Execute a L layer Deep learning model
# Input : X - Input features
#         : Y output
#         : layersDimensions - Dimension of layers
#         : hiddenActivationFunc - Activation function at hidden layer relu/tanh
#         : outputActivationFunc - Activation function at hidden layer sigmoid/softmax
#         : learning rate
#         : lambd
#         : keep_prob
#         : learning rate
#         : num of iterations
#         : initType
#output : Updated weights
L_Layer_DeepModel <- function(X, Y, layersDimensions,
                              hiddenActivationFunc='relu',
                              outputActivationFunc= 'sigmoid',
                              learningRate = 0.5,
                              lambd=0,
                              keep_prob=1,
                              numIterations = 10000,
                              initType="default",
                              print_cost=False){
  #Initialize costs vector as NULL
  costs <- NULL

  # Parameters initialization.
  if (initType=="He"){
     parameters =HeInitializeDeepModel(layersDimensions)
  } else if (initType=="Xav"){
      parameters =XavInitializeDeepModel(layersDimensions)
  }
```

```r
    else{
        print("Here")
       parameters = initializeDeepModel(layersDimensions)
    }

   # Loop (gradient descent)
    for( i in 0:numIterations){
       # Forward propagation: [LINEAR -> RELU]*(L-1) -> LINEAR -> SIGMOID/SOFTMAX.
       retvals = forwardPropagationDeep(X, parameters,keep_prob, hiddenActivationFunc,

outputActivationFunc=outputActivationFunc)
      AL <- retvals[['AL']]
      caches <- retvals[['caches']]
      dropoutMat <- retvals[['dropoutMat']]

      # Compute cost.
      if(lambd==0){
          cost <- computeCost(AL, Y,outputActivationFunc=outputActivationFunc,numClasses=layersDimensions[length(layersDimensions)])
      } else {
          cost <- computeCostWithReg(parameters, AL, Y,lambd, outputActivationFunc=outputActivationFunc,numClasses=layersDimensions[length(layersDimensions)])
      }
      # Backward propagation.
      gradients = backwardPropagationDeep(AL, Y, caches, dropoutMat, lambd, keep_prob, hiddenActivationFunc,

outputActivationFunc=outputActivationFunc,numClasses=layersDimensions[length(layersDimensions)])

      # Update parameters.
      parameters = gradientDescent(parameters, gradients, learningRate,
                                    outputActivationFunc=outputActivationFunc)


     if(i%%1000 == 0){
        costs=c(costs,cost)
        print(cost)
     }
   }

   retvals <- list("parameters"=parameters,"costs"=costs)

   return(retvals)
}

# Execute a L layer Deep learning model with Stochastic Gradient descent
# Input : X - Input features
#         : Y output
#         : layersDimensions - Dimension of layers
#         : hiddenActivationFunc - Activation function at hidden layer relu/tanh
#         : outputActivationFunc - Activation function at hidden layer sigmoid/softmax
#         : learning rate
#         : mini_batch_size
#         : num of epochs
#output : Updated weights after each  iteration
L_Layer_DeepModel_SGD <- function(X, Y, layersDimensions,
                                    hiddenActivationFunc='relu',
```

```r
                                        outputActivationFunc= 'sigmoid',
                                        learningRate = .3,
                                        mini_batch_size = 64,
                                        num_epochs = 2500,
                                        print_cost=False){

    set.seed(1)
    #Initialize costs vector as NULL
    costs <- NULL

    # Parameters initialization.
    parameters = initializeDeepModel(layersDimensions)
    seed=10

    # Loop for number of epochs
    for( i in 0:num_epochs){
        seed=seed+1
        minibatches = random_mini_batches(X, Y, mini_batch_size, seed)

        for(batch in 1:length(minibatches)){

            mini_batch_X=minibatches[[batch]][['mini_batch_X']]
            mini_batch_Y=minibatches[[batch]][['mini_batch_Y']]
            # Forward propagation:
            retvals = forwardPropagationDeep(mini_batch_X,
parameters,hiddenActivationFunc,

outputActivationFunc=outputActivationFunc)
            AL <- retvals[['AL']]
            caches <- retvals[['caches']]

            # Compute cost.
            cost <- computeCost(AL,
mini_batch_Y,outputActivationFunc=outputActivationFunc,numClasses=layersDimen
sions[length(layersDimensions)])

            # Backward propagation.
            gradients = backwardPropagationDeep(AL, mini_batch_Y,
caches,hiddenActivationFunc,

outputActivationFunc=outputActivationFunc,numClasses=layersDimensions[length(
layersDimensions)])

            # Update parameters.
            parameters = gradientDescent(parameters, gradients, learningRate,

outputActivationFunc=outputActivationFunc)
        }

        if(i%%100 == 0){
            costs=c(costs,cost)
            print(cost)
        }
    }

    retvals <- list("parameters"=parameters,"costs"=costs)

    return(retvals)
}

# Predict the output for given input
# Input : parameters
#       : X
# Output: predictions
```

```r
predict <- function(parameters, X,keep_prob=1, hiddenActivationFunc='relu'){

    fwdProp <- forwardPropagationDeep(X, parameters,keep_prob,
hiddenActivationFunc)
    predictions <- fwdProp$AL>0.5

    return (predictions)
}

# Plot a decision boundary
# This function uses ggplot2
plotDecisionBoundary <-
function(z,retvals,keep_prob=1,hiddenActivationFunc="sigmoid",lr=0.5){
    # Find the minimum and maximum for the data
    xmin<-min(z[,1])
    xmax<-max(z[,1])
    ymin<-min(z[,2])
    ymax<-max(z[,2])

    # Create a grid of values
    a=seq(xmin,xmax,length=100)
    b=seq(ymin,ymax,length=100)
    grid <- expand.grid(x=a, y=b)
    colnames(grid) <- c('x1', 'x2')
    grid1 <-t(grid)
    # Predict the output for this grid
    q <-predict(retvals$parameters,grid1,keep_prob=1, hiddenActivationFunc)
    q1 <- t(data.frame(q))
    q2 <- as.numeric(q1)
    grid2 <- cbind(grid,q2)
    colnames(grid2) <- c('x1', 'x2','q2')

    z1 <- data.frame(z)
    names(z1) <- c("x1","x2","y")
    atitle=paste("Decision boundary for learning rate:",lr)
    # Plot the contour of the boundary
    ggplot(z1) +
        geom_point(data = z1, aes(x = x1, y = x2, color = y)) +
        stat_contour(data = grid2, aes(x = x1, y = x2, z = q2,color=q2), alpha =
0.9)+
        ggtitle(atitle) + scale_colour_gradientn(colours = brewer.pal(10,
"Spectral"))
}

# Predict the probability  scores for given data set
# Input : parameters
#       : X
# Output: probability of output
computeScores <- function(parameters, X,hiddenActivationFunc='relu'){

    fwdProp <- forwardPropagationDeep(X, parameters,hiddenActivationFunc)
    scores <- fwdProp$AL

    return (scores)
}

# Create random mini batches
# Input : X - Input features
#       : Y- output
#       : miniBatchSize
#       : seed
#output : mini_batches
random_mini_batches <- function(X, Y, miniBatchSize = 64, seed = 0){

```

```r
    set.seed(seed)
    # Get number of training samples
    m = dim(X)[2]
    # Initialize mini batches
    mini_batches = list()

    # Create  a list of random numbers < m
    permutation = c(sample(m))
    # Randomly shuffle the training data
    shuffled_X = X[, permutation]
    shuffled_Y = Y[1, permutation]

    # Compute number of mini batches
    numCompleteMinibatches = floor(m/miniBatchSize)
    batch=0
    for(k in 0:(numCompleteMinibatches-1)){
         batch=batch+1
         # Set the lower and upper bound of the mini batches
         lower=(k*miniBatchSize)+1
         upper=((k+1) * miniBatchSize)
         mini_batch_X = shuffled_X[, lower:upper]
         mini_batch_Y = shuffled_Y[lower:upper]
         # Add it to the list of mini batches
         mini_batch =
list("mini_batch_X"=mini_batch_X,"mini_batch_Y"=mini_batch_Y)
         mini_batches[[batch]] =mini_batch

    }

    # If the batch size does not divide evenly with mini batc size
    if(m %% miniBatchSize != 0){
        p=floor(m/miniBatchSize)*miniBatchSize
        # Set the start and end of last batch
        q=p+m %% miniBatchSize
        mini_batch_X = shuffled_X[,(p+1):q]
        mini_batch_Y = shuffled_Y[(p+1):q]
    }
    # Return the list of mini batches
    mini_batch =
list("mini_batch_X"=mini_batch_X,"mini_batch_Y"=mini_batch_Y)
    mini_batches[[batch]]=mini_batch

    return(mini_batches)
}

# Plot a decision boundary
# This function uses ggplot2
plotDecisionBoundary1 <- function(Z,parameters,keep_prob=1){
    xmin<-min(Z[,1])
    xmax<-max(Z[,1])
    ymin<-min(Z[,2])
    ymax<-max(Z[,2])

    # Create a grid of points
    a=seq(xmin,xmax,length=100)
    b=seq(ymin,ymax,length=100)
    grid <- expand.grid(x=a, y=b)
    colnames(grid) <- c('x1', 'x2')
    grid1 <-t(grid)

    retvals = forwardPropagationDeep(grid1, parameters,keep_prob, "relu",
                                     outputActivationFunc="softmax")
```

```
        AL <- retvals$AL
        # From the  softmax probabilities pick the one with the highest 
probability
        q= apply(AL,1,which.max)

        q1 <- t(data.frame(q))
        q2 <- as.numeric(q1)
        grid2 <- cbind(grid,q2)
        colnames(grid2) <- c('x1', 'x2','q2')

        Z1 <- data.frame(Z)
        names(Z1) <- c("x1","x2","y")
        atitle=paste("Decision boundary")
        ggplot(Z1) + 
            geom_point(data = Z1, aes(x = x1, y = x2, color = y)) + 
            stat_contour(data = grid2, aes(x = x1, y = x2, z = q2,color=q2), 
alpha = 0.9)+
            ggtitle(atitle) + scale_colour_gradientn(colours = brewer.pal(10, 
"Spectral"))
}
```

6.3 Octave

```
###############################################################################
###############################
#
# File    : DLfunctions61.m
# Author  : Tinniam V Ganesh
# Date    : 16 Apr 2018
#
###############################################################################
#############################
1;
# Define sigmoid function
function [A,cache] = sigmoid(Z)
  A = 1 ./ (1+ exp(-Z));
  cache=Z;
end

# Define Relu function
function [A,cache] = relu(Z)
  A = max(0,Z);
  cache=Z;
end

# Define Relu function
function [A,cache] = tanhAct(Z)
  A = tanh(Z);
  cache=Z;
end

# Define Softmax function
function [A,cache] = softmax(Z)
    # get unnormalized probabilities
    exp_scores = exp(Z');
    # normalize them for each example
    A = exp_scores ./ sum(exp_scores,2);
    cache=Z;
end

# Define Stable Softmax function
```

```octave
function [A,cache] = stableSoftmax(Z)
    # Normalize by max value in each row
    shiftZ = Z' - max(Z',[],2);
    exp_scores = exp(shiftZ);
    # normalize them for each example
    A = exp_scores ./ sum(exp_scores,2);
    #disp("sm")
    #disp(A);
    cache=Z;
end

# Define Relu Derivative
function [dZ] = reluDerivative(dA,cache)
  Z = cache;
  dZ = dA;
  # Get elements that are greater than 0
  a = (Z > 0);
  # Select only those elements where Z > 0
  dZ = dZ .* a;
end

# Define Sigmoid Derivative
function [dZ] = sigmoidDerivative(dA,cache)
  Z = cache;
  s = 1 ./ (1+ exp(-Z));
  dZ = dA .* s .* (1-s);
end

# Define Tanh Derivative
function [dZ] = tanhDerivative(dA,cache)
  Z = cache;
  a = tanh(Z);
  dZ = dA .* (1 - a .^ 2);
end

# Populate a matrix with 1s in rows where Y=1
# This function may need to be modified if K is not 3, 10
# This function is used in computing the softmax derivative
function [Y1] = popMatrix(Y,numClasses)
    Y1=zeros(length(Y),numClasses);
    if(numClasses==3) # For 3 output classes
       Y1(Y==0,1)=1;
       Y1(Y==1,2)=1;
       Y1(Y==2,3)=1;
    elseif(numClasses==10) # For 10 output classes
       Y1(Y==0,1)=1;
       Y1(Y==1,2)=1;
       Y1(Y==2,3)=1;
       Y1(Y==3,4)=1;
       Y1(Y==4,5)=1;
       Y1(Y==5,6)=1;
       Y1(Y==6,7)=1;
       Y1(Y==7,8)=1;
       Y1(Y==8,9)=1;
       Y1(Y==9,10)=1;

    endif
end

# Define Softmax Derivative
function [dZ] = softmaxDerivative(dA,cache,Y, numClasses)
   Z = cache;
   # get unnormalized probabilities
   shiftZ = Z' - max(Z',[],2);
```

```octave
        exp_scores = exp(shiftZ);

    # normalize them for each example
    probs = exp_scores ./ sum(exp_scores,2);
    # dZ = pi- yi
    yi=popMatrix(Y,numClasses);
    dZ=probs-yi;

end

# Define Stable Softmax Derivative
function [dZ] = stableSoftmaxDerivative(dA,cache,Y, numClasses)
    Z = cache;
    # get unnormalized probabilities
    exp_scores = exp(Z');
    # normalize them for each example
    probs = exp_scores ./ sum(exp_scores,2);
    # dZ = pi- yi
    yi=popMatrix(Y,numClasses);
    dZ=probs-yi;

end

# Initialize model for L layers
# Input : List of units in each layer
# Returns: Initial weights and biases matrices for all layers
function [W b] = initializeDeepModel(layerDimensions)
      rand ("seed", 3);
      # note the Weight matrix at layer 'l' is a matrix of size (l,l-1)
      # The Bias is a vectors of size (l,1)

      # Loop through the layer dimension from 1.. L
      # Create cell arrays for Weights and biases

      for l =2:size(layerDimensions)(2)
          W{l-1} = rand(layerDimensions(l),layerDimensions(l-1))*0.01; # Multiply by .01
          b{l-1} = zeros(layerDimensions(l),1);

      endfor
end

# He Initialization for L layers
# Input : vector of units in each layer
# Returns: Initial weights and biases matrices for all layers
function [W b] = HeInitializeDeepModel(layerDimensions)
      rand ("seed", 3);
      # note the Weight matrix at layer 'l' is a matrix of size (l,l-1)
      # The Bias is a vectors of size (l,1)

      # Loop through the layer dimension from 1.. L
      # Create cell arrays for Weights and biases

      for l =2:size(layerDimensions)(2)
          W{l-1} = rand(layerDimensions(l),layerDimensions(l-1))* sqrt(2/layerDimensions(l-1)); # Multiply by .01
          b{l-1} = zeros(layerDimensions(l),1);

      endfor
end

# Xavier Initialization for L layers
# Input : vector of units in each layer
# Returns: Initial weights and biases matrices for all layers
```

```octave
function [W b] = XavInitializeDeepModel(layerDimensions)
    rand ("seed", 3);
    # note the Weight matrix at layer 'l' is a matrix of size (l,l-1)
    # The Bias is a vectors of size (l,1)

    # Loop through the layer dimension from 1.. L
    # Create cell arrays for Weights and biases

    for l =2:size(layerDimensions)(2)
         w{l-1} = rand(layerDimensions(l),layerDimensions(l-1))* sqrt(1/layerDimensions(l-1)); # Multiply by .01
         b{l-1} = zeros(layerDimensions(l),1);

    endfor
end


# Compute the activation at a layer 'l' for forward prop in a Deep Network
# Input : A_prev - Activation of previous layer
#         W,b - Weight and bias matrices and vectors
#         activationFunc - Activation function - sigmoid, tanh, relu etc
# Returns : The Activation of this layer
#         :
# Z = W * X + b
# A = sigmoid(Z), A= Relu(Z), A= tanh(Z)
function [A forward_cache activation_cache] = layerActivationForward(A_prev, W, b, activationFunc)

    # Compute Z
    Z = W * A_prev +b;
    # Create a cell array
    forward_cache = {A_prev  W   b};
    # Compute the activation for sigmoid
    if (strcmp(activationFunc,"sigmoid"))
        [A activation_cache] = sigmoid(Z);
    elseif (strcmp(activationFunc, "relu"))    # Compute the activation for Relu
        [A activation_cache] = relu(Z);
    elseif(strcmp(activationFunc,'tanh'))      # Compute the activation for tanh
        [A activation_cache] = tanhAct(Z);
    elseif(strcmp(activationFunc,'softmax'))    # Compute the activation for tanh
        #[A activation_cache] = softmax(Z);
        [A activation_cache] = stableSoftmax(Z);
    endif

end

# Compute the forward propagation for layers 1..L
# Input : X - Input Features
#         paramaters: Weights and biases
#         keep_prob
#         hiddenActivationFunc - Activation function at hidden layers Relu/tanh/sigmoid
#         outputActivationFunc- sigmoid/softmax
# Returns : AL
#           caches
# The forward propoagtion uses the Relu/tanh activation from layer 1..L-1 and sigmoid actiovation at layer L
function [AL forward_caches activation_caches dropoutMat] = forwardPropagationDeep(X, weights,biases, keep_prob=1,
                                           hiddenActivationFunc='relu', outputActivationFunc='sigmoid')
```

```octave
    # Create an empty cell array
    forward_caches = {};
    activation_caches = {};
    droputMat ={};
    # Set A to X (A0)
    A = X;
    L = length(weights); # number of layers in the neural network
    # Loop through from layer 1 to upto layer L
    for l =1:L-1
        A_prev = A;
        # Zi = Wi x Ai-1 + bi  and Ai = g(Zi)
        W = weights{l};
        b = biases{l};
        [A forward_cache activation_cache] = layerActivationForward(A_prev,
W,b, activationFunc=hiddenActivationFunc);
        D=rand(size(A)(1),size(A)(2));
        D = (D < keep_prob) ;
        # Multiply by DropoutMat
        A= A .* D;
        # Divide by keep_prob to keep expected value same
        A = A ./ keep_prob;
        # Store D
        dropoutMat{l}=D;
        forward_caches{l}=forward_cache;
        activation_caches{l} = activation_cache;
    endfor
    # Since this is binary classification use the sigmoid activation function in
    # last layer
    W = weights{L};
    b = biases{L};
    [AL, forward_cache activation_cache] = layerActivationForward(A, W,b,
activationFunc = outputActivationFunc);
    forward_caches{L}=forward_cache;
    activation_caches{L} = activation_cache;

end

# Pick columns where Y==1
# This function is used in computeCost
function [a] = pickColumns(AL,Y,numClasses)
    if(numClasses==3)
        a=[AL(Y==0,1)  ;AL(Y==1,2)  ;AL(Y==2,3)];
    elseif (numClasses==10)
        a=[AL(Y==0,1)  ;AL(Y==1,2)  ;AL(Y==2,3);AL(Y==3,4);AL(Y==4,5);
           AL(Y==5,6); AL(Y==6,7);AL(Y==7,8);AL(Y==8,9);AL(Y==9,10)];
    endif
end


# Compute the cost
# Input : Activation of last layer
#        : Output from data
#        :  outputActivationFunc- sigmoid/softmax
#        : numClasses
# Output: cost
function [cost]= computeCost(AL, Y,
outputActivationFunc="sigmoid",numClasses)
    if(strcmp(outputActivationFunc,"sigmoid"))
        numTraining= size(Y)(2);
        # Element wise multiply for logprobs
        cost = -1/numTraining * sum((Y .* log(AL)) + (1-Y) .* log(1-AL));

```

```octave
    elseif(strcmp(outputActivationFunc,'softmax'))
        numTraining = size(Y)(2);
        Y=Y';
        # Select rows where Y=0,1,and 2 and concatenate to a long vector
        #a=[AL(Y==0,1) ;AL(Y==1,2) ;AL(Y==2,3)];
        a =pickColumns(AL,Y,numClasses);

        #Select the correct column for log prob
         correct_probs = -log(a);
         #Compute log loss
         cost= sum(correct_probs)/numTraining;
     endif
end

# Compute the cost with regularization
# Input : weights
#       : AL - Activation of last layer
#       : Output from data
#       : lambd
#       : outputActivationFunc- sigmoid/softmax
#       : numClasses
# Output: cost
function [cost]= computeCostWithReg(weights, AL, Y, lambd,
outputActivationFunc="sigmoid",numClasses)
    if(strcmp(outputActivationFunc,"sigmoid"))
        numTraining= size(Y)(2);
        # Element wise multiply for logprobs
        cost = -1/numTraining * sum((Y .* log(AL)) + (1-Y) .* log(1-AL));

        # Regularization cost
        L = size(weights)(2);
        L2RegularizationCost=0;
        for l=1:L
            wtSqr = weights{l} .* weights{l};
            #disp(sum(sum(wtSqr,1)));
            L2RegularizationCost+=sum(sum(wtSqr,1));
        endfor
        L2RegularizationCost = (lambd/(2*numTraining))*L2RegularizationCost;
        cost = cost +  L2RegularizationCost ;
    elseif(strcmp(outputActivationFunc,'softmax'))
        numTraining = size(Y)(2);
        Y=Y';
        # Select rows where Y=0,1,and 2 and concatenate to a long vector
        #a=[AL(Y==0,1) ;AL(Y==1,2) ;AL(Y==2,3)];
        a =pickColumns(AL,Y,numClasses);

        #Select the correct column for log prob
         correct_probs = -log(a);
         #Compute log loss
         cost= sum(correct_probs)/numTraining;
                # Regularization cost
        L = size(weights)(2);
        L2RegularizationCost=0;
        for l=1:L
            # Compute L2 Norm
            wtSqr = weights{l} .* weights{l};
            #disp(sum(sum(wtSqr,1)));
            L2RegularizationCost+=sum(sum(wtSqr,1));
        endfor
        L2RegularizationCost = (lambd/(2*numTraining))*L2RegularizationCost;
        cost = cost +  L2RegularizationCost ;
     endif
end
```

```octave
# Compute the backpropoagation for 1 cycle
# Input : dA- Neural Network parameters
#          # cache - forward_cache & activation_cache
#          # Y-Output values
#          # outputActivationFunc- sigmoid/softmax
#          # numClasses
# Returns: Gradients
# dL/dWi= dL/dZi*Al-1
# dl/dbl = dL/dZl
# dL/dZ_prev=dL/dZl*W
function [dA_prev dW db] = layerActivationBackward(dA, forward_cache,
activation_cache, Y, activationFunc,numClasses)
    A_prev = forward_cache{1};
    W =forward_cache{2};
    b = forward_cache{3};
    numTraining = size(A_prev)(2);
    if (strcmp(activationFunc,"relu"))
        dZ = reluDerivative(dA, activation_cache);
    elseif (strcmp(activationFunc,"sigmoid"))
        dZ = sigmoidDerivative(dA, activation_cache);
    elseif(strcmp(activationFunc, "tanh"))
        dZ = tanhDerivative(dA, activation_cache);
    elseif(strcmp(activationFunc, "softmax"))
        #dZ = softmaxDerivative(dA, activation_cache,Y,numClasses);
        dZ = stableSoftmaxDerivative(dA, activation_cache,Y,numClasses);
    endif
    if (strcmp(activationFunc,"softmax"))
      W =forward_cache{2};
      b = forward_cache{3};
      # Add the regularization factor
      dW = 1/numTraining * A_prev * dZ;
      db = 1/numTraining * sum(dZ,1);
      dA_prev = dZ*W;
    else
      W =forward_cache{2};
      b = forward_cache{3};
      # Add the regularization factor
      dW = 1/numTraining * dZ * A_prev';
      db = 1/numTraining * sum(dZ,2);
      dA_prev = W'*dZ;
    endif

end

# Compute the backpropoagation with regularization for 1 cycle
# Input : dA-Neural Network parameters
#          # cache - forward_cache & activation_cache
#          # Y-Output values
#          # lambd
#          # outputActivationFunc- sigmoid/softmax
#          # numClasses
# Returns: Gradients
# dL/dWi= dL/dZi*Al-1
# dl/dbl = dL/dZl
# dL/dZ_prev=dL/dZl*W
function [dA_prev dW db] = layerActivationBackwardWithReg(dA, forward_cache,
activation_cache, Y, lambd=0, activationFunc,numClasses)
    A_prev = forward_cache{1};
    W =forward_cache{2};
    b = forward_cache{3};
    numTraining = size(A_prev)(2);
    if (strcmp(activationFunc,"relu"))
```

```octave
            dZ = reluDerivative(dA, activation_cache);
      elseif (strcmp(activationFunc,"sigmoid"))
            dZ = sigmoidDerivative(dA, activation_cache);
      elseif(strcmp(activationFunc, "tanh"))
            dZ = tanhDerivative(dA, activation_cache);
      elseif(strcmp(activationFunc, "softmax"))
           #dZ = softmaxDerivative(dA, activation_cache,Y,numClasses);
            dZ = stableSoftmaxDerivative(dA, activation_cache,Y,numClasses);
      endif
      if (strcmp(activationFunc,"softmax"))
        W =forward_cache{2};
        b = forward_cache{3};
        # Add the regularization factor
        dW = 1/numTraining * A_prev * dZ +  (lambd/numTraining) * W';
        db = 1/numTraining * sum(dZ,1);
        dA_prev = dZ*W;
      else
        W =forward_cache{2};
        b = forward_cache{3};
        # Add the regularization factor
        dW = 1/numTraining * dZ * A_prev' +  (lambd/numTraining) * W;
        db = 1/numTraining * sum(dZ,2);
        dA_prev = W'*dZ;
      endif

end


# Compute the backpropoagation for 1 cycle
# Input : AL: Output of L layer Network - weights
#         Y  Real output
#         caches -- list of caches containing:
#         every cache of layerActivationForward() with "relu"/"tanh"
#         #(it's caches[l], for l in range(L-1) i.e l = 0...L-2)
#         #the cache of layerActivationForward() with "sigmoid" (it's caches[L-1])
#         dropoutMat
#         lambd
#         keep_prob
#         hiddenActivationFunc - Activation function at hidden layers sigmoid/tanh/relu
#         outputActivationFunc- sigmoid/softmax
#         numClasses
#
#    Returns:
#     gradients -- A dictionary with the gradients
#                  gradients["dA" + str(l)] = ...
#                  gradients["dW" + str(l)] = ...
function [gradsDA gradsDW gradsDB]= backwardPropagationDeep(AL, Y, activation_caches,forward_caches,
                                    dropoutMat, lambd=0, keep_prob=1, hiddenActivationFunc='relu',outputActivationFunc="sigmoid",numClasses)

    # Set the number of layers
    L = length(activation_caches);
    m = size(AL)(2);

    if (strcmp(outputActivationFunc,"sigmoid"))
       # Initializing the backpropagation
       # dl/dAL= -(y/a + (1-y)/(1-a)) - At the output layer
       dAL = -((Y ./ AL) - (1 - Y) ./ ( 1 - AL));
    elseif (strcmp(outputActivationFunc,"softmax"))
       dAL=0;
       Y=Y';
```

```
    endif


    # Since this is a binary classification the activation at output is
sigmoid
    # Get the gradients at the last layer
    # Inputs: "AL, Y, caches".
    # Outputs: "gradients["dAL"], gradients["dWL"], gradients["dbL"]
    activation_cache = activation_caches{L};
    forward_cache = forward_caches(L);
    # Note the cell array includes an array of forward caches. To get to this
we need to include the index {1}
    if (lambd==0)
        [dA dW db] = layerActivationBackward(dAL, forward_cache{1},
activation_cache, Y, activationFunc = outputActivationFunc,numClasses);
    else
        [dA dW db] = layerActivationBackwardWithReg(dAL, forward_cache{1},
activation_cache, Y, lambd, activationFunc =
outputActivationFunc,numClasses);
    endif
    if (strcmp(outputActivationFunc,"sigmoid"))
         gradsDA{L}= dA;
    elseif (strcmp(outputActivationFunc,"softmax"))
         gradsDA{L}= dA';#Note the transpose
    endif
    gradsDW{L}= dW;
    gradsDB{L}= db;

    # Traverse in the reverse direction
    for l =(L-1):-1:1
        # Compute the gradients for L-1 to 1 for Relu/tanh
        # Inputs: "gradients["dA" + str(l + 2)], caches".
        # Outputs: "gradients["dA" + str(l + 1)] , gradients["dW" + str(l +
1)] , gradients["db" + str(l + 1)]
        activation_cache = activation_caches{l};
        forward_cache = forward_caches(l);

        #dA_prev_temp, dW_temp, db_temp =
layerActivationBackward(gradients['dA'+str(l+1)], current_cache,
activationFunc = "relu")
        # dAl the dervative of the activation of the lth layer,is the first
element
        dAl= gradsDA{l+1};
        if(lambd == 0)
           # Get the dropout mat
           D = dropoutMat{l};
           #Multiply by the dropoutMat
           dAl= dAl .* D;
           # Divide by keep_prob to keep expected value same
           dAl = dAl ./ keep_prob;
           [dA_prev_temp, dW_temp, db_temp] = layerActivationBackward(dAl,
forward_cache{1}, activation_cache, Y, activationFunc =
hiddenActivationFunc,numClasses);
        else
           [dA_prev_temp, dW_temp, db_temp] =
layerActivationBackwardWithReg(dAl, forward_cache{1}, activation_cache, Y,
lambd, activationFunc = hiddenActivationFunc,numClasses);
        endif
        gradsDA{l}= dA_prev_temp;
        gradsDW{l}= dW_temp;
        gradsDB{l}= db_temp;

    endfor
```

```octave
end


# Perform Gradient Descent
# Input  : Weights and biases
#        : gradients -gradsW,gradsB
#        : learning rate
#        : outputActivationFunc
#output : Updated weights after 1 iteration
function [weights biases] = gradientDescent(weights, biases,gradsW,gradsB,
learningRate,outputActivationFunc="sigmoid")

    L = size(weights)(2); # number of layers in the neural network

    # Update rule for each parameter.
    for l=1:(L-1)
        weights{l} = weights{l} -learningRate* gradsW{l};
        biases{l} = biases{l} -learningRate* gradsB{l};
    endfor


    if (strcmp(outputActivationFunc,"sigmoid"))
        weights{L} = weights{L} -learningRate* gradsW{L};
        biases{L} = biases{L} -learningRate* gradsB{L};
     elseif (strcmp(outputActivationFunc,"softmax"))
        weights{L} = weights{L} -learningRate* gradsW{L}';
        biases{L} = biases{L} -learningRate* gradsB{L}';
     endif


end


# Execute a L layer Deep learning model
# Input  : X - Input features
#        : Y output
#        : layersDimensions - Dimension of layers
#        : hiddenActivationFunc - Activation function at hidden layer relu
/tanh
#        : outputActivationFunc - Activation function at hidden layer
sigmoid/softmax
#        : learning rate
#        : lambd
#        : keep_prob
#        : num of iterations
#output : Updated weights and biases after each  iteration
function [weights biases costs] = L_Layer_DeepModel(X, Y, layersDimensions,
hiddenActivationFunc='relu',
             outputActivationFunc="sigmoid",learning_rate = .3, lambd=0,
keep_prob=1, num_iterations = 10000,initType="default")#lr was 0.009

    rand ("seed", 1);
    costs = [] ;
    if (strcmp(initType,"He"))
       # He Initialization
       [weights biases] = HeInitializeDeepModel(layersDimensions);
    elseif (strcmp(initType,"Xav"))
        # Xavier Initialization
       [weights biases] = XavInitializeDeepModel(layersDimensions);
    else
       # Default initialization.
       [weights biases] = initializeDeepModel(layersDimensions);
    endif

```

```octave
        # Loop (gradient descent)
        for i = 0:num_iterations
            # Forward propagation: [LINEAR -> RELU]*(L-1) -> LINEAR -> SIGMOID.
            [AL forward_caches activation_caches droputMat] =
 forwardPropagationDeep(X, weights, biases,keep_prob, hiddenActivationFunc,
 outputActivationFunc=outputActivationFunc);

                    # Regularization parameter is 0
            if (lambd==0)
              # Compute cost.
               cost = computeCost(AL,
 Y,outputActivationFunc=outputActivationFunc,numClasses=layersDimensions(size(
 layersDimensions)(2)));
             else
               # Compute cost with regularization
                cost = computeCostWithReg(weights, AL, Y, lambd,
 outputActivationFunc=outputActivationFunc,numClasses=layersDimensions(size(la
 yersDimensions)(2)));
            endif
            # Backward propagation.
            [gradsDA gradsDW gradsDB] = backwardPropagationDeep(AL, Y,
 activation_caches,forward_caches, droputMat, lambd, keep_prob,
 hiddenActivationFunc, outputActivationFunc=outputActivationFunc,

 numClasses=layersDimensions(size(layersDimensions)(2)));
            # Update parameters.
            [weights biases] = gradientDescent(weights,biases,
 gradsDW,gradsDB,learning_rate,outputActivationFunc=outputActivationFunc);


            # Print the cost every 1000 iterations
           if ( mod(i,1000) == 0)
               costs =[costs cost];
               #disp ("Cost after iteration"),
 L2RegularizationCost(i),disp(cost);
               printf("Cost after iteration i=%i cost=%d\n",i,cost);
            endif
        endfor

end

# Execute a L layer Deep learning model with Stochastic Gradient descent
# Input  : X - Input features
#        : Y output
#        : layersDimensions - Dimension of layers
#        : hiddenActivationFunc - Activation function at hidden layer relu
 /tanh
#        : outputActivationFunc - Activation function at hidden layer
 sigmoid/softmax
#        : learning rate
#        : mini_batch_size
#        : num of epochs
#output : Updated weights and biases after each  iteration
function [weights biases costs] = L_Layer_DeepModel_SGD(X, Y,
 layersDimensions, hiddenActivationFunc='relu',
 outputActivationFunc="sigmoid",learning_rate = .3,
                    mini_batch_size = 64, num_epochs = 2500)#lr was 0.009

    rand ("seed", 1);
    costs = [] ;

    # Parameters initialization.
    [weights biases] = initializeDeepModel(layersDimensions);
    seed=10;
```

```octave
        # Loop (gradient descent)
        for i = 0:num_epochs
            seed = seed + 1;
            [mini_batches_X  mini_batches_Y] = random_mini_batches(X, Y,
mini_batch_size, seed);

            minibatches=length(mini_batches_X);
            for batch=1:minibatches
                X=mini_batches_X{batch};
                Y=mini_batches_Y{batch};
                # Forward propagation: [LINEAR -> RELU]*(L-1) -> LINEAR ->
SIGMOID/SOFTMAX.
                [AL forward_caches activation_caches] =
forwardPropagationDeep(X, weights, biases,hiddenActivationFunc,
outputActivationFunc=outputActivationFunc);
                #disp(batch);
                #disp(size(X));
                #disp(size(Y));

                # Compute cost.
                cost = computeCost(AL,
Y,outputActivationFunc=outputActivationFunc,numClasses=layersDimensions(size(
layersDimensions)(2)));

                #disp(cost);
                # Backward propagation.
                [gradsDA gradsDW gradsDB] = backwardPropagationDeep(AL, Y,
activation_caches,forward_caches,hiddenActivationFunc,
outputActivationFunc=outputActivationFunc,

numClasses=layersDimensions(size(layersDimensions)(2)));
                # Update parameters.
                [weights biases] = gradientDescent(weights,biases,
gradsDW,gradsDB,learning_rate,outputActivationFunc=outputActivationFunc);

            endfor
            # Print the cost every 1000 iterations
            if ( mod(i,1000) == 0)
               costs =[costs cost];
               #disp ("Cost after iteration"), disp(i),disp(cost);
               printf("Cost after iteration i=%i cost=%d\n",i,cost);
            endif
        endfor

end

# Plot cost vs iterations
  function plotCostVsIterations(maxIterations,costs,fig1)
       iterations=[0:1000:maxIterations];
       plot(iterations,costs);
       title ("Cost vs no of iterations ");
       xlabel("No of iterations");
       ylabel("Cost");
       print -dpng figReg2-o
end;

# Compute the predicted value for a given input
# Input : Neural Network parameters
#       : Input data
function [predictions]= predict(weights, biases,
X,keep_prob=1,hiddenActivationFunc="relu")
    [AL forward_caches activation_caches] = forwardPropagationDeep(X,
weights, biases,keep_prob,hiddenActivationFunc);
    predictions = (AL>0.5);
```

```octave
743  end
744
745  # Plot the decision boundary
746  function plotDecisionBoundary(data,weights,
747  biases,keep_prob=1,hiddenActivationFunc="relu",fig2)
748      %Plot a non-linear decision boundary learned by the SVM
749      colormap ("summer");
750
751      % Make classification predictions over a grid of values
752      x1plot = linspace(min(data(:,1)), max(data(:,1)), 400)';
753      x2plot = linspace(min(data(:,2)), max(data(:,2)), 400)';
754      [X1, X2] = meshgrid(x1plot, x2plot);
755      vals = zeros(size(X1));
756      # Plot the prediction for the grid
757      for i = 1:size(X1, 2)
758          gridPoints = [X1(:, i), X2(:, i)];
759          vals(:, i)=predict(weights, biases,gridPoints',keep_prob,
760  hiddenActivationFunc=hiddenActivationFunc);
761      endfor
762
763      scatter(data(:,1),data(:,2),8,c=data(:,3),"filled");
764      % Plot the boundary
765      hold on
766      #contour(X1, X2, vals, [0 0], 'LineWidth', 2);
767      contour(X1, X2, vals,"linewidth",4);
768      title ({"3 layer Neural Network decision boundary"});
769      hold off;
770      print -dpng figReg22-o
771
772  end
773
774  #Compute scores
775  function [AL]= scores(weights, biases, X,hiddenActivationFunc="relu")
776      [AL forward_caches activation_caches] = forwardPropagationDeep(X,
777  weights, biases,hiddenActivationFunc);
778  end
779
780  # Create Random mini batches. Return cell arrays with the mini batches
781  # Input : X, Y
782  #       : Size of minibatch
783  #Output : mini batches X & Y
784  function [mini_batches_X  mini_batches_Y]= random_mini_batches(X, Y,
785  miniBatchSize = 64, seed = 0)
786
787      rand ("seed", seed);
788      # Get number of training samples
789      m = size(X)(2);
790
791
792      # Create  a list of random numbers < m
793      permutation = randperm(m);
794      # Randomly shuffle the training data
795      shuffled_X = X(:, permutation);
796      shuffled_Y = Y(:, permutation);
797
798      # Compute number of mini batches
799      numCompleteMinibatches = floor(m/miniBatchSize);
800      batch=0;
801      for k = 0:(numCompleteMinibatches-1)
802          #Set the start and end of each mini batch
803          batch=batch+1;
804          lower=(k*miniBatchSize)+1;
805          upper=(k+1) * miniBatchSize;
806          mini_batch_X = shuffled_X(:, lower:upper);
```

```
            mini_batch_Y = shuffled_Y(:, lower:upper);

            # Create cell arrays
            mini_batches_X{batch} = mini_batch_X;
            mini_batches_Y{batch} = mini_batch_Y;
    endfor

    # If the batc size does not cleanly divide with number of mini batches
    if mod(m ,miniBatchSize) != 0
        # Set the start and end of the last mini batch
        l=floor(m/miniBatchSize)*miniBatchSize;
        m=l+ mod(m,miniBatchSize);
        mini_batch_X = shuffled_X(:,(l+1):m);
        mini_batch_Y = shuffled_Y(:,(l+1):m);

        batch=batch+1;
        mini_batches_X{batch} = mini_batch_X;
        mini_batches_Y{batch} = mini_batch_Y;
    endif
end

# Plot decision boundary
function plotDecisionBoundary1( data,weights, biases,keep_prob=1, hiddenActivationFunc="relu")
    % Make classification predictions over a grid of values
    x1plot = linspace(min(data(:,1)), max(data(:,1)), 400)';
    x2plot = linspace(min(data(:,2)), max(data(:,2)), 400)';
    [X1, X2] = meshgrid(x1plot, x2plot);
    vals = zeros(size(X1));
    for i = 1:size(X1, 2)
            gridPoints = [X1(:, i), X2(:, i)];
            [AL forward_caches activation_caches] = forwardPropagationDeep(gridPoints', weights, biases,keep_prob,hiddenActivationFunc, outputActivationFunc="softmax");
            [l m] = max(AL, [ ], 2);
            vals(:, i)= m;
    endfor

    scatter(data(:,1),data(:,2),8,c=data(:,3),"filled");
    % Plot the boundary
    hold on
    contour(X1, X2, vals,"linewidth",4);
    print -dpng "fig-o1.png"
end
```

8. Appendix 7 - Gradient Descent Optimization techniques

7.1 Python

```python
# -*- coding: utf-8 -*-
################################################################################
################################
#
# File: DLfunctions7.py
# Developer: Tinniam V Ganesh
# Date : 16 Apr 2018
#
################################################################################
################################
import numpy as np
import matplotlib.pyplot as plt
import matplotlib
import matplotlib.pyplot as plt
from matplotlib import cm
import math
import sklearn
import sklearn.datasets

# Conmpute the sigmoid of a vector
def sigmoid(Z):
    A=1/(1+np.exp(-Z))
    cache=Z
    return A,cache

# Conmpute the Relu of a vector
def relu(Z):
    A = np.maximum(0,Z)
    cache=Z
    return A,cache

# Conmpute the tanh of a vector
def tanh(Z):
    A = np.tanh(Z)
    cache=Z
    return A,cache

# Conmpute the softmax of a vector
def softmax(Z):
    # get unnormalized probabilities
    exp_scores = np.exp(Z.T)
    # normalize them for each example
    A = exp_scores / np.sum(exp_scores, axis=1, keepdims=True)
    cache=Z
    return A,cache

# Conmpute the stable softmax of a vector
def stableSoftmax(Z):
    #Compute the softmax of vector x in a numerically stable way.
    shiftZ = Z.T - np.max(Z.T,axis=1).reshape(-1,1)
    exp_scores = np.exp(shiftZ)
    
    # normalize them for each example
    A = exp_scores / np.sum(exp_scores, axis=1, keepdims=True)
    cache=Z
```

```python
           return A,cache

# Compute the derivative of Relu
def reluDerivative(dA, cache):

    Z = cache
    dZ = np.array(dA, copy=True) # just converting dz to a correct object.
    # When z <= 0, you should set dz to 0 as well.
    dZ[Z <= 0] = 0
    return dZ

# Compute the derivative of sigmoid
def sigmoidDerivative(dA, cache):
    Z = cache
    s = 1/(1+np.exp(-Z))
    dZ = dA * s * (1-s)
    return dZ

# Compute the derivative of tanh
def tanhDerivative(dA, cache):
    Z = cache
    a = np.tanh(Z)
    dZ = dA * (1 - np.power(a, 2))
    return dZ

# Compute the derivative of softmax
def softmaxDerivative(dA, cache,y,numTraining):
    # Note : dA not used. dL/dZ = dL/dA * dA/dZ = pi-yi
    Z = cache
    # Compute softmax
    exp_scores = np.exp(Z.T)
    # normalize them for each example
    probs = exp_scores / np.sum(exp_scores, axis=1, keepdims=True)

    # compute the gradient on scores
    dZ = probs

    # dZ = pi- yi
    dZ[range(int(numTraining)),y[:,0]] -= 1
    return(dZ)

# Compute the derivative of Stable softmax
def stableSoftmaxDerivative(dA, cache,y,numTraining):
    # Note : dA not used. dL/dZ = dL/dA * dA/dZ = pi-yi
    Z = cache
    # Compute stable softmax
    shiftZ = Z.T - np.max(Z.T,axis=1).reshape(-1,1)
    exp_scores = np.exp(shiftZ)
    # normalize them for each example
    probs = exp_scores / np.sum(exp_scores, axis=1, keepdims=True)
    #print(probs)
    # compute the gradient on scores
    dZ = probs

    # dZ = pi- yi
    dZ[range(int(numTraining)),y[:,0]] -= 1
    return(dZ)


# Initialize the model
# Input : number of features
#         number of hidden units
#         number of units in output
# Returns: weight and bias matrices and vectors
```

```python
def initializeModel(numFeats,numHidden,numOutput):
    np.random.seed(1)
    W1=np.random.randn(numHidden,numFeats)*0.01 #   Multiply by .01
    b1=np.zeros((numHidden,1))
    W2=np.random.randn(numOutput,numHidden)*0.01
    b2=np.zeros((numOutput,1))

    # Create a dictionary of the neural network parameters
    nnParameters={'W1':W1,'b1':b1,'W2':W2,'b2':b2}
    return(nnParameters)


# Initialize model for L layers
# Input : List of units in each layer
# Returns: Initial weights and biases matrices for all layers
def initializeDeepModel(layerDimensions):
    np.random.seed(3)
    # note the Weight matrix at layer 'l' is a matrix of size (l,l-1)
    # The Bias is a vectors of size (l,1)

    # Loop through the layer dimension from 1.. L
    layerParams = {}
    for l in range(1,len(layerDimensions)):
        layerParams['W' + str(l)] = np.random.randn(layerDimensions[l],layerDimensions[l-1])*0.01 #   Multiply by .01
        layerParams['b' + str(l)] = np.zeros((layerDimensions[l],1))
        np.savetxt('W' + str(l)+'.csv',layerParams['W' + str(l)],delimiter=',')
        np.savetxt('b' + str(l)+'.csv',layerParams['b' + str(l)],delimiter=',')
    return(layerParams)
    return Z, cache

# He Initialization model for L layers
# Input : List of units in each layer
# Returns: Initial weights and biases matrices for all layers
# He initilization multiplies the random numbers with sqrt(2/layerDimensions[l-1])
def HeInitializeDeepModel(layerDimensions):
    np.random.seed(3)
    # note the Weight matrix at layer 'l' is a matrix of size (l,l-1)
    # The Bias is a vectors of size (l,1)

    # Loop through the layer dimension from 1.. L
    layerParams = {}
    for l in range(1,len(layerDimensions)):
        layerParams['W' + str(l)] = np.random.randn(layerDimensions[l],
                    layerDimensions[l-1])*np.sqrt(2/layerDimensions[l-1])
        layerParams['b' + str(l)] = np.zeros((layerDimensions[l],1))

    return(layerParams)
    return Z, cache

# Xavier Initialization model for L layers
# Input : List of units in each layer
# Returns: Initial weights and biases matrices for all layers
# Xavier initilization multiplies the random numbers with sqrt(1/layerDimensions[l-1])
def XavInitializeDeepModel(layerDimensions):
    np.random.seed(3)
    # note the Weight matrix at layer 'l' is a matrix of size (l,l-1)
    # The Bias is a vectors of size (l,1)

```

```python
        # Loop through the layer dimension from 1.. L
        layerParams = {}
        for l in range(1,len(layerDimensions)):
            layerParams['W' + str(l)] = np.random.randn(layerDimensions[l],
                            layerDimensions[l-1])*np.sqrt(1/layerDimensions[l-1])
            layerParams['b' + str(l)] = np.zeros((layerDimensions[l],1))

    return(layerParams)
    return Z, cache

# Initialize velocity of
# Input : parameters
# Returns: v - Initial velocity
def initializeVelocity(parameters):

    L = len(parameters)//2 # Create an integer
    v = {}

    # Initialize velocity with the same dimensions as W
    for l in range(L):
        v["dW" + str(l+1)] = np.zeros((parameters['W' + str(l+1)].shape[0],
                                    parameters['W' + str(l+1)].shape[1]))
        v["db" + str(l+1)] = np.zeros((parameters['b' + str(l+1)].shape[0],
                                    parameters['b' + str(l+1)].shape[1]))

    return v

# Initialize RMSProp param
# Input : List of units in each layer
# Returns: s - Initial RMSProp
def initializeRMSProp(parameters):

    L = len(parameters)//2 # Create an integer
    s = {}

    # Initialize velocity with the same dimensions as W
    for l in range(L):
        s["dW" + str(l+1)] = np.zeros((parameters['W' + str(l+1)].shape[0],
                                    parameters['W' + str(l+1)].shape[1]))
        s["db" + str(l+1)] = np.zeros((parameters['b' + str(l+1)].shape[0],
                                    parameters['b' + str(l+1)].shape[1]))

    return s

# Initialize Adam param
# Input : List of units in each layer
# Returns: v and s - Adam paramaters
def initializeAdam(parameters) :

    L = len(parameters) // 2 # number of layers in the neural networks
    v = {}
    s = {}

    # Initialize v, s.
    for l in range(L):

        v["dW" + str(l+1)] = np.zeros((parameters['W' + str(l+1)].shape[0],
                                    parameters['W' + str(l+1)].shape[1]))
        v["db" + str(l+1)] = np.zeros((parameters['b' + str(l+1)].shape[0],
                                    parameters['b' + str(l+1)].shape[1]))
        s["dW" + str(l+1)] = np.zeros((parameters['W' + str(l+1)].shape[0],
                                    parameters['W' + str(l+1)].shape[1]))
        s["db" + str(l+1)] = np.zeros((parameters['b' + str(l+1)].shape[0],
                                    parameters['b' + str(l+1)].shape[1]))
```

```
        return v, s


# Compute the activation at a layer 'l' for forward prop in a Deep Network
# Input : A_prev - Activation of previous layer
#         w,b - Weight and bias matrices and vectors
#         keep_prob
#         activationFunc - Activation function - sigmoid, tanh, relu etc
# Returns : A, cache
#         :
# Z = W * X + b
# A = sigmoid(Z), A= Relu(Z), A= tanh(Z)
def layerActivationForward(A_prev, W, b, keep_prob=1, activationFunc="relu"):

    # Compute Z
    Z = np.dot(W,A_prev) + b
    forward_cache = (A_prev, W, b)
    # Compute the activation for sigmoid
    if activationFunc == "sigmoid":
        A, activation_cache = sigmoid(Z)
    # Compute the activation for Relu
    elif activationFunc == "relu":
        A, activation_cache = relu(Z)
    # Compute the activation for tanh
    elif activationFunc == 'tanh':
        A, activation_cache = tanh(Z)
    elif activationFunc == 'softmax':
        A, activation_cache = stableSoftmax(Z)

    cache = (forward_cache, activation_cache)
    return A, cache

# Compute the forward propagation for layers 1..L
# Input : X - Input Features
#         parameters: Weights and biases
#         keep_prob
#         hiddenActivationFunc - Activation function at hidden layers Relu/tanh
#         outputActivationFunc - Activation function at output - sigmoid/softmax
# Returns : AL
#           caches
#           dropoutMat
# The forward propoagtion uses the Relu/tanh activation from layer 1..L-1 and
sigmoid actiovation at layer L
def forwardPropagationDeep(X, parameters,keep_prob=1, hiddenActivationFunc='relu',outputActivationFunc='sigmoid'):
    caches = []
    #initialize the dropout matrix
    dropoutMat = {}
    # Set A to X (A0)
    A = X
    L = len(parameters)//2 # number of layers in the neural network
    # Loop through from layer 1 to upto layer L
    for l in range(1, L):
        A_prev = A
        # Zi = Wi x Ai-1 + bi   and Ai = g(Zi)
        A, cache = layerActivationForward(A_prev, parameters['W'+str(l)], parameters['b'+str(l)], keep_prob, activationFunc = hiddenActivationFunc)

        # Randomly drop some activation units
        # Create a matrix as the same shape as A
        D = np.random.rand(A.shape[0],A.shape[1])
        D = (D < keep_prob)
```

```python
            # We need to use the same 'dropout' matrix in backward propagation
            # Save the dropout matrix for use in backprop
            dropoutMat["D" + str(l)] =D
            A= np.multiply(A,D)
            A = np.divide(A,keep_prob)

        caches.append(cache)

    # last layer
    AL, cache = layerActivationForward(A, parameters['W'+str(L)],
parameters['b'+str(L)], activationFunc = outputActivationFunc)
    caches.append(cache)

    return AL, caches, dropoutMat


# Compute the cost
# Input : parameters
#        : AL
#        : Y
#        :outputActivationFunc - Activation function at output -
sigmoid/softmax/tanh
# Output: cost
def computeCost(parameters,AL,Y,outputActivationFunc="sigmoid"):
    if outputActivationFunc=="sigmoid":
        m= float(Y.shape[1])
        # Element wise multiply for logprobs
        cost=-1/m *np.sum(Y*np.log(AL) + (1-Y)*(np.log(1-AL)))
        cost = np.squeeze(cost)
    elif outputActivationFunc=="softmax":
        # Take transpose of Y for softmax
        Y=Y.T
        m= float(len(Y))
        # Compute log probs. Take the log prob of correct class based on
output y
        correct_logprobs = -np.log(AL[range(int(m)),Y.T])
        # Conpute loss
        cost = np.sum(correct_logprobs)/m
    return cost


# Compute the cost with regularization
# Input : parameters
#        : AL
#        : Y
#        : lambd
#        :outputActivationFunc - Activation function at output -
sigmoid/softmax/tanh
# Output: cost
def computeCostWithReg(parameters,AL,Y,lambd,
outputActivationFunc="sigmoid"):


    if outputActivationFunc=="sigmoid":
        m= float(Y.shape[1])
        # Element wise multiply for logprobs
        cost=-1/m *np.sum(Y*np.log(AL) + (1-Y)*(np.log(1-AL)))
        cost = np.squeeze(cost)

        # Regularization cost
        L= int(len(parameters)/2)
        L2RegularizationCost=0
        for l in range(L):
            L2RegularizationCost+=np.sum(np.square(parameters['W'+str(l+1)]))
```

```python
            L2RegularizationCost = (lambd/(2*m))*L2RegularizationCost
            cost = cost +  L2RegularizationCost


    elif outputActivationFunc=="softmax":
        # Take transpose of Y for softmax
        Y=Y.T
        m= float(len(Y))
        # Compute log probs. Take the log prob of correct class based on output y
        correct_logprobs = -np.log(AL[range(int(m)),Y.T])
        # Conpute loss
        cost = np.sum(correct_logprobs)/m

                # Regularization cost
        L= int(len(parameters)/2)
        L2RegularizationCost=0
        for l in range(L):
            L2RegularizationCost+=np.sum(np.square(parameters['W'+str(l+1)]))

        L2RegularizationCost = (lambd/(2*m))*L2RegularizationCost
        cost = cost +  L2RegularizationCost

    return cost

# Compute the backpropoagation for 1 cycle with dropout included
# Input : Neural Network parameters - dA
#         # cache - forward_cache & activation_cache
#         # Input features
#         # keep_prob
#         # Output values Y
# Returns: Gradients
# dL/dWi= dL/dZi*Al-1
# dl/dbl = dL/dZl
# dL/dZ_prev=dL/dZl*W
def layerActivationBackward(dA, cache, Y, keep_prob=1, activationFunc="relu"):
    forward_cache, activation_cache = cache
    A_prev, W, b = forward_cache
    numtraining = float(A_prev.shape[1])
    #print("n=",numtraining)
    #print("no=",numtraining)
    if activationFunc == "relu":
        dZ = reluDerivative(dA, activation_cache)
    elif activationFunc == "sigmoid":
        dZ = sigmoidDerivative(dA, activation_cache)
    elif activationFunc == "tanh":
        dZ = tanhDerivative(dA, activation_cache)
    elif activationFunc == "softmax":
        dZ = stableSoftmaxDerivative(dA, activation_cache,Y,numtraining)

    if activationFunc == 'softmax':
        dW = 1/numtraining * np.dot(A_prev,dZ)
        db = 1/numtraining * np.sum(dZ, axis=0, keepdims=True)
        dA_prev = np.dot(dZ,W)
    else:
        #print(numtraining)
        dW = 1/numtraining *(np.dot(dZ,A_prev.T))
        #print("dW=",dW)
        db = 1/numtraining * np.sum(dZ, axis=1, keepdims=True)
        #print("db=",db)
        dA_prev = np.dot(W.T,dZ)

```

```python
        return dA_prev, dW, db


# Compute the backpropoagation with regularization for 1 cycle
# Input : dA- Neural Network parameters
#        # cache - forward_cache & activation_cache
#        # Output values Y
#        # lambd
#        # activationFunc
# Returns dA_prev, dW, db
# Returns: Gradients
# dL/dWi= dL/dZi*Al-1
# dl/dbl = dL/dZl
# dL/dZ_prev=dL/dZl*W
def layerActivationBackwardWithReg(dA, cache, Y, lambd, activationFunc):
    forward_cache, activation_cache = cache
    A_prev, W, b = forward_cache
    numtraining = float(A_prev.shape[1])
    #print("n=",numtraining)
    #print("no=",numtraining)
    if activationFunc == "relu":
        dZ = reluDerivative(dA, activation_cache)
    elif activationFunc == "sigmoid":
        dZ = sigmoidDerivative(dA, activation_cache)
    elif activationFunc == "tanh":
        dZ = tanhDerivative(dA, activation_cache)
    elif activationFunc == "softmax":
        dZ = stableSoftmaxDerivative(dA, activation_cache,Y,numtraining)

    if activationFunc == 'softmax':
        # Add the regularization factor
        dW = 1/numtraining * np.dot(A_prev,dZ) +  (lambd/numtraining) * W.T
        db = 1/numtraining * np.sum(dZ, axis=0, keepdims=True)
        dA_prev = np.dot(dZ,W)
    else:
        # Add the regularization factor
        dW = 1/numtraining *(np.dot(dZ,A_prev.T)) + (lambd/numtraining) * W
        #print("dW=",dW)
        db = 1/numtraining * np.sum(dZ, axis=1, keepdims=True)
        #print("db=",db)
        dA_prev = np.dot(W.T,dZ)


    return dA_prev, dW, db

# Compute the backpropoagation for 1 cycle
# Input : AL: Output of L layer Network - weights
#        # Y  Real output
#        # caches -- list of caches containing:
#        # dropoutMat
#        # lambd
#        # keep_prob
#        every cache of layerActivationForward() with "relu"/"tanh"
#        #(it's caches[l], for l in range(L-1) i.e l = 0...L-2)
#        #the cache of layerActivationForward() with "sigmoid" (it's caches[L-1])
#        # hiddenActivationFunc - Activation function at hidden layers - relu/sigmoid/tanh
#        #outputActivationFunc - Activation function at output - sigmoid/softmax
#
#   Returns:
#    gradients -- A dictionary with the gradients
#                 gradients["dA" + str(l)] = ...
```

```python
#                     gradients["dW" + str(l)] = ...
#                     gradients["db" + str(l)] = ...
def backwardPropagationDeep(AL, Y, caches, dropoutMat, lambd=0, keep_prob=1,
hiddenActivationFunc='relu',outputActivationFunc="sigmoid"):
    #initialize the gradients
    gradients = {}
    # Set the number of layers
    L = len(caches)
    m = float(AL.shape[1])

    if outputActivationFunc == "sigmoid":
        Y = Y.reshape(AL.shape) # after this line, Y is the same shape as AL
        # Initializing the backpropagation
        # dl/dAL= -(y/a + (1-y)/(1-a)) - At the output layer
        dAL = - (np.divide(Y, AL) - np.divide(1 - Y, 1 - AL))
    else:
        dAL =0
        Y=Y.T

    # Since this is a binary classification the activation at output is sigmoid
    # Get the gradients at the last layer
    # Inputs: "AL, Y, caches".
    # Outputs: "gradients["dAL"], gradients["dWL"], gradients["dbL"]
    current_cache = caches[L-1]
    if lambd==0:
       gradients["dA" + str(L)], gradients["dW" + str(L)], gradients["db" + str(L)] = layerActivationBackward(dAL, current_cache,
                                                        Y, activationFunc = outputActivationFunc)
    else: #Regularization
        gradients["dA" + str(L)], gradients["dW" + str(L)], gradients["db" + str(L)] = layerActivationBackwardWithReg(dAL, current_cache,
                                                        Y, lambd, activationFunc = outputActivationFunc)

    # Note dA for softmax is the transpose
    if outputActivationFunc == "softmax":
        gradients["dA" + str(L)] = gradients["dA" + str(L)].T
    # Traverse in the reverse direction
    for l in reversed(range(L-1)):
        # Compute the gradients for L-1 to 1 for Relu/tanh
        # Inputs: "gradients["dA" + str(l + 2)], caches".
        # Outputs: "gradients["dA" + str(l + 1)] , gradients["dW" + str(l + 1)] , gradients["db" + str(l + 1)]
        current_cache = caches[l]

        #dA_prev_temp, dW_temp, db_temp = layerActivationBackward(gradients['dA'+str(l+2)], current_cache,
activationFunc = "relu")
        if lambd==0:

            # In the reverse direction use the dame dropout matrix
            # Random dropout
            # Multiply dA'l' with the dropoutMat and divide to keep the expected value same
            D = dropoutMat["D" + str(l+1)]
            # Drop some dAl's
            gradients['dA'+str(l+2)]= np.multiply(gradients['dA'+str(l+2)],D)
            # Divide by keep_prob to keep expected value same
            gradients['dA'+str(l+2)] = np.divide(gradients['dA'+str(l+2)],keep_prob)
```

```python
            dA_prev_temp, dW_temp, db_temp = layerActivationBackward(gradients['dA'+str(l+2)], current_cache, Y, keep_prob=1, activationFunc = hiddenActivationFunc)

        else:
            dA_prev_temp, dW_temp, db_temp = layerActivationBackwardWithReg(gradients['dA'+str(l+2)], current_cache, Y, lambd, activationFunc = hiddenActivationFunc)

        gradients["dA" + str(l + 1)] = dA_prev_temp
        gradients["dW" + str(l + 1)] = dW_temp
        gradients["db" + str(l + 1)] = db_temp


    return gradients

# Perform Gradient Descent
# Input : Weights and biases
#       : gradients
#       : learning rate
#       : outputActivationFunc - Activation function at output - sigmoid/softmax
#output : Updated weights after 1 iteration
def gradientDescent(parameters, gradients, learningRate,outputActivationFunc="sigmoid"):

    L = int(len(parameters) / 2)
    # Update rule for each parameter.
    for l in range(L-1):
        parameters["W" + str(l+1)] = parameters['W'+str(l+1)] -learningRate* gradients['dW' + str(l+1)]
        parameters["b" + str(l+1)] = parameters['b'+str(l+1)] -learningRate* gradients['db' + str(l+1)]

    if outputActivationFunc=="sigmoid":
        parameters["W" + str(L)] = parameters['W'+str(L)] -learningRate* gradients['dW' + str(L)]
        parameters["b" + str(L)] = parameters['b'+str(L)] -learningRate* gradients['db' + str(L)]
    elif outputActivationFunc=="softmax":
        parameters["W" + str(L)] = parameters['W'+str(L)] -learningRate* gradients['dW' + str(L)].T
        parameters["b" + str(L)] = parameters['b'+str(L)] -learningRate* gradients['db' + str(L)].T

    return parameters

# Update parameters with momentum
# Input : parameters
#       : gradients
#       : v
#       : beta
#       : learningRate
#       : outputActivationFunc - softmax/sigmoid
#output : Updated parameters and velocity
def gradientDescentWithMomentum(parameters, gradients, v, beta, learningRate, outputActivationFunc="sigmoid"):

    L = len(parameters) // 2 # number of layers in the neural networks
    # Momentum update for each parameter
    for l in range(L-1):

        # Compute velocities
        # v['dWk'] = beta *v['dWk'] + (1-beta)*dWk
```

```python
            v["dw" + str(l+1)] = beta*v["dw" + str(l+1)] + (1-beta) *
gradients['dw' + str(l+1)]
            v["db" + str(l+1)] = beta*v["db" + str(l+1)] + (1-beta) *
gradients['db' + str(l+1)]
        # Update parameters with velocities
            parameters["W" + str(l+1)] = parameters['W' + str(l+1)] -
learningRate* v["dw" + str(l+1)]
            parameters["b" + str(l+1)] = parameters['b' + str(l+1)] -
learningRate* v["db" + str(l+1)]

    if outputActivationFunc=="sigmoid":
         v["dw" + str(L)] = beta*v["dw" + str(L)] + (1-beta) * gradients['dw'
+ str(L)]
         v["db" + str(L)] = beta*v["db" + str(L)] + (1-beta) * gradients['db'
+ str(L)]
         parameters["W" + str(L)] = parameters['W'+str(L)] -learningRate*
gradients['dw' + str(L)]
         parameters["b" + str(L)] = parameters['b'+str(L)] -learningRate*
gradients['db' + str(L)]
    elif outputActivationFunc=="softmax":
         v["dw" + str(L)] = beta*v["dw" + str(L)] + (1-beta) * gradients['dw'
+ str(L)].T
         v["db" + str(L)] = beta*v["db" + str(L)] + (1-beta) * gradients['db'
+ str(L)].T
         parameters["W" + str(L)] = parameters['W'+str(L)] -learningRate*
gradients['dw' + str(L)].T
         parameters["b" + str(L)] = parameters['b'+str(L)] -learningRate*
gradients['db' + str(L)].T

    return parameters, v


# Update parameters with RMSProp
# Input : parameters
#        : gradients
#        : s
#        : beta1
#        : learningRate
#        : outputActivationFunc - sigmoid/softmax
# output : Updated parameters and RMSProp
def gradientDescentWithRMSProp(parameters, gradients, s, beta1, epsilon,
learningRate, outputActivationFunc="sigmoid"):

    L = len(parameters) // 2 # number of layers in the neural networks
    # Momentum update for each parameter
    for l in range(L-1):

        # Compute RMSProp
        # s['dwk'] = beta1 *s['dwk'] + (1-beta1)*dwk**2/sqrt(s['dwk'])
        s["dw" + str(l+1)] = beta1*s["dw" + str(l+1)] + (1-beta1) * \
              np.multiply(gradients['dw' + str(l+1)],gradients['dw' +
str(l+1)])
        s["db" + str(l+1)] = beta1*s["db" + str(l+1)] + (1-beta1) * \
              np.multiply(gradients['db' + str(l+1)],gradients['db' +
str(l+1)])
        # Update parameters with  RMSProp
        parameters["W" + str(l+1)] = parameters['W' + str(l+1)] - \
              learningRate* gradients['dw' + str(l+1)]/np.sqrt(s["dw" +
str(l+1)] + epsilon)
        parameters["b" + str(l+1)] = parameters['b' + str(l+1)] - \
              learningRate* gradients['db' + str(l+1)]/np.sqrt(s["db" +
str(l+1)] + epsilon)

    if outputActivationFunc=="sigmoid":
```

```python
            s["dw" + str(L)] = beta1*s["dw" + str(L)] + (1-beta1) * \
                  np.multiply(gradients['dw' + str(L)],gradients['dw' + str(L)])
            s["db" + str(L)] = beta1*s["db" + str(L)] + (1-beta1) * \
                  np.multiply(gradients['db' + str(L)],gradients['db' + str(L)])
            parameters["W" + str(L)] = parameters['W'+str(L)] - \
                  learningRate* gradients['dW' + str(L)]/np.sqrt(s["dw" + str(L)] + epsilon)
            parameters["b" + str(L)] = parameters['b'+str(L)] - \
                  learningRate* gradients['db' + str(L)]/np.sqrt(s["db" + str(L)] + epsilon)
        elif outputActivationFunc=="softmax":
            s["dw" + str(L)] = beta1*s["dw" + str(L)] + (1-beta1) * \
                  np.multiply(gradients['dw' + str(L)].T,gradients['dw' + str(L)].T)
            s["db" + str(L)] = beta1*s["db" + str(L)] + (1-beta1) * \
                  np.multiply(gradients['db' + str(L)].T,gradients['db' + str(L)].T)
            parameters["W" + str(L)] = parameters['W'+str(L)] - \
                  learningRate* gradients['dW' + str(L)].T/np.sqrt(s["dw" + str(L)] + epsilon)
            parameters["b" + str(L)] = parameters['b'+str(L)] - \
                  learningRate* gradients['db' + str(L)].T/np.sqrt(s["db" + str(L)] + epsilon)

    return parameters, s

# Update parameters with Adam
# Input : parameters
#       : gradients
#       : v
#       : s
#       : t
#       : beta1
#       : beta2
#       : epsilon
#       : learningRate
#       : outputActivationFunc - sigmoid/softmax
# output : Updated parameters and RMSProp
def gradientDescentWithAdam(parameters, gradients, v, s, t,
                             beta1 = 0.9, beta2 = 0.999,  epsilon = 1e-8,
                             learningRate=0.1,
outputActivationFunc="sigmoid"):

    L = len(parameters) // 2
    # Initializing first moment estimate, python dictionary
    v_corrected = {}
    # Initializing second moment estimate, python dictionary
    s_corrected = {}

    # Perform Adam upto L-1
    for l in range(L-1):

        # Compute momentum
        v["dw" + str(l+1)] = beta1*v["dw" + str(l+1)] + \
                             (1-beta1) * gradients['dw' + str(l+1)]
        v["db" + str(l+1)] = beta1*v["db" + str(l+1)] + \
                             (1-beta1) * gradients['db' + str(l+1)]


        # Compute bias-corrected first moment estimate.
        v_corrected["dw" + str(l+1)] = v["dw" + str(l+1)]/(1-np.power(beta1,t))
        v_corrected["db" + str(l+1)] = v["db" + str(l+1)]/(1-np.power(beta1,t))
```

```python
            # Moving average of the squared gradients like RMSProp
            s["dw" + str(l+1)] = beta2*s["dw" + str(l+1)] + \
                    (1-beta2) * np.multiply(gradients['dw' +
str(l+1)],gradients['dw' + str(l+1)])
            s["db" + str(l+1)] = beta2*s["db" + str(l+1)] + \
                    (1-beta2) * np.multiply(gradients['db' +
str(l+1)],gradients['db' + str(l+1)])


            # Compute bias-corrected second raw moment estimate.
            s_corrected["dw" + str(l+1)] = s["dw" + str(l+1)]/(1-
np.power(beta2,t))
            s_corrected["db" + str(l+1)] = s["db" + str(l+1)]/(1-
np.power(beta2,t))

            # Update parameters.
            d1=np.sqrt(s_corrected["dw" + str(l+1)]+epsilon)
            d2=np.sqrt(s_corrected["db" + str(l+1)]+epsilon)
            parameters["W" + str(l+1)] = parameters['W' + str(l+1)]- \
                        (learningRate* v_corrected["dw" + str(l+1)]/d1)
            parameters["b" + str(l+1)] = parameters['b' + str(l+1)] - \
                        (learningRate* v_corrected["db" + str(l+1)]/d2)

        if outputActivationFunc=="sigmoid":
            #Compute 1st moment for L
            v["dw" + str(L)] = beta1*v["dw" + str(L)] + (1-beta1) *
gradients['dw' + str(L)]
            v["db" + str(L)] = beta1*v["db" + str(L)] + (1-beta1) *
gradients['db' + str(L)]
            # Compute bias-corrected first moment estimate.
            v_corrected["dw" + str(L)] = v["dw" + str(L)]/(1-
np.power(beta1,t))
            v_corrected["db" + str(L)] = v["db" + str(L)]/(1-
np.power(beta1,t))

            # Compute 2nd moment for L
            s["dw" + str(L)] = beta2*s["dw" + str(L)] + (1-beta2) * \
                        np.multiply(gradients['dw' + str(L)],gradients['dw'
+ str(L)])
            s["db" + str(L)] = beta2*s["db" + str(L)] + (1-beta2) * \
                        np.multiply(gradients['db' + str(L)],gradients['db' +
str(L)])

            # Compute bias-corrected second raw moment estimate.
            s_corrected["dw" + str(L)] = s["dw" + str(L)]/(1-
np.power(beta2,t))
            s_corrected["db" + str(L)] = s["db" + str(L)]/(1-
np.power(beta2,t))

            # Update parameters.
            d1=np.sqrt(s_corrected["dw" + str(L)]+epsilon)
            d2=np.sqrt(s_corrected["db" + str(L)]+epsilon)
            parameters["W" + str(L)] = parameters['W' + str(L)]- \
                        (learningRate* v_corrected["dw" + str(L)]/d1)
            parameters["b" + str(L)] = parameters['b' + str(L)] - \
                        (learningRate* v_corrected["db" + str(L)]/d2)

        elif outputActivationFunc=="softmax":
            # Compute 1st moment
            v["dw" + str(L)] = beta1*v["dw" + str(L)] + (1-beta1) *
gradients['dw' + str(L)].T
```

```python
                    v["db" + str(L)] = beta1*v["db" + str(L)] + (1-beta1) *
gradients['db' + str(L)].T
                    # Compute bias-corrected first moment estimate.
                    v_corrected["dw" + str(L)] = v["dw" + str(L)]/(1-
np.power(beta1,t))
                    v_corrected["db" + str(L)] = v["db" + str(L)]/(1-
np.power(beta1,t))

                    #Compute 2nd moment
                    s["dw" + str(L)] = beta2*s["dw" + str(L)] + (1-beta2) *
np.multiply(gradients['dw' + str(L)].T,gradients['dw' + str(L)].T)
                    s["db" + str(L)] = beta2*s["db" + str(L)] + (1-beta2) *
np.multiply(gradients['db' + str(L)].T,gradients['db' + str(L)].T)
                    # Compute bias-corrected second raw moment estimate.
                    s_corrected["dw" + str(L)] = s["dw" + str(L)]/(1-
np.power(beta2,t))
                    s_corrected["db" + str(L)] = s["db" + str(L)]/(1-
np.power(beta2,t))

                    # Update parameters.
                    d1=np.sqrt(s_corrected["dw" + str(L)]+epsilon)
                    d2=np.sqrt(s_corrected["db" + str(L)]+epsilon)
                    parameters["W" + str(L)] = parameters['W' + str(L)]- \
                            (learningRate* v_corrected["dw" + str(L)]/d1)
                    parameters["b" + str(L)] = parameters['b' + str(L)] - \
                            (learningRate* v_corrected["db" + str(L)]/d2)


    return parameters, v, s


#   Execute a L layer Deep learning model
# Input : X - Input features
#         : Y output
#         : layersDimensions - Dimension of layers
#         : hiddenActivationFunc - Activation function at hidden layer relu
/tanh/sigmoid
#         : outputActivationFunc - Activation function at output layer
sigmoid/softmax
#         : learning rate
#         : lambd
#         : keep_prob
#         : num of iteration
#         : initType
#output : parameters
def L_Layer_DeepModel(X1, Y1, layersDimensions, hiddenActivationFunc='relu',
outputActivationFunc="sigmoid",
                        learningRate = .3,  lambd=0, keep_prob=1,
num_iterations = 10000,initType="default",
print_cost=False,figure="figa.png"):

    np.random.seed(1)
    costs = []

    # Parameters initialization.
    if initType == "He":
        parameters = HeInitializeDeepModel(layersDimensions)
    elif initType == "Xavier" :
        parameters = XavInitializeDeepModel(layersDimensions)
    else: #Default
        parameters = initializeDeepModel(layersDimensions)
    # Loop (gradient descent)
    for i in range(0, num_iterations):

```

```python
            AL, caches, dropoutMat = forwardPropagationDeep(X1, parameters, keep_prob,
hiddenActivationFunc="relu",outputActivationFunc=outputActivationFunc)

            # Regularization parameter is 0
            if lambd==0:
                # Compute cost
                cost = computeCost(parameters,AL, Y1, outputActivationFunc=outputActivationFunc)
            # Include L2 regularization
            else:
                # Compute cost
                cost = computeCostWithReg(parameters,AL, Y1, lambd, outputActivationFunc=outputActivationFunc)

            # Backward propagation.
            gradients = backwardPropagationDeep(AL, Y1, caches, dropoutMat, lambd, keep_prob,
hiddenActivationFunc="relu",outputActivationFunc=outputActivationFunc)

            # Update parameters.
            parameters = gradientDescent(parameters, gradients, learningRate=learningRate,outputActivationFunc=outputActivationFunc)


            # Print the cost every 100 training example
            if print_cost and i % 1000 == 0:
                print ("Cost after iteration %i: %f" %(i, cost))
            if print_cost and i % 1000 == 0:
                costs.append(cost)

    # plot the cost
    plt.plot(np.squeeze(costs))
    plt.ylabel('Cost')
    plt.xlabel('No of iterations (x1000)')
    plt.title("Learning rate =" + str(learningRate))
    plt.savefig(figure,bbox_inches='tight')
    #plt.show()
    plt.clf()
    plt.close()

    return parameters

#   Execute a L layer Deep learning model Stoachastic Gradient Descent
# Input : X - Input features
#         : Y output
#         : layersDimensions - Dimension of layers
#         : hiddenActivationFunc - Activation function at hidden layer relu /tanh/sigmoid
#         : outputActivationFunc - Activation function at output - sigmoid/softmax
#         : learning rate
#         : lrDecay
#         : lambd
#         : keep_prob
#         : optimizer
#         : beta
#         : beta1
#         : beta2
#         : epsilon
#         : mini_batch_size
#         : num_epochs
#         :
#output : Updated weights and biases
```

```python
def L_Layer_DeepModel_SGD(X1, Y1, layersDimensions,
hiddenActivationFunc='relu', outputActivationFunc="sigmoid",
                          learningRate = .3, lrDecay=False, decayRate=1,
                          lambd=0, keep_prob=1,
optimizer="gd",beta=0.9,beta1=0.9, beta2=0.999,
                          epsilon = 1e-8,mini_batch_size = 64, num_epochs =
2500, print_cost=False, figure="figa.png"):

    print("lr=",learningRate)
    print("lrDecay=",lrDecay)
    print("decayRate=",decayRate)
    print("lambd=",lambd)
    print("keep_prob=",keep_prob)
    print("optimizer=",optimizer)
    print("beta=",beta)

    print("beta1=",beta1)
    print("beta2=",beta2)
    print("epsilon=",epsilon)

    print("mini_batch_size=",mini_batch_size)
    print("num_epochs=",num_epochs)
    print("epsilon=",epsilon)


    t =0 # Adam counter
    np.random.seed(1)
    costs = []

    # Parameters initialization.
    parameters = initializeDeepModel(layersDimensions)

    #Initialize the optimizer
    if optimizer == "gd":
        pass # no initialization required for gradient descent
    elif optimizer == "momentum":
        v = initializeVelocity(parameters)
    elif optimizer == "rmsprop":
        s = initializeRMSProp(parameters)
    elif optimizer == "adam":
        v,s = initializeAdam(parameters)

    seed=10
    # Loop for number of epochs
    for i in range(num_epochs):
        # Define the random minibatches. We increment the seed to reshuffle
differently the dataset after each epoch
        seed = seed + 1
        minibatches = random_mini_batches(X1, Y1, mini_batch_size, seed)

        batch=0
        # Loop through each mini batch
        for minibatch in minibatches:
            #print("batch=",batch)
            batch=batch+1
            # Select a minibatch
            (minibatch_X, minibatch_Y) = minibatch

            # Perfrom forward propagation
            AL, caches, dropoutMat = forwardPropagationDeep(minibatch_X,
parameters, keep_prob,
hiddenActivationFunc="relu",outputActivationFunc=outputActivationFunc)

            # Compute cost
```

```python
                # Regularization parameter is 0
                if lambd==0:
                   # Compute cost
                    cost = computeCost(parameters, AL, minibatch_Y, 
outputActivationFunc=outputActivationFunc)
                else: # Include L2 regularization
                              # Compute cost
                    cost = computeCostWithReg(parameters, AL, minibatch_Y, lambd, 
outputActivationFunc=outputActivationFunc)
                
                # Backward propagation.
                gradients = backwardPropagationDeep(AL, minibatch_Y, 
caches,dropoutMat, lambd, 
keep_prob,hiddenActivationFunc="relu",outputActivationFunc=outputActivationFu
nc)
   
                if optimizer == "gd":
                   # Update parameters normal gradient descent
                    parameters = gradientDescent(parameters, gradients, 
learningRate=learningRate,outputActivationFunc=outputActivationFunc)
                elif optimizer == "momentum":
                   # Update parameters for gradient descent with momentum
                    parameters, v = gradientDescentWithMomentum(parameters, 
gradients, v, beta, \
                                                
learningRate=learningRate,outputActivationFunc=outputActivationFunc) 
                elif optimizer == "rmsprop":
                   # Update parameters for gradient descent with RMSProp
                    parameters, s = gradientDescentWithRMSProp(parameters, 
gradients, s, beta1, epsilon, \
                                                
learningRate=learningRate,outputActivationFunc=outputActivationFunc) 
                elif optimizer == "adam":
                    t = t + 1 # Adam counter
                    parameters, v, s = gradientDescentWithAdam(parameters, 
gradients, v, s,
                                                                    t, beta1, 
beta2,  epsilon,
                                                
learningRate=learningRate,outputActivationFunc=outputActivationFunc)

        # Print the cost every 1000 epoch
        if print_cost and i % 100 == 0:
            print ("Cost after epoch %i: %f" %(i, cost))
        if print_cost and i % 100 == 0:
            costs.append(cost)
        if lrDecay == True:
            learningRate = np.power(decayRate,(num_epochs/1000)) * 
learningRate


        # plot the cost
        plt.plot(np.squeeze(costs))
        plt.ylabel('Cost')
        plt.xlabel('No of epochs(x100)')
        plt.title("Learning rate =" + str(learningRate))
        plt.savefig(figure,bbox_inches='tight')
        #plt.show()
        plt.clf()
        plt.close()


# Create random mini batches
# Input : X - Input features
```

```
1078  #              : Y- output
1079  #              : miniBatchSizes
1080  #              : seed
1081  #output : mini_batches
1082  def random_mini_batches(X, Y, miniBatchSize = 64, seed = 0):
1083
1084      np.random.seed(seed)
1085      # Get number of training samples
1086      m = X.shape[1]
1087      # Initialize mini batches
1088      mini_batches = []
1089
1090      # Create  a list of random numbers < m
1091      permutation = list(np.random.permutation(m))
1092      # Randomly shuffle the training data
1093      shuffled_X = X[:, permutation]
1094      shuffled_Y = Y[:, permutation].reshape((1,m))
1095
1096      # Compute number of mini batches
1097      numCompleteMinibatches = math.floor(m/miniBatchSize)
1098
1099     # For the number of mini batches
1100      for k in range(0, numCompleteMinibatches):
1101
1102          # Set the start and end of each mini batch
1103          mini_batch_X = shuffled_X[:, k*miniBatchSize : (k+1) * miniBatchSize]
1104          mini_batch_Y = shuffled_Y[:, k*miniBatchSize : (k+1) * miniBatchSize]
1105
1106          mini_batch = (mini_batch_X, mini_batch_Y)
1107          mini_batches.append(mini_batch)
1108
1109
1110      #if m % miniBatchSize != 0:. The batch does not evenly divide by the mini
1111 batch
1112      if m % miniBatchSize != 0:
1113          l=math.floor(m/miniBatchSize)*miniBatchSize
1114          # Set the start and end of last mini batch
1115          m=l+m % miniBatchSize
1116          mini_batch_X = shuffled_X[:,l:m]
1117          mini_batch_Y = shuffled_Y[:,l:m]
1118
1119          mini_batch = (mini_batch_X, mini_batch_Y)
1120          mini_batches.append(mini_batch)
1121
1122      return mini_batches
1123
1124
1125 # Plot a decision boundary
1126 # Input : Input Model,
1127 #          X
1128 #          Y
1129 #          sz - Num of hiden units
1130 #          lr - Learning rate
1131 #          Fig to be saved as
1132 # Returns Null
1133 def plot_decision_boundary(model, X, y,lr,figure1="figb.png"):
1134      print("plot")
1135      # Set min and max values and give it some padding
1136      x_min, x_max = X[0, :].min() - 1, X[0, :].max() + 1
1137      y_min, y_max = X[1, :].min() - 1, X[1, :].max() + 1
1138      colors=['black','gold']
1139      cmap = matplotlib.colors.ListedColormap(colors)
1140      h = 0.01
1141      # Generate a grid of points with distance h between them
```

```
        xx, yy = np.meshgrid(np.arange(x_min, x_max, h), np.arange(y_min, y_max,
h))
        # Predict the function value for the whole grid
        Z = model(np.c_[xx.ravel(), yy.ravel()])
        Z = Z.reshape(xx.shape)
        # Plot the contour and training examples
        plt.contourf(xx, yy, Z, cmap="coolwarm")
        plt.ylabel('x2')
        plt.xlabel('x1')
        x=X.T
        y=y.T.reshape(300,)
        plt.scatter(x[:, 0], x[:, 1], c=y, s=20);
        print(X.shape)
        plt.title("Decision Boundary for learning rate:"+lr)
        plt.savefig(figure1, bbox_inches='tight')
        #plt.show()

# Predict output
def predict(parameters,
X,keep_prob=1,hiddenActivationFunc="relu",outputActivationFunc="sigmoid"):
    A2, cache,dropoutMat = forwardPropagationDeep(X, parameters, keep_prob=1,
hiddenActivationFunc="relu",outputActivationFunc=outputActivationFunc)
    predictions = (A2>0.5)
    return predictions

# Predict probabilities
def predict_proba(parameters, X,outputActivationFunc="sigmoid"):
    A2, cache = forwardPropagationDeep(X, parameters)
    if outputActivationFunc=="sigmoid":
        proba=A2
    elif outputActivationFunc=="softmax":
        proba=np.argmax(A2, axis=0).reshape(-1,1)
        print("A2=",A2.shape)
    return proba

# Plot a decision boundary
# Input : Input Model,
#         X
#         Y
#         sz - Num of hiden units
#         lr - Learning rate
#         Fig to be saved as
# Returns Null
def plot_decision_boundary1(X, y,W1,b1,W2,b2,figure2="figc.png"):
    #plot_decision_boundary(lambda x: predict(parameters, x.T),
x1,y1.T,str(0.3),"fig2.png")
    h = 0.02
    x_min, x_max = X[:, 0].min() - 1, X[:, 0].max() + 1
    y_min, y_max = X[:, 1].min() - 1, X[:, 1].max() + 1
    xx, yy = np.meshgrid(np.arange(x_min, x_max, h),
                         np.arange(y_min, y_max, h))
    Z = np.dot(np.maximum(0, np.dot(np.c_[xx.ravel(), yy.ravel()], W1.T) +
b1.T), W2.T) + b2.T
    Z = np.argmax(Z, axis=1)
    Z = Z.reshape(xx.shape)

    fig = plt.figure()
    plt.contourf(xx, yy, Z, cmap=plt.cm.Spectral, alpha=0.8)
    print(X.shape)
    y1=y.reshape(300,)
    plt.scatter(X[:, 0], X[:, 1], c=y1, s=40, cmap=plt.cm.Spectral)
    plt.xlim(xx.min(), xx.max())
    plt.ylim(yy.min(), yy.max())
    plt.savefig(figure2, bbox_inches='tight')
```

```
1206
1207
1208 # Load the data set
1209 def load_dataset():
1210     np.random.seed(1)
1211     train_X, train_Y = sklearn.datasets.make_circles(n_samples=300,
1212 noise=.05)
1213     np.random.seed(2)
1214     test_X, test_Y = sklearn.datasets.make_circles(n_samples=100, noise=.05)
1215     # Visualize the data
1216     print(train_X.shape)
1217     print(train_Y.shape)
1218     print("load")
1219     #plt.scatter(train_X[:, 0], train_X[:, 1], c=train_Y, s=40,
1220 cmap=plt.cm.Spectral);
1221     train_X = train_X.T
1222     train_Y = train_Y.reshape((1, train_Y.shape[0]))
1223     test_X = test_X.T
1224     test_Y = test_Y.reshape((1, test_Y.shape[0]))
1225     return train_X, train_Y, test_X, test_Y
```

7.2 R

```
1  ################################################################################
2  ################################
3  #
4  # File    : DLfunctions7.R
5  # Author  : Tinniam V Ganesh
6  # Date    : 16 Apr 2018
7  #
8  ################################################################################
9  ################################
10 library(ggplot2)
11 library(PRROC)
12 library(dplyr)
13
14 # Compute the sigmoid of a vector
15 sigmoid <- function(Z){
16   A <- 1/(1+ exp(-Z))
17   cache<-Z
18   retvals <- list("A"=A,"Z"=Z)
19   return(retvals)
20
21 }
22
23 # This is the older version. Very performance intensive
24 # Compute relu
25 reluOld    <-function(Z){
26   A <- apply(Z, 1:2, function(x) max(0,x))
27   cache<-Z
28   retvals <- list("A"=A,"Z"=Z)
29   return(retvals)
30 }
31
32 # Compute the Relu of a vector (current version)
33 relu    <-function(Z){
34     # Perform relu. Set values less that equal to 0 as 0
35     Z[Z<0]=0
36     A=Z
37     cache<-Z
```

```r
38        retvals <- list("A"=A,"Z"=Z)
39        return(retvals)
40 }
41
42 # Compute the tanh activation of a vector
43 tanhActivation <- function(Z){
44    A <- tanh(Z)
45    cache<-Z
46    retvals <- list("A"=A,"Z"=Z)
47    return(retvals)
48 }
49
50 # Compute the softmax of a vector
51 softmax    <- function(Z){
52    # get unnormalized probabilities
53    exp_scores = exp(t(Z))
54    # normalize them for each example
55    A = exp_scores / rowSums(exp_scores)
56    retvals <- list("A"=A,"Z"=Z)
57    return(retvals)
58 }
59
60 # Compute the detivative of Relu
61 # g'(z) = 1 if z >0 and 0 otherwise
62 reluDerivative    <-function(dA, cache){
63    Z <- cache
64    dZ <- dA
65    # Create a logical matrix of values > 0
66    a <- Z > 0
67    # When z <= 0, you should set dz to 0 as well. Perform an element wise
68 multiply
69    dZ <- dZ * a
70    return(dZ)
71 }
72
73 # Compute the derivative of sigmoid
74 # Derivative g'(z) = a* (1-a)
75 sigmoidDerivative   <- function(dA, cache){
76    Z <- cache
77    s <- 1/(1+exp(-Z))
78    dZ <- dA * s * (1-s)
79    return(dZ)
80 }
81
82 # Compute the derivative of tanh
83 # Derivative g'(z) = 1- a^2
84 tanhDerivative    <- function(dA, cache){
85    Z = cache
86    a = tanh(Z)
87    dZ = dA * (1 - a^2)
88    return(dZ)
89 }
90
91 # This function is used in computing the softmax derivative
92 # Populate a matrix of 1s in rows where Y==1
93 # This may need to be extended for K classes. Currently
94 # supports K=3 & K=10
95 popMatrix <- function(Y,numClasses){
96     a=rep(0,times=length(Y))
97     Y1=matrix(a,nrow=length(Y),ncol=numClasses)
98     #Set the rows and columns as 1's where Y is the class value
99     if(numClasses==3){
100         Y1[Y==0,1]=1
101         Y1[Y==1,2]=1
```

```r
            Y1[Y==2,3]=1
      } else if (numClasses==10){
          Y1[Y==0,1]=1
          Y1[Y==1,2]=1
          Y1[Y==2,3]=1
          Y1[Y==3,4]=1
          Y1[Y==4,5]=1
          Y1[Y==5,6]=1
          Y1[Y==6,7]=1
          Y1[Y==7,8]=1
          Y1[Y==8,9]=1
          Y1[Y==9,0]=1
      }
      return(Y1)
}

# Compute the softmax derivative
softmaxDerivative     <- function(dA, cache ,y,numTraining,numClasses){
   # Note : dA not used. dL/dZ = dL/dA * dA/dZ = pi-yi
   Z <- cache
   # Compute softmax
   exp_scores = exp(t(Z))
   # normalize them for each example
   probs = exp_scores / rowSums(exp_scores)
   # Create a matrix of zeros
   Y1=popMatrix(y,numClasses)
   #a=rep(0,times=length(Y))
   #Y1=matrix(a,nrow=length(Y),ncol=numClasses)
   #Set the rows and columns as 1's where Y is the class value
   dZ = probs-Y1
   return(dZ)
}


# Initialize model for L layers
# Input : Vector of units in each layer
# Returns: Initial weights and biases matrices for all layers
initializeDeepModel <- function(layerDimensions){
   set.seed(2)

   # Initialize empty list
   layerParams <- list()

   # Note the Weight matrix at layer 'l' is a matrix of size (l,l-1)
   # The Bias is a vectors of size (l,1)

   # Loop through the layer dimension from 1.. L
   # Indices in R start from 1
   for(l in 2:length(layersDimensions)){
      # Initialize a matrix of small random numbers of size l x l-1
      # Create random numbers of size   l x l-1
      w=rnorm(layersDimensions[l]*layersDimensions[l-1])*0.01
      # Create a weight matrix of size l x l-1 with this initial weights and
      # Add to list W1,W2... WL
      layerParams[[paste('W',l-1,sep="")]] = matrix(w,nrow=layersDimensions[l],
                                                  ncol=layersDimensions[l-1])
      layerParams[[paste('b',l-1,sep="")]] = matrix(rep(0,layersDimensions[l]),

nrow=layersDimensions[l],ncol=1)
   }
   return(layerParams)
}
```

```r
# He Initialization model for L layers
# Input : Vector of units in each layer
# Returns: Initial weights and biases matrices for all layers
# He initilization multiplies the random numbers with
sqrt(2/layerDimensions[previouslayer])
HeInitializeDeepModel <- function(layerDimensions){
    set.seed(2)

    # Initialize empty list
    layerParams <- list()

    # Note the Weight matrix at layer 'l' is a matrix of size (l,l-1)
    # The Bias is a vectors of size (l,1)

    # Loop through the layer dimension from 1.. L
    # Indices in R start from 1
    for(l in 2:length(layersDimensions)){
        # Initialize a matrix of small random numbers of size l x l-1
        # Create random numbers of size  l x l-1
        w=rnorm(layersDimensions[l]*layersDimensions[l-1])

        # Create a weight matrix of size l x l-1 with this initial weights and
        # Add to list W1,W2... WL
        # He initialization - Divide by sqrt(2/layerDimensions[previous layer])
        layerParams[[paste('W',l-1,sep="")]] = matrix(w,nrow=layersDimensions[l],
ncol=layersDimensions[l-1])*sqrt(2/layersDimensions[l-1])
        layerParams[[paste('b',l-1,sep="")]] = matrix(rep(0,layersDimensions[l]),
nrow=layersDimensions[l],ncol=1)
    }
    return(layerParams)
}

# XavInitializeDeepModel Initialization model for L layers
# Input : Vector of units in each layer
# Returns: Initial weights and biases matrices for all layers
# He initilization multiplies the random numbers with
# sqrt(1/layerDimensions[previouslayer])
XavInitializeDeepModel <- function(layerDimensions){
    set.seed(2)

    # Initialize empty list
    layerParams <- list()

    # Note the Weight matrix at layer 'l' is a matrix of size (l,l-1)
    # The Bias is a vectors of size (l,1)

    # Loop through the layer dimension from 1.. L
    # Indices in R start from 1
    for(l in 2:length(layersDimensions)){
        # Initialize a matrix of small random numbers of size l x l-1
        # Create random numbers of size  l x l-1
        w=rnorm(layersDimensions[l]*layersDimensions[l-1])

        # Create a weight matrix of size l x l-1 with this initial weights and
        # Add to list W1,W2... WL
        # He initialization - Divide by sqrt(2/layerDimensions[previous layer])
```

```r
            layerParams[[paste('W',l-1,sep="")]] =
matrix(w,nrow=layersDimensions[l],

ncol=layersDimensions[l-1])*sqrt(1/layersDimensions[l-1])
            layerParams[[paste('b',l-1,sep="")]] =
matrix(rep(0,layersDimensions[l]),

nrow=layersDimensions[l],ncol=1)
    }
    return(layerParams)
}

# Initialize velocity
# Input : parameters
# Returns: v -Initial velocity
initializeVelocity <- function(parameters){

    L <- length(parameters)/2
    v <- list()

    # Initialize velocity with the same dimensions as W
    for(l in 1:L){
        # Get the size of weight matrix
        sz <- dim(parameters[[paste('W',l,sep="")]])
        v[[paste('dW',l,sep="")]] = matrix(rep(0,sz[1]*sz[2]),
                                        nrow=sz[1],ncol=sz[2])
        #Get the size of bias matrix
        sz <- dim(parameters[[paste('b',l,sep="")]])
        v[[paste('db',l,sep="")]] =  matrix(rep(0,sz[1]*sz[2]),
                                        nrow=sz[1],ncol=sz[2])
    }

    return(v)
}


# Initialize RMSProp
# Input : parameters
# Returns: s - Initial RMSProp
initializeRMSProp <- function(parameters){

    L <- length(parameters)/2
    s <- list()

    # Initialize velocity with the same dimensions as W
    for(l in 1:L){
        # Get the size of weight matrix
        sz <- dim(parameters[[paste('W',l,sep="")]])
        s[[paste('dW',l,sep="")]] = matrix(rep(0,sz[1]*sz[2]),
                                        nrow=sz[1],ncol=sz[2])
        #Get the size of bias matrix
        sz <- dim(parameters[[paste('b',l,sep="")]])
        s[[paste('db',l,sep="")]] =  matrix(rep(0,sz[1]*sz[2]),
                                        nrow=sz[1],ncol=sz[2])
    }

    return(s)
}

# Initialize Adam
# Input : parameters
# Returns: (v,s) - Initial Adam parameters
initializeAdam <- function(parameters){

```

```r
    L <- length(parameters)/2
    v <- list()
    s <- list()

    # Initialize velocity with the same dimensions as W
    for(l in 1:L){
        # Get the size of weight matrix
        sz <- dim(parameters[[paste('W',l,sep="")]])
        v[[paste('dW',l,sep="")]] = matrix(rep(0,sz[1]*sz[2]),
                                        nrow=sz[1],ncol=sz[2])
        s[[paste('dW',l,sep="")]] = matrix(rep(0,sz[1]*sz[2]),
                                        nrow=sz[1],ncol=sz[2])
        #Get the size of bias matrix
        sz <- dim(parameters[[paste('b',l,sep="")]])
        v[[paste('db',l,sep="")]] =  matrix(rep(0,sz[1]*sz[2]),
                                        nrow=sz[1],ncol=sz[2])
        s[[paste('db',l,sep="")]] =  matrix(rep(0,sz[1]*sz[2]),
                                        nrow=sz[1],ncol=sz[2])
    }
    retvals <- list("v"=v,"s"=s)
    return(retvals)
}

# Compute the activation at a layer 'l' for forward prop in a Deep Network
# Input : A_prev - Activation of previous layer
#         W,b - Weight and bias matrices and vectors
#         activationFunc - Activation function - sigmoid, tanh, relu etc
# Returns : The Activation of this layer
#         :
# Z = W * X + b
# A = sigmoid(Z), A= Relu(Z), A= tanh(Z)
layerActivationForward <- function(A_prev, W, b, activationFunc){

  # Compute Z
  z = W %*% A_prev
  # Broadcast the bias 'b' by column
  z <-sweep(z,1,b,'+')

  forward_cache <- list("A_prev"=A_prev, "W"=W, "b"=b)
  # Compute the activation for sigmoid
  if(activationFunc == "sigmoid"){
    vals = sigmoid(Z)
  } else if (activationFunc == "relu"){ # Compute the activation for relu
    vals = relu(Z)
  } else if(activationFunc == 'tanh'){ # Compute the activation for tanh
    vals = tanhActivation(Z)
  } else if(activationFunc == 'softmax'){
    vals = softmax(Z)
  }
  # Create a list of forward and activation cache
  cache <- list("forward_cache"=forward_cache,
"activation_cache"=vals[['Z']])
  retvals <- list("A"=vals[['A']],"cache"=cache)
  return(retvals)
}

# Compute the forward propagation for layers 1..L
# Input : X - Input Features
#         parameters: Weights and biases
#         keep_prob
#         hiddenActivationFunc - relu/sigmoid/tanh
#         outputActivationFunc - Activation function at hidden layer
sigmoid/softmax
# Returns : AL
```

```r
358  #             caches
359  #             dropoutMat
360  # The forward propoagtion uses the Relu/tanh activation from layer 1..L-1 and
361  sigmoid actiovation at layer L
362  forwardPropagationDeep <- function(X, parameters,keep_prob=1,
363  hiddenActivationFunc='relu',
364                                              outputActivationFunc='sigmoid'){
365    caches <- list()
366    dropoutMat <- list()
367    # Set A to X (A0)
368    A <- X
369    L <- length(parameters)/2 # number of layers in the neural network
370    # Loop through from layer 1 to upto layer L
371    for(l in 1:(L-1)){
372      A_prev <- A
373      # Zi = Wi x Ai-1 + bi  and Ai = g(Zi)
374      # Set W and b for layer 'l'
375      # Loop throug from W1,W2... WL-1
376      W <- parameters[[paste("W",l,sep="")]]
377      b <- parameters[[paste("b",l,sep="")]]
378      # Compute the forward propagation through layer 'l' using the activation
379  function
380      actForward <- layerActivationForward(A_prev,
381                                            W,
382                                            b,
383                                            activationFunc =
384  hiddenActivationFunc)
385      A <- actForward[['A']]
386      # Append the cache A_prev,W,b, Z
387      caches[[l]] <-actForward
388
389      # Randomly drop some activation units
390      # Create a matrix as the same shape as A
391      set.seed(1)
392      i=dim(A)[1]
393      j=dim(A)[2]
394      a<-rnorm(i*j)
395      # Normalize a between 0 and 1
396      a = (a - min(a))/(max(a) - min(a))
397      # Create a matrix of D
398      D <- matrix(a,nrow=i, ncol=j)
399      # Find D which is less than equal to keep_prob
400      D <- D < keep_prob
401      # Remove some A's
402      A <- A * D
403      # Divide by keep_prob to keep expected value same
404      A <- A/keep_prob
405      dropoutMat[[paste("D",l,sep="")]] <- D
406    }
407
408    # Since this is binary classification use the sigmoid activation function
409  in
410    # last layer
411    # Set the weights and biases for the last layer
412    W <- parameters[[paste("W",L,sep="")]]
413    b <- parameters[[paste("b",L,sep="")]]
414    # Last layer
415    actForward = layerActivationForward(A, W, b, activationFunc =
416  outputActivationFunc)
417    AL <- actForward[['A']]
418    # Append the output of this forward propagation through the last layer
419    caches[[L]] <- actForward
420    # Create a list of the final output and the caches
421    fwdPropDeep <- list("AL"=AL,"caches"=caches,"dropoutMat"=dropoutMat)
```

```r
    return(fwdPropDeep)

}

# Function pickColumns(). This function is in computeCost()
# Pick columns
# Input : AL
#         : Y
#         : numClasses
# Output: a
pickColumns <- function(AL,Y,numClasses){
    if(numClasses==3){
        a=c(AL[Y==0,1],AL[Y==1,2],AL[Y==2,3])
    }
    else if (numClasses==10){
        a=c(AL[Y==0,1],AL[Y==1,2],AL[Y==2,3],AL[Y==3,4],AL[Y==4,5],
            AL[Y==5,6],AL[Y==6,7],AL[Y==7,8],AL[Y==8,9],AL[Y==9,10])
    }
    return(a)
}


# Compute the cost
# Input : Activation of last layer
#         : Output from data
#         :outputActivationFunc - Activation function at hidden layer
sigmoid/softmax
#         : numClasses
# Output: cost
computeCost <- function(AL,Y,outputActivationFunc="sigmoid",numClasses=3){
  if(outputActivationFunc=="sigmoid"){
    m= length(Y)
    cost=-1/m*sum(Y*log(AL) + (1-Y)*log(1-AL))


  }else if (outputActivationFunc=="softmax"){
    # Select the elements where the y values are 0, 1 or 2 and make a vector
    # Pick columns
    #a=c(AL[Y==0,1],AL[Y==1,2],AL[Y==2,3])
    m= length(Y)
    a =pickColumns(AL,Y,numClasses)
    #a = c(A2[y=k,k+1])
    # Take log
    correct_probs = -log(a)

    # Compute loss
    cost= sum(correct_probs)/m
  }
  return(cost)
}


# Compute the cost with Regularization
# Input : parameters
#         : AL-Activation of last layer
#         : Y-Output from data
#         : lambd
#         : outputActivationFunc - Activation function at hidden layer
sigmoid/softmax
#         : numClasses
# Output: cost
computeCostWithReg <- function(parameters, AL,Y,lambd,
outputActivationFunc="sigmoid",numClasses=3){
```

```r
            if(outputActivationFunc=="sigmoid"){
            m= length(Y)
            cost=-1/m*sum(Y*log(AL) + (1-Y)*log(1-AL))
            
            # Regularization cost
            L <- length(parameters)/2
            L2RegularizationCost=0
            for(l in 1:L){
                L2RegularizationCost = L2RegularizationCost +
                            sum(parameters[[paste("W",l,sep="")]]^2)
            }
            L2RegularizationCost = (lambd/(2*m))*L2RegularizationCost
            cost = cost +  L2RegularizationCost
            
      }else if (outputActivationFunc=="softmax"){
          # Select the elements where the y values are 0, 1 or 2 and make a
vector
            # Pick columns
            #a=c(AL[Y==0,1],AL[Y==1,2],AL[Y==2,3])
            m= length(Y)
            a =pickColumns(AL,Y,numClasses)
            #a = c(A2[y=k,k+1])
            # Take log
            correct_probs = -log(a)
            # Compute loss
            cost= sum(correct_probs)/m
            
            # Regularization cost
            L <- length(parameters)/2
            L2RegularizationCost=0
            # Add L2 norm
            for(l in 1:L){
                L2RegularizationCost = L2RegularizationCost +
                    sum(parameters[[paste("W",l,sep="")]]^2)
            }
            L2RegularizationCost = (lambd/(2*m))*L2RegularizationCost
            cost = cost +  L2RegularizationCost
        }
    return(cost)
}

# Compute the backpropagation through a layer
# Input : Neural Network parameters - dA
#         # cache - forward_cache & activation_cache
#         # Input features
#         # Output values Y
#         # activationFunc
#         # numClasses
# Returns: Gradients
# dL/dWi= dL/dZi*Al-1
# dl/dbl = dL/dZl
# dL/dZ_prev=dL/dZl*W

layerActivationBackward  <- function(dA, cache, Y,
activationFunc,numClasses){
  # Get A_prev,w,b
  forward_cache <-cache[['forward_cache']]
  activation_cache <- cache[['activation_cache']]
  A_prev <- forward_cache[['A_prev']]
  numtraining = dim(A_prev)[2]
  # Get Z
  activation_cache <- cache[['activation_cache']]
  if(activationFunc == "relu"){
    dZ <- reluDerivative(dA, activation_cache)
```

```r
      } else if(activationFunc == "sigmoid"){
        dZ <- sigmoidDerivative(dA, activation_cache)
      } else if(activationFunc == "tanh"){
        dZ <- tanhDerivative(dA, activation_cache)
      } else if(activationFunc == "softmax"){
        dZ <- softmaxDerivative(dA,  activation_cache,Y,numtraining,numClasses)
      }

    if (activationFunc == 'softmax'){
      W <- forward_cache[['W']]
      b <- forward_cache[['b']]
      dW = 1/numtraining * A_prev%*%dZ
      db = 1/numtraining* matrix(colSums(dZ),nrow=1,ncol=numClasses)
      dA_prev = dZ %*%W
    } else {
      W <- forward_cache[['W']]
      b <- forward_cache[['b']]
      numtraining = dim(A_prev)[2]

      dW = 1/numtraining * dZ %*% t(A_prev)
      db = 1/numtraining * rowSums(dZ)
      dA_prev = t(W) %*% dZ
    }
    retvals <- list("dA_prev"=dA_prev,"dW"=dW,"db"=db)
    return(retvals)
}

# Compute the backpropagation through a layer with Regularization
# Input : dA-Neural Network parameters
#           # cache - forward_cache & activation_cache
#           # Output values Y
#           # lambd
#           # activationFunc
#           # numClasses
# Returns: Gradients
# dL/dWi= dL/dZi*Al-1
# dl/dbl = dL/dZl
# dL/dZ_prev=dL/dZl*W

layerActivationBackwardWithReg   <- function(dA, cache, Y, lambd,
activationFunc,numClasses){
    # Get A_prev,W,b
    forward_cache <-cache[['forward_cache']]
    activation_cache <- cache[['activation_cache']]
    A_prev <- forward_cache[['A_prev']]
    numtraining = dim(A_prev)[2]
    # Get Z
    activation_cache <- cache[['activation_cache']]
    if(activationFunc == "relu"){
        dZ <- reluDerivative(dA, activation_cache)
    } else if(activationFunc == "sigmoid"){
        dZ <- sigmoidDerivative(dA, activation_cache)
    } else if(activationFunc == "tanh"){
        dZ <- tanhDerivative(dA, activation_cache)
    } else if(activationFunc == "softmax"){
        dZ <- softmaxDerivative(dA,
activation_cache,Y,numtraining,numClasses)
    }

    if (activationFunc == 'softmax'){
        W <- forward_cache[['W']]
        b <- forward_cache[['b']]
        # Add the regularization factor
        dW = 1/numtraining * A_prev%*%dZ  + (lambd/numtraining) * t(W)
```

```r
            db = 1/numtraining* matrix(colSums(dZ),nrow=1,ncol=numClasses)
            dA_prev = dZ %*%W
    } else {
            W <- forward_cache[['W']]
            b <- forward_cache[['b']]
            numtraining = dim(A_prev)[2]
            # Add the regularization factor
            dW = 1/numtraining * dZ %*% t(A_prev) + (lambd/numtraining) * W
            db = 1/numtraining * rowSums(dZ)
            dA_prev = t(W) %*% dZ
    }
    retvals <- list("dA_prev"=dA_prev,"dW"=dW,"db"=db)
    return(retvals)
}

# Compute the backpropagation for 1 cycle through all layers
# Input : AL: Output of L layer Network - weights
#         Y   Real output
#         caches -- list of caches containing:
#         every cache of layerActivationForward() with "relu"/"tanh"
#         #(it's caches[l], for l in range(L-1) i.e l = 0...L-2)
#         #the cache of layerActivationForward() with "sigmoid" (it's caches[L-1])
#         dropoutMat
#         lambd
#         keep_prob
#         hiddenActivationFunc - Activation function at hidden layers - relu/tanh/sigmoid
#         outputActivationFunc - Activation function at hidden layer sigmoid/softmax
#         numClasses
#   Returns:
#     gradients -- A dictionary with the gradients
#                 gradients["dA" + str(l)]
#                 gradients["dW" + str(l)]
#                 gradients["db" + str(l)]
backwardPropagationDeep <- function(AL, Y, caches,dropoutMat, lambd=0,
keep_prob=0,   hiddenActivationFunc='relu',
                                outputActivationFunc="sigmoid",numClasses){
    #initialize the gradients
    gradients = list()
    # Set the number of layers
    L = length(caches)
    numTraining = dim(AL)[2]

    if(outputActivationFunc == "sigmoid")
        # Initializing the backpropagation
        # dl/dAL= -(y/a) - ((1-y)/(1-a)) - At the output layer
        dAL = -( (Y/AL) -(1 - Y)/(1 - AL))
    else if(outputActivationFunc == "softmax"){
        dAL=0
        Y=t(Y)
    }

    # Get the gradients at the last layer
    # Inputs: "AL, Y, caches".
    # Outputs: "gradients["dAL"], gradients["dWL"], gradients["dbL"]
    # Start with Layer L
    # Get the current cache
    current_cache = caches[[L]]$cache
    if (lambd==0){
        retvals <-  layerActivationBackward(dAL, current_cache, Y,
                                            activationFunc =
outputActivationFunc,numClasses)
```

```r
    } else {
        retvals = layerActivationBackwardWithReg(dAL, current_cache, Y, lambd,
                                        activationFunc = 
outputActivationFunc,numClasses)
    }



   #Note: Take the transpose of dA
   if(outputActivationFunc =="sigmoid")
        gradients[[paste("dA",L,sep="")]] <- retvals[['dA_prev']]
   else if(outputActivationFunc =="softmax")
        gradients[[paste("dA",L,sep="")]] <- t(retvals[['dA_prev']])

   gradients[[paste("dW",L,sep="")]] <- retvals[['dW']]
   gradients[[paste("db",L,sep="")]] <- retvals[['db']]



   # Traverse in the reverse direction
   for(l in (L-1):1){
     # Compute the gradients for L-1 to 1 for Relu/tanh
     # Inputs: "gradients["dA" + str(l + 2)], caches".
     # Outputs: "gradients["dA" + str(l + 1)] , gradients["dW" + str(l + 1)] , 
gradients["db" + str(l + 1)]
     current_cache = caches[[l]]$cache
     if (lambd==0){
         # Get the dropout matrix
         D <-dropoutMat[[paste("D",l,sep="")]]
         # Multiply gradient with dropout matrix
         gradients[[paste('dA',l+1,sep="")]] = 
gradients[[paste('dA',l+1,sep="")]] *D
         # Divide by keep_prob to keep expected value same
         gradients[[paste('dA',l+1,sep="")]] = 
gradients[[paste('dA',l+1,sep="")]]/keep_prob
         retvals = 
layerActivationBackward(gradients[[paste('dA',l+1,sep="")]],
                                         current_cache, Y,
                                         activationFunc = hiddenActivationFunc)
     } else {
         retvals = 
layerActivationBackwardWithReg(gradients[[paste('dA',l+1,sep="")]],
                                         current_cache, Y, lambd,
                                         activationFunc = 
hiddenActivationFunc)
     }

     gradients[[paste("dA",l,sep="")]] <-retvals[['dA_prev']]
     gradients[[paste("dW",l,sep="")]] <- retvals[['dW']]
     gradients[[paste("db",l,sep="")]] <- retvals[['db']]
   }

   return(gradients)
}


# Perform Gradient Descent
# Input : Weights and biases
#        : gradients
#        : learning rate
#        : outputActivationFunc - Activation function at hidden layer 
sigmoid/softmax
#output : Updated weights after 1 iteration
```

```r
gradientDescent  <- function(parameters, gradients,
learningRate,outputActivationFunc="sigmoid"){

  L = length(parameters)/2 # number of layers in the neural network
  # Update rule for each parameter. Use a for loop.
  for(l in 1:(L-1)){
    parameters[[paste("W",l,sep="")]] = parameters[[paste("W",l,sep="")]] -
      learningRate* gradients[[paste("dW",l,sep="")]]
    parameters[[paste("b",l,sep="")]] = parameters[[paste("b",l,sep="")]] -
      learningRate* gradients[[paste("db",l,sep="")]]
  }
  if(outputActivationFunc=="sigmoid"){
    parameters[[paste("W",L,sep="")]] = parameters[[paste("W",L,sep="")]] -
      learningRate* gradients[[paste("dW",L,sep="")]]
    parameters[[paste("b",L,sep="")]] = parameters[[paste("b",L,sep="")]] -
      learningRate* gradients[[paste("db",L,sep="")]]

  }else if (outputActivationFunc=="softmax"){
    parameters[[paste("W",L,sep="")]] = parameters[[paste("W",L,sep="")]] -
      learningRate* t(gradients[[paste("dW",L,sep="")]])
    parameters[[paste("b",L,sep="")]] = parameters[[paste("b",L,sep="")]] -
      learningRate* t(gradients[[paste("db",L,sep="")]])

  }
  return(parameters)
}

# Perform Gradient Descent with momentum
# Input : Weights and biases
#       : beta
#       : gradients
#       : learning rate
#       : outputActivationFunc - Activation function at hidden layer
sigmoid/softmax
#output : Updated weights after 1 iteration
gradientDescentWithMomentum  <- function(parameters, gradients,v, beta,
learningRate,outputActivationFunc="sigmoid"){

    L = length(parameters)/2 # number of layers in the neural network

    # Update rule for each parameter. Use a for loop.
    for(l in 1:(L-1)){
        # Compute velocities
        # v['dWk'] = beta *v['dWk'] + (1-beta)*dWk
        v[[paste("dW",l, sep="")]] = beta*v[[paste("dW",l, sep="")]] +
                (1-beta) * gradients[[paste('dW',l,sep="")]]
        v[[paste("db",l, sep="")]] = beta*v[[paste("db",l, sep="")]] +
            (1-beta) * gradients[[paste('db',l,sep="")]]

        parameters[[paste("W",l,sep="")]] = parameters[[paste("W",l,sep="")]]
-
            learningRate* v[[paste("dW",l, sep="")]]
        parameters[[paste("b",l,sep="")]] = parameters[[paste("b",l,sep="")]]
-
            learningRate* v[[paste("db",l, sep="")]]
    }

    # Compute for the Lth layer
    if(outputActivationFunc=="sigmoid"){
        v[[paste("dW",L, sep="")]] = beta*v[[paste("dW",L, sep="")]] +
            (1-beta) * gradients[[paste('dW',L,sep="")]]
        v[[paste("db",L, sep="")]] = beta*v[[paste("db",L, sep="")]] +
            (1-beta) * gradients[[paste('db',L,sep="")]]
```

```r
                parameters[[paste("W",L,sep="")]] = parameters[[paste("W",L,sep="")]] 
-
                    learningRate* v[[paste("dW",l, sep="")]]
                parameters[[paste("b",L,sep="")]] = parameters[[paste("b",L,sep="")]] 
-
                    learningRate* v[[paste("db",l, sep="")]]
        
        }else if (outputActivationFunc=="softmax"){
            v[[paste("dW",L, sep="")]] = beta*v[[paste("dW",L, sep="")]] +
                (1-beta) * t(gradients[[paste('dW',L,sep="")]])
            v[[paste("db",L, sep="")]] = beta*v[[paste("db",L, sep="")]] +
                (1-beta) * t(gradients[[paste('db',L,sep="")]])
            parameters[[paste("W",L,sep="")]] = parameters[[paste("W",L,sep="")]] 
-
                learningRate* t(gradients[[paste("dW",L,sep="")]])
            parameters[[paste("b",L,sep="")]] = parameters[[paste("b",L,sep="")]] 
-
                learningRate* t(gradients[[paste("db",L,sep="")]])
        }
    return(parameters)
}


# Perform Gradient Descent with RMSProp
# Input  : parameters
#        : gradients
#        : s
#        : beta1
#        : epsilon
#        : learning rate
#        : outputActivationFunc - Activation function at hidden layer
sigmoid/softmax
#output : Updated weights after 1 iteration
gradientDescentWithRMSProp   <- function(parameters, gradients,s, beta1,
epsilon, learningRate,outputActivationFunc="sigmoid"){
    L = length(parameters)/2 # number of layers in the neural network
    # Update rule for each parameter. Use a for loop.
    for(l in 1:(L-1)){
        # Compute RMSProp
        # s['dWk'] = beta1 *s['dWk'] + (1-beta1)*dWk**2/sqrt(s['dWk'])
        # Element wise multiply of gradients
        s[[paste("dW",l, sep="")]] = beta1*s[[paste("dW",l, sep="")]] +
            (1-beta1) * gradients[[paste('dW',l,sep="")]] *
gradients[[paste('dW',l,sep="")]]
        s[[paste("db",l, sep="")]] = beta1*s[[paste("db",l, sep="")]] +
            (1-beta1) * gradients[[paste('db',l,sep="")]] *
gradients[[paste('db',l,sep="")]]
        
        parameters[[paste("W",l,sep="")]] = parameters[[paste("W",l,sep="")]] 
-
            learningRate *
gradients[[paste('dW',l,sep="")]]/sqrt(s[[paste("dW",l, sep="")]]+epsilon)
        parameters[[paste("b",l,sep="")]] = parameters[[paste("b",l,sep="")]] 
-

learningRate*gradients[[paste('db',l,sep="")]]/sqrt(s[[paste("db",l,
sep="")]]+epsilon)
    }
    
    # Compute for the Lth layer
    if(outputActivationFunc=="sigmoid"){
        s[[paste("dW",L, sep="")]] = beta1*s[[paste("dW",L, sep="")]] +
            (1-beta1) * gradients[[paste('dW',L,sep="")]]
*gradients[[paste('dW',L,sep="")]]
```

```r
            s[[paste("db",L, sep="")]] = beta1*s[[paste("db",L, sep="")]] +
                (1-beta1) * gradients[[paste('db',L,sep="")]] *
gradients[[paste('db',L,sep="")]]

            parameters[[paste("W",L,sep="")]] = parameters[[paste("W",L,sep="")]]
-
                learningRate*
gradients[[paste('dW',l,sep="")]]/sqrt(s[[paste("dW",L, sep="")]]+epsilon)
            parameters[[paste("b",L,sep="")]] = parameters[[paste("b",L,sep="")]]
-
                learningRate* gradients[[paste('db',l,sep="")]]/sqrt(
s[[paste("db",L, sep="")]]+epsilon)

    }else if (outputActivationFunc=="softmax"){
        s[[paste("dW",L, sep="")]] = beta1*s[[paste("dW",L, sep="")]] +
            (1-beta1) * t(gradients[[paste('dW',L,sep="")]]) *
t(gradients[[paste('dW',L,sep="")]])
        s[[paste("db",L, sep="")]] = beta1*s[[paste("db",L, sep="")]] +
            (1-beta1) * t(gradients[[paste('db',L,sep="")]]) *
t(gradients[[paste('db',L,sep="")]])

            parameters[[paste("W",L,sep="")]] = parameters[[paste("W",L,sep="")]]
-
                learningRate*
t(gradients[[paste("dW",L,sep="")]])/sqrt(s[[paste("dW",L, sep="")]]+epsilon)
            parameters[[paste("b",L,sep="")]] = parameters[[paste("b",L,sep="")]]
-
                learningRate* t(gradients[[paste("db",L,sep="")]])/sqrt(
s[[paste("db",L, sep="")]]+epsilon)
    }
    return(parameters)
}


# Perform Gradient Descent with Adam
# Input : parameters
#        : gradients
#        : v
#        : s
#        : t
#        : beta1
#        : beta2
#        : epsilon
#        : learning rate
#        : outputActivationFunc - Activation function at hidden layer
sigmoid/softmax
#output : Updated weights after 1 iteration
gradientDescentWithAdam  <- function(parameters, gradients,v, s, t,
                        beta1=0.9, beta2=0.999, epsilon=10^-8,
learningRate=0.1,outputActivationFunc="sigmoid"){

    L = length(parameters)/2 # number of layers in the neural network
    v_corrected <- list()
    s_corrected <- list()
    # Update rule for each parameter. Use a for loop.
    for(l in 1:(L-1)){
        # v['dWk'] = beta *v['dWk'] + (1-beta)*dWk
        v[[paste("dW",l, sep="")]] = beta1*v[[paste("dW",l, sep="")]] +
            (1-beta1) * gradients[[paste('dW',l,sep="")]]
        v[[paste("db",l, sep="")]] = beta1*v[[paste("db",l, sep="")]] +
            (1-beta1) * gradients[[paste('db',l,sep="")]]


        # Compute bias-corrected first moment estimate.
```

```
            v_corrected[[paste("dw",l, sep="")]] = v[[paste("dw",l, sep="")]]/(1-beta1^t)
            v_corrected[[paste("db",l, sep="")]] = v[[paste("db",l, sep="")]]/(1-beta1^t)


            # Element wise multiply of gradients
            s[[paste("dW",l, sep="")]] = beta2*s[[paste("dW",l, sep="")]] +
                (1-beta2) * gradients[[paste('dW',l,sep="")]] * gradients[[paste('dW',l,sep="")]]
            s[[paste("db",l, sep="")]] = beta2*s[[paste("db",l, sep="")]] +
                (1-beta2) * gradients[[paste('db',l,sep="")]] * gradients[[paste('db',l,sep="")]]

            # Compute bias-corrected second moment estimate.
            s_corrected[[paste("dW",l, sep="")]] = s[[paste("dW",l, sep="")]]/(1-beta2^t)
            s_corrected[[paste("db",l, sep="")]] = s[[paste("db",l, sep="")]]/(1-beta2^t)

            # Update parameters.
            d1=sqrt(s_corrected[[paste("dW",l, sep="")]]+epsilon)
            d2=sqrt(s_corrected[[paste("db",l, sep="")]]+epsilon)

            parameters[[paste("W",l,sep="")]] = parameters[[paste("W",l,sep="")]] -
                learningRate * v_corrected[[paste("dW",l, sep="")]]/d1
            parameters[[paste("b",l,sep="")]] = parameters[[paste("b",l,sep="")]] -
                learningRate*v_corrected[[paste("db",l, sep="")]]/d2
    }

    # Compute for the Lth layer
    if(outputActivationFunc=="sigmoid"){
        v[[paste("dW",L, sep="")]] = beta1*v[[paste("dW",L, sep="")]] +
            (1-beta1) * gradients[[paste('dW',L,sep="")]]
        v[[paste("db",L, sep="")]] = beta1*v[[paste("db",L, sep="")]] +
            (1-beta1) * gradients[[paste('db',L,sep="")]]


        # Compute bias-corrected first moment estimate.
        v_corrected[[paste("dW",L, sep="")]] = v[[paste("dW",L, sep="")]]/(1-beta1^t)
        v_corrected[[paste("db",L, sep="")]] = v[[paste("db",L, sep="")]]/(1-beta1^t)


        # Element wise multiply of gradients
        s[[paste("dW",L, sep="")]] = beta2*s[[paste("dW",L, sep="")]] +
            (1-beta2) * gradients[[paste('dW',L,sep="")]] * gradients[[paste('dW',L,sep="")]]
        s[[paste("db",L, sep="")]] = beta2*s[[paste("db",L, sep="")]] +
            (1-beta2) * gradients[[paste('db',L,sep="")]] * gradients[[paste('db',L,sep="")]]

        # Compute bias-corrected second moment estimate.
        s_corrected[[paste("dW",L, sep="")]] = s[[paste("dW",L, sep="")]]/(1-beta2^t)
        s_corrected[[paste("db",L, sep="")]] = s[[paste("db",L, sep="")]]/(1-beta2^t)

        # Update parameters.
        d1=sqrt(s_corrected[[paste("dW",L, sep="")]]+epsilon)
        d2=sqrt(s_corrected[[paste("db",L, sep="")]]+epsilon)
```

```
            parameters[[paste("W",L,sep="")]] = parameters[[paste("W",L,sep="")]] -
                learningRate * v_corrected[[paste("dw",L, sep="")]]/d1
            parameters[[paste("b",L,sep="")]] = parameters[[paste("b",L,sep="")]] -
                learningRate*v_corrected[[paste("db",L, sep="")]]/d2

        }else if (outputActivationFunc=="softmax"){
            v[[paste("dw",L, sep="")]] = beta1*v[[paste("dw",L, sep="")]] +
                (1-beta1) * t(gradients[[paste('dw',L,sep="")]])
            v[[paste("db",L, sep="")]] = beta1*v[[paste("db",L, sep="")]] +
                (1-beta1) * t(gradients[[paste('db',L,sep="")]])


            # Compute bias-corrected first moment estimate.
            v_corrected[[paste("dw",L, sep="")]] = v[[paste("dw",L, sep="")]]/(1-beta1^t)
            v_corrected[[paste("db",L, sep="")]] = v[[paste("db",L, sep="")]]/(1-beta1^t)


            # Element wise multiply of gradients
            s[[paste("dw",L, sep="")]] = beta2*s[[paste("dw",L, sep="")]] +
                (1-beta2) * t(gradients[[paste('dw',L,sep="")]]) * t(gradients[[paste('dw',L,sep="")]])
            s[[paste("db",L, sep="")]] = beta2*s[[paste("db",L, sep="")]] +
                (1-beta2) * t(gradients[[paste('db',L,sep="")]]) * t(gradients[[paste('db',L,sep="")]])

            # Compute bias-corrected second moment estimate.
            s_corrected[[paste("dw",L, sep="")]] = s[[paste("dw",L, sep="")]]/(1-beta2^t)
            s_corrected[[paste("db",L, sep="")]] = s[[paste("db",L, sep="")]]/(1-beta2^t)

            # Update parameters.
            d1=sqrt(s_corrected[[paste("dw",L, sep="")]]+epsilon)
            d2=sqrt(s_corrected[[paste("db",L, sep="")]]+epsilon)

            parameters[[paste("W",L,sep="")]] = parameters[[paste("W",L,sep="")]] -
                learningRate * v_corrected[[paste("dw",L, sep="")]]/d1
            parameters[[paste("b",L,sep="")]] = parameters[[paste("b",L,sep="")]] -
                learningRate*v_corrected[[paste("db",L, sep="")]]/d2
        }
    return(parameters)
}

# Execute a L layer Deep learning model
# Input : X - Input features
#       : Y output
#       : layersDimensions - Dimension of layers
#       : hiddenActivationFunc - Activation function at hidden layer relu /tanh
#       : outputActivationFunc - Activation function at hidden layer sigmoid/softmax
#       : learning rate
#       : lambd
#       : keep_prob
#       : learning rate
#       : num of iterations
#       : initType
```

```r
#output : Updated weights
L_Layer_DeepModel <- function(X, Y, layersDimensions,
                                    hiddenActivationFunc='relu',
                                    outputActivationFunc= 'sigmoid',
                                    learningRate = 0.5,
                                    lambd=0,
                                    keep_prob=1,
                                    numIterations = 10000,
                                    initType="default",
                                    print_cost=False){
    #Initialize costs vector as NULL
    costs <- NULL

    # Parameters initialization.
    if (initType=="He"){
       parameters =HeInitializeDeepModel(layersDimensions)
    } else if (initType=="Xav"){
        parameters =XavInitializeDeepModel(layersDimensions)
    }
    else{
        parameters = initializeDeepModel(layersDimensions)
    }


    # Loop (gradient descent)
    for( i in 0:numIterations){
       # Forward propagation: [LINEAR -> RELU]*(L-1) -> LINEAR -> SIGMOID/SOFTMAX.
        retvals = forwardPropagationDeep(X, parameters,keep_prob, hiddenActivationFunc,

outputActivationFunc=outputActivationFunc)
       AL <- retvals[['AL']]
       caches <- retvals[['caches']]
       dropoutMat <- retvals[['dropoutMat']]

       # Compute cost.
       if(lambd==0){
           cost <- computeCost(AL, Y,outputActivationFunc=outputActivationFunc,numClasses=layersDimensions[length(layersDimensions)])
       } else {
           cost <- computeCostWithReg(parameters, AL, Y,lambd, outputActivationFunc=outputActivationFunc,numClasses=layersDimensions[length(layersDimensions)])
       }
       # Backward propagation.
       gradients = backwardPropagationDeep(AL, Y, caches, dropoutMat, lambd, keep_prob, hiddenActivationFunc,

outputActivationFunc=outputActivationFunc,numClasses=layersDimensions[length(layersDimensions)])

       # Update parameters.
       parameters = gradientDescent(parameters, gradients, learningRate,
                                    outputActivationFunc=outputActivationFunc)


       if(i%%1000 == 0){
         costs=c(costs,cost)
         print(cost)
       }
    }
```

```r
    retvals <- list("parameters"=parameters,"costs"=costs)

    return(retvals)
}

# Execute a L layer Deep learning model with Stochastic Gradient descent
# Input : X - Input features
#       : Y output
#       : layersDimensions - Dimension of layers
#       : hiddenActivationFunc - Activation function at hidden layer relu /tanh
#       : outputActivationFunc - Activation function at hidden layer sigmoid/softmax
#       : learning rate
#       : lrDecay
#       : decayRate
#       : lambd
#       : keep_prob
#       : optimizer
#       : beta
#       : beta1
#       : beta2
#       : epsilon
#       : mini_batch_size
#       : num of epochs
#output : Updated weights after each  iteration
L_Layer_DeepModel_SGD <- function(X, Y, layersDimensions,
                                  hiddenActivationFunc='relu',
                                  outputActivationFunc= 'sigmoid',
                                  learningRate = .3,
                                  lrDecay=FALSE,
                                  decayRate=1,
                                  lambd=0,
                                  keep_prob=1,
                                  optimizer="gd",
                                  beta=0.9,
                                  beta1=0.9,
                                  beta2=0.999,
                                  epsilon=10^-8,
                                  mini_batch_size = 64,
                                  num_epochs = 2500,
                                  print_cost=False){
    # Check the values
    cat("learningRate= ",learningRate)
    cat("\n")
    cat("lambd=",lambd)
    cat("\n")
    cat("keep_prob=",keep_prob)
    cat("\n")
    cat("optimizer=",optimizer)
    cat("\n")
    cat("lrDecay=",lrDecay)
    cat("\n")
    cat("decayRate=",decayRate)
    cat("\n")
    cat("beta=",beta)
    cat("\n")
    cat("beta1=",beta1)
    cat("\n")
    cat("beta2=",beta2)
    cat("\n")
    cat("epsilon=",epsilon)
    cat("\n")
    cat("mini_batch_size=",mini_batch_size)
```

```r
        cat("\n")
        cat("num_epochs=",num_epochs)
        cat("\n")
        set.seed(1)
        #Initialize costs vector as NULL
        costs <- NULL
        t <- 0
        # Parameters initialization.
        parameters = initializeDeepModel(layersDimensions)

        #Initialize the optimizer

        if(optimizer == "momentum"){
            v <-initializeVelocity(parameters)
        } else if(optimizer == "rmsprop"){
            s <-initializeRMSProp(parameters)
        } else if (optimizer == "adam"){
            adamVals <-initializeAdam(parameters)
        }


        seed=10

        # Loop for number of epochs
        for( i in 0:num_epochs){
            seed=seed+1
            minibatches = random_mini_batches(X, Y, mini_batch_size, seed)

            for(batch in 1:length(minibatches)){

                mini_batch_X=minibatches[[batch]][['mini_batch_X']]
                mini_batch_Y=minibatches[[batch]][['mini_batch_Y']]
                # Forward propagation:
                retvals = forwardPropagationDeep(mini_batch_X,
parameters,keep_prob, hiddenActivationFunc,

outputActivationFunc=outputActivationFunc)
                AL <- retvals[['AL']]
                caches <- retvals[['caches']]
                dropoutMat <- retvals[['dropoutMat']]

                # Compute cost.
                # Compute cost.
                if(lambd==0){
                    cost <- computeCost(AL,
mini_batch_Y,outputActivationFunc=outputActivationFunc,numClasses=layersDimen
sions[length(layersDimensions)])
                } else {
                    cost <- computeCostWithReg(parameters, AL, Y,lambd,
outputActivationFunc=outputActivationFunc,numClasses=layersDimensions[length(
layersDimensions)])
                }
                # Backward propagation.
                gradients = backwardPropagationDeep(AL, mini_batch_Y, caches,
dropoutMat, lambd, keep_prob, hiddenActivationFunc,

outputActivationFunc=outputActivationFunc,numClasses=layersDimensions[length(
layersDimensions)])

                if(optimizer == "gd"){
                    # Update parameters.
                    parameters = gradientDescent(parameters, gradients,
learningRate,

outputActivationFunc=outputActivationFunc)
```

```r
                    }else if(optimizer == "momentum"){
                        # Update parameters with Momentum
                        parameters = gradientDescentWithMomentum(parameters,
gradients,v,beta, learningRate,
                                                                 
outputActivationFunc=outputActivationFunc)

                    } else if(optimizer == "rmsprop"){
                        # Update parameters with RMSProp
                        parameters = gradientDescentWithRMSProp(parameters,
gradients,s,beta1, epsilon,learningRate,
                                                                
outputActivationFunc=outputActivationFunc)

                    } else if(optimizer == "adam"){
                        # Update parameters with Adam
                        #Get v and s
                        t <- t+1
                        v <- adamVals[['v']]
                        s <- adamVals[['s']]
                        parameters = gradientDescentWithAdam(parameters, gradients,v,
s,t, beta1,beta2, epsilon,learningRate,
                                                             
outputActivationFunc=outputActivationFunc)
                    }
                }

            if(i%%1000 == 0){
                costs=c(costs,cost)
                print(cost)
            }
            if(lrDecay==TRUE){
                learningRate = decayRate^(num_epochs/1000) * learningRate
            }
        }

    retvals <- list("parameters"=parameters,"costs"=costs)

    return(retvals)
}

# Predict the output for given input
# Input : parameters
#       : X
# Output: predictions
predict <- function(parameters, X,keep_prob=1, hiddenActivationFunc='relu'){

  fwdProp <- forwardPropagationDeep(X, parameters,keep_prob,
hiddenActivationFunc)
  predictions <- fwdProp$AL>0.5

  return (predictions)
}

# Plot a decision boundary
# This function uses ggplot2
plotDecisionBoundary <-
function(z,retvals,keep_prob=1,hiddenActivationFunc="sigmoid",lr=0.5){
  # Find the minimum and maximum for the data
  xmin<-min(z[,1])
  xmax<-max(z[,1])
  ymin<-min(z[,2])
  ymax<-max(z[,2])
```

```r
    # Create a grid of values
    a=seq(xmin,xmax,length=100)
    b=seq(ymin,ymax,length=100)
    grid <- expand.grid(x=a, y=b)
    colnames(grid) <- c('x1', 'x2')
    grid1 <-t(grid)
    # Predict the output for this grid
    q <-predict(retvals$parameters,grid1,keep_prob=1, hiddenActivationFunc)
    q1 <- t(data.frame(q))
    q2 <- as.numeric(q1)
    grid2 <- cbind(grid,q2)
    colnames(grid2) <- c('x1', 'x2','q2')

    z1 <- data.frame(z)
    names(z1) <- c("x1","x2","y")
    atitle=paste("Decision boundary for learning rate:",lr)
    # Plot the contour of the boundary
    ggplot(z1) +
       geom_point(data = z1, aes(x = x1, y = x2, color = y)) +
       stat_contour(data = grid2, aes(x = x1, y = x2, z = q2,color=q2), alpha = 0.9)+
       ggtitle(atitle) + scale_colour_gradientn(colours = brewer.pal(10,
"Spectral"))
}

# Predict the probability  scores for given data set
# Input : parameters
#         : X
# Output: probability of output
computeScores <- function(parameters, X,hiddenActivationFunc='relu'){

    fwdProp <- forwardPropagationDeep(X, parameters,hiddenActivationFunc)
    scores <- fwdProp$AL

    return (scores)
}

# Create random mini batches
# Input : X - Input features
#         : Y- output
#         : miniBatchSize
#         : seed
#output : mini_batches
random_mini_batches <- function(X, Y, miniBatchSize = 64, seed = 0){


    set.seed(seed)
    # Get number of training samples
    m = dim(X)[2]
    # Initialize mini batches
    mini_batches = list()

    # Create  a list of random numbers < m
    permutation = c(sample(m))
    # Randomly shuffle the training data
    shuffled_X = X[, permutation]
    shuffled_Y = Y[1, permutation]

    # Compute number of mini batches
    numCompleteMinibatches = floor(m/miniBatchSize)
    batch=0
    for(k in 0:(numCompleteMinibatches-1)){
         batch=batch+1
         # Set the lower and upper bound of the mini batches
```

```r
            lower=(k*miniBatchSize)+1
            upper=((k+1) * miniBatchSize)
            mini_batch_X = shuffled_X[, lower:upper]
            mini_batch_Y = shuffled_Y[lower:upper]
            # Add it to the list of mini batches
            mini_batch =
list("mini_batch_X"=mini_batch_X,"mini_batch_Y"=mini_batch_Y)
            mini_batches[[batch]] =mini_batch



    }

    # If the batch size does not divide evenly with mini batc size
    if(m %% miniBatchSize != 0){
        p=floor(m/miniBatchSize)*miniBatchSize
        # Set the start and end of last batch
        q=p+m %% miniBatchSize
        mini_batch_X = shuffled_X[,(p+1):q]
        mini_batch_Y = shuffled_Y[(p+1):q]
    }
    # Return the list of mini batches
    mini_batch =
list("mini_batch_X"=mini_batch_X,"mini_batch_Y"=mini_batch_Y)
    mini_batches[[batch]]=mini_batch

    return(mini_batches)
}

# Plot a decision boundary
# This function uses ggplot2
plotDecisionBoundary1 <- function(Z,parameters,keep_prob=1){
    xmin<-min(Z[,1])
    xmax<-max(Z[,1])
    ymin<-min(Z[,2])
    ymax<-max(Z[,2])

    # Create a grid of points
    a=seq(xmin,xmax,length=100)
    b=seq(ymin,ymax,length=100)
    grid <- expand.grid(x=a, y=b)
    colnames(grid) <- c('x1', 'x2')
    grid1 <-t(grid)

    retvals = forwardPropagationDeep(grid1, parameters,keep_prob, "relu",
                                    outputActivationFunc="softmax")


    AL <- retvals$AL
    # From the  softmax probabilities pick the one with the highest
probability
    q= apply(AL,1,which.max)

    q1 <- t(data.frame(q))
    q2 <- as.numeric(q1)
    grid2 <- cbind(grid,q2)
    colnames(grid2) <- c('x1', 'x2','q2')

    Z1 <- data.frame(Z)
    names(Z1) <- c("x1","x2","y")
    atitle=paste("Decision boundary")
    ggplot(Z1) +
        geom_point(data = Z1, aes(x = x1, y = x2, color = y)) +
        stat_contour(data = grid2, aes(x = x1, y = x2, z = q2,color=q2),
alpha = 0.9)+
```

7.3 Octave

```
##############################################################################
##############################
#
# File    : DLfunctions7.R
# Author  : Tinniam V Ganesh
# Date    : 16 Apr 2018
#
##############################################################################
##############################
1;
# Define sigmoid function
function [A,cache] = sigmoid(Z)
    A = 1 ./ (1+ exp(-Z));
    cache=Z;
end

# Define Relu function
function [A,cache] = relu(Z)
    A = max(0,Z);
    cache=Z;
end

# Define Relu function
function [A,cache] = tanhAct(Z)
    A = tanh(Z);
    cache=Z;
end

# Define Softmax function
function [A,cache] = softmax(Z)
    # get unnormalized probabilities
    exp_scores = exp(Z');
    # normalize them for each example
    A = exp_scores ./ sum(exp_scores,2);
    cache=Z;
end

# Define Stable Softmax function
function [A,cache] = stableSoftmax(Z)
    # Normalize by max value in each row
    shiftZ = Z' - max(Z',[],2);
    exp_scores = exp(shiftZ);
    # normalize them for each example
    A = exp_scores ./ sum(exp_scores,2);
    #disp("sm")
    #disp(A);
    cache=Z;
end

# Define Relu Derivative
function [dZ] = reluDerivative(dA,cache)
    Z = cache;
    dZ = dA;
    # Get elements that are greater than 0
```

```octave
55    a = (Z > 0);
56    # Select only those elements where Z > 0
57    dZ = dZ .* a;
58  end
59
60  # Define Sigmoid Derivative
61  function [dZ] = sigmoidDerivative(dA,cache)
62    Z = cache;
63    s = 1 ./ (1+ exp(-Z));
64    dZ = dA .* s .* (1-s);
65  end
66
67  # Define Tanh Derivative
68  function [dZ] = tanhDerivative(dA,cache)
69    Z = cache;
70    a = tanh(Z);
71    dZ = dA .* (1 - a .^ 2);
72  end
73
74  # Populate a matrix with 1s in rows where Y=1
75  # This function may need to be modified if K is not 3, 10
76  # This function is used in computing the softmax derivative
77  function [Y1] = popMatrix(Y,numClasses)
78      Y1=zeros(length(Y),numClasses);
79      if(numClasses==3) # For 3 output classes
80         Y1(Y==0,1)=1;
81         Y1(Y==1,2)=1;
82         Y1(Y==2,3)=1;
83      elseif(numClasses==10) # For 10 output classes
84         Y1(Y==0,1)=1;
85         Y1(Y==1,2)=1;
86         Y1(Y==2,3)=1;
87         Y1(Y==3,4)=1;
88         Y1(Y==4,5)=1;
89         Y1(Y==5,6)=1;
90         Y1(Y==6,7)=1;
91         Y1(Y==7,8)=1;
92         Y1(Y==8,9)=1;
93         Y1(Y==9,10)=1;
94
95        endif
96  end
97
98  # Define Softmax Derivative
99  function [dZ] = softmaxDerivative(dA,cache,Y, numClasses)
100    Z = cache;
101    # get unnormalized probabilities
102    shiftZ = Z' - max(Z',[],2);
103    exp_scores = exp(shiftZ);
104
105    # normalize them for each example
106    probs = exp_scores ./ sum(exp_scores,2);
107    # dZ = pi- yi
108    yi=popMatrix(Y,numClasses);
109    dZ=probs-yi;
110
111  end
112
113  # Define Stable Softmax Derivative
114  function [dZ] = stableSoftmaxDerivative(dA,cache,Y, numClasses)
115    Z = cache;
116    # get unnormalized probabilities
117    exp_scores = exp(Z');
118    # normalize them for each example
```

```octave
    probs = exp_scores ./ sum(exp_scores,2);
    # dZ = pi- yi
    yi=popMatrix(Y,numClasses);
    dZ=probs-yi;

end

# Initialize model for L layers
# Input : Vector of units in each layer
# Returns: Initial weights and biases matrices for all layers
function [W b] = initializeDeepModel(layerDimensions)
    rand ("seed", 3);
    # note the Weight matrix at layer 'l' is a matrix of size (l,l-1)
    # The Bias is a vectors of size (l,1)

    # Loop through the layer dimension from 1.. L
    # Create cell arrays for Weights and biases

    for l =2:size(layerDimensions)(2)
         W{l-1} = rand(layerDimensions(l),layerDimensions(l-1))*0.01; # Multiply by .01
         b{l-1} = zeros(layerDimensions(l),1);

    endfor
end

# He Initialization for L layers
# Input : Vector of units in each layer
# Returns: Initial weights and biases matrices for all layers
function [W b] = HeInitializeDeepModel(layerDimensions)
    rand ("seed", 3);
    # note the Weight matrix at layer 'l' is a matrix of size (l,l-1)
    # The Bias is a vectors of size (l,1)

    # Loop through the layer dimension from 1.. L
    # Create cell arrays for Weights and biases

    for l =2:size(layerDimensions)(2)
         W{l-1} = rand(layerDimensions(l),layerDimensions(l-1))* sqrt(2/layerDimensions(l-1)); #  Multiply by .01
         b{l-1} = zeros(layerDimensions(l),1);

    endfor
end

# Xavier Initialization for L layers
# Input : Vector of units in each layer
# Returns: Initial weights and biases matrices for all layers
function [W b] = XavInitializeDeepModel(layerDimensions)
    rand ("seed", 3);
    # note the Weight matrix at layer 'l' is a matrix of size (l,l-1)
    # The Bias is a vectors of size (l,1)

    # Loop through the layer dimension from 1.. L
    # Create cell arrays for Weights and biases

    for l =2:size(layerDimensions)(2)
         W{l-1} = rand(layerDimensions(l),layerDimensions(l-1))* sqrt(1/layerDimensions(l-1)); #  Multiply by .01
         b{l-1} = zeros(layerDimensions(l),1);

    endfor
end
```

```octave
# Initialize velocity
# Input : weights, biases
# Returns: vdW, vdB - Initial velocity
function[vdW vdB] = initializeVelocity(weights, biases)

    L = size(weights)(2) # Create an integer
    # Initialize a cell array
    v = {}

    # Initialize velocity with the same dimensions as W
    for l=1:L
        sz = size(weights{l});
        vdW{l} = zeros(sz(1),sz(2));
        sz = size(biases{l});
        vdB{l} =zeros(sz(1),sz(2));
    endfor;
end

# Initialize RMSProp
# Input : weights, biases
# Returns: sdW, sdB - Initial RMSProp
function[sdW sdB] = initializeRMSProp(weights, biases)

    L = size(weights)(2) # Create an integer
    # Initialize a cell array
    s = {}

    # Initialize velocity with the same dimensions as W
    for l=1:L
        sz = size(weights{l});
        sdW{l} = zeros(sz(1),sz(2));
        sz = size(biases{l});
        sdB{l} =zeros(sz(1),sz(2));
    endfor;
end

# Initialize Adam
# Input : parameters
# Returns: vdW, vdB, sdW, sdB -Initial Adam
function[vdW vdB sdW sdB] = initializeAdam(weights, biases)

    L = size(weights)(2) # Create an integer
    # Initialize a cell array
    s = {}

    # Initialize velocity with the same dimensions as W
    for l=1:L
        sz = size(weights{l});
        vdW{l} = zeros(sz(1),sz(2));
        sdW{l} = zeros(sz(1),sz(2));
        sz = size(biases{l});
        sdB{l} =zeros(sz(1),sz(2));
        vdB{l} =zeros(sz(1),sz(2));
    endfor;
end

# Compute the activation at a layer 'l' for forward prop in a Deep Network
# Input : A_prev - Activation of previous layer
#         W,b - Weight and bias matrices and vectors
#         activationFunc - Activation function - sigmoid, tanh, relu etc
# Returns : The Activation of this layer
#            :
# Z = W * X + b
# A = sigmoid(Z), A= Relu(Z), A= tanh(Z)
```

```octave
function [A forward_cache activation_cache] = layerActivationForward(A_prev,
w, b, activationFunc)

    # Compute Z
    Z = w * A_prev +b;
    # Create a cell array
    forward_cache = {A_prev  W  b};
    # Compute the activation for sigmoid
    if (strcmp(activationFunc,"sigmoid"))
        [A activation_cache] = sigmoid(Z);
    elseif (strcmp(activationFunc, "relu"))   # Compute the activation for Relu
        [A activation_cache] = relu(Z);
    elseif(strcmp(activationFunc,'tanh'))       # Compute the activation for tanh
        [A activation_cache] = tanhAct(Z);
    elseif(strcmp(activationFunc,'softmax'))      # Compute the activation for tanh
        #[A activation_cache] = softmax(Z);
        [A activation_cache] = stableSoftmax(Z);
    endif

end

# Compute the forward propagation for layers 1..L
# Input : X - Input Features
#         parameters: Weights and biases
#         keep_prob
#         hiddenActivationFunc - Activation function at hidden layers Relu/tanh/sigmoid
#         outputActivationFunc- sigmoid/softmax
# Returns : AL, forward,_caches, activation_caches, dropoutMat
# The forward propoagtion uses the Relu/tanh activation from layer 1..L-1 and
sigmoid actiovation at layer L
function [AL forward_caches activation_caches dropoutMat] =
forwardPropagationDeep(X, weights,biases, keep_prob=1,
                                                hiddenActivationFunc='relu',
outputActivationFunc='sigmoid')
    # Create an empty cell array
    forward_caches = {};
    activation_caches = {};
    droputMat ={};
    # Set A to X (A0)
    A = X;
    L = length(weights); # number of layers in the neural network
    # Loop through from layer 1 to upto layer L
    for l =1:L-1
        A_prev = A;
        # Zi = Wi x Ai-1 + bi   and Ai = g(Zi)
        w = weights{l};
        b = biases{l};
        [A forward_cache activation_cache] = layerActivationForward(A_prev,
w,b, activationFunc=hiddenActivationFunc);
        D=rand(size(A)(1),size(A)(2));
        D = (D < keep_prob) ;
        # Multiply by DropoutMat
        A= A .* D;
        # Divide by keep_prob to keep expected value same
        A = A ./ keep_prob;
        # Store D
        dropoutMat{l}=D;
        forward_caches{l}=forward_cache;
        activation_caches{l} = activation_cache;
    endfor
```

```octave
        # Since this is binary classification use the sigmoid activation function
in
        # last layer
        W = weights{L};
        b = biases{L};
        [AL, forward_cache activation_cache] = layerActivationForward(A, W,b,
activationFunc = outputActivationFunc);
        forward_caches{L}=forward_cache;
        activation_caches{L} = activation_cache;

end

# Pick columns where Y==1
# This function is used in computeCost
function [a] = pickColumns(AL,Y,numClasses)
     if(numClasses==3)
        a=[AL(Y==0,1) ;AL(Y==1,2) ;AL(Y==2,3)];
     elseif (numClasses==10)
        a=[AL(Y==0,1) ;AL(Y==1,2) ;AL(Y==2,3);AL(Y==3,4);AL(Y==4,5);
           AL(Y==5,6); AL(Y==6,7);AL(Y==7,8);AL(Y==8,9);AL(Y==9,10)];
     endif
end


# Compute the cost
# Input : AL-Activation of last layer
#        : Y-Output from data
#        : outputActivationFunc- sigmoid/softmax
#        : numClasses
# Output: cost
function [cost]= computeCost(AL, Y,
outputActivationFunc="sigmoid",numClasses)
    if(strcmp(outputActivationFunc,"sigmoid"))
        numTraining= size(Y)(2);
        # Element wise multiply for logprobs
        cost = -1/numTraining * sum((Y .* log(AL)) + (1-Y) .* log(1-AL));


    elseif(strcmp(outputActivationFunc,'softmax'))
        numTraining = size(Y)(2);
        Y=Y';
        # Select rows where Y=0,1,and 2 and concatenate to a long vector
        #a=[AL(Y==0,1) ;AL(Y==1,2) ;AL(Y==2,3)];
        a =pickColumns(AL,Y,numClasses);

        #Select the correct column for log prob
         correct_probs = -log(a);
         #Compute log loss
         cost= sum(correct_probs)/numTraining;
      endif
end

# Compute the cost with regularization
# Input : weights
#        : AL - Activation of last layer
#        : Output from data
#        : lambd
#        : outputActivationFunc- sigmoid/softmax
#        : numClasses
# Output: cost
function [cost]= computeCostWithReg(weights, AL, Y, lambd,
outputActivationFunc="sigmoid",numClasses)

    if(strcmp(outputActivationFunc,"sigmoid"))
```

```octave
            numTraining= size(Y)(2);
            # Element wise multiply for logprobs
            cost = -1/numTraining * sum((Y .* log(AL)) + (1-Y) .* log(1-AL));

            # Regularization cost
            L = size(weights)(2);
            L2RegularizationCost=0;
            for l=1:L
                wtSqr = weights{l} .* weights{l};
                #disp(sum(sum(wtSqr,1)));
                L2RegularizationCost+=sum(sum(wtSqr,1));
            endfor
            L2RegularizationCost = (lambd/(2*numTraining))*L2RegularizationCost;
            cost = cost +  L2RegularizationCost ;


       elseif(strcmp(outputActivationFunc,'softmax'))
            numTraining = size(Y)(2);
            Y=Y';
            # Select rows where Y=0,1,and 2 and concatenate to a long vector
            #a=[AL(Y==0,1) ;AL(Y==1,2)  ;AL(Y==2,3)];
            a =pickColumns(AL,Y,numClasses);

            #Select the correct column for log prob
             correct_probs = -log(a);
             #Compute log loss
             cost= sum(correct_probs)/numTraining;
                    # Regularization cost
            L = size(weights)(2);
            L2RegularizationCost=0;
            for l=1:L
                # Compute L2 Norm
                wtSqr = weights{l} .* weights{l};
                #disp(sum(sum(wtSqr,1)));
                L2RegularizationCost+=sum(sum(wtSqr,1));
            endfor
            L2RegularizationCost = (lambd/(2*numTraining))*L2RegularizationCost;
            cost = cost +  L2RegularizationCost ;
        endif
end



# Compute the backpropoagation for 1 cycle
# Input : dA- Neural Network parameters
#         # cache - forward_cache & activation_cache
#         # Y-Output values
#         # outputActivationFunc- sigmoid/softmax
#         # numClasses
# Returns: Gradients
# dL/dWi= dL/dZi*Al-1
# dl/dbl = dL/dZl
# dL/dZ_prev=dL/dZl*W
function [dA_prev dW db] = layerActivationBackward(dA, forward_cache,
activation_cache, Y, activationFunc,numClasses)

    A_prev = forward_cache{1};
    W =forward_cache{2};
    b = forward_cache{3};
    numTraining = size(A_prev)(2);
    if (strcmp(activationFunc,"relu"))
        dZ = reluDerivative(dA, activation_cache);
    elseif (strcmp(activationFunc,"sigmoid"))
        dZ = sigmoidDerivative(dA, activation_cache);
```

```octave
        elseif(strcmp(activationFunc, "tanh"))
            dZ = tanhDerivative(dA, activation_cache);
        elseif(strcmp(activationFunc, "softmax"))
            #dZ = softmaxDerivative(dA, activation_cache,Y,numClasses);
            dZ = stableSoftmaxDerivative(dA, activation_cache,Y,numClasses);
        endif


        if (strcmp(activationFunc,"softmax"))
          W =forward_cache{2};
          b = forward_cache{3};
          # Add the regularization factor
          dW = 1/numTraining * A_prev * dZ;
          db = 1/numTraining * sum(dZ,1);
          dA_prev = dZ*W;
        else
          W =forward_cache{2};
          b = forward_cache{3};
          # Add the regularization factor
          dW = 1/numTraining * dZ * A_prev';
          db = 1/numTraining * sum(dZ,2);
          dA_prev = W'*dZ;
        endif

end

# Compute the backpropoagation with regularization for 1 cycle
# Input : dA-Neural Network parameters
#         # cache - forward_cache & activation_cache
#         # Y-Output values
#         # lambd
#         # outputActivationFunc- sigmoid/softmax
#         # numClasses
# Returns: Gradients
# dL/dWi= dL/dzi*Al-1
# dl/dbl = dL/dzl
# dL/dZ_prev=dL/dzl*W
function [dA_prev dW db] = layerActivationBackwardWithReg(dA, forward_cache,
activation_cache, Y, lambd=0, activationFunc,numClasses)

    A_prev = forward_cache{1};
    W =forward_cache{2};
    b = forward_cache{3};
    numTraining = size(A_prev)(2);
    if (strcmp(activationFunc,"relu"))
        dZ = reluDerivative(dA, activation_cache);
    elseif (strcmp(activationFunc,"sigmoid"))
        dZ = sigmoidDerivative(dA, activation_cache);
    elseif(strcmp(activationFunc, "tanh"))
        dZ = tanhDerivative(dA, activation_cache);
    elseif(strcmp(activationFunc, "softmax"))
        #dZ = softmaxDerivative(dA, activation_cache,Y,numClasses);
        dZ = stableSoftmaxDerivative(dA, activation_cache,Y,numClasses);
    endif

    if (strcmp(activationFunc,"softmax"))
      W =forward_cache{2};
      b = forward_cache{3};
      # Add the regularization factor
      dW = 1/numTraining * A_prev * dZ +  (lambd/numTraining) * W';
      db = 1/numTraining * sum(dZ,1);
      dA_prev = dZ*W;
    else
      W =forward_cache{2};
```

```octave
            b = forward_cache{3};
            # Add the regularization factor
            dW = 1/numTraining * dZ * A_prev' +  (lambd/numTraining) * W;
            db = 1/numTraining * sum(dZ,2);
            dA_prev = W'*dZ;
       endif
    
end


# Compute the backpropoagation for 1 cycle
# Input : AL: Output of L layer Network - weights
#         Y  Real output
#         caches -- list of caches containing:
#         every cache of layerActivationForward() with "relu"/"tanh"
#         #(it's caches[l], for l in range(L-1) i.e l = 0...L-2)
#         #the cache of layerActivationForward() with "sigmoid" (it's caches[L-1])
#         dropoutMat
#         lambd
#         keep_prob
#         hiddenActivationFunc - Activation function at hidden layers sigmoid/tanh/relu
#         outputActivationFunc- sigmoid/softmax
#         numClasses
#
#    Returns:
#     gradients -- A dictionary with the gradients
#                  gradients["dA" + str(l)] = ...
#                  gradients["dW" + str(l)] = ...
#                  gradients["db" + str(l)] = ...
function [gradsDA gradsDW gradsDB]= backwardPropagationDeep(AL, Y,
activation_caches,forward_caches,
                              dropoutMat, lambd=0, keep_prob=1,
hiddenActivationFunc='relu',outputActivationFunc="sigmoid",numClasses)


    # Set the number of layers
    L = length(activation_caches);
    m = size(AL)(2);
    
    if (strcmp(outputActivationFunc,"sigmoid"))
        # Initializing the backpropagation
        # dl/dAL= -(y/a + (1-y)/(1-a)) - At the output layer
        dAL = -((Y ./ AL) - (1 - Y) ./ ( 1 - AL));
    elseif (strcmp(outputActivationFunc,"softmax"))
        dAL=0;
        Y=Y';
    endif
    
    
    # Since this is a binary classification the activation at output is sigmoid
    # Get the gradients at the last layer
    # Inputs: "AL, Y, caches".
    # Outputs: "gradients["dAL"], gradients["dWL"], gradients["dbL"]
    activation_cache = activation_caches{L};
    forward_cache = forward_caches(L);
    # Note the cell array includes an array of forward caches. To get to this we need to include the index {1}
    if (lambd==0)
        [dA dW db] = layerActivationBackward(dAL, forward_cache{1},
activation_cache, Y, activationFunc = outputActivationFunc,numClasses);
    else
```

```octave
            [dA dW db] = layerActivationBackwardWithReg(dAL, forward_cache{1},
activation_cache, Y, lambd, activationFunc =
outputActivationFunc,numClasses);
        endif
        if (strcmp(outputActivationFunc,"sigmoid"))
            gradsDA{L}= dA;
        elseif (strcmp(outputActivationFunc,"softmax"))
            gradsDA{L}= dA';#Note the transpose
        endif
        gradsDW{L}= dW;
        gradsDB{L}= db;

        # Traverse in the reverse direction
        for l =(L-1):-1:1
            # Compute the gradients for L-1 to 1 for Relu/tanh
            # Inputs: "gradients["dA" + str(l + 2)], caches".
            # Outputs: "gradients["dA" + str(l + 1)] , gradients["dW" + str(l +
1)] , gradients["db" + str(l + 1)]
            activation_cache = activation_caches{l};
            forward_cache = forward_caches(l);

            #dA_prev_temp, dW_temp, db_temp =
layerActivationBackward(gradients['dA'+str(l+1)], current_cache,
activationFunc = "relu")
            # dAl the dervative of the activation of the lth layer,is the first
element
            dAl= gradsDA{l+1};
            if(lambd == 0)
               # Get the dropout mat
               D = dropoutMat{l};
               #Multiply by the dropoutMat
               dAl= dAl .* D;
               # Divide by keep_prob to keep expected value same
               dAl = dAl ./ keep_prob;
               [dA_prev_temp, dW_temp, db_temp] = layerActivationBackward(dAl,
forward_cache{1}, activation_cache, Y, activationFunc =
hiddenActivationFunc,numClasses);
            else
               [dA_prev_temp, dW_temp, db_temp] =
layerActivationBackwardWithReg(dAl, forward_cache{1}, activation_cache, Y,
lambd, activationFunc = hiddenActivationFunc,numClasses);
            endif
            gradsDA{l}= dA_prev_temp;
            gradsDW{l}= dW_temp;
            gradsDB{l}= db_temp;

        endfor

end


# Perform Gradient Descent
# Input : Weights and biases
#        : gradients -gradsW,gradsB
#        : learning rate
#        : outputActivationFunc
#output : Updated weights after 1 iteration
function [weights biases] = gradientDescent(weights, biases,gradsW,gradsB,
learningRate,outputActivationFunc="sigmoid")

    L = size(weights)(2); # number of layers in the neural network
    # Update rule for each parameter.
    for l=1:(L-1)
        weights{l} = weights{l} -learningRate* gradsW{l};
```

```octave
            biases{l} = biases{l} -learningRate* gradsB{l};
        endfor


        if (strcmp(outputActivationFunc,"sigmoid"))
            weights{L} = weights{L} -learningRate* gradsW{L};
            biases{L} = biases{L} -learningRate* gradsB{L};
         elseif (strcmp(outputActivationFunc,"softmax"))
            weights{L} = weights{L} -learningRate* gradsW{L}';
            biases{L} = biases{L} -learningRate* gradsB{L}';
        endif


end


# Update parameters with momentum
# Input : parameters
#       : gradients -gradsDW,gradsDB
#       : v -vdW, vdB
#       : beta
#       : learningRate
#       : outputActivationFunc
#output : Updated weights, biases
function [weights biases] = gradientDescentWithMomentum(weights,
biases,gradsDW,gradsDB, vdW, vdB, beta,
learningRate,outputActivationFunc="sigmoid")
    L = size(weights)(2); # number of layers in the neural network
    # Update rule for each parameter.
    for l=1:(L-1)
        # Compute velocities
        # v['dwk'] = beta *v['dwk'] + (1-beta)*dwk
        vdW{l} =  beta*vdW{l} + (1 -beta) * gradsDW{l};
        vdB{l} =  beta*vdB{l} + (1 -beta) * gradsDB{l};
        weights{l} = weights{l} -learningRate* vdW{l};
        biases{l} = biases{l} -learningRate* vdB{l};
    endfor

    if (strcmp(outputActivationFunc,"sigmoid"))
        vdW{L} =  beta*vdW{L} + (1 -beta) * gradsDW{L};
        vdB{L} =  beta*vdB{L} + (1 -beta) * gradsDB{L};
        weights{L} = weights{L} -learningRate* vdW{L};
        biases{L} = biases{L} -learningRate* vdB{L};
     elseif (strcmp(outputActivationFunc,"softmax"))
        vdW{L} =  beta*vdW{L} + (1 -beta) * gradsDW{L}';
        vdB{L} =  beta*vdB{L} + (1 -beta) * gradsDB{L}';
        weights{L} = weights{L} -learningRate* vdW{L};
        biases{L} = biases{L} -learningRate* vdB{L};
    endif


end


# Update parameters with RMSProp
# Input : parameters - weights, biases
#       : gradients - gradsDW,gradsDB
#       : s -sdW, sdB
#       : beta1
#       : epsilon
#       : learningRate
#       : outputActivationFunc
#output : Updated weights and biases RMSProp
```

```octave
function [weights biases] = gradientDescentWithRMSProp(weights,
biases,gradsDW,gradsDB, sdW, sdB, beta1, epsilon,
learningRate,outputActivationFunc="sigmoid")
    L = size(weights)(2); # number of layers in the neural network
    # Update rule for each parameter.
    for l=1:(L-1)
        sdW{l} =  beta1*sdW{l} + (1 -beta1) * gradsDW{l} .* gradsDW{l};
        sdB{l} =  beta1*sdB{l} + (1 -beta1) * gradsDB{l} .* gradsDB{l};
        weights{l} = weights{l} - learningRate* gradsDW{l} ./ sqrt(sdW{l} + epsilon);
        biases{l} = biases{l} -  learningRate* gradsDB{l} ./ sqrt(sdB{l} + epsilon);
    endfor

    if (strcmp(outputActivationFunc,"sigmoid"))
        sdW{L} =  beta1*sdW{L} + (1 -beta1) * gradsDW{L} .* gradsDW{L};
        sdB{L} =  beta1*sdB{L} + (1 -beta1) * gradsDB{L} .* gradsDB{L};
        weights{L} = weights{L} -learningRate* gradsDW{L} ./ sqrt(sdW{L} +epsilon);
        biases{L} = biases{L} -learningRate* gradsDB{L} ./ sqrt(sdB{L} + epsilon);
     elseif (strcmp(outputActivationFunc,"softmax"))
        sdW{L} =  beta1*sdW{L} + (1 -beta1) * gradsDW{L}' .* gradsDW{L}';
        sdB{L} =  beta1*sdB{L} + (1 -beta1) * gradsDB{L}' .* gradsDB{L}';
        weights{L} = weights{L} -learningRate* gradsDW{L}' ./ sqrt(sdW{L} +epsilon);
        biases{L} = biases{L} -learningRate* gradsDB{L}' ./ sqrt(sdB{L} + epsilon);
     endif


end


# Update parameters with Adam
# Input : parameters - weights, biases
#        : gradients -gradsDW,gradsDB
#        : v - vdW, vdB
#        : s - sdW, sdB
#        : t
#        : beta1
#        : beta2
#        : epsilon
#        : learningRate
#        : epsilon
#output : Updated weights and biases
function [weights biases] = gradientDescentWithAdam(weights,
biases,gradsDW,gradsDB,
                  vdW, vdB, sdW, sdB, t, beta1, beta2, epsilon,
learningRate,epsilon="sigmoid")
    vdW_corrected = {};
    vdB_corrected = {};
    sdW_corrected = {};
    sdB_corrected = {};
    L = size(weights)(2); # number of layers in the neural network
    # Update rule for each parameter.
    for l=1:(L-1)
        vdW{l} =  beta1*vdW{l} + (1 -beta1) * gradsDW{l};
        vdB{l} =  beta1*vdB{l} + (1 -beta1) * gradsDB{l};

        # Compute bias-corrected first moment estimate.
        vdW_corrected{l} = vdW{l}/(1-beta1^t);
        vdB_corrected{l} = vdB{l}/(1-beta1^t);

```

```
            sdW{l} =   beta2*sdW{l} + (1 -beta2) * gradsDW{l} .* gradsDW{l};
            sdB{l} =   beta2*sdB{l} + (1 -beta2) * gradsDB{l} .* gradsDB{l};

            # Compute bias-corrected second moment estimate.
            sdW_corrected{l} = sdW{l}/(1-beta2^t);
            sdB_corrected{l} = sdB{l}/(1-beta2^t);

            # Update parameters.
            d1=sqrt(sdW_corrected{l}+epsilon);
            d2=sqrt(sdB_corrected{l}+epsilon);

            weights{l} = weights{l} - learningRate* vdW_corrected{l} ./ d1;
            biases{l} = biases{l} -learningRate* vdB_corrected{l} ./ d2;
        endfor

        if (strcmp(outputActivationFunc,"sigmoid"))
            vdW{L} =   beta1*vdW{L} + (1 -beta1) * gradsDW{L};
            vdB{L} =   beta1*vdB{L} + (1 -beta1) * gradsDB{L};

            # Compute bias-corrected first moment estimate.
            vdW_corrected{L} = v{L}/(1-beta1^t);
            vdB_corrected{L} = v{L}/(1-beta1^t);

            sdW{L} =   beta2*sdW{L} + (1 -beta2) * gradsDW{L} .* gradsDW{L};
            sdB{L} =   beta2*sdB{L} + (1 -beta2) * gradsDB{L} .* gradsDB{L};

            # Compute bias-corrected second moment estimate.
            sdW_corrected{L} = s{L}/(1-beta2^t);
            sdB_corrected{L} = s{L}/(1-beta2^t);

            # Update parameters.
            d1=sqrt(sdW_corrected{L}+epsilon);
            d2=sqrt(sdB_corrected{L}+epsilon);

            weights{L} = weights{L} - learningRate* vdW_corrected{L} ./ d1;
            biases{L} = biases{L} -learningRate* vdB_corrected{L} ./ d2;
        elseif (strcmp(outputActivationFunc,"softmax"))
            vdW{L} =   beta1*vdW{L} + (1 -beta1) * gradsDW{L}';
            vdB{L} =   beta1*vdB{L} + (1 -beta1) * gradsDB{L}';

            # Compute bias-corrected first moment estimate.
            vdW_corrected{L} = vdW{L}/(1-beta1^t);
            vdB_corrected{L} = vdB{L}/(1-beta1^t);

            sdW{L} =   beta2*sdW{L} + (1 -beta2) * gradsDW{L}' .* gradsDW{L}';
            sdB{L} =   beta2*sdB{L} + (1 -beta2) * gradsDB{L}' .* gradsDB{L}';

            # Compute bias-corrected second moment estimate.
            sdW_corrected{L} = sdW{L}/(1-beta2^t);
            sdB_corrected{L} = sdB{L}/(1-beta2^t);

            # Update parameters.
            d1=sqrt(sdW_corrected{L}+epsilon);
            d2=sqrt(sdB_corrected{L}+epsilon);

            weights{L} = weights{L} - learningRate* vdW_corrected{L} ./ d1;
            biases{L} = biases{L} -learningRate* vdB_corrected{L} ./ d2;
        endif


end

# Execute a L layer Deep learning model
# Input : X - Input features
```

```octave
#              : Y output
#              : layersDimensions - Dimension of layers
#              : hiddenActivationFunc - Activation function at hidden layer relu
/tanh
#              : outputActivationFunc - Activation function at hidden layer
sigmoid/softmax
#              : learning rate
#              : lambd
#              : keep_prob
#              : num of iterations
#output : Updated weights and biases after each  iteration
function [weights biases costs] = L_Layer_DeepModel(X, Y, layersDimensions,
hiddenActivationFunc='relu',
                outputActivationFunc="sigmoid",learning_rate = .3, lambd=0,
keep_prob=1, num_iterations = 10000,initType="default")#lr was 0.009

    rand ("seed", 1);
    costs = [] ;
    if (strcmp(initType,"He"))
       # He Initialization
       [weights biases] = HeInitializeDeepModel(layersDimensions);
    elseif (strcmp(initType,"Xav"))
        # Xavier Initialization
       [weights biases] = XavInitializeDeepModel(layersDimensions);
    else
       # Default initialization.
       [weights biases] = initializeDeepModel(layersDimensions);
    endif

    # Loop (gradient descent)
    for i = 0:num_iterations
        # Forward propagation: [LINEAR -> RELU]*(L-1) -> LINEAR -> SIGMOID.
        [AL forward_caches activation_caches droputMat] =
forwardPropagationDeep(X, weights, biases,keep_prob, hiddenActivationFunc,
outputActivationFunc=outputActivationFunc);

                 # Regularization parameter is 0
        if (lambd==0)
          # Compute cost.
          cost = computeCost(AL,
Y,outputActivationFunc=outputActivationFunc,numClasses=layersDimensions(size(
layersDimensions)(2)));
        else
          # Compute cost with regularization
          cost = computeCostWithReg(weights, AL, Y, lambd,
outputActivationFunc=outputActivationFunc,numClasses=layersDimensions(size(la
yersDimensions)(2)));
        endif
        # Backward propagation.
        [gradsDA gradsDW gradsDB] = backwardPropagationDeep(AL, Y,
activation_caches,forward_caches, droputMat, lambd, keep_prob,
hiddenActivationFunc, outputActivationFunc=outputActivationFunc,

numClasses=layersDimensions(size(layersDimensions)(2)));
        # Update parameters.
        [weights biases] = gradientDescent(weights,biases,
gradsDW,gradsDB,learning_rate,outputActivationFunc=outputActivationFunc);


        # Print the cost every 1000 iterations
       if ( mod(i,1000) == 0)
            costs =[costs cost];
            #disp ("Cost after iteration"),
L2RegularizationCost(i),disp(cost);
```

```octave
                    printf("Cost after iteration i=%i cost=%d\n",i,cost);
            endif
        endfor

end

# Execute a L layer Deep learning model with Stochastic Gradient descent
# Input : X - Input features
#         : Y output
#         : layersDimensions - Dimension of layers
#         : hiddenActivationFunc - Activation function at hidden layer relu
/tanh/sigmoid
#         : outputActivationFunc - Activation function at hidden layer
sigmoid/softmax
#         : learning rate
#         : lrDecay
#         : decayRate
#         : lambd
#         : keep_prob
#         : optimizer
#         : beta
#         : beta1
#         : beta2
#         : epsilon
#         : mini_batch_size
#         : num of epochs
#output : Updated weights and biases after each iteration
function [weights biases costs] = L_Layer_DeepModel_SGD(X, Y,
layersDimensions, hiddenActivationFunc='relu',

outputActivationFunc="sigmoid",learningRate = .3,
                                                    optimizer
lrDecay=false,decayRate=1,
                                                lambd=0, keep_prob=1,
                                                optimizer="gd", beta=0.9, beta1=0.9,
beta2=0.999,epsilon=10^-8,
                                                mini_batch_size = 64, num_epochs =
2500)

    disp("Values");
    printf("learningRate=%f ",learningRate);
    printf("lrDecay=%d ",lrDecay);
    printf("decayRate=%f ",decayRate);
    printf("lamd=%d ",lambd);
    printf("keep_prob=%f ",keep_prob);
    printf("optimizer=%s ",optimizer);
    printf("beta=%f ",beta);
    printf("beta1=%f  ",beta1);
    printf("beta2=%f  ",beta2);
    printf("epsilon=%f ",epsilon);
    printf("mini_batch_size=%d ",mini_batch_size);
    printf("num_epochs=%d ",num_epochs);
    t=0;
    rand ("seed", 1);
    costs = [] ;
    # Parameters initialization.
    [weights biases] = initializeDeepModel(layersDimensions);

    if (strcmp(optimizer,"momentum"))
        [vdW vdB] = initializeVelocity(weights, biases);

    elseif(strcmp(optimizer,"rmsprop"))
        [sdW sdB] = initializeRMSProp(weights, biases);

```

```octave
        elseif(strcmp(optimizer,"adam"))
            [vdW vdB sdW sdB] = initializeAdam(weights, biases);
        endif
        seed=10;
        # Loop (gradient descent)
        for i = 0:num_epochs
            seed = seed + 1;
            [mini_batches_X  mini_batches_Y] = random_mini_batches(X, Y, mini_batch_size, seed);

            minibatches=length(mini_batches_X);
            for batch=1:minibatches
                X=mini_batches_X{batch};
                Y=mini_batches_Y{batch};
                # Forward propagation: [LINEAR -> RELU]*(L-1) -> LINEAR -> SIGMOID/SOFTMAX.
                [AL forward_caches activation_caches droputMat] = forwardPropagationDeep(X, weights, biases, keep_prob,hiddenActivationFunc, outputActivationFunc=outputActivationFunc);
                #disp(batch);
                #disp(size(X));
                #disp(size(Y));
                if (lambd==0)
                    # Compute cost.
                    cost = computeCost(AL, Y,outputActivationFunc=outputActivationFunc,numClasses=layersDimensions(size(layersDimensions)(2)));
                else
                    # Compute cost with regularization
                    cost = computeCostWithReg(weights, AL, Y, lambd, outputActivationFunc=outputActivationFunc,numClasses=layersDimensions(size(layersDimensions)(2)));
                endif
                #disp(cost);
                # Backward propagation.
                [gradsDA gradsDW gradsDB] = backwardPropagationDeep(AL, Y, activation_caches,forward_caches, droputMat, lambd, keep_prob, hiddenActivationFunc, outputActivationFunc=outputActivationFunc,

numClasses=layersDimensions(size(layersDimensions)(2)));

                if (strcmp(optimizer,"gd"))
                    # Update parameters.
                    [weights biases] = gradientDescent(weights,biases, gradsDW,gradsDB,learningRate,outputActivationFunc=outputActivationFunc);
                elseif (strcmp(optimizer,"momentum"))
                    [weights biases] = gradientDescentWithMomentum(weights, biases,gradsDW,gradsDB, vdW, vdB, beta, learningRate,outputActivationFunc);
                elseif (strcmp(optimizer,"rmsprop"))
                    [weights biases] = gradientDescentWithRMSProp(weights, biases,gradsDW,gradsDB, sdW, sdB, beta1, epsilon, learningRate,outputActivationFunc);

                elseif (strcmp(optimizer,"adam"))
                    t=t+1;
                    [weights biases] = gradientDescentWithAdam(weights, biases,gradsDW,gradsDB,vdW, vdB, sdW, sdB, t, beta1, beta2, epsilon, learningRate,outputActivationFunc);
                endif
            endfor
            # Print the cost every 1000 iterations
            if ( mod(i,1000) == 0)
               costs =[costs cost];
               #disp ("Cost after iteration"), disp(i),disp(cost);
```

```octave
            printf("Cost after iteration i=%i cost=%d\n",i,cost);
         endif
         if(lrDecay==true)
              learningRate=decayRate^(num_epochs/1000)*learningRate;
         endif
    endfor

end

# Plot cost vs iterations
function plotCostVsIterations(maxIterations,costs,fig1)
    iterations=[0:1000:maxIterations];
    plot(iterations,costs);
    title ("Cost vs no of iterations ");
    xlabel("No of iterations");
    ylabel("Cost");
    print -dpng figReg2-o
end;

# Plot cost vs epochs
function plotCostVsEpochs(maxEpochs,costs,fig1)
    epochs=[0:1000:maxEpochs];
    plot(epochs,costs);
    title ("Cost vs no of epochs ");
    xlabel("No of epochs");
    ylabel("Cost");
    print -dpng fig5-o
end;

# Compute the predicted value for a given input
# Input : Neural Network parameters
#       : Input data
function [predictions]= predict(weights, biases,
X,keep_prob=1,hiddenActivationFunc="relu")
    [AL forward_caches activation_caches] = forwardPropagationDeep(X,
weights, biases,keep_prob,hiddenActivationFunc);
    predictions = (AL>0.5);
end

# Plot the decision boundary
function plotDecisionBoundary(data,weights,
biases,keep_prob=1,hiddenActivationFunc="relu",fig2)
    %Plot a non-linear decision boundary learned by the SVM
    colormap ("summer");

    % Make classification predictions over a grid of values
    x1plot = linspace(min(data(:,1)), max(data(:,1)), 400)';
    x2plot = linspace(min(data(:,2)), max(data(:,2)), 400)';
    [X1, X2] = meshgrid(x1plot, x2plot);
    vals = zeros(size(X1));
    # Plot the prediction for the grid
    for i = 1:size(X1, 2)
       gridPoints = [X1(:, i), X2(:, i)];
       vals(:, i)=predict(weights, biases,gridPoints',keep_prob,
hiddenActivationFunc=hiddenActivationFunc);
    endfor

    scatter(data(:,1),data(:,2),8,c=data(:,3),"filled");
    % Plot the boundary
    hold on
    #contour(X1, X2, vals, [0 0], 'LineWidth', 2);
    contour(X1, X2, vals,"linewidth",4);
    title ({"3 layer Neural Network decision boundary"});
    hold off;
```

```octave
            print -dpng figReg22-o

end


# Compute scores
function [AL]= scores(weights, biases, X,hiddenActivationFunc="relu")
     [AL forward_caches activation_caches] = forwardPropagationDeep(X,
weights, biases,hiddenActivationFunc);
end


# Create Random mini batches. Return cell arrays with the mini batches
# Input : X, Y
#         : Size of minibatch
#Output : mini batches X & Y
function [mini_batches_X  mini_batches_Y]= random_mini_batches(X, Y,
miniBatchSize = 64, seed = 0)

    rand ("seed", seed);
    # Get number of training samples
    m = size(X)(2);


    # Create  a list of random numbers < m
    permutation = randperm(m);
    # Randomly shuffle the training data
    shuffled_X = X(:, permutation);
    shuffled_Y = Y(:, permutation);

    # Compute number of mini batches
    numCompleteMinibatches = floor(m/miniBatchSize);
    batch=0;
    for k = 0:(numCompleteMinibatches-1)
        #Set the start and end of each mini batch
        batch=batch+1;
        lower=(k*miniBatchSize)+1;
        upper=(k+1) * miniBatchSize;
        mini_batch_X = shuffled_X(:, lower:upper);
        mini_batch_Y = shuffled_Y(:, lower:upper);
        # Create cell arrays
        mini_batches_X{batch} = mini_batch_X;
        mini_batches_Y{batch} = mini_batch_Y;
    endfor

    # If the batc size does not cleanly divide with number of mini batches
    if mod(m ,miniBatchSize) != 0
        # Set the start and end of the last mini batch
        l=floor(m/miniBatchSize)*miniBatchSize;
        m=l+ mod(m,miniBatchSize);
        mini_batch_X = shuffled_X(:,(l+1):m);
        mini_batch_Y = shuffled_Y(:,(l+1):m);

        batch=batch+1;
        mini_batches_X{batch} = mini_batch_X;
        mini_batches_Y{batch} = mini_batch_Y;
    endif
end

# Plot decision boundary
function plotDecisionBoundary1( data,weights, biases,keep_prob=1,
hiddenActivationFunc="relu")
    % Make classification predictions over a grid of values
    x1plot = linspace(min(data(:,1)), max(data(:,1)), 400)';
    x2plot = linspace(min(data(:,2)), max(data(:,2)), 400)';
    [X1, X2] = meshgrid(x1plot, x2plot);
```

```octave
        vals = zeros(size(X1));
        for i = 1:size(X1, 2)
               gridPoints = [X1(:, i), X2(:, i)];
               [AL forward_caches activation_caches] =
forwardPropagationDeep(gridPoints', weights,
biases,keep_prob,hiddenActivationFunc, outputActivationFunc="softmax");
               [l m] = max(AL, [ ], 2);
               vals(:, i)= m;
        endfor

        scatter(data(:,1),data(:,2),8,c=data(:,3),"filled");
        % Plot the boundary
        hold on
        contour(X1, X2, vals,"linewidth",4);
        print -dpng "fig-o1.png"
end
```

9. Appendix 8 – Gradient Check

8.1 Python

```python
# -*- coding: utf-8 -*-
###########################################################################
################################
#
# File: DLfunctions8.py
# Developer: Tinniam V Ganesh
# Date : 6 May 2018
#
###########################################################################
##############################
import numpy as np
import matplotlib.pyplot as plt
import matplotlib
import matplotlib.pyplot as plt
from matplotlib import cm
import math
import sklearn
import sklearn.datasets

# Conmpute the sigmoid of a vector
def sigmoid(Z):
    A=1/(1+np.exp(-Z))
    cache=Z
    return A,cache

# Conmpute the Relu of a vector
def relu(Z):
    A = np.maximum(0,Z)
    cache=Z
    return A,cache

# Conmpute the tanh of a vector
def tanh(Z):
    A = np.tanh(Z)
```

```python
35        cache=Z
36        return A,cache
37
38 # Conmpute the softmax of a vector
39 def softmax(Z):
40     # get unnormalized probabilities
41     exp_scores = np.exp(Z.T)
42     # normalize them for each example
43     A = exp_scores / np.sum(exp_scores, axis=1, keepdims=True)
44     cache=Z
45     return A,cache
46
47 # Conmpute the Stable softmax of a vector
48 def stableSoftmax(Z):
49     #Compute the softmax of vector x in a numerically stable way.
50     shiftZ = Z.T - np.max(Z.T,axis=1).reshape(-1,1)
51     exp_scores = np.exp(shiftZ)
52
53     # normalize them for each example
54     A = exp_scores / np.sum(exp_scores, axis=1, keepdims=True)
55     cache=Z
56     return A,cache
57
58 # Compute the derivative of Relu
59 def reluDerivative(dA, cache):
60
61     Z = cache
62     dZ = np.array(dA, copy=True) # just converting dz to a correct object.
63     # When z <= 0, you should set dz to 0 as well.
64     dZ[Z <= 0] = 0
65     return dZ
66
67 # Compute the derivative of sigmoid
68 def sigmoidDerivative(dA, cache):
69     Z = cache
70     s = 1/(1+np.exp(-Z))
71     dZ = dA * s * (1-s)
72     return dZ
73
74 # Compute the derivative of tanh
75 def tanhDerivative(dA, cache):
76     Z = cache
77     a = np.tanh(Z)
78     dZ = dA * (1 - np.power(a, 2))
79     return dZ
80
81 # Compute the derivative of softmax
82 def softmaxDerivative(dA, cache,y,numTraining):
83       # Note : dA not used. dL/dZ = dL/dA * dA/dZ = pi-yi
84       Z = cache
85       # Compute softmax
86       exp_scores = np.exp(Z.T)
87       # normalize them for each example
88       probs = exp_scores / np.sum(exp_scores, axis=1, keepdims=True)
89
90       # compute the gradient on scores
91       dZ = probs
92
93       # dZ = pi- yi
94       dZ[range(int(numTraining)),y[:,0]] -= 1
95       return(dZ)
96
97 # Compute the derivative of Stable softmax
98 def stableSoftmaxDerivative(dA, cache,y,numTraining):
```

```python
        # Note : dA not used. dL/dZ = dL/dA * dA/dZ = pi-yi
        Z = cache
        # Compute stable softmax
        shiftZ = Z.T - np.max(Z.T,axis=1).reshape(-1,1)
        exp_scores = np.exp(shiftZ)
        # normalize them for each example
        probs = exp_scores / np.sum(exp_scores, axis=1, keepdims=True)
        #print(probs)
        # compute the gradient on scores
        dZ = probs

        # dZ = pi- yi
        dZ[range(int(numTraining)),y[:,0]] -= 1
        return(dZ)


# Initialize the model
# Input : number of features
#         number of hidden units
#         number of units in output
# Returns: Weight and bias matrices and vectors
def initializeModel(numFeats,numHidden,numOutput):
    np.random.seed(1)
    W1=np.random.randn(numHidden,numFeats)*0.01 #  Multiply by .01
    b1=np.zeros((numHidden,1))
    W2=np.random.randn(numOutput,numHidden)*0.01
    b2=np.zeros((numOutput,1))

    # Create a dictionary of the neural network parameters
    nnParameters={'W1':W1,'b1':b1,'W2':W2,'b2':b2}
    return(nnParameters)


# Initialize model for L layers
# Input : List of units in each layer
# Returns: Initial weights and biases matrices for all layers
def initializeDeepModel(layerDimensions):
    np.random.seed(3)
    # note the Weight matrix at layer 'l' is a matrix of size (l,l-1)
    # The Bias is a vectors of size (l,1)

    # Loop through the layer dimension from 1.. L
    layerParams = {}
    for l in range(1,len(layerDimensions)):
        layerParams['W' + str(l)] =
np.random.randn(layerDimensions[l],layerDimensions[l-1])*0.01 #  Multiply by
.01
        layerParams['b' + str(l)] = np.zeros((layerDimensions[l],1))
            np.savetxt('W' + str(l)+'.csv',layerParams['W' +
str(l)],delimiter=',')
            np.savetxt('b' + str(l)+'.csv',layerParams['b' +
str(l)],delimiter=',')
    return(layerParams)
    return Z, cache

# He Initialization model for L layers
# Input : List of units in each layer
# Returns: Initial weights and biases matrices for all layers
# He initilization multiplies the random numbers with
sqrt(2/layerDimensions[l-1])
def HeInitializeDeepModel(layerDimensions):
    np.random.seed(3)
    # note the Weight matrix at layer 'l' is a matrix of size (l,l-1)
    # The Bias is a vectors of size (l,1)
```

```python
        # Loop through the layer dimension from 1.. L
        layerParams = {}
        for l in range(1,len(layerDimensions)):
                layerParams['W' + str(l)] = np.random.randn(layerDimensions[l],
                            layerDimensions[l-1])*np.sqrt(2/layerDimensions[l-1])
                layerParams['b' + str(l)] = np.zeros((layerDimensions[l],1))

    return(layerParams)
    return Z, cache

# Xavier Initialization model for L layers
# Input : List of units in each layer
# Returns: Initial weights and biases matrices for all layers
# Xavier initilization multiplies the random numbers with
sqrt(1/layerDimensions[l-1])
def XavInitializeDeepModel(layerDimensions):
    np.random.seed(3)
    # note the Weight matrix at layer 'l' is a matrix of size (l,l-1)
    # The Bias is a vectors of size (l,1)

    # Loop through the layer dimension from 1.. L
    layerParams = {}
    for l in range(1,len(layerDimensions)):
            layerParams['W' + str(l)] = np.random.randn(layerDimensions[l],
                        layerDimensions[l-1])*np.sqrt(1/layerDimensions[l-1])
            layerParams['b' + str(l)] = np.zeros((layerDimensions[l],1))

    return(layerParams)
    return Z, cache

# Initialize velocity of
# Input : parameters
# Returns: v - Initial velocity
def initializeVelocity(parameters):

    L = len(parameters)//2 # Create an integer
    v = {}

    # Initialize velocity with the same dimensions as W
    for l in range(L):
        v["dW" + str(l+1)] = np.zeros((parameters['W' + str(l+1)].shape[0],
                                        parameters['W' + str(l+1)].shape[1]))
        v["db" + str(l+1)] = np.zeros((parameters['b' + str(l+1)].shape[0],
                                        parameters['b' + str(l+1)].shape[1]))

    return v

# Initialize RMSProp param
# Input : List of units in each layer
# Returns: s - Initial RMSProp
def initializeRMSProp(parameters):

    L = len(parameters)//2 # Create an integer
    s = {}

    # Initialize velocity with the same dimensions as W
    for l in range(L):
        s["dW" + str(l+1)] = np.zeros((parameters['W' + str(l+1)].shape[0],
                                        parameters['W' + str(l+1)].shape[1]))
        s["db" + str(l+1)] = np.zeros((parameters['b' + str(l+1)].shape[0],
                                        parameters['b' + str(l+1)].shape[1]))

    return s
```

```python
# Initialize Adam param
# Input : List of units in each layer
# Returns: v and s - Adam paramaters
def initializeAdam(parameters) :

    L = len(parameters) // 2 # number of layers in the neural networks
    v = {}
    s = {}

    # Initialize v, s.
    for l in range(L):

        v["dW" + str(l+1)] = np.zeros((parameters['W' + str(l+1)].shape[0],
                                        parameters['W' + str(l+1)].shape[1]))
        v["db" + str(l+1)] = np.zeros((parameters['b' + str(l+1)].shape[0],
                                        parameters['b' + str(l+1)].shape[1]))
        s["dW" + str(l+1)] = np.zeros((parameters['W' + str(l+1)].shape[0],
                                        parameters['W' + str(l+1)].shape[1]))
        s["db" + str(l+1)] = np.zeros((parameters['b' + str(l+1)].shape[0],
                                        parameters['b' + str(l+1)].shape[1]))
    return v, s

# Compute the activation at a layer 'l' for forward prop in a Deep Network
# Input : A_prev - Activation of previous layer
#         W,b - Weight and bias matrices and vectors
#         keep_prob
#         activationFunc - Activation function - sigmoid, tanh, relu etc
# Returns : A, cache
#         :
# Z = W * X + b
# A = sigmoid(Z), A= Relu(Z), A= tanh(Z)
def layerActivationForward(A_prev, W, b, keep_prob=0, activationFunc="relu"):

    # Compute Z
    Z = np.dot(W,A_prev) + b
    forward_cache = (A_prev, W, b)
    # Compute the activation for sigmoid
    if activationFunc == "sigmoid":
        A, activation_cache = sigmoid(Z)
    # Compute the activation for Relu
    elif activationFunc == "relu":
        A, activation_cache = relu(Z)
    # Compute the activation for tanh
    elif activationFunc == 'tanh':
        A, activation_cache = tanh(Z)
    elif activationFunc == 'softmax':
        A, activation_cache = stableSoftmax(Z)

    cache = (forward_cache, activation_cache)
    return A, cache

# Compute the forward propagation for layers 1..L
# Input : X - Input Features
#         parameters: Weights and biases
#         keep_prob
#         hiddenActivationFunc - Activation function at hidden layers
Relu/tanh
#         outputActivationFunc - Activation function at output -
sigmoid/softmax
# Returns : AL
#           caches
#           dropoutMat
```

```python
# The forward propoagtion uses the Relu/tanh activation from layer 1..L-1 and
# sigmoid actiovation at layer L
def forwardPropagationDeep(X, parameters,keep_prob=0,
hiddenActivationFunc='relu',outputActivationFunc='sigmoid'):
    caches = []
    #initialize the dropout matrix
    dropoutMat = {}
    # Set A to X (A0)
    A = X
    L = len(parameters)//2 # number of layers in the neural network
    # Loop through from layer 1 to upto layer L
    for l in range(1, L):
        A_prev = A
        # Zi = Wi x Ai-1 + bi   and Ai = g(Zi)
        A, cache = layerActivationForward(A_prev, parameters['W'+str(l)],
parameters['b'+str(l)], keep_prob, activationFunc = hiddenActivationFunc)

        # Randomly drop some activation units
        # Create a matrix as the same shape as A
        D = np.random.rand(A.shape[0],A.shape[1])
        D = (D < keep_prob)
        # We need to use the same 'dropout' matrix in backward propagation
        # Save the dropout matrix for use in backprop
        dropoutMat["D" + str(l)] =D
        A= np.multiply(A,D)
        A = np.divide(A,keep_prob)

        caches.append(cache)


    # last layer
    AL, cache = layerActivationForward(A, parameters['W'+str(L)],
parameters['b'+str(L)], activationFunc = outputActivationFunc)
    caches.append(cache)

    return AL, caches, dropoutMat


# Compute the cost
# Input : Activation of last layer
#       : Output from data
#       : Y
#       :outputActivationFunc - Activation function at output -
sigmoid/softmax
# Output: cost
def computeCost(AL,Y,outputActivationFunc="sigmoid"):
    if outputActivationFunc=="sigmoid":
        m= float(Y.shape[1])
        # Element wise multiply for logprobs
        cost=-1/m *np.sum(Y*np.log(AL) + (1-Y)*(np.log(1-AL)))
        cost = np.squeeze(cost)
    elif outputActivationFunc=="softmax":
        # Take transpose of Y for softmax
        Y=Y.T
        m= float(len(Y))
        # Compute log probs. Take the log prob of correct class based on
output y
        correct_logprobs = -np.log(AL[range(int(m)),Y.T])
        # Conpute loss
        cost = np.sum(correct_logprobs)/m
    return cost


# Compute the cost with regularization
```

```python
# Input : parameters
#        : AL
#        : Y
#        : lambd
#        :outputActivationFunc - Activation function at output - sigmoid/softmax/tanh
# Output: cost
def computeCostWithReg(parameters,AL,Y,lambd,
outputActivationFunc="sigmoid"):


    if outputActivationFunc=="sigmoid":
        m= float(Y.shape[1])
        # Element wise multiply for logprobs
        cost=-1/m *np.sum(Y*np.log(AL) + (1-Y)*(np.log(1-AL)))
        cost = np.squeeze(cost)

        # Regularization cost
        L= int(len(parameters)/2)
        L2RegularizationCost=0
        for l in range(L):
            L2RegularizationCost+=np.sum(np.square(parameters['W'+str(l+1)]))

        L2RegularizationCost = (lambd/(2*m))*L2RegularizationCost
        cost = cost +  L2RegularizationCost


    elif outputActivationFunc=="softmax":
        # Take transpose of Y for softmax
        Y=Y.T
        m= float(len(Y))
        # Compute log probs. Take the log prob of correct class based on output y
        correct_logprobs = -np.log(AL[range(int(m)),Y.T])
        # Conpute loss
        cost = np.sum(correct_logprobs)/m

                # Regularization cost
        L= int(len(parameters)/2)
        L2RegularizationCost=0
        for l in range(L):
            L2RegularizationCost+=np.sum(np.square(parameters['W'+str(l+1)]))

        L2RegularizationCost = (lambd/(2*m))*L2RegularizationCost
        cost = cost +  L2RegularizationCost

    return cost

# Compute the backpropoagation for 1 cycle
# Input : Neural Network parameters - dA
#         # cache - forward_cache & activation_cache
#         # Input features
#         # keep_prob
#         # Output values Y
# Returns: Gradients
# dL/dWi= dL/dZi*Al-1
# dl/dbl = dL/dZl
# dL/dZ_prev=dL/dZl*W
def layerActivationBackward(dA, cache, Y, keep_prob=1,
activationFunc="relu"):
    forward_cache, activation_cache = cache
    A_prev, W, b = forward_cache
    numtraining = float(A_prev.shape[1])
    if activationFunc == "relu":
```

```python
            dZ = reluDerivative(dA, activation_cache)
        elif activationFunc == "sigmoid":
            dZ = sigmoidDerivative(dA, activation_cache)
        elif activationFunc == "tanh":
            dZ = tanhDerivative(dA, activation_cache)
        elif activationFunc == "softmax":
            dZ = stableSoftmaxDerivative(dA, activation_cache,Y,numtraining)

        if activationFunc == 'softmax':
            dW = 1/numtraining * np.dot(A_prev,dZ)
            db = 1/numtraining * np.sum(dZ, axis=0, keepdims=True)
            dA_prev = np.dot(dZ,W)
        else:

            dW = 1/numtraining *(np.dot(dZ,A_prev.T))
            db = 1/numtraining * np.sum(dZ, axis=1, keepdims=True)
            dA_prev = np.dot(W.T,dZ)

        return dA_prev, dW, db


# Compute the backpropoagation with regularization for 1 cycle
# Input : dA- Neural Network parameters
#         # cache - forward_cache & activation_cache
#         # Output values Y
#         # lambd
#         # activationFunc
# Returns dA_prev, dw, db
# Returns: Gradients
# dL/dWi= dL/dZi*Al-1
# dl/dbl = dL/dZl
# dL/dZ_prev=dL/dZl*W
def layerActivationBackwardWithReg(dA, cache, Y, lambd, activationFunc):
    forward_cache, activation_cache = cache
    A_prev, W, b = forward_cache
    numtraining = float(A_prev.shape[1])

    #print("n=",numtraining)
    #print("no=",numtraining)
    if activationFunc == "relu":
        dZ = reluDerivative(dA, activation_cache)
    elif activationFunc == "sigmoid":
        dZ = sigmoidDerivative(dA, activation_cache)
    elif activationFunc == "tanh":
        dZ = tanhDerivative(dA, activation_cache)
    elif activationFunc == "softmax":
        dZ = stableSoftmaxDerivative(dA, activation_cache,Y,numtraining)

    if activationFunc == 'softmax':
        # Add the regularization factor
        dW = 1/numtraining * np.dot(A_prev,dZ) +  (lambd/numtraining) * W.T
        db = 1/numtraining * np.sum(dZ, axis=0, keepdims=True)
        dA_prev = np.dot(dZ,W)
    else:

        # Add the regularization factor
        dW = 1/numtraining *(np.dot(dZ,A_prev.T)) + (lambd/numtraining) * W
        #print("dW=",dW)
        db = 1/numtraining * np.sum(dZ, axis=1, keepdims=True)
        #print("db=",db)
        dA_prev = np.dot(W.T,dZ)


    return dA_prev, dW, db
```

```python
# Compute the backpropoagation for 1 cycle
# Input : AL: Output of L layer Network - weights
#        # Y  Real output
#        # caches -- list of caches containing:
#        # dropoutMat
#        # lambd
#        # keep_prob
#        every cache of layerActivationForward() with "relu"/"tanh"
#        #(it's caches[l], for l in range(L-1) i.e l = 0...L-2)
#        #the cache of layerActivationForward() with "sigmoid" (it's caches[L-1])
#        # hiddenActivationFunc - Activation function at hidden layers - relu/sigmoid/tanh
#        #outputActivationFunc - Activation function at output - sigmoid/softmax
#
#     Returns:
#      gradients -- A dictionary with the gradients
#                   gradients["dA" + str(l)] = ...
#                   gradients["dW" + str(l)] = ...
#                   gradients["db" + str(l)] = ...
def backwardPropagationDeep(AL, Y, caches, dropoutMat, lambd=0, keep_prob=1,
hiddenActivationFunc='relu',outputActivationFunc="sigmoid"):
    #initialize the gradients
    gradients = {}
    # Set the number of layers
    L = len(caches)
    m = float(AL.shape[1])

    if outputActivationFunc == "sigmoid":
        Y = Y.reshape(AL.shape) # after this line, Y is the same shape as AL
        # Initializing the backpropagation
        # dl/dAL= -(y/a + (1-y)/(1-a)) - At the output layer
        dAL = - (np.divide(Y, AL) - np.divide(1 - Y, 1 - AL))
    else:
        dAL =0
        Y=Y.T

    # Since this is a binary classification the activation at output is sigmoid
    # Get the gradients at the last layer
    # Inputs: "AL, Y, caches".
    # Outputs: "gradients["dAL"], gradients["dWL"], gradients["dbL"]
    current_cache = caches[L-1]
    if lambd==0:
        gradients["dA" + str(L)], gradients["dW" + str(L)], gradients["db" + str(L)] = layerActivationBackward(dAL, current_cache,
                                                    Y, activationFunc = outputActivationFunc)
    else: #Regularization
        gradients["dA" + str(L)], gradients["dW" + str(L)], gradients["db" + str(L)] = layerActivationBackwardWithReg(dAL, current_cache,
                                                    Y, lambd, activationFunc = outputActivationFunc)

    # Note dA for softmax is the transpose
    if outputActivationFunc == "softmax":
        gradients["dA" + str(L)] = gradients["dA" + str(L)].T
    # Traverse in the reverse direction
    for l in reversed(range(L-1)):

        # Compute the gradients for L-1 to 1 for Relu/tanh
        # Inputs: "gradients["dA" + str(l + 2)], caches".
```

```python
            # Outputs: "gradients["dA" + str(l + 1)] , gradients["dW" + str(l + 1)] , gradients["db" + str(l + 1)]
            current_cache = caches[l]

            #dA_prev_temp, dW_temp, db_temp = layerActivationBackward(gradients['dA'+str(l+2)], current_cache, activationFunc = "relu")
            if lambd==0:
                # In the reverse direction use the dame dropout matrix
                # Random dropout
                # Multiply dA'l' with the dropoutMat and divide to keep the expected value same
                D = dropoutMat["D" + str(l+1)]
                # Drop some dAl's
                gradients['dA'+str(l+2)]= np.multiply(gradients['dA'+str(l+2)],D)
                # Divide by keep_prob to keep expected value same
                gradients['dA'+str(l+2)] = np.divide(gradients['dA'+str(l+2)],keep_prob)

                dA_prev_temp, dW_temp, db_temp = layerActivationBackward(gradients['dA'+str(l+2)], current_cache, Y, keep_prob=1, activationFunc = hiddenActivationFunc)

            else:
                dA_prev_temp, dW_temp, db_temp = layerActivationBackwardWithReg(gradients['dA'+str(l+2)], current_cache, Y, lambd, activationFunc = hiddenActivationFunc)
            gradients["dA" + str(l + 1)] = dA_prev_temp
            gradients["dW" + str(l + 1)] = dW_temp
            gradients["db" + str(l + 1)] = db_temp

    return gradients

# Perform Gradient Descent
# Input : Weights and biases
#       : gradients
#       : learning rate
#       : outputActivationFunc - Activation function at output - sigmoid/softmax
#output : Updated weights after 1 iteration
def gradientDescent(parameters, gradients, learningRate,outputActivationFunc="sigmoid"):

    L = int(len(parameters) / 2)
    # Update rule for each parameter.
    for l in range(L-1):
        parameters["W" + str(l+1)] = parameters['W'+str(l+1)] -learningRate* gradients['dW' + str(l+1)]
        parameters["b" + str(l+1)] = parameters['b'+str(l+1)] -learningRate* gradients['db' + str(l+1)]

    if outputActivationFunc=="sigmoid":
        parameters["W" + str(L)] = parameters['W'+str(L)] -learningRate* gradients['dW' + str(L)]
        parameters["b" + str(L)] = parameters['b'+str(L)] -learningRate* gradients['db' + str(L)]
    elif outputActivationFunc=="softmax":
        parameters["W" + str(L)] = parameters['W'+str(L)] -learningRate* gradients['dW' + str(L)].T
        parameters["b" + str(L)] = parameters['b'+str(L)] -learningRate* gradients['db' + str(L)].T

    return parameters
```

```python
# Update parameters with momentum
# Input  : parameters
#        : gradients
#        : v
#        : beta
#        : learningRate
#        : outputActivationFunc - softmax/sigmoid
#output : Updated parameters and velocity
def gradientDescentWithMomentum(parameters, gradients, v, beta, learningRate,
outputActivationFunc="sigmoid"):

    L = len(parameters) // 2 # number of layers in the neural networks
    # Momentum update for each parameter
    for l in range(L-1):

        # Compute velocities
        # v['dWk'] = beta *v['dWk'] + (1-beta)*dWk
        v["dW" + str(l+1)] = beta*v["dW" + str(l+1)] + (1-beta) * gradients['dW' + str(l+1)]
        v["db" + str(l+1)] = beta*v["db" + str(l+1)] + (1-beta) * gradients['db' + str(l+1)]
        # Update parameters with velocities
        parameters["W" + str(l+1)] = parameters['W' + str(l+1)] - learningRate* v["dW" + str(l+1)]
        parameters["b" + str(l+1)] = parameters['b' + str(l+1)] - learningRate* v["db" + str(l+1)]

    if outputActivationFunc=="sigmoid":
        v["dW" + str(L)] = beta*v["dW" + str(L)] + (1-beta) * gradients['dW' + str(L)]
        v["db" + str(L)] = beta*v["db" + str(L)] + (1-beta) * gradients['db' + str(L)]
        parameters["W" + str(L)] = parameters['W'+str(L)] -learningRate* gradients['dW' + str(L)]
        parameters["b" + str(L)] = parameters['b'+str(L)] -learningRate* gradients['db' + str(L)]
    elif outputActivationFunc=="softmax":
        v["dW" + str(L)] = beta*v["dW" + str(L)] + (1-beta) * gradients['dW' + str(L)].T
        v["db" + str(L)] = beta*v["db" + str(L)] + (1-beta) * gradients['db' + str(L)].T
        parameters["W" + str(L)] = parameters['W'+str(L)] -learningRate* gradients['dW' + str(L)].T
        parameters["b" + str(L)] = parameters['b'+str(L)] -learningRate* gradients['db' + str(L)].T

    return parameters, v


# Update parameters with RMSProp
# Input  : parameters
#        : gradients
#        : s
#        : beta1
#        : learningRate
#        : outputActivationFunc - sigmoid/softmax
# output : Updated parameters and RMSProp
def gradientDescentWithRMSProp(parameters, gradients, s, beta1, epsilon,
learningRate, outputActivationFunc="sigmoid"):

    L = len(parameters) // 2 # number of layers in the neural networks
    # Momentum update for each parameter
    for l in range(L-1):

```

```python
            # Compute RMSProp
            # s['dwk'] = beta1 *s['dwk'] + (1-beta1)*dwk**2/sqrt(s['dwk'])
            s["dw" + str(l+1)] = beta1*s["dw" + str(l+1)] + (1-beta1) * \
                    np.multiply(gradients['dw' + str(l+1)],gradients['dw' + str(l+1)])
            s["db" + str(l+1)] = beta1*s["db" + str(l+1)] + (1-beta1) * \
                    np.multiply(gradients['db' + str(l+1)],gradients['db' + str(l+1)])
            # Update parameters with RMSProp
            parameters["W" + str(l+1)] = parameters['W' + str(l+1)] - \
                    learningRate* gradients['dw' + str(l+1)]/np.sqrt(s["dw" + str(l+1)] + epsilon)
            parameters["b" + str(l+1)] = parameters['b' + str(l+1)] - \
                    learningRate* gradients['db' + str(l+1)]/np.sqrt(s["db" + str(l+1)] + epsilon)

        if outputActivationFunc=="sigmoid":
            s["dw" + str(L)] = beta1*s["dw" + str(L)] + (1-beta1) * \
                    np.multiply(gradients['dw' + str(L)],gradients['dw' + str(L)])
            s["db" + str(L)] = beta1*s["db" + str(L)] + (1-beta1) * \
                    np.multiply(gradients['db' + str(L)],gradients['db' + str(L)])
            parameters["W" + str(L)] = parameters['W'+str(L)] - \
                    learningRate* gradients['dw' + str(L)]/np.sqrt(s["dw" + str(L)] + epsilon)
            parameters["b" + str(L)] = parameters['b'+str(L)] - \
                    learningRate* gradients['db' + str(L)]/np.sqrt(s["db" + str(L)] + epsilon)
        elif outputActivationFunc=="softmax":
            s["dw" + str(L)] = beta1*s["dw" + str(L)] + (1-beta1) * \
                    np.multiply(gradients['dw' + str(L)].T,gradients['dw' + str(L)].T)
            s["db" + str(L)] = beta1*s["db" + str(L)] + (1-beta1) * \
                    np.multiply(gradients['db' + str(L)].T,gradients['db' + str(L)].T)
            parameters["W" + str(L)] = parameters['W'+str(L)] - \
                    learningRate* gradients['dw' + str(L)].T/np.sqrt(s["dw" + str(L)] + epsilon)
            parameters["b" + str(L)] = parameters['b'+str(L)] - \
                    learningRate* gradients['db' + str(L)].T/np.sqrt(s["db" + str(L)] + epsilon)

    return parameters, s

# Update parameters with Adam
# Input : parameters
#       : gradients
#       : v
#       : s
#       : t
#       : beta1
#       : beta2
#       : epsilon
#       : learningRate
#       : outputActivationFunc - sigmoid/softmax
# output : Updated parameters and RMSProp
def gradientDescentWithAdam(parameters, gradients, v, s, t,
                                    beta1 = 0.9, beta2 = 0.999,  epsilon = 1e-8,
                                    learningRate=0.1,
outputActivationFunc="sigmoid"):


    L = len(parameters) // 2
    # Initializing first moment estimate, python dictionary
    v_corrected = {}
```

```python
        # Initializing second moment estimate, python dictionary
        s_corrected = {}

        # Perform Adam upto L-1
        for l in range(L-1):

            # Compute momentum
            v["dW" + str(l+1)] = beta1*v["dW" + str(l+1)] + \
                            (1-beta1) * gradients['dW' + str(l+1)]
            v["db" + str(l+1)] = beta1*v["db" + str(l+1)] + \
                            (1-beta1) * gradients['db' + str(l+1)]


            # Compute bias-corrected first moment estimate.
            v_corrected["dW" + str(l+1)] = v["dW" + str(l+1)]/(1-np.power(beta1,t))
            v_corrected["db" + str(l+1)] = v["db" + str(l+1)]/(1-np.power(beta1,t))


            # Moving average of the squared gradients like RMSProp
            s["dW" + str(l+1)] = beta2*s["dW" + str(l+1)] + \
                     (1-beta2) * np.multiply(gradients['dW' + str(l+1)],gradients['dW' + str(l+1)])
            s["db" + str(l+1)] = beta2*s["db" + str(l+1)] + \
                     (1-beta2) * np.multiply(gradients['db' + str(l+1)],gradients['db' + str(l+1)])


            # Compute bias-corrected second raw moment estimate.
            s_corrected["dW" + str(l+1)] = s["dW" + str(l+1)]/(1-np.power(beta2,t))
            s_corrected["db" + str(l+1)] = s["db" + str(l+1)]/(1-np.power(beta2,t))

            # Update parameters.
            d1=np.sqrt(s_corrected["dW" + str(l+1)]+epsilon)
            d2=np.sqrt(s_corrected["db" + str(l+1)]+epsilon)
            parameters["W" + str(l+1)] = parameters['W' + str(l+1)]- \
                            (learningRate* v_corrected["dW" + str(l+1)]/d1)
            parameters["b" + str(l+1)] = parameters['b' + str(l+1)] - \
                            (learningRate* v_corrected["db" + str(l+1)]/d2)

        if outputActivationFunc=="sigmoid":
            #Compute 1st moment for L
            v["dW" + str(L)] = beta1*v["dW" + str(L)] + (1-beta1) * gradients['dW' + str(L)]
            v["db" + str(L)] = beta1*v["db" + str(L)] + (1-beta1) * gradients['db' + str(L)]
            # Compute bias-corrected first moment estimate.
            v_corrected["dW" + str(L)] = v["dW" + str(L)]/(1-np.power(beta1,t))
            v_corrected["db" + str(L)] = v["db" + str(L)]/(1-np.power(beta1,t))

            # Compute 2nd moment for L
            s["dW" + str(L)] = beta2*s["dW" + str(L)] + (1-beta2) * \
                            np.multiply(gradients['dW' + str(L)],gradients['dW' + str(L)])
            s["db" + str(L)] = beta2*s["db" + str(L)] + (1-beta2) * \
                            np.multiply(gradients['db' + str(L)],gradients['db' + str(L)])

            # Compute bias-corrected second raw moment estimate.
```

```python
            s_corrected["dw" + str(L)] = s["dw" + str(L)]/(1-np.power(beta2,t))
            s_corrected["db" + str(L)] = s["db" + str(L)]/(1-np.power(beta2,t))

            # Update parameters.
            d1=np.sqrt(s_corrected["dw" + str(L)]+epsilon)
            d2=np.sqrt(s_corrected["db" + str(L)]+epsilon)
            parameters["W" + str(L)] = parameters['W' + str(L)]- \
                        (learningRate* v_corrected["dw" + str(L)]/d1)
            parameters["b" + str(L)] = parameters['b' + str(L)] - \
                        (learningRate* v_corrected["db" + str(L)]/d2)

        elif outputActivationFunc=="softmax":
            # Compute 1st moment
            v["dw" + str(L)] = beta1*v["dw" + str(L)] + (1-beta1) * gradients['dw' + str(L)].T
            v["db" + str(L)] = beta1*v["db" + str(L)] + (1-beta1) * gradients['db' + str(L)].T
            # Compute bias-corrected first moment estimate.
            v_corrected["dw" + str(L)] = v["dw" + str(L)]/(1-np.power(beta1,t))
            v_corrected["db" + str(L)] = v["db" + str(L)]/(1-np.power(beta1,t))

            #Compute 2nd moment
            s["dw" + str(L)] = beta2*s["dw" + str(L)] + (1-beta2) * np.multiply(gradients['dw' + str(L)].T,gradients['dw' + str(L)].T)
            s["db" + str(L)] = beta2*s["db" + str(L)] + (1-beta2) * np.multiply(gradients['db' + str(L)].T,gradients['db' + str(L)].T)
            # Compute bias-corrected second raw moment estimate.
            s_corrected["dw" + str(L)] = s["dw" + str(L)]/(1-np.power(beta2,t))
            s_corrected["db" + str(L)] = s["db" + str(L)]/(1-np.power(beta2,t))

            # Update parameters.
            d1=np.sqrt(s_corrected["dw" + str(L)]+epsilon)
            d2=np.sqrt(s_corrected["db" + str(L)]+epsilon)
            parameters["W" + str(L)] = parameters['W' + str(L)]- \
                        (learningRate* v_corrected["dw" + str(L)]/d1)
            parameters["b" + str(L)] = parameters['b' + str(L)] - \
                        (learningRate* v_corrected["db" + str(L)]/d2)


    return parameters, v, s


#   Execute a L layer Deep learning model
# Input : X - Input features
#         : Y output
#         : layersDimensions - Dimension of layers
#         : hiddenActivationFunc - Activation function at hidden layer relu /tanh/sigmoid
#         : outputActivationFunc - Activation function at output layer sigmoid/softmax
#         : learning rate
#         : lambd
#         : keep_prob
#         : num of iteration
#         : initType
#output : parameters
```

```python
def L_Layer_DeepModel(X1, Y1, layersDimensions, hiddenActivationFunc='relu',
outputActivationFunc="sigmoid",
                        learningRate = .3,   lambd=0, keep_prob=1,
num_iterations = 10000,initType="default",
print_cost=False,figure="figa.png"):

    np.random.seed(1)
    costs = []

    # Parameters initialization.
    if initType == "He":
        parameters = HeInitializeDeepModel(layersDimensions)
    elif initType == "Xavier" :
        parameters = XavInitializeDeepModel(layersDimensions)
    else: #Default
        parameters = initializeDeepModel(layersDimensions)
    # Loop (gradient descent)
    for i in range(0, num_iterations):

        AL, caches, dropoutMat = forwardPropagationDeep(X1, parameters,
keep_prob,
hiddenActivationFunc="relu",outputActivationFunc=outputActivationFunc)

        # Regularization parameter is 0
        if lambd==0:
            # Compute cost
            cost = computeCost(parameters,AL, Y1,
outputActivationFunc=outputActivationFunc)
        # Include L2 regularization
        else:
            # Compute cost
            cost = computeCostWithReg(parameters,AL, Y1, lambd,
outputActivationFunc=outputActivationFunc)

        # Backward propagation.
        gradients = backwardPropagationDeep(AL, Y1, caches, dropoutMat,
lambd, keep_prob,
hiddenActivationFunc="relu",outputActivationFunc=outputActivationFunc)

        # Update parameters.
        parameters = gradientDescent(parameters, gradients,
learningRate=learningRate,outputActivationFunc=outputActivationFunc)


        # Print the cost every 100 training example
        if print_cost and i % 1000 == 0:
            print ("Cost after iteration %i: %f" %(i, cost))
        if print_cost and i % 1000 == 0:
            costs.append(cost)

    # plot the cost
    plt.plot(np.squeeze(costs))
    plt.ylabel('Cost')
    plt.xlabel('No of iterations (x1000)')
    plt.title("Learning rate =" + str(learningRate))
    plt.savefig(figure,bbox_inches='tight')
    #plt.show()
    plt.clf()
    plt.close()

    return parameters

#   Execute a L layer Deep learning model Stoachastic Gradient Descent
# Input : X - Input features
```

```
#          : Y output
#          : layersDimensions - Dimension of layers
#          : hiddenActivationFunc - Activation function at hidden layer relu
/tanh/sigmoid
#          : outputActivationFunc - Activation function at output -
sigmoid/softmax
#          : learning rate
#          : lrDecay
#          : lambd
#          : keep_prob
#          : optimizer
#          : beta
#          : beta1
#          : beta2
#          : epsilon
#          : mini_batch_size
#          : num_epochs
#          :
#output : Updated weights and biases

def L_Layer_DeepModel_SGD(X1, Y1, layersDimensions,
hiddenActivationFunc='relu', outputActivationFunc="sigmoid",
                          learningRate = .3, lrDecay=False, decayRate=1,
                          lambd=0, keep_prob=1,
optimizer="gd",beta=0.9,beta1=0.9, beta2=0.999,
                          epsilon = 1e-8,mini_batch_size = 64, num_epochs =
2500, print_cost=False, figure="figa.png"):

    print("lr=",learningRate)
    print("lrDecay=",lrDecay)
    print("decayRate=",decayRate)
    print("lambd=",lambd)
    print("keep_prob=",keep_prob)
    print("optimizer=",optimizer)
    print("beta=",beta)

    print("beta1=",beta1)
    print("beta2=",beta2)
    print("epsilon=",epsilon)

    print("mini_batch_size=",mini_batch_size)
    print("num_epochs=",num_epochs)
    print("epsilon=",epsilon)


    t =0 # Adam counter
    np.random.seed(1)
    costs = []

    # Parameters initialization.
    parameters = initializeDeepModel(layersDimensions)

    #Initialize the optimizer
    if optimizer == "gd":
        pass # no initialization required for gradient descent
    elif optimizer == "momentum":
        v = initializeVelocity(parameters)
    elif optimizer == "rmsprop":
        s = initializeRMSProp(parameters)
    elif optimizer == "adam":
        v,s = initializeAdam(parameters)

    seed=10
    # Loop for number of epochs
```

```python
for i in range(num_epochs):
    # Define the random minibatches. We increment the seed to reshuffle
    # differently the dataset after each epoch
    seed = seed + 1
    minibatches = random_mini_batches(X1, Y1, mini_batch_size, seed)

    batch=0
    # Loop through each mini batch
    for minibatch in minibatches:
        #print("batch=",batch)
        batch=batch+1
        # Select a minibatch
        (minibatch_X, minibatch_Y) = minibatch

        # Perfrom forward propagation
        AL, caches, dropoutMat = forwardPropagationDeep(minibatch_X,
parameters, keep_prob,
hiddenActivationFunc="relu",outputActivationFunc=outputActivationFunc)

        # Compute cost
        # Regularization parameter is 0
        if lambd==0:
            # Compute cost
            cost = computeCost(parameters, AL, minibatch_Y,
outputActivationFunc=outputActivationFunc)
        else: # Include L2 regularization
                            # Compute cost
            cost = computeCostWithReg(parameters, AL, minibatch_Y, lambd,
outputActivationFunc=outputActivationFunc)

        # Backward propagation.
        gradients = backwardPropagationDeep(AL, minibatch_Y,
caches,dropoutMat, lambd,
keep_prob,hiddenActivationFunc="relu",outputActivationFunc=outputActivationFunc)

        if optimizer == "gd":
            # Update parameters normal gradient descent
            parameters = gradientDescent(parameters, gradients,
learningRate=learningRate,outputActivationFunc=outputActivationFunc)
        elif optimizer == "momentum":
            # Update parameters for gradient descent with momentum
            parameters, v = gradientDescentWithMomentum(parameters,
gradients, v, beta, \

learningRate=learningRate,outputActivationFunc=outputActivationFunc)
        elif optimizer == "rmsprop":
            # Update parameters for gradient descent with RMSProp
            parameters, s = gradientDescentWithRMSProp(parameters,
gradients, s, beta1, epsilon, \

learningRate=learningRate,outputActivationFunc=outputActivationFunc)
        elif optimizer == "adam":
            t = t + 1 # Adam counter
            parameters, v, s = gradientDescentWithAdam(parameters,
gradients, v, s,
                                                        t, beta1,
beta2,  epsilon,

learningRate=learningRate,outputActivationFunc=outputActivationFunc)

    # Print the cost every 1000 epoch
    if print_cost and i % 100 == 0:
        print ("Cost after epoch %i: %f" %(i, cost))
```

```python
            if print_cost and i % 100 == 0:
                costs.append(cost)
            if lrDecay == True:
                learningRate = np.power(decayRate,(num_epochs/1000)) * learningRate


        # plot the cost
        plt.plot(np.squeeze(costs))
        plt.ylabel('Cost')
        plt.xlabel('No of epochs(x100)')
        plt.title("Learning rate =" + str(learningRate))
        plt.savefig(figure,bbox_inches='tight')
        #plt.show()
        plt.clf()
        plt.close()


# Create random mini batches
# Input : X - Input features
#       : Y- output
#       : miniBatchSizes
#       : seed
#output : mini_batches
def random_mini_batches(X, Y, miniBatchSize = 64, seed = 0):

    np.random.seed(seed)
    # Get number of training samples
    m = X.shape[1]
    # Initialize mini batches
    mini_batches = []

    # Create  a list of random numbers < m
    permutation = list(np.random.permutation(m))
    # Randomly shuffle the training data
    shuffled_X = X[:, permutation]
    shuffled_Y = Y[:, permutation].reshape((1,m))

    # Compute number of mini batches
    numCompleteMinibatches = math.floor(m/miniBatchSize)

   # For the number of mini batches
    for k in range(0, numCompleteMinibatches):

        # Set the start and end of each mini batch
        mini_batch_X = shuffled_X[:, k*miniBatchSize : (k+1) * miniBatchSize]
        mini_batch_Y = shuffled_Y[:, k*miniBatchSize : (k+1) * miniBatchSize]

        mini_batch = (mini_batch_X, mini_batch_Y)
        mini_batches.append(mini_batch)


    #if m % miniBatchSize != 0:. The batch does not evenly divide by the mini batch
    if m % miniBatchSize != 0:
        l=math.floor(m/miniBatchSize)*miniBatchSize
        # Set the start and end of last mini batch
        m=l+m % miniBatchSize
        mini_batch_X = shuffled_X[:,l:m]
        mini_batch_Y = shuffled_Y[:,l:m]

        mini_batch = (mini_batch_X, mini_batch_Y)
        mini_batches.append(mini_batch)
```

```python
             return mini_batches


# Plot a decision boundary
# Input : Input Model,
#            X
#            Y
#            sz - Num of hiden units
#            lr - Learning rate
#            Fig to be saved as
# Returns Null
def plot_decision_boundary(model, X, y,lr,figure1="figb.png"):
    print("plot")
    # Set min and max values and give it some padding
    x_min, x_max = X[0, :].min() - 1, X[0, :].max() + 1
    y_min, y_max = X[1, :].min() - 1, X[1, :].max() + 1
    colors=['black','gold']
    cmap = matplotlib.colors.ListedColormap(colors)
    h = 0.01
    # Generate a grid of points with distance h between them
    xx, yy = np.meshgrid(np.arange(x_min, x_max, h), np.arange(y_min, y_max, h))
    # Predict the function value for the whole grid
    Z = model(np.c_[xx.ravel(), yy.ravel()])
    Z = Z.reshape(xx.shape)
    # Plot the contour and training examples
    plt.contourf(xx, yy, Z, cmap="coolwarm")
    plt.ylabel('x2')
    plt.xlabel('x1')
    x=X.T
    y=y.T.reshape(300,)
    plt.scatter(x[:, 0], x[:, 1], c=y, s=20);
    print(X.shape)
    plt.title("Decision Boundary for learning rate:"+lr)
    plt.savefig(figure1, bbox_inches='tight')
    #plt.show()

# Predict output
def predict(parameters,
X,keep_prob=1,hiddenActivationFunc="relu",outputActivationFunc="sigmoid"):
    A2, cache,dropoutMat = forwardPropagationDeep(X, parameters, keep_prob=1,
hiddenActivationFunc="relu",outputActivationFunc=outputActivationFunc)
    predictions = (A2>0.5)
    return predictions

# Predict probability
def predict_proba(parameters, X,outputActivationFunc="sigmoid"):
    A2, cache = forwardPropagationDeep(X, parameters)
    if outputActivationFunc=="sigmoid":
        proba=A2
    elif outputActivationFunc=="softmax":
        proba=np.argmax(A2, axis=0).reshape(-1,1)
        print("A2=",A2.shape)
    return proba

# Plot a decision boundary
# Input : Input Model,
#            X
#            Y
#            sz - Num of hiden units
#            lr - Learning rate
#            Fig to be saved as
# Returns Null
def plot_decision_boundary1(X, y,W1,b1,W2,b2,figure2="figc.png"):
```

```python
        #plot_decision_boundary(lambda x: predict(parameters, x.T),
x1,y1.T,str(0.3),"fig2.png")
        h = 0.02
        x_min, x_max = X[:, 0].min() - 1, X[:, 0].max() + 1
        y_min, y_max = X[:, 1].min() - 1, X[:, 1].max() + 1
        xx, yy = np.meshgrid(np.arange(x_min, x_max, h),
                             np.arange(y_min, y_max, h))
        Z = np.dot(np.maximum(0, np.dot(np.c_[xx.ravel(), yy.ravel()], W1.T) + b1.T), W2.T) + b2.T
        Z = np.argmax(Z, axis=1)
        Z = Z.reshape(xx.shape)

        fig = plt.figure()
        plt.contourf(xx, yy, Z, cmap=plt.cm.Spectral, alpha=0.8)
        print(X.shape)
        y1=y.reshape(300,)
        plt.scatter(X[:, 0], X[:, 1], c=y1, s=40, cmap=plt.cm.Spectral)
        plt.xlim(xx.min(), xx.max())
        plt.ylim(yy.min(), yy.max())
        plt.savefig(figure2, bbox_inches='tight')

# Load the circles dataset
def load_dataset():
    np.random.seed(1)
    train_X, train_Y = sklearn.datasets.make_circles(n_samples=300, noise=.05)
    np.random.seed(2)
    test_X, test_Y = sklearn.datasets.make_circles(n_samples=100, noise=.05)
    # Visualize the data
    print(train_X.shape)
    print(train_Y.shape)
    #plt.scatter(train_X[:, 0], train_X[:, 1], c=train_Y, s=40, cmap=plt.cm.Spectral);
    train_X = train_X.T
    train_Y = train_Y.reshape((1, train_Y.shape[0]))
    test_X = test_X.T
    test_Y = test_Y.reshape((1, test_Y.shape[0]))
    return train_X, train_Y, test_X, test_Y

#############
# Note: Using dictionary_to_vector followed by vector_to_dictionary =>
original dictionary
#############
# Convert a weight,biases dictionary to a vector
# Input : parameter dictionary
# Returns : vector
def dictionary_to_vector(parameters):
    """
    Roll all our parameters dictionary into a single vector satisfying our
specific required shape.
    """
    keys = []
    count = 0
    for key in parameters:
        # flatten parameter
        new_vector = np.reshape(parameters[key], (-1,1))
        keys = keys + [key]*new_vector.shape[0]

        if count == 0:
            theta = new_vector
        else:
            theta = np.concatenate((theta, new_vector), axis=0)
        count = count + 1

```

```python
            return theta, keys


# Convert a gradient dictionary to a vector
# Input : parameter
#         : gradient dictionary
# Returns : gradient vector
def gradients_to_vector(parameters, gradients):

    #Roll all our gradients dictionary into a single vector satisfying our
specific required shape.

    keyvals=[]
    L=len(parameters)//2
    count = 0
    for l in range(L):
        # flatten parameter
        keyvals.append('dW'+str(l+1))
        keyvals.append('db'+str(l+1))

    for key in keyvals:
        new_vector = np.reshape(gradients[key], (-1,1))

        if count == 0:
            theta = new_vector
        else:
            theta = np.concatenate((theta, new_vector), axis=0)
        count = count + 1

    return theta

# Convert a vector  to a dictionary
# Input : parameter
#         : theta
# Returns : parameters1 (dictionary)
def vector_to_dictionary(parameters,theta):
    #Unroll all our parameters dictionary from a single vector satisfying our
specific required shape.

    start=0
    parameters1 = {}
    #For key
    for key in parameters:
        (a,b) = parameters[key].shape
        # Create a dictionary
        parameters1[key]= theta[start:start+a*b].reshape((a,b))
        start=start+a*b

    return parameters1

# Convert a vector  to a dictionary
# Input : parameter
#         : theta
# Returns : parameters1 (dictionary)
def vector_to_dictionary2(parameters,theta):
    #Unroll all our parameters dictionary from a single vector satisfying our
specific required shape.

    start=0
    parameters2= {}
    # For key
    for key in parameters:
        (a,b) = parameters[key].shape
        # Create a key value pair
```

```python
            parameters2['d'+key]= theta[start:start+a*b].reshape((a,b))
            start=start+a*b

    return parameters2

#   Perform a gradient check
# Input : parameters
#        : gradients
#        : train_X
#        : train_Y
#        : epsilon
#        : outputActivationFunc
# Returns :
def gradient_check_n(parameters, gradients, train_X, train_Y, epsilon = 1e-7,outputActivationFunc="sigmoid"):
    # Set-up variables
    parameters_values, _ = dictionary_to_vector(parameters)
    grad = gradients_to_vector(parameters,gradients)
    num_parameters = parameters_values.shape[0]
    J_plus = np.zeros((num_parameters, 1))
    J_minus = np.zeros((num_parameters, 1))
    gradapprox = np.zeros((num_parameters, 1))

    # Compute gradapprox using 2 sided derivative
    for i in range(num_parameters):
        # Compute J_plus[i]. Inputs: "parameters_values, epsilon". Output = "J_plus[i]".
        thetaplus = np.copy(parameters_values)
        thetaplus[i][0] = thetaplus[i][0] + epsilon
        AL, caches, dropoutMat = forwardPropagationDeep(train_X, vector_to_dictionary(parameters,thetaplus), keep_prob=1, hiddenActivationFunc="relu",outputActivationFunc=outputActivationFunc)
        J_plus[i] = computeCost(AL, train_Y, outputActivationFunc=outputActivationFunc)


        # Compute J_minus[i]. Inputs: "parameters_values, epsilon". Output = "J_minus[i]".
        thetaminus = np.copy(parameters_values)
        thetaminus[i][0] = thetaminus[i][0] - epsilon
        AL, caches, dropoutMat  = forwardPropagationDeep(train_X, vector_to_dictionary(parameters,thetaminus), keep_prob=1, hiddenActivationFunc="relu",outputActivationFunc=outputActivationFunc)
        J_minus[i] = computeCost(AL, train_Y, outputActivationFunc=outputActivationFunc)


        # Compute gradapprox[i]
        gradapprox[i] = (J_plus[i] - J_minus[i])/(2*epsilon)

    # Compare gradapprox to backward propagation gradients by computing difference.
    numerator = np.linalg.norm(grad-gradapprox)
    denominator = np.linalg.norm(grad) +  np.linalg.norm(gradapprox)
    difference =  numerator/denominator


    if difference > 1e-5:
        print ("\033[93m" + "There is a mistake in the backward propagation! difference = " + str(difference) + "\033[0m")
    else:
```

```
                print ("\033[92m" + "Your backward propagation works perfectly fine!
difference = " + str(difference) + "\033[0m")
    print(difference)
    print("\n")
    # Covert grad to dictionary
    m=vector_to_dictionary2(parameters,grad)
    print("Gradients from backprop")
    print(m)
    print("\n")
    # Convert gradapprox to dictionary
    n=vector_to_dictionary2(parameters,gradapprox)
    print("Gradapprox from gradient check")
    print(n)

```

8.2 R

```r
###########################################################################
###############################
#
# File    : DLfunctions8.R
# Author  : Tinniam V Ganesh
# Date    : 6 May 2018
#
###########################################################################
##############################
library(ggplot2)
library(PRROC)
library(dplyr)

# Compute the sigmoid of a vector
sigmoid <- function(Z){
  A <- 1/(1+ exp(-Z))
  cache<-Z
  retvals <- list("A"=A,"Z"=Z)
  return(retvals)

}

# This is the older version. Very performance intensive
reluOld    <-function(Z){
  A <- apply(Z, 1:2, function(x) max(0,x))
  cache<-Z
  retvals <- list("A"=A,"Z"=Z)
  return(retvals)
}

# Compute the Relu of a vector (current version)
relu    <-function(Z){
    # Perform relu. Set values less that equal to 0 as 0
    Z[Z<0]=0
    A=Z
    cache<-Z
    retvals <- list("A"=A,"Z"=Z)
    return(retvals)
}

# Compute the tanh activation of a vector
tanhActivation <- function(Z){
```

```r
43      A <- tanh(Z)
44      cache<-Z
45      retvals <- list("A"=A,"Z"=Z)
46      return(retvals)
47  }
48
49  # Conmpute the softmax of a vector
50  softmax    <- function(Z){
51      # get unnormalized probabilities
52      exp_scores = exp(t(Z))
53      # normalize them for each example
54      A = exp_scores / rowSums(exp_scores)
55      retvals <- list("A"=A,"Z"=Z)
56      return(retvals)
57  }
58
59  # Compute the derivative of Relu
60  # g'(z) = 1 if z >0 and 0 otherwise
61  reluDerivative   <-function(dA, cache){
62      Z <- cache
63      dZ <- dA
64      # Create a logical matrix of values > 0
65      a <- Z > 0
66      # When z <= 0, you should set dz to 0 as well. Perform an element wise
67  multiply
68      dZ <- dZ * a
69      return(dZ)
70  }
71
72  # Compute the derivative of sigmoid
73  # Derivative g'(z) = a* (1-a)
74  sigmoidDerivative   <- function(dA, cache){
75      Z <- cache
76      s <- 1/(1+exp(-Z))
77      dZ <- dA * s * (1-s)
78      return(dZ)
79  }
80
81  # Compute the derivative of tanh
82  # Derivative g'(z) = 1- a^2
83  tanhDerivative    <- function(dA, cache){
84      Z = cache
85      a = tanh(Z)
86      dZ = dA * (1 - a^2)
87      return(dZ)
88  }
89
90  # Populate a matrix of 1s in rows where Y==1
91  # This may need to be extended for K classes. Currently
92  # supports K=3 & K=10
93  popMatrix <- function(Y,numClasses){
94       a=rep(0,times=length(Y))
95       Y1=matrix(a,nrow=length(Y),ncol=numClasses)
96       #Set the rows and columns as 1's where Y is the class value
97       if(numClasses==3){
98           Y1[Y==0,1]=1
99           Y1[Y==1,2]=1
100          Y1[Y==2,3]=1
101      } else if (numClasses==10){
102          Y1[Y==0,1]=1
103          Y1[Y==1,2]=1
104          Y1[Y==2,3]=1
105          Y1[Y==3,4]=1
106          Y1[Y==4,5]=1
```

```r
           Y1[Y==5,6]=1
           Y1[Y==6,7]=1
           Y1[Y==7,8]=1
           Y1[Y==8,9]=1
           Y1[Y==9,0]=1
       }
    return(Y1)
}

# Compute the softmax derivative
softmaxDerivative    <- function(dA, cache ,y,numTraining,numClasses){
    # Note : dA not used. dL/dZ = dL/dA * dA/dZ = pi-yi
    Z <- cache
    # Compute softmax
    exp_scores = exp(t(Z))
    # normalize them for each example
    probs = exp_scores / rowSums(exp_scores)
    # Create a matrix of zeros
    Y1=popMatrix(y,numClasses)
    #a=rep(0,times=length(Y))
    #Y1=matrix(a,nrow=length(Y),ncol=numClasses)
    #Set the rows and columns as 1's where Y is the class value
    dZ = probs-Y1
    return(dZ)
}


# Initialize model for L layers
# Input : List of units in each layer
# Returns: Initial weights and biases matrices for all layers
initializeDeepModel <- function(layerDimensions){
   set.seed(2)

   # Initialize empty list
   layerParams <- list()

   # Note the Weight matrix at layer 'l' is a matrix of size (l,l-1)
   # The Bias is a vectors of size (l,1)

   # Loop through the layer dimension from 1.. L
   # Indices in R start from 1
   for(l in 2:length(layersDimensions)){
      # Initialize a matrix of small random numbers of size l x l-1
      # Create random numbers of size  l x l-1
      w=rnorm(layersDimensions[l]*layersDimensions[l-1])*0.01
      # Create a weight matrix of size l x l-1 with this initial weights and
      # Add to list W1,W2... WL
      layerParams[[paste('W',l-1,sep="")]] = matrix(w,nrow=layersDimensions[l],
                                               ncol=layersDimensions[l-1])
      layerParams[[paste('b',l-1,sep="")]] = matrix(rep(0,layersDimensions[l]),

nrow=layersDimensions[l],ncol=1)
   }
   return(layerParams)
}



# He Initialization model for L layers
# Input : List of units in each layer
# Returns: Initial weights and biases matrices for all layers
# He initilization multiplies the random numbers with
sqrt(2/layerDimensions[previouslayer])
HeInitializeDeepModel <- function(layerDimensions){
```

```r
    set.seed(2)

    # Initialize empty list
    layerParams <- list()

    # Note the Weight matrix at layer 'l' is a matrix of size (l,l-1)
    # The Bias is a vectors of size (l,1)

    # Loop through the layer dimension from 1.. L
    # Indices in R start from 1
    for(l in 2:length(layersDimensions)){
        # Initialize a matrix of small random numbers of size l x l-1
        # Create random numbers of size  l x l-1
        w=rnorm(layersDimensions[l]*layersDimensions[l-1])

        # Create a weight matrix of size l x l-1 with this initial weights and
        # Add to list W1,W2... WL
        # He initialization - Divide by sqrt(2/layerDimensions[previous layer])
        layerParams[[paste('W',l-1,sep="")]] = matrix(w,nrow=layersDimensions[l],
ncol=layersDimensions[l-1])*sqrt(2/layersDimensions[l-1])
        layerParams[[paste('b',l-1,sep="")]] = matrix(rep(0,layersDimensions[l]),
nrow=layersDimensions[l],ncol=1)
    }
    return(layerParams)
}

# XavInitializeDeepModel Initialization model for L layers
# Input : List of units in each layer
# Returns: Initial weights and biases matrices for all layers
# He initilization multiplies the random numbers with
sqrt(1/layerDimensions[previouslayer])
XavInitializeDeepModel <- function(layerDimensions){
    set.seed(2)

    # Initialize empty list
    layerParams <- list()

    # Note the Weight matrix at layer 'l' is a matrix of size (l,l-1)
    # The Bias is a vectors of size (l,1)

    # Loop through the layer dimension from 1.. L
    # Indices in R start from 1
    for(l in 2:length(layersDimensions)){
        # Initialize a matrix of small random numbers of size l x l-1
        # Create random numbers of size  l x l-1
        w=rnorm(layersDimensions[l]*layersDimensions[l-1])

        # Create a weight matrix of size l x l-1 with this initial weights and
        # Add to list W1,W2... WL
        # He initialization - Divide by sqrt(2/layerDimensions[previous layer])
        layerParams[[paste('W',l-1,sep="")]] = matrix(w,nrow=layersDimensions[l],
ncol=layersDimensions[l-1])*sqrt(1/layersDimensions[l-1])
        layerParams[[paste('b',l-1,sep="")]] = matrix(rep(0,layersDimensions[l]),
```

```r
                                nrow=layersDimensions[l],ncol=1)
    }
    return(layerParams)
}

# Initialize velocity
# Input : parameters
# Returns: v -Initial velocity
initializeVelocity <- function(parameters){
    
    L <- length(parameters)/2
    v <- list()
    
    # Initialize velocity with the same dimensions as W
    for(l in 1:L){
        # Get the size of weight matrix
        sz <- dim(parameters[[paste('W',l,sep="")]])
        v[[paste('dW',l,sep="")]] = matrix(rep(0,sz[1]*sz[2]),
                                           nrow=sz[1],ncol=sz[2])
        #Get the size of bias matrix
        sz <- dim(parameters[[paste('b',l,sep="")]])
        v[[paste('db',l,sep="")]] =  matrix(rep(0,sz[1]*sz[2]),
                                            nrow=sz[1],ncol=sz[2])
    }
    
    return(v)
}


# Initialize RMSProp
# Input : parameters
# Returns: s - Initial RMSProp
initializeRMSProp <- function(parameters){
    
    L <- length(parameters)/2
    s <- list()
    
    # Initialize velocity with the same dimensions as W
    for(l in 1:L){
        # Get the size of weight matrix
        sz <- dim(parameters[[paste('W',l,sep="")]])
        s[[paste('dW',l,sep="")]] = matrix(rep(0,sz[1]*sz[2]),
                                           nrow=sz[1],ncol=sz[2])
        #Get the size of bias matrix
        sz <- dim(parameters[[paste('b',l,sep="")]])
        s[[paste('db',l,sep="")]] =  matrix(rep(0,sz[1]*sz[2]),
                                            nrow=sz[1],ncol=sz[2])
    }
    
    return(s)
}

# Initialize Adam
# Input : parameters
# Returns: (v,s) - Initial Adam parameters
initializeAdam <- function(parameters){
    
    L <- length(parameters)/2
    v <- list()
    s <- list()
    
    # Initialize velocity with the same dimensions as W
    for(l in 1:L){
```

```r
            # Get the size of weight matrix
            sz <- dim(parameters[[paste('W',l,sep="")]])
            v[[paste('dW',l,sep="")]] = matrix(rep(0,sz[1]*sz[2]),
                                        nrow=sz[1],ncol=sz[2])
            s[[paste('dW',l,sep="")]] = matrix(rep(0,sz[1]*sz[2]),
                                        nrow=sz[1],ncol=sz[2])
            #Get the size of bias matrix
            sz <- dim(parameters[[paste('b',l,sep="")]])
            v[[paste('db',l,sep="")]] =  matrix(rep(0,sz[1]*sz[2]),
                                         nrow=sz[1],ncol=sz[2])
            s[[paste('db',l,sep="")]] = matrix(rep(0,sz[1]*sz[2]),
                                         nrow=sz[1],ncol=sz[2])
    }
    retvals <- list("v"=v,"s"=s)
    return(retvals)
}

# Compute the activation at a layer 'l' for forward prop in a Deep Network
# Input : A_prev - Activation of previous layer
#         W,b - Weight and bias matrices and vectors
#         activationFunc - Activation function - sigmoid, tanh, relu etc
# Returns : The Activation of this layer
#         :
# Z = W * X + b
# A = sigmoid(Z), A= Relu(Z), A= tanh(Z)
layerActivationForward <- function(A_prev, W, b, activationFunc){

  # Compute Z
  z = W %*% A_prev
  # Broadcast the bias 'b' by column
  Z <-sweep(z,1,b,'+')

  forward_cache <- list("A_prev"=A_prev, "W"=W, "b"=b)
  # Compute the activation for sigmoid
  if(activationFunc == "sigmoid"){
    vals = sigmoid(Z)
  } else if (activationFunc == "relu"){ # Compute the activation for relu
    vals = relu(Z)
  } else if(activationFunc == 'tanh'){ # Compute the activation for tanh
    vals = tanhActivation(Z)
  } else if(activationFunc == 'softmax'){
    vals = softmax(Z)
  }
  # Create a list of forward and activation cache
  cache <- list("forward_cache"=forward_cache,
"activation_cache"=vals[['Z']])
  retvals <- list("A"=vals[['A']],"cache"=cache)
  return(retvals)
}

# Compute the forward propagation for layers 1..L
# Input : X - Input Features
#         parameters: Weights and biases
#         keep_prob
#         hiddenActivationFunc - relu/sigmoid/tanh
#         outputActivationFunc - Activation function at hidden layer
sigmoid/softmax
# Returns : AL
#           caches
#           dropoutMat
# The forward propoagtion uses the Relu/tanh activation from layer 1..L-1 and
sigmoid actiovation at layer L
forwardPropagationDeep <- function(X, parameters,keep_prob=1,
hiddenActivationFunc='relu',
```

```r
                                              outputActivationFunc='sigmoid'){
  caches <- list()
  dropoutMat <- list()
  # Set A to X (A0)
  A <- X
  L <- length(parameters)/2 # number of layers in the neural network
  # Loop through from layer 1 to upto layer L
  for(l in 1:(L-1)){
    A_prev <- A
    # Zi = Wi x Ai-1 + bi   and Ai = g(Zi)
    # Set W and b for layer 'l'
    # Loop throug from W1,W2... WL-1
    W <- parameters[[paste("W",l,sep="")]]
    b <- parameters[[paste("b",l,sep="")]]
    # Compute the forward propagation through layer 'l' using the activation function
    actForward <- layerActivationForward(A_prev,
                                          W,
                                          b,
                                          activationFunc = hiddenActivationFunc)
    A <- actForward[['A']]
    # Append the cache A_prev,W,b, Z
    caches[[l]] <-actForward

    # Randomly drop some activation units
    # Create a matrix as the same shape as A
    set.seed(1)
    i=dim(A)[1]
    j=dim(A)[2]
    a<-rnorm(i*j)
    # Normalize a between 0 and 1
    a = (a - min(a))/(max(a) - min(a))
    # Create a matrix of D
    D <- matrix(a,nrow=i, ncol=j)
    # Find D which is less than equal to keep_prob
    D <- D < keep_prob
    # Remove some A's
    A <- A * D
    # Divide by keep_prob to keep expected value same
    A <- A/keep_prob
    dropoutMat[[paste("D",l,sep="")]] <- D
  }

  # Since this is binary classification use the sigmoid activation function in
  # last layer
  # Set the weights and biases for the last layer
  W <- parameters[[paste("W",L,sep="")]]
  b <- parameters[[paste("b",L,sep="")]]
  # Last layer
  actForward = layerActivationForward(A, W, b, activationFunc = outputActivationFunc)
  AL <- actForward[['A']]
  # Append the output of this forward propagation through the last layer
  caches[[L]] <- actForward
  # Create a list of the final output and the caches
  fwdPropDeep <- list("AL"=AL,"caches"=caches,"dropoutMat"=dropoutMat)
  return(fwdPropDeep)

}

# Function pickColumns(). This function is in computeCost()
# Pick columns
```

```r
# Input : AL
#       : Y
#       : numClasses
# Output: a
pickColumns <- function(AL,Y,numClasses){
    if(numClasses==3){
        a=c(AL[Y==0,1],AL[Y==1,2],AL[Y==2,3])
    }
    else if (numClasses==10){
        a=c(AL[Y==0,1],AL[Y==1,2],AL[Y==2,3],AL[Y==3,4],AL[Y==4,5],
            AL[Y==5,6],AL[Y==6,7],AL[Y==7,8],AL[Y==8,9],AL[Y==9,10])
    }
    return(a)
}


# Compute the cost
# Input : Activation of last layer
#       : Output from data
#       :outputActivationFunc - Activation function at hidden layer sigmoid/softmax
#       : numClasses
# Output: cost
computeCost <- function(AL,Y,outputActivationFunc="sigmoid",numClasses=3){
  if(outputActivationFunc=="sigmoid"){
    m= length(Y)
    cost=-1/m*sum(Y*log(AL) + (1-Y)*log(1-AL))


  }else if (outputActivationFunc=="softmax"){
    # Select the elements where the y values are 0, 1 or 2 and make a vector
    # Pick columns
    #a=c(AL[Y==0,1],AL[Y==1,2],AL[Y==2,3])
    m= length(Y)
    a =pickColumns(AL,Y,numClasses)
    #a = c(A2[y=k,k+1])
    # Take log
    correct_probs = -log(a)

    # Compute loss
    cost= sum(correct_probs)/m
  }
  return(cost)
}



# Compute the cost with Regularization
# Input : parameters
#       : AL-Activation of last layer
#       : Y-Output from data
#       : lambd
#       : outputActivationFunc - Activation function at hidden layer sigmoid/softmax
#       : numClasses
# Output: cost
computeCostWithReg <- function(parameters, AL,Y,lambd,
outputActivationFunc="sigmoid",numClasses=3){

        if(outputActivationFunc=="sigmoid"){
        m= length(Y)
        cost=-1/m*sum(Y*log(AL) + (1-Y)*log(1-AL))

        # Regularization cost
```

```r
            L <- length(parameters)/2
            L2RegularizationCost=0
            for(l in 1:L){
                L2RegularizationCost = L2RegularizationCost +
                        sum(parameters[[paste("W",l,sep="")]]^2)
            }
            L2RegularizationCost = (lambd/(2*m))*L2RegularizationCost
            cost = cost +  L2RegularizationCost

    }else if (outputActivationFunc=="softmax"){
         # Select the elements where the y values are 0, 1 or 2 and make a 
vector
         # Pick columns
         #a=c(AL[Y==0,1],AL[Y==1,2],AL[Y==2,3])
         m= length(Y)
         a =pickColumns(AL,Y,numClasses)
         #a = c(A2[y=k,k+1])
         # Take log
         correct_probs = -log(a)
         # Compute loss
         cost= sum(correct_probs)/m

         # Regularization cost
         L <- length(parameters)/2
         L2RegularizationCost=0
         # Add L2 norm
         for(l in 1:L){
                L2RegularizationCost = L2RegularizationCost +
                   sum(parameters[[paste("W",l,sep="")]]^2)
         }
         L2RegularizationCost = (lambd/(2*m))*L2RegularizationCost
         cost = cost +  L2RegularizationCost
    }
    return(cost)
}

# Compute the backpropagation through a layer
# Input : Neural Network parameters - dA
#       # cache - forward_cache & activation_cache
#       # Input features
#       # Output values Y
#       # activationFunc
#       # numClasses
# Returns: Gradients
# dL/dWi= dL/dZi*Al-1
# dl/dbl = dL/dZl
# dL/dZ_prev=dL/dZl*W

layerActivationBackward  <- function(dA, cache, Y, 
activationFunc,numClasses){
  # Get A_prev,W,b
  forward_cache <-cache[['forward_cache']]
  activation_cache <- cache[['activation_cache']]
  A_prev <- forward_cache[['A_prev']]
  numtraining = dim(A_prev)[2]
  # Get Z
  activation_cache <- cache[['activation_cache']]
  if(activationFunc == "relu"){
    dZ <- reluDerivative(dA, activation_cache)
  } else if(activationFunc == "sigmoid"){
    dZ <- sigmoidDerivative(dA, activation_cache)
  } else if(activationFunc == "tanh"){
    dZ <- tanhDerivative(dA, activation_cache)
  } else if(activationFunc == "softmax"){
```

```r
      dZ <- softmaxDerivative(dA,  activation_cache,Y,numtraining,numClasses)
   }

   if (activationFunc == 'softmax'){
     W <- forward_cache[['W']]
     b <- forward_cache[['b']]
     dW = 1/numtraining * A_prev%*%dZ
     db = 1/numtraining* matrix(colSums(dZ),nrow=1,ncol=numClasses)
     dA_prev = dZ %*%W
   } else {
     W <- forward_cache[['W']]
     b <- forward_cache[['b']]
     numtraining = dim(A_prev)[2]
     dW = 1/numtraining * dZ %*% t(A_prev)
     db = 1/numtraining * rowSums(dZ)
     dA_prev = t(W) %*% dZ
   }
   retvals <- list("dA_prev"=dA_prev,"dW"=dW,"db"=db)
   return(retvals)
}

# Compute the backpropagation through a layer with Regularization
# Input : dA-Neural Network parameters
#        # cache - forward_cache & activation_cache
#        # Output values Y
#        # lambd
#        # activationFunc
#        # numClasses
# Returns: Gradients
# dL/dWi= dL/dzi*Al-1
# dl/dbl = dL/dzl
# dL/dZ_prev=dL/dzl*W

layerActivationBackwardWithReg  <- function(dA, cache, Y, lambd,
activationFunc,numClasses){
    # Get A_prev,W,b
    forward_cache <-cache[['forward_cache']]
    activation_cache <- cache[['activation_cache']]
    A_prev <- forward_cache[['A_prev']]
    numtraining = dim(A_prev)[2]
    # Get Z
    activation_cache <- cache[['activation_cache']]
    if(activationFunc == "relu"){
        dZ <- reluDerivative(dA, activation_cache)
    } else if(activationFunc == "sigmoid"){
        dZ <- sigmoidDerivative(dA, activation_cache)
    } else if(activationFunc == "tanh"){
        dZ <- tanhDerivative(dA, activation_cache)
    } else if(activationFunc == "softmax"){
        dZ <- softmaxDerivative(dA,
activation_cache,Y,numtraining,numClasses)
    }

    if (activationFunc == 'softmax'){
        W <- forward_cache[['W']]
        b <- forward_cache[['b']]
        # Add the regularization factor
        dW = 1/numtraining * A_prev%*%dZ   + (lambd/numtraining) * t(W)
        db = 1/numtraining* matrix(colSums(dZ),nrow=1,ncol=numClasses)
        dA_prev = dZ %*%W
    } else {
        W <- forward_cache[['W']]
        b <- forward_cache[['b']]
        numtraining = dim(A_prev)[2]
```

```r
                  # Add the regularization factor
                  dW = 1/numtraining * dZ %*% t(A_prev) + (lambd/numtraining) * W
                  db = 1/numtraining * rowSums(dZ)
                  dA_prev = t(W) %*% dZ
        }
    retvals <- list("dA_prev"=dA_prev,"dW"=dW,"db"=db)
    return(retvals)
}

# Compute the backpropagation for 1 cycle through all layers
# Input : AL: Output of L layer Network - weights
#         Y   Real output
#         caches -- list of caches containing:
#         every cache of layerActivationForward() with "relu"/"tanh"
#         #(it's caches[l], for l in range(L-1) i.e l = 0...L-2)
#         #the cache of layerActivationForward() with "sigmoid" (it's caches[L-1])
#         dropoutMat
#         lambd
#         keep_prob
#         hiddenActivationFunc - Activation function at hidden layers - relu/tanh/sigmoid
#         outputActivationFunc - Activation function at hidden layer sigmoid/softmax
#         numClasses
#   Returns:
#     gradients -- A dictionary with the gradients
#                  gradients["dA" + str(l)]
#                  gradients["dW" + str(l)]
#                  gradients["db" + str(l)]
backwardPropagationDeep <- function(AL, Y, caches,dropoutMat, lambd=0,
keep_prob=0,  hiddenActivationFunc='relu',
                                     outputActivationFunc="sigmoid",numClasses){
    #initialize the gradients
    gradients = list()
    # Set the number of layers
    L = length(caches)
    numTraining = dim(AL)[2]

    if(outputActivationFunc == "sigmoid")
        # Initializing the backpropagation
        # dl/dAL= -(y/a) - ((1-y)/(1-a)) - At the output layer
        dAL = -( (Y/AL) -(1 - Y)/(1 - AL))
    else if(outputActivationFunc == "softmax"){
        dAL=0
        Y=t(Y)
    }

    # Get the gradients at the last layer
    # Inputs: "AL, Y, caches".
    # Outputs: "gradients["dAL"], gradients["dWL"], gradients["dbL"]
    # Start with Layer L
    # Get the current cache
    current_cache = caches[[L]]$cache
    if (lambd==0){
       retvals <-  layerActivationBackward(dAL, current_cache, Y,
                                            activationFunc =
outputActivationFunc,numClasses)
    } else {
        retvals = layerActivationBackwardWithReg(dAL, current_cache, Y, lambd,
                                            activationFunc =
outputActivationFunc,numClasses)
    }

```

```r
    #Note: Take the transpose of dA
    if(outputActivationFunc =="sigmoid")
        gradients[[paste("dA",L,sep="")]] <- retvals[['dA_prev']]
    else if(outputActivationFunc =="softmax")
        gradients[[paste("dA",L,sep="")]] <- t(retvals[['dA_prev']])

    gradients[[paste("dW",L,sep="")]] <- retvals[['dW']]
    gradients[[paste("db",L,sep="")]] <- retvals[['db']]



    # Traverse in the reverse direction
    for(l in (L-1):1){
      # Compute the gradients for L-1 to 1 for Relu/tanh
      # Inputs: "gradients["dA" + str(l + 2)], caches".
      # Outputs: "gradients["dA" + str(l + 1)] , gradients["dW" + str(l + 1)] , gradients["db" + str(l + 1)]
      current_cache = caches[[l]]$cache
      if (lambd==0){
          cat("l=",l)
          # Get the dropout matrix
          D <-dropoutMat[[paste("D",l,sep="")]]
          # Multiply gradient with dropout matrix
          gradients[[paste('dA',l+1,sep="")]] = gradients[[paste('dA',l+1,sep="")]] *D
          # Divide by keep_prob to keep expected value same
          gradients[[paste('dA',l+1,sep="")]] = gradients[[paste('dA',l+1,sep="")]]/keep_prob
          retvals = layerActivationBackward(gradients[[paste('dA',l+1,sep="")]],
                                      current_cache, Y,
                                      activationFunc = hiddenActivationFunc)
      } else {
          retvals = layerActivationBackwardWithReg(gradients[[paste('dA',l+1,sep="")]],
                                      current_cache, Y, lambd,
                                      activationFunc = hiddenActivationFunc)
      }

      gradients[[paste("dA",l,sep="")]] <-retvals[['dA_prev']]
      gradients[[paste("dW",l,sep="")]] <- retvals[['dW']]
      gradients[[paste("db",l,sep="")]] <- retvals[['db']]
   }



   return(gradients)
}


# Perform Gradient Descent
# Input : Weights and biases
#       : gradients
#       : learning rate
#       : outputActivationFunc - Activation function at hidden layer sigmoid/softmax
#output : Updated weights after 1 iteration
gradientDescent  <- function(parameters, gradients, learningRate,outputActivationFunc="sigmoid"){

   L = length(parameters)/2 # number of layers in the neural network
```

```r
    # Update rule for each parameter. Use a for loop.
    for(l in 1:(L-1)){
      parameters[[paste("W",l,sep="")]] = parameters[[paste("W",l,sep="")]] -
        learningRate* gradients[[paste("dW",l,sep="")]]
      parameters[[paste("b",l,sep="")]] = parameters[[paste("b",l,sep="")]] -
        learningRate* gradients[[paste("db",l,sep="")]]
    }
    if(outputActivationFunc=="sigmoid"){
      parameters[[paste("W",L,sep="")]] = parameters[[paste("W",L,sep="")]] -
        learningRate* gradients[[paste("dW",L,sep="")]]
      parameters[[paste("b",L,sep="")]] = parameters[[paste("b",L,sep="")]] -
        learningRate* gradients[[paste("db",L,sep="")]]

    }else if (outputActivationFunc=="softmax"){
      parameters[[paste("W",L,sep="")]] = parameters[[paste("W",L,sep="")]] -
        learningRate* t(gradients[[paste("dW",L,sep="")]])
      parameters[[paste("b",L,sep="")]] = parameters[[paste("b",L,sep="")]] -
        learningRate* t(gradients[[paste("db",L,sep="")]])

    }
    return(parameters)
}

#  Perform Gradient Descent with momentum
# Input : Weights and biases
#        : beta
#        : gradients
#        : learning rate
#        : outputActivationFunc - Activation function at hidden layer
sigmoid/softmax
#output : Updated weights after 1 iteration
gradientDescentWithMomentum  <- function(parameters, gradients,v, beta,
learningRate,outputActivationFunc="sigmoid"){

    L = length(parameters)/2 # number of layers in the neural network

    # Update rule for each parameter. Use a for loop.
    for(l in 1:(L-1)){
        # Compute velocities
        # v['dWk'] = beta *v['dWk'] + (1-beta)*dWk
        v[[paste("dW",l, sep="")]] = beta*v[[paste("dW",l, sep="")]] +
                  (1-beta) * gradients[[paste('dW',l,sep="")]]
        v[[paste("db",l, sep="")]] = beta*v[[paste("db",l, sep="")]] +
            (1-beta) * gradients[[paste('db',l,sep="")]]

        parameters[[paste("W",l,sep="")]] = parameters[[paste("W",l,sep="")]]
-
            learningRate* v[[paste("dW",l, sep="")]]
        parameters[[paste("b",l,sep="")]] = parameters[[paste("b",l,sep="")]]
-
            learningRate* v[[paste("db",l, sep="")]]
    }

    # Compute for the Lth layer
    if(outputActivationFunc=="sigmoid"){
        v[[paste("dW",L, sep="")]] = beta*v[[paste("dW",L, sep="")]] +
            (1-beta) * gradients[[paste('dW',L,sep="")]]
        v[[paste("db",L, sep="")]] = beta*v[[paste("db",L, sep="")]] +
            (1-beta) * gradients[[paste('db',L,sep="")]]

        parameters[[paste("W",L,sep="")]] = parameters[[paste("W",L,sep="")]]
-
            learningRate* v[[paste("dW",l, sep="")]]
```

```r
            parameters[[paste("b",L,sep="")]] = parameters[[paste("b",L,sep="")]]
-
                learningRate* v[[paste("db",l, sep="")]]

    }else if (outputActivationFunc=="softmax"){
          v[[paste("dW",L, sep="")]] = beta*v[[paste("dW",L, sep="")]] +
              (1-beta) * t(gradients[[paste('dW',L,sep="")]])
          v[[paste("db",L, sep="")]] = beta*v[[paste("db",L, sep="")]] +
              (1-beta) * t(gradients[[paste('db',L,sep="")]])
          parameters[[paste("W",L,sep="")]] = parameters[[paste("W",L,sep="")]]
-
              learningRate* t(gradients[[paste("dW",L,sep="")]])
          parameters[[paste("b",L,sep="")]] = parameters[[paste("b",L,sep="")]]
-
              learningRate* t(gradients[[paste("db",L,sep="")]])
    }
    return(parameters)
}


# Perform Gradient Descent with RMSProp
# Input : parameters
#        : gradients
#        : s
#        : beta1
#        : epsilon
#        : learning rate
#        : outputActivationFunc - Activation function at hidden layer
sigmoid/softmax
#output : Updated weights after 1 iteration
gradientDescentWithRMSProp  <- function(parameters, gradients,s, beta1,
epsilon, learningRate,outputActivationFunc="sigmoid"){
    L = length(parameters)/2 # number of layers in the neural network
    # Update rule for each parameter. Use a for loop.
    for(l in 1:(L-1)){
        # Compute RMSProp
        # s['dWk'] = beta1 *s['dWk'] + (1-beta1)*dwk**2/sqrt(s['dWk'])
        # Element wise multiply of gradients
        s[[paste("dW",l, sep="")]] = beta1*s[[paste("dW",l, sep="")]] +
            (1-beta1) * gradients[[paste('dW',l,sep="")]] *
gradients[[paste('dW',l,sep="")]]
        s[[paste("db",l, sep="")]] = beta1*s[[paste("db",l, sep="")]] +
            (1-beta1) * gradients[[paste('db',l,sep="")]] *
gradients[[paste('db',l,sep="")]]

        parameters[[paste("W",l,sep="")]] = parameters[[paste("W",l,sep="")]]
-
            learningRate *
gradients[[paste('dW',l,sep="")]]/sqrt(s[[paste("dW",l, sep="")]]+epsilon)
        parameters[[paste("b",l,sep="")]] = parameters[[paste("b",l,sep="")]]
-

learningRate*gradients[[paste('db',l,sep="")]]/sqrt(s[[paste("db",l,
sep="")]]+epsilon)
    }

    # Compute for the Lth layer
    if(outputActivationFunc=="sigmoid"){
        s[[paste("dW",L, sep="")]] = beta1*s[[paste("dW",L, sep="")]] +
            (1-beta1) * gradients[[paste('dW',L,sep="")]]
*gradients[[paste('dW',L,sep="")]]
        s[[paste("db",L, sep="")]] = beta1*s[[paste("db",L, sep="")]] +
            (1-beta1) * gradients[[paste('db',L,sep="")]] *
gradients[[paste('db',L,sep="")]]
```

```r
            parameters[[paste("W",L,sep="")]] = parameters[[paste("W",L,sep="")]] -
                learningRate* gradients[[paste('dW',l,sep="")]]/sqrt(s[[paste("dW",L, sep="")]]+epsilon)
            parameters[[paste("b",L,sep="")]] = parameters[[paste("b",L,sep="")]] -
                learningRate* gradients[[paste('db',l,sep="")]]/sqrt( s[[paste("db",L, sep="")]]+epsilon)

        }else if (outputActivationFunc=="softmax"){
            s[[paste("dW",L, sep="")]] = beta1*s[[paste("dW",L, sep="")]] +
                (1-beta1) * t(gradients[[paste('dW',L,sep="")]]) * t(gradients[[paste('dW',L,sep="")]])
            s[[paste("db",L, sep="")]] = beta1*s[[paste("db",L, sep="")]] +
                (1-beta1) * t(gradients[[paste('db',L,sep="")]]) * t(gradients[[paste('db',L,sep="")]])

            parameters[[paste("W",L,sep="")]] = parameters[[paste("W",L,sep="")]] -
                learningRate* t(gradients[[paste("dW",L,sep="")]])/sqrt(s[[paste("dW",L, sep="")]]+epsilon)
            parameters[[paste("b",L,sep="")]] = parameters[[paste("b",L,sep="")]] -
                learningRate* t(gradients[[paste("db",L,sep="")]])/sqrt( s[[paste("db",L, sep="")]]+epsilon)
        }
    return(parameters)
}


# Perform Gradient Descent with Adam
# Input : parameters
#         : gradients
#         : v
#         : s
#         : t
#         : beta1
#         : beta2
#         : epsilon
#         : learning rate
#         : outputActivationFunc - Activation function at hidden layer sigmoid/softmax
#output : Updated weights after 1 iteration
gradientDescentWithAdam   <- function(parameters, gradients,v, s, t,
                            beta1=0.9, beta2=0.999, epsilon=10^-8,
learningRate=0.1,outputActivationFunc="sigmoid"){

    L = length(parameters)/2 # number of layers in the neural network
    v_corrected <- list()
    s_corrected <- list()
    # Update rule for each parameter. Use a for loop.
    for(l in 1:(L-1)){
        # v['dWk'] = beta *v['dWk'] + (1-beta)*dwk
        v[[paste("dW",l, sep="")]] = beta1*v[[paste("dW",l, sep="")]] +
            (1-beta1) * gradients[[paste('dW',l,sep="")]]
        v[[paste("db",l, sep="")]] = beta1*v[[paste("db",l, sep="")]] +
            (1-beta1) * gradients[[paste('db',l,sep="")]]


        # Compute bias-corrected first moment estimate.
        v_corrected[[paste("dW",l, sep="")]] = v[[paste("dW",l, sep="")]]/(1-beta1^t)
```

```
            v_corrected[[paste("db",l, sep="")]] = v[[paste("db",l, sep="")]]/(1-
beta1^t)


        # Element wise multiply of gradients
        s[[paste("dw",l, sep="")]] = beta2*s[[paste("dw",l, sep="")]] +
            (1-beta2) * gradients[[paste('dw',l,sep="")]] *
gradients[[paste('dw',l,sep="")]]
        s[[paste("db",l, sep="")]] = beta2*s[[paste("db",l, sep="")]] +
            (1-beta2) * gradients[[paste('db',l,sep="")]] *
gradients[[paste('db',l,sep="")]]

        # Compute bias-corrected second moment estimate.
        s_corrected[[paste("dw",l, sep="")]] = s[[paste("dw",l, sep="")]]/(1-
beta2^t)
        s_corrected[[paste("db",l, sep="")]] = s[[paste("db",l, sep="")]]/(1-
beta2^t)

        # Update parameters.
        d1=sqrt(s_corrected[[paste("dw",l, sep="")]]+epsilon)
        d2=sqrt(s_corrected[[paste("db",l, sep="")]]+epsilon)

        parameters[[paste("W",l,sep="")]] = parameters[[paste("W",l,sep="")]] -
            learningRate * v_corrected[[paste("dw",l, sep="")]]/d1
        parameters[[paste("b",l,sep="")]] = parameters[[paste("b",l,sep="")]] -
            learningRate*v_corrected[[paste("db",l, sep="")]]/d2
    }

    # Compute for the Lth layer
    if(outputActivationFunc=="sigmoid"){
        v[[paste("dw",L, sep="")]] = beta1*v[[paste("dw",L, sep="")]] +
            (1-beta1) * gradients[[paste('dw',L,sep="")]]
        v[[paste("db",L, sep="")]] = beta1*v[[paste("db",L, sep="")]] +
            (1-beta1) * gradients[[paste('db',L,sep="")]]


        # Compute bias-corrected first moment estimate.
        v_corrected[[paste("dw",L, sep="")]] = v[[paste("dw",L, sep="")]]/(1-
beta1^t)
        v_corrected[[paste("db",L, sep="")]] = v[[paste("db",L, sep="")]]/(1-
beta1^t)


        # Element wise multiply of gradients
        s[[paste("dw",L, sep="")]] = beta2*s[[paste("dw",L, sep="")]] +
            (1-beta2) * gradients[[paste('dw',L,sep="")]] *
gradients[[paste('dw',L,sep="")]]
        s[[paste("db",L, sep="")]] = beta2*s[[paste("db",L, sep="")]] +
            (1-beta2) * gradients[[paste('db',L,sep="")]] *
gradients[[paste('db',L,sep="")]]

        # Compute bias-corrected second moment estimate.
        s_corrected[[paste("dw",L, sep="")]] = s[[paste("dw",L, sep="")]]/(1-
beta2^t)
        s_corrected[[paste("db",L, sep="")]] = s[[paste("db",L, sep="")]]/(1-
beta2^t)

        # Update parameters.
        d1=sqrt(s_corrected[[paste("dw",L, sep="")]]+epsilon)
        d2=sqrt(s_corrected[[paste("db",L, sep="")]]+epsilon)
```

```
            parameters[[paste("W",L,sep="")]] = parameters[[paste("W",L,sep="")]] -
                learningRate * v_corrected[[paste("dW",L, sep="")]]/d1
            parameters[[paste("b",L,sep="")]] = parameters[[paste("b",L,sep="")]] -
                learningRate*v_corrected[[paste("db",L, sep="")]]/d2

      }else if (outputActivationFunc=="softmax"){
          v[[paste("dW",L, sep="")]] = beta1*v[[paste("dW",L, sep="")]] +
              (1-beta1) * t(gradients[[paste('dW',L,sep="")]])
          v[[paste("db",L, sep="")]] = beta1*v[[paste("db",L, sep="")]] +
              (1-beta1) * t(gradients[[paste('db',L,sep="")]])


          # Compute bias-corrected first moment estimate.
          v_corrected[[paste("dW",L, sep="")]] = v[[paste("dW",L, sep="")]]/(1-beta1^t)
          v_corrected[[paste("db",L, sep="")]] = v[[paste("db",L, sep="")]]/(1-beta1^t)


          # Element wise multiply of gradients
          s[[paste("dW",L, sep="")]] = beta2*s[[paste("dW",L, sep="")]] +
              (1-beta2) * t(gradients[[paste('dW',L,sep="")]]) * t(gradients[[paste('dW',L,sep="")]])
          s[[paste("db",L, sep="")]] = beta2*s[[paste("db",L, sep="")]] +
              (1-beta2) * t(gradients[[paste('db',L,sep="")]]) * t(gradients[[paste('db',L,sep="")]])

          # Compute bias-corrected second moment estimate.
          s_corrected[[paste("dW",L, sep="")]] = s[[paste("dW",L, sep="")]]/(1-beta2^t)
          s_corrected[[paste("db",L, sep="")]] = s[[paste("db",L, sep="")]]/(1-beta2^t)

          # Update parameters.
          d1=sqrt(s_corrected[[paste("dW",L, sep="")]]+epsilon)
          d2=sqrt(s_corrected[[paste("db",L, sep="")]]+epsilon)

          parameters[[paste("W",L,sep="")]] = parameters[[paste("W",L,sep="")]] -
              learningRate * v_corrected[[paste("dW",L, sep="")]]/d1
          parameters[[paste("b",L,sep="")]] = parameters[[paste("b",L,sep="")]] -
              learningRate*v_corrected[[paste("db",L, sep="")]]/d2
      }
    return(parameters)
}

# Execute a L layer Deep learning model
# Input : X - Input features
#       : Y output
#       : layersDimensions - Dimension of layers
#       : hiddenActivationFunc - Activation function at hidden layer relu /tanh
#       : outputActivationFunc - Activation function at hidden layer sigmoid/softmax
#       : learning rate
#       : lambd
#       : keep_prob
#       : learning rate
#       : num of iterations
#       : initType
#output : Updated weights
```

```r
L_Layer_DeepModel <- function(X, Y, layersDimensions,
                              hiddenActivationFunc='relu',
                              outputActivationFunc= 'sigmoid',
                              learningRate = 0.5,
                              lambd=0,
                              keep_prob=1,
                              numIterations = 10000,
                              initType="default",
                              print_cost=False){
    #Initialize costs vector as NULL
    costs <- NULL

    # Parameters initialization.
    if (initType=="He"){
       parameters =HeInitializeDeepModel(layersDimensions)
    } else if (initType=="Xav"){
        parameters =XavInitializeDeepModel(layersDimensions)
    }
    else{
        parameters = initializeDeepModel(layersDimensions)
    }


    # Loop (gradient descent)
    for( i in 0:numIterations){
       # Forward propagation: [LINEAR -> RELU]*(L-1) -> LINEAR -> SIGMOID/SOFTMAX.
       retvals = forwardPropagationDeep(X, parameters,keep_prob, hiddenActivationFunc,

outputActivationFunc=outputActivationFunc)
       AL <- retvals[['AL']]
       caches <- retvals[['caches']]
       dropoutMat <- retvals[['dropoutMat']]

       # Compute cost.
       if(lambd==0){
           cost <- computeCost(AL, Y,outputActivationFunc=outputActivationFunc,numClasses=layersDimensions[length(layersDimensions)])
       } else {
           cost <- computeCostWithReg(parameters, AL, Y,lambd,
outputActivationFunc=outputActivationFunc,numClasses=layersDimensions[length(layersDimensions)])
       }
       # Backward propagation.
       gradients = backwardPropagationDeep(AL, Y, caches, dropoutMat, lambd, keep_prob, hiddenActivationFunc,

outputActivationFunc=outputActivationFunc,numClasses=layersDimensions[length(layersDimensions)])

       # Update parameters.
       parameters = gradientDescent(parameters, gradients, learningRate,
                                    outputActivationFunc=outputActivationFunc)


       if(i%%1000 == 0){
         costs=c(costs,cost)
         print(cost)
       }
    }
```

```r
    retvals <- list("parameters"=parameters,"costs"=costs)

    return(retvals)
}

# Execute a L layer Deep learning model with Stochastic Gradient descent
# Input : X - Input features
#         : Y output
#         : layersDimensions - Dimension of layers
#         : hiddenActivationFunc - Activation function at hidden layer relu/tanh
#         : outputActivationFunc - Activation function at hidden layer sigmoid/softmax
#         : learning rate
#         : lrDecay
#         : decayRate
#         : lambd
#         : keep_prob
#         : optimizer
#         : beta
#         : beta1
#         : beta2
#         : epsilon
#         : mini_batch_size
#         : num of epochs
#output : Updated weights after each  iteration
L_Layer_DeepModel_SGD <- function(X, Y, layersDimensions,
                                   hiddenActivationFunc='relu',
                                   outputActivationFunc= 'sigmoid',
                                   learningRate = .3,
                                   lrDecay=FALSE,
                                   decayRate=1,
                                   lambd=0,
                                   keep_prob=1,
                                   optimizer="gd",
                                   beta=0.9,
                                   beta1=0.9,
                                   beta2=0.999,
                                   epsilon=10^-8,
                                   mini_batch_size = 64,
                                   num_epochs = 2500,
                                   print_cost=False){



    print("Values")
    cat("learningRate= ",learningRate)
    cat("\n")
    cat("lambd=",lambd)
    cat("\n")
    cat("keep_prob=",keep_prob)
    cat("\n")
    cat("optimizer=",optimizer)
    cat("\n")
    cat("lrDecay=",lrDecay)
    cat("\n")
    cat("decayRate=",decayRate)
    cat("\n")
    cat("beta=",beta)
    cat("\n")
    cat("beta1=",beta1)
    cat("\n")
    cat("beta2=",beta2)
    cat("\n")
```

```r
        cat("epsilon=",epsilon)
        cat("\n")
        cat("mini_batch_size=",mini_batch_size)
        cat("\n")
        cat("num_epochs=",num_epochs)
        cat("\n")
        set.seed(1)
        #Initialize costs vector as NULL
        costs <- NULL
        t <- 0
        # Parameters initialization.
        parameters = initializeDeepModel(layersDimensions)


        #Initialize the optimizer

        if(optimizer == "momentum"){
            v <-initializeVelocity(parameters)
        } else if(optimizer == "rmsprop"){
            s <-initializeRMSProp(parameters)
        } else if (optimizer == "adam"){
            adamVals <-initializeAdam(parameters)
        }

        seed=10

        # Loop for number of epochs
        for( i in 0:num_epochs){
            seed=seed+1
            minibatches = random_mini_batches(X, Y, mini_batch_size, seed)

            for(batch in 1:length(minibatches)){

                mini_batch_X=minibatches[[batch]][['mini_batch_X']]
                mini_batch_Y=minibatches[[batch]][['mini_batch_Y']]
                # Forward propagation:
                retvals = forwardPropagationDeep(mini_batch_X,
parameters,keep_prob, hiddenActivationFunc,

outputActivationFunc=outputActivationFunc)
                AL <- retvals[['AL']]
                caches <- retvals[['caches']]
                dropoutMat <- retvals[['dropoutMat']]

                # Compute cost.
                # Compute cost.
                if(lambd==0){
                    cost <- computeCost(AL,
mini_batch_Y,outputActivationFunc=outputActivationFunc,numClasses=layersDimen
sions[length(layersDimensions)])
                } else {
                    cost <- computeCostWithReg(parameters, AL, Y,lambd,
outputActivationFunc=outputActivationFunc,numClasses=layersDimensions[length(
layersDimensions)])
                }
                # Backward propagation.
                gradients = backwardPropagationDeep(AL, mini_batch_Y, caches,
dropoutMat, lambd, keep_prob, hiddenActivationFunc,

outputActivationFunc=outputActivationFunc,numClasses=layersDimensions[length(
layersDimensions)])

                if(optimizer == "gd"){
                    # Update parameters.
```

```r
                        parameters = gradientDescent(parameters, gradients, learningRate,

outputActivationFunc=outputActivationFunc)
            }else if(optimizer == "momentum"){
                # Update parameters with Momentum
                parameters = gradientDescentWithMomentum(parameters, gradients,v,beta, learningRate,

outputActivationFunc=outputActivationFunc)

            } else if(optimizer == "rmsprop"){
                # Update parameters with RMSProp
                parameters = gradientDescentWithRMSProp(parameters, gradients,s,beta1, epsilon,learningRate,

outputActivationFunc=outputActivationFunc)

            } else if(optimizer == "adam"){
                # Update parameters with Adam
                #Get v and s
                t <- t+1
                v <- adamVals[['v']]
                s <- adamVals[['s']]
                parameters = gradientDescentWithAdam(parameters, gradients,v,s,t, beta1,beta2, epsilon,learningRate,

outputActivationFunc=outputActivationFunc)
            }
        }

        if(i%%1000 == 0){
            costs=c(costs,cost)
            print(cost)
        }
        if(lrDecay==TRUE){
            learningRate = decayRate^(num_epochs/1000) * learningRate
        }
    }

    retvals <- list("parameters"=parameters,"costs"=costs)

    return(retvals)
}

# Predict the output for given input
# Input : parameters
#       : X
# Output: predictions
predict <- function(parameters, X,keep_prob=1, hiddenActivationFunc='relu'){

   fwdProp <- forwardPropagationDeep(X, parameters,keep_prob, hiddenActivationFunc)
   predictions <- fwdProp$AL>0.5

   return (predictions)
}

# Plot a decision boundary
# This function uses ggplot2
plotDecisionBoundary <- function(z,retvals,keep_prob=1,hiddenActivationFunc="sigmoid",lr=0.5){
   # Find the minimum and maximum for the data
   xmin<-min(z[,1])
```

```r
    xmax<-max(z[,1])
    ymin<-min(z[,2])
    ymax<-max(z[,2])

    # Create a grid of values
    a=seq(xmin,xmax,length=100)
    b=seq(ymin,ymax,length=100)
    grid <- expand.grid(x=a, y=b)
    colnames(grid) <- c('x1', 'x2')
    grid1 <-t(grid)
    # Predict the output for this grid
    q <-predict(retvals$parameters,grid1,keep_prob=1, hiddenActivationFunc)
    q1 <- t(data.frame(q))
    q2 <- as.numeric(q1)
    grid2 <- cbind(grid,q2)
    colnames(grid2) <- c('x1', 'x2','q2')

    z1 <- data.frame(z)
    names(z1) <- c("x1","x2","y")
    atitle=paste("Decision boundary for learning rate:",lr)
    # Plot the contour of the boundary
    ggplot(z1) +
       geom_point(data = z1, aes(x = x1, y = x2, color = y)) +
       stat_contour(data = grid2, aes(x = x1, y = x2, z = q2,color=q2), alpha =
0.9)+
       ggtitle(atitle) + scale_colour_gradientn(colours = brewer.pal(10,
"Spectral"))
}

# Predict the probability  scores for given data set
# Input : parameters
#         : X
# Output: probability of output
computeScores <- function(parameters, X,hiddenActivationFunc='relu'){

   fwdProp <- forwardPropagationDeep(X, parameters,hiddenActivationFunc)
   scores <- fwdProp$AL

   return (scores)
}

# Create random mini batches
# Input : X - Input features
#         : Y- output
#         : miniBatchSize
#         : seed
#output : mini_batches
random_mini_batches <- function(X, Y, miniBatchSize = 64, seed = 0){

    set.seed(seed)
    # Get number of training samples
    m = dim(X)[2]
    # Initialize mini batches
    mini_batches = list()

    # Create  a list of random numbers < m
    permutation = c(sample(m))
    # Randomly shuffle the training data
    shuffled_X = X[, permutation]
    shuffled_Y = Y[1, permutation]

    # Compute number of mini batches
    numCompleteMinibatches = floor(m/miniBatchSize)
    batch=0
```

```r
        for(k in 0:(numCompleteMinibatches-1)){
            batch=batch+1
            # Set the lower and upper bound of the mini batches
            lower=(k*miniBatchSize)+1
            upper=((k+1) * miniBatchSize)
            mini_batch_X = shuffled_X[, lower:upper]
            mini_batch_Y = shuffled_Y[lower:upper]
            # Add it to the list of mini batches
            mini_batch =
list("mini_batch_X"=mini_batch_X,"mini_batch_Y"=mini_batch_Y)
            mini_batches[[batch]] =mini_batch


        }

        # If the batch size does not divide evenly with mini batc size
        if(m %% miniBatchSize != 0){
            p=floor(m/miniBatchSize)*miniBatchSize
            # Set the start and end of last batch
            q=p+m %% miniBatchSize
            mini_batch_X = shuffled_X[,(p+1):q]
            mini_batch_Y = shuffled_Y[(p+1):q]
        }
        # Return the list of mini batches
        mini_batch =
list("mini_batch_X"=mini_batch_X,"mini_batch_Y"=mini_batch_Y)
        mini_batches[[batch]]=mini_batch

        return(mini_batches)
}

# Plot a decision boundary
# This function uses ggplot2
plotDecisionBoundary1 <- function(Z,parameters,keep_prob=1){
    xmin<-min(Z[,1])
    xmax<-max(Z[,1])
    ymin<-min(Z[,2])
    ymax<-max(Z[,2])

    # Create a grid of points
    a=seq(xmin,xmax,length=100)
    b=seq(ymin,ymax,length=100)
    grid <- expand.grid(x=a, y=b)
    colnames(grid) <- c('x1', 'x2')
    grid1 <-t(grid)

    retvals = forwardPropagationDeep(grid1, parameters,keep_prob, "relu",
                                        outputActivationFunc="softmax")

    AL <- retvals$AL
    # From the  softmax probabilities pick the one with the highest
probability
    q= apply(AL,1,which.max)

    q1 <- t(data.frame(q))
    q2 <- as.numeric(q1)
    grid2 <- cbind(grid,q2)
    colnames(grid2) <- c('x1', 'x2','q2')

    Z1 <- data.frame(Z)
    names(Z1) <- c("x1","x2","y")
    atitle=paste("Decision boundary")
    ggplot(Z1) +
        geom_point(data = Z1, aes(x = x1, y = x2, color = y)) +
```

```r
            stat_contour(data = grid2, aes(x = x1, y = x2, z = q2,color=q2),
alpha = 0.9)+
            ggtitle(atitle) + scale_colour_gradientn(colours = brewer.pal(10,
"Spectral"))
}

#############
# Note: Using list_to_vector followed by vector_to_list => original list
#############
# Convert a weight,biases as a list to a vector
# Input : parameter dictionary
# Returns : vector
list_to_vector <- function(parameters){
    vec <- NULL
    L=length(parameters)/2
    for(l in 1:L){
        vec1= as.vector(t(parameters[[paste('W',l,sep="")]])) #Take transpose
        vec1=as.matrix(vec1,nrow=length(vec1),ncol=1)
        vec2= as.vector(t(parameters[[paste('b',l,sep="")]])) #Take transpose
        vec2=as.matrix(vec2,nrow=length(vec2),ncol=1)
        vec <- rbind(vec,vec1)
        vec <- rbind(vec,vec2)
    }
    return(vec)
}

# Convert a list of gradients to a vector
# Input : parameter
#        : gradient list
# Returns : gradient vector
gradients_to_vector <- function(parameters,gradients){
    vec <- NULL
    L=length(parameters)/2
    for(l in 1:L){
        vec1= as.vector(t(gradients[[paste('dW',l,sep="")]])) #Take transpose
        vec1=as.matrix(vec1,nrow=length(vec1),ncol=1)
        vec2= as.vector(t(gradients[[paste('db',l,sep="")]])) #Take transpose
        vec2=as.matrix(vec2,nrow=length(vec2),ncol=1)
        vec <- rbind(vec,vec1)
        vec <- rbind(vec,vec2)
    }
    return(vec)
}

# Convert vector to a list
# This should be a mirror copy of list_to_vector
# Input : parameters
#        : theta
# Returns : parameters1 (list)
vector_to_list    <- function(parameters,theta){
    L<-length(parameters)/2
    start<-1
    parameters1 <- list()
    for(l in 1:L){
        m = dim(parameters[[paste('W',l,sep="")]])
        a = theta[start:(start+m[1]*m[2]-1),1]
        parameters1[[paste('W',l,sep="")]] = t(matrix(a,nrow=m[2],ncol=m[1]))
        start=start+m[1]*m[2]
        n = dim(parameters[[paste('b',l,sep="")]])
        b= theta[start:(start+n[1]*n[2]-1),1]
        parameters1[[paste('b',l,sep="")]]=t(matrix(b,nrow=n[2],ncol=n[1]))
        start=start+n[1]*n[2]
    }
```

```r
            return(parameters1)
}

# Convert vector  of gradients to list of gradients
# Input : parameters
#       : grads
# Returns : gradients1 (list)
vector_to_list2    <- function(parameters,grads){
    L<-length(parameters)/2
    start<-1
    gradients1 <- list()
    for(l in 1:L){
        m = dim(parameters[[paste('W',l,sep="")]])
        a = grads[start:(start+m[1]*m[2]-1),1]
        gradients1[[paste('dW',l,sep="")]] = matrix(a,nrow=m[1],ncol=m[2])
        start=start+m[1]*m[2]
        n = dim(parameters[[paste('b',l,sep="")]])
        b= grads[start:(start+n[1]*n[2]-1),1]
        gradients1[[paste('db',l,sep="")]]=matrix(b,nrow=n[1],ncol=n[2])
        start=start+n[1]*n[2]
    }

    return(gradients1)
}

# Compute L2Norm
L2NormVec <- function(x) {
    sqrt(sum(x^2))
}

# Perform Gradient check
# Input : parameters
#       : gradients
#       : X
#       : Y
#       : epsilon
#       : outputActivationFunc
# Returns :
gradient_check_n <- function(parameters, gradients, X, Y,
                             epsilon = 1e-7,outputActivationFunc="sigmoid"){
    # Convert parameters to a vector
    parameters_values = list_to_vector(parameters)
    # Convert gradients to a vector
    grad = gradients_to_vector(parameters,gradients)
    num_parameters = dim(parameters_values)[1]
    #Initialize
    J_plus = matrix(rep(0,num_parameters),
                    nrow=num_parameters,ncol=1)
    J_minus = matrix(rep(0,num_parameters),
                     nrow=num_parameters,ncol=1)
    gradapprox = matrix(rep(0,num_parameters),
                        nrow=num_parameters,ncol=1)

    # Compute gradapprox
    for(i in 1:num_parameters){
        # Compute J_plus[i].
        thetaplus = parameters_values
        thetaplus[i][1] = thetaplus[i][1] + epsilon
        retvals = forwardPropagationDeep(X,
vector_to_list(parameters,thetaplus), keep_prob=1,

hiddenActivationFunc="relu",outputActivationFunc=outputActivationFunc)

        AL <- retvals[['AL']]
```

```
            J_plus[i] = computeCost(AL, Y,
outputActivationFunc=outputActivationFunc)


        # Compute J_minus[i].
        thetaminus = parameters_values
        thetaminus[i][1] = thetaminus[i][1] - epsilon
        retvals  = forwardPropagationDeep(X,
vector_to_list(parameters,thetaminus), keep_prob=1,

hiddenActivationFunc="relu",outputActivationFunc=outputActivationFunc)
        AL <- retvals[['AL']]
        J_minus[i] = computeCost(AL, Y,
outputActivationFunc=outputActivationFunc)


        # Compute gradapprox[i]
        gradapprox[i] = (J_plus[i] - J_minus[i])/(2*epsilon)
    }
    # Compare gradapprox to backward propagation gradients by computing
difference.
    numerator = L2NormVec(grad-gradapprox)
    denominator = L2NormVec(grad) +   L2NormVec(gradapprox)
    difference =  numerator/denominator
    if(difference > 1e-5){
       cat("There is a mistake, the difference is too high",difference)
    } else{
       cat("The implementations works perfectly", difference)
    }


    # This can be used to check the structure of gradients and gradapprox
    print("Gradients from backprop")
    m=vector_to_list2(parameters,grad)
    print(m)
    print("Grad approx from gradient check")
    n=vector_to_list2(parameters,gradapprox)
    print(n)
}
```

8.3 Octave

```
###########################################################################
###############################
#
# File    : DLfunctions8.R
# Author  : Tinniam V Ganesh
# Date    : 6 May 2018
#
###########################################################################
############################
1;
# Define sigmoid function
function [A,cache] = sigmoid(Z)
  A = 1 ./ (1+ exp(-Z));
  cache=Z;
end

# Define Relu function
function [A,cache] = relu(Z)
  A = max(0,Z);
```

```octave
20    cache=Z;
21  end
22
23  # Define Relu function
24  function [A,cache] = tanhAct(Z)
25    A = tanh(Z);
26    cache=Z;
27  end
28
29  # Define Softmax function
30  function [A,cache] = softmax(Z)
31      # get unnormalized probabilities
32      exp_scores = exp(Z');
33      # normalize them for each example
34      A = exp_scores ./ sum(exp_scores,2);
35      cache=Z;
36  end
37
38  # Define Stable Softmax function
39  function [A,cache] = stableSoftmax(Z)
40      # Normalize by max value in each row
41      shiftZ = Z' - max(Z',[],2);
42      exp_scores = exp(shiftZ);
43      # normalize them for each example
44      A = exp_scores ./ sum(exp_scores,2);
45      #disp("sm")
46      #disp(A);
47      cache=Z;
48  end
49
50  # Define Relu Derivative
51  function [dZ] = reluDerivative(dA,cache)
52    Z = cache;
53    dZ = dA;
54    # Get elements that are greater than 0
55    a = (Z > 0);
56    # Select only those elements where Z > 0
57    dZ = dZ .* a;
58  end
59
60  # Define Sigmoid Derivative
61  function [dZ] = sigmoidDerivative(dA,cache)
62    Z = cache;
63    s = 1 ./ (1+ exp(-Z));
64    dZ = dA .* s .* (1-s);
65  end
66
67  # Define Tanh Derivative
68  function [dZ] = tanhDerivative(dA,cache)
69    Z = cache;
70    a = tanh(Z);
71    dZ = dA .* (1 - a .^ 2);
72  end
73
74  # Populate a matrix with 1s in rows where Y=1
75  # This function may need to be modified if K is not 3, 10
76  # This function is used in computing the softmax derivative
77  function [Y1] = popMatrix(Y,numClasses)
78      Y1=zeros(length(Y),numClasses);
79      if(numClasses==3) # For 3 output classes
80          Y1(Y==0,1)=1;
81          Y1(Y==1,2)=1;
82          Y1(Y==2,3)=1;
83      elseif(numClasses==10) # For 10 output classes
```

```octave
            Y1(Y==0,1)=1;
            Y1(Y==1,2)=1;
            Y1(Y==2,3)=1;
            Y1(Y==3,4)=1;
            Y1(Y==4,5)=1;
            Y1(Y==5,6)=1;
            Y1(Y==6,7)=1;
            Y1(Y==7,8)=1;
            Y1(Y==8,9)=1;
            Y1(Y==9,10)=1;

        endif
end

# Define Softmax Derivative
function [dZ] = softmaxDerivative(dA,cache,Y, numClasses)
   Z = cache;
   # get unnormalized probabilities
   shiftZ = Z' - max(Z',[],2);
   exp_scores = exp(shiftZ);

   # normalize them for each example
   probs = exp_scores ./ sum(exp_scores,2);
   # dZ = pi- yi
   yi=popMatrix(Y,numClasses);
   dZ=probs-yi;

end

# Define Stable Softmax Derivative
function [dZ] = stableSoftmaxDerivative(dA,cache,Y, numClasses)
   Z = cache;
   # get unnormalized probabilities
   exp_scores = exp(Z');
   # normalize them for each example
   probs = exp_scores ./ sum(exp_scores,2);
   # dZ = pi- yi
   yi=popMatrix(Y,numClasses);
   dZ=probs-yi;

end

# Initialize model for L layers
# Input : List of units in each layer
# Returns: Initial weights and biases matrices for all layers
function [W b] = initializeDeepModel(layerDimensions)
    rand ("seed", 3);
    # note the Weight matrix at layer 'l' is a matrix of size (l,l-1)
    # The Bias is a vectors of size (l,1)

    # Loop through the layer dimension from 1.. L
    # Create cell arrays for Weights and biases

    for l =2:size(layerDimensions)(2)
        W{l-1} = rand(layerDimensions(l),layerDimensions(l-1))*0.01; #
Multiply by .01
        b{l-1} = zeros(layerDimensions(l),1);

    endfor
end

# He Initialization for L layers
# Input : List of units in each layer
# Returns: Initial weights and biases matrices for all layers
```

```octave
148  function [W b] = HeInitializeDeepModel(layerDimensions)
149      rand ("seed", 3);
150      # note the Weight matrix at layer 'l' is a matrix of size (l,l-1)
151      # The Bias is a vectors of size (l,1)
152
153      # Loop through the layer dimension from 1.. L
154      # Create cell arrays for Weights and biases
155
156      for l =2:size(layerDimensions)(2)
157           W{l-1} = rand(layerDimensions(l),layerDimensions(l-1))*
158  sqrt(2/layerDimensions(l-1)); #  Multiply by .01
159           b{l-1} = zeros(layerDimensions(l),1);
160
161      endfor
162  end
163
164  # Xavier Initialization for L layers
165  # Input : List of units in each layer
166  # Returns: Initial weights and biases matrices for all layers
167  function [W b] = XavInitializeDeepModel(layerDimensions)
168      rand ("seed", 3);
169      # note the Weight matrix at layer 'l' is a matrix of size (l,l-1)
170      # The Bias is a vectors of size (l,1)
171
172      # Loop through the layer dimension from 1.. L
173      # Create cell arrays for Weights and biases
174
175      for l =2:size(layerDimensions)(2)
176           W{l-1} = rand(layerDimensions(l),layerDimensions(l-1))*
177  sqrt(1/layerDimensions(l-1)); #  Multiply by .01
178           b{l-1} = zeros(layerDimensions(l),1);
179
180      endfor
181  end
182
183  # Initialize velocity
184  # Input : weights, biases
185  # Returns: vdW, vdB - Initial velocity
186  function[vdW vdB] =  initializeVelocity(weights, biases)
187
188      L = size(weights)(2) # Create an integer
189      # Initialize a cell array
190      v = {}
191
192      # Initialize velocity with the same dimensions as W
193      for l=1:L
194          sz = size(weights{l});
195          vdW{l} = zeros(sz(1),sz(2));
196          sz = size(biases{l});
197          vdB{l} =zeros(sz(1),sz(2));
198      endfor;
199  end
200
201  # Initialize RMSProp
202  # Input : weights, biases
203  # Returns: sdW, sdB - Initial RMSProp
204  function[sdW sdB] =  initializeRMSProp(weights, biases)
205
206      L = size(weights)(2) # Create an integer
207      # Initialize a cell array
208      s = {}
209
210      # Initialize velocity with the same dimensions as W
211      for l=1:L
```

```
            sz = size(weights{l});
            sdW{l} = zeros(sz(1),sz(2));
            sz = size(biases{l});
            sdB{l} =zeros(sz(1),sz(2));
        endfor;
end

# Initialize Adam
# Input : parameters
# Returns: vdW, vdB, sdW, sdB -Initial Adam
function[vdW vdB sdW sdB] = initializeAdam(weights, biases)

    L = size(weights)(2) # Create an integer
    # Initialize a cell array
    s = {}

    # Initialize velocity with the same dimensions as W
    for l=1:L
        sz = size(weights{l});
        vdW{l} = zeros(sz(1),sz(2));
        sdW{l} = zeros(sz(1),sz(2));
        sz = size(biases{l});
        sdB{l} =zeros(sz(1),sz(2));
        vdB{l} =zeros(sz(1),sz(2));
    endfor;
end

# Compute the activation at a layer 'l' for forward prop in a Deep Network
# Input : A_prec - Activation of previous layer
#         W,b - Weight and bias matrices and vectors
#         activationFunc - Activation function - sigmoid, tanh, relu etc
# Returns : The Activation of this layer
#         :
# Z = W * X + b
# A = sigmoid(Z), A= Relu(Z), A= tanh(Z)
function [A forward_cache activation_cache] = layerActivationForward(A_prev,
w, b, activationFunc)

    # Compute Z
    Z = W * A_prev +b;
    # Create a cell array
    forward_cache = {A_prev  W  b};
    # Compute the activation for sigmoid
    if (strcmp(activationFunc,"sigmoid"))
        [A activation_cache] = sigmoid(Z);
    elseif (strcmp(activationFunc, "relu"))   # Compute the activation for Relu
        [A activation_cache] = relu(Z);
    elseif(strcmp(activationFunc,'tanh'))     # Compute the activation for tanh
        [A activation_cache] = tanhAct(Z);
    elseif(strcmp(activationFunc,'softmax'))   # Compute the activation for tanh
        #[A activation_cache] = softmax(Z);
        [A activation_cache] = stableSoftmax(Z);
    endif

end

# Compute the forward propagation for layers 1..L
# Input : X - Input Features
#         parameters: Weights and biases
#         keep_prob
```

```octave
275  #              hiddenActivationFunc - Activation function at hidden layers
276  Relu/tanh/sigmoid
277  #              outputActivationFunc- sigmoid/softmax
278  # Returns : AL, forward,_caches, activation_caches, dropoutMat
279  # The forward propoagtion uses the Relu/tanh activation from layer 1..L-1 and
280  sigmoid actiovation at layer L
281  function [AL forward_caches activation_caches dropoutMat] =
282  forwardPropagationDeep(X, weights,biases, keep_prob=1,
283                                                     hiddenActivationFunc='relu',
284  outputActivationFunc='sigmoid')
285      # Create an empty cell array
286      forward_caches = {};
287      activation_caches = {};
288      droputMat ={};
289      # Set A to X (A0)
290      A = X;
291      L = length(weights); # number of layers in the neural network
292      # Loop through from layer 1 to upto layer L
293      for l =1:L-1
294          A_prev = A;
295          # Zi = Wi x Ai-1 + bi   and Ai = g(Zi)
296          W = weights{l};
297          b = biases{l};
298          [A forward_cache activation_cache] = layerActivationForward(A_prev,
299  W,b, activationFunc=hiddenActivationFunc);
300          D=rand(size(A)(1),size(A)(2));
301          D = (D < keep_prob) ;
302          # Multiply by DropoutMat
303          A= A .* D;
304          # Divide by keep_prob to keep expected value same
305          A = A ./ keep_prob;
306          # Store D
307          dropoutMat{l}=D;
308          forward_caches{l}=forward_cache;
309          activation_caches{l} = activation_cache;
310      endfor
311      # Since this is binary classification use the sigmoid activation function
312  in
313      # last layer
314      W = weights{L};
315      b = biases{L};
316      [AL, forward_cache activation_cache] = layerActivationForward(A, W,b,
317  activationFunc = outputActivationFunc);
318      forward_caches{L}=forward_cache;
319      activation_caches{L} = activation_cache;
320
321  end
322
323  # Pick columns where Y==1
324  # This function is used in computeCost
325  function [a] = pickColumns(AL,Y,numClasses)
326      if(numClasses==3)
327          a=[AL(Y==0,1)  ;AL(Y==1,2)  ;AL(Y==2,3)];
328      elseif (numClasses==10)
329          a=[AL(Y==0,1)  ;AL(Y==1,2)  ;AL(Y==2,3);AL(Y==3,4);AL(Y==4,5);
330             AL(Y==5,6);  AL(Y==6,7);AL(Y==7,8);AL(Y=8,9);AL(Y==9,10)];
331      endif
332  end
333
334
335  # Compute the cost
336  # Input : AL-Activation of last layer
337  #       : Y-Output from data
338  #       : outputActivationFunc- sigmoid/softmax
```

```octave
#         : numClasses
# Output: cost
function [cost]= computeCost(AL, Y,
outputActivationFunc="sigmoid",numClasses)
    if(strcmp(outputActivationFunc,"sigmoid"))
        numTraining= size(Y)(2);
        # Element wise multiply for logprobs
        cost = -1/numTraining * sum((Y .* log(AL)) + (1-Y) .* log(1-AL));
        #disp(cost);

    elseif(strcmp(outputActivationFunc,'softmax'))
        numTraining = size(Y)(2);
        Y=Y';
        # Select rows where Y=0,1,and 2 and concatenate to a long vector
        #a=[AL(Y==0,1) ;AL(Y==1,2) ;AL(Y==2,3)];
        a =pickColumns(AL,Y,numClasses);

        #Select the correct column for log prob
         correct_probs = -log(a);
         #Compute log loss
         cost= sum(correct_probs)/numTraining;
    endif
end

# Compute the cost with regularization
# Input : weights
#       : AL - Activation of last layer
#       : Output from data
#       : lambd
#       : outputActivationFunc- sigmoid/softmax
#       : numClasses
# Output: cost
function [cost]= computeCostWithReg(weights, AL, Y, lambd,
outputActivationFunc="sigmoid",numClasses)

    if(strcmp(outputActivationFunc,"sigmoid"))
        numTraining= size(Y)(2);
        # Element wise multiply for logprobs
        cost = -1/numTraining * sum((Y .* log(AL)) + (1-Y) .* log(1-AL));

        # Regularization cost
        L = size(weights)(2);
        L2RegularizationCost=0;
        for l=1:L
            wtSqr = weights{l} .* weights{l};
            #disp(sum(sum(wtSqr,1)));
            L2RegularizationCost+=sum(sum(wtSqr,1));
        endfor
        L2RegularizationCost = (lambd/(2*numTraining))*L2RegularizationCost;
        cost = cost +  L2RegularizationCost ;


    elseif(strcmp(outputActivationFunc,'softmax'))
        numTraining = size(Y)(2);
        Y=Y';
        # Select rows where Y=0,1,and 2 and concatenate to a long vector
        #a=[AL(Y==0,1) ;AL(Y==1,2) ;AL(Y==2,3)];
        a =pickColumns(AL,Y,numClasses);

        #Select the correct column for log prob
         correct_probs = -log(a);
         #Compute log loss
         cost= sum(correct_probs)/numTraining;
                # Regularization cost
```

```octave
            L = size(weights)(2);
            L2RegularizationCost=0;
            for l=1:L
                # Compute L2 Norm
                wtSqr = weights{l} .* weights{l};
                #disp(sum(sum(wtSqr,1)));
                L2RegularizationCost+=sum(sum(wtSqr,1));
            endfor
            L2RegularizationCost = (lambd/(2*numTraining))*L2RegularizationCost;
            cost = cost +  L2RegularizationCost ;
        endif
end



# Compute the backpropoagation for 1 cycle
# Input : Neural Network parameters - dA
#         # cache - forward_cache & activation_cache
#         # Input features
#         # Output values Y
#         # outputActivationFunc- sigmoid/softmax
#         # numClasses
# Returns: Gradients
# dL/dWi= dL/dZi*Al-1
# dl/dbl = dL/dZl
# dL/dZ_prev=dL/dZl*W
function [dA_prev dW db] = layerActivationBackward(dA, forward_cache,
activation_cache, Y, activationFunc,numClasses)

    A_prev = forward_cache{1};
    W = forward_cache{2};
    b = forward_cache{3};
    numTraining = size(A_prev)(2);
    if (strcmp(activationFunc,"relu"))
        dZ = reluDerivative(dA, activation_cache);
    elseif (strcmp(activationFunc,"sigmoid"))
        dZ = sigmoidDerivative(dA, activation_cache);
    elseif(strcmp(activationFunc, "tanh"))
        dZ = tanhDerivative(dA, activation_cache);
    elseif(strcmp(activationFunc, "softmax"))
        #dZ = softmaxDerivative(dA, activation_cache,Y,numClasses);
        dZ = stableSoftmaxDerivative(dA, activation_cache,Y,numClasses);
    endif


    if (strcmp(activationFunc,"softmax"))
      W = forward_cache{2};
      b = forward_cache{3};
      # Add the regularization factor
      dW = 1/numTraining * A_prev * dZ;
      db = 1/numTraining * sum(dZ,1);
      dA_prev = dZ*W;
    else
      W = forward_cache{2};
      b = forward_cache{3};
      # Add the regularization factor
      dW = 1/numTraining * dZ * A_prev';
      db = 1/numTraining * sum(dZ,2);
      dA_prev = W'*dZ;
    endif

end

# Compute the backpropoagation for 1 cycle
```

```octave
# Input : dA- Neural Network parameters
#         # cache - forward_cache & activation_cache
#         # Y-Output values
#         # outputActivationFunc- sigmoid/softmax
#         # numClasses
# Returns: Gradients
# dL/dWi= dL/dzi*Al-1
# dl/dbl = dL/dZl
# dL/dZ_prev=dL/dZl*W
function [dA_prev dW db] = layerActivationBackwardWithReg(dA, forward_cache,
activation_cache, Y, lambd=0, activationFunc,numClasses)

    A_prev = forward_cache{1};
    W =forward_cache{2};
    b = forward_cache{3};
    numTraining = size(A_prev)(2);
    if (strcmp(activationFunc,"relu"))
        dZ = reluDerivative(dA, activation_cache);
    elseif (strcmp(activationFunc,"sigmoid"))
        dZ = sigmoidDerivative(dA, activation_cache);
    elseif(strcmp(activationFunc, "tanh"))
        dZ = tanhDerivative(dA, activation_cache);
    elseif(strcmp(activationFunc, "softmax"))
        #dZ = softmaxDerivative(dA, activation_cache,Y,numClasses);
        dZ = stableSoftmaxDerivative(dA, activation_cache,Y,numClasses);
    endif

    if (strcmp(activationFunc,"softmax"))
      W =forward_cache{2};
      b = forward_cache{3};
      # Add the regularization factor
      dW = 1/numTraining * A_prev * dZ +  (lambd/numTraining) * W';
      db = 1/numTraining * sum(dZ,1);
      dA_prev = dZ*W;
    else
      W =forward_cache{2};
      b = forward_cache{3};
      # Add the regularization factor
      dW = 1/numTraining * dZ * A_prev' +  (lambd/numTraining) * W;
      db = 1/numTraining * sum(dZ,2);
      dA_prev = w'*dZ;
    endif

end

# Compute the backpropoagation with regularization for 1 cycle
# Input : dA-Neural Network parameters
#         # cache - forward_cache & activation_cache
#         # Y-Output values
#         # lambd
#         # outputActivationFunc- sigmoid/softmax
#         # numClasses
# Returns: Gradients
# dL/dWi= dL/dzi*Al-1
# dl/dbl = dL/dZl
# dL/dZ_prev=dL/dZl*W
function [dA_prev dW db] = layerActivationBackwardWithReg(dA, forward_cache,
activation_cache, Y, lambd=0, activationFunc,numClasses)

    A_prev = forward_cache{1};
    W =forward_cache{2};
    b = forward_cache{3};
    numTraining = size(A_prev)(2);
    if (strcmp(activationFunc,"relu"))
```

```octave
            dZ = reluDerivative(dA, activation_cache);
        elseif (strcmp(activationFunc,"sigmoid"))
            dZ = sigmoidDerivative(dA, activation_cache);
        elseif(strcmp(activationFunc, "tanh"))
            dZ = tanhDerivative(dA, activation_cache);
        elseif(strcmp(activationFunc, "softmax"))
            #dZ = softmaxDerivative(dA, activation_cache,Y,numClasses);
            dZ = stableSoftmaxDerivative(dA, activation_cache,Y,numClasses);
        endif

        if (strcmp(activationFunc,"softmax"))
           W =forward_cache{2};
           b = forward_cache{3};
           # Add the regularization factor
           dW = 1/numTraining * A_prev * dZ +  (lambd/numTraining) * W';
           db = 1/numTraining * sum(dZ,1);
           dA_prev = dZ*W;
        else
           W =forward_cache{2};
           b = forward_cache{3};
           # Add the regularization factor
           dW = 1/numTraining * dZ * A_prev' +  (lambd/numTraining) * W;
           db = 1/numTraining * sum(dZ,2);
           dA_prev = W'*dZ;
        endif

end

# Compute the backpropoagation for 1 cycle
# Input : AL: Output of L layer Network - weights
#         Y  Real output
#         caches -- list of caches containing:
#         every cache of layerActivationForward() with "relu"/"tanh"
#         #(it's caches[l], for l in range(L-1) i.e l = 0...L-2)
#         #the cache of layerActivationForward() with "sigmoid" (it's caches[L-1])
#         dropoutMat
#         lambd
#         keep_prob
#         hiddenActivationFunc - Activation function at hidden layers
sigmoid/tanh/relu
#         outputActivationFunc- sigmoid/softmax
#         numClasses
#
#    Returns:
#     gradients -- A dictionary with the gradients
#                  gradients["dA" + str(l)] = ...
#                  gradients["dW" + str(l)] = ...
#                  gradients["db" + str(l)] = ...

function [gradsDA gradsDW gradsDB]= backwardPropagationDeep(AL, Y,
activation_caches,forward_caches,
                                  dropoutMat, lambd=0, keep_prob=1,
hiddenActivationFunc='relu',outputActivationFunc="sigmoid",numClasses)


    # Set the number of layers
    L = length(activation_caches);
    m = size(AL)(2);

    if (strcmp(outputActivationFunc,"sigmoid"))
        # Initializing the backpropagation
        # dl/dAL= -(y/a + (1-y)/(1-a)) - At the output layer
        dAL = -((Y ./ AL) - (1 - Y) ./ ( 1 - AL));
```

```octave
        elseif (strcmp(outputActivationFunc,"softmax"))
            dAL=0;
            Y=Y';
        endif


    # Since this is a binary classification the activation at output is
sigmoid
    # Get the gradients at the last layer
    # Inputs: "AL, Y, caches".
    # Outputs: "gradients["dAL"], gradients["dWL"], gradients["dbL"]
    activation_cache = activation_caches{L};
    forward_cache = forward_caches(L);
    # Note the cell array includes an array of forward caches. To get to this
we need to include the index {1}
    if (lambd==0)
        [dA dW db] = layerActivationBackward(dAL, forward_cache{1},
activation_cache, Y, activationFunc = outputActivationFunc,numClasses);
    else
        [dA dW db] = layerActivationBackwardWithReg(dAL, forward_cache{1},
activation_cache, Y, lambd, activationFunc =
outputActivationFunc,numClasses);
    endif
    if (strcmp(outputActivationFunc,"sigmoid"))
         gradsDA{L}= dA;
    elseif (strcmp(outputActivationFunc,"softmax"))
         gradsDA{L}= dA';#Note the transpose
    endif
    gradsDW{L}= dW;
    gradsDB{L}= db;

    # Traverse in the reverse direction
    for l =(L-1):-1:1
        # Compute the gradients for L-1 to 1 for Relu/tanh
        # Inputs: "gradients["dA" + str(l + 2)], caches".
        # Outputs: "gradients["dA" + str(l + 1)] , gradients["dW" + str(l +
1)] , gradients["db" + str(l + 1)]
        activation_cache = activation_caches{l};
        forward_cache = forward_caches(l);

        #dA_prev_temp, dW_temp, db_temp =
layerActivationBackward(gradients['dA'+str(l+1)], current_cache,
activationFunc = "relu")
        # dAl the dervative of the activation of the lth layer,is the first
element
        dAl= gradsDA{l+1};
        if(lambd == 0)
            # Get the dropout mat
            D = dropoutMat{l};
            #Multiply by the dropoutMat
            dAl= dAl .* D;
            # Divide by keep_prob to keep expected value same
            dAl = dAl ./ keep_prob;
            [dA_prev_temp, dW_temp, db_temp] = layerActivationBackward(dAl,
forward_cache{1}, activation_cache, Y, activationFunc =
hiddenActivationFunc,numClasses);
        else
            [dA_prev_temp, dW_temp, db_temp] =
layerActivationBackwardWithReg(dAl, forward_cache{1}, activation_cache, Y,
lambd, activationFunc = hiddenActivationFunc,numClasses);
        endif
        gradsDA{l}= dA_prev_temp;
        gradsDW{l}= dW_temp;
        gradsDB{l}= db_temp;
```

```octave
        endfor

end


# Perform Gradient Descent
# Input : Weights and biases
#        : gradients -gradsW,gradsB
#        : learning rate
#        : outputActivationFunc
#output : Updated weights after 1 iteration
function [weights biases] = gradientDescent(weights, biases,gradsW,gradsB,
learningRate,outputActivationFunc="sigmoid")

    L = size(weights)(2); # number of layers in the neural network
    # Update rule for each parameter.
    for l=1:(L-1)
        weights{l} = weights{l} -learningRate* gradsW{l};
        biases{l} = biases{l} -learningRate* gradsB{l};
    endfor


    if (strcmp(outputActivationFunc,"sigmoid"))
        weights{L} = weights{L} -learningRate* gradsW{L};
        biases{L} = biases{L} -learningRate* gradsB{L};
     elseif (strcmp(outputActivationFunc,"softmax"))
        weights{L} = weights{L} -learningRate* gradsW{L}';
        biases{L} = biases{L} -learningRate* gradsB{L}';
     endif


end


# Update parameters with momentum
# Input : parameters
#        : gradients -gradsDW,gradsDB
#        : v -vdW, vdB
#        : beta
#        : learningRate
#        : outputActivationFunc
#output : Updated weights, biases
function [weights biases] = gradientDescentWithMomentum(weights,
biases,gradsDW,gradsDB, vdW, vdB, beta,
learningRate,outputActivationFunc="sigmoid")
    L = size(weights)(2); # number of layers in the neural network
    # Update rule for each parameter.
    for l=1:(L-1)
        # Compute velocities
        # v['dwk'] = beta *v['dwk'] + (1-beta)*dwk
        vdW{l} =  beta*vdW{l} + (1 -beta) * gradsDW{l};
        vdB{l} =  beta*vdB{l} + (1 -beta) * gradsDB{l};
        weights{l} = weights{l} -learningRate* vdW{l};
        biases{l} = biases{l} -learningRate* vdB{l};
    endfor

    if (strcmp(outputActivationFunc,"sigmoid"))
        vdW{L} =  beta*vdW{L} + (1 -beta) * gradsDW{L};
        vdB{L} =  beta*vdB{L} + (1 -beta) * gradsDB{L};
        weights{L} = weights{L} -learningRate* vdW{L};
        biases{L} = biases{L} -learningRate* vdB{L};
     elseif (strcmp(outputActivationFunc,"softmax"))
        vdW{L} =  beta*vdW{L} + (1 -beta) * gradsDW{L}';
```

```octave
            vdB{L} =  beta*vdB{L} + (1 -beta) * gradsDB{L}';
            weights{L} = weights{L} -learningRate* vdW{L};
            biases{L} = biases{L} -learningRate* vdB{L};
        endif


end


# Update parameters with RMSProp
# Input : parameters - weights, biases
#       : gradients - gradsDW,gradsDB
#       : s -sdW, sdB
#       : beta1
#       : epsilon
#       : learningRate
#       : outputActivationFunc
#output : Updated weights and biases RMSProp
function [weights biases] = gradientDescentWithRMSProp(weights,
biases,gradsDW,gradsDB, sdW, sdB, beta1, epsilon,
learningRate,outputActivationFunc="sigmoid")
    L = size(weights)(2); # number of layers in the neural network
    # Update rule for each parameter.
    for l=1:(L-1)
        sdW{l} =  beta1*sdW{l} + (1 -beta1) * gradsDW{l} .* gradsDW{l};
        sdB{l} =  beta1*sdB{l} + (1 -beta1) * gradsDB{l} .* gradsDB{l};
        weights{l} = weights{l} - learningRate* gradsDW{l} ./ sqrt(sdW{l} +
epsilon);
        biases{l} = biases{l} -  learningRate* gradsDB{l} ./ sqrt(sdB{l} +
epsilon);
    endfor

    if (strcmp(outputActivationFunc,"sigmoid"))
        sdW{L} =  beta1*sdW{L} + (1 -beta1) * gradsDW{L} .* gradsDW{L};
        sdB{L} =  beta1*sdB{L} + (1 -beta1) * gradsDB{L} .* gradsDB{L};
        weights{L} = weights{L} -learningRate* gradsDW{L} ./ sqrt(sdW{L}
+epsilon);
        biases{L} = biases{L} -learningRate* gradsDB{L} ./ sqrt(sdB{L} +
epsilon);
    elseif (strcmp(outputActivationFunc,"softmax"))
        sdW{L} =  beta1*sdW{L} + (1 -beta1) * gradsDW{L}' .* gradsDW{L}';
        sdB{L} =  beta1*sdB{L} + (1 -beta1) * gradsDB{L}' .* gradsDB{L}';
        weights{L} = weights{L} -learningRate* gradsDW{L}' ./ sqrt(sdW{L}
+epsilon);
        biases{L} = biases{L} -learningRate* gradsDB{L}' ./ sqrt(sdB{L} +
epsilon);
    endif


end


# Update parameters with Adam
# Input : parameters - weights, biases
#       : gradients -gradsDW,gradsDB
#       : v - vdW, vdB
#       : s - sdW, sdB
#       : t
#       : beta1
#       : beta2
#       : epsilon
#       : learningRate
#       : epsilon
#output : Updated weights and biases
```

```octave
function [weights biases] = gradientDescentwithAdam(weights,
biases,gradsDW,gradsDB,
                    vdW, vdB, sdW, sdB, t, beta1, beta2, epsilon,
learningRate,outputActivationFunc="sigmoid")
    vdW_corrected = {};
    vdB_corrected = {};
    sdW_corrected = {};
    sdB_corrected = {};
    L = size(weights)(2); # number of layers in the neural network
    # Update rule for each parameter.
    for l=1:(L-1)
        vdW{l} =  beta1*vdW{l} + (1 -beta1) * gradsDW{l};
        vdB{l} =  beta1*vdB{l} + (1 -beta1) * gradsDB{l};

        # Compute bias-corrected first moment estimate.
        vdW_corrected{l} = vdW{l}/(1-beta1^t);
        vdB_corrected{l} = vdB{l}/(1-beta1^t);

        sdW{l} =  beta2*sdW{l} + (1 -beta2) * gradsDW{l} .* gradsDW{l};
        sdB{l} =  beta2*sdB{l} + (1 -beta2) * gradsDB{l} .* gradsDB{l};

        # Compute bias-corrected second moment estimate.
        sdW_corrected{l} = sdW{l}/(1-beta2^t);
        sdB_corrected{l} = sdB{l}/(1-beta2^t);

        # Update parameters.
        d1=sqrt(sdW_corrected{l}+epsilon);
        d2=sqrt(sdB_corrected{l}+epsilon);

        weights{l} = weights{l} - learningRate* vdW_corrected{l} ./ d1;
        biases{l} = biases{l} -learningRate* vdB_corrected{l} ./ d2;
    endfor

    if (strcmp(outputActivationFunc,"sigmoid"))
        vdW{L} =  beta1*vdW{L} + (1 -beta1) * gradsDW{L};
        vdB{L} =  beta1*vdB{L} + (1 -beta1) * gradsDB{L};

        # Compute bias-corrected first moment estimate.
        vdW_corrected{L} = v{L}/(1-beta1^t);
        vdB_corrected{L} = v{L}/(1-beta1^t);

        sdW{L} =  beta2*sdW{L} + (1 -beta2) * gradsDW{L} .* gradsDW{L};
        sdB{L} =  beta2*sdB{L} + (1 -beta2) * gradsDB{L} .* gradsDB{L};

        # Compute bias-corrected second moment estimate.
        sdW_corrected{L} = s{L}/(1-beta2^t);
        sdB_corrected{L} = s{L}/(1-beta2^t);

        # Update parameters.
        d1=sqrt(sdW_corrected{L}+epsilon);
        d2=sqrt(sdB_corrected{L}+epsilon);

        weights{L} = weights{L} - learningRate* vdW_corrected{L} ./ d1;
        biases{L} = biases{L} -learningRate* vdB_corrected{L} ./ d2;
    elseif (strcmp(outputActivationFunc,"softmax"))
        vdW{L} =  beta1*vdW{L} + (1 -beta1) * gradsDW{L}';
        vdB{L} =  beta1*vdB{L} + (1 -beta1) * gradsDB{L}';

        # Compute bias-corrected first moment estimate.
        vdW_corrected{L} = vdW{L}/(1-beta1^t);
        vdB_corrected{L} = vdB{L}/(1-beta1^t);

        sdW{L} =  beta2*sdW{L} + (1 -beta2) * gradsDW{L}' .* gradsDW{L}';
        sdB{L} =  beta2*sdB{L} + (1 -beta2) * gradsDB{L}' .* gradsDB{L}';
```

```octave
            # Compute bias-corrected second moment estimate.
            sdW_corrected{L} = sdW{L}/(1-beta2^t);
            sdB_corrected{L} = sdB{L}/(1-beta2^t);

            # Update parameters.
            d1=sqrt(sdW_corrected{L}+epsilon);
            d2=sqrt(sdB_corrected{L}+epsilon);

            weights{L} = weights{L} - learningRate* vdW_corrected{L} ./ d1;
            biases{L} = biases{L} -learningRate* vdB_corrected{L} ./ d2;
       endif



end

# Execute a L layer Deep learning model
# Input : X - Input features
#       : Y output
#       : layersDimensions - Dimension of layers
#       : hiddenActivationFunc - Activation function at hidden layer relu
/tanh
#       : outputActivationFunc - Activation function at hidden layer
sigmoid/softmax
#       : learning rate
#       : lambd
#       : keep_prob
#       : num of iterations
#output : Updated weights and biases after each  iteration
function [weights biases costs] = L_Layer_DeepModel(X, Y, layersDimensions,
hiddenActivationFunc='relu',
                 outputActivationFunc="sigmoid",learning_rate = .3, lambd=0,
keep_prob=1, num_iterations = 10000,initType="default")#lr was 0.009

    rand ("seed", 1);
    costs = [] ;
    if (strcmp(initType,"He"))
       # He Initialization
       [weights biases] = HeInitializeDeepModel(layersDimensions);
    elseif (strcmp(initType,"Xav"))
        # Xavier Initialization
       [weights biases] = XavInitializeDeepModel(layersDimensions);
    else
       # Default initialization.
       [weights biases] = initializeDeepModel(layersDimensions);
    endif

    # Loop (gradient descent)
    for i = 0:num_iterations
        # Forward propagation: [LINEAR -> RELU]*(L-1) -> LINEAR -> SIGMOID.
        [AL forward_caches activation_caches droputMat] =
forwardPropagationDeep(X, weights, biases,keep_prob, hiddenActivationFunc,
outputActivationFunc=outputActivationFunc);

                # Regularization parameter is 0
        if (lambd==0)
           # Compute cost.
           cost = computeCost(AL,
Y,outputActivationFunc=outputActivationFunc,numClasses=layersDimensions(size(
layersDimensions)(2)));
        else
           # Compute cost with regularization
```

```octave
                cost = computeCostWithReg(weights, AL, Y, lambd,
outputActivationFunc=outputActivationFunc,numClasses=layersDimensions(size(la
yersDimensions)(2)));
            endif
            # Backward propagation.
            [gradsDA gradsDW gradsDB] = backwardPropagationDeep(AL, Y,
activation_caches,forward_caches, droputMat, lambd, keep_prob,
hiddenActivationFunc, outputActivationFunc=outputActivationFunc,

numClasses=layersDimensions(size(layersDimensions)(2)));
            # Update parameters.
            [weights biases] = gradientDescent(weights,biases,
gradsDW,gradsDB,learning_rate,outputActivationFunc=outputActivationFunc);


            # Print the cost every 1000 iterations
            if ( mod(i,1000) == 0)
                costs =[costs cost];
                #disp ("Cost after iteration"),
L2RegularizationCost(i),disp(cost);
                printf("Cost after iteration i=%i cost=%d\n",i,cost);
            endif
        endfor

end

# Execute a L layer Deep learning model with Stochastic Gradient descent
# Input : X - Input features
#       : Y output
#       : layersDimensions - Dimension of layers
#       : hiddenActivationFunc - Activation function at hidden layer relu
/tanh/sigmoid
#       : outputActivationFunc - Activation function at hidden layer
sigmoid/softmax
#       : learning rate
#       : lrDecay
#       : decayRate
#       : lambd
#       : keep_prob
#       : optimizer
#       : beta
#       : beta1
#       : beta2
#       : epsilon
#       : mini_batch_size
#       : num of epochs
#output : Updated weights and biases after each   iteration
function [weights biases costs] = L_Layer_DeepModel_SGD(X, Y,
layersDimensions, hiddenActivationFunc='relu',

outputActivationFunc="sigmoid",learningRate = .3,
                                            lrDecay=false,decayRate=1,
                                            lambd=0, keep_prob=1,
                                            optimizer="gd", beta=0.9, beta1=0.9,
beta2=0.999,epsilon=10^-8,
                                            mini_batch_size = 64, num_epochs =
2500)

    disp("here");
    printf("learningRate=%f ",learningRate);
    printf("lrDecay=%d ",lrDecay);
    printf("decayRate=%f ",decayRate);
    printf("lamd=%d ",lambd);
    printf("keep_prob=%f ",keep_prob);
```

```octave
        printf("optimizer=%s ",optimizer);
        printf("beta=%f ",beta);
        printf("beta1=%f ",beta1);
        printf("beta2=%f ",beta2);
        printf("epsilon=%f ",epsilon);
        printf("mini_batch_size=%d ",mini_batch_size);
        printf("num_epochs=%d ",num_epochs);
        t=0;
       rand ("seed", 1);
       costs = [] ;
       # Parameters initialization.
       [weights biases] = initializeDeepModel(layersDimensions);

       if (strcmp(optimizer,"momentum"))
           [vdW vdB] = initializeVelocity(weights, biases);

       elseif(strcmp(optimizer,"rmsprop"))
           [sdW sdB] = initializeRMSProp(weights, biases);

       elseif(strcmp(optimizer,"adam"))
           [vdW vdB sdW sdB] = initializeAdam(weights, biases);
       endif
       seed=10;
       # Loop (gradient descent)
       for i = 0:num_epochs
           seed = seed + 1;
           [mini_batches_X  mini_batches_Y] = random_mini_batches(X, Y,
mini_batch_size, seed);

           minibatches=length(mini_batches_X);
           for batch=1:minibatches
                X=mini_batches_X{batch};
                Y=mini_batches_Y{batch};
                # Forward propagation: [LINEAR -> RELU]*(L-1) -> LINEAR ->
SIGMOID/SOFTMAX.
                [AL forward_caches activation_caches droputMat] =
forwardPropagationDeep(X, weights, biases, keep_prob,hiddenActivationFunc,
outputActivationFunc=outputActivationFunc);
                #disp(batch);
                #disp(size(X));
                #disp(size(Y));
                if (lambd==0)
                    # Compute cost.
                     cost = computeCost(AL,
Y,outputActivationFunc=outputActivationFunc,numClasses=layersDimensions(size(
layersDimensions)(2)));
                else
                    # Compute cost with regularization
                    cost = computeCostWithReg(weights, AL, Y, lambd,
outputActivationFunc=outputActivationFunc,numClasses=layersDimensions(size(la
yersDimensions)(2)));
                endif
                #disp(cost);
                # Backward propagation.
                [gradsDA gradsDW gradsDB] = backwardPropagationDeep(AL, Y,
activation_caches,forward_caches, droputMat, lambd, keep_prob,
hiddenActivationFunc, outputActivationFunc=outputActivationFunc,

numClasses=layersDimensions(size(layersDimensions)(2)));

                if (strcmp(optimizer,"gd"))
                    # Update parameters.
                    [weights biases] = gradientDescent(weights,biases,
gradsDW,gradsDB,learningRate,outputActivationFunc=outputActivationFunc);
```

```octave
                    elseif (strcmp(optimizer,"momentum"))
                        [weights biases] = gradientDescentWithMomentum(weights,
biases,gradsDW,gradsDB, vdW, vdB, beta, learningRate,outputActivationFunc);
                    elseif (strcmp(optimizer,"rmsprop"))
                        [weights biases] = gradientDescentWithRMSProp(weights,
biases,gradsDW,gradsDB, sdW, sdB, beta1, epsilon,
learningRate,outputActivationFunc);

                    elseif (strcmp(optimizer,"adam"))
                        t=t+1;
                        [weights biases] = gradientDescentWithAdam(weights,
biases,gradsDW,gradsDB,vdW, vdB, sdW, sdB, t, beta1, beta2, epsilon,
learningRate,outputActivationFunc);
                    endif
              endfor
              # Print the cost every 1000 iterations
              if ( mod(i,1000) == 0)
                 costs =[costs cost];
                 #disp ("Cost after iteration"), disp(i),disp(cost);
                 printf("Cost after iteration i=%i cost=%d\n",i,cost);
              endif
              if(lrDecay==true)
                   learningRate=decayRate^(num_epochs/1000)*learningRate;
              endif
        endfor

end

 # Plot cost vs iterations
 function plotCostVsIterations(maxIterations,costs,fig1)
      iterations=[0:1000:maxIterations];
      plot(iterations,costs);
      title ("Cost vs no of iterations ");
      xlabel("No of iterations");
      ylabel("Cost");
      print -dpng figReg2-o
end;

 # Plot cost vs number of epochs
 function plotCostVsEpochs(maxEpochs,costs,fig1)
      epochs=[0:1000:maxEpochs];
      plot(epochs,costs);
      title ("Cost vs no of epochs ");
      xlabel("No of epochs");
      ylabel("Cost");
      print -dpng fig5-o
end;

# Compute the predicted value for a given input
# Input : Neural Network parameters
#       : Input data
function [predictions]= predict(weights, biases,
X,keep_prob=1,hiddenActivationFunc="relu")
    [AL forward_caches activation_caches] = forwardPropagationDeep(X,
weights, biases,keep_prob,hiddenActivationFunc);
    predictions = (AL>0.5);
end

# Plot the decision boundary
function plotDecisionBoundary(data,weights,
biases,keep_prob=1,hiddenActivationFunc="relu",fig2)
    %Plot a non-linear decision boundary learned by the SVM
    colormap ("summer");
```

```octave
    % Make classification predictions over a grid of values
    x1plot = linspace(min(data(:,1)), max(data(:,1)), 400)';
    x2plot = linspace(min(data(:,2)), max(data(:,2)), 400)';
    [X1, X2] = meshgrid(x1plot, x2plot);
    vals = zeros(size(X1));
    # Plot the prediction for the grid
    for i = 1:size(X1, 2)
       gridPoints = [X1(:, i), X2(:, i)];
       vals(:, i)=predict(weights, biases,gridPoints',keep_prob,
hiddenActivationFunc=hiddenActivationFunc);
    endfor

    scatter(data(:,1),data(:,2),8,c=data(:,3),"filled");
    % Plot the boundary
    hold on
    #contour(X1, X2, vals, [0 0], 'LineWidth', 2);
    contour(X1, X2, vals,"linewidth",4);
    title ({"3 layer Neural Network decision boundary"});
    hold off;
    print -dpng figReg22-o

end

# Compute scores
function [AL]= scores(weights, biases, X,hiddenActivationFunc="relu")
    [AL forward_caches activation_caches] = forwardPropagationDeep(X,
weights, biases,hiddenActivationFunc);
end

# Create Random mini batches. Return cell arrays with the mini batches
# Input : X, Y
#        : Size of minibatch
#Output : mini batches X & Y
function [mini_batches_X  mini_batches_Y]= random_mini_batches(X, Y,
miniBatchSize = 64, seed = 0)

    rand ("seed", seed);
    # Get number of training samples
    m = size(X)(2);


    # Create  a list of random numbers < m
    permutation = randperm(m);
    # Randomly shuffle the training data
    shuffled_X = X(:, permutation);
    shuffled_Y = Y(:, permutation);

    # Compute number of mini batches
    numCompleteMinibatches = floor(m/miniBatchSize);
    batch=0;
    for k = 0:(numCompleteMinibatches-1)
       #Set the start and end of each mini batch
       batch=batch+1;
       lower=(k*miniBatchSize)+1;
       upper=(k+1) * miniBatchSize;
       mini_batch_X = shuffled_X(:, lower:upper);
       mini_batch_Y = shuffled_Y(:, lower:upper);

       # Create cell arrays
       mini_batches_X{batch} = mini_batch_X;
       mini_batches_Y{batch} = mini_batch_Y;
    endfor

    # If the batc size does not cleanly divide with number of mini batches
```

```
        if mod(m ,miniBatchSize) != 0
            # Set the start and end of the last mini batch
            l=floor(m/miniBatchSize)*miniBatchSize;
            m=l+ mod(m,miniBatchSize);
            mini_batch_X = shuffled_X(:,(l+1):m);
            mini_batch_Y = shuffled_Y(:,(l+1):m);

            batch=batch+1;
            mini_batches_X{batch} = mini_batch_X;
            mini_batches_Y{batch} = mini_batch_Y;
        endif
end

# Plot decision boundary
function plotDecisionBoundary1( data,weights, biases,keep_prob=1,
hiddenActivationFunc="relu")
    % Make classification predictions over a grid of values
    x1plot = linspace(min(data(:,1)), max(data(:,1)), 400)';
    x2plot = linspace(min(data(:,2)), max(data(:,2)), 400)';
    [X1, X2] = meshgrid(x1plot, x2plot);
    vals = zeros(size(X1));
    for i = 1:size(X1, 2)
            gridPoints = [X1(:, i), X2(:, i)];
            [AL forward_caches activation_caches] =
forwardPropagationDeep(gridPoints', weights,
biases,keep_prob,hiddenActivationFunc, outputActivationFunc="softmax");
            [l m] = max(AL, [ ], 2);
            vals(:, i)= m;
    endfor

    scatter(data(:,1),data(:,2),8,c=data(:,3),"filled");
    % Plot the boundary
    hold on
    contour(X1, X2, vals,"linewidth",4);
    print -dpng "fig-o1.png"
end

#############
# Note: Using cellArray_to_vector followed by vector_to_cellArray => original
cellArray
#############
# Convert a weight,biases as a cell array to a vector
# Input : weight and biases cell array
# Returns : vector
function [vec] = cellArray_to_vector(weights,biases)
        vec=[];
        for i = 1: size(weights)(2)
            w= weights{i};
            sz=size(w);
            # Take transpose before reshaping
            l=reshape(w',sz(1)*sz(2),1);

            b=biases{i};
            sz1=size(b);
            m=reshape(b',sz1(1)*sz1(2),1);
            #Concatenate
            vec=[vec;l;m];
        endfor
end

# Convert gradients cell array to a vector
# Input : gradients cell array
# Returns : vector
function [vec] = gradients_to_vector(gradsDW,gradsDB)
```

```
            vec=[];
            for i = 1: size(gradsDW)(2)
                gW= gradsDW{i};
                sz=size(gW);
                # Take transpose before reshaping
                l=reshape(gW',sz(1)*sz(2),1);

                gB=gradsDB{i};
                sz1=size(gB);
                m=reshape(gB',sz1(1)*sz1(2),1);
                #Concatenate
                vec=[vec;l;m];
             endfor
end

# Convert a vector to a cell array
# Input : vector
# Returns : cell array
function [weights1 biases1] = vector_to_cellArray(weights, biases,params)
          vec=[];
          weights1 = {};
          biases1 ={};
          start=1;
          for i = 1: size(weights)(2)
              w= weights{i};
              sz=size(w);
              # Take transpose before reshaping
              a = params(start:start+sz(1)*sz(2)-1,1);
              b = reshape(a,sz(2),sz(1));
              weights1{i}= b';
              start=start+sz(1)*sz(2);
              b=biases{i};
              sz=size(b);
              c = params(start:start+sz(1)*sz(2)-1,1);
              d = reshape(c,sz(2),sz(1));
              biases1{i}= d';
              start=start+sz(1)*sz(2);

          endfor
end

# Convert a vector to a cell array
# Input : vector
# Returns : cell array
function [weights1 biases1] = vector_to_cellArray1(weights, biases,gradients)
          vec=[];
          weights1 = {};
          biases1 ={};
          start=1;
          for i = 1: size(weights)(2)
              w= weights{i};
              sz=size(w);
              # Take transpose before reshaping
              a = grads(start:start+sz(1)*sz(2)-1,1);
              b = reshape(a,sz(2),sz(1));
              weights1{i}= b';
              start=start+sz(1)*sz(2);
              b=biases{i};
              sz=size(b);
              c = grads(start:start+sz(1)*sz(2)-1,1);
              d = reshape(c,sz(2),sz(1));
              biases1{i}= d';
              start=start+sz(1)*sz(2);
```

```octave
        endfor
end

# Perform Gradient check
# Input : weights,biases
#       : gradsDW,gradsDB
#       : X
#       : Y
#       : epsilon
#       : outputActivationFunc
#       : numClasses
# Returns :
function [difference]=  gradient_check_n(weights,biases,gradsDW,gradsDB, X,
Y, epsilon = 1e-7,outputActivationFunc="sigmoid",numClasses)
   # Convert cell array to vector
   parameters_values = cellArray_to_vector(weights, biases);
   # Convert gradient cell array to vector
   grad = gradients_to_vector(gradsDW,gradsDB);
   num_parameters = size(parameters_values)(1);
   #Initialize
   J_plus = zeros(num_parameters, 1);
   J_minus = zeros(num_parameters, 1);
   gradapprox = zeros(num_parameters, 1);


   # Compute gradapprox
   for i = 1:num_parameters
       # Compute J_plus[i]. Inputs: "parameters_values, epsilon". Output = "J_plus[i]".
       thetaplus = parameters_values;
       thetaplus(i,1) = thetaplus(i,1) + epsilon;
       [weights1 biases1] =vector_to_cellArray(weights, biases,thetaplus);
       [AL forward_caches activation_caches droputMat] = forwardPropagationDeep(X', weights1, biases1, keep_prob=1,

hiddenActivationFunc="relu",outputActivationFunc=outputActivationFunc);
       J_plus(i) = computeCost(AL, Y',
outputActivationFunc=outputActivationFunc,numClasses);


       # Compute J_minus[i]. Inputs: "parameters_values, epsilon". Output = "J_minus[i]".
       thetaminus = parameters_values;
       thetaminus(i,1) = thetaminus(i,1) - epsilon ;
       [weights1 biases1] = vector_to_cellArray(weights, biases,thetaminus);
       [AL forward_caches activation_caches droputMat]   = forwardPropagationDeep(X',weights1, biases1, keep_prob=1,

hiddenActivationFunc="relu",outputActivationFunc=outputActivationFunc);
       J_minus(i) = computeCost(AL, Y',
outputActivationFunc=outputActivationFunc,numClasses);

       # Compute gradapprox[i]
       gradapprox(i) = (J_plus(i) - J_minus(i))/(2*epsilon);

   endfor

   # Compute L2Norm
   numerator = L2NormVec(grad-gradapprox);
   denominator = L2NormVec(grad) +   L2NormVec(gradapprox);
   difference =  numerator/denominator;
;
   if difference > 1e-04
      printf("There is a mistake in the implementation ");
```

```octave
        disp(difference);
    else
        printf("The implementation works perfectly");
            disp(difference);
    endif
    # This can be used to compare the gradients from backprop and gradapprox
    [weights1 biases1] = vector_to_cellArray(weights, biases,grad);
    printf("Gradients from back propagation");
    disp(weights1);
    disp(biases1);
    [weights2 biases2] = vector_to_cellArray(weights, biases,gradapprox);
    printf("Gradients from gradient check");
    disp(weights2);
    disp(biases2);

end

# Compute L2Norm
function [l2norm] = L2NormVec(x)
     l2norm=sqrt(sum(x .^ 2));
end
```

References

1. Deep Learning Specialization - https://www.coursera.org/specializations/deep-learning
2. Neural Networks for Machine Learning - https://www.coursera.org/learn/neural-networks
3. Deep Learning by Ian Goodfellow, Yoshua Bengio and Aaron Courville - http://www.deeplearningbook.org/
4. Neural Networks: The mechanics of backpropagation - https://gigadom.wordpress.com/2017/01/21/neural-networks-the-mechanics-of-backpropagation/
5. Machine Learning - https://www.coursera.org/learn/machine-learning
6. CS231n Convolutional Neural Networks for Visual Recognition -http://cs231n.github.io/neural-networks-case-study/
7. The Softmax function and its derivative - https://eli.thegreenplace.net/2016/the-softmax-function-and-its-derivative/
8. Cross Validated - https://stats.stackexchange.com/questions/235528/backpropagation-with-softmax-cross-entropy
9. CS231n: How to calculate gradient for Softmax loss function? - https://stackoverflow.com/questions/41663874/cs231n-how-to-calculate-gradient-for-softmax-loss-function
10. Derivative of Softmax loss function - https://math.stackexchange.com/questions/945871/derivative-of-softmax-loss-function
11. The Matrix Calculus You Need For Deep Learning - https://arxiv.org/abs/1802.01528
12. A Step by Step Backpropagation Example - https://mattmazur.com/2015/03/17/a-step-by-step-backpropagation-example/
13. The Backpropagation Algorithm - https://page.mi.fu-berlin.de/rojas/neural/chapter/K7.pdf
14. Backpropagation Learning- https://www.cs.cmu.edu/afs/cs/academic/class/15883-f15/slides/backprop.pdf
15. Practical Machine Learning with R and Python – Machine Learning in stereo - https://www.amazon.com/dp/1973443503

www.ingramcontent.com/pod-product-compliance
Lightning Source LLC
Chambersburg PA
CBHW081552220526
45468CB00010B/2643